What ISLAM Is All About

Yahiya Emerick

Previous ISBN: 9781933269023
    First printing: June 1997
    Second printing: January 1999
    Third printing: January 2001
    Fourth printing (Revised): August 2002
    Fifth printing (Revised): June 2004
    Sixth printing: June 2005
    Seventh printing: March 2007
    Eighth printing: August 2008
    Ninth printing: May 2010
    Tenth printing: June 2011

Current ISBN: 9781933269160
    First printing: July 2014
    Second printing: July 2017

Published and distributed by:

E-mail: *info@noorart.com*
          www.noorart.com

Printed By Mega Printing in Turkey

Dedicated to my mother-in-law,
Mrs. Suraiya Baig,
for all her strength and inspiration.

In the Name of Allah, The Most Gracious,
The Most Merciful

Author:
Yahiya Emerick

Chief Editor:
Noor Saadeh

Religious Content Editor:
Sheikh Amin Amer, PhD

Content Editors:
Shaza Khan, PhD
Lena Dirbashi
Farheen Khan

Language Editors:
Carole Strum
Britanie Wilson
Kara Brunson

Production Manager:
Ammar Saadeh

Designers:
Mohammad A.Shream
Wafa'a Abu-Hilaleh

A Note from Noorart

Noorart is dedicated to providing quality Islamic educational materials for English-speaking Muslims.

What Islam Is All About was conceived of to support English-language readers with an interest in the religion and those Muslims who are new to the faith. This text presents materials only from the authentic Islamic sources: the Holy Qur'an, Sunnah, and Ahadith. Accurate information is paramount in fulfilling our mission to share the true message of Islam. Consequently, Noorart collaborated closely with religious scholars to authenticate all Islamic information in this text. While legitimate differences of opinion do exist across the spectrum of Islam, the material presented in this text coincides with the majority opinion of religious scholars. Noorart, however, trusts that those seeking religious knowledge are capable of exploring the differences of opinion conveyed in this book. By following this approach, we pray that respect and tolerance for differences in opinions and schools of thought will be fostered among our readers.

In circulation since 1997, What Islam Is All About has undergone significant revisions targeting the information needs of today's readers. To that end, this new edition features:

- Streamlined layout and design elements
- Accessible and clear language style
- Rich, full color, images
- Comprehensive coverage of the basic tenets of Islam
- Concise account of Islamic history
- Full Arabic text and translation of selections from Qur'an, Hadith and dua'
- Transliteration and translation of dua', Islamic phrases and words

We welcome your comments at textbookfeedback@noorart.com to guide us in continued textbook development.

Author's Foreword

Welcome to the World of Islam! The book you hold in your hands is your guidepost and companion in exploration of this important and often misunderstood religion. It seeks to present the worldview and practices of Islam in a straightforward and logical manner. In today's world people are seeking knowledge about all things spiritual. **What Islam is All About** aims to fill that need.

In our rapidly changing lives, we don't find the time to educate ourselves in things that truly matter—faith, spirituality and teachings—that give us purpose to carry on. Often too late we discover that a life spent in endless pursuit of material objects and comforts masks an inner hunger for something more—for some meaning that can give life purpose, and ultimately, satisfaction.

The way of life known as **Islam** is a path and a lifestyle that seeks to instill this sense of satisfaction in every aspect of our lives, holding out the assurance of justice here on earth and the promise of something even better beyond this short existence—the forgiveness and acceptance of the Supreme Power of the Universe.

There are many who claim to be spokespersons for this great religion, but as is often the case, many use religion as a mere window dressing to hide motives that may be political or self serving. Sadly, the teachings of any religion or secular ideology can be warped or misinterpreted in the service of something with which it has no real relation.

So how does a one strip away the layers of complexity and disguise that are wrapped around the pillars of light, the core of any true religion? Some pursue a self-study of a variety of sources. Others prefer to listen to the words of orators, and yet others prefer to engage in those activities that put the teachings into practice.

I would recommend a combination of all three approaches coupled with an open and curious mind. Do not feel threatened by ideas that challenge what you think you may know. Only in allowing ourselves to be flexible and to be open to the possibility of accepting new and better ideas, can we truly grow. This revolution in personal growth is one of the core principles of the Islamic program for the heart and the mind. Our Creator gave us a mind to think, to understand, to doubt, to question, to explore and to adopt what is ever closer to His truth. When our ideas are challenged, Allah, (literally The God) is opening the door for growth.

Indeed, we are the creatures who agreed to accept the burden of consciousness and self-awareness. We have chosen to be the ones granted the ability to reason and choose the course of our actions. God did not force us to be self-aware. Indeed, He offered this blessing and burden to the rest of creation first. But there were no takers. This is a mighty responsibility which rests upon our shoulders. "We did indeed offer the Trust to the Heavens and the Earth and the mountains, but they refused to undertake it, being afraid thereof; but man undertook it - He was indeed unjust and foolish." Al-Ahzab 33: 72

Our task in this life is clear: surrender our wills to the perfect will of Allah, and then do what is morally right in relating to our fellow living beings. In order to facilitate our understanding and acceptance of this way of life, Allah conferred His guidance on humans from time to time, and at times revealed messages to the hearts of people to be recited then written down. Only one of these messages, the Holy Qur'an, has been preserved in its original form.

Islam is the last installment of divine, codified guidance by its Creator to humanity. There will be no new prophets or legitimate faiths to follow. The Blessed Prophet Muhammad assured us of that. Consequently, any group that has arisen in the world since then claiming to have the truth, is, in fact, not only deceived but deceivers. Allah has said, "This day have I perfected your way of life for you and completed My favor upon you. I have chosen Islam as your way of life." (5:3)

We hope and pray for the mercy and reward of our Lord. May He grant us the best in this short life. May He grant us the best in the Next Life, not according to what we deserve—a mere trifling—but according to His mercy and compassion. May your exploration be fruitful and may you arise every morning with a desire to draw ever nearer to the ultimate meaning and purpose of your life.

'Oh Allah, increase me in knowledge.' Ameen.

Yahiya Emerick

Tips for Readers

1. The most useful translations used in this book are ranked as follows:

1. *The Noble Qur'an* by Mufti Taqi Usmani
2. *The Meaning of the Holy Qur'an in Today's English* by Yahiya Emerick
3. *The Noble Qur'an* by Dr. Muhsin Khan & Taqi-Ud-Din Hilali
4. *The Noble Qur'an* by Abdalhaqq and Aisha Bewley
5. *The Holy Qur'an* by 'Abdallah Yusuf 'Ali

2. Selections from the Qur'an and hadith have been presented in a specific font and style for easy recognition:

- **Qur'an:**

Truly the way of life that Allah accepts is Islam. Surat Al 'Imran (The Family of 'Imran) 3:19

﴿إِنَّ ٱلدِّينَ عِندَ ٱللَّهِ ٱلْإِسْلَٰمُ﴾ سُورَةُ آلِ عِمْرَان 19:3

- **Hadith:**

Abu Hurayrah ﵁ narrated that the Blessed Prophet ﷺ said, "Every child is born following their Fitrah (i.e. they are a natural Muslim). It is the parents who make them a Jew, Christian or Zoroastrian (ancient Persian religion)." (Al Bukhari & Muslim)

عَنِ أَبِي هُرَيْرَةَ ﵁، أَنَّ رَسُولَ اللهِ ﷺ: «كُلُّ مَوْلُودٍ يُولَدُ عَلَى الْفِطْرَةِ، فَأَبَوَاهُ يُهَوِّدَانِهِ أَوْ يُنَصِّرَانِهِ أَوْ يُمَجِّسَانِهِ». رَوَاهُ الْبُخَارِيُّ وَمُسْلِمٌ

3. Glorifications used in this book:

- (Arabic: ﷿ عَزَّ وَجَلَّ 'azza wa jal). "Glorified and Sublime be He." This phrase usually appears after the name of Allah in Islamic texts. Saying this phrase is seen as an act of reverence and devotion towards Allah among Muslims. It can also be translated in English as: "Mighty and Majestic be He" or "May His Majesty be Exalted."
- (Arabic: ﷺ صَلَّى اللهُ عَلَيْهِ وَسَلَّمَ salla Allahu 'alay-he wa-sallam). "Peace and blessings of Allah be upon him." This expression follows specifically after uttering the name of Prophet Muhammad, although the phrase "May Allah bless him and grant him peace" may also be used.
- (Arabic: ﵇ عَلَيْهِ السَّلام, 'alayhi as-salam). "Peace be upon him." Muslims say this phrase after uttering or hearing the name of any of the prophets.
- (Arabic: ﵁ رَضِيَ اللهُ عَنْهُ Radhiallahu 'anhu). "May Allah be pleased with him." This phrase is usually uttered after a Companion's name. There are grammatical variations used after the names of female Companions or when more than one person is mentioned at the same time. For females, it is (Arabic: ﵂ رَضِيَ اللهُ عَنْهَا Radhiallahu 'anha) and for more than one person, it is (Arabic: ﵄ رَضِيَ اللهُ عَنْهُمْ Radhiallahu 'anhum).

Contents

Chapter 5: Islamic Beliefs: Part One

Chapter 6: Islamic Beliefs: Part Two

Chapter 7: Prayer

Chapter 8: Other Practices and Duties

Chapter 9: Tales of Ancient Days

Chapter 10: Bani Isra'il

Chapter 11: The Legacy of Prophet 'Isa

Chapter 12: The Final Prophet

Chapter 17: Fiqh and Shari'ah

Chapter 18: Islam in Society

Reference

Chapter 1
Qur'anic Research Skills

What Is Islam?

Islam is the way of life that is followed by approximately one billion people around the world. Muslims, or people who follow the Islamic way of life, comprise the majority in over 50 countries. In addition, the global Muslim population is growing rapidly every year. In the United States, for example, Islam is considered the fastest growing religion in the country.

The word Islam إسلام comes from the Arabic word that means peace and surrender. The full religious definition implies that when you submit your life to God, you can find peace in your soul. Living Islam helps you learn to be patient when you face tests and trials in your life. The word Muslim مُسْلِم means a person who submits to God by following the guidance of the Qur'an and the Sunnah of Prophet Muhammad ﷺ, thereby finding inner peace.

Many of the spiritual traditions in the world are merely philosophies. Islam, however, is a complete way of life that fulfills physical, spiritual, emotional and psychological needs of mankind. The goal in Islam is more than praying five times a day. Islam helps people live in harmony with nature and with the society around them. Additionally, Islam provides a blueprint and a set of principles for how to turn societies into God-oriented communities; this sets Islam apart from all other faith traditions.

The basis of Islam is the belief in the Creator, or God, known as Allah الله in the Arabic language. The name Allah literally means "the God." Allah is not a God distinct from that of the Judeo-Christian tradition. Arabic-speaking Christians also use the name Allah when they refer to God. In fact, the name Allah is directly related to the ancient Hebrew term for God, Eloh. Both languages (Arabic and Hebrew) are Semitic and spring from the same ancient roots. Muslims who speak English will use both terms, God and Allah, when they talk about their faith, but most prefer to use the name Allah.

What Is Our Purpose?

Untold years ago, Allah caused the Universe to come into existence. He created natural laws and ordered every particle to move in accordance with His will. Therefore, the actions of atoms and other matter were determined by Allah rather than by some random occurrence.

On some planets, Allah allowed living organisms to develop. For example, Earth supports a highly complex ecosystem of plants and animals. After untold years later, Allah created human beings. They would be unlike any other creatures before them, as they were given the ability to choose their actions.

Everything Allah created functions according to its instincts and natural tendencies. Humans, however, are allowed to make their own decisions about how to live their lives. With this privilege, however, came great responsibility. Allah created a Universe free of disorder and chaos. As human societies developed, people could choose whether to use their sophisticated thinking skills for good or to misuse their intelligence and abilities by creating chaos and disorder all around them.

The way of life that Allah wants humans to choose is the one in which we use our intellect and emotions in the pursuit of the higher truth of Allah's Universe. There must be no giving in to anger, hatred, violence and greed. All of these emotions are to be controlled, lest we become similar to or worse than the animals.

And Allah created the heavens and earth in truth and so that every soul may be recompensed for what it has earned, and they will not be wronged. Surat Al Jatheyah (The Crouching) 45: 22

﴿وَخَلَقَ ٱللَّهُ ٱلسَّمَٰوَٰتِ وَٱلۡأَرۡضَ بِٱلۡحَقِّ وَلِتُجۡزَىٰ كُلُّ نَفۡسٍۭ بِمَا كَسَبَتۡ وَهُمۡ لَا يُظۡلَمُونَ﴾ سُورَةُ الجاثِيَة 45:22

To aid us in this quest, Allah chose righteous men, or prophets, and communicated messages to them. They were like lighthouses in a storm, calling people to salvation in a troubled world. Sometimes Allah would send a prophet a message that He intended to survive for later generations to understand and practice. Yet all too often, people allowed themselves to be tempted by their desires, resulting in war, hatred and chaos on Earth.

Those, however, who follow Allah's guidance are promised a reward in the next life. Those who deny this truth will receive a punishment for turning their backs on God's message. They reject not only Allah's prophets but also human nature, which prompts them to be good.

They prefer to cover themselves in shame and evil. When the Universe comes to an end, and Allah collapses all matter back into its origins, all humans will be assembled together on the Day of Judgment to be judged for their actions. Of course, human beings are not perfect, and they never will be; Allah knows what He created. So for those who have sincerity and faith, Allah promises to forgive their sins and encompass them in His Mercy.

Allah made us, and He knows best how we can be good to others and protected from our inner weaknesses. Those people who recognize this truth and wish only to serve Allah are the ones who try their best to live their lives in accordance with the laws He revealed.

Previous prophets were sent to people throughout the world at different points in history. They include Ibrahim (Abraham), Musa (Moses), Salih and 'Isa (Jesus), may Allah be pleased with them all, to name a few. The last message that Allah sent to humanity was given to Muhammad ﷺ, who was born in Arabia in the year 570 CE. (40:78)

This final message is in the form of the Qur'an قُرآن. It is a book that elevates a person's mind and spirit to a higher level — a stage from which they can escape the hold of their baser instincts to stand up for what is right and to forbid what is wrong. (17: 9) The person whose goal in life is serving his Creator will come to understand that the Islamic way is also the natural way.

How Do I Study Islam?

To study Islam, one must begin with the Qur'an and refer to it at every stage. Only then can a true understanding of Islam and our ultimate destiny be achieved. Today, many Muslims have become disconnected from the message of the Qur'an and have not applied its lessons as they should. One reason is a weakened commitment to faith due to materialism. This has transformed many societies around the world into wasteful consumer cultures.

Within only the past few hundred years, the Muslim civilization declined from the most advanced in the world to being among the least advanced. It is encouraging to know that this trend can be reversed. In fact, Allah has promised in the Qur'an that those who uphold its message will be successful, both in this world and in the next.

Islam is the way of life that Allah established from the very beginning of time. If you examine the teachings of Islam, you realize that it is the same way of life that has been taught by all the prophets and righteous persons throughout history. This lifestyle has been given various names and has included different rituals according to the customs of the people to whom it was revealed. However, the core teachings of God's true prophets were always the same: submit to the universal teachings of God and do what is approved as right and good.

If we want to improve the condition of Muslims, and even those who are not yet Muslim, then we must reconnect with the message of the Qur'an. Of all of the previous messages, only the Qur'an has survived to this day, unchanged as a guide for people as they journey through this brief stage of life. Allah said, *We (Allah) have made this Qur'an easy to remember. Is there anyone who would receive a reminder? Surat Al Qamar (The Moon) 54: 40*

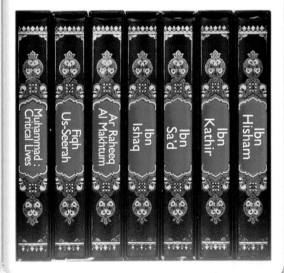

History books about the Blessed Prophet ﷺ are called books of seerah. Below are the names of the most important history books about the Blessed Prophet ﷺ.

﴿وَلَقَدْ يَسَّرْنَا ٱلْقُرْءَانَ لِلذِّكْرِ فَهَلْ مِن مُّدَّكِرٍ﴾ سُورَةُ الْقَمَر 40:54

The Qur'an is the source of guidance. The life of the prophet who bore it, Muhammad ﷺ, is our example of how to put it into practice. The example of Prophet Muhammad ﷺ, including everything about how he lived his life, is referred to as the **Sunnah** سُنَّة. This book uses both the Qur'an and the Sunnah as the primary sources for understanding Islam. If you learn how to understand the Qur'an and Sunnah, and live by what they mean, you can become a living example of the Qur'an.

Vocabulary of the Qur'an

The Qur'an has special vocabulary related to it. When we talk about the Qur'an, or parts of it, we use these words because they have special meanings. Look at the list below and learn the vocabulary and when to use it.

Ayat: آيَـة
One verse from the Qur'an

Ayaat: آيـات
More than one ayah

Surah: سُورَة
One chapter of the Qur'an

Suwar: سُور
More than one
chapter of the Qur'an

Juz': جُزْء
One part of the Qur'an out of thirty
equal parts

Kitaab: كِتاب
A book

Rasul: رَسُول
Messenger of Allah

Mus-haf: مُصحَف
The written Arabic text of the
Qur'an

Qari': قارِئ
A special reciter of the Qur'an

Hafith: حافِظ
Someone who memorized the
whole Qur'an by heart

Tarjamah: تَرْجَمَة
Translation in a different language

How Do I Find That Ayah?

How would you find an ayah, or verse, about a certain subject in the Qur'an? Flipping through the pages of the entire book would be time-consuming. It would be more efficient to look at the table of contents found at the front of the Qur'an or the index found at the back.

The Qur'an is comprised of suwar and ayaat. So, for example, 4:64 would indicate the fourth chapter or Surah An-Nisa' (The Women), verse or ayah 64.

The table of contents lists the suwar or chapters that comprise the Qur'an. Alternatively, the index lists topics alphabetically and the specific ayaat that mention them. The most complete indexes of English meaning are found in the editions by:

The Meaning of the Holy Qur'an by 'Abdallah Yusuf 'Ali
The Noble Qur'an by Abdalhaqq and Aisha Bewley
The Meaning of the Qur'an by Abul 'Ala Maududi
The Message of the Qur'an by Muhammad Asad
The Gracious Qur'an (the Parallel Edition: English and Arabic side-by-side) by Ahmad Zaki Hammad
The Glorious Qur'an by Adbul Majid Daryabadi
Interpretation of the Meaning of the Noble Qur'an by Darrussalam
The Qur'an by Oxford University Press

Today, online sites abound with easy search engines that use English meanings or even transliterated Arabic words to search with. Examples are: www.searchtruth.com, www.islamicity.com, www.quranexplorer.com and corpus.quran.com.

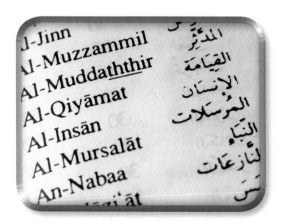

1730   INDEX

Charity (cont'd.)
    objects of, 2:273; 9:60;
    meaning of, n. 5001 to 61:19. Children, 2:233; 42:49-50.
Christ, see Jesus. Christians, 2:138-140; 5:14;
    who became Muslims, n. 3385 to 28:53; n. 3476 to 29:47;
    nearest in love to Islam, 5:82-85.
Chronology of Early Years of Islam, App. IX, pp. 1031-1032.
Cities overthrown, 69:9, n. 5644.
Cleanliness, 4:43; 5:6.
Commentaries, on the Qur'an, pp. ix-xii.
Commerce that will never fail, 35:29.
Confederates, Intro. S. 33, pp. 1053-1054; 33:9-20, 22-27.
Consultation, mutual, 42:38, nn. 4578-4579.
Courtesy, 4:86.
Covetousness, 3:180; 4:32; 57:24.

Why Was the Arabic Language Chosen for Revelation?

If a person doesn't know the Arabic language, or knows only a little, then a translation of the meaning of the Qur'an is necessary to understand what Allahﷻ is saying to us. "Why Arabic?" you might ask. An obvious reason that the Qur'an is in the Arabic language is that Allahﷻ revealed it to an Arab prophet and to an Arabic-speaking people.

We have sent it down, as an Arabic Qur'an, so that you may understand. Surat Yusuf 12: 2

﴿إِنَّا أَنزَلْنَٰهُ قُرْءَٰنًا عَرَبِيًّا لَّعَلَّكُمْ تَعْقِلُونَ﴾ سُورَةُ يُوسُفَ 2:12

Arabic was also the most advanced and comprehensive language of its time when the Qur'an was revealed. It remains today a very specific and comprehensive language. Due to the breadth and depth of the Arabic language, the chapters and verses offer great drama, poetic and lyrical beauty, designed to catch and hold the readers' hearts and minds.

The mission of Prophet Muhammad ﷺ led many Arabs to accept Islam. Due to their strategic location in the Middle East (the crossroads of the world), they were in a position to spread the message of Islam to millions of Romans, Asians, East Indians, Africans and others who then accepted the message of Islam.

The Arabs carried Islam with them in their expansion beyond Arabia. Although both the mighty Persians and the Byzantine Romans repeatedly attacked the new Islamic State, the Muslims were able to successfully drive back the armies of both empires.

Today not everyone has access to a teacher of Arabic, so translations of the Qur'an are often used. Even though translations are helpful for understanding the meaning of the Qur'an, it must be emphasized that a translation of the Qur'an can never fully represent the original Arabic text. Translations are only a learning tool, as there is no perfect translation from one language to another.

Arabic Is a Living Language

Sanskrit, ancient Greek, Aramaic and Hebrew are no longer in use today as when they were spoken and written long ago. Yet, the Arabic of the Qur'an continues to live on through continued study and use by millions in their daily lives. The form of Arabic still spoken today includes **Fus-ha** فُصْحَى, the pure Arabic of the Qur'an, as well as informal dialects that have developed over time. Thus, Islam is quite distinguished from other religions in that both the original book, the Qur'an, and the original language, Arabic, are still widely used today.

The complete Qur'an was written down in the lifetime of Prophet Muhammad ﷺ. It was personally arranged by him under the instruction of Angel Jibreel﷿, and Muslims have always memorized it in the same order. 'Uthman﷐ reported that whenever a new verse was revealed, the Prophet ﷺ would call a scribe who was appointed to write down the revealed words of the Qur'an. The scribe would write what was revealed to the Prophet on leather, paper or any other material that could be used to record the words of the Holy Qur'an. Then the Blessed Prophet ﷺ would instruct the scribe to put this ayah or verse in the correct surah.

Additionally, each year during the month of Ramadan, the Prophet ﷺ would recite the entire Qur'an from beginning to end with Angel Jibreel﷿. Its proper order was therefore no mystery.

Many of the **Sahaba** صَحَابَة **Companions of Prophet Muhammad** ﷺ, not only memorized it completely, they also wrote it down and even added **Tafseer** تَفْسِير **Commentary**. Thus, scholarship in Islam existed from the very beginning. When the Prophet ﷺ passed away, the whole Qur'an had already been written down on pieces of paper and leather. However, it was not yet gathered in book form.

Compare these two translations of the same chapter in the Qur'an:

- **'Abdallah Yusuf 'Ali translation:** To you have We granted the Fount (of Abundance). Therefore to your Lord turn in Prayer and Sacrifice. For he who hates you, he will be cut off (from future Hope). 108: 1-3
- **Pickthall translation:** Lo! We have given thee Abundance; So pray unto thy Lord and sacrifice. Lo! It is thy insulter (and not thou) who is without posterity. 108: 1-3

List of Translated Editions of the Qur'an

- Marmaduke Pickthall, 1930, *The Meaning of the Glorious Qur'an*
- 'Abdallah Yusuf 'Ali, 1934, *The Meaning of the Holy Qur'an*
- Muhammad Asad, 1980, *The Message of The Qur'an*
- Zafar Ishaq Ansari, 1988, *Towards Understanding the Qur'an.*
- T. B. Irving, 1991, *Noble Qur'an: Arabic Text & English Translation*
- AbdalHaqq & Aisha B., 1999, *The Noble Qur'an: A New Rendering of its Meaning in English*
- Dr. Muhammad Muhsin Khan and Dr. M. Taqi-ud-Din Al-Hilali, 1999, *The Noble Qur'an.*
- Justice Mufti Taqi Usmani, 2008, *Translation of Qur'an*

The Only Unchanged Revelation

Allah promised to protect and preserve His Book, and all Muslims seek to learn it in its original language to understand it directly. **Al hamdulillah الحَمْدُلِله Praise be to Allah**, there are millions of Arabic copies of the Qur'an all over the world, and all of them have precisely the same text. No other religious tradition can make this claim.

Indeed, it is We who sent down the Qur'an and indeed, We will be its guardian. Surat Al Hijr (The Rocky Tract) 15:9

﴿ إِنَّا نَحْنُ نَزَّلْنَا ٱلذِّكْرَ وَ إِنَّا لَهُ لَحَٰفِظُونَ ﴾ سُورَةُ الحِجْرِ 9:15

Other religious traditions have incomplete compilations of their holy books, many of which have been altered in successive translations. The original books were lost a long time ago. Since then, many additions, changes and deletions have occurred. For example, there are numerous versions of the Holy Bible, with significant differences among them. Thanks to the dedication of early Muslims, the Holy Qur'an was preserved in its original form, ensuring that such variations do not occur.

How Do I Read Other Languages?

For non-Arabic speakers it may be difficult to pronounce some of the Arabic letters while learning a **Surah سُورَة Chapter** from the Qur'an. Maybe the student does not know how to read Arabic and does not yet know how to join the letters together. A student perhaps has forgotten how a letter sounds. Until we can learn to read the Arabic language correctly and with ease, this problem can be solved with a useful tool called transliteration.

Transliteration means taking a word written in one alphabet and writing it in another. For example, the word for house in Arabic is بَيْت. If you are unable to pronounce it written in the Arabic characters, you can use transliteration. The three letters used in Arabic are ت , ب , ي , and it is pronounced **bayt**. So even if you don't read Arabic well yet, you can use the transliteration of words to help you pronounce just about anything.

> Bismi Allahi Ar-Rahmani Ar-Rahim.
> Qul Huwa Al-Lahu Ahad.
> Allahu As-samad.
> Lam Yalid Wa Lam Yulad.
> Walam Yakun Lahu Kufuan Ahad.

Surat Al Ikhlaas (The Sincerity) 112: 1-4 in Transliteration

بِسْمِ ٱللَّهِ ٱلرَّحْمَٰنِ ٱلرَّحِيمِ
﴿ قُلْ هُوَ ٱللَّهُ أَحَدٌ ﴾ ﴿ ٱللَّهُ ٱلصَّمَدُ ﴾
﴿ لَمْ يَلِدْ وَلَمْ يُولَدْ ﴾ ﴿ وَلَمْ يَكُن لَّهُ كُفُوًا أَحَدٌ ﴾
سُورَةُ الإِخلاص 1:112- 4

Many volumes of the Qur'an offer the transliteration of the suwar so that those unfamiliar with the Arabic language can learn them easily. In this way, a Muslim can then offer his daily prayers in Arabic. These volumes also include the transliteration of **Dua'** دُعاء, a request we make of Allah. There are many dua' within the Qur'an and also those that Prophet Muhammad ﷺ advised us to recite for specific needs and occasions.

View the transliteration of *Surat Al Ikhlaas (The Sincerity, chapter 112)* and compare it to the Arabic text. Try pronouncing the Arabic words using the English transliteration provided. Transliterated copies of the Qur'an contain both the Arabic text and the transliteration, side-by-side. These books often include the English meaning as well.

Our goal, however, must always be to learn to read and pronounce the Arabic language of the Qur'an to the best of our ability. As beginners, we can rely for a short time on transliteration to help us make the transition. There are many hadith that cite the rewards for those who even just try to read the original text.

What Is a Roman Transliteration?

The technical term for a transliteration into English is 'Roman transliteration.' This is a reference to the use of the Latin alphabet used by the Romans, which forms the basis of the English language.*

There are many rules for transliteration between languages. For example, the sounds in the Chinese language for 'j' are often transliterated as 'zh' in English because the Chinese 'j' also has some of the 'zh' sound in it. Arabic, too, must be transliterated in a certain way because its sounds are slightly different from English sounds. For example, ق, ض, غ and ح are not found in English. You may see these letters transliterated as 'q,' 'dh,' 'gh' and 'kha,' respectively.

Surat Al Bayyinah (The Clear Proof) - Verse/Ayah 4

وَمَا تَفَرَّقَ ٱلَّذِينَ أُوتُوا۟ ٱلْكِتَٰبَ إِلَّا مِنۢ بَعْدِ مَا جَآءَتْهُمُ ٱلْبَيِّنَةُ ﴿٤﴾

4- Nor did those who were given the Scripture become divided until after there had come to them clear evidence.

4- Wama tafarraqa allatheena ootooalkitaba illa min baAAdi ma jaat-humualbayyina

---

The Qur'an: Treat It with Respect

Now proof has come to you from your Lord. If anyone cares to see, it will be for (the good) of his own soul. If anyone would be blind, it will be for (the bad) of his own soul. Surat Al An'aam (The Cattle) 6:104

﴿قَدْ جَآءَكُم بَصَآئِرُ مِن رَّبِّكُمْ فَمَنْ أَبْصَرَ فَلِنَفْسِهِۦ وَمَنْ عَمِيَ فَعَلَيْهَا﴾ سُورَةُ الأنعام 6:104

The proof Allah speaks about is the Qur'an and all the miraculous statements within it. Allah informs us that we can either open our eyes to the truth or be blind to it.

The Qur'an is not like any other book. Therefore to benefit from the Qur'an, it must be approached with a certain reverence and respect, and be treated and used in a certain manner. The Qur'an is an instruction manual from Allah on how to live the best life and to prepare our souls for the life to come.

To proceed, then, we must become aware of the proper manners for using the Qur'an. It's not hard to learn, and if you feel in your heart that the Qur'an is a special book, then you will naturally treat it with respect.

Manners When Reading the Qur'an

Internal

1. You should recognize that you are holding the words of Allah in your hands and proceed with a humble heart. (7:204)
2. Whenever a description of Judgment Day or Hellfire is mentioned, you should recognize the importance of that real event. (16:107)
3. You should pay attention to understanding the meaning of the text since Allah encourages us to ponder the meaning of the Qur'an. (47:24)
4. After reading the Qur'an, you should reflect on the lessons learned. It is reported that the Blessed Prophet once remarked that a person's reward is increased if they understand the meaning of what they are doing.

External

1. If you are in a state of major impurity, then you must take a purifying bath before reading the Qur'an. (56:79)
2. Muslims are permitted to read and teach the Qur'an without ablution, **wudu'**, although it is preferred to be in the state of ablution. When one is teaching and reading from the Mus-haf, which is the physical, actual Qur'an in book form, then wudu' is compulsory.
3. You are recommended to face the Qiblah, the direction of Ka'ba in Makkah, when reading.
4. You should not eat or drink while reading the Qur'an.
5. If the Arabic text is recited in **Tilawah** تِلاوَة, or read out loud, you should try to read along as correctly as you can. Don't be afraid to read it, even if you can't yet recite it well. The Blessed Prophet said the person who recites the Qur'an with difficulty receives twice the reward of a person who says it without difficulty, because of the greater effort.
6. Before reciting, you should say, **A'udhu billahi min ash-shaytaan ar-rajeem** أَعُوذُ بِاللهِ مِنَ الشَّيْطَانِ الرَّجِيم. This means "I seek Allah's protection from the rejected Satan."
7. After seeking protection from Shaytan, you are highly recommended to recite **Bismi Allahi Ar-Rahmani Ar-Rahim** بِسْمِ اللهِ الرَّحْمَنِ الرَّحِيم "In the Name of Allah, The Most Gracious, The Most Merciful" except at the beginning of Surat At-Tawbah (The Repentance), chapter 9.
8. After the reading is finished, you can say, **Sadaqa Allaahu Al 'atheem** صَدَقَ اللهُ العَظِيُم. This means, "Allah the Exalted, has spoken the truth."
9. The best time to read the Qur'an is after the early morning prayer. (17:78)
10. Keep the Qur'an in a respectful place, but do not leave it merely as a decoration in your home that will go unused.

Selected Sayings
Regarding the Qur'an

1. 'Umar bin Al Khattab reported that the Messenger of Allah said, "Allah will raise some people up with this book (those who follow it) and bring down others (those who ignore it)." (Muslim)

قَالَ عُمَرَ بْنَ الْخَطَّابِ: أَمَا إِنَّ نَبِيَّكُمْ ، قَدْ قَالَ: «إِنَّ اللهَ يَرْفَعُ بِهَذَا الْكِتَابِ أَقْوَامًا وَ يَضَعُ بِهِ آخَرِينَ». رَوَاهُ مُسْلِمٌ

2. Abu Musa reported that the Messenger of Allah said, "The example of the believer who reads the Qur'an is like that of a citrus fruit whose smell is nice and taste is good. The example of the believer who does not read the Qur'an is like that of a fresh date which has no scent but whose taste is still sweet. The example of the hypocrite who does not read the Qur'an is like that of a basil leaf which has no smell and whose taste is bitter. The example of the hypocrite who reads the Qur'an is like that of a fragrant flower which has a nice smell but whose taste is terrible." (Al Bukhari & Muslim)

عَنْ أَبِي مُوسَى الْأَشْعَرِيِّ قَالَ: قَالَ رَسُولُ الله : «مَثَلُ الْمُؤْمِنِ الَّذِي يَقْرَأُ الْقُرْآنَ كَمَثَلِ الأُتْرُجَّةِ؛ رِيحُهَا طَيِّبٌ وَ طَعْمُهَا طَيِّبٌ, وَ مَثَلُ الْمُؤْمِنِ الَّذِي لَا يَقْرَأُ الْقُرْآنَ؛ كَمَثَلِ التَّمْرَةِ لَا رِيحَ لَهَا وَ طَعْمُهَا حُلْوٌ, وَ مَثَلُ الْمُنَافِقِ الَّذِي يَقْرَأُ الْقُرْآنَ مَثَلُ الرَّيْحَانَةِ؛ رِيحُهَا طَيِّبٌ وَ طَعْمُهَا مُرٌّ, وَ مَثَلُ الْمُنَافِقِ الَّذِي لَا يَقْرَأُ الْقُرْآنَ كَمَثَلِ الْحَنْظَلَةِ لَيْسَ لَهَا رِيحٌ وَ طَعْمُهَا مُرٌّ». رَوَاهُ الْبُخَارِيُّ وَمُسْلِمٌ

3. 'Aishah reported that the Messenger of Allah said, "A person who has expert knowledge of the Qur'an will be with the honorable writers (angels), and the one who reads the Qur'an and struggles with it in difficulty will get twice the reward." (Al Bukhari & Muslim)

عَنْ عَائِشَةَ، قَالَتْ: قَالَ رَسُولُ الله : «الْمَاهِرُ بِالْقُرْآنِ مَعَ السَّفَرَةِ الْكِرَامِ الْبَرَرَةِ، وَ الَّذِي يَقْرَأُ الْقُرْآنَ وَ يَتَتَعْتَعُ فِيهِ وَ هُوَ عَلَيْهِ شَاقٌّ لَهُ أَجْرَانِ». رَوَاهُ الْبُخَارِيُّ وَمُسْلِمٌ

4. The Messenger of Allah once said, "There is no envy (allowed in Islam) except for two cases: a person to whom Allah has given knowledge of the Qur'an and who lives by it through the night and day and a person to whom Allah has given wealth and who spends from it (in the Cause of Allah) through the night and day." (Al Bukhari & Muslim)

عَنِ النَّبِيِّ ، قال: «لَا حَسَدَ إِلَّا فِي اثْنَتَيْنِ: رَجُلٌ أَتَاهُ اللهُ الْكِتَابَ فَهُوَ يَقُومُ بِهِ آنَاءَ اللَّيْلِ وَ آنَاءَ النَّهَارِ، وَ رَجُلٌ أَتَاهُ اللهُ مَالًا فَهُوَ يَتَصَدَّقُ بِهِ آنَاءَ اللَّيْلِ وَ آنَاءَ النَّهَارِ». رَوَاهُ الْبُخَارِيُّ وَمُسْلِمٌ

The Blessed Prophet once remarked, "Whoever has nothing of the Qur'an in their heart is like a ruined house." (At-Tirmidhi)

قَالَ رَسُولُ الله : «إِنَّ الَّذِي لَيْسَ فِي جَوْفِهِ شَيْءٌ مِنَ الْقُرْآنِ كَالْبَيْتِ الْخَرِبِ». رَوَاهُ التِّرْمَذِيُّ

'Uthman narrated that the Prophet said, "The best among you (Muslims) are those who learn the Qur'an and teach it." (Al Bukhari)

عَنْ عُثْمَانَ، عَنِ النَّبِيِّ قَالَ: «خَيْرُكُمْ مَنْ تَعَلَّمَ الْقُرْآنَ وَ عَلَّمَهُ». رَوَاهُ الْبُخَارِيُّ

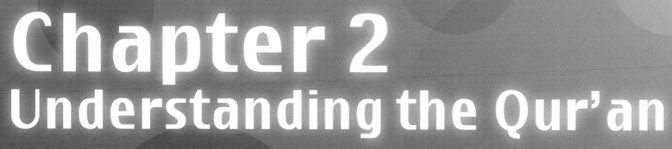

Chapter 2
Understanding the Qur'an

Who Received the Revelation of the Qur'an?

The Holy Qur'an is Allah's final message to this world. It was revealed between the years 610 CE and 632 CE to a person who lived in Arabia. The one who received this Book of Light was Muhammad ﷺ, the son of 'Abdallah and Aminah. Muhammad ﷺ was known for honesty and wisdom, a reputation that later earned him the respect of even his enemies. Allah chose Muhammad ﷺ to be His last prophet for all of humanity.

Although at times it seemed Muhammad's ﷺ mission was doomed to fail due to the overwhelming odds against him, Allah protected him and granted him the final victory. Today, Muslims love and respect Prophet Muhammad ﷺ and ask Allah to send peace upon his soul countless times every day.

Whenever we hear or read his name, we should say, either silently or aloud, **Salla Allahu 'Alay-he Wa-sallam** صَلَّى اللهُ عَلَيْهِ وَسَلَّم, **Peace and Blessings of Allah be upon him,** which will be notated throughout the book as: ﷺ.

To understand the Blessed Prophet's ﷺ mission is to understand the purpose of life for every human being. To learn about his noble and honorable example is to come to love him more than any other human being who ever lived.

One Night, Alone in the Dark…

"Iqra! Read!" commanded a voice out of nowhere.

The sudden appearance of an Angel, a creature of light, startled Muhammad ﷺ out of his deep sleep. He had come to this lonely mountain cave to think about the meaning of his life. Suddenly, he was faced with something so fantastic that he could hardly move or breathe. He was frozen in place. "I can't read," he muttered to the strange presence that seemed to encircle him.

The Angel then embraced Muhammad's ﷺ body and nearly squeezed the breath out of him, commanding him to read. Muhammad ﷺ protested again, so the Angel repeated the strange embrace a third time. He commanded once more, "Read!" Muhammad ﷺ cried out, "What should I read?"

Then, the Angel began to recite, *Read in the Name of your Lord Who created humans from a clinging (embryo). Read, for your Lord is Generous. He is the One Who taught people with the pen, taught them things they didn't know before. Surat Al 'Alaq (The Clot) 96:1-5*

﴿اقْرَأْ بِاسْمِ رَبِّكَ الَّذِي خَلَقَ﴾ ﴿خَلَقَ الْإِنْسَانَ مِنْ عَلَقٍ﴾ ﴿اقْرَأْ وَرَبُّكَ الْأَكْرَمُ﴾ ﴿الَّذِي عَلَّمَ بِالْقَلَمِ﴾ ﴿عَلَّمَ الْإِنْسَانَ مَا لَمْ يَعْلَمْ﴾ سُورَةُ الْعَلَق 96:1-5

Muhammad ﷺ rushed out of the cave, flustered and frightened. He ran back down the mountain as fast as he could. All he wanted to do was to get home, to escape this strange sensation that he didn't understand. Then, as he paused for breath, he looked up at the horizon and saw the Angel who confronted him in the cave in his actual form. Muhammad ﷺ turned around, and again the Angel was there, larger than the mountains and staring at him, saying his name was Jibreel جِبْرِيل. Overwhelmed, Muhammad ﷺ ran back to his home in Makkah without looking back.

When he burst through the front door of his house, he fell into the arms of his beloved wife, Khadijah ﷺ. As he shook with fear, she held her husband tightly and wondered frantically what was happening. "Cover me! Cover me!" he cried. So Khadijah ﷺ took him to their room and covered him with a sheet. She watched over him the whole night, sometimes holding his hands, other times wiping his moistened brow. What could have happened? What could she do? She would know soon.

Later that night, Muhammad ﷺ wondered aloud if trouble was coming for him. Khadijah ﷺ, who knew him to be a man of integrity, comforted him and explained that Allah would never let anything evil befall him. He was honest, charitable and upright. If something was to come, it surely would not be bad.

After some time, Angel Jibreel again came to Muhammad ﷺ. This time, he was more prepared for the otherworldly experience. When the Angel finished speaking, Muhammad ﷺ memorized the revelation from Allah.

You, wrapped up in sheets! Stand (in prayer) at night, but not all night, maybe half, or a little less or more. Recite the Qur'an in slow, measured tones. Soon, We (Allah) will give you a heavy Message. Truly, getting up late at night is powerful for controlling (one's soul) and the best for forming words (of prayer and praise). Surat Al Muzzammil (The Enshrouded One) 73: 1-6

﴿يَا أَيُّهَا الْمُزَّمِّلُ﴾ ﴿قُمِ اللَّيْلَ إِلَّا قَلِيلًا﴾ ﴿نِصْفَهُ أَوِ انْقُصْ مِنْهُ قَلِيلًا﴾ ﴿أَوْ زِدْ عَلَيْهِ وَرَتِّلِ الْقُرْآنَ تَرْتِيلًا﴾ ﴿إِنَّا سَنُلْقِي عَلَيْكَ قَوْلًا ثَقِيلًا﴾ ﴿إِنَّ نَاشِئَةَ اللَّيْلِ هِيَ أَشَدُّ وَطْئًا وَأَقْوَمُ قِيلًا﴾ سُورَةُ الْمُزَّمِّل 73:1-6

Muhammad ﷺ had been a simple man in a remote and dusty trading town. Now, he was about to embark on a mission which would change the face of the world forever. Little did he know what hardships and adventures lay ahead.

Surat Al Muddaththir (The Cloaked One) سُورَةُالمُدَّثِّر

In the Name of Allah, The Most Gracious, The Most Merciful

O you who covers himself (Muhammad), don't lay there, wrapped up under your blanket! Get out of bed and warn your people! Glorify your Lord and keep your clothes clean and pure and stay far away from the idols. Don't confer favor to acquire more. For your Lord's sake, keep struggling onward. A mighty horn blast will blow (when the world finally comes to its end). That Day will be a difficult one (full of fear and stress). It certainly won't be easy for the disbelievers (people who hid the truth).

Leave me alone (to deal) with the one whom I created lonely and gave him extensive wealth and sons present before (his) eyes! I even made living in the world smooth and easy for him! Yet he was greedy and wanted Me to give more and more. No way! He was stubborn about Our signs! I will soon bring a load of trouble on him! He thought and he plotted against Me so ruin to him! Oh, how he schemed! Yes! Ruin to him! Oh, how he planned! He looked around and saw all the proof in the world about God but then frowned and scowled. He turned away in arrogance and said, "This (Qur'an) is nothing more than ancient magic. This is nothing but the word of a mortal man!" We'll soon throw him into Saqar (the Hellfire)! And how can you understand what Saqar (Hellfire) really is? It doesn't let anything survive nor does it leave anything alone! It darkens and warps people's skins! Watching over it are nineteen angels.

We put angels as guards in charge of the Fire and chose their exact number only as a test for the faithless so that the recipients of earlier revelation (the Jews and Christians) can know for sure, so that the believers can increase their faith and also so that no doubts can remain with the recipients of earlier revelation and the believers. Those who have twisted hearts and are the faithless will say, "What does God mean by this number?" This is how God leaves to wander whoever He wants and how He guides whoever He wants. No one can know the forces of the Lord except Him, and this message is nothing more than a warning to all people. No way! By the moon (as it arises) and the night as it closes and by the dawn as it shines ever and ever brighter, this (Qur'an) is only one of the tremendous signs and a warning to humanity, to any one of you who chooses to press forward on the path to heaven or to follow behind and fall into ruin. Every soul will be held as collateral for its actions, all except the companions of the Right. They will rest in beautiful gardens, asking (each other how anyone could have refused to enter Paradise. Then they will be allowed to ask) the sinners far below them, "What led you to Hell?" The sinners will answer, "We weren't the kind of people who prayed or fed the poor. Instead, we used to gossip with useless people and we denied the Day of Judgement all the way up until the Promised Day came upon us."

(On that Day), no one's words will help them get out of trouble. So what's the matter with them that they turn away from being reminded, as if they were scared donkeys running from a lion? To be sure, every one of them wants to be given unrolled scrolls of revelation tailored just for them! But no way! They aren't afraid of the next life. But this is a reminder nonetheless! Anyone who wants to be reminded will remember it! But no one will remember it except as God wills. He is the Lord of Goodness and the Lord of Forgiveness.

Surat Al Muddaththir (The Cloaked One) 74:1-56

The Qur'an Is Protected

Allah has said in the Qur'an that He is the One Who will protect His Book. No mortals will ever be allowed to lose or change this last message as previous messages were lost or changed.

Indeed, Allah has kept His promise. The Qur'an that we read today contains the same words and the same letters that were revealed directly to Prophet Muhammad over 1400 years ago. The Qur'an is again unique in this regard compared to all other religions.

Evidence that other religious books have been changed can be seen in the numerous variations of their texts. For example, the Protestant Bible contains a total of 66 books, while the Catholic Bible has 73 books. Some versions of the Bible contain chapters and verses that are not included in other versions. Other religions, including Buddhism and Hinduism, have sacred books whose authors are unknown. Only the Qur'an has survived through the centuries unchanged as even today, it is still read the original language.

Leaf from a 14th–15th century Qur'an manuscript (Iraq or Iran).

Who Recorded the Words of the Qur'an?

As the Blessed Prophet Muhammad received the revelations from Allah, he memorized the ayaat and then taught them to other people. In this way, the Qur'an was safeguarded because so many people immediately learned and discussed its message.

Additionally, the Prophet received help from scribes, who were trained to write. Just as the Blessed Prophet himself was receiving and speaking the revelation, these scribes would record the words on paper, leather or whatever else was available to write on.

An early source of Islamic history states that at one time, there was a total of 24 different scribes. The most important of these was Zayd bin Thabit, who also memorized the entire Qur'an.

We know the Qur'an was written down in the lifetime of the Blessed Prophet and personally arranged by him under the instruction of Angel Jibreel. Many copies of the text were used for studying and teaching before and after **Al Hijrah الهِجْرَة Migration from Makkah to Al Madinah.**

The Danger of Losing the Qur'an

Abu Bakr was the first **Khalifa خَلِيفَة Leader of the Muslim nation**. During his rule, a rebellion arose among some distant Arab tribes who wanted to leave the Islamic community and alter Islam to suit their needs. The Muslim leadership knew that this amounted to treason, so they organized armies to stop the sedition. During one battle with the rebels, at a place called Yamamah, nearly 70 of those who had memorized the Qur'an were killed.

'Umar worried that if more of those who memorized the Qur'an were killed or died, then the Qur'an might be lost. He convinced Abu Bakr that the Qur'an should be gathered in book form to preserve it permanently. Zayd bin Thabit was responsible for overseeing this task. He was the Prophet's chief scribe and was himself a **Hafith (Hafiz) حافظ, One who has Memorized the Entire Qur'an.** He arranged the text of the Qur'an into its agreed-upon order and assembled it into one complete book.

Zayd followed strict methods in his compilation, enlisting dozens of other huffath (plural of hafith) to verify his work to make sure everything was perfectly accurate. Abu Bakr, who was also a hafith, confirmed that everything was correct. After Abu Bakr passed away, 'Umar took charge of the book, and when he passed away, the copy was kept with his daughter, Hafsah, a widow of Prophet Muhammad.

In addition to transcribing the Qur'an, thousands of Muslims were committing it to memory. As a result, the number of huffath was growing every year. Every Muslim memorized some part of the Qur'an, and most people learned very large portions of it. The written copy of the Qur'an did not have the current day vowel markings above and below letters, nor were the ayaat separated and numbered. It was written in the Arabic letters of old, which any literate Arab then could read easily without such aids.

But as the Muslim world expanded into lands where the people learned Arabic as a second language, these new Muslims had difficulty learning the correct pronunciation of the text. During the rule of 'Uthman﷽, the third Khalifa, serious differences arose between the Syrians and Iraqis about how to pronounce the letters and words correctly. One Sahaba by the name of Hudhayfah﷽ complained about this to Khalifa 'Uthman﷽. 'Uthman﷽ consulted with the other Sahaba, and they agreed that something should be done to prevent such confusion.

The Official Qur'an Is Authenticated and Circulated

'Uthman﷽, responding to this concern, charged that all copies of the Qur'an that represented different dialects be collected and destroyed. He again called upon Zayd bin Thabit﷽ and three other trusted Companions to reproduce and rewrite one copy of the Qur'an in the dialect that was best known at the time: the Qurayshi dialect.

Together, the four guardians borrowed the original complete copy of the Qur'an from Hafsah﷽ and transcribed many more copies of the Qur'an from it. Thus, the Qur'an was compiled in one pure and complete form, exactly as it was recited at the time of Prophet Muhammad﷽.

Each major Muslim city was then sent a copy from which they could make more copies and spread the written Qur'an to other areas. At least two of these original copies of the Qur'an exist today. One is housed in the Topkapi Museum in Istanbul, Turkey; the other is in the city of Tashkent in Central Asia. Allah﷽ miraculously protected His book through the actions of motivated and dedicated people. The Qur'an we use today is the same as the one circulated over 1,400 years ago.

During the rule of Khalifa Malik bin Marwan, **Tashkeel تَشْكِيل Dots and vowel markings** were added by Hajjaj bin Yusuf. He did this to make it easier for non-Arabs to learn and pronounce the words correctly.

We have been blessed by the fact that the revelation of Allah﷽ has been preserved and remains intact for everyone all over the world. To this day, Muslims memorize the Qur'an and study its meaning. Every Muslim child learns at least a small part of the Qur'an. Many educated speakers of Arabic from all over the world use the style of Arabic in the Qur'an as a model to learn the language.

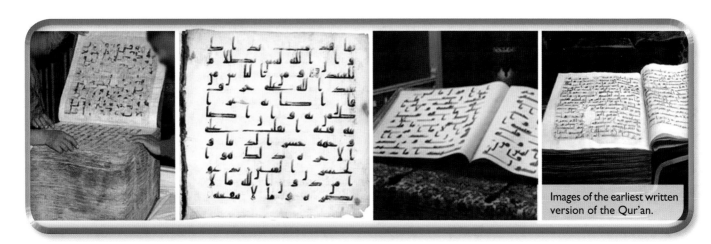

Images of the earliest written version of the Qur'an.

The Qur'an Is Unique

Allah declares, *If this Qur'an were bestowed upon a mountain, it would crumble.* Surat Al Hashr (The Exile) 59:21

﴿لَوْ أَنزَلْنَا هَٰذَا الْقُرْآنَ عَلَىٰ جَبَلٍ لَّرَأَيْتَهُ خَاشِعًا مُّتَصَدِّعًا مِّنْ خَشْيَةِ اللَّهِ وَتِلْكَ الْأَمْثَالُ نَضْرِبُهَا لِلنَّاسِ لَعَلَّهُمْ يَتَفَكَّرُونَ﴾ سُورَةُ الْحَشْرِ 59:21

Indeed, the Holy Qur'an is a book of great power and miracles. No other book has been read or memorized more than the Qur'an. It moves people to action and brings joy and happiness to the hearts of the young and old, rich and poor. Many books have been written about the amazing qualities of the Holy Qur'an, from its perfect use of analogies and expressions to its melodic rhythm when recited aloud.

There are no mistakes or errors in the Qur'an. It is a perfect book, and people have spent their entire lives studying merely one aspect of it. Some examine the many scientific statements, while others marvel at the perfect grammar. Some look for the hidden meanings of its verses, while others ponder the solutions provided for the problems of mankind.

Allah uses many words to describe the Qur'an, such as 'the Guidance الْهُدَى,' 'the Good News الْبُشْرَى,' 'the Noble Message الرِّسَالَةُ النَّبِيلَة,' 'the Standard الْمِنْهَاج' 'the Clear Book الْكِتَابُ الْوَاضِح' and 'the Glorious Book الْمَجِيد.' It was revealed gradually to the Blessed Prophet Muhammad, who could neither read nor write, over a period of 23 years.

The Prophet memorized the entire message and thousands of his Companions did so as well. The Qur'an was committed to writing within his lifetime, and was checked and rechecked for accuracy in the earliest days of Islam. After the Prophet's death, the message was gradually distributed in book form all over the world.

It has 114 chapters, or suwar, comprising approximately 6,208 ayaat, or verses. The verses cover a wide range of topics and themes that relate to the life of the present world and in the next life. Some verses are clear in meaning, while others are mystical or allegorical. (3:7) The ayaat are often referred to as **Makkan** مَكِّي or **Madinan** مَدَنِّي revelations. That is, any revelations that came to the Prophet while he was in the first phase of his mission, in Makkah, are called Makkan suwar. Any revelations that came to the Prophet after his migration to Al Madinah are called Madinan suwar. The Makkan suwar deal primarily with Islamic beliefs and teachings, while Madinan suwar emphasize how to form and live within an Islamic society ruled by Islamic law (Shariah).

A Guide for the Heart

The Qur'an is the most widely read and memorized book in the world, surpassing even the Bible, which has been in circulation far longer. It contains scientific details of which no human being knew at the time of Prophet Muhammad. These facts did not come to light until more than a thousand years later.

As Allah indicates, *We have already sent down to you verses making things clear, an illustration from (the story of) people who passed away before you, and an admonition for those who fear (Allah).* Surat An-Noor (The Light) 24:34

﴿وَلَقَدْ أَنزَلْنَا إِلَيْكُمْ آيَاتٍ مُّبَيِّنَاتٍ وَمَثَلًا مِّنَ الَّذِينَ خَلَوْا مِن قَبْلِكُمْ وَمَوْعِظَةً لِّلْمُتَّقِينَ﴾ سُورَةُ النُّور 24:34

Through the study of this book, millions have found a renewed sense of purpose in their lives. It is the book of guidance, direction and healing. No man or woman could have ever produced it, and no one can ever claim to understand all of its teachings. It is the book that provides a clear and noble path for people to follow in both their personal and spiritual affairs. It is the final message given to us by the Creator of the Universe and is unlike any other book in existence. Those who pay attention to what it says and implement its teachings are promised success in this life and the next, while those who reject it will ultimately fail.

Allah ﷻ Describes the Qur'an...

If it were a Book from anyone else besides Allah, you would have found many mistakes in it.
Surat An-Nisa' (The Women) 4:82

﴿وَلَوْ كَانَ مِنْ عِندِ غَيْرِ ٱللَّهِ لَوَجَدُوا۟ فِيهِ ٱخْتِلَٰفًا كَثِيرًا﴾ سُورَةُ النِّسَاءِ 4:82

When the Qur'an is read, listen to it with attention and hold your peace so you can receive Mercy. And bring your Lord to remembrance in your (very) soul, with humility and in reverence, without loudness in words in the mornings and evenings, and don't be negligent. Those who are near to your Lord don't hesitate to do Him service. They celebrate His praises and bow down before Him. *Surat Al 'Araaf (The Heights) 7:204-206*

﴿وَإِذَا قُرِئَ ٱلْقُرْءَانُ فَٱسْتَمِعُوا۟ لَهُۥ وَأَنصِتُوا۟ لَعَلَّكُمْ تُرْحَمُونَ﴾﴿وَٱذْكُر رَّبَّكَ فِى نَفْسِكَ تَضَرُّعًا وَخِيفَةً وَدُونَ ٱلْجَهْرِ مِنَ ٱلْقَوْلِ بِٱلْغُدُوِّ وَٱلْءَاصَالِ
وَلَا تَكُن مِّنَ ٱلْغَٰفِلِينَ﴾﴿إِنَّ ٱلَّذِينَ عِندَ رَبِّكَ لَا يَسْتَكْبِرُونَ عَنْ عِبَادَتِهِۦ وَيُسَبِّحُونَهُۥ وَلَهُۥ يَسْجُدُونَ۩﴾ سُورَةُ الْأَعْرَافِ 7:204-206

And We sent down the book to you so that you can make clear (to people) those things in which they differ and that it should be a guide and a mercy to those who believe.
Surat An-Nahl (The Bees) 16:64

﴿وَمَا أَنزَلْنَا عَلَيْكَ ٱلْكِتَٰبَ إِلَّا لِتُبَيِّنَ لَهُمُ ٱلَّذِى ٱخْتَلَفُوا۟ فِيهِ وَهُدًى وَرَحْمَةً لِّقَوْمٍ يُؤْمِنُونَ﴾ سُورَةُ النَّحْلِ 16:64

Read what is revealed to you of the (Qur'an) and establish prayer because prayer restrains (a person from doing) shameful deeds. Remembering Allah is the greatest (thing in life). And Allah knows what you do. Don't argue with the People of the Book (the Jews and Christians) except in a better way, unless it be with the ones who are doing wrong, but even then, only say: "We believe in the revelation that came down to us and in the one that came down to you. Our God and your God is one, and it's to Him we bow."
And so We have sent down the book to you and some of the People of the book believe in it, even as some of these (Arabs do). Only the faithless reject Our signs. And you (Muhammad) were not (able) to recite a book before this (book came) nor are you (able) to write it with your own right hand (because you don't know how to write). If you (were a known writer before the Qur'an was revealed), then the vain people could have doubted.
Indeed, here are proven signs in the hearts of those who understand. Only the unjust reject Our signs. Yet they say: "Why are there no (miracles) sent down to him from his Lord?"
Tell them, "The signs are indeed with Allah, and I am indeed a clear warner." Isn't it enough for them that We sent down to you the Book that is read to them? Indeed, in it is a mercy and reminder to those who believe. *Surat Al 'Ankabut (The Spider) 29:45-51*

﴿ٱتْلُ مَا أُوحِىَ إِلَيْكَ مِنَ ٱلْكِتَٰبِ وَأَقِمِ ٱلصَّلَوٰةَ إِنَّ ٱلصَّلَوٰةَ تَنْهَىٰ عَنِ ٱلْفَحْشَاءِ وَٱلْمُنكَرِ وَلَذِكْرُ ٱللَّهِ أَكْبَرُ وَٱللَّهُ يَعْلَمُ مَا تَصْنَعُونَ﴾﴿وَلَا
تُجَٰدِلُوا۟ أَهْلَ ٱلْكِتَٰبِ إِلَّا بِٱلَّتِى هِىَ أَحْسَنُ إِلَّا ٱلَّذِينَ ظَلَمُوا۟ مِنْهُمْ وَقُولُوا۟ ءَامَنَّا بِٱلَّذِى أُنزِلَ إِلَيْنَا وَأُنزِلَ إِلَيْكُمْ وَإِلَٰهُنَا وَإِلَٰهُكُمْ وَٰحِدٌ
وَنَحْنُ لَهُۥ مُسْلِمُونَ﴾﴿وَكَذَٰلِكَ أَنزَلْنَا إِلَيْكَ ٱلْكِتَٰبَ فَٱلَّذِينَ ءَاتَيْنَٰهُمُ ٱلْكِتَٰبَ يُؤْمِنُونَ بِهِۦ وَمِنْ هَٰؤُلَاءِ مَن يُؤْمِنُ بِهِۦ وَمَا يَجْحَدُ بِـَٔايَٰتِنَا إِلَّا
ٱلْكَٰفِرُونَ﴾﴿وَمَا كُنتَ تَتْلُوا۟ مِن قَبْلِهِۦ مِن كِتَٰبٍ وَلَا تَخُطُّهُۥ بِيَمِينِكَ إِذًا لَّٱرْتَابَ ٱلْمُبْطِلُونَ﴾﴿بَلْ هُوَ ءَايَٰتٌۢ بَيِّنَٰتٌ فِى صُدُورِ ٱلَّذِينَ أُوتُوا۟ ٱلْعِلْمَ
وَمَا يَجْحَدُ بِـَٔايَٰتِنَا إِلَّا ٱلظَّٰلِمُونَ﴾﴿وَقَالُوا۟ لَوْلَا أُنزِلَ عَلَيْهِ ءَايَٰتٌ مِّن رَّبِّهِۦ قُلْ إِنَّمَا ٱلْءَايَٰتُ عِندَ ٱللَّهِ وَإِنَّمَا أَنَا۠ نَذِيرٌ مُّبِينٌ﴾﴿أَوَلَمْ يَكْفِهِمْ أَنَّا أَنزَلْنَا
عَلَيْكَ ٱلْكِتَٰبَ يُتْلَىٰ عَلَيْهِمْ إِنَّ فِى ذَٰلِكَ لَرَحْمَةً وَذِكْرَىٰ لِقَوْمٍ يُؤْمِنُونَ﴾ سُورَةُ الْعَنْكَبُوتِ 29:45-51

A Scientist Speaks

"The relationship between the Qur'an and science is... a surprise, especially when it turns out to be one of harmony and not of discord." –Dr. Maurice Bucaille, *The Bible, the Qur'an and Science. (p. 110)*

After studying verses from the Qur'an that make reference to scientific subjects, the French scientist, Dr. Maurice Bucaille, was astounded. He noticed no discrepancies between the Qur'anic ayaat and modern scientific knowledge.

Indeed, the Qur'an is a book that not only provides guidance but also speaks of the natural world around us. Many studies prove that everything said in the Qur'an about science is accurate and consistent with what we know in science today. While this may not initially seem surprising or special, we must remember that the Qur'an was revealed to Prophet Muhammad ﷺ nearly 1,435 years ago! It then becomes a rather spectacular miracle.

Many of the ayaat in the Qur'an referencing plants, animals, the Earth, space and humans were unknown at that time—it was completely new information. What is even more spectacular is that the Blessed Prophet ﷺ lived in the center of Arabia; an area with limited exposure to the outside world. There were no schools, no universities nor any scientific thought. But Allah ﷻ uses scientific statements in the Qur'an as a means for us to believe in Him and to follow the way of life that He wants for us. This is Islam.

In this chapter, we will explore a few of the many scientific statements in the Qur'an. If you are wondering what Muslims must have thought about these verses, those we are only beginning to understand today, remember that we are taught to believe in the Qur'an completely. If there is a part we don't fully understand yet, then we must, exercise patience and ask Allah ﷻ to help us to discover the meaning.

Allah ﷻ explained this point in Surat Al 'Imran (The Family of 'Imran). *He it is Who has sent down to thee the Book. In it are verses basic or fundamental (of established meaning); they are the foundation of the Book: others are allegorical. But those in whose hearts is perversity follow the part thereof that is allegorical, seeking discord, and searching for its hidden meanings, but no one knows its hidden meanings except Allah. And those who are firmly grounded in knowledge say: "We believe in the Book; the whole of it is from our Lord" and none will grasp the Message except men of understanding. "Our Lord!" (They say), "Let not our hearts deviate now after Thou hast guided us, but grant us mercy from Thine own Presence; for Thou art the Grantor of bounties without measure. Our Lord! Thou art He that will gather mankind Together against a day about which there is no doubt; for Allah never fails in His promise."*
Surat Al 'Imran (The Family of 'Imran) 3: 7-9

﴿هُوَ ٱلَّذِىٓ أَنزَلَ عَلَيْكَ ٱلْكِتَـٰبَ مِنْهُ ءَايَـٰتٌ مُّحْكَمَـٰتٌ هُنَّ أُمُّ ٱلْكِتَـٰبِ وَأُخَرُ مُتَشَـٰبِهَـٰتٌ فَأَمَّا ٱلَّذِينَ فِى قُلُوبِهِمْ زَيْغٌ فَيَتَّبِعُونَ مَا تَشَـٰبَهَ مِنْهُ ٱبْتِغَآءَ ٱلْفِتْنَةِ وَٱبْتِغَآءَ تَأْوِيلِهِۦ وَمَا يَعْلَمُ تَأْوِيلَهُۥٓ إِلَّا ٱللَّهُ وَٱلرَّٰسِخُونَ فِى ٱلْعِلْمِ يَقُولُونَ ءَامَنَّا بِهِۦ كُلٌّ مِّنْ عِندِ رَبِّنَا وَمَا يَذَّكَّرُ إِلَّآ أُوْلُوا ٱلْأَلْبَـٰبِ ﴾ ﴿رَبَّنَا لَا تُزِغْ قُلُوبَنَا بَعْدَ إِذْ هَدَيْتَنَا وَهَبْ لَنَا مِن لَّدُنكَ رَحْمَةً إِنَّكَ أَنتَ ٱلْوَهَّابُ ﴾ ﴿رَبَّنَآ إِنَّكَ جَامِعُ ٱلنَّاسِ لِيَوْمٍ لَّا رَيْبَ فِيهِ إِنَّ ٱللَّهَ لَا يُخْلِفُ ٱلْمِيعَادَ ﴾ سُورَةُ آلِ عِمْرَان 3:7-9

Muslims throughout history have embraced science and sought knowledge about the natural world. Allah ﷻ commands us to study the Universe so that we can recognize His power and strengthen our faith through this understanding. (2:164) The next time you learn something fascinating about the world you live in, remember that it's a sign of Allah's ﷻ power, and that, insha'Allah, your dedication and faith in your Creator will increase because of it.

"Our Lord! Let not our hearts deviate (from the truth) after You have guided us and grant us mercy from You. Truly, You are the Bestower. Our Lord! Verily, it is You Who will gather mankind together on the Day about which there is no doubt. Verily Allah never breaks His Promise." Surat Al 'Imran (The Family of 'Imran) 3: 8-9

﴿رَبَّنَا لَا تُزِغْ قُلُوبَنَا بَعْدَ إِذْ هَدَيْتَنَا وَهَبْ لَنَا مِن لَّدُنكَ رَحْمَةً إِنَّكَ أَنتَ ٱلْوَهَّابُ﴾ ﴿رَبَّنَا إِنَّكَ جَامِعُ ٱلنَّاسِ لِيَوْمٍ لَّا رَيْبَ فِيهِ إِنَّ ٱللَّهَ لَا يُخْلِفُ ٱلْمِيعَادَ﴾ سُورَةُ آلِ عِمْرَانَ 3:8-9

Some Scientific Marvels of the Qur'an

Nearly all ants are females. Male ants are infrequently produced and quickly die after mating. All worker ants, as well as the queen, are females. Ants also communicate in their own 'language.' The Arabic word for 'ant' is النَّمَل, which is a masculine noun. Gender differences in the insect community were unknown at this time. In the Qur'an we are told that Prophet Sulayman ﷺ was given the ability to understand the speech of animals. Prophet Sulayman ﷺ overheard an ant speaking to 'her' fellow ants قَالَتْ نَمْلَةٌ, telling them to run and hide to avoid being trampled by his approaching army. The feminine form of the verb قَالَ is قَالَتْ is used in ayah 27:18. Thus, the ant is clearly described as female. Prophet Sulayman ﷺ is said to have been amused at "her speech." (27:19)

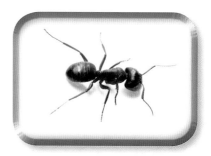

Allah ﷻ compares the state of an unbeliever to that of a person in the dark depths of the ocean. He cannot see his hand in front of his face and is under layers of darkness. Remember that the Prophet ﷺ had never even seen the ocean, nor had anyone at that time ever explored the deep recesses of the seas to know that it was in pitch darkness. (24:40)

There is life on some other planets. Allah ﷻ says that every creature in space and on Earth has to follow Him and that He spread life throughout space and Earth. (3:83; 19:93-95; 24:41; 23:17; 42:29; 30:26; 55:29; 65:12)

The action of the wind over the seas pulls moisture along and collects it in the clouds. The clouds are spread again by wind currents and then break up as rain falls down from them. (24:43; 30:48)

Salt water and fresh water do not mix easily. There is a 'barrier' between them. (27:61; 55:19-22)

Many species of spiders are solitary. The female may even eat the male after mating. Allah mentions that spiders have the weakest homes of all. That doesn't mean just the webs. Their entire family structure definitely needs improvement! (29:41)

The moon is referred to as munir or 'light reflector,' while the sun is referred to as siraj or 'light producer.' (25:61; 71:15-16; 78:12-13.)

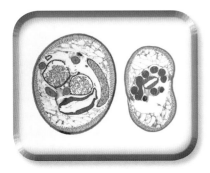

A pregnancy occurs only when the ova and sperm unite. Then the fertilized egg 'clings,' or 'alaq, in the womb. The fetus grows in stages until it is ready to be born. (23:14; 40:67; 75:37-38)

Water is the basis of all life. Allah created all life from water. (24:45)

Everything was compacted together and then split apart. Gases spread throughout the Universe, and stars, planets and other entities were formed. (21:30; 41:11)

Plants have both male and female reproductive organs. All plants were created with paired organs. (13:3; 20:53; 22:5; 31:10; 36:36)

People have trouble breathing when they ascend to very high elevations. Their lungs become constricted. Even planes need pressurized cabins so people can breathe easily. (6:125)

Humans can only break free of Earth's gravity and enter space with modern technology and powerful engines. Allah says humans can only venture into space with powerful tools to use. (55:33)

Literature Selection

Surat Ash-Shura
(The Consultations)

Adapted from *The Holy Qur'an*
Arranged by Yahiya Emerick
(Explanatory words added in parentheses)

In the Name of Allah,
The Most Gracious, The Most Merciful

Ha Mim (1) 'Ayn Seen Qaf.* (2) And so, He's inspiring you (Muhammad), as He inspired the (ancient Prophets) who came before you, and Allah is All-Mighty and the Wise. (3) Whatever is in the Heavens and on Earth belongs to Him, He's the Exalted and the Most Great One. (4) The skies are nearly ripped to shreds above them, and the angels praise their Lord and pray for the forgiveness for all creatures on Earth. He is indeed the Forgiving and the Merciful, (5) but whoever looks for protector allies other than Him—Allah is Guardian over them—and you're not responsible for them at all. (6) And so, We've revealed to you a Qur'an in Arabic so you can warn "Um Al Qurah," most important city (of Makkah), and all of the other (cities) beyond it, about the Day of Assembly that will arrive without any doubt. Some of them will be in Paradise, while the rest of them will be in the Raging Blaze. (7) If Allah had wanted to, He could have made all (the people of the Earth) into a single nation, but He (lets them differ and divide in order to test them), and also so that He can be merciful to whomever He wants, though the wrongdoers certainly aren't going to find any protector or rescuer to save them. (8)

Are they taking allies other than Him? Allah is the (only) One who can protect you, and He's the One who will bring the dead to life, for He has power over everything. (9) Whatever you're all arguing about, Allah will be the One to solve it. That is my Lord, Allah. I trust in Him and I turn myself towards Him (for guidance). (10) (He's) the Creator of the Heavens and the Earth, and He made you all into pairs (of male and female) among your own kind, even as He made cattle in pairs. That's how He made it possible for you to multiply. There's really nothing like Him at all, for He's the Listening and the Watchful. (11) The keys of the Heavens and the Earth belong to Him, and He extends or restricts the provision of whoever He wants to, for He knows about everything. (12) He has established the same way of life for you that He introduced to Noah—it's the same one that We're revealing to you, and the same one that We introduced to Abraham, Moses, and Jesus, namely to establish the (moral) way of life and not to be divided about it. The idol-worshippers find that what you're asking of them is hard, though Allah directs to Himself whoever He wants to, and He guides to Himself (all) who turn (their hopes towards Him). (13) (The people of the past) divided up (into many competing sects)—and that was after they already had knowledge (from Allah)! (They did it solely) out of selfish envy among themselves. If it wasn't for an order that your Lord had already decreed that gave (humanity) a fixed time limit, then the situation would have been resolved between them. (Later generations), who have inherited the Scriptures since then, are filled with uncertainty about

---

* Al Huruf Al Muqatta'h الحروف المقطعة are unique letters that appear in the beginning of 29 suwar of the Qur'an. Muqatta'h means disjointed or unconnected letters. Their real meanings remain unknown and are considered by most Muslims to be known to Allah alone.

(them). (14) So, on account of that, do continue to call them (to believe in the Qur'an), and remain committed (to the Cause) as you're commanded to and don't follow their whims. Tell them, "I believe in the Book that Allah has sent down. I am commanded to judge fairly between you. Allah is our Lord and your Lord. To us, are our deeds, and to you, are your deeds. There is no argument between us and you. Allah will bring us all together and the final return is back with Him." (15)

Whoever argues about Allah after His (existence) has already been accepted (by all parties concerned) as arguing over nothing in Allah's sight. His anger is drawn over them and a strong punishment lies in reserve. (16) Allah's the One Who sent down the Book in all honesty and well-balanced (principles). And what will make you perceive? Perhaps the Hour is near. (17) The only ones who want it to come sooner are the ones who don't believe in it, but the faithful are in awe of it and know that it's a reality. Isn't it (true) that those who disregard the Hour are grossly mistaken? (18) Allah is More than Fair to His Servants. Allah is gracious to His servants; He gives the necessities of life to whoever He wants to, and He has the strength to do whatever He wants. (19) Whoever desires the harvest of the next life, We add to his harvest. Whoever desires the harvest of this world, We'll give him some of it, but he'll have no share of the next life. (20) Do they have "partners" (as powerful as Allah) who can make a religion for them without Allah's permission? If it wasn't for the order of Judgement , the issue would've already been decided between them, but the wrongdoers have a terrible punishment waiting for them. (21)

You're going to see the wrongdoers trembling in fear for all the (sins) they've earned, and that is something they'll have to bear. The believers, however, who did what was morally right, will rest in the luxuries of Paradise. In their Lord's presence, they're going to have everything they wish for, and that's the greatest bounty! (22) That's the same one that Allah is giving the good news of to His servants who believe and do what's morally right. Say to them, "I'm not asking you for any reward for this, but at least extend to me the love that is due to a member of your own family!" Whoever accumulates any good (deeds), We will multiply the goodness within it, for Allah is Forgiving and Appreciative. (23) Are they saying, "He's making up lies about Allah?" If Allah had wanted to, He could have sealed up even your heart, but Allah blots out falsehood and proves, by His Own words, that the Truth is true, for He knows the secrets that lurk within (people's) hearts. (24) He's the One Who accepts repentance from His servants, and He also forgives sins, and He certainly knows whatever you're doing. (25)

He listens to the believers who do what's morally right and gives them an increase (in their fortune) from His largess—but, for the faithless, there is nothing but a terrible punishment. (26) If He ever increased the (financial) resources of His servants, they would surely go out of control all over the world, but He sends it down in increments as He wills, for He is ever aware and observant of His servants. (27) He's the One who sends down rain even after (people) have given up all hope for it, and He scatters His mercy (in every direction), for He is the Protector and the Praiseworthy. (28) Among His signs is the creation of the Heavens and the Earth, and all the living creatures that He scattered about, and He has the ability to collect them all together again when He wants to. (29)

Never Overlook Personal Responsibility

No misfortune comes upon you without it being the result of your own actions, but for many (of your mishaps) there is forgiveness. (30) And you can't escape (the results of your bad decisions) by running all over the world, for you have no one else who can help or protect you besides Allah. (31) Among His signs are the smooth sailing ships that ply through the oceans, looking like mountain peaks. (32) If He wanted to, He could stop the wind (that propels them), and they would be rendered immobile on the (ocean's) surface. Truly, there are signs in this (example) for all who persevere patiently and give thanks. (33) Or (if He wanted to), He could (sink those ships) as a (punishment) for (the sins) that (people) have earned, but He forgives many things.

(34) and those who argue about Our signs, they will have no escape! (35) Whatever you're given in this world is only a trifle to use in this life, but whatever is with Allah is better and more lasting—(a reward) for the believers who put their trust in their Lord. (36) They avoid the most serious sins and shameful acts and forgive others, even when they're angry. (37) They respond to their Lord and establish prayers. They decide their communal affairs by consulting each other and spend (in Allah's Cause) out of what We have given them, (38) and they also defend themselves when they are wronged. (39) The payback for an evil (done to you) is (to get back) an equal (amount of compensation) from the (one who wronged you), unless a person forgives (the one who wronged them) and reconciles with him. His compensation is with Allah, for He does not love the wrongdoers. (40) If anyone defends themselves after they were wronged, they will not be blamed for it. (41) Blame will only be assigned against those who oppress people and defy all norms of justice in the Earth against all that is right, and a terrible punishment awaits them! (42) Whoever is patient and forgives (the wrongs that were done against them) is truly courageous, and that is worth considering deeply. (43)

Let Them Decide for Themselves

Whoever Allah leaves astray, there is no protector for them after that. You are going to see the wrongdoers say, just as they eye the punishment (ahead of them), "Isn't there any way to go back?" (44)

And You are going to see them brought to the front in utter humility for their shame, with eyes darting about. The believers will exclaim, "The losers are the ones who lost their own selves and their families on this Day of Judgement. Oh, how lasting a punishment the wrongdoers must endure!" (45) They will not have any protectors to help them in the sight of Allah, and anyone whom Allah leaves to stray will have no way (to escape). (46) Respond to your Lord before the Day comes when there will be no way to delay it, by Allah's (will). On that Day there will be no place for you to hide, nor will there be any chance for you to deny (your guilt). (47) If (people) turn away, then (it's not your fault), for We have not made you to be their keeper. Your duty is only to deliver (the message). And isn't it the case that whenever We give someone a taste of Our mercy, he celebrates, but when some misfortune befalls him, as a result of his own handiwork, he is truly thankless! (48) The control of the Heavens and the Earth belongs to Allah. He creates whatever He wants to, and bestows female children upon whom He pleases and male children upon whom He pleases, (49) or He bestows both males and females, while he leaves barren whom He wills, for He is full of knowledge and powerful. (50) It's beyond the majesty of Allah to speak to a human being, unless it's through inspired revelation, or from behind a veil, or through the agency of a message-bearer (like an Angel), who will reveal, with Allah's permission, whatever Allah wills him to, for He is highly exalted and wise. (51) And thus We've directed revelation to you by Our command. You didn't know what revelation and faith were (before being made a prophet), but We have sent down to you a light which you can use to guide whichever of Our servants that We will, and you are giving guidance towards a straight path (52) —the path of Allah—the One to Whom belongs whatever is in the Heavens and whatever is on Earth, and all affairs certainly will come back to Allah. (53)

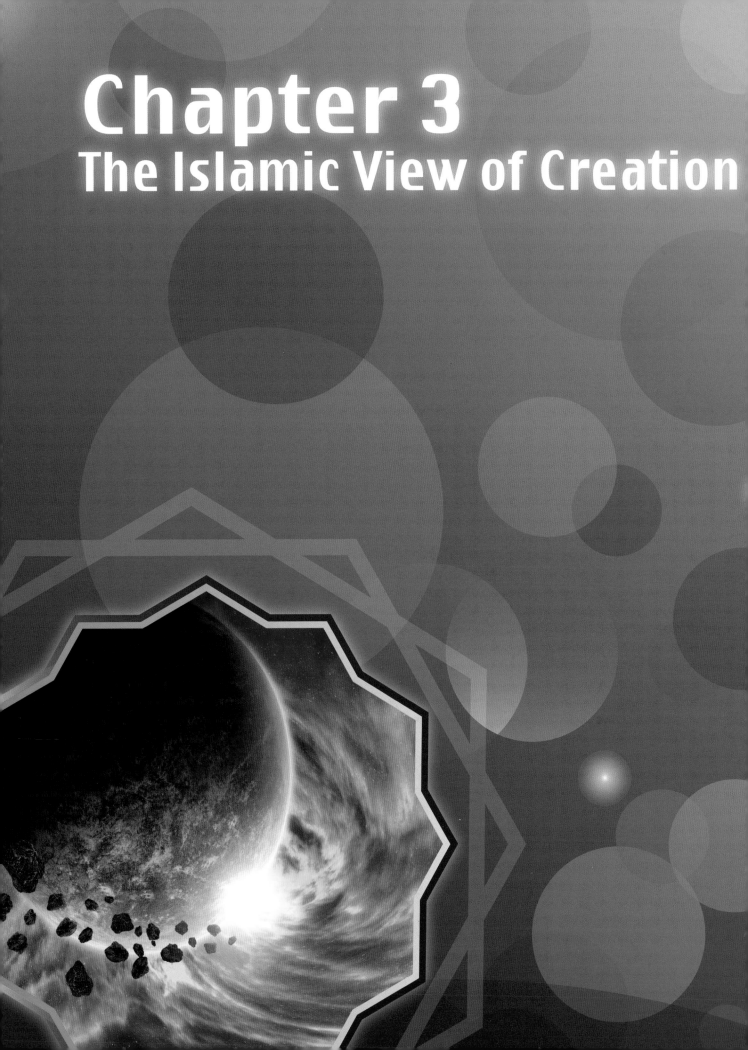

Chapter 3
The Islamic View of Creation

Why Does Allah ﷻ Tell Us about Creating the Universe?

The Holy Qur'an is the book given to us by the Creator of the Universe. Allah ﷻ as our Creator knows us best and knows that humans can be very skeptical creatures.

Allah ﷻ said, *If their aversion is too hard on you, then seek, if you can, a tunnel into the earth or a ladder unto the sky in order to bring them a sign. Had Allah so willed, He would have brought all of them to the right path. So never be one of the ignorant.* Surat Al An'aam (The Cattle) 6: 35

﴿وَإِن كَانَ كَبُرَ عَلَيْكَ إِعْرَاضُهُمْ فَإِنِ ٱسْتَطَعْتَ أَن تَبْتَغِيَ نَفَقًا فِي ٱلْأَرْضِ أَوْ سُلَّمًا فِي ٱلسَّمَاءِ فَتَأْتِيَهُم بِآيَةٍ وَلَوْ شَاءَ ٱللَّهُ لَجَمَعَهُمْ عَلَى ٱلْهُدَى فَلَا تَكُونَنَّ مِنَ ٱلْجَاهِلِينَ﴾ سُورَةُ الأنعام ٦:٣٥

Allah ﷻ, the Keeper of Wisdom, purposely provides many proofs in the Qur'an about His existence and creativity in guiding humanity. The diversity of all the proof strengthens the belief in Allah ﷻ. We need proof, and Allah ﷻ gives us that proof.

Assuredly the creation of the heavens and the earth is a greater (matter) than the creation of humans: Yet most humans understand not. Surat Ghafir (The Forgiver) 40:57

﴿لَخَلْقُ ٱلسَّمَوَاتِ وَٱلْأَرْضِ أَكْبَرُ مِنْ خَلْقِ ٱلنَّاسِ وَلَكِنَّ أَكْثَرَ ٱلنَّاسِ لَا يَعْلَمُونَ﴾ سُورَةُ غَافِر ٥٧:٤٠

Allah ﷻ, of course, does not need us to follow Him or believe in Him. As He stated, *Allah can do without them and Allah is free of all needs.* Surat At-Taghabun (The Mutual Disillusion) 64:6

﴿وَٱسْتَغْنَى ٱللَّهُ وَٱللَّهُ غَنِيٌّ حَمِيدٌ﴾ سُورَةُ التَّغَابُن ٦:٦٤

Allah ﷻ merely provides proofs so that those who wish to, can believe in Him. In turn, Allah ﷻ can reward them for their choice. Allah ﷻ is ready to forgive even those who act wrongly if they but ask for His forgiveness.

Abu Hurayrah ﷺ narrated that Allah's Messenger ﷺ said, "When Allah completed the creation, He wrote in His Book which is with Him on His Throne, 'My Mercy overpowers My Anger.'" (Al Bukhari & Muslim)

عَنْ أَبِي هُرَيْرَةَ ﷺ قَالَ قَالَ رَسُولُ اللهِ ﷺ: «لَمَّا قَضَى اللهُ الْخَلْقَ كَتَبَ فِي كِتَابِهِ، فَهُوَ عِنْدَهُ فَوْقَ الْعَرْشِ إِنَّ رَحْمَتِي غَلَبَتْ غَضَبِي». رَوَاهُ الْبُخَارِيُّ وَمُسْلِمٌ

Among the proofs given in the Qur'an is a very detailed explanation of how the Universe was fashioned and how the planets and stars were formed. Those who lived during the revelation of the Qur'an would not have understood the scientific basis of the ayaat, but they accepted them and interpreted them as best they could.

Allah ﷻ instructs us to accept everything in the Qur'an, even if we don't yet understand its meaning. Our understanding of the Qur'an grows with each passing generation as we gain more scientific knowledge about the Earth and its surrounding space and galaxies. As Allah ﷻ said, *But those firm in knowledge say, "We believe in it. All [of it] is from our Lord." And no one will be reminded except those of understanding.* Surat Al 'Imran (The Family of 'Imran) 3:7

﴿وَٱلرَّاسِخُونَ فِي ٱلْعِلْمِ يَقُولُونَ ءَامَنَّا بِهِ كُلٌّ مِّنْ عِندِ رَبِّنَا وَمَا يَذَّكَّرُ إِلَّا أُوْلُوا ٱلْأَلْبَابِ﴾ سُورَةُ آلِ عِمْرَان ٧:٣

Modern Science and Islam

Modern day scientists are amazed by the complexity of the Universe. The sciences of astronomy, chemistry, astrophysics and molecular biology have pushed the limits of our knowledge ever further.

Who has created seven skies, one over the other. You will see nothing out of proportion in the creation of the Rahman (the All-Merciful Allah). So, cast your eye again. Do you see any rifts? Then cast your eye again and again, and the eye will come back to you abased, in a state of weariness. *Surat Al Mulk (The Dominion) 67:3-4*

﴿ٱلَّذِي خَلَقَ سَبْعَ سَمَٰوَٰتٍ طِبَاقًا مَّا تَرَىٰ فِي خَلْقِ ٱلرَّحْمَٰنِ مِن تَفَٰوُتٍ فَٱرْجِعِ ٱلْبَصَرَ هَلْ تَرَىٰ مِن فُطُورٍ﴾ ﴿ثُمَّ ٱرْجِعِ ٱلْبَصَرَ كَرَّتَيْنِ يَنقَلِبْ إِلَيْكَ ٱلْبَصَرُ خَاسِئًا وَهُوَ حَسِيرٌ﴾ سُورَةُ الْمُلْكِ 4-3:67

These new discoveries have helped us better understand many Qur'anic ayaat. For example, Allah mentions that humans begin their life as an 'alaq in their mother's womb. The word 'alaq literally means 'a clinging thing.' No one, however, in centuries past understood the process of human development.

Created man from a clinging substance. Surat Al 'Alaq (The Clot) 96:2

﴿خَلَقَ ٱلْإِنسَٰنَ مِنْ عَلَقٍ﴾ سُورَةُ الْعَلَقِ 2:96

New discoveries in the last century have shown that in the early stages of pregnancy, the fertilized egg actually attaches itself to the uterine wall and clings there as it is growing. Thus, modern knowledge unlocks another mystery that previous Muslims could only guess at.

To a startling degree, the same holds true in other Qur'anic revelations. When we study the ayaat of the Qur'an relating to the creation of the Universe, we pause astounded, as the verses agree with what has been only recently discovered.

The Qur'an does not give a single, unified essay on how the Universe began. Instead, in keeping with the Qur'anic method of teaching, different aspects of creation are mentioned in various suwar in order to give authority to the particular lesson.

For example, in *Surat At-Tariq (The Nightcommer) (86)*, Allah begins by mentioning the brightest star that appears in the sky at night. He then uses it as a metaphor for how every human has an angel watching over them. In this manner, Allah uses physical aspects of nature to illustrate spiritual principles.

I swear by the sky and by the Night-Comer. And what may let you know what the Night-Comer is? The star of piercing brightness! There is no human being, but there is a watcher over him. So, let man consider of which stuff he is created. Surat At-tariq (The Nightcommer) 86:1-5

﴿وَٱلسَّمَآءِ وَٱلطَّارِقِ﴾ ﴿وَمَآ أَدْرَىٰكَ مَا ٱلطَّارِقُ﴾ ﴿ٱلنَّجْمُ ٱلثَّاقِبُ﴾ ﴿إِن كُلُّ نَفْسٍ لَّمَّا عَلَيْهَا حَافِظٌ﴾ ﴿فَلْيَنظُرِ ٱلْإِنسَٰنُ مِمَّ خُلِقَ﴾ سُورَةُ الطَّارِقِ 5-1:86

The Qur'anic History of Creation

Each of the individual references to creation in the Qur'an can be pieced together to get a complete picture of how Allah's revelation explains the beginning of the Universe. As Muslims, however, we must not forget to look into the lesson within each passage. We must remember that the purpose for including these signs in the Qur'an is spiritual as well as mental enlightenment. Allah begins by stating that the Universe and planet Earth took six 'days' to create.

Indeed, your Lord is Allah , who created the heavens and earth in six days and then established Himself above the Throne. He covers the night with the day, [another night] chasing it rapidly; and [He created] the sun, the moon, and the stars, subjected by His command. Unquestionably, His is the creation and the command; blessed is Allah, Lord of the worlds. Surat Al 'Araaf (The Heights) 7:54

﴿إِنَّ رَبَّكُمُ ٱللَّهُ ٱلَّذِي خَلَقَ ٱلسَّمَٰوَٰتِ وَٱلْأَرْضَ فِي سِتَّةِ أَيَّامٍ ثُمَّ ٱسْتَوَىٰ عَلَى ٱلْعَرْشِ يُغْشِي ٱلَّيْلَ ٱلنَّهَارَ يَطْلُبُهُ حَثِيثًا وَٱلشَّمْسَ وَٱلْقَمَرَ وَٱلنُّجُومَ مُسَخَّرَٰتٍ بِأَمْرِهِ أَلَا لَهُ ٱلْخَلْقُ وَٱلْأَمْرُ تَبَارَكَ ٱللَّهُ رَبُّ ٱلْعَٰلَمِينَ﴾ سُورَةُ الْأَعْرَافِ 54:7

However, in Arabic, the word يوم can mean **a day** as we know it, or it can mean any stage or period of time. As

Allah points out, a day to Him can be 1,000 years, 50,000 years or infinitely more. [1]

The creation of the planets, including Earth, took place in the last two periods of time. As Allah said, *Declare (O Muhammad): Do you disbelieve in the One Who created the Earth in two stages? Do you make others equal to Him? He is the Lord of all the worlds.* Surat Fussilat (Explained in Detail) 41:9

﴿قُلْ أَئِنَّكُمْ لَتَكْفُرُونَ بِالَّذِي خَلَقَ الْأَرْضَ فِي يَوْمَيْنِ وَتَجْعَلُونَ لَهُ أَندَادًا ذَٰلِكَ رَبُّ الْعَالَمِينَ﴾ سُورَةُ فُصِّلَت 9:41

The process of creation can be summarized as follows: all matter in the Universe was compacted together in one place. Then Allah gave the command and it blew apart, scattering molecules and gases in all directions. This theory is what scientists refer to as the Big Bang. The force of this initial explosion keeps the Universe expanding.

Space was filled with matter, anti-matter and gases, which eventually combined into larger particles. These bits of matter eventually grew into asteroids, planets, stars and moons. Each object in interstellar space conformed to a set of physical laws that governed the trajectory of their orbits, so a regular pattern of rotation could be seen. (13:2, 21:33)

Stars ignited in a fury of radioactive fusion. They gave off light and heat, which brought warmth to those planets near them. (86:3) Small moons were captured in the orbit of larger planets. These moons developed a regular orbit around the planets, often reflecting light from the sun. Finally, the planets themselves developed in a variety of ways, with fantastic geological formations and movements both above and below the surface.

Or the One who made the earth a place to settle and made rivers amidst it and made mountains for (making) it (firm), and made a barrier between two seas? Is there any god along with Allah? No, but most of them do not have knowledge. Surat An-Naml (The Ants) 27:61

﴿أَمَّن جَعَلَ الْأَرْضَ قَرَارًا وَجَعَلَ خِلَالَهَا أَنْهَارًا وَجَعَلَ لَهَا رَوَاسِيَ وَجَعَلَ بَيْنَ الْبَحْرَيْنِ حَاجِزًا أَإِلَٰهٌ مَّعَ اللَّهِ بَلْ أَكْثَرُهُمْ لَا يَعْلَمُونَ﴾ سُورَةُ النَّمل 61:27

The planet Earth, in particular, cooled near its outer layers, forming a thin crust made up of plates that moved and grated against each other. This allowed the Earth's surface to constantly erase the damage caused by occasional asteroid impacts. But the plate collisions also had the side effect of raising tall mountains and exposing the geological history of the planet. Escaping gases from the ground and water warmed in the sunlight and eventually ascended to a high altitude where they formed a protective layer. This ozone layer shielded Earth from the harmful radiation and ultraviolet rays of the sun.

It is amazing that this scientific narrative is so similar to what Allah revealed in the Holy Qur'an. Always remember that Allah mentioned these things to convince us to be believers in Him. If He proves His words with things we have only recently discovered, how can we deny His message?

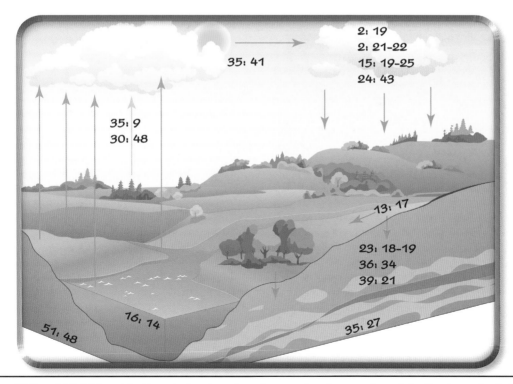

The Earth and its ecosystems are extremely complex. Look up the ayah for each stage of this hydrology diagram.

1 See 32:5 and 70:4. Many Muslim scholars have long known that the creation of the Earth was in six long stages and not in what we humans consider to be six days.

Qur'anic History of the Universe

Everything was compacted together and then Allah﷾ made it split apart. Gases, matter and anti-matter spread throughout the Universe and stars, planets, black holes, anti-matter geysers and other things were formed.
This is called the Big Bang. (21:30; 41:11)

Allah﷾ spread the Earth out and caused the crust to form like a carpet over the surface of the planet. Then He created mountains in the Earth to keep it stable. The formation of mountains acts as a kind of 'brake' or 'buffer zone' between the tectonic plates that make up Earth's crust. (71:19-20; 88:19-20; 78:6-7)

Allah is expanding the size of the Universe, everything in it is constantly moving away from each other. (51:47)

Allah created a protective canopy over the Earth that we call the ozone layer. It is constantly shielding us from harmful ultraviolet radiation. (21:32)

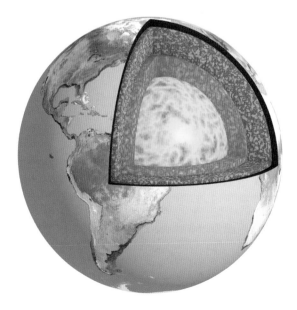

The Earth came into existence far before humans ever appeared. The different colored layers in the rock table provide us with a geological time line of our planet's history. (35:27-28, 40:64)

How Can We Know the World around Us?

As we have learned, Islamic teachings imply that Earth and the Universe are very old. In addition, the Qur'an clearly states that one of the reasons Allah made us intelligent and self-aware is so that we can discover the wonders of the natural world around us. In short, Allah gave us a mission to investigate what He created.

There is so much we don't know or understand, even about how our own bodies work. With all these fantastic areas of knowledge to pursue, the work of a Master Creator seems apparent. However, some still choose to keep their eyes closed. As Allah said, *He created man from a drop, and soon he turned into a debating person, expressing himself openly.* Surat An-Nahl (The Bees) 16:4

﴿خَلَقَ ٱلْإِنسَـٰنَ مِن نُّطْفَةٍ فَإِذَا هُوَ خَصِيمٌ مُّبِينٌ﴾ سُورَةُ النَّحْلِ 16:4

Thankfully, there are plenty of highly intelligent individuals that face life and learning with open minds and recent scientific discoveries are helping to complete our picture of the Universe, both past and present.

What Do We Know about the Origins of Life?

Today, scientists tell us that life began in the sea when simple molecules bonded together and became self-replicating, or self-producing. These single-celled organisms quickly took on the characteristics of what we know as algae. They received their energy from the sun in a process termed photosynthesis. As a result of this activity, new gases formed in the air, creating a viable environment for more complex forms of life.

Muslims can accept this theory, reject it or modify it according to what is known of Allah's revelation. In this instance, it may be easier to accept the theory, as Allah speaks of His creation of all life from water then raised a protective canopy over the Earth. For theories that are not referenced in the Qur'an, study, research, testing, and reflection are needed, followed by the faith that Allah knows best.

Scientists further tell us that over millions of years, the first organisms blossomed gradually into many different types and shapes, resulting in plant life, plankton, arthropods and simple fishes. Dinosaurs, higher creatures and mammals followed.

What Is the Islamic Perspective Evolution and Creationism?

You may be surprised to learn that Muslims can agree with aspects of both sides of the debate on evolution and that these discoveries do not necessarily undermine a healthy belief in Allah's power as the Creator of all things.

Islam teaches that Allah's creation is vast and beyond our comprehension. We also learn that the more we explore and learn, the more we will come to believe in Allah. That is the Islamic position.

So, we assert without any hesitation, that Allah caused the creation of the Universe and set up the laws for its functioning. As Allah said, *Behold! In the creation of space and the Earth and in the changing of night into day are indeed signs for people of understanding. Those who remember Allah standing, sitting and lying down and contemplate the (wonders) of creation in space and Earth. (They declare) "Our Lord! You didn't create all of this for nothing. So save us from the punishment of the fire."*
Surat Al 'Imran (The Family of 'Imran) 3: 190-191

﴿إِنَّ فِي خَلْقِ ٱلسَّمَٰوَٰتِ وَٱلْأَرْضِ وَٱخْتِلَٰفِ ٱلَّيْلِ وَٱلنَّهَارِ لَأَيَٰتٍ لِّأُوْلِي ٱلْأَلْبَٰبِ﴾﴿ٱلَّذِينَ يَذْكُرُونَ ٱللَّهَ قِيَٰمًا وَقُعُودًا وَعَلَىٰ جُنُوبِهِمْ وَيَتَفَكَّرُونَ فِي خَلْقِ ٱلسَّمَٰوَٰتِ وَٱلْأَرْضِ رَبَّنَا مَا خَلَقْتَ هَٰذَا بَٰطِلًا سُبْحَٰنَكَ فَقِنَا عَذَابَ ٱلنَّارِ﴾ سُورَةُ آل عمران 190-191:3

Science, then, increases our faith. People have discovered fossils, bones and ancient artifacts, which point to a hidden past we don't know much about. Allah commands us to travel and learn from what we see.

We know that Earth existed long before the appearance of humans. Allah said, *Wasn't there a long period of time before humans were even mentioned? Al 'Insaan (The Man) 76:1*

﴿هَلْ أَتَىٰ عَلَى ٱلْإِنسَٰنِ حِينٌ مِّنَ ٱلدَّهْرِ لَمْ يَكُن شَيْئًا مَّذْكُورًا﴾ سُورَةُ الإنسان 76:1

We also know from the geological timetable that Earth went through many ages before the advent of humans. In the following ayaat , we are given a very strong clue about the adaptability of life forms to their environment.

Allah said, *Don't you see that Allah sends rain from the sky? With it We produce plants of various colors. And in the mountains are colored layers, white and red, of various tones and some black in hue. And so too, among humans, and crawling creatures, and cattle. They are of various colors. Those among Allah's servants who have knowledge truly fear Him, for Allah is Mighty and Forgiving.*
Surat Faatir (The Originator) 35:27-28

﴿أَلَمْ تَرَ أَنَّ ٱللَّهَ أَنزَلَ مِنَ ٱلسَّمَآءِ مَآءً فَأَخْرَجْنَا بِهِۦ ثَمَرَٰتٍ مُّخْتَلِفًا أَلْوَٰنُهَا وَمِنَ ٱلْجِبَالِ جُدَدٌ بِيضٌ وَحُمْرٌ مُّخْتَلِفٌ أَلْوَٰنُهَا وَغَرَابِيبُ سُودٌ﴾﴿وَمِنَ ٱلنَّاسِ وَٱلدَّوَآبِّ وَٱلْأَنْعَٰمِ مُخْتَلِفٌ أَلْوَٰنُهُۥ كَذَٰلِكَ إِنَّمَا يَخْشَى ٱللَّهَ مِنْ عِبَادِهِ ٱلْعُلَمَٰٓؤُاْ إِنَّ ٱللَّهَ عَزِيزٌ غَفُورٌ﴾ سُورَةُ فاطر 27-28:35

So while Muslims agree with the Creationists who say Allah made the Universe, we disagree with how quickly it was constructed and with the position that Earth is the center of focus for the Creator. Allah declares Himself to be **Rabb Al 'Alameen** رَبُّ الْعَالَمِين **Lord of All the Universe**. Importantly, the word 'alameen in Arabic is plural, indicating more than one world or planet.

Because we do not reject the evidence presented to us by paleontologists or other scientists, we can accept some of what is theorized about the origins of life on Earth. However, we disagree with those who claim creation occurred by chance and without Divine purpose. Allah tells us in the Qur'an that He is the Source of all things.

To Allah belongs the control of space and the Earth and Allah has power over all things. Surat Al 'Imran (The Family of 'Imran) 3: 189

﴿وَلِلَّهِ مُلْكُ ٱلسَّمَٰوَٰتِ وَٱلْأَرْضِ وَٱللَّهُ عَلَىٰ كُلِّ شَيْءٍ قَدِيرٌ﴾ سُورَةُ آل عمران 189:3

Islam takes the moderate position; Allah said we were created to be the middle community—never going to extremes.

And thus We have made you a medium (just) nation. Surat Al Baqarah (The Cow) 2:143

﴿وَكَذَٰلِكَ جَعَلْنَٰكُمْ أُمَّةً وَسَطًا﴾ سُورَةُ البقرة 143:2

The Qur'an is our standard, our determiner. For a Muslim, then, the evidence of dinosaurs, trilobites and ancient algae is not a threat to belief. Rather, it is a confirmation of the power of Allah.

Allah created every creature from water. Of them are some that creep on their bellies, some that walk on two legs and some that walk on four. Allah creates what He wills, for He has power over all things. We have indeed sent signs that make things clear and Allah guides whom He wills to the straight way.
Surat An-Noor (The Light) 24: 45-46

The Earth may be as old as 4.5 billion years!

﴿وَٱللَّهُ خَلَقَ كُلَّ دَآبَّةٍ مِّن مَّآءٍ فَمِنْهُم مَّن يَمْشِي عَلَىٰ بَطْنِهِۦ وَمِنْهُم مَّن يَمْشِي عَلَىٰ رِجْلَيْنِ وَمِنْهُم مَّن يَمْشِي عَلَىٰٓ أَرْبَعٍ يَخْلُقُ ٱللَّهُ مَا يَشَآءُ إِنَّ ٱللَّهَ عَلَىٰ كُلِّ شَيْءٍ قَدِيرٌ﴾ ﴿لَّقَدْ أَنزَلْنَآ ءَايَٰتٍ مُّبَيِّنَٰتٍ وَٱللَّهُ يَهْدِي مَن يَشَآءُ إِلَىٰ صِرَٰطٍ مُّسْتَقِيمٍ﴾ سُورَةُ النُّور 24:45 - 46

Who else but Allah could have made such a complex and mysterious Universe?
Even the miraculous fertilization of an egg cannot convince some people to believe in the ingenuity of the Creator of the Universe. Allah asked, *Then what message will they believe in after this? Surat Al Mursalat (Those Sent Forth) 77:50*

﴿فَبِأَيِّ حَدِيثٍ بَعْدَهُۥ يُؤْمِنُونَ﴾ سُورَةُ المُرْسَلات 77:50

The fossil record is like a timeline. The deeper one digs into the Earth, the older and less complex the fossils get.

A Trilobite.

Dinosaurs lived from 220 million years ago until 65 million years ago. We know of their existence through the discovery of fossils, bones and rock imprints. They are a sign of Allah's creative will.

The early surface of Earth suffered frequent volcanic eruptions and earthquakes.

Who Are We?

Who are we? How did we get here? What is our purpose? Why are we here and where are we going?

Philosophers have spent thousands of years trying to answer these questions. When one philosopher believed that an answer was found, another would criticize the theory and replace it with something different. How can we know what it all means? How can we understand our origins?

Why not ask the One Who made us? Allah, the Creator of the Universe and Builder of Life, knows us best. So in order to understand why Allah chose humans over any other type of intelligent creature, we can consult the guidebook Allah left in our hands. In this book, we have the answers to all of our most important questions. The Qur'an is where we will return again and again as we explore the origin of humankind.

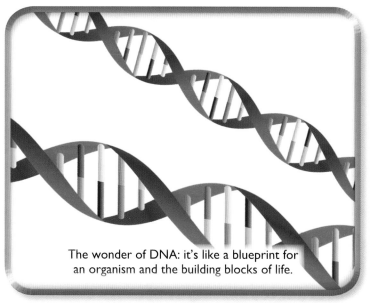

The wonder of DNA: it's like a blueprint for an organism and the building blocks of life.

Oh Mankind! Have awareness of your Lord Who created you from a single person and created for him a mate of similar nature. From the two He scattered countless men and women. Be aware of Allah, by Whom you demand your (human) rights. Respect the womb (of mothers) for Allah watches over you.
Surat An-Nisa' (The Women) 4:1

﴿يَا أَيُّهَا ٱلنَّاسُ ٱتَّقُوا۟ رَبَّكُمُ ٱلَّذِى خَلَقَكُم مِّن نَّفْسٍ وَٰحِدَةٍ وَخَلَقَ مِنْهَا زَوْجَهَا وَبَثَّ مِنْهُمَا رِجَالًا كَثِيرًا وَنِسَاءً وَٱتَّقُوا۟ ٱللَّهَ ٱلَّذِى تَسَاءَلُونَ بِهِۦ وَٱلْأَرْحَامَ إِنَّ ٱللَّهَ كَانَ عَلَيْكُمْ رَقِيبًا﴾ سُورَةُ النِّسَاء:1:4

What Other Intelligent Life Exists?

Before humanity existed on Earth. Allah had already formed the physical Universe and populated it with angels and jinn. **Angels** مَلَائِكَة are made from the elements of light and are created for carrying out Allah's will. The **Jinn** جِن are made from the elements of fire and have a very limited interaction with mankind. They are intelligent like humans and generally exist only in their own dimension.

In time, Allah willed the creation of a third type of being. Before He initiated this new life form that would be called **Human** بَشَر, He first posed a question to everything else in the Universe: Was anything willing to take responsibility for its actions? No. No other creation agreed. Only man accepted the responsibility.

Allah said, *We did offer the Trust to the heavens and the earth and the mountains, but they refused to bear its burden and were afraid of it, and man picked it up. Indeed he is unjust (to himself), unaware (of the end).* Surat Al Ahzab (The Confederates) 33:72

﴿إِنَّا عَرَضْنَا ٱلْأَمَانَةَ عَلَى ٱلسَّمَوَٰتِ وَٱلْأَرْضِ وَٱلْجِبَالِ فَأَبَيْنَ أَن يَحْمِلْنَهَا وَأَشْفَقْنَ مِنْهَا وَحَمَلَهَا ٱلْإِنسَنُ إِنَّهُ كَانَ ظَلُومًا جَهُولًا﴾ سُورَةُ الأحزاب:72:33

Thus, the human spirit accepted His challenge, and so Allah created man. The angels initially objected, understanding the full extent of man's ability to choose to accept or reject Allah's guidance. The angels, who only do Allah's bidding, argued that men would create disorder and chaos.

But Allah knew exactly what He intended to create, and He fashioned men in the form that He willed. Afterwards, He gave mankind the faculties of sight, speech, hearing and reason. As Allah declared, *He is the One Who created for you hearing, sight, feeling and understanding. Yet you are not very thankful.* Surat Al Mu'minun (The Believers) 23: 78

﴿وَهُوَ ٱلَّذِى أَنشَأَ لَكُمُ ٱلسَّمْعَ وَٱلْأَبْصَرَ وَٱلْأَفْـِٔدَةَ قَلِيلًا مَّا تَشْكُرُونَ﴾ سُورَةُ المُؤمِنون:78:23

Allah then demonstrated to the angels that humans were created with superior qualities. He ordered the angels to bow to the first human, Adam, in respect. All the angels bowed as they only obey their Creator. A jinn, however, named Iblis refused.

When Allah questioned Iblis as to why he refused to bow, Iblis responded with pride and arrogance. He exclaimed that he was made from the elements of fire, while the humans were made from mere elements of earth (clay).

Allah then banished Iblis for his disobedience and pride, as well as those jinn who followed him. In retaliation, Iblis requested to mislead all humans into error and chaos if given the opportunity. Allah the Master of all granted the request of Iblis with the condition that only those who rejected Him (Allah) could be misled by Iblis.

Recall when your Lord said to the angels, "I am going to create a human being from a ringing clay made of decayed mud. When I form him perfect, and blow in him of My spirit, then you must fall down before him in prostration." So the angels prostrated themselves, all together, Except Iblis (Satan). He refused to join those who prostrated. He (Allah) said, "O Iblis, what is the matter with you that you did not join those who prostrated?" He said, "I am not such that I should prostrate myself before a mortal whom You have created from a ringing clay made of decayed mud." He said, "Then, get out of here, for you are an outcast, And upon you is the curse up to the Day of Judgement." He said, "My Lord, then give me respite up to the day they (the dead) shall be raised." He (Allah) said, "Well, respite is given to you until the day of the Appointed Time." He said, "My Lord, since You made me go astray, I swear that I shall beautify for them (evils) on the earth, and shall lead all of them astray, Except those of Your servants from among them who are chosen (by You)." He (Allah) said, "This is the straight path leading to Me (that a person is chosen by Me through his good deeds). My servants are such that you have no power over them except those of the deviators who will follow you. And Jahannam (Hell) is the promised place for them all." *Surat Al Hijr (The Rocky Tract) 15:28-43*

﴿وَإِذْ قَالَ رَبُّكَ لِلْمَلَٰٓئِكَةِ إِنِّى خَٰلِقٌۢ بَشَرًا مِّن صَلْصَٰلٍ مِّنْ حَمَإٍ مَّسْنُونٍ﴾﴿فَإِذَا سَوَّيْتُهُۥ وَنَفَخْتُ فِيهِ مِن رُّوحِى فَقَعُواْ لَهُۥ سَٰجِدِينَ﴾ ﴿فَسَجَدَ ٱلْمَلَٰٓئِكَةُ كُلُّهُمْ أَجْمَعُونَ﴾﴿إِلَّآ إِبْلِيسَ أَبَىٰٓ أَن يَكُونَ مَعَ ٱلسَّٰجِدِينَ﴾﴿قَالَ يَٰٓإِبْلِيسُ مَا لَكَ أَلَّا تَكُونَ مَعَ ٱلسَّٰجِدِينَ﴾﴿قَالَ لَمْ أَكُن لِّأَسْجُدَ لِبَشَرٍ خَلَقْتَهُۥ مِن صَلْصَٰلٍ مِّنْ حَمَإٍ مَّسْنُونٍ﴾﴿قَالَ فَٱخْرُجْ مِنْهَا فَإِنَّكَ رَجِيمٌ﴾﴿وَإِنَّ عَلَيْكَ ٱللَّعْنَةَ إِلَىٰ يَوْمِ ٱلدِّينِ﴾ ﴿قَالَ رَبِّ فَأَنظِرْنِىٓ إِلَىٰ يَوْمِ يُبْعَثُونَ﴾﴿قَالَ فَإِنَّكَ مِنَ ٱلْمُنظَرِينَ﴾﴿إِلَىٰ يَوْمِ ٱلْوَقْتِ ٱلْمَعْلُومِ﴾﴿قَالَ رَبِّ بِمَآ أَغْوَيْتَنِى لَأُزَيِّنَنَّ لَهُمْ فِى ٱلْأَرْضِ وَلَأُغْوِيَنَّهُمْ أَجْمَعِينَ﴾﴿إِلَّا عِبَادَكَ مِنْهُمُ ٱلْمُخْلَصِينَ﴾﴿قَالَ هَٰذَا صِرَٰطٌ عَلَىَّ مُسْتَقِيمٌ﴾﴿إِنَّ عِبَادِى لَيْسَ لَكَ عَلَيْهِمْ سُلْطَٰنٌ إِلَّا مَنِ ٱتَّبَعَكَ مِنَ ٱلْغَاوِينَ﴾﴿وَإِنَّ جَهَنَّمَ لَمَوْعِدُهُمْ أَجْمَعِينَ﴾ سُورَةُ الْحِجْرِ 15:28-43

Adam and Hawwa

Allah placed Adam and his mate Hawwa and they lived carefree in a garden paradise. Allah gave them only one ruling: that they should not approach one particular tree. This tree was neither special nor magical, but merely a test.[2]

Iblis, who was then referred to as **Shaytan شَيْطَان Devil**, came into the garden and tempted the pair to eat from the tree. For their disobedience, Allah expelled them from the garden paradise and into the precarious world where they would have to fend for themselves.

---

2 It was Iblis who told Adam and Hawwa that the tree was magical and contained powers. There are some other religious traditions that teach that the woman misled the man and that the pain of childbirth is punishment on the women for this sin. Still other traditions teach that this was the original sin, and the guilt of that sin is still carried by each human on earth. Islam, on the other hand, says that both Adam and Hawwa were equally responsible for disobeying Allah. Muslims believe that they asked for forgiveness, and Allah forgave them. No soul is ever responsible for the sins of another. (See 7:19-27)

The humans asked for Allah's forgiveness. Allah said, They (Adam and Eve) said, Our Lord! We have wronged our own souls. If you forgive us not and bestow not upon us your Mercy, we shall certainly be lost. Surat Al 'Araaf (The Heights) 7:23.

﴿قَالَا رَبَّنَا ظَلَمْنَا أَنفُسَنَا وَإِن لَّمْ تَغْفِرْ لَنَا وَتَرْحَمْنَا لَنَكُونَنَّ مِنَ الْخَاسِرِينَ﴾ سُورَةُ الأَعْرَاف 7:23

Allah accepted their repentance and forgave them. He then informed them that whoever follows the guidance of Allah will be protected. Those who disbelieve in His signs will be punished. (2:38-39) Where was the garden paradise? How long ago did they live expelled in the untouched wilderness? For these answers, we can turn to what archeologists and anthropologists have discovered. (16:43)

Scientists are in virtual agreement that every human being alive today can be traced back to the same ancestor couple. Genetic tests and DNA studies have confirmed that we are all one large extended family. The oldest known humanoid remains have been found in East Africa and date back about 3,000,000 years.

Those remains, however, are not entirely human in comparison to us today. Scientists have classified modern humans as Homo Sapiens, and the earliest bones of our particular species are around 150,000 to 200,000 years old. These first humans are said to have migrated out of Africa and into the Middle East and Europe about 60,000 years ago. They replaced earlier species and came to dominate the land completely.

Around 35,000 years ago, people began to form small communities. Then, approximately 7,000 years ago, people started to farm and cultivate the land they lived on, leading to the start of civilization as we know it today.

Why Did Humans Separate?

All men and women today originate from these first two people, Adam and Hawwa. Allah explains that the earliest humans began as part of one small community but soon multiplied. Allah's plan for the creation of mankind was that races would differ, yet those very differences would intrigue men and women to know each other. Unfortunately, mankind eventually split because of those differences and due to pride and arrogance. Men created and populated many nations that persistently rebelled against each other and against the guidance of Allah. Allah sent prophets to guide them, but most of them ignored the messages and continued in their prideful disobedience. Many ancient societies were destroyed for their wrongdoings.

All men used to be a single community (of a single faith). Then (after they differed in matters of faith), Allah sent prophets carrying good news and warnings and sent down with them the Book of Truth to judge between people in matters of their dispute. But it was none other than those to whom it (the Book) was given who, led by envy against each other, disputed it after the clear signs had come to them. Then Allah, by His will, guided those who believed to the truth over which they disputed; and Allah guides whom He wills to the straight path. Surat Al Baqarah (The Cow) 2:213

﴿كَانَ النَّاسُ أُمَّةً وَاحِدَةً فَبَعَثَ اللَّهُ النَّبِيِّينَ مُبَشِّرِينَ وَمُنذِرِينَ وَأَنزَلَ مَعَهُمُ الْكِتَابَ بِالْحَقِّ لِيَحْكُمَ بَيْنَ النَّاسِ فِيمَا اخْتَلَفُوا فِيهِ وَمَا اخْتَلَفَ فِيهِ إِلَّا الَّذِينَ أُوتُوهُ مِن بَعْدِ مَا جَاءَتْهُمُ الْبَيِّنَاتُ بَغْيًا بَيْنَهُمْ فَهَدَى اللَّهُ الَّذِينَ آمَنُوا لِمَا اخْتَلَفُوا فِيهِ مِنَ الْحَقِّ بِإِذْنِهِ وَاللَّهُ يَهْدِي مَن يَشَاءُ إِلَى صِرَاطٍ مُّسْتَقِيمٍ﴾ سُورَةُ البَقَرَة 2:213

How were Adam and Hawwa, the first of this species, created? The ability of modern humans to think, shape, plan, create art and change their environment is unprecedented in Earth's natural history. Anthropologists are constantly debating our origins. Muslims find the answers to the current pressing debates within the Qur'an.

We have created man in the best composition. Surat At-Tin (The Fig) 95: 4

We have abilities that make us aware of our surroundings, and the gift of reasoning, so we can understand and make sense of the world around us.

Allah has brought you forth from your mothers' wombs when you knew nothing, and He made for you ears, eyes and hearts, so that you may be grateful. Surat An-Nahl (The Bees) 16:78

﴿وَٱللَّهُ أَخْرَجَكُم مِّنۢ بُطُونِ أُمَّهَٰتِكُمْ لَا تَعْلَمُونَ شَيْـًٔا وَجَعَلَ لَكُمُ ٱلسَّمْعَ وَٱلْأَبْصَٰرَ وَٱلْأَفْـِٔدَةَ لَعَلَّكُمْ تَشْكُرُونَ﴾ سُورَةُ ٱلنَّحْلِ 78:16

Additionally, we were made with a disposition to know Allah. Specifically, our basic natural way or **Fitrah** فِطْرَة prompts us towards belief in Allah. Allah created Adam by shaping him from the clay of the earth and then breathing the **Ruh** رُوح **Spirit** into him. The ruh is created by Allah. (15:29)

At the same time, humans have an earthly response system that compels us to satisfy our basic instincts. We are gifted with intelligence, but we can be seduced by our base desires. Shaytan also promised to whisper into the hearts and mind of mankind to lead people astray through pride and arrogance. Yet Allah revealed His guidance to chosen people, prophets and messengers, who would call them back to the straight way.

Through Allah's guidance and with the divine messages and character of messengers and prophets, we learn how to fulfill our responsibilities, particularly in worshipping Allah. If we choose to surrender to and obey Allah, then we become worthy of reward. If, however, we reject our Creator and instead follow only our desires, we develop many vices, including greed, gluttony, hatred, envy and anger. In this instance, we will incur a punishment possibly in this life and in the Hereafter. (4:147)

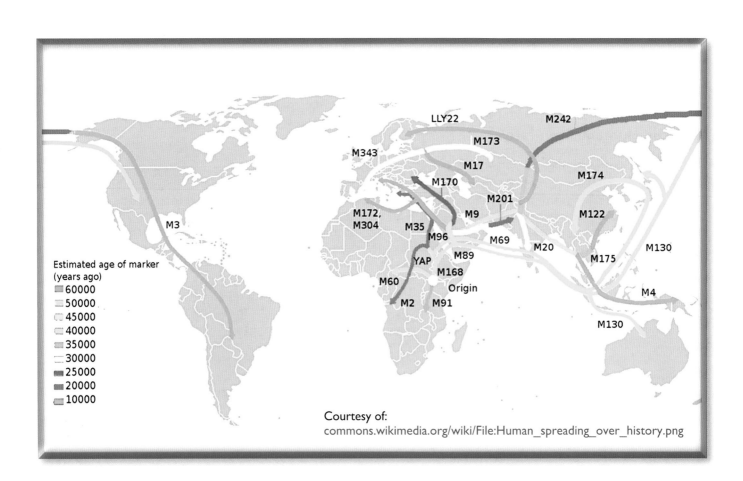

Courtesy of:
commons.wikimedia.org/wiki/File:Human_spreading_over_history.png

What Is Our Nature?

Humans were created with certain qualities of strength such as self-awareness, intelligence, sight and feeling. At the same time, humans have weaknesses, earthly desires and motivations that prompt us to seek satisfaction and fulfillment at any cost. These two competing forces operate in all of us. When combined together in a balanced way, they can create what we call the human spirit.

Our basic nature is one of good, and our hearts are constantly directing us to seek the higher power outside of ourselves. But Shaytan seeks to corrupt and to drive us towards our base natures and desires. Small thoughts, faint whispers, an urge, a flash of emotion—these are the means by which we can fall into the clutches of the Shaytan and help him fulfill his promise.

Why is Shaytan allowed to tempt us? Yet, we have an instinct which calls us back towards Allah? Allah has declared that He created humans and jinn only to worship Him and obey His laws.

I have only created jinn and humans so they can worship Me. Surat Ath- Thaariyaat (The Winds that Scatter) 51:56

﴿وَمَا خَلَقْتُ الْجِنَّ وَالْإِنسَ إِلَّا لِيَعْبُدُونِ﴾ سُورَةُ الذَّارِيَات 56:51

Allah gave mankind the ability to choose whether or not to worship and obey Him. The jinn on the other hand have very limited interaction with mankind and are prone to arrogance, which leads them to disobedience.

To Him will be the return of all of you. The promise of Allah is sure. He is the One Who began the process of creation and then repeats it, so He can reward with justice those who believe and do good. But those who reject Him will have boiling fluid and a painful punishment because they rejected Him. Surat Yunus (Jonah) 10:4

﴿إِلَيْهِ مَرْجِعُكُمْ جَمِيعًا وَعْدَ اللهِ حَقًّا إِنَّهُ يَبْدَؤُا الْخَلْقَ ثُمَّ يُعِيدُهُ لِيَجْزِيَ الَّذِينَ ءَامَنُوا وَعَمِلُوا الصَّلِحَتِ بِالْقِسْطِ وَالَّذِينَ كَفَرُوا لَهُمْ شَرَابٌ مِّنْ حَمِيمٍ وَعَذَابٌ أَلِيمٌ بِمَا كَانُوا يَكْفُرُونَ﴾ سُورَةُ يُونُس 4:10

You who believe, shall I lead you to a bargain that will save you from an awful punishment? It is that you believe in Allah and His Messenger and that you struggle in the Cause of Allah with your property and your selves. That is the best for you if you only knew. Then He will forgive you your sins and admit you to gardens beneath which rivers flow and to beautiful mansions in gardens of eternity. That is the supreme achievement! Surat As-Saff (The Rank) 61:10-12

﴿يَٰٓأَيُّهَا الَّذِينَ ءَامَنُوا هَلْ أَدُلُّكُمْ عَلَىٰ تِجَٰرَةٍ تُنجِيكُم مِّنْ عَذَابٍ أَلِيمٍ﴾ ﴿تُؤْمِنُونَ بِاللهِ وَرَسُولِهِ وَتُجَٰهِدُونَ فِي سَبِيلِ اللهِ بِأَمْوَٰلِكُمْ وَأَنفُسِكُمْ ذَٰلِكُمْ خَيْرٌ لَّكُمْ إِن كُنتُمْ تَعْلَمُونَ﴾ ﴿يَغْفِرْ لَكُمْ ذُنُوبَكُمْ وَيُدْخِلْكُمْ جَنَّٰتٍ تَجْرِي مِن تَحْتِهَا الْأَنْهَٰرُ وَمَسَٰكِنَ طَيِّبَةً فِي جَنَّٰتِ عَدْنٍ ذَٰلِكَ الْفَوْزُ الْعَظِيمُ﴾

سُورَةُ الصَّفّ 12-10:61

Life Is a Great Test

Islam tells us that our purpose in life is to worship Allah, work in His cause and spread the message to those who still don't know or believe. By doing so, we will be rewarded with an existence in a place of eternal delight.

But what about the person who denies the existence of Allah and His manifold signs? And also the one who lives a life filled with selfish pleasure, only seeking to satisfy his desires? Do these two deserve the same consequence or fate?

Those who don't place their hope in their meeting with Us (Allah), but are instead satisfied with the life of this world, and those who don't pay attention to Our signs, will be in the home of the fire because of what they earned. Those who believe and do good will be guided by their Lord because of their faith. Beneath them will flow rivers in gardens of happiness. They will call out, "Glory to You, Allah!" Their greeting will be "Peace." Their call will end with, "Praise be to Allah, the Lord of the Universe!"
Surat Yunus (Jonah) 10:7-10

﴿إِنَّ ٱلَّذِينَ لَا يَرْجُونَ لِقَاءَنَا وَرَضُوا بِٱلْحَيَوٰةِ ٱلدُّنْيَا وَٱطْمَأَنُّوا بِهَا وَٱلَّذِينَ هُمْ عَنْ ءَايَٰتِنَا غَٰفِلُونَ ۝ أُوْلَٰٓئِكَ مَأْوَىٰهُمُ ٱلنَّارُ بِمَا كَانُوا يَكْسِبُونَ ۝ إِنَّ ٱلَّذِينَ ءَامَنُوا وَعَمِلُوا ٱلصَّٰلِحَٰتِ يَهْدِيهِمْ رَبُّهُم بِإِيمَٰنِهِمْ تَجْرِي مِن تَحْتِهِمُ ٱلْأَنْهَٰرُ فِي جَنَّٰتِ ٱلنَّعِيمِ ۝ دَعْوَىٰهُمْ فِيهَا سُبْحَٰنَكَ ٱللَّهُمَّ وَتَحِيَّتُهُمْ فِيهَا سَلَٰمٌ وَءَاخِرُ دَعْوَىٰهُمْ أَنِ ٱلْحَمْدُ لِلَّهِ رَبِّ ٱلْعَٰلَمِينَ﴾ سُورَةُ يُونُس 10-7:10

It is clear that our life is a test. Allah knows our capacities as He is the one who created us, and He knows both the future and the past. We, however live and undergo life that in many way is like a series of test culminating in a final exam. At the same time our lives are short, and we never know if we will live beyond tomorrow.

Our duty is to surrender to Allah's perfect will and to do what is right. Even Shaytan cannot force us to fall into error. We choose it for ourselves. Allah said, But (Shaytan) had no authority over them, other than what We (allowed him to have), to test them to distinguish the one who believes in the next life from the one who doubts it. Your Lord watches over all things. Surat Saba' (Sheba) 34:21

﴿وَمَا كَانَ لَهُۥ عَلَيْهِم مِّن سُلْطَٰنٍ إِلَّا لِنَعْلَمَ مَن يُؤْمِنُ بِٱلْءَاخِرَةِ مِمَّنْ هُوَ مِنْهَا فِي شَكٍّ وَرَبُّكَ عَلَىٰ كُلِّ شَيْءٍ حَفِيظٌ﴾ سُورَةُ سَبَأ 21:34

Allah asks us to enter Islam whole-heartedly. Allah made us khalifa, successors, in implementing Allah's message on this earth. We are here to create order and harmony—not to cause disorder and chaos. Allah warned us of this when He said Know, all of you, that the life of this world is only play and amusement, partying and bragging, and racing for more wealth and children. Here is an example: The rain and what it grows brings happiness to the gardeners. But soon (the plants) wither. You will see them become yellow and dry, eventually crumbling to dust. But in the next life, the destruction is even greater (for those who do wrong.) The forgiveness of Allah and the best reward (is better). What is the life of this world but materials of deception? Surat Al Hadid (The Iron) 57:20

﴿ٱعْلَمُوٓا أَنَّمَا ٱلْحَيَوٰةُ ٱلدُّنْيَا لَعِبٌ وَلَهْوٌ وَزِينَةٌ وَتَفَاخُرٌۢ بَيْنَكُمْ وَتَكَاثُرٌ فِي ٱلْأَمْوَٰلِ وَٱلْأَوْلَٰدِ كَمَثَلِ غَيْثٍ أَعْجَبَ ٱلْكُفَّارَ نَبَاتُهُۥ ثُمَّ يَهِيجُ فَتَرَىٰهُ مُصْفَرًّا ثُمَّ يَكُونُ حُطَٰمًا وَفِي ٱلْءَاخِرَةِ عَذَابٌ شَدِيدٌ وَمَغْفِرَةٌ مِّنَ ٱللَّهِ وَرِضْوَٰنٌ وَمَا ٱلْحَيَوٰةُ ٱلدُّنْيَآ إِلَّا مَتَٰعُ ٱلْغُرُورِ﴾ سُورَةُ الحديد 20:57

How Should We Look at Our Lives?

The Blessed Prophet Muhammad once remarked, "Be in the world as though you were a stranger or a traveler." (Al Bukhari)

قَالَ رَسُولُ اللهِ ﷺ : «كُنْ فِي الدُّنْيَا كَأَنَّكَ غَرِيبٌ أَوْ عَابِرُ سَبِيلٍ». رَوَاهُ الْبُخَارِيُّ

Take, for another example, the story "The Owner of the Garden" contained in Surat Al Kahf (The Cave) (18:32-49). In this story, a man owned a huge tract of land and grew very wealthy. So much so that He even boasted, "I don't think this good life will ever end nor will I be brought back to account." But it did end. A raging storm destroyed his land and ruined him. He was grief-stricken and cried out in sorrow.

The French writer Montaigne once remarked, "Fortune can destroy in a second what has taken long years to build." Sometimes it becomes difficult to remember that fortune and wealth can be destroyed in an instant, without warning. Allah remarked, Wealth and children are the attractive things of this life, but good deeds are the things which last in the sight of your Lord, as the basis for reward and the best thing to rest your hopes on. Surat Al Kahf (The Cave) 18:46

﴿ٱلْمَالُ وَٱلْبَنُونَ زِينَةُ ٱلْحَيَوٰةِ ٱلدُّنْيَا وَٱلْبَٰقِيَٰتُ ٱلصَّٰلِحَٰتُ خَيْرٌ عِندَ رَبِّكَ ثَوَابًا وَخَيْرٌ أَمَلًا﴾ سُورَةُ الكهف 46:18

Islam teaches that when you leave this life, you only take your **Emaan** إِيمَان **Faith** and our record of deeds. If we have faith in Allah and try our best to lead a moral life, then we will be rewarded by Allah. Even those who make mistakes or do wrong are able to receive Allah's rewards, if they sincerely ask Allah for forgiveness by making **Tawbah** تَوْبَة **Repentance**. (48:13-14,)

Those who persistently disobey Allah﷾ should listen carefully to His warnings. Allah﷾ said clearly, *Warn humanity of the day when the wrath will reach them. Then the sinners will say, "Our Lord, give us more time, even just a little. Then we'll listen to Your call and follow the prophets!" What?! Didn't you used to swear before that you would never perish?* Surat Ibrahim (Abraham) 14:44

﴿وَأَنذِرِ ٱلنَّاسَ يَوْمَ يَأْتِيهِمُ ٱلْعَذَابُ فَيَقُولُ ٱلَّذِينَ ظَلَمُوا۟ رَبَّنَآ أَخِّرْنَآ إِلَىٰٓ أَجَلٍ قَرِيبٍ نُّجِبْ دَعْوَتَكَ وَنَتَّبِعِ ٱلرُّسُلَ ۗ أَوَلَمْ تَكُونُوٓا۟ أَقْسَمْتُم مِّن قَبْلُ مَالَكُم مِّن
زَوَالٍ﴾ سُورَةُ إِبْرَاهِيم 14:44

Once this short life is over, there will be no more chances left to do things differently. Allah﷾ reminds us that there are individuals who live their lives as if they will never die. But indeed, we will all die one day, even if we choose not to think about it. (56:57-62)

The Reality

Whatever we choose to do in life, the fact of the matter remains: life is short and temporary. Indeed, we are not permanent residents of the world. To further bring this truth home to our hearts, what if it were possible to know the year in which you were going to die? How would such knowledge affect you? Would you think a little differently? Would your lifestyle change? Would your goals suddenly appear a little foolish or meaningless? Would you suddenly have an overwhelming desire to follow Islamic teachings and believe in the Mercy of Allah﷾? Allah﷾ says, *The example of those who deny their Lord is that their accomplishments are like ashes upon which the wind blows furiously on a stormy day. They have no power over what they earned. They were far from the real goal.* Surat Ibrahim (Abraham) 14:18

﴿مَّثَلُ ٱلَّذِينَ كَفَرُوا۟ بِرَبِّهِمْ ۖ أَعْمَٰلُهُمْ كَرَمَادٍ ٱشْتَدَّتْ بِهِ ٱلرِّيحُ فِى يَوْمٍ عَاصِفٍ ۖ لَّا يَقْدِرُونَ عَلَىٰ شَىْءٍ مِّمَّا كَسَبُوا۟ ۚ ذَٰلِكَ هُوَ ٱلضَّلَٰلُ ٱلْبَعِيدُ﴾
سُورَةُ إِبْرَاهِيم 14:18

We are created to surrender our will to Allah﷾. (39:11-12) To undergo a set of tests to determine if we are worthy of eternal rewards or eternal punishment. What we see before our eyes glitters but is temporal. Only those who seek to please Allah﷾ in all that they do will ultimately succeed in the next life. (98:8)

'Ali bin Abi Talibﷺ once said, "People are asleep, and when they die, they will wake up." Some people are not aware of their purpose and thus appear as though they are 'sleeping-walking' through life.

Consider this example: Once the Blessed Prophet ﷺ was organizing an army to fight the idol-worshippers, but several people came forward asking to be excused from military duty.

Have you not seen those to whom it was said, "Hold your hands (from fighting) and be steadfast in Salah and pay Zakah." However, when fighting is enjoined upon them, then surprisingly, a group from them starts fearing people, as one would fear Allah, or fearing even more. They say, "Our Lord, why have you enjoined fighting upon us? Would you have not spared us for a little more time?" Say, "The enjoyment of the world is but a little, and the Hereafter is far better for the one who fears Allah, and you shall not be wronged, even to the measure of a fiber. *Surat An-Nisa' (The Women) 4: 77*

﴿أَلَمْ تَرَ إِلَى ٱلَّذِينَ قِيلَ لَهُمْ كُفُّوٓا۟ أَيْدِيَكُمْ وَأَقِيمُوا۟ ٱلصَّلَوٰةَ وَءَاتُوا۟ ٱلزَّكَوٰةَ فَلَمَّا كُتِبَ عَلَيْهِمُ ٱلْقِتَالُ إِذَا فَرِيقٌ مِّنْهُمْ يَخْشَوْنَ ٱلنَّاسَ كَخَشْيَةِ ٱللَّهِ أَوْ أَشَدَّ خَشْيَةً ۚ وَقَالُوا۟ رَبَّنَا لِمَ كَتَبْتَ عَلَيْنَا ٱلْقِتَالَ لَوْلَآ أَخَّرْتَنَآ إِلَىٰٓ أَجَلٍ قَرِيبٍ ۗ قُلْ مَتَٰعُ ٱلدُّنْيَا قَلِيلٌ وَٱلْءَاخِرَةُ خَيْرٌ لِّمَنِ ٱتَّقَىٰ وَلَا تُظْلَمُونَ فَتِيلًا﴾ سُورَةُ ٱلنِّسَاء 4:77

What is with you shall perish and what is with Allah shall last. And certainly, We shall bless those who observed patience, with their reward for the best of what they used to do. *Surat An-Nahl (The Bees) 16:96*

We are all warned that, *Wherever you are, death will find you; even if you are in mighty towers.* Surat An-Nisa' (The Women) 4: 78

﴿أَيْنَمَا تَكُونُوا يُدْرِككُّمُ الْمَوْتُ وَلَوْ كُنتُمْ فِي بُرُوجٍ مُّشَيَّدَةٍ﴾ سُورَةُ النِّسَاء 4:78

No can escape death. According to Islam, this is not the final nor permanent residence—that is the next life. Our purpose is to be tested, and through those tests build emaan so that the eventual outcome is the desired one—eternal paradise. (2:160 & 41:34)

And do not lose hope in the mercy of Allah. In fact, only the infidels lose hope in Allah's mercy. Surat Yusuf (Joseph) 12:87

﴿وَلَا تَأْيَسُوا مِن رَّوْحِ اللَّهِ إِنَّهُ لَا يَأْيَسُ مِن رَّوْحِ اللَّهِ إِلَّا الْقَوْمُ الْكَافِرُونَ﴾ سُورَةُ يُوسُف 12:87

Life does not end with death. Our physical bodies perish and decay, but the spirit, the ruh, that was breathed into us, is quickly released into the next world. It crosses over and quickly learns the outcome of the actions of the present life. Allah declared, *Indeed, Allah is the reality. It is He Who gives life to the dead, and it is He Who has power over all things.* Surat Al Hajj (The Pilgrimage) 22:6

﴿ذَٰلِكَ بِأَنَّ اللَّهَ هُوَ الْحَقُّ وَأَنَّهُ يُحْيِ الْمَوْتَىٰ وَأَنَّهُ عَلَىٰ كُلِّ شَيْءٍ قَدِيرٌ﴾ سُورَةُ الْحَج 22:6

The purpose of our lives can best be summed up in the few words of a man who reflected much and realized the truth: *I wouldn't be reasonable if I didn't worship the One Who created me and to Whom I will return.* Surat Ya-sin 36:22

﴿وَمَا لِيَ لَا أَعْبُدُ الَّذِي فَطَرَنِي وَإِلَيْهِ تُرْجَعُونَ﴾ سُورَةُ يس 36:22

Which do we choose? Gardens of eternity and a life of contentment or the pain and punishment of eternal fire? The Qur'an provides all the tools to help us to successfully complete the test of life. (3:90-91) We only have one chance to get our the record straight. (6:30-32)

Our beloved Prophet once said, "Allah forgives the person who commits a sin (then feels ashamed of it), purifies himself, offers a prayer and seeks His forgiveness." Then the Prophet recited these verses from the Qur'an: *Those who, when they do an evil thing or wrong themselves, but then remember Allah and implore forgiveness for their sins—and who can forgive sins except Allah?—And who do not knowingly repeat (the bad deed) they did, the reward for that kind of person will be forgiveness from their Lord and gardens underneath which rivers flow. They will live there forever, a bountiful reward for those who work (in Allah's way).* (3:135-136) (Abu Dawud)

قَالَ حَبِيبُنَا ﷺ: «مَا مِنْ عَبْدٍ يُذْنِبُ ذَنْبًا فَيُحْسِنُ الطُّهُورَ ثُمَّ يَقُومُ فَيُصَلِّي رَكْعَتَيْنِ ثُمَّ يَسْتَغْفِرُ اللهَ إِلَّا غَفَرَ اللهُ لَهُ». ثُمَّ قَرَأَ هَذِهِ الْآيَةَ:
﴿وَالَّذِينَ إِذَا فَعَلُوا فَاحِشَةً أَوْ ظَلَمُوا أَنْفُسَهُمْ ذَكَرُوا اللهَ فَاسْتَغْفَرُوا لِذُنُوبِهِمْ وَمَن يَغْفِرُ الذُّنُوبَ إِلَّا اللهُ وَلَمْ يُصِرُّوا عَلَى مَا فَعَلُوا وَهُمْ يَعْلَمُونَ ۞ أُولَٰئِكَ جَزَاؤُهُم مَّغْفِرَةٌ مِّن رَّبِّهِمْ وَجَنَّاتٌ تَجْرِي مِن تَحْتِهَا الْأَنْهَارُ خَالِدِينَ فِيهَا وَنِعْمَ أَجْرُ الْعَامِلِينَ﴾ 3:135-136. رَوَاهُ أَبُو دَاوُد

If anyone does good deeds, be they male or female, and has emaan, they will enter Paradise and no injustice will be done to them at all. Surat An-Nisa' (The Women) 4: 124

﴿وَمَن يَعْمَلْ مِنَ الصَّالِحَاتِ مِن ذَكَرٍ أَوْ أُنثَىٰ وَهُوَ مُؤْمِنٌ فَأُولَٰئِكَ يَدْخُلُونَ الْجَنَّةَ وَلَا يُظْلَمُونَ نَقِيرًا﴾ سُورَةُ النِّسَاء 4:124

The Blessed Prophet once said, "Whoever intends to do something good is rewarded by Allah with one good deed for it. If he or she then does that good thing, Allah rewards him or her from ten to seven hundred times. Whoever intends to do something wrong, but doesn't do it, is also rewarded by Allah one good reward. If he or she does that bad thing, he or she is accounted with only one bad deed." (Al Bukhari & Muslim)

عَنْ رَسُولِ اللهِ ﷺ: «مَنْ هَمَّ بِحَسَنَةٍ فَلَمْ يَعْمَلْهَا كَتَبَهَا اللهُ عِنْدَهُ حَسَنَةً كَامِلَةً، وَإِنْ هَمَّ بِهَا فَعَمِلَهَا كَتَبَهَا اللهُ عِنْدَهُ عَشْرَ حَسَنَاتٍ إِلَى سَبْعِمِائَةِ ضِعْفٍ إِلَى أَضْعَافٍ كَثِيرَةٍ، وَإِنْ هَمَّ بِسَيِّئَةٍ فَلَمْ يَعْمَلْهَا كَتَبَهَا اللهُ عِنْدَهُ حَسَنَةً كَامِلَةً، وَإِنْ هَمَّ بِهَا فَعَمِلَهَا كَتَبَهَا اللهُ سَيِّئَةً وَاحِدَةً». رَوَاهُ الْبُخَارِيُّ وَمُسْلِم

Say (on My behalf), "O servants of Mine who have acted recklessly against their own selves, do not despair of Allah's mercy. Surely, Allah will forgive all sins. Surely, He is the One who is the Most-Forgiving, the Very-Merciful. Turn passionately towards your Lord, and submit to Him before the punishment comes to you, after which you will not be helped. And follow the best of what has been sent down to you from your Lord before the punishment comes to you suddenly when you do not even expect." Lest someone should say, "Pity on me, because I fell short in respect of (observing the rights of) Allah and, in fact, I was one of those who mocked," Or (lest) someone should say, "If Allah were to show me the way, I would have surely been among those who fear Allah," Or (lest) someone should say when he sees the punishment, "Would that I have a chance to return, so that I may become one of those who are good in their deeds." No! My verses had reached you, but you called them untrue, and waxed proud and became of those who disbelieved. And on the Day of Judgement , you will see those who had forged lies against Allah (in a state) that their faces are turned black. Is it not that in Jahannam there is an abode for the arrogant? And Allah will save the God-fearing (from Jahannam), with utmost success granted to them such so as no evil will touch them, nor will they grieve. Surat Az-Zumar (The Groups) 39:53-61

• • • • • • •●●●●●●●●●●●• • • • • •

The Blessed Prophet ﷺ once said, "'Hearts can get rusty, just like metal.' When the people asked how that can be prevented, the Prophet replied, 'By remembering that you will die someday and by reading the Qur'an.'" (Al Baihaqi)

قَالَ رَسُولُ اللهِ ﷺ : «إِنَّ هَذِهِ الْقُلُوبَ تَصْدَأُ، كَمَا يَصْدَأُ الْحَدِيدُ إِذَا أَصَابَهُ الْمَاءُ، قِيلَ: يَا رَسُولَ اللهِ، وَمَا جِلاَؤُهَا؟ قَالَ: كَثْرَةُ ذِكْرِ الْمَوْتِ، وَتِلاَوَةُ الْقُرْآنِ». رَوَاهُ الْبَيْهَقِيُّ

Literature Selection

Surat Az-Zukhruf (The Ornaments of Gold)

Adapted from *The Holy Qur'an*
Arranged by Yahiya Emerick
(Explanatory words added in parentheses)

In the Name of Allah, The Most Gracious, The Most Merciful.

Ha Mim.* (1) By the Book that makes things clear. (2) We made it an Arabic Qur'an so you could understand it. (3) It (originated) in the Mother of the Book "Umm Al Kitab," which is kept in Our presence, transcendent and full of wisdom. (4) Should we take Our message away from you (Arabs), simply because you're transgressing people? (5)

Yet how many Prophets did we send to earlier civilizations? (6) No Prophet ever went anywhere without being mocked and ridiculed. (7) And so We destroyed (those nations), which were even mightier than this (one of yours). Thus, the example of earlier civilizations passes on. (8) Recognizing His Favors If you asked them, "Who created the Heavens and the Earth?" They would most likely reply, "They were created by the most Powerful and the most Knowledgeable One." (9) (And they would be right, for) He's the One Who spread the earth out for you and made many pathways throughout it so you can find the right direction. (10) (And He's the One Who) sends down sufficient rain from the sky to revive the dead land—and that's also how you'll be raised (up at the resurrection).(11) (He's also the One Who) created all living things in pairs, and He sent down (the knowledge of shipbuilding) so you could sail in ships, and (He's the One Who gave you) cattle, as well, so you could ride them, (12) sitting securely on their flat backs. Whenever you're sitting on (some mode of travel) you can say, "Glory be to the One Who subjected this to our (use), for we never could have mastered this by ourselves,(13) and we will certainly return to our Lord." (14)

They Claim Ignorance

Yet they have attributed to Him from His servants a portion.! Indeed, humanity is clearly (guilty of) suppressing (the truth)! (15) Has He given Himself daughters, (out of everything) He created, and then gave you the choice to have sons? (16) When one of them is told the good news of (the birth of a daughter)—the same thing that he so readily adds to the likeness of the Compassionate (God)—his face becomes downcast, and he's filled with terrible disappointment. (17) (Is it right that you would ascribe

---

* Al Huruf Al Muqatta'h الحروف المقطعة are unique letters that appear in the beginning of 29 suwar of the Qur'an. Muqatta'h means disjointed or unconnected letters. Their real meanings remain unknown and are considered by most Muslims to be known to Allah alone.

the qualities of a female), whom (you consider) to be raised merely as an ornament (for a man's life), and (whom you consider) to be incapable of speaking with directness, (with the qualities of God)? (18) And so they turn the angels into females, even though (the angels were made) only to serve God. Were they there when they were created? (If they were) then their evidence will be noted, and they will be questioned about it. (19) And then (the idol-worshippers) say, "If it had been the Compassionate (God's) will, then we would have never worshipped (any false gods)." However, they don't know what (they're saying), and they do nothing but guess. (20) Did We ever give them some scripture in the past that they're committed to? (21) No way! They're only (excuse is to) say, "This is the (religion) we found our forefathers following, so we're guiding ourselves according to their footsteps." (22)

And this is how it's always been: whenever We sent a warner before you to any nation, the well-to-do among them said, "This is the (religion) we found our forefathers following, so we're going to follow in their footsteps." (23) (And their warner would always) say, "What! Even though I'm bringing you better guidance than what you inherited from your forefathers?" (To which the people would always) reply, "As far as we're concerned, we don't (believe) that you've been sent (on any mission at all)."(24) And so We took payback from them—and oh, how (stunning) was the closure of those who rejected (the truth)! (25) Abraham told his father and his people, "I'm free of what you're worshipping! (26) (I'm only going to serve) the One Who made me, for He's the One Who's going to guide me." (27) And (Abraham) left this doctrine to posterity so that (people) after his time could turn back (to God). (28)

The Myth of Silver and Gold

But no! I've given (the luxuries of this world) to these (ungrateful people), as well as to their forefathers, until even now when a clear Messenger (has come to them) bringing them the truth. (29) So now that the truth has come to them, they (deny it), saying, "It's just some kind of magic, and we reject it." (30) (These idol-worshippers of Makkah go one step further by) asking, "Why isn't this Qur'an being sent down to someone important from either of the two (largest) cities (in the area)?" (31) Are they the ones who parcel out your Lord's mercy? In fact, We're the One who parcels out among them their resources in the life of this world. We promote some (people) above the rest in status so they can coerce labor from them, but the mercy of your Lord is far better than what they accumulate. (32) And if it wasn't for the fact that all (people) would (merge together) into one community (of greedy misers), then We would've given everyone who blasphemes against the Compassionate (God) silver roofs for their houses, and (silver) stairs upon which to climb, (33) and (silver) doors on their houses, and thrones (made of silver) to rest upon, (34) and golden ornament as well! But all of those are nothing but things to use in the life of this world. The next life, in God's view, is for those who were aware (of the difference). (35) Separation from God is the Root of All Evil. Whoever blinds himself to the remembrance of the Compassionate will have a devil assigned to him by Us to be his close companion.(36) They steer them away from the path even as they think they're being rightly guided. (37) (This goes on) until he comes back to Us and then says (to his devil), "If only we were as far apart as the east and then another east!" What a terrible companion (he had)!" (38)

(Knowing then that) you were wrong won't help you at all on that Day, for you both will (have an equal) share in the punishment! (39) Can you make the deaf hear or show the way to the blind or to someone who is clearly wrong? (40) Even if We took you away from

them, (as they wish to get rid of you), We would still get our due out of them, (41) and We might just show you what We've promised is coming to them, for We indeed have power over them. (42) So hold tight to the revelation that's coming down to you, for you're on a straight path. (43) Truly this (revelation) is the remembrance (intended) for you and your people, and soon you'll have to give an accounting (of how well you lived it). (44)

The Example of Moses

You should ask Our messengers who We sent before your time if We ever set up any gods for worship other than the Compassionate. (45) In the past, We sent Moses with Our signs to Pharaoh and his officials, and he said, "I'm a Messenger from the Lord of All the Worlds." (46) But (even though) He went to them with Our signs, they laughed at them. (47) We showed them sign after sign, with each one being more impressive than the last, until We finally seized them with (plagues) so they could (at least have a chance) to return (to God's path). (48) (In their fear) they cried out, "You wizard! Call upon your Lord for us by your covenant with Him (and remove these plagues from us), then we'll accept (your) guidance." (49) But (every time) We took away a punishment from them, they went back on their word. (50) And Pharaoh declared to his nation, "My people! Doesn't the kingdom of Egypt belong to me? Look at these rivers flowing underneath me. Don't you see them? (51) Aren't I better than (Moses), that vagabond who can't even speak properly? (52) Why isn't he wearing gold bracelets, and why isn't he flanked by angels in conjunction?" (53) This is how he made fools out of his people, for they obeyed him and were truly a rebellious nation. (54) When they provoked Us, We took Our due from them and drowned them all. (55) We caused them (to recede into history) and made them an example for those who would follow. (56)

The Example of Jesus

When the son of Mary is held up as an example, your people complain loudly (57) saying, "Are our gods better, (or that Jesus, whom the Christians worship)?" They're offering this (objection) against you for no other reason than (they like) to argue, or they're a very argumentative people. (58) (Jesus) was nothing more than a servant to whom We granted Our favor, and We made him an example for the Children of Israel. (59) If We had wanted to, We could've sent angels to live among you in the Earth who would've replaced you. (60) (Jesus) is a portent of the Hour (of Judgement), so don't doubt Its (coming), rather you should follow Me, for that is a straight path. (61) Don't let Satan steer you away, for he is your declared enemy. (62) When Jesus came with clear evidence (of the truth) he said (to his people),

"I've come to you with wisdom so I can resolve those issues that cause you to differ, therefore be mindful of God and obey me. (63) Truly God is my Lord and your Lord, so serve Him alone, for that is a straight path." (64) However, sects arose over differences among them, (in spite of Jesus' best efforts), so ruin upon those who do wrong, (for they're going to suffer) from the punishment of a Dreadful Day. (65)

Paradise Described

Are they waiting for the Hour to come upon them all of a sudden, without their knowing? (66) Brothers will be enemies on that Day, except among those who were mindful (of God). (67) My servants! You won't have any fear on that Day, nor will you feel sorrow. (68) You're the ones who have believed in Our signs and surrendered (to Us) (69) so enter into Paradise—you and your spouses both—in jubilation. (70)

Dishes (of food) and golden cups will be passed around among them! Everything that a soul could want will be there; everything that eyes could take pleasure in, and you will get to stay there forever! (71) This is the Paradise that you'll inherit (as a reward) for what you used to do (in the world), (72) and there will be an endless supply of delicious fruits for you to partake of. (73) Hellfire Described The wicked will remain in the punishment of Hellfire, (74) and its (torments) won't be lightened for them, even as they're engulfed by sorrow and despair. (75) But it's not that We're being unfair to them, rather, they're the ones who were unfair to themselves. (76) "Oh Master!" They will cry out (to the Warden of Hell), "If only your Lord would put an end to us!" But they'll be told, "(No), for you must remain." (77) People Say Incredible Things About God And so We've brought the truth to you, (people of Earth), yet most of you have an aversion to reality. (78) Have they made some kind of plan (to thwart Us), when We're the One Who decides matters, (79) or do they think that We didn't hear their secrets and private meetings? Certainly not! Our messengers (angels) are very close, watching them (as they talk). (80) Tell them, "If the Compassionate had a son, then I would be the first to worship him." (81)

Glory to the Lord of the Heavens and the Earth; the Lord of the Throne is (far removed) from what they're ascribing (to Him). (82) So leave them to quibble and play until they come upon their Day that they've been promised. (83) He's the One Who is God in the Heavens, and God on the Earth, and He is the Wise and the Knowing. (84) Blessed is the One Who controls the Heavens and the Earth and all in between them! He has the knowledge of the Hour, and you're all going to return back to Him. (85) The ones that they call upon besides God have no power to intercede, except for those who testified to the truth, and (God) knows who they were. (86) If you were to ask them who created them, they would be sure to say, "God did." So how come they're so far off the mark? (87) And (the Prophet) said, "My Lord Truly these are a people who won't believe!" (88) Then turn away from them and say, "Peace," but soon they'll know (the truth). (89)

Chapter 4
What Is Islam?

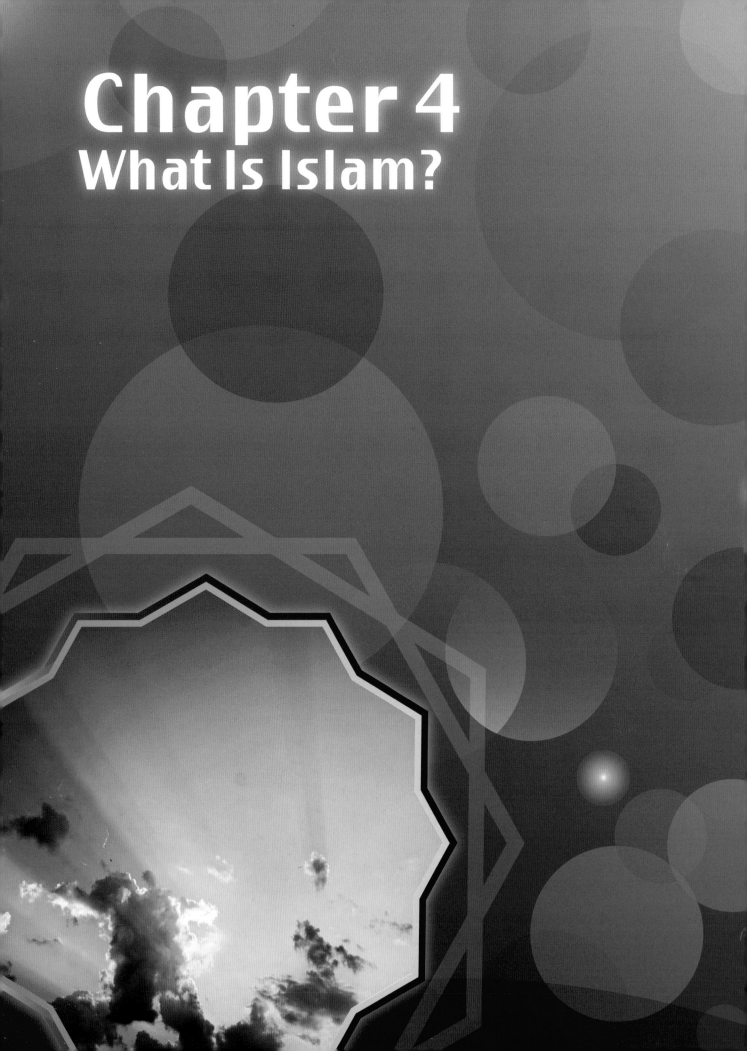

What Is the Definition of Islam?

Islam comes from the Arabic root word **Salima** سَلِمَ, which means both 'surrender' and 'peace.' Judaism, Christianity, Sikhism, Buddhism, Hinduism and all the other beliefs were named for either a person, a place or an ideology. The way of life Muslims follow was given the name by Allah himself. (6:162-163, 3:19)

The word Islam implies the following concept: by surrendering to Allah, one can let go of all fears and earthly temptations to have peace in the soul. Thus, Islam is surrendering one's will to Allah and by doing so, you find peace. The synonym 'surrender' is also used sometimes in place of 'submission.'

Our fitrah, or basic natural way, prompts us towards Allah, so when we answer His call, we find contentment in our hearts. In contrast, wealth and riches do not offer this total sense of harmony and balance. Only by submitting ourselves to our Creator and His guidance can we experience true feelings of contentment.

The Blessed Prophet once remarked, "True wealth does not come from an abundance of things. True wealth comes from a contented heart." (Al Bukhari & Muslim)

قال النبي ﷺ: «لَيْسَ الْغِنَى عَنْ كَثْرَةِ الْعَرَضِ وَلَكِنَّ الْغِنَى غِنَى النَّفْسِ». رَوَاهُ الْبُخَارِيُّ وَمُسْلِم

According to the Qur'an, Islam, submission to Allah's will, is the way of life that Allah designated for humanity, just as the rest of the Universe submits to His will. (41:11) The task of mankind is to choose whether to choose to submit or not. Allah declared, *Certainly the way of life acceptable to Allah is Islam (surrender to His Will) and those to whom the Book had been given did not show opposition until after knowledge had come to them, out of envy among themselves, and whoever disbelieves in the communications of Allah then surely Allah is quick in reckoning. Surat Al 'Imran (The Family of 'Imran) 3:19*

﴿إِنَّ الدِّينَ عِندَ اللَّهِ الْإِسْلَامُ وَمَا اخْتَلَفَ الَّذِينَ أُوتُوا الْكِتَابَ إِلَّا مِن بَعْدِ مَا جَاءَهُمُ الْعِلْمُ بَغْيًا بَيْنَهُمْ وَمَن يَكْفُرْ بِآيَاتِ اللَّهِ فَإِنَّ اللَّهَ سَرِيعُ الْحِسَابِ﴾ سُورَةُ آلِ عِمران

19:3

Anyone who follows his heart and intellect and seeks to submit to Allah as his Creator is called a Muslim. Therefore, a Muslim is a person seeking peace by submitting to Allah. It is Allah Who revealed His messages to chosen guides throughout human history. Most of the names of these prophets, messengers, sages and seers are unknown to us today. (7:35) The culture in which they lived and the rituals they taught varied from place-to-place and time-to-time. Yet, no matter what various rituals the people were given to practice, the core message was always the same. It was always, Islam, submission to the will of the Creator. (6:42-45, 14:4, 42:13)

For every Ummah (religious community) We have appointed a way of worship they are to observe. Therefore, they should never quarrel with you in the matter. And do call (them) to your Lord. Surely, you are on straight Guidance. Surat Al Hajj (The Pilgrimage) 22:67

﴿لِّكُلِّ أُمَّةٍ جَعَلْنَا مَنسَكًا هُمْ نَاسِكُوهُ فَلَا يُنَازِعُنَّكَ فِي الْأَمْرِ وَادْعُ إِلَىٰ رَبِّكَ إِنَّكَ لَعَلَىٰ هُدًى مُّسْتَقِيمٍ﴾ سُورَةُ الْحَجِّ 22:67

Every prophet brought Islam, or willing self-surrender to Allah. Each taught the practice of good deeds and forbade the evil ones. (40:78) Although various religions in times past were not officially named 'Islam,' each taught the same basic principles—labeled 'Islam' in the Qur'an. Previous messages were either lost or changed by human intervention throughout the centuries, resulting in the current mosaic of religions that we find throughout the world today. (42:14)

The Final Message

The final installment of Allah's divine revelation to humanity began in the year 610 CE. This guidance, the Qur'an, contains a complete summation of the way of life ordained by Allah. Muhammad bin 'Abdallah ﷺ, the prophet who bore this message, not only delivered it but was a living example of how to implement its guidance throughout life.

When asked how he lived his life, 'Aishah, who was the wife of Prophet Muhammad ﷺ, replied, "His character was the Qur'an." (Ahmad)

عَنْ أُمِّ الْمُؤْمِنِينَ عَائِشَةَ لَمَّا سُئِلَتْ عَنْ خُلُقِ رَسُولِ اللهِ ﷺ، قَالَتْ: «كَانَ خُلُقُهُ الْقُرْآنَ». رَوَاهُ أَحْمَد

So when we discuss Islam, we must consult the Qur'an and the Sunnah each and every step of the way. Islam can be understood best by dividing it into three areas: Islamic beliefs, Islamic practices and Islamic duties.

The Six-Five-Three Program

There are six main beliefs, five main practices and three main duties. The six beliefs of Islam are listed in what is known as the **Arkan Al Emaan** أَرْكَانُ الإِيمَان **Pillars of Belief**. In Arabic it is said as follows:

1. Belief in Allah الإِيمَانُ بِاللهِ عَزَّ وَجَلَّ.
2. Belief in the angels الإِيمَانُ بِالمَلَائِكَة.
3. Belief in the revealed books الإِيمَانُ بِالكُتُبِ السَّمَاوِيَّة.
4. Belief in the commissioned Messengers (peace be upon them) الإِيمَانُ بِالرُّسُل.
5. Belief in the resurrection and the events of Qiyamah الإِيمَانُ بِاليَومِ الآخَر.
6. Belief in the predestination by Allah of all things, both the good and the bad الإِيمَانُ بِالقَدَرِ خَيِّرِهِ وَشَرِّه.

O you who have believed, believe in Allah and His Messenger and the Book that He sent down upon His Messenger and the Scripture which He sent down before. And whoever disbelieves in Allah, His angels, His books, His messengers, and the Last Day has certainly gone far astray. Surat An-Nisa' (The Women) 4: 136

﴿يَٰٓأَيُّهَا ٱلَّذِينَ ءَامَنُوٓاْ ءَامِنُواْ بِٱللَّهِ وَرَسُولِهِۦ وَٱلۡكِتَٰبِ ٱلَّذِى نَزَّلَ عَلَىٰ رَسُولِهِۦ وَٱلۡكِتَٰبِ ٱلَّذِىٓ أَنزَلَ مِن قَبۡلُ وَمَن يَكۡفُرۡ بِٱللَّهِ وَمَلَٰٓئِكَتِهِۦ وَكُتُبِهِۦ وَرُسُلِهِۦ وَٱلۡيَوۡمِ ٱلۡءَاخِرِ فَقَدۡ ضَلَّ ضَلَٰلَۢا بَعِيدًا﴾ سُورَةُ النِّسَاء 136:4

The five practices, also known as the **Arkan Al Islam** أَرْكَانُ الإِسْلام **Pillars of Islam**, are given in detail. In Arabic it is said as follows:

1. The declaration, "There is no God but Allah and Muhammad is His prophet" Shahadah. الشَّهَادَةُ أَنْ لا إِلَهَ إِلاَّ الله، وَأَنَّ مُحَمَّدًا رَسُولُ الله.
2. Prayer الصَّلاة Salat.
3. Giving charity الزَّكَاة Zakah.
4. Fasting الصَّوْم Siyam.
5. Pilgrimage الحَجّ Hajj.

The Prophet ﷺ once said, "Islam is founded on five things: Declaring that there is no god but Allah and that Muhammad is the Messenger of Allah, establishing Salah (prayer), giving Zakah (Charity), making Hajj (pilgrimage) to the House (the Ka'bah in Makkah) and fasting in Ramadan." (Al Bukhari & Muslim)

قَالَ رَسُولُ اللهِ ﷺ: «بُنِيَ الإِسْلاَمُ عَلَى خَمْسٍ شَهَادَةِ أَنْ لاَ إِلَهَ إِلاَّ اللهُ وَأَنَّ مُحَمَّدًا عَبْدُهُ وَرَسُولُهُ وَإِقَامِ الصَّلاَةِ وَإِيتَاءِ الزَّكَاةِ وَحَجِّ البَيْتِ وَصَوْمِ رَمَضَانَ». رَوَاهُ البُخَارِيُّ وَمُسْلِمٌ

There are several duties that a Muslim must do based on the commandments of Allah ﷻ in the Qur'an. Three main ones are described in this book:

1. Calling others to Islam الدَّعْوَة Da'wah
2. Striving in Allah's ﷻ Cause الجِهاد Jihad
3. Encouraging good while forbidding evil الأَمْرُ بِالمَعْرُوفِ وَالنَّهْيُ عَنِ المُنْكَر

These are the features that make up the basic Islamic way of life. To be a practicing Muslim and to enjoy the benefits of peace through submission, one needs to know and implement these pillars and duties. Allah ﷻ declared, *Oh you who believe! Enter Islam wholeheartedly, and don't follow the path of the Shaytan. He is your declared enemy.* Surat Al Baqarah (The Cow) 2: 208

﴿يَٰٓأَيُّهَا ٱلَّذِينَ ءَامَنُواْ ٱدْخُلُواْ فِي ٱلسِّلْمِ كَآفَّةً وَلَا تَتَّبِعُواْ خُطُوَٰتِ ٱلشَّيْطَٰنِۚ إِنَّهُۥ لَكُمْ عَدُوٌّ مُّبِينٌ﴾ سُورَةُ ٱلْبَقَرَةِ 2:208

Islam teaches that we approach the relationship with our Lord individually. In Islam, there are no intermediaries between the individual person and Allah. (2:186)

Will they wait until Allah comes to them in canopies of clouds with angels, and the issue is decided? Indeed, to Allah do all issues return. *Surat Al Baqarah (The Cow) 2: 210*

﴿هَلْ يَنظُرُونَ إِلَّآ أَن يَأْتِيَهُمُ ٱللَّهُ فِي ظُلَلٍ مِّنَ ٱلْغَمَامِ وَٱلْمَلَٰٓئِكَةُ وَقُضِيَ ٱلْأَمْرُۚ وَإِلَى ٱللَّهِ تُرْجَعُ ٱلْأُمُورُ﴾ سُورَةُ ٱلْبَقَرَةِ 2:210

Islam is a complete way of life to follow. It speaks to our intellect, emotions, senses, and spirit. Allah said, Declare to them (Muhammad), "If you love Allah, then follow me. Allah will love you and forgive you your sins." For Allah is the Forgiving and Merciful. *Surat Al 'Imran (The Family of 'Imran) 3:31*

﴿قُلْ إِن كُنتُمْ تُحِبُّونَ ٱللَّهَ فَٱتَّبِعُونِي يُحْبِبْكُمُ ٱللَّهُ وَيَغْفِرْ لَكُمْ ذُنُوبَكُمْۗ وَٱللَّهُ غَفُورٌ رَّحِيمٌ﴾ سُورَةُ آلِ عِمْرَانَ 3:31

The Importance of Following Islamic Teachings

The effects of following this way of life are summed up best by our Creator. Allah tells us: Those (are the ones) who say, "Our Lord, surely we have believed, so forgive us our sins and save us from the punishment of the Fire," And those who are the patient, the truthful and the devout, who spend (in Allah's way) and who seek forgiveness in pre-dawn hours. *Surat Al 'Imran (The Family of 'Imran) 3:16-17*

﴿ٱلَّذِينَ يَقُولُونَ رَبَّنَآ إِنَّنَآ ءَامَنَّا فَٱغْفِرْ لَنَا ذُنُوبَنَا وَقِنَا عَذَابَ ٱلنَّارِ﴾ ﴿ٱلصَّٰبِرِينَ وَٱلصَّٰدِقِينَ وَٱلْقَٰنِتِينَ وَٱلْمُنفِقِينَ وَٱلْمُسْتَغْفِرِينَ بِٱلْأَسْحَارِ﴾ سُورَةُ آلِ عِمْرَانَ 3:

16-17

Prophet Muhammad was the last and the 'seal' in a long line of messengers. In his final sermon, the Blessed Prophet confirmed what Allah confirmed what is said in the Qur'an— after this, there will be no more revelations from Allah.

Muhammad is not a father of any of your men, but he is a messenger of Allah and the last of the prophets. And Allah has the Knowledge of every thing. *Surat Al Ahzab 33:40*

﴿مَّا كَانَ مُحَمَّدٌ أَبَآ أَحَدٍ مِّن رِّجَالِكُمْ وَلَٰكِن رَّسُولَ ٱللَّهِ وَخَاتَمَ ٱلنَّبِيِّۦنَۗ وَكَانَ ٱللَّهُ بِكُلِّ شَيْءٍ عَلِيمًا﴾ سُورَةُ ٱلْأَحْزَابِ 33:40

Prophet Muhammad advised that mankind would never go astray if they held onto two sources: the Qur'an and his Sunnah. Islam is to be followed based on what these two sources contain. Allah promises that Islam is the way of life that He will make prevail over all other ways of life. (61:8-9) Allah will look at our efforts and see how we balanced our lives with Islam. Anyone who learns of this message is offered the chance to discover it for himself. No one can be forced to follow Islam. (2:256) True belief will not exist through compulsion. Those who, when presented with the truth, knowingly reject it, will be losers on the Day of Judgment. (53:31)

Who is more wrong than the person who is reminded of the signs of his Lord but turns away from them, forgetting the deeds which his hands have done? *Surat Al Kahf (The Cave) 18:57*

﴿وَمَنْ أَظْلَمُ مِمَّن ذُكِّرَ بِـَٔايَٰتِ رَبِّهِۦ فَأَعْرَضَ عَنْهَا وَنَسِيَ مَا قَدَّمَتْ يَدَاهُ﴾ سُورَةُ ٱلْكَهْفِ 18:57

Islam, the way of life, for mankind is perfect and complete. To follow it is to be successful. To deny it is to fail in the definitive decision of your life.

Whoever seeks a faith other than Islam, it will never be accepted from him, and he, in the Hereafter, will be among the losers. *Surat Al 'Imran (The Family of 'Imran) 3:85*

﴿وَمَن يَبْتَغِ غَيْرَ ٱلْإِسْلَٰمِ دِينًا فَلَن يُقْبَلَ مِنْهُ وَهُوَ فِي ٱلْءَاخِرَةِ مِنَ ٱلْخَٰسِرِينَ﴾ سُورَةُ آلِ عِمْرَانَ 3:85

How I Chose Islam!

- SubhanAllah, I went from being an atheist to (alhamdulillah) being a God-fearing person who implements Islam into every aspect of my life.

- I converted September the 21st 2011. Islam was the total opposite of how I lived my life before. It was a HUGE turning point in my life.

- I accepted Islam. It began when I was alone and chanced onto a conversion story online, becoming captivated with the sincerity and genuine feelings I witnessed. I began to read more about Islam, feeling all along a powerful transitional calm. I found the location for jumah (Friday Prayer) in a nearby city and attended, returning home to read, think. Later that night I said my Shahadah (declaration of faith) to a brother by phone. I can't remember feeling greater happiness or peace. I bathed and prayed, convinced I'd made the most important decision of my life.

- In my senior year of high school, I made a decision that I was going to read the Quran. I felt as though a book which guided so many people and influenced so many world events deserved my reading at the least. When I later read the Quran, I found many of my questions answered and found Islam to be the one pure guidance for mankind.

- What surprised me (more) was that I found teachings of love, brotherhood, charity and forgiveness. I found verses regarding the adoption of orphans, protection of women and children, feeding of the poor and even of mercy in times of war. These writings touched me deeply and I found myself beginning to form a very new opinion of Muslims and the religion of Islam.

- I was at that point in my life a racist, but only because that is how I was raised and I didn't know any different. Years later after school and after college I met someone who started teaching me about Islam and it wowed me. I kept learning continually, becoming more and more fascinated by it. I Love Islam.

- I am Malaysian. I started being interested in Islam last year when I started my first year in high school. My high school is very religious as majority of the students are Muslims. My Muslim friends started sharing stories about Islam to me. I found out the truth about Islam. Islam isn't like what stereotypical people would say about it. It is a very great and peaceful religion.

- I'm a Filipino. I reverted to Islam when I was 21 while working in Qatar in the Middle East. I am proud that being so coward led me to embrace ALLAH and the Deen that made me so strong.

- I never felt secure growing up as I never had a religious routine. I always used to research Islam and think about converting. Researching Islam was like second nature to me; I found myself reading into it more and more. Not a day went by without reading about people's stories on reverting to Islam and what their daily routines involve. I began to fall in love with this beautiful religion. I admire how modestly the women dress from wearing a simple headscarf to the niqab/burqa. I said my Shahadah in August and have not and never will look back.

- I lived in a really anti-Islam area which, basically after research, drove me to Islam. So I wanted to research the anti-Islam in my city and was dazed by Islam. I wanted to learn more about it. My friends encouraged me to convert because I loved it so I took Shahadah a few months later. I started to take roles of a muslim by fasting and praying. I have to say, I feel at peace when praying and fasting has made me look deep into myself.

- I wanted to belong and believe with a community. The **Community أمة Ummah**- where I now belong- is a worldwide community, that share the same beliefs. I found my way to Islam on a summer holiday to Egypt, the devotion of the people, made me find my path to Allah. One day in a field near my house I felt a presence; at once I became aware that I had been with Allah. I had been enlightened!

- As Christian Jew, I was undecided on my religious path. I felt I had found the one true faith, even though I, as a Christian Jew, knew Islam, Judaism and Christianity shared the same God. God, HaShem and Allah are one of the same. I researched it over the years and finally I decided to take the plunge when I was 16.

- Sometimes the answer becomes so clear. Sometimes something happens deep within that can't be explained. Even though you might have been introduced to Islam in (such) a simple way, but then a moment of incredible clarity overcame me. I felt like for once in my life I knew what Allah has intended for me. He provided the guiding light on my path. I finally felt complete and whole with Him.

- I am very young. Not even a teenager yet. I experimented in Wicca, but found that I was never truly happy. I had left Christianity long before. I learned about Islam from a mutual friend, and have been very devout ever since.

- I was born in a traditional Hindu family in Panchthar, a far eastern district of Nepal. I came to know about Islam which enforced me towards study. I studied Quran in Hindi and other Islamic books for three years and at last when I came to be clear about the scientific facts in Quran I was unable to live out of the boundary of Islam. So in the year 2007, I became a Muslim.

- I found a book of the Koran at the library and it was that simple.

- I converted to Islam in 2010 during Ramadan. I spent time searching for the right religion, and I found peace and real people in the Muslim community. Now I am a very happy Muslim woman, and obey all the rules of Islam which made me a better person.

- I always turned to God for guidance, but I did not feel that Christianity was the right religion. It wasn't right to me, so I decided to search for answers. I read about Islam and learned as much as I could. About two years ago, I met a gentleman from Pakistan. He and his brother answered the many questions I had, and this year I made my decision to officially convert. As I read over the last few years, everything felt right, and it has been the best decision of my life. Al humdulillah.

- My path to Islam was quite unexpected. I met a young Muslim woman. She kept telling me how clean and peaceful she felt when she attended the mosque and how worshiping Allah brought her peace. I was desperately seeking a faith that brought me peace, I realize I was making a huge decision and a change in my former way of life. I converted at a beautiful mosque and was surrounded by many sisters who welcomed me into Islam. I read the Quran, the hadiths, and the qudsi hadiths for guidance. I struggled at first with the five obligatory prayers, but as soon as I remember I make up the prayers. When I attend Jumah on Friday, I leave feeling happy and at peace with my life.

What Makes One a Muslim?

Abu Hurayrah۞ narrated that the Blessed Prophet۞ said, "Every child is born following their Fitrah (i.e. they are a natural Muslim). It is the parents who make them a Jew, Christian or Zoroastrian (ancient Persian religion)." (Al Bukhari & Muslim)

عَنْ أَبِي هُرَيْرَةَ۞، أَنَّ رَسُولَ اللهِ ۞ : « كُلُّ مَوْلُودٍ يُولَدُ عَلَى الْفِطْرَةِ، فَأَبَوَاهُ يُهَوِّدَانِهِ أَوْ يُنَصِّرَانِهِ أَوْ يُمَجِّسَانِهِ». رَوَاهُ الْبُخَارِيُّ وَمُسْلِم

In other words, the culture we live in and the people around us have a strong influence on how our identity is formed. We have already explored what Islam means and some of the features of this way of life. Anyone who accepts Allah۞ without partners, believes in Allah۞ as the Creator, and then determines to live a life seeking the straight path towards their Lord, can be called a Muslim. (16:9)

We live in a world of varying cultures, languages, ideologies and social customs. Every day, children are born and the process of indoctrination into his culture begins. What makes each of them a Muslim? A Muslim name? The clothes they wear? The food they eat? The language they speak?

The world abounds with people who call themselves adherents of one faith or another. In truth their identity is based on cultural traditions rather than the teachings of the faith. Muslims are no exception. Islam is not passed from one generation to another through genetics. It is not a footnote attached to someone's name. It is not sustained because of one's attire, the food one eats, or the culture in which one lives.

Who Is a Muslim?

To be a Muslim, a person must profess his or her belief and learn what this way of life requires. Each person must gain knowledge of the teachings of Islam and know how to behave in their daily life. A person who never sincerely declared that *There is no god but Allah, and that Muhammad is His Messenger* has never even entered Islam!

Not everyone with a Muslim name or from a traditional Muslim country is a Muslim. A Muslim understands what Islam teaches and practices those teachings.

The **Shahadah** شَهَادَة **Statement of Faith**, contains two parts that signify something unique. The first part, *I declare that there is no God but Allah*, affirms the truth that nothing in this life, be it money, idols or fame, deserves our allegiance other than Allah۞.

The second part, *and I declare that Muhammad is the Messenger of Allah*, indicates that we accept the Prophet ۞ as our model, guide and spiritual leader. We must emulate the way he lived life and interacted in all his relationships and positions. These are the basic understandings that every Muslim must have.

There is indeed a good model for you in the Messenger of Allah—for the one who has hope in Allah and the Last Day and remembers Allah profusely. Surat Al Ahzab (The Confederates) 33:21

﴿لَقَدْ كَانَ لَكُمْ فِي رَسُولِ اللَّهِ أُسْوَةٌ حَسَنَةٌ لِمَنْ كَانَ يَرْجُو اللَّهَ وَالْيَوْمَ الْآخِرَ وَذَكَرَ اللَّهَ كَثِيرًا﴾ سُورَةُ الأَحْزَاب 21:33

Who Is a Kafir?

The word **Kafir** (plural Kuffar or Kafiroon) comes from the Arabic term **Kafara** كَفَرَ, which means to cover up or to hide something. A kafir is a person who covers up the truth and tries to hide it. So, a person who rejects the message of the Shahadah is called a kafir. Allah۞ stated emphatically, *Therefore, avoid those who turn away from Our Message and who desire nothing but the life of this world. That is as far as knowledge will reach them. Certainly, your Lord knows best those who are astray from His path and, He knows those who are guided.* An-Najm (The Star) 53:29-30

﴿فَأَعْرِضْ عَن مَّن تَوَلَّى عَن ذِكْرِنَا وَلَمْ يُرِدْ إِلَّا الْحَيَوةَ الدُّنْيَا﴾ ﴿ذَلِكَ مَبْلَغُهُم مِّنَ الْعِلْمِ إِنَّ رَبَّكَ هُوَ أَعْلَمُ بِمَن ضَلَّ عَن سَبِيلِهِ وَهُوَ أَعْلَمُ بِمَنِ اهْتَدَى﴾ سُورَةُ النَّجْم

30-29:53

While Allah۞ advises us to stay away from those who desire only this life, He reminds us that He Alone knows who is and is not guided. Therefore, it is not acceptable for Muslims to try to categorize other people. We never know who will become Muslim before their death or what might be in their hearts. These are secrets that only Allahﷻ knows and He Alone is the Judge of all matters.

Allahﷻ clearly points out that one can have different levels of faith. Allahﷻ describes these different levels of faith with this example: The (Bedouin) Arabs say, "We believe!" Declare to them, "You have no faith, but you only say, 'We are surrendered to Allah,' because emaan has not yet entered your hearts. But if you obey Allah and His Messenger, He will not lower any of your deeds, for Allah is the Forgiving, the Merciful." Only those are believers who have believed in Allah and His Messenger and have never since doubted. They have struggled with their wealth and their selves in the Cause of Allah. They are the sincere ones. Surat Al Hujurat (The Dwellings) 49:14-15

﴿قَالَتِ ٱلْأَعْرَابُ ءَامَنَّا قُل لَّمْ تُؤْمِنُوا۟ وَلَٰكِن قُولُوٓا۟ أَسْلَمْنَا وَلَمَّا يَدْخُلِ ٱلْإِيمَٰنُ فِى قُلُوبِكُمْ وَإِن تُطِيعُوا۟ ٱللَّهَ وَرَسُولَهُۥ لَا يَلِتْكُم مِّنْ أَعْمَٰلِكُمْ شَيْـًٔا إِنَّ ٱللَّهَ غَفُورٌ رَّحِيمٌ﴾ ﴿إِنَّمَا ٱلْمُؤْمِنُونَ ٱلَّذِينَ ءَامَنُوا۟ بِٱللَّهِ وَرَسُولِهِۦ ثُمَّ لَمْ يَرْتَابُوا۟ وَجَٰهَدُوا۟ بِأَمْوَٰلِهِمْ وَأَنفُسِهِمْ فِى سَبِيلِ ٱللَّهِ أُو۟لَٰٓئِكَ هُمُ ٱلصَّٰدِقُونَ﴾ سُورَةُ الْحُجُرَات 49:14-15

These ayaat demonstrate that there is a vast difference between saying that one surrenders to Allahﷻ and behaving as such. The most sincere of believers never waver in their faith and put all their resources into the Cause of Allahﷻ.

To become a 'sincere believer,' as Allahﷻ describes in the Qur'an, one must have belief, knowledge and actions that reflect those beliefs and teachings. Muslims are admonished to gently invite those who are astray back to the straight path of guidance. If we know of someone who is near Islam but is not following it the way it should be followed, we should call them to come closer to their Lord. We must use compassion, understanding and respect in our interaction with them because this was the way of Prophet Muhammad ﷺ and the main way in which we can reach their heart.

Invite others to the way of your Lord with wisdom and inspiring speech. Reason with them in a superior manner. Certainly, your Lord knows who has strayed from His path and who is guided.
Surat An-Nahl (The Bees) 16:125

﴿ٱدْعُ إِلَىٰ سَبِيلِ رَبِّكَ بِٱلْحِكْمَةِ وَٱلْمَوْعِظَةِ ٱلْحَسَنَةِ وَجَٰدِلْهُم بِٱلَّتِى هِىَ أَحْسَنُ إِنَّ رَبَّكَ هُوَ أَعْلَمُ بِمَن ضَلَّ عَن سَبِيلِهِۦ وَهُوَ أَعْلَمُ بِٱلْمُهْتَدِينَ﴾ سُورَةُ النَّجْل 16:125

What Is a Munaafiq?

Another class of people who fall short of being believers are the **Munaafiqoon** مُنَافِقُون **Hypocrites**. These are people who claim to be believers in front of other Muslims. However, they disobey the commandments of Allahﷻ and spend their energy in trying to divide people. (5:41, 9:124-125)

The Blessed Prophetﷺ once said, "There are four signs which, if present in a person, show him to be a hypocrite. If someone has one of them, then he has one part of hypocrisy until he gets rid of it. These are: when he is trusted with something, he cheats; when he talks, he lies; when he promises, he breaks his promise; and when he argues, he insults." (Al Bukhari, Muslim)

قَالَ رَسُولُ اللهِ ﷺ : «أَرْبَعٌ مَنْ كُنَّ فِيهِ كَانَ مُنَافِقًا خَالِصًا، وَمَنْ كَانَتْ فِيهِ خَصْلَةٌ مِنْهُنَّ كَانَتْ فِيهِ خَصْلَةٌ مِنَ النِّفَاقِ حَتَّى يَدَعَهَا إِذَا اؤْتُمِنَ خَانَ وَ إِذَا حَدَّثَ كَذَبَ وَ إِذَا عَاهَدَ غَدَرَ، وَ إِذَا خَاصَمَ فَجَرَ». رَوَاهُ الْبُخَارِيُّ وَمُسْلِم

Allahﷻ describes them this way, Among people are some who say, "We believe in Allah and the last day." But they don't really believe. They try to fool Allah and the believers, but they only fool themselves without realizing it. Their hearts are diseased, and Allah increases their disease because they were false to themselves. When they're told not to make trouble in the world, they answer, "We only want to make peace." But they're making trouble without realizing it. When they're told to believe like the other people believe, they say, "Should we believe like the fools?" But they're the fools without knowing it. When they meet the believers, they also say, "We believe." But when they're alone with their evil friends they say, "We're with you; we were only fooling them." Surat Al Baqarah (The Cow) 2:8-14

﴿وَمِنَ ٱلنَّاسِ مَن يَقُولُ ءَامَنَّا بِٱللَّهِ وَبِٱلْيَوْمِ ٱلْءَاخِرِ وَمَا هُم بِمُؤْمِنِينَ﴾ ﴿يُخَٰدِعُونَ ٱللَّهَ وَٱلَّذِينَ ءَامَنُوا۟ وَمَا يَخْدَعُونَ إِلَّآ أَنفُسَهُمْ وَمَا يَشْعُرُونَ﴾ ﴿فِى قُلُوبِهِم مَّرَضٌ فَزَادَهُمُ ٱللَّهُ مَرَضًا وَلَهُمْ عَذَابٌ أَلِيمٌۢ بِمَا كَانُوا۟ يَكْذِبُونَ﴾ ﴿وَإِذَا قِيلَ لَهُمْ لَا تُفْسِدُوا۟ فِى ٱلْأَرْضِ قَالُوٓا۟ إِنَّمَا نَحْنُ مُصْلِحُونَ﴾ ﴿أَلَآ إِنَّهُمْ هُمُ ٱلْمُفْسِدُونَ وَلَٰكِن لَّا يَشْعُرُونَ﴾ ﴿وَإِذَا قِيلَ لَهُمْ ءَامِنُوا۟ كَمَآ ءَامَنَ ٱلنَّاسُ قَالُوٓا۟ أَنُؤْمِنُ كَمَآ ءَامَنَ ٱلسُّفَهَآءُ أَلَآ إِنَّهُمْ هُمُ ٱلسُّفَهَآءُ وَلَٰكِن لَّا يَعْلَمُونَ﴾ ﴿وَإِذَا لَقُوا۟ ٱلَّذِينَ ءَامَنُوا۟ قَالُوٓا۟ ءَامَنَّا وَإِذَا خَلَوْا۟ إِلَىٰ شَيَٰطِينِهِمْ قَالُوٓا۟ إِنَّا مَعَكُمْ إِنَّمَا نَحْنُ مُسْتَهْزِءُونَ﴾ سُورَةُ الْبَقَرَة 2:8-14

Hypocrisy is a dangerous thing as it involves being a two-faced liar. Allahﷻ warns Muslims against descending into hypocrisy in these words: *Oh you who believe! Why do you say what you don't do? It's a hateful thing in Allah's sight to say what you don't do. Surat As-Saff (The Rank) 61: 2-3*

﴿يَٰٓأَيُّهَا ٱلَّذِينَ ءَامَنُوا لِمَ تَقُولُونَ مَا لَا تَفْعَلُونَ﴾ ﴿كَبُرَ مَقْتًا عِندَ ٱللَّهِ أَن تَقُولُوا مَا لَا تَفْعَلُونَ﴾ سُورَةُ الصَّفِّ 61:2-3

Allah has promised to punish the hypocrites unless they repent of their **Nifaaq** نفاق **Hypocrisy**. (4:142-146) He declared to them, *Make no excuses. You became disbelievers (by mocking at Allah and His Messenger) after you had professed Faith. If We forgive some of you (who repent and believe), We shall punish others (who carry on their hypocrisy) because they were guilty. Surat Al Tawbah (Repentance) 9:66*

﴿لَا تَعْتَذِرُوا قَدْ كَفَرْتُم بَعْدَ إِيمَٰنِكُمْ إِن نَّعْفُ عَن طَآئِفَةٍ مِّنكُمْ نُعَذِّبْ طَآئِفَةَۢ بِأَنَّهُمْ كَانُوا مُجْرِمِينَ﴾ سُورَةُ التَّوْبَةِ 9:66

The Blessed Prophet said, "The worst people in the sight of Allah on the Day of Resurrection will be the two-faced people. They appear to some people with one face and to other people with another face." (Al Bukhari)

قَالَ النَّبِيُّ : «تَجِدُ مِنْ شَرِّ النَّاسِ يَوْمَ الْقِيَامَةِ عِنْدَ اللهِ ذَا الْوَجْهَيْنِ، الَّذِي يَأْتِي هَؤُلَاءِ بِوَجْهٍ وَهَؤُلَاءِ بِوَجْهٍ». رَوَاهُ الْبُخَارِيُّ

With these statements from Allah and the Blessed Prophet , we can determine that a practicing Muslim is one who knows the Islamic teachings, follows those teachings and believes and practices them sincerely. He or she have faith in Allah and place their hope in Him. Muslims make Islamic practices a part of their life, and they remain a unified group. (3:102-103)

Whoever voluntarily believes in and practices Islam, and submits his whole heart and mind, is promised entrance into Paradise. (9:71-72) Allah asks only for gratitude and good words as per the example of Prophet Muhammad , not perfection. That is the message of Islam: believe and try one's best. (63:1-3)

Handling Objections

People have basic objections to Allah's call that can be summarized and answered intelligently, but to overcome them and offer explanations, one must have knowledge of the Qur'an and other religions. See the chart on the following page for some of those objections and answers. Look up the ayaat from the Qur'an to see how Allah answers these objections with utmost eloquence.

As you can see from the chart, there are a large number of objections to faith put forward by those who don't believe. The objections that have been raised from the most ancient days of human history are the same as those that are raised today. These objectors have chosen to disobey their hearts and their prophets and to leave this life losing the most important challenge of all. (7:174-177) Allah stated, *Those who reject faith, and die rejecting it, on them is the curse of Allah, the angels and of all humanity!* Surat Al Baqarah (The Cow) 2:161

﴿إِنَّ ٱلَّذِينَ كَفَرُوا۟ وَمَاتُوا۟ وَهُمْ كُفَّارٌ أُو۟لَٰٓئِكَ عَلَيْهِمْ لَعْنَةُ ٱللَّهِ وَٱلْمَلَٰٓئِكَةِ وَٱلنَّاسِ أَجْمَعِينَ﴾ سُورَةُ ٱلْبَقَرَةِ 161:2

The same situation occurred in the lifetime of the Blessed Prophet Muhammad ﷺ. The non-believers opposed him at every turn and made life unbearable at times. The idol-worshippers even resorted to incredible violence to try and silence the new message. But they were ultimately unsuccessful, for within a few years, people all over the world were flocking to this way of life.

Even though the message of Islam triumphed in the Middle East and much of Asia and Africa, the struggle with the disbelievers continued, as it does today. Hardly a moment goes by where the faith of a Muslim is not challenged by those around him or her. At every turn and in every hour, someone or something seeks to turn us from our Lord.

There is a great challenge faced by Muslims who live in non-Muslim countries. We are under the twin-pressures of external conflict and internal disunity. We are constrained to do things that compromise our faith, our morals, our family values and our faith in Allah.

Many of the people of the Scripture (Jews and Christians) wish that if they could turn you away as disbelievers after you have believed, out of envy from their own selves even after the truth has become manifest unto them. But forgive and overlook till Allah brings His Command. Verily, Allah is Able to do all things. Surat Al Baqarah (The Cow) 2:109

﴿وَدَّ كَثِيرٌ مِّنْ أَهْلِ ٱلْكِتَٰبِ لَوْ يَرُدُّونَكُم مِّنۢ بَعْدِ إِيمَٰنِكُمْ كُفَّارًا حَسَدًا مِّنْ عِندِ أَنفُسِهِم مِّنۢ بَعْدِ مَا تَبَيَّنَ لَهُمُ ٱلْحَقُّ فَٱعْفُوا۟ وَٱصْفَحُوا۟ حَتَّىٰ يَأْتِيَ ٱللَّهُ بِأَمْرِهِ إِنَّ ٱللَّهَ عَلَىٰ كُلِّ شَىْءٍ قَدِيرٌ﴾ سُورَةُ ٱلْبَقَرَةِ 109:2

At the same time, many of us have relatives who want us to make ethnic or national pride the basis of our identity rather than Islam. (2:272) It is as if we are stuck between two moving walls that are trying to crush us. (3:176)

If we understand and live Islam sincerely, Allah will provide us with an iron bar to place between the moving walls. The key is **Taqwa** تَقْوى **Awareness of Allah**. The more taqwa we develop, the stronger and more unyielding we will become. Solid taqwa is the one thing that bullets, bombs, torture, music videos, fashion and sin will never be able to destroy. So if you're wondering what to do when you're faced with people who refuse to listen to the message of Islam, remember that the Blessed Prophet ﷺ had to face the same things—and worse.

Allah instructed him, *If they argue with you, tell them, "I have surrendered my whole self to Allah and so have those who follow me." And declare to the People of the Book (Jews and Christians) and to those who don't know, "Will you also surrender yourself (to Allah)?" If they do, then they will be on the right guidance. But if they turn away, your duty is only to convey the message. Allah sees all of His servants.* Surat Al 'Imran (The Family of 'Imran) 3:20

﴿فَإِنْ حَآجُّوكَ فَقُلْ أَسْلَمْتُ وَجْهِيَ لِلَّهِ وَمَنِ ٱتَّبَعَنِ وَقُل لِّلَّذِينَ أُوتُوا۟ ٱلْكِتَٰبَ وَٱلْأُمِّيِّينَ ءَأَسْلَمْتُمْ فَإِنْ أَسْلَمُوا۟ فَقَدِ ٱهْتَدَوا۟ وَّإِن تَوَلَّوْا۟ فَإِنَّمَا عَلَيْكَ ٱلْبَلَٰغُ وَٱللَّهُ بَصِيرٌۢ بِٱلْعِبَادِ﴾ سُورَةُ آلِ عِمْرَانَ 20:3

To better understand how to deal with those who reject Allah at every turn, it is a good idea to learn about the prophets, messengers and wise men and women Allah mentions in the Qur'an. By reading their stories, we can gain a greater appreciation of the struggle ahead of us. We can remove worry from our minds, knowing that even better people than us had a hard time. Pay careful attention to how Allah brought peace to the hearts of His servants and know that Allah's message can bring peace to yours. (10:57-58)

"Some Answers"
To the Objections of Non-Muslims

Allah only spoke to the Jews and only sent revelation to Jewish prophets.
Allah did give His message to the Jews, but He also sent messages to all the other nations. (2:83-85, 5:18, 5:41, 5:44, 61:5-8)

No belief in Allah or in an omnipotent creator of the Universe.
Allah gave us life, and signs in nature point to His existence. Only the blind refuse to see. Whether we believe in Him or not, He's there. (2:28-29, 6:104, 2:99, 11:13, 69:38-43, 34:31-32, 14:15, 10:4-20, 30:52-53)

Muhammad must have learned his message from someone or somewhere or copied it from the Bible.
Muhammad was illiterate; he neither knew how to read or write. The Qur'an mentions things that no one in that place or at that time could have known. There are similarities between the Bible and Old Testament because each revelation is from the same source. The other revelations either no longer exist or have been changed. (11:13, 16:103, 39:28, 62:2, 10:37-41)

'Isa (Jesus) was the last prophet sent to Earth. 'Isa was the son of God and/or God and that he came to die for man's sins, so no new prophets would be needed.
'Isa was a man. Allah was neither born not bears children. Allah forgives directly without an intermediary. 'Isa taught people to believe in one God and to do right (i.e., Islam). Christians broke up into sects because they lost the true teachings of 'Isa. Prophet 'Isa foretold the coming of Muhammad. (6:101, 6:159, 5:18, 5:116-117, 5:172, 9:30-31, 61:6, 112:1-4, 4:116, 17:42, 21:21-22, 13:16)

Faith has no place in the modern world where technology performs miracles everyday.
They only remember Allah when they're in trouble and afterwards they forget Him. People can only find real peace with Allah. (3:180, 10:12, 3:14-15, 2:212, 3:188, 13:28, 3:190, 2:204-206, 70:42, 2:257)

Eat, drink and live life to the fullest. Tomorrow we will die and that is the end. There is no afterlife nor a Day of Judgment.
It is only Shaytan which bids them to follow their lusts. All evil conduct will be paid back in the next life. Immoral people and the willfully disobedient will be stressed in this life and losers in the next. (2:168-169, 4:118-119, 2:15-16, 18, 3:185, 16:111, 2:256, 74:38, 7:33, 50:16-19, 2:204-206, 70:42, 2:257, 18:57, 7:28, 21:38-40, 7:53, 7:187, 18:55, 18:58-59, 14:10, 2:170, 5:104, 28:78-82, 15:13, 67:15-18, 90:4-7, 17:66-70, 13:26, 19:77-80, 5:100, 10:7-8, 10:48-56)

Why did Allah send a mortal man and not an angel or other supernatural forces to convey His message?
They can't believe a man would be chosen to bring Allah's messages, but who better to communicate on the rational level with other humans? How would there be a fair testing ground in any other case? If the world was populated by angels, He would have sent an angel to them as a messenger. (14:11, 14:17, 14:94-95, 13:43, 15:6-9, 64:56, 2:118, 21:2, 10:2-6)

They don't believe in a next life or that a Day of Judgement will come.
Allah gave us life to begin with. He can make us again and judge us. (17:49-50, 19:66-67, 17:9, 2:28, 6:94, 75:36-40, 50:1-15, 17:71-73, 10:37, 10:24, 10:31-36, 30:54)

They want to see supernatural proof such as angels, magic or miracles before they're convinced.
The Qur'an and nature are the greatest signs of all. Even if angels came or books appeared magically, they would only say it's magic or illusion anyway. (17:92-93, 13:27, 15:6-15, 6:7-9, 6:103, 21:5)

Suggested Qur'anic Wisdom

1:1-7	The best surat and prayer.	17:66-72	Who really is in control?
6:1-50	Answering the unbelievers.	18:32-44	The gardener who forgot Allah.
13:8-17	What nature can teach us about Allah.	18:60-82	Prophet Musa and the Wise Man.
14:9-27	The Messengers call us to good.	24:35-40	Allah is the light.
35:1-26	Realizing our true relationship with Allah.	27:83-93	Reward or punishment?
49:1-15	How to be a true Muslim.	29:56-69	Gratitude to Allah.
56:1-98	A summary of the next life and what will happen to all.	34:37-39	How to get closer to Allah.
7:44-52	Conversations between those in Heaven and those in Hell.	40:28-44	The man who stood up to a pharaoh.
81:1-29	A final call to our hearts.	6:155-165	There are no excuses.
10:11-40	Here is your proof!	3:133-139	A message of hope.
59:18-24	The attributes of Allah.		

Chapter 5
Islamic Beliefs: Part One

Primitive Beliefs

Throughout human existence, people have pondered the meaning of their lives. As we have learned in previous lessons, humans have been given a chance in this life to accept or reject belief in Allah﷾. But Who and What is Allah﷾? How do we understand the One Who has the power to create a billion galaxies by just saying one word, "Be!"

The Originator of the heavens and the earth. When He decrees a matter, He only says to it : "Be!"—And it is.
Surat Al Baqarah (The Cow) 2:117

﴿بَدِيعُ ٱلسَّمَٰوَٰتِ وَٱلۡأَرۡضِ وَإِذَا قَضَىٰٓ أَمۡرًا فَإِنَّمَا يَقُولُ لَهُۥ كُن فَيَكُونُ﴾ سُورَةُ الْبَقَرَةِ 2:117

Quetzalcoatl as depicted by Aztec priests.

People have often wondered about their Creator. Many have even been tempted to draw pictures or make statues of what they imagined was God. (16:74) Others thought that there were many gods, each with unique powers, moving about in their own spiritual world while meddling in the affairs of people here on earth. (16:73)

The Aztecs had Quetzalcoatl, the Greeks had Cronus, the Romans had Jupiter, and the Chinese had Ti. In fact, most cultures have, at some point, attempted to put a face on God. The earliest archeological remains uncovered ancient belief systems that centered on primitive earth-mother statues. (4:117) These small idols, found all across the routes of early humans from Africa to Europe and Asia, symbolize the fertility of the Earth and the power of women to bear children.

The First Communities

If you remember, Adam﷨ and Hawwa were the first human beings like us to walk the Earth. They were expelled from their garden paradise as a consequence of their disobedience to Allah﷾, and their descendants spread out over the Earth in later generations. This eventually led to different ethnic groups and races. Many reasons can explain why humans split into different groups: power, lack of resources, even contrasting belief systems. As Allah﷾ remarked, *Mankind were but one community, then they differed (later), and had not it been for a Word that went forth before from your Lord, it would have been settled between them regarding what they differed.* Surat Yunus (Jonah) 10:19

﴿وَمَا كَانَ ٱلنَّاسُ إِلَّآ أُمَّةً وَٰحِدَةً فَٱخۡتَلَفُوا۟ وَلَوۡلَا كَلِمَةٌ سَبَقَتۡ مِن رَّبِّكَ لَقُضِيَ بَيۡنَهُمۡ فِيمَا فِيهِ يَخۡتَلِفُونَ﴾ سُورَةُ يُونُسَ 10:19

Allah﷾ had told Adam﷨ and Hawwa that prophets would be sent to later generations. (2:38-39) If the people accepted their prophets' teachings, then they would prosper. If the people split into different groups and ignored Allah﷾, they would become unbelievers and lost. (10:17-18) Whenever people would break up into groups and move away, they would then be sent some form of guidance from Allah﷾. These early hunter-gatherers moved from place to place and lived on a subsistence diet. Allah﷾ declared that He sent a warner to every nation. (10:47)

We did raise a messenger among every people, with the message: "Worship Allah and stay away from the Rebel (the Satan)." Then, there were some among them whom Allah guided, and there were others against whom deviation (from the right path) was established. So, travel on earth and see how was the fate of those who rejected. Surat An-Nahl (The Bees) 16:36

﴿وَلَقَدۡ بَعَثۡنَا فِي كُلِّ أُمَّةٍ رَّسُولًا أَنِ ٱعۡبُدُوا۟ ٱللَّهَ وَٱجۡتَنِبُوا۟ ٱلطَّٰغُوتَ فَمِنۡهُم مَّنۡ هَدَى ٱللَّهُ وَمِنۡهُم مَّنۡ حَقَّتۡ عَلَيۡهِ ٱلضَّلَٰلَةُ فَسِيرُوا۟ فِي ٱلۡأَرۡضِ فَٱنظُرُوا۟ كَيۡفَ كَانَ عَٰقِبَةُ ٱلۡمُكَذِّبِينَ﴾ سُورَةُ النَّحۡلِ 16:36

Clearly, many of these primitive cultures did not remain true to Islamic teachings. They entered into disbelief despite having a more basic form of Islam to follow. This is evidenced by the saying of the Blessed Prophet Muhammad ﷺ: "Among the earliest words of revelation were, 'If you feel no shame, then do as you wish.'" (Al Bukhari)

قَالَ رَسُولُ اللهِ ﷺ: «إِنَّ مِمَّا أَدْرَكَ النَّاسُ مِنْ كَلَامِ النُّبُوَّةِ الْأُولَى: إِذَا لَمْ تَسْتَحِ فَاصْنَعْ مَا شِئْتَ». رَوَاهُ الْبُخَارِيُّ

Human Civilization on the Rise

Historians have charted the beginnings of human civilization with advancements in tool-making and farming. They measure the time of the Neolithic Era, or Stone Age, as between 8,000-5,000 BCE. Based on this measurement, the Stone Age is thought to have been at least 5,000 years before Prophet 'Isa's ﷺ birth.

As people progressed through the Neolithic Era, they developed more organized social structures and beliefs. When prophets came to them, the people either accepted or rejected them. What would make a person create an idol and say that it was their god? Humans have an inner nature that prompts them towards the Higher Power. If a person rejects Allah's ﷻ guidance, they often replace the love that should be for Allah ﷻ with something else. This makes it easier for people to create idols of stone, seeking their blessings or favors instead of asking for these things from Allah ﷻ.

A primitive shelter.

Say (O Muhammad): Shall we invoke others besides Allah, that can do us neither good nor harm, and shall we turn back on our heels after Allah has guided us? Like one whom the devils have made to go astray, in the land in confusion, his companions calling him to guidance: Come to us. Say (O Muhammad): Verily, Allah's Guidance is the only guidance, and we have been commanded to submit to the Lord of mankind. Surat Al An'aam (The Cattle) 6:71

﴿قُلْ أَنَدْعُوا مِن دُونِ ٱللَّهِ مَا لَا يَنفَعُنَا وَلَا يَضُرُّنَا وَنُرَدُّ عَلَىٰٓ أَعْقَابِنَا بَعْدَ إِذْ هَدَىٰنَا ٱللَّهُ كَٱلَّذِي ٱسْتَهْوَتْهُ ٱلشَّيَٰطِينُ فِي ٱلْأَرْضِ حَيْرَانَ لَهُۥٓ أَصْحَٰبٌ يَدْعُونَهُۥٓ إِلَى ٱلْهُدَى ٱئْتِنَا قُلْ إِنَّ هُدَى ٱللَّهِ هُوَ ٱلْهُدَىٰ وَأُمِرْنَا لِنُسْلِمَ لِرَبِّ ٱلْعَٰلَمِينَ﴾ سُورَةُ الْأَنْعَامِ 6:71

The end of the Neolithic era saw the development of established farming communities in Egypt and the Fertile Crescent. These communities had strong oral traditions, making it easy for a prophet's teachings to survive for many generations. Yet, only some communities believed, while many others continued to worship idols.

With the rise of cities and empires in Mesopotamia, India, China and Egypt, idol-worship became the official religion. Huge temples were built, and elaborate and often bloody rituals were instituted. Allah's ﷻ prophets perhaps had a harder time convincing people of the truth because the state authorities (kings, officials and soldiers) could be mobilized to destroy a particular prophet and his followers. It was during these instances when Allah ﷻ would decree the destruction of such an evil and unrepentant people.

Allah ﷻ said, *We destroyed generations before you when they practiced evil. Their Messengers came to them with clear signs, but they would not believe. This is how we deal with*

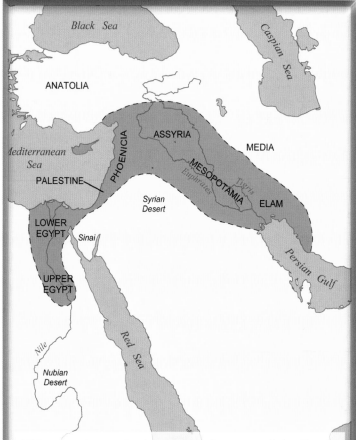

This map shows the location and extent of the Fertile Crescent, a region in the Middle East incorporating Ancient Egypt, the Levant and Mesopotamia.

those who sin. *Surat Yunus (Jonah) 10: 13*

﴿وَلَقَدْ أَهْلَكْنَا الْقُرُونَ مِن قَبْلِكُمْ لَمَّا ظَلَمُوا وَجَاءَتْهُمْ رُسُلُهُم بِالْبَيِّنَتِ وَمَا كَانُوا لِيُؤْمِنُوا كَذَلِكَ نَجْزِي الْقَوْمَ الْمُجْرِمِينَ﴾ سُورَةُ يُونُس 10:13

Mighty civilizations, such as the Roman and Greek, were harder to persuade against the worship of idols. Prophets 'Isa and Musa are great examples of prophets who were sent to these powerful civilizations. The new Christian religion emerged with the decline of the last great empire, the Romans. Christianity combined the true teachings of Prophet 'Isa with ideas from the local culture and Greek philosophy. The result was a religion that likened God with a human; a religion that said God was three: a father, a son and a spirit.

O people of the Book, be not excessive in your Faith, and do not say about Allah anything but the truth. The Masih 'Isa, the son of Maryam, is only a Messenger of Allah, and His Word that He had delivered to Maryam, and a spirit from Him. So, believe in Allah and His Messengers. Do not say "Three." Stop it. That is good for you. Allah is the only One God. He is far too pure to have a son. To Him belongs what is in the heavens and what is in the earth. And Allah is enough to trust in. Surat An-Nisa' (The Women) 4:171

﴿يَأَهْلَ الْكِتَبِ لَا تَغْلُوا فِي دِينِكُمْ وَلَا تَقُولُوا عَلَى اللَّهِ إِلَّا الْحَقَّ إِنَّمَا الْمَسِيحُ عِيسَى ابْنُ مَرْيَمَ رَسُولُ اللَّهِ وَكَلِمَتُهُ أَلْقَاهَا إِلَى مَرْيَمَ وَرُوحٌ مِّنْهُ فَامِنُوا بِاللَّهِ وَرُسُلِهِ وَلَا تَقُولُوا ثَلَثَةٌ انتَهُوا خَيْرًا لَّكُمْ إِنَّمَا اللَّهُ إِلَهٌ وَحِدٌ سُبْحَنَهُ أَن يَكُونَ لَهُ وَلَدٌ لَّهُ مَا فِي السَّمَوَتِ وَمَا فِي الْأَرْضِ وَكَفَى بِاللَّهِ وَكِيلًا﴾ سُورَةُ النِّسَاءِ 4:171

With the blending of all these ideas, much of Prophet 'Isa's true teachings were irreparably corrupted and lost. (3:55) However, Allah declared that every age would have access to His Truth. This is so people can know Who and What Allah is and why they must surrender their wills to Him. (10:47) The final message He sent to the world, the Qur'an, contains the only existing and accurate description of Allah for us today. This is because Allah Himself explained His own nature and qualities to us in the Qur'an.

Therefore, all other descriptions of the Creator, whether they be from myths, legends, ancient religions, or modern trends, must be put aside in favor of Allah's direct words. Different cultures, even those that worshipped idols, have known the Supreme Being by different names: Jehovah, Orenda, Ti, Great Spirit, Mott, Cronus, Elah, Manitou, Dios and God. But these cultures did not have the correct understanding of Allah's nature. Many portrayed Him as a man, as a spirit or as an image. (16:62)

The name that God revealed to humanity in His last revelation is **Allah الله**. This is a unique name in the Arabic language. It cannot be made plural, masculine, feminine or altered in any way. For example, the word 'god' can be changed into goddess, godling, demi–god and so forth. The word Allah is not open to grammatical alteration. The name of Allah is unique and sublime, and Allah clearly states that people have known Him by different names through previous prophets.

Say to them, "Call upon Allah, call upon the Merciful. By whatever name you call upon Him, for to Him belong the most beautiful names." And offer your prayer neither aloud nor in a low voice, but follow a way between. Surat Al Isra' (The Night Journey) 17:110

Some early idols looked like this earth mother statue.

﴿قُلِ ادْعُوا اللَّهَ أَوِ ادْعُوا الرَّحْمَنَ أَيًّا مَّا تَدْعُوا فَلَهُ الْأَسْمَاءُ الْحُسْنَى وَلَا تَجْهَرْ بِصَلَاتِكَ وَلَا تُخَافِتْ بِهَا وَابْتَغِ بَيْنَ ذَلِكَ سَبِيلًا﴾ سُورَةُ الإِسْرَاءِ 17:110

What Are Allah's Names?

Our Creator has many names, Allah being chief among them. His other names, which He revealed to us in His last book, are known collectively as the **Asma'u Allah Al Husna أَسْمَاءُ اللَّهِ الْحُسْنَى Most Beautiful Names**. They are a group of perfect attributes that describe what Allah is like. These are important to us because Allah has no form we can see nor any shape we can comprehend.

He is the Creator of the heavens and the earth. He has made for you pairs from among yourselves, and pairs from the cattle. He makes you expand in this way. Nothing is like Him. And He is the All-Hearing, the All-Seeing. Surat Ash-Shura (The Consultation) 42:11

﴿فَاطِرُ ٱلسَّمَٰوَٰتِ وَٱلْأَرْضِ جَعَلَ لَكُم مِّنْ أَنفُسِكُمْ أَزْوَٰجًا وَمِنَ ٱلْأَنْعَٰمِ أَزْوَٰجًا يَذْرَؤُكُمْ فِيهِ لَيْسَ كَمِثْلِهِ شَىْءٌ وَهُوَ ٱلسَّمِيعُ ٱلْبَصِيرُ﴾ سُورَةُ ٱلشُّورَى 42:11

Although we can never imagine exactly what Allah﷾ is, or how He is so powerful, we can better understand what Allah's﷾ qualities are like by learning His 99 Names. (10:31-34) People will keep asking who made things until they begin to ask who made Allah﷾. At that point, the Prophet ﷺ advised that we should stop questioning. We will never know the answer and may enter disbelief. Instead, we must say, "Glory to Allah." This advice prevents us from going astray by questioning things in life that we cannot comprehend. Allah﷾ has revealed more than enough about His creation for us to be convinced of His power and authority.

O you who believe, do not ask about things which, if disclosed, would displease you. If you ask about them while the Qur'an is being revealed, they will be disclosed to you. Allah has pardoned you for it. Allah is Most-Forgiving, Forbearing. People before you asked such questions, and then, as a result, became disbelievers. Surat Al Ma'idah (The Table) 5:101-102

﴿يَٰٓأَيُّهَا ٱلَّذِينَ ءَامَنُوا لَا تَسْـَٔلُوا عَنْ أَشْيَآءَ إِن تُبْدَ لَكُمْ تَسُؤْكُمْ وَإِن تَسْـَٔلُوا عَنْهَا حِينَ يُنَزَّلُ ٱلْقُرْءَانُ تُبْدَ لَكُمْ عَفَا ٱللَّهُ عَنْهَا وَٱللَّهُ غَفُورٌ حَلِيمٌ﴾ ﴿قَدْ سَأَلَهَا قَوْمٌ مِّن قَبْلِكُمْ ثُمَّ أَصْبَحُوا بِهَا كَٰفِرِينَ﴾ سُورَةُ ٱلْمَائِدَة 5:101-102

One of the most important qualities of God is that He is One—unique. He has no partner, son, daughter, wife or helper of any kind. (16:22) **Tawhid** تَوْحِيد is one of the clearest lines of separation between Islam and all other ways of life. All prophets have taught that God is One, but later generations mixed their own fables, whims and skewed understandings into their belief systems, resulting in all kinds of chaos. (16:51-56)

The doctrine of tawhid, as explained in the Qur'an, overcomes the false ideas people have about Allah﷾. In fact, there are so many ayaat that explain what Allah﷾ is and is not that it would take pages to list them all! Clearly, Allah﷾ wants us to be free of all superstition and misinformation about our Creator. (6:56)

Perhaps the best known surat that summarizes Islamic teachings is Surat Al Ikhlaas (The Sincerity). It states, Declare: He is One God; Allah, the Self-Sufficient Master, Whom all creatures need. He neither begets, nor was He begotten, and there is nothing comparable to Him. Surat Al Ikhlaas (The Sincerity) (112:1-4)

﴿قُلْ هُوَ ٱللَّهُ أَحَدٌ﴾ ﴿ٱللَّهُ ٱلصَّمَدُ﴾ ﴿لَمْ يَلِدْ وَلَمْ يُولَدْ﴾ ﴿وَلَمْ يَكُن لَّهُ كُفُوًا أَحَدٌ﴾ سُورَةُ ٱلْإِخْلَاص 112:1-4

Another oft-quoted passage is the famous, Ayat Al Kursi (Verse of the Throne).

Allah! There is no god but He—the Living, Eternal and Self-subsisting. No slumber takes Him, nor does He rest. Everything in space and on Earth belongs to Him. Who can intercede in His presence without His permission? He knows what happens before, after and behind them. No one can gain anything of His knowledge except as He wills. His throne extends over space and the Earth. He does not tire in guarding and protecting them. He is the Most High, the Supreme. Surat Al Baqarah (The Cow) 2: 255

﴿ٱللَّهُ لَآ إِلَٰهَ إِلَّا هُوَ ٱلْحَىُّ ٱلْقَيُّومُ لَا تَأْخُذُهُ سِنَةٌ وَلَا نَوْمٌ لَّهُ مَا فِي ٱلسَّمَٰوَٰتِ وَمَا فِي ٱلْأَرْضِ مَن ذَا ٱلَّذِي يَشْفَعُ عِندَهُ إِلَّا بِإِذْنِهِ يَعْلَمُ مَا بَيْنَ أَيْدِيهِمْ وَمَا خَلْفَهُمْ وَلَا يُحِيطُونَ بِشَىْءٍ مِّنْ عِلْمِهِ إِلَّا بِمَا شَآءَ وَسِعَ كُرْسِيُّهُ ٱلسَّمَٰوَٰتِ وَٱلْأَرْضَ وَلَا يَـُٔودُهُ حِفْظُهُمَا وَهُوَ ٱلْعَلِيُّ ٱلْعَظِيمُ﴾ سُورَةُ ٱلْبَقَرَة 2:255

The Lord of the Universe

Allah's﷾ relationship with His creation is unique. He describes Himself as the **Rabb Al 'Alameen** رَبُّ الْعَالَمِين **Lord of All the Universe**. (1:2) The word 'Rabb' is often translated as Lord, as we have translated it in this book, too. But in Arabic, this term actually means something deeper. It means 'the One

الله

Allah ﷻ **is One**

74

who takes care of, watches over, preserves and provides for something in a loving way.'

Everything in the Universe depends on Allah, and He is the Guardian and Preserver of all He created. He keeps order in the Universe and applies His will as the basis of all natural law, whether governing animate or inanimate objects. He needs nothing from His creation. Laws of energy and motion function in a certain way and this is their task. Humans also are told to follow Allah's law and create order, but we have a choice about whether or not to follow this order. (10:31-32) Goodness, justice, fairness and peace are the laws all humans must strive toward. Allah commands justice, as the Qur'an declares: *Verily! Allah commands that you should render back the*

trusts to those to whom they are due and that, when you judge between men, you judge with justice. Verily, how excellent is the teaching which He (Allah) gives you! Surely, Allah is All-Hearing, All-Seeing. Surat An-Nisa' (The Women) 4:58

﴿إِنَّ ٱللَّهَ يَأْمُرُكُمْ أَن تُؤَدُّوا۟ ٱلْأَمَٰنَٰتِ إِلَىٰٓ أَهْلِهَا وَإِذَا حَكَمْتُم بَيْنَ ٱلنَّاسِ أَن تَحْكُمُوا۟ بِٱلْعَدْلِ إِنَّ ٱللَّهَ نِعِمَّا يَعِظُكُم بِهِۦٓ إِنَّ ٱللَّهَ كَانَ سَمِيعًۢا بَصِيرًا﴾ سُورَةُ النِّسَاءِ 4:58

But is Allah a Lord who feels too powerful to have anything to do with us? Through the centuries, people invented idols, saints or other intermediaries to establish a connection between Allah and themselves. Yet this was the wrong approach, and it led people away from their Creator. The prophets and messengers declared this to their people and informed them that Allah listens to us directly. Indeed, Allah's knowledge is present everywhere and knows everything that is happening. (6:59) He declared that He is too exalted to show himself to mere humans, but He also declared that He knows what is in our hearts and He listens to everyone who calls on Him.

When My servants ask you (Muhammad) about Me, I am indeed close. I listen to the prayer of everyone who calls on Me. Let whoever wants to, then, listen to My call and believe in Me so they can walk in the right way. Surat Al Baqarah (The Cow) 2: 186

﴿وَإِذَا سَأَلَكَ عِبَادِى عَنِّى فَإِنِّى قَرِيبٌ أُجِيبُ دَعْوَةَ ٱلدَّاعِ إِذَا دَعَانِ فَلْيَسْتَجِيبُوا۟ لِى وَلْيُؤْمِنُوا۟ بِى لَعَلَّهُمْ يَرْشُدُونَ﴾ سُورَةُ الْبَقَرَةِ 2:186

Muslims believe in what Allah revealed about Himself in His last revelation, the Holy Qur'an. He is not a created being; He is the most Loving and Merciful yet stern in punishment. He is never unfair to anyone and never does any injustice in the least to His creation. He was never born and will never die. He is the Lord of the Universe! (27:62)

The Biggest Sin

Allah told us: *Say, "Praise belongs to Allah who has neither had a son, nor is there any partner to Him in His kingdom nor is anyone (needed) to protect Him from (any) weakness." And proclaim His greatness an open proclamation.* Surat Al Isra' (The Night Journey) 17:111

﴿وَقُلِ ٱلْحَمْدُ لِلَّهِ ٱلَّذِى لَمْ يَتَّخِذْ وَلَدًا وَلَمْ يَكُن لَّهُۥ شَرِيكٌ فِى ٱلْمُلْكِ وَلَمْ يَكُن لَّهُۥ وَلِىٌّ مِّنَ ٱلذُّلِّ وَكَبِّرْهُ تَكْبِيرًا﴾ سُورَةُ الْإِسْرَاءِ 17:111

Allah has declared it a terrible sin to make others equal to Him. This great sin is known as **Shirk شرك Associating Others with Allah**. It is such a horrendous sin that Allah declared it the one sin He will not forgive if a person dies while committing it. A person who commits shirk is called a **Mushrik مُشْرك Polytheist**. A common translation of this word is idol-worshipper. (4:116) The people who worship idols made the mistake of thinking that they needed some supernatural spirit or lesser god to go to Allah for them. (36:74-75)

Verily, Allah forgives not that partners should be set up with Him (in worship), but He forgives except that (anything else) to whom He wills, and whoever sets up partners with Allah in worship, he has indeed invented a tremendous sin. Surat An-Nisa' (The Women) 4:48

﴿إِنَّ ٱللَّهَ لَا يَغْفِرُ أَن يُشْرَكَ بِهِۦ وَيَغْفِرُ مَا دُونَ ذَٰلِكَ لِمَن يَشَآءُ وَمَن يُشْرِكْ بِٱللَّهِ فَقَدِ ٱفْتَرَىٰٓ إِثْمًا عَظِيمًا﴾ سُورَةُ النِّسَاءِ 4:48

Some of the Jews and the Christians made the mistake of worshipping one of Allah's creatures. They call this person an intercessor, or someone who acts on behalf of another in difficulty or trouble. They will pray to this person to intercede for them with Allah, as a sort of go-between. Some Christians even worship other, lesser men, whom they call saints. They believe that saints somehow also convey their prayers to Allah. Other Christians even pray to Maryam, the mother of Prophet 'Isa, believing that as she is the mother of 'God' (Jesus), she also can answer their prayers or intercede with Allah for them. (9: 30-31)

The Jews say Allah is a wrathful, stern God, while the Christians claim He is all love and came to Earth to be killed by us to show us how much He loves us. They believe these strange things because they too, like so many before them, lost their original prophet's teachings.

Allah told us, *The Jews say: "The Christians have nothing to stand on" and the Christians say "The Jews have nothing to stand on" while they both read the Book! Similarly, those who do not know have said like they (the Jews and the Christians) say. So, Allah will judge between them on the Day of Resurrection in what they used to dispute.* Surat Al Baqarah (The Cow) 2:113

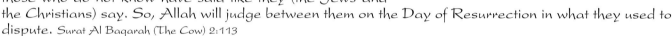

﴿وَقَالَتِ ٱلْيَهُودُ لَيْسَتِ ٱلنَّصَـٰرَىٰ عَلَىٰ شَىْءٍ وَقَالَتِ ٱلنَّصَـٰرَىٰ لَيْسَتِ ٱلْيَهُودُ عَلَىٰ شَىْءٍ وَهُمْ يَتْلُونَ ٱلْكِتَـٰبَ كَذَٰلِكَ قَالَ ٱلَّذِينَ لَا يَعْلَمُونَ مِثْلَ قَوْلِهِمْ فَٱللَّهُ يَحْكُمُ بَيْنَهُمْ يَوْمَ ٱلْقِيَـٰمَةِ فِيمَا كَانُوا فِيهِ يَخْتَلِفُونَ﴾ سُورَةُ الْبَقَرَةِ 2:113

Although we learn of some of the wrongdoings of Jews and Christians in the Qur'an, Allah still sets them apart from idol-worshippers or other disbelievers. This is because they have some understanding about Him and have fragments of the ancient wisdom of the true prophets remaining in their current scriptures. (5:44)

May Allah give us the will to continue seeking knowledge of Him, and may He help us to seek His forgiveness for our wrongs. God promised to forgive those who seek His pardon. Allah said it in the most concise way: *Tell My servants that I am indeed Forgiving and Merciful. And also that My punishment will be a terrible punishment.* Surat Al-Hijr (15:49-50)

﴿نَبِّئْ عِبَادِي أَنِّي أَنَا ٱلْغَفُورُ ٱلرَّحِيمُ﴾ ﴿وَأَنَّ عَذَابِي هُوَ ٱلْعَذَابُ ٱلْأَلِيمُ﴾ سُورَةُ الْحِجْرِ 15:49-50

What Allah Is and Is Not

Allah is One. He has no partner, wife or son.	*Allah is not divided up into parts or a trinity. He sometimes refers to Himself as 'We' or 'Us' because, in Arabic as well as English, these pronouns can be used by a single being to emphasize power and majesty.*
Allah is above all His creations.	*Allah is not a male or female. In Arabic, words are either male or female, and there is no term for 'it.' However, we use the English pronoun 'He' because it is generic. 'He' in this context doesn't imply any gender.*
Allah is the One Who answers prayers.	*Allah is not in need of any intercessors or intermediaries.*
Allah is aware of everything simultaneously.	*Allah is not a part of any physical objects.*
He will gather all of us together on Judgement Day.	*Allah is not a passive force in the Universe.*

The Most Beautiful Names

The 99 Names of Allah عَزَّوَجَلَّ

The Compassionate	The Merciful	The Sovereign	The Holy	The Source of Peace	The Guardian of Faith
الرّحمن	الرّحيم	الملك	القدّوس	السّلام	المؤمن

The Protector	The Mighty	The Compeller	The Majestic	The Creator	The Evolver
المهيمن	العزيز	الجبّار	المتكبّر	الخالق	البارئ

The Fashioner	The Great Forgiver	The Subduer	The Giver	The Provider	The Opener
المصوّر	الغفّار	القهّار	الوهّاب	الرّزّاق	الفتّاح

The All-Knowing	The Constrictor	The Expander	The Abaser	The Exalter	The Honorer
العليم	القابض	الباسط	الخافض	الرّافع	المعزّ

The Dishonorer	The Hearing	The Seeing	The Judge	The Just	The Most Subtle
المذلّ	السّميع	البصير	الحكم	العدل	اللّطيف

The Aware	The Forbearing	The Great One	The Forgiving	The Thankful	The Most High
الخبير	الحليم	العظيم	الغفور	الشكور	العليّ

The Most Great	The Preserver	The Maintainer	The Accounter	The Sublime	The Generous
الكبير	الحفيظ	المقيت	الحسيب	الجليل	الكريم

The Watchful	The Responsive	The All-Embracing	The Wise	The Loving	The Most Glorious
الرّقيب	المجيب	الواسع	الحكيم	الودود	المجيد

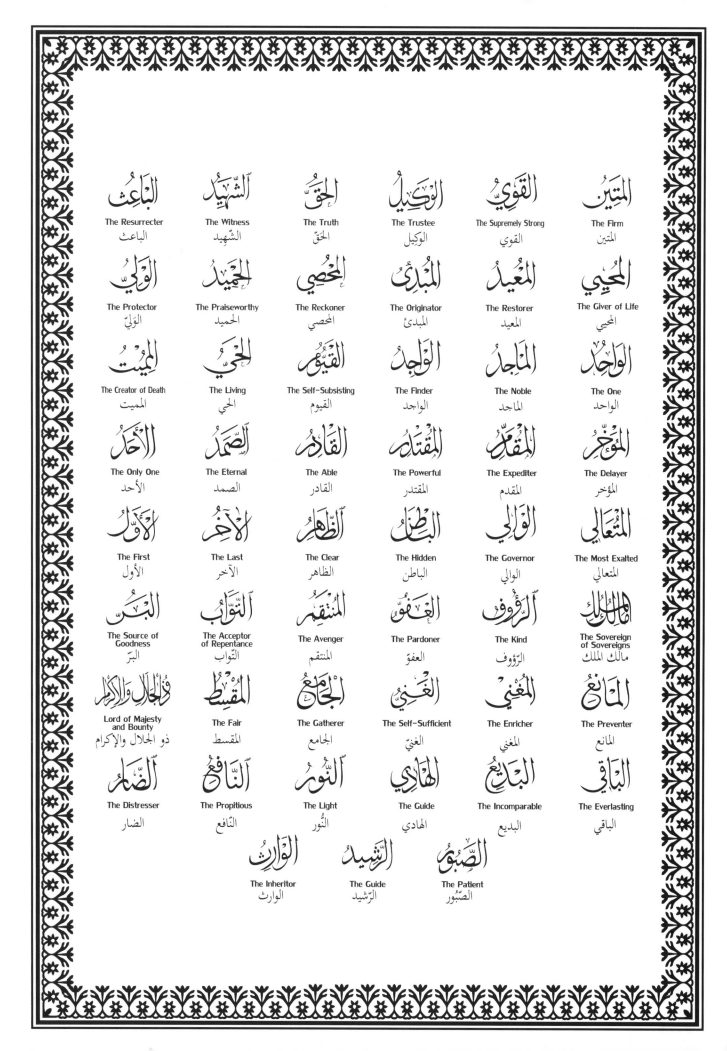

الْبَاعِث	الشَّهِيْد	الْحَقُّ	الْوَكِيْل	الْقَوِيُّ	الْمَتِيْن
The Resurrecter	The Witness	The Truth	The Trustee	The Supremely Strong	The Firm
الباعث	الشّهيد	الحقّ	الوكيل	القوي	المتين

الْوَلِيُّ	الْحَمِيْد	الْمُحْصِي	الْمُبْدِئُ	الْمُعِيْد	الْمُحْيِي
The Protector	The Praiseworthy	The Reckoner	The Originator	The Restorer	The Giver of Life
الوَلِيّ	الحميد	المحصي	المبدئ	المعيد	المحيي

الْمُمِيْت	الْحَيُّ	الْقَيُّوم	الْوَاجِدُ	الْمَاجِدُ	الْوَاحِدُ
The Creator of Death	The Living	The Self-Subsisting	The Finder	The Noble	The One
المميت	الحي	القيوم	الواجد	الماجد	الواحد

الْأَحَدُ	الصَّمَدُ	الْقَادِرُ	الْمُقْتَدِرُ	الْمُقَدِّمُ	الْمُؤَخِّرُ
The Only One	The Eternal	The Able	The Powerful	The Expediter	The Delayer
الأحد	الصمد	القادر	المقتدر	المقدم	المؤخر

الْأَوَّلُ	الْآخِرُ	الظَّاهِرُ	الْبَاطِنُ	الْوَالِي	الْمُتَعَالِي
The First	The Last	The Clear	The Hidden	The Governor	The Most Exalted
الأول	الآخر	الظاهر	الباطن	الوالي	المتعالي

الْبَرُّ	التَّوَّابُ	الْمُنْتَقِمُ	الْعَفْوُ	الرَّؤُوف	مَالِكُ الْمُلْكِ
The Source of Goodness	The Acceptor of Repentance	The Avenger	The Pardoner	The Kind	The Sovereign of Sovereigns
البرّ	التّواب	المنتقم	العفوّ	الرّؤوف	مالك الملك

ذُوالْجَلَالِ وَالإِكْرَام	الْمُقْسِطُ	الْجَامِعُ	الْغَنِيُّ	الْمُغْنِي	الْمَانِعُ
Lord of Majesty and Bounty	The Fair	The Gatherer	The Self-Sufficient	The Enricher	The Preventer
ذو الجلال والإكرام	المقسط	الجامع	الغنيّ	المغني	المانع

الضَّارُّ	النَّافِعُ	النُّورُ	الْهَادِي	الْبَدِيعُ	الْبَاقِي
The Distresser	The Propitious	The Light	The Guide	The Incomparable	The Everlasting
الضار	النّافع	النُّور	الهادي	البديع	الباقي

الْوَارِث	الرَّشِيد	الصَّبُور
The Inheritor	The Guide	The Patient
الوارث	الرّشيد	الصّبور

What Angels Are Not

Islam teaches that there are intelligent beings in the Universe in addition to us. One type of creature, which was made specifically by Allah to carry out His commands, are the **Mala'ikah** مَلَائِكَة **Angels**. In non-Islamic nations, angels are usually portrayed according to Christians and secularists, often resulting in contradictions.

Centuries of myths, legends, tall-tales and folklore combined to paint a picture of angels that is, according to Islam, far from the truth. Some Christians believe that angels can communicate with humans, commit sins and act in weak and fickle ways like us. Movies and television shows depict angels as fun-loving people with magical powers. Many believe that Shaytan and his devils are merely angels that went bad.

Allah warned us that, *They have no knowledge about (the angels). They follow nothing but guesses. Guessing is nothing in the face of truth. Surat An-Najm (The Star) 53:28*

﴿وَمَا لَهُم بِهِۦ مِنْ عِلْمٍ إِن يَتَّبِعُونَ إِلَّا ٱلظَّنَّ وَإِنَّ ٱلظَّنَّ لَا يُغْنِي مِنَ ٱلْحَقِّ شَيْـًٔا﴾ سُورَةُ النَّجْم 53:28

Muslims must protect themselves from picking up these false ideas. Instead, we must learn what Allah and His Messenger told us about them. That is the most accurate and truthful picture. According to Islam, angels were made from the elements of light. They have metaphorical wings and can travel at the speed of light. (70:4) They can assume physical form, and when they do appear as humans, they have perfect features. However, to humans they may seem a little too perfect and usually dazzle the eyes of those who see them. (19:17)

Angels are neither male or female nor are they the children of Allah. They are, rather, like intelligent servants who have definite tasks and duties to perform. They never fail in their missions, and they see everything we do although we cannot see them. They have no independent desires or whims, and they never disobey Allah.

We don't descend except by the command of our Lord. To Him belongs what is in front of us and what is behind us and everything in between. Your Lord never forgets. He is the Lord of space and the Earth and all in between. So serve Him and be firm in serving Him. Do you know any other who is worthy of the same name as He? Surat Maryam (Mary) 19: 64 - 65

﴿وَمَا نَتَنَزَّلُ إِلَّا بِأَمْرِ رَبِّكَ لَهُۥ مَا بَيْنَ أَيْدِينَا وَمَا خَلْفَنَا وَمَا بَيْنَ ذَٰلِكَ وَمَا كَانَ رَبُّكَ نَسِيًّا﴾ ﴿رَبُّ ٱلسَّمَٰوَٰتِ وَٱلْأَرْضِ وَمَا بَيْنَهُمَا فَٱعْبُدْهُ وَٱصْطَبِرْ لِعِبَٰدَتِهِۦ هَلْ تَعْلَمُ لَهُۥ سَمِيًّا﴾ سُورَةُ مَرْيَم 19:64-65

What Do Angels Do?

One of the most important jobs of the angels is to record the deeds and actions of humans. Allah does not need them to do this; He merely wills it so. The angels that record our deeds are stationed to our right and left and are described as the **Kiraman Katibeen** كِرَامًا كَاتِبِين **Noble Writers**. They take note of what we do and record everything as if they had a camera on us at every moment. (50:17-18)

Other angels intervene in nature when Allah wills. For example, if Allah was going to punish a people for their wickedness, He might send angels to cause a natural disaster. On the other hand, if some people were going to be shown mercy, Allah might send angels for protection from harm. (79:1-5) Multitudes of angels fill the cosmos and perform a variety of functions, both in this world and in the next. There are groups of angels that stand at each of the eight gates of Paradise. They greet those who are about to enter with the greetings of peace. (13:23-24 & 39:73-75)

Munkar and Nakir مُنْكَر وَنَكِير are angels that question the soul of the dead person as he is awaiting resurrection. Based on the answers, either punishment or peace will be visited upon that soul until that person is raised for Judgement. **Malaku Al Mawt** مَلَكُ الْمَوْت the Angel of Death, is in charge of taking people's souls when they die. (32:11) The soul of a good person will be gently removed at death, while an evil person's soul will be ripped violently away.

Hellfire, too, has angels standing guard. (74:30-31) They throw the wrong-doers into the pit of Hell. (19:86) Then, they push them back as they try to escape. They tell them that this is the fate they deserve for leading such a sinful life before. The chief of the angels of Hellfire is named Malik.

The unbelievers will be led to Hellfire in crowds. When they arrive there, its gates will be opened and its keepers will say, "Didn't Messengers come to you from among your own kind, explaining to you the signs of your Lord and warning you of the meeting on this Day of yours?" Then (the keepers will) answer their own question thus, "It is true. The order of punishment has been proved against the unbelievers." Then (the unbelievers will be told), "Enter the gates of Hell and dwell inside. Terrible is the home of the arrogant!" Surat Az-Zumar (The Groups) 39:71-72

﴿وَسِيقَ ٱلَّذِينَ كَفَرُوٓاْ إِلَىٰ جَهَنَّمَ زُمَرًا حَتَّىٰٓ إِذَا جَآءُوهَا فُتِحَتْ أَبْوَٰبُهَا وَقَالَ لَهُمْ خَزَنَتُهَآ أَلَمْ يَأْتِكُمْ رُسُلٌ مِّنكُمْ يَتْلُونَ عَلَيْكُمْ ءَايَٰتِ رَبِّكُمْ وَيُنذِرُونَكُمْ لِقَآءَ يَوْمِكُمْ هَٰذَا قَالُوٓاْ بَلَىٰ وَلَٰكِنْ حَقَّتْ كَلِمَةُ ٱلْعَذَابِ عَلَى ٱلْكَٰفِرِينَ﴾ قِيلَ ٱدْخُلُوٓاْ أَبْوَٰبَ جَهَنَّمَ خَٰلِدِينَ فِيهَا فَبِئْسَ مَثْوَى ٱلْمُتَكَبِّرِينَ﴾ سُورَةُ الزُّمَر 39: 71-72

Jibreel صلى الله is the angel that brings Allah's صلى الله messages to human prophets. He is the one who brought revelation to all the prophets, and he is considered to be the most important of all the angels. He is named Ruh ul Quddus or the Spirit of Holiness for his role in bringing the good news to the people of the world. (16:102)

There is also a special angel named Israfil إِسْرَافِيل whose only job is to sound the notes that will signal the end of the world and the beginning of the Day of Judgement. The sound will reverberate all over the Earth and cause people to stare in awe.

They don't fully estimate the (power of Allah) as they should. On the Day of Judgement the entire Earth will be but His handful, and space will be rolled up in His right hand. Glory to Him! He is high above the partners they associate with Him. The horn will be sounded, and then all beings in space and on Earth will faint, except as Allah wills. Then a second sound will be sent forth and everyone will be standing, looking on (in the Plain of Judgement). Surat Az-Zumar (The Groups) 39:67-68

﴿وَسِيقَ ٱلَّذِينَ كَفَرُوٓاْ إِلَىٰ جَهَنَّمَ زُمَرًا حَتَّىٰٓ إِذَا جَآءُوهَا فُتِحَتْ أَبْوَٰبُهَا وَقَالَ لَهُمْ خَزَنَتُهَآ أَلَمْ يَأْتِكُمْ رُسُلٌ مِّنكُمْ يَتْلُونَ عَلَيْكُمْ ءَايَٰتِ رَبِّكُمْ وَيُنذِرُونَكُمْ لِقَآءَ يَوْمِكُمْ هَٰذَا قَالُوٓاْ بَلَىٰ وَلَٰكِنْ حَقَّتْ كَلِمَةُ ٱلْعَذَابِ عَلَى ٱلْكَٰفِرِينَ﴾ قِيلَ ٱدْخُلُوٓاْ أَبْوَٰبَ جَهَنَّمَ خَٰلِدِينَ فِيهَا فَبِئْسَ مَثْوَى ٱلْمُتَكَبِّرِينَ﴾ سُورَةُ الزُّمَر 39: 67-68

Angels not only watch our actions and perform the multiple tasks that Allah صلى الله assigns them, but they can also implant peace within our minds and cause a feeling of tranquility to come over us when we're afraid or worried. Only those who have emaan and taqwa and who sincerely look towards their Lord can hope for this tranquility to come. They can also cause terror in the hearts of those who are enemies of Allah صلى الله. (8:9-10)

This is a nearly-complete picture of what angels are and what they do. There is no magic. They are not intermingling with us in restaurants and street-corners like they show in the movies and on television.

Angels don't feel pride; they don't disobey Allah صلى الله, nor do they operate as independent agents. They can appear in human form, by Allah's صلى الله command, when there is a pressing need to be performed. Movie producers and songwriters often portray angels as the spirits of dead people who made it to Heaven. This is a false notion.

The next time you see an image of an angel that looks like a person, maybe wearing a gold and blue gown, or a halo of light and blond hair in a painting, remember, it's not an accurate depiction of true angels. Rather, it is the imagination and false ideas of people who have no authority from Allah صلى الله.

Literature Selection
Allah ﷻ Is the Most Merciful!

The Messenger of Allah ﷺ once said, "Allah has some angels who look for those who are praising Allah on the roads and paths.

When they find someone praising Allah, they call to each other saying, 'Come to what you're looking for!' Then the angels encircle them with their wings up to the top of the world. When the angels return to Allah, their Lord asks them, though He knows better than them, 'What are My servants saying?'

The angels will reply, 'They are saying: Glory to Allah, Allah is the Greatest and Praise be to Allah.'

Allah will ask, 'Have they ever seen Me?'

The angels answer, 'No! By Allah they've never seen You!'

Allah will declare, 'How would it be if they had seen Me?'

The angels will answer, 'If they ever saw You, they would serve You more devoutly and praise You more deeply. They would declare that You're not like anything in creation much more often.'

Allah will say to the angels, 'What are they asking Me for?'

The angels will answer, 'They are asking for Paradise.'

Allah will say, 'Have they ever seen it?'

The angels will answer, 'No! By Allah, Oh Lord, They've never seen it!'

Allah will say, 'How would it be if they had seen it?'

The angels will answer, 'If they had seen it, they would have a greater desire for it and would seek it with more enthusiasm and longing.'

Then Allah will ask, 'What do they want to be protected from?'

The angels will answer, 'They want to be protected from the fire.'

Allah will say, 'Have they ever seen it?'

The angels will answer, 'No! By Allah, Oh Lord, they have never seen it!'

Allah will say, 'How would it be if they had seen it?'

The angels will answer, 'If they ever saw it, they would run from it at top speed and would be terrified of it.' Then Allah will declare, 'I make you witnesses that I have forgiven (the people who were praising Me).'

One of the angels will say, 'There was another person with them who wasn't doing any praising. He was just there.' Allah will answer, 'The companions of the praising people will also not be reduced to misery.'" (Al Bukhari)

قَالَ رَسُولُ اللهِ ﷺ : « إِنَّ لِلهِ مَلَائِكَةً يَطُوفُونَ فِي الطُّرُقِ ، يَلْتَمِسُونَ أَهْلَ الذِّكْرِ ، فَإِذَا وَجَدُوا قَوْمًا يَذْكُرُونَ اللهَ تَنَادَوْا اهْلُمُّوا إِلَى حَاجَتِكُمْ. قَالَ فَيَحُفُّونَهُمْ بِأَجْنِحَتِهِمْ إِلَى السَّمَاءِ الدُّنْيَا. قَالَ فَيَسْأَلُهُمْ رَبُّهُمْ وَهُوَ أَعْلَمُ مِنْهُمْ مَا يَقُولُ عِبَادِي قَالُوا يَقُولُونَ يُسَبِّحُونَكَ ، وَ يُكَبِّرُونَكَ ، وَ يَحْمَدُونَكَ ، وَ يُمَجِّدُونَكَ. قَالَ فَيَقُولُ هَلْ رَأَوْنِي قَالَ فَيَقُولُونَ لَا وَ اللهِ مَا رَأَوْكَ. قَالَ فَيَقُولُ كَيْفَ لَوْ رَأَوْنِي قَالَ يَقُولُونَ لَوْ رَأَوْكَ كَانُوا أَشَدَّ لَكَ عِبَادَةً ، وَأَشَدَّ لَكَ تَمْجِيدًا ، وَأَكْثَرَ لَكَ تَسْبِيحًا. قَالَ يَقُولُ فَمَا يَسْأَلُونِي قَالَ يَسْأَلُونَكَ الْجَنَّةَ. قَالَ يَقُولُ وَهَلْ رَأَوْهَا قَالَ يَقُولُونَ لَا وَ اللهِ يَا رَبِّ مَا رَأَوْهَا. قَالَ يَقُولُ فَكَيْفَ لَوْ أَنَّهُمْ رَأَوْهَا قَالَ يَقُولُونَ لَوْ أَنَّهُمْ رَأَوْهَا كَانُوا أَشَدَّ عَلَيْهَا حِرْصًا ، وَأَشَدَّ لَهَا طَلَبًا ، وَأَعْظَمَ فِيهَا رَغْبَةً. قَالَ فَمِمَّ يَتَعَوَّذُونَ قَالَ يَقُولُونَ مِنَ النَّارِ. قَالَ يَقُولُ وَهَلْ رَأَوْهَا قَالَ يَقُولُونَ لَا وَ اللهِ مَا رَأَوْهَا. قَالَ يَقُولُ فَكَيْفَ لَوْ رَأَوْهَا قَالَ يَقُولُونَ لَوْ رَأَوْهَا كَانُوا أَشَدَّ مِنْهَا فِرَارًا ، وَأَشَدَّ لَهَا مَخَافَةً. قَالَ فَيَقُولُ فَأُشْهِدُكُمْ أَنِّي قَدْ غَفَرْتُ لَهُمْ. قَالَ يَقُولُ مَلَكٌ مِنَ الْمَلَائِكَةِ فِيهِمْ فُلَانٌ لَيْسَ مِنْهُمْ إِنَّمَا جَاءَ لِحَاجَةٍ. قَالَ هُمُ الْجُلَسَاءُ لَا يَشْقَى بِهِمْ جَلِيسُهُمْ » . رَوَاهُ الْبُخَارِيُّ

What Is a Jinn?

In addition to angels, there is another type of creature in our Universe that came into existence before us. Known as the jinn, these beings exist in another dimension, which is not open to us. They can see us and are aware of us, but we cannot see them. We can sometimes feel their presence, however, usually in a way which makes us uncomfortable.

O children of Adam, do not let Satan put you in trouble the way he had your parents expelled from Paradise, having their dress removed from them, so that he could show them their shame. Indeed, he sees you, he and his company, from where you do not see them. Surely, We have made the devils friends to those who do not believe.
Surat Al A'raf (The Heights) 7: 27

﴿يَٰبَنِيٓ ءَادَمَ لَا يَفْتِنَنَّكُمُ ٱلشَّيْطَٰنُ كَمَآ أَخْرَجَ أَبَوَيْكُم مِّنَ ٱلْجَنَّةِ يَنزِعُ عَنْهُمَا لِبَاسَهُمَا لِيُرِيَهُمَا سَوْءَٰتِهِمَآ إِنَّهُۥ يَرَىٰكُمْ هُوَ وَقَبِيلُهُۥ مِنْ حَيْثُ لَا تَرَوْنَهُمْ إِنَّا جَعَلْنَا ٱلشَّيَٰطِينَ أَوْلِيَآءَ لِلَّذِينَ لَا يُؤْمِنُونَ﴾ سُورَةُ الأعراف 27:7

Allah created their kind from the elements of fire. (55:15) Scientists have long wondered what shape other life forms would take in our Universe. All Earth-born creatures are carbon-based life forms. Perhaps those on other planets are silicon-based, ether-based or, as in the case of the jinn, fire-based. They cannot travel as fast as the angels, nor do they have any power over them.

The jinn were given a limited form of free-will. Like us, they live, die, procreate and can choose to surrender their wills to Allah or not. (51:56) But their fiery temper and arrogance can lead them astray far faster than our own animal desires can affect us. Those jinn who accept Allah as their Lord are generally peaceful and leave the world of humans alone.

Other jinn, those who choose to reject Allah, become what we call **devils** or **evil spirits**. The first jinn to turn against Allah was **Iblis** إِبْلِيس. He was present when Allah commanded the angels to bow to Adam in respect. All the angels bowed, but Iblis arrogantly refused. **3**

He (Allah) said, "O Iblis, what is the matter with you that you did not join those who prostrated?" He said, "I'm not going to bow to any humans that You made from dried clay of altered mud!"
Surat Al Hijr (The Rocky Tract) 15: 32-33

Then, he vainly boasted, *...I'm better than him, for You made me from fire and him you created from clay.* Surat Al A'raf (The Heights) 7:12

The Arrogance of Iblis

As a punishment for disobeying Allah and showing such pride, Allah commanded Iblis to leave the heavens. However, Iblis asked Allah to give him until the Day of Judgement to prove that humans were inferior to him; Allah granted Iblis his request.

Iblis said, "Allow me respite till the Day they are raised up (i.e. The Day of Resurrection)." Allah said, "You are of those respited." Surat Al A'raf (The Heights) 7:14-15

Iblis then blamed Allah for his own mistake. He said to Allah, *Because You have sent me astray, I'll lie in ambush for them on Your straight way. I'll attack them from their front and back, from their right and left, and (in the end), you will find most of them to be thankless.* Surat Al A'raf (The Heights) 7:16-17

---

3 Some sects of Christianity teach that Iblis, whom they call Lucifer, was an angel who went bad and that all the devils are bad angels. Islam teaches that angels can only obey Allah and that Iblis was a jinn who refused to bow to Adam as the angels had done. Allah clearly states that Iblis was a jinn in ayah 18:50.

Allah﷽ commanded Iblis, *Get out of here. You are cursed and rejected. If any of them follow you, I will fill Hell with you all!* Surat Al A'raf (The Heights) 7:18

Iblis was renamed Shaytan, which means to stay away from the truth, and this is what Shaytan wants to do with people and their relationship to Allah﷽. Allah﷽ placed the first two humans, Adam﷽ and Hawwa, in a garden paradise. They were good and lived a simple and wholesome life. But Shaytan began to whisper suggestions into their minds in an effort to pull them away from Allah﷽.

Allah﷽ had commanded Adam﷽ and Hawwa to live in the Garden in peace and to eat anything they wished. However, they were told to avoid one certain tree. There was nothing magical about the tree; it was merely a test to see if the pair would obey the only limitation placed on them.

Shaytan suggested that the tree could make them live forever or become angels. (7:20) After a while, he succeeded in tempting them to eat from the tree. Yet Adam﷽ and Hawwa didn't live forever nor did they gain any magical powers. Instead, they immediately realized that they had done wrong, and their sense of shame was awakened with a sudden, compelling force. (7:20-22)

Consequently, Adam﷽ and Hawwa were expelled out into the open land of Earth, and from them descended all human beings. Although Shaytan was able to tempt Adam﷽ and Hawwa, they had a capacity he didn't count on: feeling sorry and asking for forgiveness from Allah﷽. So Allah﷽ forgave the two, wiping their sins clean.

Shaytan's Plans Are Thwarted

Shaytan, in his frustration, must have realized that trying to corrupt humans would be a full-time job. As often as he would corrupt them, Allah﷽ would send prophets to call them back to purity and goodness. Thus began the struggle for the human soul.

Shaytan succeeded in influencing other jinn to join him, and they too became evil. They joined together to cause corruption among humans and the good jinn who had not yet joined them. (35:6) Allah﷽ has also sent messengers to the jinn, and some surrendered their wills to Him. But many are still seduced by their worldly lives and in need of guidance. (6:130)

You might have heard stories related to the jinn from family or friends: doors closing by themselves, haunted houses, voices in the dark or mysteriously lost items. However, jinn do not usually assume physical form and tamper with our property, though they can if they want to. **4**

They work primarily on the mind and seek to corrupt a person's morals and values. (4:120) Most stories and accounts that people tell are merely folklore or even natural events that people like to blame on the jinn. If you think you have been involved in a real jinn encounter, recite Surat Al Falaq and Surat An-Nas for protection. (Suwar 113 and 114)

The Tricks of Some Jinn

If you've ever had a powerful urge to do wrong, one that you didn't know how to silence, then it is possible that you felt the effects of a bad jinn. In addition, some jinn have succeeded in getting people to consult astrologers, soothsayers, psychics and tarot cards for guidance. These evil occult practices come from bad jinn who whisper secret knowledge to humans. Psychics and astrologers think that they're talking to the dead or predicting the future, but they're really sinking lower and lower into unbelief. The information is sometimes correct but not always.

The jinn can steal information from the angels, whom they spy on. (72:8-10) But the secrets of the jinn are not accurate. Most people don't pay attention to the errors of professional predictors because they are so programmed to believe in fortune-tellers, ouija boards and the like. (72:6)

Muslims are warned to avoid astrology, witchcraft, palm-reading and seeking hidden knowledge of the future because it is the tool of Shaytan to turn us away from our Lord. (20:69) When we attempt to learn about our future

---

4 Prophets could sometimes see the jinn and warned their people against the suggestions of the evil ones. Prophet Sulayman﷽ actually had control over the jinn and made them serve him in war, construction and other things. (See Qur'an 27:17 and 34:12)

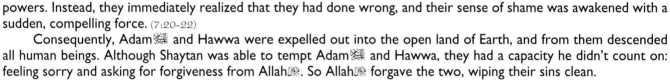

and what it holds, this indicates a weakness in our faith and trust in Allah. (34:41) We become impatient and fall for Shaytan's tricks. It is such a serious crime that the Prophet once remarked, "Whoever consults a fortune-teller will not have his or her prayers accepted for forty nights." (Muslim)

عَنِ النَّبِيِّ ﷺ : «مَنْ أَتَى عَرَّافًا فَسَأَلَهُ عَنْ شَيْءٍ لَمْ تُقْبَلْ لَهُ صَلَاةٌ أَرْبَعِينَ لَيْلَةً». رَوَاهُ مُسْلِمٌ

The Blessed Prophet ﷺ once said, "While the Angels talk among the clouds about things that are going to happen on Earth, the Shayaateen hear a word of what they say and pour it into the ears of a fortune-teller like pouring something into a bottle. Then they add one hundred lies to it." (Al Bukhari and Muslim)

Stories of ghouls and ghosts could be the jinn at work.

سَمِعْتُ رَسُولَ اللهِ ﷺ يَقُولُ: «إِنَّ الْمَلَائِكَةَ تَنْزِلُ فِي الْعَنَانِ ـ وَهُوَ السَّحَابُ ـ فَتَذْكُرُ الْأَمْرَ قُضِيَ فِي السَّمَاءِ، فَتَسْتَرِقُ الشَّيَاطِينُ السَّمْعَ، فَتَسْمَعُهُ فَتُوحِيهِ إِلَى الْكُهَّانِ، فَيَكْذِبُونَ مَعَهَا مِائَةَ كَذْبَةٍ مِنْ عِنْدِ أَنْفُسِهِمْ». رَوَاهُ الْبُخَارِيُّ وَمُسْلِمٌ

The other tools of Shaytan are alcohol, drugs and gambling. He preys upon the worries, frustrations and insecurities of people, promising them salvation in a bottle or instant riches from a slot machine. Allah warns us against them thus, Oh you who believe! Liquor and gambling and games of chance are the tools of Shaytan. Avoid them so you may prosper. The plan of Shaytan is to arouse hatred and envy between you with liquor and gambling and to block you from remembering Allah and from prayer. Won't you avoid them?
Surat Al Ma'idah (The Table) 5:90-91

﴿يَا أَيُّهَا الَّذِينَ آمَنُوا إِنَّمَا الْخَمْرُ وَالْمَيْسِرُ وَالْأَنْصَابُ وَالْأَزْلَامُ رِجْسٌ مِنْ عَمَلِ الشَّيْطَانِ فَاجْتَنِبُوهُ لَعَلَّكُمْ تُفْلِحُونَ ۞ إِنَّمَا يُرِيدُ الشَّيْطَانُ أَنْ يُوقِعَ بَيْنَكُمُ الْعَدَاوَةَ وَالْبَغْضَاءَ فِي الْخَمْرِ وَالْمَيْسِرِ وَيَصُدَّكُمْ عَنْ ذِكْرِ اللَّهِ وَعَنِ الصَّلَاةِ فَهَلْ أَنْتُمْ مُنْتَهُونَ﴾ سُورَةُ الْمَائِدَةِ 5: 90-91

But Allah will counter the effects of Shaytan for any who would listen. Shaytan attacks our fitrah, or natural instincts, and calls to our lower, animal desires. Allah, therefore, sent prophets and messengers to human societies to appeal to people's intelligence and intellect. The one thing that Shaytan can never accept is humanity's superior intelligence. If we open our eyes, then we can fend off the prompting of our lower desires. That is our defense against the evil one and his cohorts.

Allah gives us an example of the effects of the Qur'an upon the jinn. In a chapter aptly entitled Surat Al Jinn, Allah recounts the story of a group of jinn who came near Prophet Muhammad ﷺ and heard him reciting Allah's revelation. (72:1-15) They were enthralled by it and became Muslims. Thereafter, they started preaching Islam to their fellow jinn. (46:29-32)

In the end, those jinn who accept their mission and surrender their wills to Allah will be rewarded with Allah's Paradise. In contrast, those who reject their own nature, whether jinn or human, will be punished. Even if you faithfully follow Shaytan, on the Day of Judgement, he will disown you. He will say that he didn't make you stray, but that you chose to listen and obey him. (59:16)

The day He will assemble all of them together, (Allah will say to jinn) "O species of jinn, you have done too much against mankind." Their friends from among the human beings will say, "Our Lord, some of us have benefited from others, and we have reached our term that You had appointed for us." He will say, "The Fire is your Abode wherein you will remain for ever, unless Allah wills (otherwise). Surely, your Lord is All-Wise, All-Knowing." Surat Al An'aam (The Cattle) 6:128

﴿وَيَوْمَ يَحْشُرُهُمْ جَمِيعًا يَا مَعْشَرَ الْجِنِّ قَدِ اسْتَكْثَرْتُمْ مِنَ الْإِنْسِ وَقَالَ أَوْلِيَاؤُهُمْ مِنَ الْإِنْسِ رَبَّنَا اسْتَمْتَعَ بَعْضُنَا بِبَعْضٍ وَبَلَغْنَا أَجَلَنَا الَّذِي أَجَّلْتَ لَنَا قَالَ النَّارُ مَثْوَاكُمْ خَالِدِينَ فِيهَا إِلَّا مَا شَاءَ اللَّهُ إِنَّ رَبَّكَ حَكِيمٌ عَلِيمٌ﴾ سُورَةُ الْأَنْعَامِ 6: 128

The Earliest Revelations of Allah ﷻ

The earliest human societies had no knowledge of reading and writing. In fact, language itself was very limited and confined to simple commands, gestures and intonations. If you remember from the story in the Qur'an, the first humans had very little dialogue. Allah ﷻ gave simple commands to Adam ﷺ and Hawwa and they were tempted by the simple suggestions of Shaytan. They had all the capabilities of advanced speech, but it would not develop to full capacity until later generations.

When Allah ﷻ mentions that He taught Adam ﷺ the names of all things, it doesn't mean that Adam ﷺ knew the title of every insect, fish, reptile, bird, mammal and other creatures on the face of the Earth. The Arabic term اِسْم, or **name**, can also be used to describe the qualities or characteristics within something. So, as many scholars have pointed out, Allah ﷻ gave Adam ﷺ the understanding of the environment around him and gave him status through knowledge of the nature of his world.

Remember that Adam ﷺ and Hawwa disobeyed their one prime directive: not to go close to a certain tree. They were then dismissed from the heavens as a consequence. Shaytan thought he had fulfilled his vow and had caused the first humans to slip up. But Allah ﷻ knew the capacity of the creatures He made, and He ﷻ knew their intellect could save them and future humans from the low suggestions of Shaytan.

We said, "Go down from here, all of you. Then, should some guidance come to you from Me, those who follow My guidance shall have no fear, nor shall they grieve. As for those who disbelieve and deny Our signs, they are the people of the Fire. They shall dwell in it forever." Surat Al Baqarah (The Cow) 2:38-39

﴿قُلْنَا اهْبِطُوا مِنْهَا جَمِيعًا فَإِمَّا يَأْتِيَنَّكُم مِّنِّي هُدًى فَمَن تَبِعَ هُدَايَ فَلَا خَوْفٌ عَلَيْهِمْ وَلَا هُمْ يَحْزَنُونَ﴾ ﴿وَالَّذِينَ كَفَرُوا وَكَذَّبُوا بِآيَاتِنَا أُولَٰئِكَ أَصْحَابُ النَّارِ هُمْ فِيهَا خَالِدُونَ﴾ سُورَةُ البَقَرَة 38-39:2

Allah ﷻ informed Adam ﷺ that future generations were going to be granted Allah's ﷻ guidance for their protection against Shaytan. To accomplish this task, Allah ﷻ chose humans to be His prophets, messengers, teachers and wise leaders, so people could be guided to the truth.

And We sent not before you (O Muhammad) any but men to whom We sent revelation. So ask of those who know the Scripture, if you know not. With clear signs and Books, and We have also sent down unto you the Thikr (the Qur'an), that you may explain clearly to men what is sent down to them and that they may give thought. Surat An-Nahl (The Bees) 16:43-44

﴿وَمَا أَرْسَلْنَا مِن قَبْلِكَ إِلَّا رِجَالًا نُّوحِي إِلَيْهِمْ فَاسْأَلُوا أَهْلَ الذِّكْرِ إِن كُنتُمْ لَا تَعْلَمُونَ﴾ ﴿بِالْبَيِّنَاتِ وَالزُّبُرِ وَأَنزَلْنَا إِلَيْكَ الذِّكْرَ لِتُبَيِّنَ لِلنَّاسِ مَا نُزِّلَ إِلَيْهِمْ وَلَعَلَّهُمْ يَتَفَكَّرُونَ﴾ سُورَةُ النَّحْل 43-44:16

The First Prophets

Almost all of the first prophets had limited missions, which were really only for their local areas, and their message wasn't remembered for more than a couple of generations. But a few, whom we call messengers, were given a legacy that survived long after they were gone. Allah ﷻ gave each of these special messengers a book. (2:213)

The term for messenger in the Qur'anic language is **Rasul** رَسُول **Messenger**. It literally means 'message-bearer.' This title is for those whom Allah ﷻ chose to receive organized teachings that were meant to be preserved after the messengers had passed away. There were hundreds of such messengers in history.

A **Nabi** نَبِيّ **Prophet**, on the other hand, received teachings, guidance and prophecies, but not a book. There were thousands of them throughout world history. What is the source for these messages? Allah has a record that He keeps with Him of all wisdom, knowledge and truth. This special record is called the **Umm Al Kitab** أُمّ الكِتاب **Mother of the Book**, from which all earthly revelations are derived.

Certainly, (the Qur'an) is in the Mother of the Book, which is in Our presence, raised high and full of wisdom. Surat Az-Zukhruf (The Gold Adornment) 43:4

﴿وَإِنَّهُۥ فِىٓ أُمِّ ٱلۡكِتَٰبِ لَدَيۡنَا لَعَلِيٌّ حَكِيمٌ﴾ سُورَةُ الزُّخۡرُف 43:4

When Allah determined that a person should receive **Wahi** وَحي **Revelation**, He would order Angel Jibreel to deliver it and strengthen the spirit of the chosen one. (22:75) Both men and women could receive revelation from Allah, but men were chosen to be messengers. This may be based on the need for strength in the face of the extreme opposition and physical punishment they would have to go through, and Allah knows best. **5**

When the revelation was intended for generations to come, either the messenger would write it down himself, or it would be revealed to him so that others would write it someday. Each of these writings is known as a 'Book of Allah.' We don't know how many books Allah sent to the world in the last 6,000 years of literacy. Allah declares that He told us the stories of some of our forefathers, but has chosen not to tell us about all of them. (40:78) That is because the Qur'an is not meant to be a book of stories. Rather it is a book of lessons that helps us understand our relationship with our Creator and what our purpose is here on Earth.

We did not send before you (Messengers) other than men from the people of the towns whom We inspired with revelation. Have they not traveled in the land where they could have seen how was the fate of those before them? And surely the abode of the Hereafter is much better for those who fear Allah. Would you, then, still not understand? Surat Yusuf 12:109

﴿وَمَآ أَرۡسَلۡنَا مِن قَبۡلِكَ إِلَّا رِجَالٗا نُّوحِىٓ إِلَيۡهِم مِّنۡ أَهۡلِ ٱلۡقُرَىٰٓ أَفَلَمۡ يَسِيرُوا۟ فِى ٱلۡأَرۡضِ فَيَنظُرُوا۟ كَيۡفَ كَانَ عَٰقِبَةُ ٱلَّذِينَ مِن قَبۡلِهِمۡ وَلَدَارُ ٱلۡءَاخِرَةِ خَيۡرٞ لِّلَّذِينَ ٱتَّقَوۡا۟ أَفَلَا تَعۡقِلُونَ﴾ سُورَةُ يُوسُف 12:109

What about Previous Revelations?

The Qur'an mentions only five books of Allah by name, but it is likely that there were others which simply did not survive the tide of history. The five books and to whom they were given are in historical order:

1. The Suhuf (Scrolls) الصُّحُف, Ibrahim
2. The Tawrah (Law) التَّوۡرَاة, Musa
3. The Zabur (Sacred Poems) الزَّبُور, Dawud
4. The Injeel (Gospel) الإنۡجِيل, 'Isa
5. The Qur'an (Recitation) القُرۡآن الكَرِيم, Prophet Muhammad

All of these revelations have been lost or altered, except the Qur'an. The Jews and the Christians, who are called the 'People of the Book,' believe they have some of the first four books. While some elements have survived, the Bible only contains fragments of the original revelations mixed with others' writings and stories. (5:66-68)

What Is the Bible?

The Bible has two main parts: the Old Testament and the New Testament. The Old Testament was compiled around the year 100 CE by rabbis in Palestine. It is a collection of Jewish writings about their tribe, culture and thoughts spanning thousands of years. Various groups of Christians wrote what was later to be called the New Testament part of the Bible. It comprises letters, advice, biographies, theological essays, supernatural stories and history that was written some 50 to 100 years after the time of Prophet 'Isa. None of the authors of these texts thought they were writing revelations, nor did they know that later people were going to collect their writings in a holy book. They were merely writing letters to record their beliefs, and many of the writers didn't even agree with each other.

To understand how the Bible came to be, remember that after Prophet 'Isa left the world, his followers

---

5 Maryam received a visit from Angel Jibreel, who came to explain her mission and that of her son, 'Isa. (19:17-21, 24-26) The mother of Prophet Musa also received revelation from Allah instructing her to set him adrift in the Nile River. (20:38-39, 28:7) Although neither woman was a prophet, this shows that Allah sends His revelation to whomsoever He pleases.

immediately broke up into different groups. These groups had contrasting ideas of how they understood the teachings of 'Isa﷽. (98:1-6)

Many of these new Christians were successful in spreading their personal interpretations across the pagan Roman world. Soon, they made temples of their own that they later called churches. Eventually, flourishing communities and active movements sprang up all around the coasts of the Mediterranean Sea. Because every church had its own beliefs, they all began writing books and letters that reflected their own positions and opinions about Christianity. (6:159)

Some writers, who wanted to tell the story of 'Isa﷽ from their own points of view, wrote biographies that were later labeled the Injeel Gospel, which means 'good news' in English. However, they were merely poorly-researched biographies of Prophet 'Isa﷽—not his message or his Injeel.

There was no unity among the Christians, and for 300 years, they were fighting and arguing about what 'Isa﷽ taught. (3:79-80) They had this problem because no one had written down 'Isa's﷽ message while he was in the world. When people finally began to write something, so many years had passed that there was really nothing left that wasn't already mixed up with other people's ideas, opinions and wishful thinking.

Colossal marble head of Emperor Constantine the Great, Rome, 4th century.

From the people who call themselves Christians, We (Allah) took an agreement. But they forgot most of the Message that was sent to them. So We let them become disunited in envy and hatred between each other, up to the Day of Judgement. Soon Allah will show them what they have done. Surat Al Ma'idah (The Table) 5:14

﴿وَمِنَ ٱلَّذِينَ قَالُوٓاْ إِنَّا نَصَٰرَىٰٓ أَخَذۡنَا مِيثَٰقَهُمۡ فَنَسُواْ حَظًّا مِّمَّا ذُكِّرُواْ بِهِۦ فَأَغۡرَيۡنَا بَيۡنَهُمُ ٱلۡعَدَاوَةَ وَٱلۡبَغۡضَآءَ إِلَىٰ يَوۡمِ ٱلۡقِيَٰمَةِ وَسَوۡفَ يُنَبِّئُهُمُ ٱللَّهُ بِمَا كَانُواْ يَصۡنَعُونَ﴾ سُورَةُ المَائدَة 5:14

How Did the Christians Invent a Holy Book of Their Own?

In the year 325 CE, Roman Emperor Constantine called for a conference of all Christians. He ordered them to bring all their books and writings with them. He then commanded them to agree on something and left them alone to argue.

The majority of the Christian representatives were from Europe. Many agreed that 'Isa﷽ was God and God's son at the same time. They called their belief the 'Trinity' to explain that God was divided into three parts (5:17). The minority, who were from Africa and the Middle East, believed that 'Isa﷽ was a prophet and not God. Constantine accepted the European opinion.

O people of the Book, be not excessive in your Faith, and do not say about Allah anything but the truth. The Masih 'Isa, the son of Maryam is only a Messenger of Allah, and His Word that He had delivered to Maryam, and a spirit from Him. So believe in Allah and His Messengers. Do not say "Three." Stop it. That is good for you. Allah is the only One God. He is far too pure to have a son. To Him belongs what is in the heavens and what is in the earth. And Allah is enough to trust in. Surat An-Nisa' (The Women) 4:171

﴿يَٰٓأَهۡلَ ٱلۡكِتَٰبِ لَا تَغۡلُواْ فِي دِينِكُمۡ وَلَا تَقُولُواْ عَلَى ٱللَّهِ إِلَّا ٱلۡحَقَّ إِنَّمَا ٱلۡمَسِيحُ عِيسَى ٱبۡنُ مَرۡيَمَ رَسُولُ ٱللَّهِ وَكَلِمَتُهُۥٓ أَلۡقَىٰهَآ إِلَىٰ مَرۡيَمَ وَرُوحٌ مِّنۡهُ فَـَٔامِنُواْ بِٱللَّهِ وَرُسُلِهِۦ وَلَا تَقُولُواْ ثَلَٰثَةٌ ٱنتَهُواْ خَيۡرًا لَّكُمۡ إِنَّمَا ٱللَّهُ إِلَٰهٌ وَٰحِدٌ سُبۡحَٰنَهُۥٓ أَن يَكُونَ لَهُۥ وَلَدٌ لَّهُۥ مَا فِي ٱلسَّمَٰوَٰتِ وَمَا فِي ٱلۡأَرۡضِ وَكَفَىٰ بِٱللَّهِ وَكِيلًا﴾ سُورَةُ النِّسَاء 4:171

They took all the letters and writings that agreed with their Trinity theories and put them together in a book, which they called a Bible, a Latin word meaning simply 'book.' They ordered all the other writings to be burned.

The Time Line of Known Books

Prophet Ibrahim & the Suhuf	Prophet Musa & the Tawrah	Prophet Dawud & the Zabur		Prophet 'Isa & the Injeel	Prophet Muhammad & the Qur'an
ca. 1900	ca. 1250	ca. 900	BCE 0 CE	ca. 30	610-632
Place: Mesopotamia, Palestine & Arabia	Place: Egypt, Palestine & Arabia	Place: Palestine & Ancient Isra'il		Place: Palestine	Place: Arabia
Language: Chaldean	Languages: Egyptian & Hebrew	Language: Hebrew		Languages: Aramaic & Hebrew	Language: Arabic

The Christians from Africa and the Middle East refused to accept the majority position and went home in disgust. **6** Ever since that time, European Christians have believed in the Trinity theory that Allah has a son. The Christians divide the Bible between the Old and New Testaments. The New Testament is a collection of notes, letters to friends, biographies and stories. One of the main points of contention between the Christians and the Jews is that the Christians now believe that they are the only ones that will receive Allah's mercy.

The Scrolls of Ibrahim, which were written on leather, disintegrated long ago and were not preserved by later generations. The Law of Musa, which was sent to guide the Jews after escaping Egypt, was rewritten, changed, corrupted, and parts were lost throughout the centuries, leaving only a little of the original message intact today. (7:144-145) The Zabur, known in the Bible as the Psalms, is now mixed in with so many other poems and writings that it's impossible to know who wrote what.

Understanding the Place of the Bible in Christian History

The Injeel of 'Isa was never written down, and eventually most of it was lost. All that remains are some of his sayings and speeches as well as letters written by Greek and Jewish Christians about his message. Many of their own personal opinions were accepted by others rather than the exact words or teachings of 'Isa. For the next 1,200 years, the Christian leaders of Europe ruled over the spiritual life of their flock with a dark and evil hand. Poor people were not taught how to read, nor were they allowed to read their holy book. The Catholic Church, or Universal Church, was eventually consumed by corruption.

The Catholic Church also intimidated people who disagreed with the way it functioned. Anybody who disagreed with the church authorities could be called a heretic and punished. Torture was an essential part of the interrogation process, and few were ever found innocent. While there were good Christian leaders, there were many more who cared only for power and therefore oppressed their people.

Meanwhile, many of the Christians in North Africa and the Middle East accepted Islam within a few years of its arrival. Even scholars acknowledge that there was little to no force or coercion used. The people chose Islam themselves. The few who remained Christians lived peacefully as equal citizens with Muslim counterparts. The Christians, however, had to pay a special tax called the jizyah because they were not obligated to enlist in the army.

In the 16th century, a major split between Christians occurred, and a new group who called themselves Protestants emerged. They altered the Bible with a new understanding of Christianity, adding different chapters, writings, and verses inside. This became known as the Protestant Bible, and it is found most commonly in America and Northern Europe. The Protestants rejected large portions of the original Catholic Bible and removed what they didn't feel was authentic.

Allah sent His revelations to humanity to be followed and passed on. (3:3-4) He put the power into the hands of people to carry out this responsibility. Through the passage of time, people lost, made up or changed the revelations, resulting in the many religions and scriptures that we have today. (23:53-56)

So, woe to those who write the Book with their hands and then say, "This is from Allah," so that they may gain thereby a trifling price. Then, woe to them for what their hands have written, and woe to them for what they earn. Surat Al Baqarah 2:79

﴿فَوَيْلٌ لِّلَّذِينَ يَكْتُبُونَ الْكِتَابَ بِأَيْدِيهِمْ ثُمَّ يَقُولُونَ هَٰذَا مِنْ عِندِ اللَّهِ لِيَشْتَرُوا بِهِ ثَمَنًا قَلِيلًا فَوَيْلٌ لَّهُم مِّمَّا كَتَبَتْ أَيْدِيهِمْ وَوَيْلٌ لَّهُم مِّمَّا يَكْسِبُونَ﴾ سُورَةُ الْبَقَرَةِ 2:79

---

6 Two books have survived that were written by original disciples of Prophet 'Isa. They tell the story of Prophet 'Isa like we know from Islamic teachings. They are called the Gospel of Barnabas and the Gospel of Thomas. The Christian leaders at the council in 325 CE rejected these two books because they didn't contain Trinity teachings, so they ordered them all to be burned!

Allah promised to protect one of His Books, however. That Book is the Qur'an. This was His last Message to the world and therefore, He would ensure that it would be left unchanged for all future generations. It was a correction of all the misinformation that people had accumulated over the last 6,000 years and is the only perfect book. (10:37)

Don't they consider the Qur'an with care? Had it been from any other besides Allah, they would have found many problems in it. Surat An-Nisa' (The Women) 4:82

﴿أَفَلَا يَتَدَبَّرُونَ ٱلْقُرْءَانَ وَلَوْ كَانَ مِنْ عِندِ غَيْرِ ٱللَّهِ لَوَجَدُوا۟ فِيهِ ٱخْتِلَٰفًا كَثِيرًا﴾ سُورَةُ النِّسَاء 4:82

This is the teaching the Blessed Prophet Muhammad ﷺ instilled in his followers: the previous revelations were lost, so protect the Qur'an and let no change enter it. This is the mission Muslims accepted and have remained faithful to. We must recognize that Allah revealed messages to people in the past and that the Qur'an is the only accurate message to follow. (3:84-85)

Oh you who believe! Believe in Allah and His Messenger and in the book which He sent to His Messenger. And in the books which He sent to those before. Anyone who denies Allah, His angels, His Books, His Messengers and the Day of Judgement has gone into great error. Surat An-Nisa' (The Women) 4:136

﴿يَٰٓأَيُّهَا ٱلَّذِينَ ءَامَنُوٓا۟ ءَامِنُوا۟ بِٱللَّهِ وَرَسُولِهِ وَٱلْكِتَٰبِ ٱلَّذِى نَزَّلَ عَلَىٰ رَسُولِهِ وَٱلْكِتَٰبِ ٱلَّذِىٓ أَنزَلَ مِن قَبْلُ وَمَن يَكْفُرْ بِٱللَّهِ وَمَلَٰٓئِكَتِهِ وَكُتُبِهِ وَرُسُلِهِ وَٱلْيَوْمِ ٱلْءَاخِرِ فَقَدْ ضَلَّ ضَلَٰلًۢا بَعِيدًا﴾ سُورَةُ النِّسَاء 4:136

The Jews and the Christians are invited by Allah to examine and accept His last revelation. (5:15) If any do so, they will be fulfilling the ultimate purpose of all the prophets. (4:172-175) If they reject it and only accept the revelation that Allah sent to them, then they close their hearts and invite destruction upon themselves.

Those whom Allah wills to guide, He opens their heart to Islam. Those whom He wills to leave straying, He makes their hearts closed and constricted as if they were climbing up into the skies. Allah (increases) the penalty on those who refuse to believe. Surat Al An'aam (The Cattle) 6:125

﴿فَمَن يُرِدِ ٱللَّهُ أَن يَهْدِيَهُ يَشْرَحْ صَدْرَهُۥ لِلْإِسْلَٰمِ وَمَن يُرِدْ أَن يُضِلَّهُۥ يَجْعَلْ صَدْرَهُۥ ضَيِّقًا حَرَجًا كَأَنَّمَا يَصَّعَّدُ فِى ٱلسَّمَآءِ كَذَٰلِكَ يَجْعَلُ ٱللَّهُ ٱلرِّجْسَ عَلَى ٱلَّذِينَ لَا يُؤْمِنُونَ﴾ سُورَةُ الأَنعام 6:125

This is the way of your Lord leading straight. We have given detailed signs for those who accept advice. Surat Al An'aam (The Cattle) 6:126

﴿وَهَٰذَا صِرَٰطُ رَبِّكَ مُسْتَقِيمًا قَدْ فَصَّلْنَا ٱلْءَايَٰتِ لِقَوْمٍ يَذَّكَّرُونَ﴾ سُورَةُ الأَنعام 6:126

Abu Hurayrah narrated that the Prophet ﷺ said, "Every Prophet was given miracles because of which people believed, but what I have been given, is Divine Inspiration which Allah has revealed to me. So I hope that my followers will outnumber the followers of the other Prophets on the Day of Resurrection." (Al Bukhari)

عَنْ أَبِي هُرَيْرَةَ ، قَالَ قَالَ النَّبِيُّ ﷺ : «مَا مِنَ الأَنْبِيَاءِ نَبِيٌّ إِلاَّ أُعْطِيَ مَا مِثْلُهُ آمَنَ عَلَيْهِ الْبَشَرُ، وَإِنَّمَا كَانَ الَّذِي أُوتِيتُ وَحْيًا أَوْحَاهُ اللهُ إِلَيَّ فَأَرْجُو أَنْ أَكُونَ أَكْثَرَهُمْ تَابِعًا يَوْمَ الْقِيَامَةِ». رَوَاهُ الْبُخَارِيُّ

Religious Symbols.

Why Are There So Many Religions in the World?

Islam has a unique answer to this question! This subject immediately comes to mind when you pass by temples, churches, synagogues and masaajid. Some people take the easy way out and say that all religions are correct. Others take the opposite approach and say they don't need to follow any one of them. Both groups of people will be losers in the next life.

It's true that there are many different religions in the world. But all of them began from the same source: a prophet or messenger from Allah. Only Islam, the last revealed way of life, has survived intact and without change. All other messages that went before it were changed beyond recognition, away from the truth that was originally revealed.

According to Islamic teachings, Allah chose people in every nation to teach their communities to serve Allah and to do what is right. After these guides passed away, the people often forgot the message, or they altered the teachings, advice and example of their prophet. After many generations, they were so confused in their belief that it was no longer a true way of life from Allah. Thus, man-made religions were born. (8:31)

For every people there is a messenger. So, when their messenger comes, the matter is decided between them with justice, and they are not wronged. Surat Yunus (Jonah) 10:47

﴿وَلِكُلِّ أُمَّةٍ رَّسُولٌ فَإِذَا جَاءَ رَسُولُهُمْ قُضِيَ بَيْنَهُم بِالْقِسْطِ وَهُمْ لَا يُظْلَمُونَ﴾ سُورَةُ يُونُس 10:47

For example, some Hindu teachings say that women should be burned alive along with their deceased husband's body, or that it is good to become a beggar and sleep on a bed of nails. These are ideas that have nothing to do with what a prophet from Allah would teach, yet Hindus are taught to believe in these ideas, generation after generation. (5:103-104)

At the same time, Hinduism teaches that good is better than evil and that the soul of a person lives on after the body has died. To this, though, they add the concept of reincarnation, wherein the deceased person returns to earth as another creature. Thus, while some authentic teachings of prophets have survived over time, others have been transformed far from what is correct.

The Growth of Society and Spiritual Awareness

Humanity's origins go back thousands of years. The first two humans were Adam and Hawwa. Adam is considered to be the first prophet of Allah. A prophet, or nabi, is 'one who gives prophecies and news about Allah and the way of life he wants us to follow.' (16:36) In ancient times, humans were very primitive and lived a simple life of gathering and later, hunting. Although they developed a well-defined social structure, there was also a need for spiritual and moral guidance.

As Allah had promised Adam and Hawwa, prophets and guided people were raised up to teach their descendants the truth. But the call of Shaytan was strong, and many people allowed themselves to be led away from their Lord and moral living. (21:1-3) They quarreled with each other and fell into disputes. (10:19) Eventually, the first human communities separated into different groups, each going their own unique way. Some went south, deeper into Africa. Others migrated east into Asia, and then the Americas, while others moved north into the Middle East and Europe. (16:93)

Oh humanity! Be aware of your Lord Who created you from a single person and from him created his mate of a similar nature. From those two He scattered countless men and women. Surat An-Nisa' (The Women) 4:1

﴿يَا أَيُّهَا النَّاسُ اتَّقُوا رَبَّكُمُ الَّذِي خَلَقَكُم مِّن نَّفْسٍ وَاحِدَةٍ وَخَلَقَ مِنْهَا زَوْجَهَا وَبَثَّ مِنْهُمَا رِجَالًا كَثِيرًا وَنِسَاءً﴾ سُورَةُ النِّسَاء 4:1

These early nomads lived a difficult existence and had to adapt to their local environments or perish. But Allah was not going to leave them adrift spiritually. He guided them by sending one of their own kind to reveal His messages to the people. (14:4) If people accepted the teachings, then Allah would protect them. If people rejected their guides, then they were left to their ignorant ways until Judgement Day. (6:42-45)

Some peoples were destroyed if they were overly cruel and wicked. (22:48) Either Allah would allow natural disasters to obliterate them, (29:40) or He would let them be conquered by other stronger peoples. (2:251) Idol and spirit worship became rampant through the Earth, and more and more prophets were sent to bring people back to the right path. (23:63-65)

We didn't send before you, (Muhammad) except that they were humans like you who We inspired. They lived in human dwellings as well. Don't they travel over the Earth and see what happened to those who went before them? But the home of the next life is best for those who do right. Won't you understand? Surat Yusuf (Joseph) 12:109

﴿وَمَآ أَرْسَلْنَا مِن قَبْلِكَ إِلَّا رِجَالًا نُّوحِىٓ إِلَيْهِم مِّنْ أَهْلِ ٱلْقُرَىٰٓ أَفَلَمْ يَسِيرُوا۟ فِى ٱلْأَرْضِ فَيَنظُرُوا۟ كَيْفَ كَانَ عَٰقِبَةُ ٱلَّذِينَ مِن قَبْلِهِمْ وَلَدَارُ ٱلْءَاخِرَةِ خَيْرٌ لِّلَّذِينَ ٱتَّقَوْا۟ أَفَلَا تَعْقِلُونَ﴾

سُورَةُ يُوسُف 12:109

Nomads had to adapt to their local environments.

The message in ancient prehistoric times was passed on through oral traditions. People did not yet know how to read or write. In time, they learned how to draw pictures and record important events with stone carvings. Archeologists have discovered cave paintings in Africa, Australia, Europe, North America and Asia that date back tens of thousands of years.

Although many of these paintings are of animals and the hunt, many had spiritual meanings, like drawings that appeared to be spirits and idols. Most of human history passed by in this way. Countless prophets and guides were raised up, although their names may never be known to us.

Some time after the last Ice Age, which ended some 10,000 years ago, people discovered how to farm and raise animals. Before this, they moved about as nomads, always seeking new sources of food to gather. Therefore, human settlements were often small and usually temporary.

But when people learned that they could grow food, and do it year-after-year, more permanent villages were established. The earliest such farming communities date back to about 8000 BCE. Allah﷾ gives many descriptions in the Qur'an about the miracle of farming and what it means to human societies. (13:3-4)

Organized Groups and Spiritual Practices

Along with the growth of villages came the development of trade. Initially, it was established through bartering. During this period, something interesting happened. Surplus food became available, thus freeing others from the process of food production. Consequently, craftsmanship developed along with innovations in tools, baskets, weapons and even jewelry.

Allah's﷾ prophets still depended upon oral traditions to carry on their message after they were gone. But, with stable villages where generations could be raised in relative safety, it became easier for divine teachings to survive for longer periods of time. At the same time, it also became easier, unfortunately, for false ideas to grow and multiply as well.

Many cultures developed elaborate idol-worshipping practices and could now build shrines and small temples in which to worship their gods. Surplus food meant that villagers could afford to support full-time priests and other religious officials. These small farming villages were mainly clustered along the fertile river valleys in Egypt, Mesopotamia, India and China. From these four places sprang civilization. (16:80-81)

With abundant food supplies, fewer children and adults died from diseases and malnutrition. Thus, with healthier people and consistent provisions, villages would eventually transform into cities after only a few hundred years. Cities were ruled by strong leaders who were oftentimes priests. One of the earliest known cities was Ur, located on the Euphrates River in Mesopotamia.

Trade between people and cities grew to such an extent that simple writing, called 'cuneiform,' was developed around 3100 BCE to keep track of business. Official scribes, or writers, were present in every city. Eventually, this writing system was used to record stories and history as well. One of the oldest surviving stories today is called "The Epic of Gilgamesh," written in ancient Sumer, sometime before 2000 BCE.

Empires were created by powerful leaders invading and establishing control over new cities and areas. This process of conquest continued until a mighty state was created which unified all the villages and people within it. The first organized cities in human history were built by the Sumerians, such as Sargon of Akkad who conquered a vast region and ruled them by his own hand. He reigned until about 2279 BCE. From that time on, empire-builders would dominate human history. (11:100-102) With the invention of writing, humans had a way to record events, and Allah's﷾ guidance, for future generations. (68:1)

The Impact of the Written Word

Writing greatly aided the cause of truth since Allah's chosen prophets could now leave permanent records behind. (96:1-5) Prophets who received formalized messages from Allah, which were sometimes compiled in the form of books, are called messengers.

The earliest known messenger was Ibrahim, who lived in the city of Ur, in Mesopotamia. He was persecuted for confronting the idol-worship among his people. (21:51-71) Allah commanded him to leave with his followers and settle in a new land. Ibrahim recorded his revelation on clay tablets and leather scrolls in the Chaldean language. This message, written almost 4,000 years ago, did not survive.

Other known messengers named in the Qur'an are Musa, Dawud, 'Isa and Muhammad. A messenger

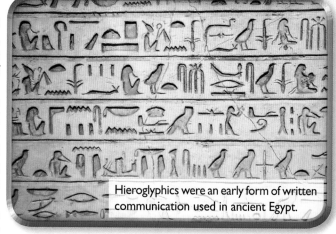

Hieroglyphics were an early form of written communication used in ancient Egypt.

can also be a prophet, because they also bring news of Allah and the truth. According to a well-known saying of the Blessed Prophet Muhammad, there were many thousands of prophets and messengers raised up throughout human history.

The Qur'an explains that Allah chose to give us the story of some of His prophets, but not of others. There are a total of 25 mentioned by name in the Qur'an, along with many others whose identities were not given. The Qur'an names prophets that lived in Africa, Mesopotamia and the Middle East. It also states that Allah sent prophets to all ancient peoples all over the world.

We have told you the story of some Messengers and others We have not. Surat An-Nisa' (The Women) 4:164

﴿وَرُسُلًا قَدْ قَصَصْنَٰهُمْ عَلَيْكَ مِن قَبْلُ وَرُسُلًا لَّمْ نَقْصُصْهُمْ عَلَيْكَ وَكَلَّمَ ٱللَّهُ مُوسَىٰ تَكْلِيمًا﴾ سُورَةُ النِّسَاء 4:164

The Muslim attitude upon learning of another's beliefs should be one of interest and curiosity. Every nation in the past received prophets from Allah. Later generations lost, corrupted or changed those teachings, resulting in the thousands of different religious systems we have today. (7:51-53)

We recognize that each religion might have begun with a true prophet, and then we investigate how that prophet's message was changed. (4:136) In some cases, later generations even took to worshipping their prophets as gods. We must understand what misled them so we can avoid falling into the same trap. (21:29)

Allah says: *O you who believe, do believe in Allah and His Messenger and in the Book He has revealed to His Messenger and in the Books He has revealed earlier. Whoever disbelieves in Allah and His angels and His Books and His Messengers and the Last Day has indeed gone far astray.* Surat An-Nisa' (The Women) 4: 136

﴿يَٰٓأَيُّهَا ٱلَّذِينَ ءَامَنُوٓا۟ ءَامِنُوا۟ بِٱللَّهِ وَرَسُولِهِۦ وَٱلْكِتَٰبِ ٱلَّذِى نَزَّلَ عَلَىٰ رَسُولِهِۦ وَٱلْكِتَٰبِ ٱلَّذِىٓ أَنزَلَ مِن قَبْلُ وَمَن يَكْفُرْ بِٱللَّهِ وَمَلَٰٓئِكَتِهِۦ وَكُتُبِهِۦ وَرُسُلِهِۦ وَٱلْيَوْمِ ٱلْءَاخِرِ فَقَدْ ضَلَّ ضَلَٰلًۢا بَعِيدًا﴾ سُورَةُ النِّسَاء 4:136

What we must do is explain to others that Islam is the last message Allah gave to humans. It is the only accurate standard to go by, because nothing was ever changed or added to it. (16:125) Then we must invite them to examine the Qur'an and the history of Prophet Muhammad and to look for any evidence in their own teachings that confirms the truth of what we say. Allah says: *We have sent you revelation, as We sent it to Nuh and the prophets after him; also We sent revelation to Ibrahim, Isma'il, Ishaq, Yaqub and the clans, 'Isa, Ayyub, Yunus, Harun, Sulayman and to Dawud we gave the Zabur.* Surat An-Nisa' (The Women) 4: 163

﴿إِنَّآ أَوْحَيْنَآ إِلَيْكَ كَمَآ أَوْحَيْنَآ إِلَىٰ نُوحٍ وَٱلنَّبِيِّـۧنَ مِنۢ بَعْدِهِۦ وَأَوْحَيْنَآ إِلَىٰٓ إِبْرَٰهِيمَ وَإِسْمَٰعِيلَ وَإِسْحَٰقَ وَيَعْقُوبَ وَٱلْأَسْبَاطِ وَعِيسَىٰ وَأَيُّوبَ وَيُونُسَ وَهَٰرُونَ وَسُلَيْمَٰنَ وَءَاتَيْنَا دَاوُۥدَ زَبُورًا﴾ سُورَةُ النِّسَاء 4:163

Identifying Allah's Prophets

Muslim scholars have tried to identify past prophets and their possible books. Some say that Guatama Buddha was a prophet; others claim Confucius and Lao Tzu were ancient Chinese prophets from Allah, while yet others say that Socrates was an ancient prophet to the Greeks.

On these issues, only Allah﷾ knows. But the principle remains: We must respect the beliefs of others while calling them to the truth. (4:174-175)

We sent every Messenger before you, (Muhammad) with this revelation sent by Us to him, that there is no god but I, so serve Me. Surat Al Anbiya' (The Prophets) 21: 25

﴿وَمَآ أَرْسَلْنَا مِن قَبْلِكَ مِن رَّسُولٍ إِلَّا نُوحِيٓ إِلَيْهِ أَنَّهُۥ لَآ إِلَٰهَ إِلَّآ أَنَا۠ فَٱعْبُدُونِ﴾ سُورَةُ الأنبياء 25:21

Every prophet's story is unique and contains the record of his fight against ignorance and falsehood. Prophets were sent to the Egyptians, Greeks, Jews, Chinese, Africans and to all other peoples. The story of history is the story of humanity's acceptance or rejection of Allah's﷾ guidance. This is what it all comes down to. (18:54-59)

Don't they travel over the world and see the end of those before them? They were even superior to them in strength! (Consider) the traces (and ruins they left) in the land. Allah called them to account for their sins and none of them had any defense against Allah. That is because there came to them Messengers with clear proof but they rejected them. Surat Ghaafir (The Forgiver) 40:21-22

﴿أَوَلَمْ يَسِيرُوا۟ فِى ٱلْأَرْضِ فَيَنظُرُوا۟ كَيْفَ كَانَ عَٰقِبَةُ ٱلَّذِينَ كَانُوا۟ مِن قَبْلِهِمْ كَانُوٓا۟ هُمْ أَشَدَّ مِنْهُمْ قُوَّةً وَءَاثَارًا فِى ٱلْأَرْضِ فَأَخَذَهُمُ ٱللَّهُ بِذُنُوبِهِمْ وَمَا كَانَ لَهُم مِّنَ ٱللَّهِ مِن وَاقٍ﴿ذَٰلِكَ بِأَنَّهُمْ كَانَت تَّأْتِيهِمْ رُسُلُهُم بِٱلْبَيِّنَٰتِ فَكَفَرُوا۟ فَأَخَذَهُمُ ٱللَّهُ إِنَّهُۥ قَوِىٌّ شَدِيدُ ٱلْعِقَابِ﴾ سُورَةُ غافر 22-21:40

Prophets Named in the Qur'an

Idris	إدْرِيس	Adam	آدَم
Salih	صَالِح	Hud	هُود
'Isa	عِيسَى	Isma'il	إسْمَاعِيل
Yusuf	يُوسُف	Ya'qub	يَعْقُوب
Yunus	يُونُس	Shu'ayb	شُعَيْب
Musa	مُوسَى	Ayyoub	أَيُّوب
Dawud	دَاوُود	Dhu'l Kifl	ذُو الكِفْل
Zakariyya	زَكَرِيَّا	Al Yasa'	اليَسَع
Nuh	نُوح	Ibrahim	إبْرَاهِيم
Is-haq	إسْحَاق	Lut	لُوط
Ilyas	إلْيَاس	Harun	هَارُون
Sulayman	سُلَيْمَان	Yahya	يَحْيى

Peace be upon them all

After the mention of any prophet's name, say ﷺ Peace be upon him.

and

Muhammad ﷺ محَمَّد

The prophets were chosen by Allah﷾ and never failed to uphold to their trust. They exemplified the best morals, habits and the finest character. They were not gods or angels or immortal. (21:8) Some were granted miracles, but none claimed to have power within themselves. They all taught the same basic message, but the form and rituals were different according to the time and place. (21:25 & 22:34) Some were successful, yet others were killed by their own people. In the end, the world advanced enough for one final revelation to descend from Allah﷾, which will last until the end of humanity itself.

The Blessed Prophet Muhammad ﷺ is the last of the guides sent from Allah﷾ to humanity. (34:28) Allah﷾ calls him the **Seal of the Prophets** خَاتَمُ النَّبِيِّين, meaning that Allah's﷾ revelation to the world has been completed. (33:40) The message that we know as Islam came at a time when the world had developed a sophisticated social, political and economic network. This enabled Islam to spread quickly from nation-to-nation. (34:28 & 61:9) On the Day of Judgement, everyone will either be standing behind Allah's﷾ prophets, or standing behind the ideas that they believed in. (18:48 & 10:47) Those who accepted Islam, as taught by Prophet Muhammad ﷺ, will be standing behind him. (40:51)

Although multitudes of prophets and messengers were sent throughout all of human history, only a fraction of humanity listened to their teachings. (2:213) Shaytan will succeed in corrupting many of us. (40:48-50, 7:202, 23:103-111) But with Allah's﷾ assistance, there will also be many who listened to His guides and who will join them in Paradise. Pray that you will be among them. (29:48-52, 18:59)

Oh Humanity! The Messenger has come to you in truth from Allah. Believe in him because it's best for you. But if you reject (this message, then know that) to Allah belongs all things in space and on Earth. Allah is the All-Knowing, the All-Wise. Surat An-Nisa' (The Women) 4:170

﴿يَٰٓأَيُّهَا ٱلنَّاسُ قَدْ جَآءَكُمُ ٱلرَّسُولُ بِٱلْحَقِّ مِن رَّبِّكُمْ فَـَٔامِنُوا۟ خَيْرًا لَّكُمْ وَإِن تَكْفُرُوا۟ فَإِنَّ لِلَّهِ مَا فِى ٱلسَّمَٰوَٰتِ وَٱلْأَرْضِ وَكَانَ ٱللَّهُ عَلِيمًا حَكِيمًا﴾ سُورَةُ النِّسَاء 170:4

Literature Selection

Surat Al Anbiya'

Adapted from *The Holy Qur'an*
Arranged by Yahiya Emerick
(Explanatory words added in parentheses)

In the Name of Allah, The Most Gracious, The Most Merciful

People are coming closer to their accounting, but they're careless about it, so they just turn away. (1) No fresh message ever comes to them from their Lord without them listening to it like it was a joke (2)—all the while their hearts are occupied (with trivial things). The wrongdoers hide their secret discussions: "Is this (man) any different than the rest of you? Are you going to succumb to (his) magic while you see it (for what it is)?" (3) Say to them, "My Lord knows what's being said in the Heavens and on the Earth, for He's the Listener and the Knower." (4) "No way!" they say. "Just a bunch of jumbled dreams! No way! He made it up! No way! He's just a poet! So let him bring us a miracle like the ones that were sent down in ancient times!" (5) None of those previous civilizations that We destroyed ever believed, so will these (people) ever believe? (6) And before you, We sent Messengers who were (ordinary) men—they (just had the added blessing of) receiving Our revelations. If you're not sure about it, then ask those who (already) have (previously revealed) messages. (7) We didn't give (any previous prophets) bodies that could go without food, nor were they immortal. (8) In the end We fulfilled Our promise to them and saved them, and whoever else We wanted to, and We destroyed those who went out of control (in their wickedness). (9) And so it is that We've revealed a Book for (all of) you that contains a message directed towards you, so won't you at least reflect (upon it)? (10)

History Is Proof of God's Will

How many civilizations have We destroyed completely on account of their corruption, and then established other peoples in their place? (11) And whenever they sensed Our punishment (coming for them), they tried to escape it! (12) Oh, don't run away now! Go back to your luxuries and your dwellings so you can have your accounting! (13)
They would cry out, "We're doomed! We were truly wrong!" (14) And their cry never ceased until We mowed them down and reduced them to silent embers. (15)
We didn't create the Heavens and the Earth and everything in between them for some kind of passing entertainment. (16) If We would've wanted to play a game, then We could've chosen (Our entertainment) from things that are near to Us if ever We were so inclined! (17) No way! We throw the truth against falsehood and knock out its brains! And thus falsehood passes away—so you're going to be doomed on account of how you try to (falsely) define (God), (18) for everyone in the heavens and the Earth belongs to Him—even those (angels) who are very near to Him are not too proud or weary (to serve him). (19) They glorify Him throughout the night and the day, and they never pause nor falter. (20)

The Claim of Many Equals with God Is Preposterous

Or have they taken gods from the earth who can raise the dead to life? (21) If there were other gods in the heavens and the earth besides God, then there would've been chaos in both! Glory be to God, the Lord of the Throne, for He's high above what they attribute to Him! (22) He can't be questioned for what He does, but they will be questioned (for what they do). (23) Or have they taken other gods for worship besides Him? Say to them, "Bring me your evidence. This (Qur'an) is the (proven) message of those with me, and the (proven) message of those who came before me." But no! Most of them don't know the truth, and so they just turn away. (24)

We never sent any Messenger before you without giving him this (exact same) inspired message that: 'there is no god besides Me, so serve Me.' (25) But then they say, "The Compassionate (God) has given birth to children." Glory be to Him! No way! The (beings that you say are His children) are only honored servants. (26) They don't speak before He speaks, and they do what He commands. (27) He knows what's (coming) ahead of them and what's (happened) behind them, and they can't intercede unless they're acceptable to Him, and they hold Him in fear and reverence. (28) If any of them should ever say, "I'm a god in place of Him," then We would reward him with Hellfire, and that's how We reward the wrongdoers. (29)

Isn't Nature Proof Enough of God?

Don't the faithless see that the heavens and the earth were once fused together in a single piece until We split them apart, and don't they see that We made every living thing from water? So why won't they believe? (30) We placed the mountains firmly rooted in the earth so it wouldn't shake along with them, and We made broad passes (between the mountains) for them to travel through, so that (through these landmarks) you could be guided (in your travels). (31) And We even made the sky as a sheltering canopy (over you), yet they turn away from (these) miracles (that prove Our existence). (32) Moreover, He's the One Who created the night and the day, and the sun and the moon, and each of these swims gently along in its rounded (orbit). (33)

We didn't grant eternal life to any human being before you, so if you died suddenly, would they get to live forever? (34) Every soul will have a taste of death, and We're testing you through both evil and good, and you will return back to Us. (35)

The Foolish Reject Faith

When the faithless see you, they treat you with nothing but contempt, saying, "Is this the one who's talking (against) your gods?" And (worse still) they reject The Compassionate whenever He's mentioned! (36) How hasty are human beings! But I will soon show you My signs, and then you'll beg Me not to hurry them on! (37)

"So when will all of this come to pass," they ask, "if you're really telling the truth?" (38) Oh, if only the faithless knew (for sure about the time) when they'll be powerless to keep the Fire off their faces and their backs and when they'll be quite beyond help! (39) But no! It's going to come upon them all of a sudden, leaving them perplexed! They won't have any power to keep it away, nor will they be given a break! (40) Many Messengers were ridiculed before you, but their critics were surrounded by the very thing they scoffed at! (41)

Heed the Warning Before It's Too Late

Ask them, "Who can keep you safe throughout the night and the day from (the will) of the Compassionate?" Yet still they turn away from the remembrance of their Lord. (42) Or is it because they have gods that can guard them from Us? They don't even have the power to help themselves, nor can anyone protect them from Us! (43)

No way! We've given the luxuries of this life to these (people), and to their ancestors, until their time period grew long for them. Don't they see that We're gradually reducing the land (that they hold influence over) from its outer borders? (Do they think that) they're going to be victorious? (44) Say to them, "I'm only warning you as the revelation (dictates me to)." But the deaf can't hear the call, even when they're given a warning! (45)

If only a slight breath of your Lord's punishment were to touch them, they would surely cry out, "We're doomed! We were truly wrong!" (46) On the Day of Judgement, We're going to erect scales of justice, so no soul will be treated unfairly in the least, and if there's (a deed) even as light as the weight of a mustard seed, We're going to bring it (to the scale), and We're quite able enough to take an account (of everything). (47) In the past We gave the Standard (of Judgement) to Moses and Aaron as well as a bright light (the Torah) and a reminder for those who would be mindful (of God). (49) And this (Qur'an) is a blessed message that We've sent down (to you people), so are you just going to dismiss it? (50)

Abraham Had a Similar Challenge

In the past We gave right direction to Abraham, and We knew all about him. (51) He had said to his father and his people, "What are these images that you're so devoted to?" (52)

"We found our ancestors worshipping them," they replied. (53)
"And so both you and your ancestors have been clearly mistaken!" (Abraham) answered. (54) "Have you really brought the truth to us," they asked, "or are you only joking?" (55) "Certainly not!" he answered. "Your Lord is the Lord of the Heavens and the Earth, and He's the One Who began them (in the beginning)! I'm just a witness to this (truth). (56) By God! I have a plan for your idols after you've turned your backs!" (57) So later he broke them all to pieces—all except for the biggest one—so they could return (and find it standing alone amidst the rubble). (58)

(When the people returned to the temple and saw what had happened), they said, "Who did this to our gods? He must have been a criminal!" (59) (Some of the people) said, "We heard a young man named Abraham talking out against them." (60) So the (others) said, "Then bring him before the eyes of the people so they can witness (his confession)." (61)

(When he was brought), they asked him, "Are you the one who did this to our gods, Abraham?" (62) "Surely not!" (Abraham) answered. "The biggest (idol) did it. Ask (the broken idols) if they can speak!" (63) Then (the people) turned to (talk amongst) themselves, and they said, "You were all certainly wrong (in trying to get a confession from him, for the biggest idol must have done it)." (64) Then their thought became muddled, and they said (to Abraham), "You know full well that they can't speak!" (65)

"So are you worshipping, besides God," (Abraham) asked, "things that can't do you any good or harm? (66) To heck with you, and the things that you're worshipping besides God! Don't you have any sense?" (67) "Burn him!" they shouted. "Protect your gods if you must do something!" (68) We said, "Fire be cool and safe for Abraham!" (69) Then they made a plan against him, but We made them lose, (70) and We saved him and Lot (and sent them) to the land that We've blessed for all the worlds. (71)

And We granted him (his son) Isaac and (his grandson) Jacob, as an extra gift, and We made each of them righteous. (72) We also made them into leaders to guide (people) by Our command, and We inspired them to do good, to establish prayer, and to give in charity, and they always served Us. (73) And We gave common sense and knowledge to Lot, and We saved him from the civilization that behaved immorally, and they really were an evil and rebellious people, (74) and We admitted him into Our mercy, for he was one of the righteous. (75)

On Noah, David and Solomon

When Noah called upon (Us) in the past, We listened to him and saved him and his family from the massive disaster. (76) We helped him against the people who denied Our signs, and they really were an evil people, so We drowned them all together! (77)

And when David and Solomon rendered their verdict concerning the case of some person's sheep who wandered by night into the field (of someone else, causing crop loss), We witnessed their verdict. (78) We endowed Solomon with a clear understanding of the matter, for to each of them We gave common sense and knowledge. We caused both the mountains and the birds to glorify Us along with David, and We caused it to happen. (79) And We also taught (David) how to make coats of armor for your benefit, so you could be protected from each other's violence, so won't you be thankful? (80)

Solomon had command of the rushing winds, and he used them (to propel his ships) towards blessed lands, and We know about everything. (81) (And Solomon had control) over some evil jinn who (were forced) to dive (in the sea for pearls) for him and who did other work, besides and We were guarding them. (82)

There Were Other Prophets Who Were Blessed

When Job cried out to his Lord, saying, "Misery has come upon me! But You're the most merciful of the merciful," (83) We listened to him and took away his misery and restored his family to him and doubled their number, as a mercy from Our presence and a reminder for those who serve Us. (84)

And Ishmael, Idris and Ezekiel—each of them was patient, (85) so We admitted them into Our mercy, for they were among the righteous. (86) And the Fish Master, (Jonah)! He left in anger and thought We had no power over him, but he cried out in the darkened (belly of the fish), "There is no god but You! Glory to You! I was truly wrong!" (87) So We listened to him and saved him from his misery, and that's how We save those who have faith! (88)

And when Zachariah called upon his Lord, saying, "My Lord! Don't leave me childless, though

You're the best inheritor (of the future)," (89) We listened to him too and granted him (a son named) John, and thus We cured his wife's infertility! (All of) these Prophets were quick to do good, and they used to call upon Us in hope and trepidation, and they were humble to Us. (90) And (Mary), who had maintained her virginity—We breathed Our spirit into her and made her and her son a sign for all the worlds. (91)

This fellowship of yours is a single fellowship (of believing people), and I am your Lord, so serve me. (92) (Later generations after these righteous people) divided their affairs among them (by breaking up into competing factions), but they're all going to return to Us. (93)

What Will Happen When They Return

Whoever does a moral deed and has faith won't have his effort rejected, for We're going to record it. (94) It's forbidden for any civilization that We destroyed to ever return (to life) (95) until (the people of) Gog and Magog are let loose, and they swoop down from every hill. (96) And when the true promise draws near, that's when the eyes of the faithless will stare unblinking in horror. "We're doomed! We never thought about any of this! We were totally wrong!" (97)

Truly, both you and (the false gods) you used to worship besides God will be nothing more than fuel for Hellfire—and you're going to reach it! (98) If those (idols) were really gods, then they would've never reached it, but they're going to stay in there! (99) For them there is nothing more than weeping and crushing silence within. (100)

But those who already had a good (record) from Us will be far removed from there, (101) nor will they hear even the faintest sound of Hellfire, for they're going to remain in the place that their souls had hoped for. (102) They're not going to be troubled at all by the Great Terror but will instead be met by angels (who will say), "This is your day that you've been promised!" (103)

(This will happen on the) Day when We roll up the sky like a written scroll, and even as We began creation in the beginning, We're going to produce a new one, and that's a promise binding upon Us, and We can certainly fulfill it! (104)

This Is a Message for All People to Consider

And so We've written in the Scriptures (sent to the Messengers of the past, and also in this) message (that We're sending to you) now after them, that the Earth shall be inherited by My righteous servants. (105) There is instruction in this for people who serve (God). (106)

We didn't send you except to be a mercy to all the worlds. (107) So say to them, "It's been revealed to me that your God is One God, so will you now submit to Him?" (108) But if they turn back, then tell them, "I've delivered the message to you evenly, and I don't know if what you've been promised is near or far. (109) He knows what's being spoken aloud and what's hidden. (110) I don't know if (God's delay in punishment) is meant to be a test for you and merely a time for you to enjoy yourselves." (111) Then say to them, "My Lord! Judge truthfully (between us). Our Compassionate Lord is the One to Whom We should look to for help against all (the false things) you attribute (to Him)." (112)

Chapter 6
Islamic Beliefs: Part 2

Why Do Things Happen the Way They Do?

Why do we do the things we do? If Allah knows what I'm going to do, then why does He need to punish or reward me later? If Allah already knows everything that is going to happen, why did He create the Universe to begin with? Do I have any free choice in my life?

These are the tough questions that people sometimes ask when they try to make sense of their note about four things: lives. "If we are being tested," they ask, "then what are the rules? Does Allah make people do good or bad things?"

The answers to these questions are easily and logically answered by Allah in the Holy Qur'an. It is important to recount that the Universe was created by Allah according to His will, along with everything else. He allows the Universe to function in a certain way. Within this Universe, Allah created humans with a limited free will to choose whether to serve and obey Him or to defy and disobey him. (18:29)

With that said, what about our choices in this life? What about our freedom and Allah's knowledge of the future? To clear up any mistaken ideas, we must understand that Islam does not teach destiny or fatalism. It does not teach that you are automatically saved or doomed without any say in the matter. Instead, Islam has a unique message that combines both sides of the coin. Simply put, human beings have control over some things and no control over other things in their lives. Our test is in how we react in both those circumstances.

What Do and Don't We Control?

We primarily control our attitudes, intentions, feelings, goals, desires and motivations. We can choose to believe in something or not. We can choose to do right or wrong. We can choose to control our anger or let it loose. We can choose to learn from our life experiences or to remain ignorant. We can even decide whether to love or hate those around us.

On the other hand, we are part of a whole web of relationships in this world. Sometimes we have no control over the flow of events. You cannot stop an earthquake or a tornado. You cannot prevent meeting someone, nor change what other people do, even though their actions may affect your life in ways you never imagined. You can't force someone to hire you for a job. You can't prevent an accident from happening. You can't force others to like or hate you; they decide for themselves. All of these things are quite beyond your control and are external events in your life.

Indeed the knowledge of the Hour is with Allah. And He sends down rain and knows what is in the wombs. No one knows what he will earn tomorrow, nor does anyone know what land he will die in. Surely Allah knows and is aware of everything. Surat Luqman (Luqman) 31:34

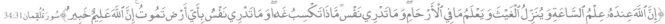

﴿إِنَّ ٱللَّهَ عِندَهُۥ عِلْمُ ٱلسَّاعَةِ وَيُنَزِّلُ ٱلْغَيْثَ وَيَعْلَمُ مَا فِى ٱلْأَرْحَامِ وَمَا تَدْرِى نَفْسٌ مَّاذَا تَكْسِبُ غَدًا وَمَا تَدْرِى نَفْسٌ بِأَيِّ أَرْضٍ تَمُوتُ إِنَّ ٱللَّهَ عَلِيمٌ خَبِيرٌ﴾ سُورَةُ لُقْمَان ٣٤:٣١

So we can see that the events of our lives are not under our complete control. But at the same time, we can decide how we feel and react to what happens around us. This is exactly how Islam describes our relationship to this life and to Allah and His Knowledge.

The Blessed Prophet once said, "How excellent is a believer's situation, unlike all others. There is good in everything he does. If he is prosperous, he thanks Allah, which is good. But if some bad thing happens, he endures it with patience, and that is best for him." (Muslim)

قَالَ رَسُولُ اللهِ ﷺ: «عَجَبًا لِأَمْرِ الْمُؤْمِنِ إِنَّ أَمْرَهُ كُلَّهُ خَيْرٌ وَلَيْسَ ذَاكَ لِأَحَدٍ إِلَّا لِلْمُؤْمِنِ إِنْ أَصَابَتْهُ سَرَّاءُ شَكَرَ فَكَانَ خَيْرًا لَهُ وَإِنْ أَصَابَتْهُ ضَرَّاءُ صَبَرَ فَكَانَ خَيْرًا لَهُ». رَوَاهُ مُسْلِمٌ

What Is Measurement?

Islam teaches a unique concept known as **Qada' and Qadar** قَضَاءٌ وَقَدَرٌ **Determination and Predestination**. Allah has determined the course of the entire Universe and measured everything, including the time you will spend on Earth, whether you will be rich or poor and the land in which you will die.

In a sense, these are all the things you have no control over anyway. Yet, importantly, this measurement doesn't include every step you take or bite you eat. Instead, it is the overall boundary or parameters of your life here on Earth.

It is not the choice of a person to die without the will of Allah, death being a time-bound destiny. Whoever seeks a reward in this world, We shall give him out of it, and whoever seeks a reward in the Hereafter, We shall give him out of it. We shall soon reward the grateful. Surat Al 'Imran (The Family of 'Imran) 3: 145

﴿وَمَا كَانَ لِنَفْسٍ أَنْ تَمُوتَ إِلَّا بِإِذْنِ اللَّهِ كِتَابًا مُؤَجَّلًا وَمَنْ يُرِدْ ثَوَابَ الدُّنْيَا نُؤْتِهِ مِنْهَا وَمَنْ يُرِدْ ثَوَابَ الْآخِرَةِ نُؤْتِهِ مِنْهَا وَسَنَجْزِي الشَّاكِرِينَ﴾ سُورَةُ آلِ عِمْرَان 3:145

Within that framework of measured things, you have all the choice in the world about how to react to circumstances in your life. You are given the five senses, plus intelligence, reasoning and a spiritual motivation that you can choose to employ, seeking Allah. Or you can choose to ignore what your own senses tell you and live a life filled with foul habits and meaningless pleasure. (42:20)

Whatever good happens to you, it is from Allah. But whatever wickedness (you perform) is from your own self. We have sent you to be a Messenger for the people. Allah is enough to be a witness. Surat An-Nisa' (The Women) 4: 79

﴿مَا أَصَابَكَ مِنْ حَسَنَةٍ فَمِنَ اللَّهِ وَمَا أَصَابَكَ مِنْ سَيِّئَةٍ فَمِنْ نَفْسِكَ وَأَرْسَلْنَاكَ لِلنَّاسِ رَسُولًا وَكَفَى بِاللَّهِ شَهِيدًا﴾ سُورَةُ النِّسَاء:79

The choice is yours. (73:19) Anyone who is born blind, deaf, mute or physically handicapped merely has gotten a tougher test (and perhaps an easier Judgement) than the rest of us. (2:286) Those who are mentally deficient or who die as children are not held accountable at all and go straight to Paradise. Remember from previous chapters that this life is a testing ground. (29:2) We have our base desires and Shaytan pulling us towards this worldly life. Then we have our fitrah and Allah's prophets with their revelations calling us towards the next life. We can decide for ourselves which way we want to go. (91:7-10)

We have tied up every human's fortune to his neck, and on the Day of Resurrection, We will bring forth a book for him that he will find wide open. And We will say to him) "Read your book. Enough are you today to take your own account." Whoever adopts the right path does so for his own benefit, and whoever goes astray does so to his own detriment, and no bearer of burden shall bear the burden of another, and it is not Our way to punish (anyone) unless We send a Messenger. Surat Al Isra' (The Night Journey) 17: 13-15

The Prophet ﷺ once said, and he is the Truthful, the Believed, "Indeed, the creation of each one of you is brought together in his or her mother's womb for forty days in the form of a seed. Then he or she is a clinging (embryo) for a like period, then a morsel of flesh for a like period. Then an angel is sent who blows the breath of life into him or her.

(The angel) is then commanded to take note of four things: the person's livelihood, life span, actions and whether he or she will be happy or miserable.

By Allah, Who is the only God, one of you will act like a person of Paradise until there is only an arm's length between it and him, but then what is recorded will overtake him as he begins to act like a person of Hell and finally enters it.

One of you will behave like a person of Hell until there is only an arm's length between it and him, but then what is recorded will overtake him as he begins to act like a person of Paradise and finally enters it." (Al Bukhari & Muslim)

قَالَ الرَّسُولُ ﷺ -وَهُوَ الصَّادِقُ الْمَصْدُوقُ:

«إِنَّ أَحَدَكُمْ يُجْمَعُ خَلْقُهُ فِي بَطْنِ أُمِّهِ أَرْبَعِينَ يَوْمًا نُطْفَةً، ثُمَّ يَكُونُ عَلَقَةً مِثْلَ ذَلِكَ، ثُمَّ يَكُونُ مُضْغَةً مِثْلَ ذَلِكَ، ثُمَّ يُرْسَلُ إِلَيْهِ الْمَلَكُ فَيَنْفُخُ فِيهِ الرُّوحَ، وَيُؤْمَرُ بِأَرْبَعِ كَلِمَاتٍ: بِكَتْبِ رِزْقِهِ، وَأَجَلِهِ، وَعَمَلِهِ، وَشَقِيٌّ أَمْ سَعِيدٌ؛ فَوَاللهِ الَّذِي لَا إِلَهَ غَيْرُهُ إِنَّ أَحَدَكُمْ لَيَعْمَلُ بِعَمَلِ أَهْلِ الْجَنَّةِ حَتَّى مَا يَكُونُ بَيْنَهُ وَبَيْنَهَا إِلَّا ذِرَاعٌ فَيَسْبِقُ عَلَيْهِ الْكِتَابُ فَيَعْمَلُ بِعَمَلِ أَهْلِ النَّارِ فَيَدْخُلُهَا. وَإِنَّ أَحَدَكُمْ لَيَعْمَلُ بِعَمَلِ أَهْلِ النَّارِ حَتَّى مَا يَكُونُ بَيْنَهُ وَبَيْنَهَا إِلَّا ذِرَاعٌ فَيَسْبِقُ عَلَيْهِ الْكِتَابُ فَيَعْمَلُ بِعَمَلِ أَهْلِ الْجَنَّةِ فَيَدْخُلُهَا». رَوَاهُ الْبُخَارِيُّ وَمُسْلِمٌ

﴿وَكُلَّ إِنسَانٍ أَلْزَمْنَهُ طَٰئِرَهُۥ فِى عُنُقِهِۦ وَنُخْرِجُ لَهُۥ يَوْمَ ٱلْقِيَٰمَةِ كِتَٰبًا يَلْقَىٰهُ مَنشُورًا ﴾ ﴿ٱقْرَأْ كِتَٰبَكَ كَفَىٰ بِنَفْسِكَ ٱلْيَوْمَ عَلَيْكَ حَسِيبًا ﴾ ﴿مَّنِ ٱهْتَدَىٰ فَإِنَّمَا يَهْتَدِى لِنَفْسِهِۦ وَمَن ضَلَّ فَإِنَّمَا يَضِلُّ عَلَيْهَا وَلَا تَزِرُ وَازِرَةٌ وِزْرَ أُخْرَىٰ وَمَا كُنَّا مُعَذِّبِينَ حَتَّىٰ نَبْعَثَ رَسُولًا ﴾ سُورَةُ الإسراء 13-15:17

This means that every action we do is added to our record, and it is almost like a chain hanging around our neck. In other words, we are completely responsible for what we do, and every action is recorded. These actions will reveal themselves on the Day of Judgement when we have to confront them.

(All this will happen) on the day when everyone will come pleading for himself, and everyone will be given in full what he did, and they will not be wronged. Surat An-Nahl (The Bees) 16:111

﴿يَوْمَ تَأْتِى كُلُّ نَفْسٍ تُجَٰدِلُ عَن نَّفْسِهَا وَتُوَفَّىٰ كُلُّ نَفْسٍ مَّا عَمِلَتْ وَهُمْ لَا يُظْلَمُونَ ﴾ سُورَةُ النَّحْل 16:111

How Do We Look at Life?

How are we to live? What should our attitude be towards life? It's really quite simple: if we take responsibility for all our actions and remember that we will have to face Allah ﷻ in the end, then we can act without fear or apprehension. (4:110-111) We don't have to answer for other people's sins, and we don't give up, nor do we forget our own ultimate destiny. A balance is achieved. (42:15)

This point is illustrated in a story from the Prophet's ﷺ life. Anas bin Malik ﷺ narrated that a man said, "O Messenger of Allah! Shall I tie it (his camel) and rely (upon Allah), or leave it loose and rely (upon Allah)?' He said, "Tie it and rely (upon Allah)." (At-Tirmidhi)

عَنْ أَنَسِ بْنِ مَالِكٍ ﷺ: «قَالَ رَجُلٌ يَا رَسُولَ اللهِ أَعْقِلُهَا وَأَتَوَكَّلُ أَوْ أُطْلِقُهَا وَأَتَوَكَّلُ؟ قَالَ: اعْقِلْهَا وَتَوَكَّلْ». رَوَاهُ التِّرْمِذِيُّ

In an apparent misinterpretation of the meaning of qadar, the man felt that if it were in his destiny, then Allah ﷻ would keep the camel near, and if it was not in his destiny, the camel would roam free. Yet, he did not understand that he too had a role in his destiny, as illustrated by the Prophet's ﷺ response. This is a clear sign that we are responsible for our lives and livelihood, even while we place our trust in Allah ﷻ to take care of things.

On another occasion, the Blessed Prophet ﷺ declared, "Get a hold of five things before five things happen: your youth before your old age, your health before your sickness, your money before your

poverty, your free time before you get busy and your life before your death." (At-Tirmidhi)

قَالَ رَسُولُ الله ﷺ : «اغْتَنِمْ خَمْسًا قَبْلَ خَمْسٍ: شَبَابَكَ قَبْلَ هَرِمِكَ، وَصِحَّتَكَ قَبْلَ سَقَمِكَ، وَغِنَاكَ قَبْلَ فَقْرِكَ، وَفَرَاغَكَ قَبْلَ شُغْلِكَ، وَحَيَاتَكَ قَبْلَ مَوْتِكَ». رَوَاهُ
التِّرْمِذِيّ

Why should Allah ﷺ make Paradise and just put us there if we didn't do anything to deserve it? We are the only creatures Allah ﷺ made that could choose to serve Him or reject Him. If you choose Allah ﷺ, then He will reward you. But you have to take the test in order to earn the reward.

Of course, Allah ﷺ knows the future and the past. He knows when you will die and if you will be a believer or a wrong-doer. But that is because Allah ﷺ created time. He is not trapped in a time line like we are. He is outside of time and sees everything happening at once. So He knows what you will do, but He is not making you do it. It's tough to imagine, but we have to accept that Allah ﷺ is not bound by time. He knows the past, present and future and has all the information recorded. (57:22)

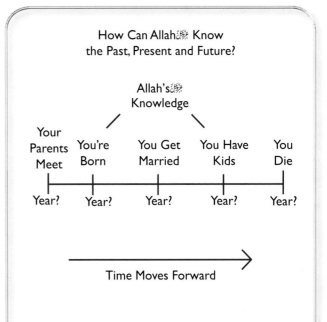

How Can Allah ﷺ Know the Past, Present and Future?

Allah's ﷺ Knowledge

Your Parents Meet — You're Born — You Get Married — You Have Kids — You Die

Year? — Year? — Year? — Year? — Year?

Time Moves Forward

Allah ﷺ sees it all happening at once. He is outside the time line. He created time; He is not bound by it.

Abu Hurayrah ﷺ narrated that Allah's Messenger ﷺ said, "Allah said, 'The son of Adam hurts me for he abuses Time though I am Time: in My Hands are all things, and I cause the revolution of day and night." (Al Bukhari & Muslim)

عَنْ أَبِي هُرَيْرَةَ ﷺ، قَالَ قَالَ النَّبِيُّ ﷺ : «قَالَ اللهُ تَعَالَى يُؤْذِينِي ابْنُ آدَمَ، يَسُبُّ الدَّهْرَ وَأَنَا الدَّهْرُ، بِيَدِي الأَمْرُ، أُقَلِّبُ اللَّيْلَ وَالنَّهَارَ». رَوَاهُ الْبُخَارِيُّ وَمُسْلِمٌ

Trusting in Allah ﷺ, Not the Occult

Those who place their trust in Allah ﷺ and surrender their wills to Him do not worry about the future. They know that everything will eventually happen as Allah ﷺ has planned in the end. They are even taught to say, **Insha'Allah** إِنْ شَاءَ الله **If Allah Wills** while planning any important action. (18:23-24) Those who deny Allah ﷺ are gripped with fear when they think about their death and ultimate end.

Astrology, fortune-tellers and tarot card readers are popular all over the world because many people are afraid of the future. They are uneasy, unsure and worried about the unknown, leading them to these forbidden alternatives. They pay huge amounts of money to try to find out where their lives are headed, but they still never know for sure. That's why they go back and spend even more money to know.

They reject the easier solution of accepting Allah's ﷺ guidance and living life the best way they can according to Islamic teachings. That is why magic and fortune-telling are such major crimes in Islam. It's a sign of lack of faith in the Creator.

The Prophet ﷺ said, "Whoever talks about (their) predestination will have to answer for it on the Day of Judgement, while whoever was silent about it will not." (Ibn Majah)

DANGER!

قَالَ رَسُولُ الله ﷺ : «مَنْ تَكَلَّمَ فِي شَيْءٍ مِنَ الْقَدَرِ سُئِلَ عَنْهُ يَوْمَ الْقِيَامَةِ وَمَنْ لَمْ يَتَكَلَّمْ فِيهِ لَمْ يُسْأَلْ عَنْهُ». رَوَاهُ ابْنُ مَاجَهْ

Allah ﷺ also does not make you an unbeliever or a believer. We decide that. (16:35-37) Allah ﷺ gave us hearing, sight and a heart to understand so we can be thankful to Him. (16:78) One of the things Allah ﷺ willed was for us to have a choice in our belief, and He is holding us accountable for the choices we make with it. (53:39)

The Blessed Prophetﷺ said, "there are two groups of (Muslims) who have no part of Islam. The Murji'ah (those who say there is no predestination), and the Qadariyyah (those who say that there is nothing but destiny and that human action is fruitless)." (At-Tirmidhi)

قَالَ رَسُولُ الله ﷺ : «صِنْفَانِ مِنْ أُمَّتِي لَيْسَ لَهُمَا فِي الإِسْلَامِ نَصِيبٌ الْمُرْجِئَةُ وَ الْقَدَرِيَّة». رَوَاهُ التَّرْمَذِي

The Blessed Prophetﷺ said, "Do (good) deeds which are within your capacity as Allah never gets tired of giving rewards till you get tired of doing good deeds." (Al Bukhari & Muslim)

قَالَ رَسُولُ الله ﷺ : «عَلَيْكُمْ مَا تُطِيقُونَ مِنَ الأَعْمَالِ، فَإِنَّ اللهَ لَا يَمَلُّ حَتَّى تَمَلُّوا». رَوَاهُ الْبُخَارِيُّ وَمُسْلِمْ

The Prophetﷺ said, "If Allah wants to do good to somebody, He afflicts him with trials." (Al Bukhari)

قَالَ رَسُولُ الله ﷺ : «مَنْ يُرِدِ اللهُ بِهِ خَيْرًا يُصِبْ مِنْه». رَوَاهُ الْبُخَارِيُّ

The Prophetﷺ said, "Affliction will continue to befall believing men and women in their body, family and property until they meet Allah weighed down by no sins." (At-Tirmidhi)

قَالَ رَسُولُ الله ﷺ : «مَا يَزَالُ الْبَلَاءُ بِالْمُؤْمِنِ وَ الْمُؤْمِنَةِ فِي نَفْسِهِ وَ وَلَدِهِ وَ مَالِهِ حَتَّى يَلْقَى اللهَ وَمَا عَلَيْهِ خَطِيئَةٌ». رَوَاهُ التَّرْمَذِي

It was We Who created man and We know what dark suggestions his lower self makes to him. We are nearer to him than his jugular vein. Two (angels) are assigned to learn (his actions), one on the right and one on the left. Every word he says is noted by a ready watcher. The haze of coming death will bring the realization: This was what you were trying to avoid. *Surat Q'aaf (The Letter Q'aaf) 50:16-19*

﴿وَلَقَدْ خَلَقْنَا الْإِنسَانَ وَنَعْلَمُ مَا تُوَسْوِسُ بِهِ نَفْسُهُ وَنَحْنُ أَقْرَبُ إِلَيْهِ مِنْ حَبْلِ الْوَرِيدِ﴾﴿إِذْ يَتَلَقَّى الْمُتَلَقِّيَانِ عَنِ الْيَمِينِ وَعَنِ الشِّمَالِ قَعِيدٌ﴾﴿مَا يَلْفِظُ مِن قَوْلٍ إِلَّا لَدَيْهِ رَقِيبٌ عَتِيدٌ﴾﴿وَجَاءَتْ سَكْرَةُ الْمَوْتِ بِالْحَقِّ ذَلِكَ مَا كُنتَ مِنْهُ تَحِيدُ﴾ سُورَةُ ق 50:16-19

There are many passages in the Qur'an where Allahﷻ mentions that He leads some people astray. Many people become confused by this and think that Allahﷻ makes people unbelievers. This is the thinking of people who want to put the blame for their own wrong-doing on someone else. In fact, Allahﷻ has said that He only leads those astray who first rejected Him. (39:36-37)

Allah will not guide those who reject (Him). *Surat An-Nahl (The Bees) 16:107*

﴿وَأَنَّ اللهَ لَا يَهْدِي الْقَوْمَ الْكَافِرِينَ﴾ سُورَةُ النَّجْل 16:107

If a person rejects Allahﷻ first, then He will let him or her wander in ignorance as much as he or she wants, straying further and further away from the path. Shaytan succeeds in corrupting them, and Allahﷻ will not make any effort to guide them. This is what the 'leading astray' means. (6:122-125)

The Shaytan has got the better of them. He got them to lose the remembrance of Allah. *Surat Al Mujadala (The Disputation) 58:19*

﴿اسْتَحْوَذَ عَلَيْهِمُ الشَّيْطَانُ فَأَنسَاهُمْ ذِكْرَ اللهِ﴾ سُورَةُ الْمُجَادَلَة 58:19

After our minds and hearts have denied our Creator, Allahﷻ lets one of Shaytan's minions loose upon us as a punishment. (41:25) Then it becomes even harder to reform ourselves. But we deserve what we get because we rejected our Lord first. (4:115)

If anyone withdraws himself from remembering the Most Gracious, We appoint for him an evil one to be his close companion. *Surat Az-Zukhruf (The Gold Adornment) 43:36*

﴿وَمَن يَعْشُ عَن ذِكْرِ الرَّحْمَنِ نُقَيِّضْ لَهُ شَيْطَانًا فَهُوَ لَهُ قَرِينٌ﴾ سُورَةُ الزُّخْرُف 43:36

On the other hand, if we can manage to break free of Shaytan's influence and come towards Allahﷻ again, Allahﷻ will come towards us, too.

On the authority of Abu Hurayrah☺, who said that the Prophet☺ said, "Allah the Almighty said, 'I am as my servant expects Me to be, and I am with him when he remembers me. If he thinks of Me, I think of him. If he mentions Me in company, I mention him in an even better company. When he comes closer to Me by a hands pan, I come closer to him an arm's length. If he draws closer to Me by an arm's length, I draw closer by a distance of two outstretched arms nearer to him. If my servant comes to Me walking, I go to him running.'"(Al Bukhari)

عَنْ أَبِي هُرَيْرَةَ قَالَ: قَالَ النَّبِيُّ ﷺ: «يَقُولُ اللهُ تَعَالَى: أَنَا عِنْدَ ظَنِّ عَبْدِي بِي، وَأَنَا مَعَهُ إِذَا ذَكَرَنِي، فَإِنْ ذَكَرَنِي فِي نَفْسِهِ، ذَكَرْتُهُ فِي نَفْسِي، وَإِنْ ذَكَرَنِي فِي مَلَإٍ، ذَكَرْتُهُ فِي مَلَإٍ خَيْرٍ مِنْهُمْ، وَإِنْ تَقَرَّبَ إِلَيَّ بِشِبْرٍ، تَقَرَّبْتُ إِلَيْهِ ذِرَاعًا، وَإِنْ تَقَرَّبَ إِلَيَّ ذِرَاعًا، تَقَرَّبْتُ إِلَيْهِ بَاعًا وَإِنْ أَتَانِي يَمْشِي، أَتَيْتُهُ هَرْوَلَةً». رَوَاهُ الْبُخَارِيُّ وَمُسْلِم

Certainly, Allah will not deal unjustly with anyone in anything. It is a person who wrongs his own soul.
Surat Yunus (Jonah) 10:44

﴿إِنَّ اللَّهَ لَا يَظْلِمُ النَّاسَ شَيْئًا وَلَٰكِنَّ النَّاسَ أَنْفُسَهُمْ يَظْلِمُونَ﴾ سُورَةُ يُونُس 10:44

Say, "O people, the truth has come to you from your Lord. So, whoever accepts guidance accepts it to his own benefit, and whoever goes astray does so to his own detriment. And I am not responsible for you." Surat Yunus (Jonah) 10:108

﴿قُلْ يَا أَيُّهَا النَّاسُ قَدْ جَاءَكُمُ الْحَقُّ مِنْ رَبِّكُمْ فَمَنِ اهْتَدَىٰ فَإِنَّمَا يَهْتَدِي لِنَفْسِهِ وَمَنْ ضَلَّ فَإِنَّمَا يَضِلُّ عَلَيْهَا وَمَا أَنَا عَلَيْكُمْ بِوَكِيلٍ﴾ سُورَةُ يُونُس 10:108

Everything important is measured by Allah☺, such as our life span, our place of death and our happiness and sadness in life. Our lives are filled with events that are, likewise, beyond our control. Within that framework, we have some freedom of movement, but the direction our hearts and soul will eventually take is known only to Allah☺.

'Umar bin Al Khattab☺ reported that the Apostle of Allah☺ said, "Actions are to be judged only by intentions and a man will have only what he intended. When one's emigration is to Allah and His Apostle, his emigration is to Allah and His Apostle but his emigration is to a worldly end at which he aims or to a woman whom he marries, his emigration is to that for which he emigrated." (Al Bukhari and Muslim)

عَنْ عُمَرَ بْنِ الْخَطَّابِ، يَقُولُ قَالَ رَسُولُ الله ﷺ: «إِنَّمَا الْأَعْمَالُ بِالنِّيَّاتِ وَإِنَّمَا لِكُلِّ امْرِئٍ مَا نَوَى فَمَنْ كَانَتْ هِجْرَتُهُ إِلَى الله وَرَسُولِهِ فَهِجْرَتُهُ إِلَى الله وَرَسُولِهِ وَمَنْ كَانَتْ هِجْرَتُهُ لِلدُّنْيَا يُصِيبُهَا أَوِ امْرَأَةٍ يَتَزَوَّجُهَا فَهِجْرَتُهُ إِلَى مَا هَاجَرَ إِلَيْهِ». رَوَاهُ الْبُخَارِيُّ وَمُسْلِم

Choose what you do wisely and know that you are responsible for your actions. You only have one lifetime to get it right.

Death Is the Great Equalizer

Every living creature that walks the Earth will leave this world one day. No matter how much we learn, gain or understand, it will all be over with our last breath. Death is the greatest certainty of life and the thing many people fear the most. (56:83-87)

In previous lessons, we learned that Allah ﷻ gave us life, why He gave it to us and what He wants us to do with it. We have also learned that our death date is fixed, and death will come for us whether we are ready or not.

But what happens to us when our body dies? Are we gone to dust? Do we, as individuals, cease to exist? These are the questions everyone wants answered. Islam is very clear on this issue. Though you will die, you will live again in a new reality. (56:60-62)

Every person has to taste death; then to Us you are to be returned. Surat Al 'Ankabut (The Spider) 29: 57

﴿كُلُّ نَفْسٍ ذَآئِقَةُ ٱلْمَوْتِ ۖ ثُمَّ إِلَيْنَا تُرْجَعُونَ﴾ سُورَةُ العَنكَبوت 29:57

Islam teaches that there are four definite stages of every human life. The first is our existence in the womb of our mothers. There, the flesh is united with the spirit or soul. (15:29 & 32:9) According to the saying of the Blessed Prophet ﷺ, this joining takes place sometime around the fourth month of pregnancy. (23:13-14)

'Abdallah bin Mas'ud ﷺ reported that Allah's Messenger ﷺ who is the most truthful (of the human beings) and his being truthful (is a fact) said, "Verily your creation is on this wise. The constituents of one of you are collected for forty days in his mother's womb in the form of blood, after which it becomes a clot of blood in another period of forty days. Then it becomes a lump of flesh and forty days later Allah sends His Angel to it with instructions concerning four things, so the Angel writes down his livelihood, his death, his deeds, his fortune and misfortune. By Him, besides Whom there is no God, that one amongst you acts like the people deserving Paradise until between him and Paradise there remains but the distance of a cubit, when suddenly the writing of destiny overcomes him and he begins to act like the denizens of Hell and thus enters Hell, and another one acts in the way of the denizens of Hell, until there remains between him and Hell a distance of a cubit that the writing of destiny overcomes him and then he begins to act like the people of Paradise and enters Paradise." (Muslim)

عَنْ عَبْدِ اللهِ بْنِ مَسْعُودٍ، قَالَ حَدَّثَنَا رَسُولُ اللهِ ﷺ وَهُوَ الصَّادِقُ الْمَصْدُوقُ: «إِنَّ أَحَدَكُمْ يُجْمَعُ خَلْقُهُ فِي بَطْنِ أُمِّهِ أَرْبَعِينَ يَوْمًا ثُمَّ يَكُونُ فِي ذَلِكَ عَلَقَةً مِثْلَ ذَلِكَ ثُمَّ يَكُونُ فِي ذَلِكَ مُضْغَةً مِثْلَ ذَلِكَ ثُمَّ يُرْسَلُ الْمَلَكُ فَيَنْفُخُ فِيهِ الرُّوحَ وَيُؤْمَرُ بِأَرْبَعِ كَلِمَاتٍ بِكَتْبِ رِزْقِهِ وَأَجَلِهِ وَعَمَلِهِ وَشَقِيٌّ أَوْ سَعِيدٌ فَوَالَّذِي لاَ إِلَهَ غَيْرُهُ إِنَّ أَحَدَكُمْ لَيَعْمَلُ بِعَمَلِ أَهْلِ الْجَنَّةِ حَتَّى مَا يَكُونَ بَيْنَهُ وَبَيْنَهَا إِلاَّ ذِرَاعٌ فَيَسْبِقُ عَلَيْهِ الْكِتَابُ فَيَعْمَلُ بِعَمَلِ أَهْلِ النَّارِ فَيَدْخُلُهَا وَإِنَّ أَحَدَكُمْ لَيَعْمَلُ بِعَمَلِ أَهْلِ النَّارِ حَتَّى مَا يَكُونَ بَيْنَهُ وَبَيْنَهَا إِلاَّ ذِرَاعٌ فَيَسْبِقُ عَلَيْهِ الْكِتَابُ فَيَعْمَلُ بِعَمَلِ أَهْلِ الْجَنَّةِ فَيَدْخُلُهَا». رَوَاهُ مُسْلِم

The second stage is our life on Earth in the **Dunya دُنْيَا World**. We are born, grow as children into adults and then reach an old age where we gradually decline in strength and awareness. Although some people die in their youth and others live longer, it is a time of testing for all who make it past the age of puberty. (22:5)

The third stage begins after our death. When we take our last breath of air and then close our eyes for the last time, we cross over into the first stage of the next life. We enter the life in the grave, which can be peaceful or violent.

That part of you that is released the moment your physical body dies is the real you. It is your ruh, which makes up your essence, your individuality. Everything you are, including your deeds, intentions, beliefs, convictions and nature are contained in your soul. The ruh you were given before birth was transformed by your individuality and has become customized by you.

The Angel of Death

When you die, your soul is taken from your body by the Angel of Death. (79:1-2) If Allah☀ was pleased with you, it is gently drawn out from the flesh. If He was displeased with you, then your soul is ripped violently from your body. (47:27-28) You are made to hover near your body. Although you can see and hear everything around you, you cannot communicate with the living. You see the people mourning your death, and you see yourself being buried. You even hear the footsteps of the people as they leave your grave.

The Blessed Prophet☀ explained how the deceased responds during this time. Abu Sa'id Al-Khudri☀ narrated that Allah's Messenger☀ said, "When the funeral is ready and the men carry it on their shoulders, if the deceased was righteous it will say, 'Present me (hurriedly),' and if he was not righteous, it will say, 'Woe to it (me)! Where are they taking it (me)?' Its voice is heard by everything except man and if he heard it he would fall unconscious." (Al Bukhari)

What Happens in the Grave

Abu Hurayrah☀ reported that the Messenger of Allah☀ said, "When the deceased is buried, two angels, black and blue eyed, come to him. One of them is called Al-Munkar, and the other An-Nakir. They say: 'What did you used to say about this man?' So he says what he was saying (before death): 'He is Allah's slave and His Messenger. I testify that none has the right to be worshipped but Allah and that Muhammad is His slave and His Messenger.' So they say: 'We knew that you would say this.' Then his grave is expanded to seventy by seventy cubits, then it is illuminated for him. Then it is said to him: 'Sleep.' So he said: 'Can I return to my family to inform them?' They say: 'Sleep as a newlywed, whom none awakens but the dearest of his family.' Until Allah resurrects him from his resting place. If he was a hypocrite he would say: 'I heard people saying something, so I said the same; I do not know.' So they said: 'We knew you would say that.' So the earth is told: 'Constrict him.' So it constricts around him, squeezing his ribs together. He continues being punished like that until Allah resurrects him from his resting place." (At-Tirmidhi)

عَنْ أَبِى هُرَيْرَةَ قَالَ قَالَ رَسُولُ اللهِ ﷺ: «إِذَا قُبِرَ الْمَيِّتُ - أَتَاهُ مَلَكَانِ أَسْوَدَانِ أَزْرَقَانِ يُقَالُ لِأَحَدِهِمَا الْمُنْكَرُ وَالآخَرُ النَّكِيرُ فَيَقُولَانِ مَا كُنْتَ تَقُولُ فِى هَذَا الرَّجُلِ فَيَقُولُ مَا كَانَ يَقُولُ هُوَ عَبْدُ اللهِ وَرَسُولُهُ أَشْهَدُ أَنْ لاَ إِلَهَ إِلاَّ اللهُ وَأَنَّ مُحَمَّدًا عَبْدُهُ وَرَسُولُهُ. فَيَقُولاَنِ قَدْ كُنَّا نَعْلَمُ أَنَّكَ تَقُولُ هَذَا. ثُمَّ يُفْسَحُ لَهُ فِى قَبْرِهِ سَبْعُونَ ذِرَاعًا فِى سَبْعِينَ ثُمَّ يُنَوَّرُ لَهُ فِيهِ ثُمَّ يُقَالُ لَهُ نَمْ. فَيَقُولُ أَرْجِعُ إِلَى أَهْلِى فَأُخْبِرُهُمْ فَيَقُولاَنِ نَمْ كَنَوْمَةِ الْعَرُوسِ الَّذِى لاَ يُوقِظُهُ إِلاَّ أَحَبُّ أَهْلِهِ إِلَيْهِ. حَتَّى يَبْعَثَهُ اللهُ مِنْ مَضْجَعِهِ ذَلِكَ. وَإِنْ كَانَ مُنَافِقًا قَالَ سَمِعْتُ النَّاسَ يَقُولُونَ فَقُلْتُ مِثْلَهُ لاَ أَدْرِى. فَيَقُولاَنِ قَدْ كُنَّا نَعْلَمُ أَنَّكَ تَقُولُ ذَلِكَ. فَيُقَالُ لِلأَرْضِ الْتَئِمِى عَلَيْهِ. فَتَلْتَئِمُ عَلَيْهِ. فَتَخْتَلِفُ فِيهَا أَضْلاَعُهُ فَلاَ يَزَالُ فِيهَا مُعَذَّبًا حَتَّى يَبْعَثَهُ اللهُ مِنْ مَضْجَعِهِ ذَلِكَ». رَوَاهُ التِّرْمَذِى

عَنْ أَبِي سَعِيدٍ الْخُدْرِيِّ ﷺ أَنَّ رَسُولَ اللهِ ﷺ قَالَ «إِذَا وُضِعَتِ الْجِنَازَةُ وَاحْتَمَلَهَا الرِّجَالُ عَلَى أَعْنَاقِهِمْ، فَإِنْ كَانَتْ صَالِحَةً قَالَتْ قَدِّمُونِي. وَإِنْ كَانَتْ غَيْرَ صَالِحَةٍ قَالَتْ يَا وَيْلَهَا أَيْنَ يَذْهَبُونَ بِهَا يَسْمَعُ صَوْتَهَا كُلُّ شَيْءٍ إِلَّا الْإِنْسَانَ، وَلَوْ سَمِعَهُ صَعِقَ». رَوَاهُ الْبُخَارِيُّ

Your soul is no longer a physical part of your body but will remain near it. Next, two angels named Munkar and Nakir visit you and raise your soul to an upright position. They ask you the following questions: Who is your Lord? What was your deen? Who is your prophet? If you were a believer in Allah﷾ and followed the teachings of your prophet, then you will answer the questions correctly. Your surroundings will then be softly lit. Your resting place in the spiritual dimension will be made roomy and comfortable, allowing you to sleep and dream gently until the Day of Judgement.

But if you didn't believe in Allah﷾, or were a hypocrite, then the angels will become horrifying. They will strike you and cause your soul's resting place to close in on you until you feel suffocated. Then you will be tormented until the Day of Judgement. This is called the 'punishment of the grave.' The Blessed Prophet ﷺ advised us to ask Allah﷾ to save us from it.

The period between your death and being raised up on the Day of Judgement is called the **Barzakh** بَرْزَخ **Partition**. Time has no meaning there. According to the Prophet ﷺ, the Barzakh is the first step to the next life, and whoever finds safety there will have an easy time later on.

The fourth and final stage of our existence begins when the end of the world has come. The appointed Angel Israfil﷩ will sound the trumpet, and fantastic events will engulf the globe. The Earth will be destroyed in a great catastrophe before it is transformed into a new Earth. Every human being alive at that time will swoon and die instantly. This is called **Al Yaum Al Akhir** اليَوْمُ الآخِر **the Last Day**. (20:102-104, 79:13-14, 81:1-14)

The term **Ghayb** غَيْب means anything that is beyond our senses or our ability to realize it by using our minds. Believing in what we can't see right now is a sign of our emaan. It shows we truly trust Allah﷾. (See 2:3)

The Day of Judgement

Allah﷾ will raise up the souls of people and recreate them again for the **Yaum ul Qiyamah** يَوْمُ القِيامَة **Resurrection Day**. (79:10-14) The Qur'an gives additional names for this day: the **Day of Assembly** and the **Day of Judgement**. Then all of humanity—including our generation, earlier generations and the generations that came later—will stand for Judgement. (19:66-69) Good people will be instinctively anticipating Allah's﷾ presence, while those who did wrong will be quaking with fear. For example, a greedy person will find his wealth has assumed physical form and is worth nothing.

Everyone will be sorted into groups based on a variety of factors, the most important one being belief. Then they will advance on a flat plain, standing behind the people or objects that they used to follow in the world. Whoever followed a prophet's teachings will be standing behind that prophet. Likewise, whoever followed idols, ideologies or false teachers will be behind them. Muslims will be standing behind Prophet Muhammad ﷺ. Allah﷾ calls this 'The Sorting.' (39:67-75)

And the day when the Hour (Qiyamah: the Day of Judgement) will take place; it will be on that day that they will turn into separate groups. Then, those who had believed and had done righteous deeds—they will be in a garden, extremely delighted. As for those who had disbelieved and rejected Our verses and the meeting of the Hereafter, they will be brought for punishment. Surat Ar-Rum (The Romans) (30:14-16)

﴿وَيَوْمَ تَقُومُ السَّاعَةُ يَوْمَئِذٍ يَتَفَرَّقُونَ﴾﴿فَأَمَّا الَّذِينَ ءَامَنُوا۟ وَعَمِلُوا۟ الصَّٰلِحَٰتِ فَهُمْ فِي رَوْضَةٍ يُحْبَرُونَ﴾﴿وَأَمَّا الَّذِينَ كَفَرُوا۟ وَكَذَّبُوا۟ بِـَٔايَٰتِنَا وَلِقَآئِ الْءَاخِرَةِ فَأُو۟لَٰئِكَ فِي الْعَذَابِ مُحْضَرُونَ﴾ سُورَةُ الرُّومِ 14-16

People who have near-death experiences often tell of being taken through a tunnel towards a light at the other end. If it wasn't their time to die, however, the angels put the soul back in their body. Some felt punishment coming while others felt peace.

Each person will be brought forward and shown the complete record of what he or she did while alive. (50:21-29) People who have done well will receive their record in their right hand, while those who have done poorly will receive it in their left or behind their backs. (69:19- 25) We will see with our own eyes the truth of what we did. (64:9) Nothing will be hidden, and every good deed, evil deed, thought and motivation will be made apparent. (54:52-53) We will be amazed that our record leaves out nothing. Even our body parts will testify against us! (24:24) Then Allah's blessings upon us will be explained, and we will be questioned about what we did with those bounties. (102:8)

After the truth is made clear to us, Allah will decide what sins He will or will not forgive. Allah is fair to everyone, and has promised to forgive the sins for those who sought His forgiveness and made repentance. If we never did this, though, then we are on our own. According to a hadith, the Messenger of Allah ﷺ said, "Allah, Blessed is He and Most High, said, 'O son of Adam! Verily as long as you called upon Me and hoped in Me, I forgave you, despite whatever may have occurred from you, and I did not mind. O son of Adam! Were your sins to reach the clouds of the sky, then you sought forgiveness from Me, I would forgive you, and I would not mind. So son of Adam! If you came to me with sins nearly as great as the earth, and then you met Me not associating anything with Me, I would come to you with forgiveness nearly as great as it.'" (At-Tirmidhi)

سَمِعْتُ رَسُولَ اللهِ ﷺ يَقُولُ: «قَالَ اللهُ يَا ابْنَ آدَمَ إِنَّكَ مَا دَعَوْتَنِي وَرَجَوْتَنِي غَفَرْتُ لَكَ عَلَى مَا كَانَ فِيكَ وَلَا أُبَالِي يَا ابْنَ آدَمَ لَوْ بَلَغَتْ ذُنُوبُكَ عَنَانَ السَّمَاءِ ثُمَّ اسْتَغْفَرْتَنِي غَفَرْتُ لَكَ وَلَا أُبَالِي يَا ابْنَ آدَمَ إِنَّكَ لَوْ أَتَيْتَنِي بِقُرَابِ الْأَرْضِ خَطَايَا ثُمَّ لَقِيتَنِي لَا تُشْرِكُ بِي شَيْئًا لَأَتَيْتُكَ بِقُرَابِهَا مَغْفِرَةً». رَوَاهُ التِّرْمَذِيّ

Those who worshipped men or idols will be ordered to call upon their false gods for help. (18:52, 28:64) Of course, these things will be of no assistance to them, but this will make them realize how foolish they were to serve those who could never really benefit them. Even Shaytan will abandon them and say that they made their own mistakes. (14:21-22) The wrong-doers will beg for forgiveness, but it will be a waste of time. (5:36) They will be overwhelmed with shame, and their heads will hang low in sorrow over their utter helplessness. (42:45) They associated other things with Allah or gave in to their own lusts in the world, and they now will be held accountable. Now it is too late.

If only you could see when the guilty ones will bend their heads low before their Lord (saying), "Our Lord! We have seen and we have heard. Now please send us back (to the world) so we can do good this time, for we now believe." If We had so willed We could certainly have brought every soul to true guidance, but the Word from Me will come true. I will fill Hell with jinn and people all together. Taste (the fire) for you forgot the meeting on this Day of yours, and We too will forget you! Taste the penalty for eternity for your (evil) deeds! Surat As-Sajdah (The Prostration) 32:12-14.

﴿وَلَوْ تَرَىٰ إِذِ ٱلْمُجْرِمُونَ نَاكِسُوا۟ رُءُوسِهِمْ عِندَ رَبِّهِمْ رَبَّنَآ أَبْصَرْنَا وَسَمِعْنَا فَٱرْجِعْنَا نَعْمَلْ صَٰلِحًا إِنَّا مُوقِنُونَ﴾ ﴿وَلَوْ شِئْنَا لَءَاتَيْنَا كُلَّ نَفْسٍ هُدَىٰهَا وَلَٰكِنْ حَقَّ ٱلْقَوْلُ مِنِّي لَأَمْلَأَنَّ جَهَنَّمَ مِنَ ٱلْجِنَّةِ وَٱلنَّاسِ أَجْمَعِينَ﴾ ﴿فَذُوقُوا۟ بِمَا نَسِيتُمْ لِقَآءَ يَوْمِكُمْ هَٰذَآ إِنَّا نَسِينَٰكُمْ وَذُوقُوا۟ عَذَابَ ٱلْخُلْدِ بِمَا كُنتُمْ تَعْمَلُونَ﴾ سُورَةُ السَّجْدَةِ 12-14

The Balance

Our good and bad deeds will be sorted. (17:71-72) If we ever wronged anyone or harmed any creature, we may end up losing some of our good deeds to them by way of compensation. (4:112) Then our deeds will be weighed on a scale, finally showing our true conduct. (101:6-11)

The worst people will be dragged and thrown to the gates of Hellfire right away, while everyone else will wait. (39:71-72) Then, when the Judgement is finished, a bridge will be stretched over the top of the pit of Hell. This bridge, called the **Sirat** صراط, will lead to Paradise on the other side. Everyone will have to cross this bridge over the roar of Hellfire below. (19:71-72)

The bridge will be razor thin and be studded with sharp and jagged edges. The prophets and most righteous people will zoom right over it and enter the gates of Paradise, where they will receive their rewards and delights. (39:73-75) After that, all other humans will begin to cross. As they move over it, they will be cut or hurt by the rough edges, according to their actions in during their lives on Earth. If they were good, they'll get across without too much trouble and enter Paradise as well. If they weigh evenly in good and bad deeds, they may cross over in tatters, but will also enter Paradise. But if their bad deeds outweigh the good, and their sins are not forgiven, they then will tumble into the dark pit of Hell. (67:6-8)

Some of the worst people will stay in Hellfire forever. Others will stay only as long as it takes to punish them for their sins. Whoever completes their punishment will be taken out by the angels, who will recognize them by the marks of their prostrations for the prayers they did while alive. The water of life will be poured over their burnt bones, and they will become whole again. Then they will be admitted to Paradise with purified souls, free from stain. But even one moment in Hellfire is the most unimaginable torture!

Abu Hurayrah ﷺ narrated that the Prophet ﷺ said, "Allah will give shade to seven on the Day when there will be no shade but His. (These seven persons are) a just ruler, a youth who has been brought up in the worship of Allah (i.e. worships Allah sincerely from childhood), a man whose heart is attached to the mosques (i.e. to pray the compulsory prayers in the mosque in congregation), two persons who love each other only for Allah's sake and they meet and part in Allah's cause only, a man who refuses the call of a charming woman of noble birth for illicit intercourse with her and says: I am afraid of Allah, a man who gives charitable gifts so secretly that his left hand does not know what his right hand has given (i.e. nobody knows how much he has given in charity), and a person who remembers Allah in seclusion and his eyes are then flooded with tears." (Al Bukhari)

عَنْ أَبِي هُرَيْرَةَ ﷺ، عَنِ النَّبِيِّ ﷺ قَالَ: «سَبْعَةٌ يُظِلُّهُمُ اللهُ فِي ظِلِّهِ يَوْمَ لاَ ظِلَّ إِلاَّ ظِلُّهُ الإِمَامُ الْعَادِلُ، وَشَابٌّ نَشَأَ فِي عِبَادَةِ رَبِّهِ، وَرَجُلٌ قَلْبُهُ مُعَلَّقٌ فِي الْمَسَاجِدِ، وَرَجُلاَنِ تَحَابَّا فِي اللهِ اجْتَمَعَا عَلَيْهِ وَتَفَرَّقَا عَلَيْهِ، وَرَجُلٌ طَلَبَتْهُ امْرَأَةٌ ذَاتُ مَنْصِبٍ وَجَمَالٍ فَقَالَ إِنِّي أَخَافُ اللهَ. وَرَجُلٌ تَصَدَّقَ أَخْفَى حَتَّى لاَ تَعْلَمَ شِمَالُهُ مَا تُنْفِقُ يَمِينُهُ، وَرَجُلٌ ذَكَرَ اللهَ خَالِيًا فَفَاضَتْ عَيْنَاهُ». رَوَاهُ الْبُخَارِيُّ.

There is a place between Paradise and Hell called **Al A'raf الأعراف**, or **the Heights**, where some will wait before they are allowed to enter Paradise. They don't deserve to enter right away on account of their deeds, but Allah ﷺ has decreed they don't deserve Hellfire either. They will see Paradise and long for it, while they will also see Hellfire and fear it. When their wait is over, they will be admitted to **Jannah جنّة Paradise**. (7:46-51)

Those who enter Paradise stay in it forever and never want to leave. It is a place of eternal peace, happiness and delight. (32:17) This is the ultimate achievement and where we want to end up, not in Hellfire. (40:7-9)

The Blessed Prophet ﷺ said, "Whoever loves his present life does damage to his next life. Whoever loves his next life does damage to his present life. So prefer what is lasting to what is fleeting." (Ahmad & Al Baihaqi)

قَالَ رَسُولُ اللهِ ﷺ: «مَنْ أَحَبَّ دُنْيَاهُ أَضَرَّ بِآخِرَتِهِ، وَمَنْ أَحَبَّ آخِرَتَهُ أَضَرَّ بِدُنْيَاهُ، فَآثِرُوا مَا يَبْقَى عَلَى مَا يَفْنَى». رَوَاهُ أَحْمَدُ وَالْبَيْهَقِيُّ

A bridge, the Sirat, will lead us to Paradise. We will have to cross this bridge with the roar of Hellfire below.

Our whole life is a test which determines what will happen to us in **Al Akhirah الآخرة** the **Next Life**. Our few years on this planet will be gone in an instant. Do you want to live as if there were no tomorrow, even though it will surely come? (41:49-51) Remember why you are alive, and what will happen to you after you die. It is in this remembrance that you will truly lose all fear of death. (39:53-59) Instead, you will make the focus of your life to seek Allah's ﷺ forgiveness and to live by the way of life He ordained for all mankind—Islam. (32:18-20)

You have come to Us all alone, just as We had first created you. Surat Al An'aam (The Cattle) 6:94

﴿وَلَقَدْ جِئْتُمُونَا فُرَادَى كَمَا خَلَقْنَاكُمْ أَوَّلَ مَرَّةٍ﴾ سُورَةُ الأَنعام:94:6

There is none among you who does not have to arrive at it. This is undertaken by your Lord as an absolute decree, bound to be enforced. Then We will save those who feared Allah, and will leave the wrongdoers in it, fallen on their knees. Surat Maryam (Mary) 19: 71-72

﴿وَإِن مِّنكُمْ إِلَّا وَارِدُهَا كَانَ عَلَى رَبِّكَ حَتْمًا مَّقْضِيًّا۝ ثُمَّ نُنَجِّي الَّذِينَ اتَّقَوا وَّنَذَرُ الظَّالِمِينَ فِيهَا جِثِيًّا﴾ سُورَةُ مَريَم 19:71-72

The Names of the Day of Judgement

Day of Judgement	يَوْمُ الدِّين	(1:4)
Last Day	الْيَوْمُ الآخِر	(2:8)
Day of Resurrection	يَوْمُ القِيَامَة	(2:85)
A Day about Which There Is No Doubt	يَوْمٌ لا رَيْبَ فيه	(3:9)
A Distressful Day	يَوْمٌ عَصِيب	(11:77)
A Day Where Mankind Will Be Gathered Together	يَوْمٌ مَجْموع	(11:103)
A Day When All Will Be Present	يَوْمٌ مَشْهود	(11:103)
A Day on Which There Will Be No Mutual Bargaining or Befriending	يَوْمٌ لا بَيْعَ فيهِ ولا خِلال	(14:31)
Day of the Time Appointed	يَوْمُ الوَقْتِ المَعْلوم	(15:38)
Day of Distress	يَوْمُ الحَسْرَة	(19:39)
Day of Disaster	يَوْمٌ عَقِيم	(22:55)
A Day Which None Can Avert	يَوْمٌ لا مَرَدَّ لَهُ	(30:43)
Day of Resurrection	يَوْمُ البَعْث	(30:56)
Day of Decision	يَوْمُ الفَتْح	(32:29)
Day of Sorting Out	يَوْمُ الفَصْل	(37:21)
Day of Account	يَوْمُ الحِساب	(38:16)
Day of Mutual Meeting	يَوْمُ التَّلاق	(40:15)
The Day That Is Drawing Near	يَوْمُ الآزِفَة	(40:18)
The Day When There Will Be Mutual Calling	يَوْمُ التَّناد	(40:32)
Day of Gathering	يَوْمُ الجَمْع	(42:7)
Day of Warning	يَوْمُ الوَعيد	(50:20)
Day of Eternal Life	يَوْمُ الخُلود	(50:34)
Day of Coming Out	يَوْمُ الخُروج	(50:42)
A Hard Day	يَوْمٌ عَسِر	(54:9)
A Violent Day	يَوْمٌ نَحْسٍ مُسْتَمِر	(54:19)
Day of Mutual Loss & Gain	يَوْمُ التَّغابُن	(64:9)
A Hard Day	يَوْمٌ عَسِير	(74:9)
Day of Truth	يَوْمُ الحَقّ	(78:39)
Promised Day	الْيَوْمُ المَوْعود	(85:2)
The Hour	السّاعَة	(6:31)
The Event	الواقِعَة	(56:1)
The Reality	الحاقَّة	(69:1)
The Striking Hour	القارِعَة	(69:4)
The Greatest Catastrophe	الطّامَةُ الكُبْرى	(79:34)
The Trumpet Blast	الصّاخَّة	(80:33)
The Overwhelming	الغاشِيَة	(88:1)

Literature Selection

The Last Man of Paradise

From Sahih Al Bukhari

Abu Hurayrah reported that some people asked the Messenger of Allah, "Will we see our Lord on the Day of Resurrection?" "Do you have any doubts about seeing a full moon on a clear night?" he replied.

They answered, "No, oh Messenger of Allah." He then said, "Do you have any doubts about seeing the sun on a cloudless day?" They again answered in the negative. Then Allah's Messenger announced, "You will see Allah in a similar way. On the Day of Resurrection, when people will be grouped together, He will command them to serve what they used to worship. Hence, some of them will worship the sun, others the moon and yet others various assorted deities. Finally, only this community will be left, along with the hypocrites in its ranks. Allah will approach them and declare, 'I am your Lord,' to which they will reply, 'We shall remain here until our Lord comes to us and we recognize Him.' Then Allah will approach closer and declare, 'I am your Lord,' to which they will reply, 'Indeed, You are our Lord.' Then, Allah will call them out, and a bridge will be laid over the chasm of Hell. I, Muhammad, will be the first among the Messengers to cross over it with my followers. No one save the Messengers will be able to speak, and they will be saying, 'Allah protect us. Allah protect us.' There will be jagged hooks on the bridge, like the thorns of the Sa'dan bush. Have you seen those thorns?" The people around the Prophet answered, "Yes," and then he continued. "Those jagged hooks will be like the thorns of the Sa'dan, but none save Allah knows their enormity of size. They will ensnare people according to their life's actions; some will tumble into Hell and remain forever, while others will be torn, though they will eventually be taken out of Hell when Allah intends mercy on whom He pleases amongst Hell's inmates. For those, He will command that the angels remove from Hell those who served nothing except Allah.

"The angels will draw them out by recognizing the traces of their prostrations, for Allah has forbidden the fire to consume those marks. Thus, they will be removed from the fire, but it will have eaten away their flesh, save the prostration marks. When they are pulled from the fire, they will be mere skeletons. The Water of Life will be poured over them, and they will regenerate, as a seed on a river bank. Then, when Allah has finished making judgements among His creations, only one person will remain between Hell and Paradise, and he will be the last dweller of Hell to enter Paradise. He will be facing Hell and crying, 'Allah! Turn my face from the fire, for its scorching wind has baked me, and its scalding steam has seared me.' Allah will then ask him, 'Will you request anything else if I grant you this

favor?' 'No, by Your Might!' He will reply. Then he will give His Lord promises and oaths. So Allah will turn his face from the fire, but when he is facing Paradise, and will see its delights, he shall remain silent as long as Allah wills. 'My Lord,' he will ask, 'Let me go to the gate of Paradise.' Allah will ask him, 'Didn't you give promises and make oaths that you would not ask for anything more than what you requested before?' He will reply, 'My Lord, don't make me the poorest among Your creatures.'

"Allah will answer, 'If this request is granted, will you request anything else?' 'No,' he will cry, 'By Your Might I will not ask for anymore.' Then he will give to His Lord (as He will) promises and oaths, and Allah will allow him to approach the gate of Paradise. When he reaches it, and after he has seen its vitality, allurement and delights, he will remain silent for as long as Allah wills. Then he will say, 'My Lord, let me enter Paradise.'

"Allah will then declare, 'May Allah (Me) be merciful towards you, son of Adam! How devious you are! Have you not made oaths and given promises that you will not request anything beyond what you have been given?' The man will answer, 'My Lord, do not make me the poorest among Your creatures.' So Allah will laugh and then allow him to enter Paradise, telling him to request whatever he likes. The man will do so until all his desires are fulfilled. Then Allah will say, 'Request more of these things.' And Allah will remind him, and after all his desires and wishes have been met, Allah will announce, 'All this is granted to you and a similar amount besides.'"

An Exclusive Place

Islam teaches that there is a place where there is no pain, sadness or worry—a place in which it is always pleasant and where no one grows old or dies. It is a magical and mystical land in which all desires are fulfilled, and no one ever grows bored.

(They will enter) the Gardens of eternity, promised by the All-Merciful (Allah) to His servants, in the unseen world. They will surely reach (the places of) His promise. They will not hear anything absurd therein but a word of peace, and there they will have their provision at morn and eve. That is the Paradise We will give as inheritance to those of Our servants who have been God-fearing. Surat Maryam (Mary) 19: 61-63

﴿جَنَّٰتِ عَدۡنٍ ٱلَّتِي وَعَدَ ٱلرَّحۡمَٰنُ عِبَادَهُۥ بِٱلۡغَيۡبِ إِنَّهُۥ كَانَ وَعۡدُهُۥ مَأۡتِيّٗا﴾ ﴿لَّا يَسۡمَعُونَ فِيهَا لَغۡوًا إِلَّا سَلَٰمٗا وَلَهُمۡ رِزۡقُهُمۡ فِيهَا بُكۡرَةٗ وَعَشِيّٗا﴾ ﴿تِلۡكَ ٱلۡجَنَّةُ ٱلَّتِي نُورِثُ مِنۡ عِبَادِنَا مَن كَانَ تَقِيّٗا﴾ سُورَةُ مَرۡيَمَ 19: 61-63

That place is quite beyond the reach of any technology known to mankind. But everyone has the chance to go there, and everyone will, except those who refuse the offer. Yet, you can't get there in your lifetime; it is a place reserved for the life after death.

Of course, people must earn their way to this place. The person who was a believer, worked hard, remembered his Creator and asked for His forgiveness will be eligible to enter the realm of Jannah. Your belief and actions will be the ticket to Paradise. However, those combined may not even be enough. It is entirely up to Allah﷾ to open the doors to anyone who demonstrates that they want to enter.

Paradise is the reward for what we did in this lifetime. It is the gift Allah﷾ gives to those who avoided what He said to avoid, who did what He said to do and who remembered that they were going to have to face Allah﷾ in the end.

If anyone does good deeds, whether male or female, and has faith, they will enter Paradise and not the least injustice will be done to them. Surat An-Nisa' (The Women) 4: 124

﴿وَمَن يَعۡمَلۡ مِنَ ٱلصَّٰلِحَٰتِ مِن ذَكَرٍ أَوۡ أُنثَىٰ وَهُوَ مُؤۡمِنٞ فَأُوْلَٰٓئِكَ يَدۡخُلُونَ ٱلۡجَنَّةَ وَلَا يُظۡلَمُونَ نَقِيرٗا﴾ سُورَةُ النِّسَاءِ 4:124

The Key to Entry

The Qur'an gives some very vivid descriptions of what Jannah will be like, just as it gives us instructions on how to get there. (16:30-32) Allah﷾ gave Prophet Muhammad ﷺ the honor of looking into both Paradise and Hellfire while he was still alive. Thus, the sayings of the Prophet ﷺ are also rich with its description.

Abu Hurayrah﷦ narrated that the Prophet ﷺ said, "All my followers will enter Paradise except those who refuse." They said, "O Allah's Messenger! Who will refuse?" He said, "Whoever obeys me will enter Paradise, and whoever disobeys me is the one who refuses (to enter it)." (Al Bukhari)

عَنۡ أَبِي هُرَيۡرَةَ ﷺ، أَنَّ النَّبِيَّ ﷺ، قَالَ: «كُلُّ أُمَّتِي يَدۡخُلُونَ الۡجَنَّةَ، إِلَّا مَنۡ أَبَى وَمَنۡ يَأۡبَى قَالُوا: يَا رَسُولَ اللهِ وَمَنۡ يَأۡبَى قَالَ: مَنۡ أَطَاعَنِي دَخَلَ الۡجَنَّةَ، وَمَنۡ عَصَانِي فَقَدۡ أَبَى». رَوَاهُ الۡبُخَارِيُّ

To understand how we can choose our ultimate fate through our beliefs and actions, read the following passage from the Holy Qur'an: *Is a person who knows that what was revealed to you is the truth from your Lord the same as the person who is blind to it? Only those who understand will remember. Those who fulfill the agreement of Allah and who don't fail in their promise. They join together what Allah commands to be joined, hold their Lord in awe and fear the terrible accounting (of deeds). Those who have patience, seeking the gaze of Allah, who establish prayer, give in charity from what We gave them both openly and secretly and turn away evil with good. For these is the gaining of the (best) home.* Surat Ar-Ra'd (The Thunder) 13:19-22

﴿ أَفَمَن يَعْلَمُ أَنَّمَآ أُنزِلَ إِلَيْكَ مِن رَّبِّكَ ٱلْحَقُّ كَمَنْ هُوَ أَعْمَىٰٓ إِنَّمَا يَتَذَكَّرُ أُوْلُواْ ٱلْأَلْبَٰبِ ﴾ ﴿ ٱلَّذِينَ يُوفُونَ بِعَهْدِ ٱللَّهِ وَلَا يَنقُضُونَ ٱلْمِيثَٰقَ ﴾ ﴿ وَٱلَّذِينَ يَصِلُونَ مَآ أَمَرَ ٱللَّهُ بِهِۦٓ أَن يُوصَلَ وَيَخْشَوْنَ رَبَّهُمْ وَيَخَافُونَ سُوٓءَ ٱلْحِسَابِ ﴾ ﴿ وَٱلَّذِينَ صَبَرُواْ ٱبْتِغَآءَ وَجْهِ رَبِّهِمْ وَأَقَامُواْ ٱلصَّلَوٰةَ وَأَنفَقُواْ مِمَّا رَزَقْنَٰهُمْ سِرًّا وَعَلَانِيَةً وَيَدْرَءُونَ بِٱلْحَسَنَةِ ٱلسَّيِّئَةَ أُوْلَٰٓئِكَ لَهُمْ عُقْبَى ٱلدَّارِ ﴾ سُورَةُ الرَّعْد 13:19 - 22

The opposing type of people are described in this way, *But those who break the agreement of Allah, after accepting it and who divide what Allah ordered joined and cause trouble in the world, a curse is on them, and they will have the terrible home.* Surat Ar-Ra'd (The Thunder) 13:25

﴿ وَٱلَّذِينَ يَنقُضُونَ عَهْدَ ٱللَّهِ مِنۢ بَعْدِ مِيثَٰقِهِۦ وَيَقْطَعُونَ مَآ أَمَرَ ٱللَّهُ بِهِۦٓ أَن يُوصَلَ وَيُفْسِدُونَ فِى ٱلْأَرْضِ أُوْلَٰٓئِكَ لَهُمُ ٱللَّعْنَةُ وَلَهُمْ سُوٓءُ ٱلدَّارِ ﴾ سُورَةُ الرَّعْد 13:25

When we read about Jannah in the Qur'an and Hadith, we must keep one thing in our minds: we are humans who cannot fully understand the power of the One Who created the Universe. When Allah﷾ tells us there are rivers, trees and silk in Paradise, He is merely providing examples of what is really there. But even then, the trees and silk will not be like the ones we are familiar with in this life. They are descriptive pictures and metaphors to help us understand how perfect Jannah will be. (2:25)

As Allah﷾ said in a **Hadith Qudsi** حَدِيثٌ قُدْسِيٌّ, which is the words of Allah﷾ reported by Prophet Muhammad ﷺ, Abu Hurayrah﵁ said that the Prophet ﷺ said, "Allah said, 'I have prepared for My pious worshippers such things as no eye has ever seen, no ear has ever heard of, and nobody has ever thought of. All that is reserved, besides which, all that you have seen, is nothing.' Then he recited, 'No soul knows what is kept hidden (in reserve) for them of joy as a reward for what they used to do.'" Surat As-Sajdah (The Prostration) 32:17. (Al Bukhari & Muslim)

عَنْ أَبِي هُرَيْرَةَ﵁ عَنِ ٱلنَّبِيِّ ﷺ: «يَقُولُ ٱللهُ تَعَالَى أَعْدَدْتُ لِعِبَادِي ٱلصَّالِحِينَ مَا لاَ عَيْنٌ رَأَتْ، وَلاَ أُذُنٌ سَمِعَتْ، وَلاَ خَطَرَ عَلَى قَلْبِ بَشَرٍ، ذُخْرًا، بَلْهَ مَا أُطْلِعْتُمْ عَلَيْهِ». ثُمَّ قَرَأَ:
﴿ فَلَا تَعْلَمُ نَفْسٌ مَّآ أُخْفِيَ لَهُم مِّن قُرَّةِ أَعْيُنٍ جَزَآءًۢ بِمَا كَانُواْ يَعْمَلُونَ ﴾ سُورَةُ السَّجْدَة 32:17. رَوَاهُ ٱلْبُخَارِيُّ وَمُسْلِمٌ

The Entry to Paradise

Those who are granted entrance into Jannah will be told by Allah﷾, *O soul at rest, come back to your Lord well pleased and well pleasing to Him. Enter among My servants! Enter My Paradise!* Surat Al Fajr (The Dawn) 89:27-30

﴿ يَٰٓأَيَّتُهَا ٱلنَّفْسُ ٱلْمُطْمَئِنَّةُ ﴾ ﴿ ٱرْجِعِىٓ إِلَىٰ رَبِّكِ رَاضِيَةً مَّرْضِيَّةً ﴾ ﴿ فَٱدْخُلِى فِى عِبَٰدِى ﴾ ﴿ وَٱدْخُلِى جَنَّتِى ﴾ سُورَةُ الفَجْر 89:27-30

The fortunate and grateful people who will make it over the Sirat will be relieved and joyful. They will approach a gleaming, sparkling realm beyond all imagination. The amazement and wonder will be more intense than we could ever comprehend right now. (47:15)

There are many gates into Paradise, each with its own name. The gate of Prayers, the gate of Jihad, the gate of Charity, the gate of Rayyan (Fasting), the gate of Truth, the gate of Supplication, the gate of Swallowing Anger and Forgiving People and the Right Gate (the gate of depending on Allah)

Each one of these gates will call to the person who performed that activity the most or the best. Some people will be called by more than one gate, and in that case, they can enter through whichever one they like! There are angels that will stand outside of each gate. As you enter, they will call out to you and tell you the good news of your success. (39:73-74)

The Wonder of Wonders

As we enter the gates of Paradise, we will be met with a wonderland of fresh scents, lights, colors, sounds and delights. The scene will be unimaginable and compelling. (76:20) Everyone will be fully healthy, in perfect bodies that are in the prime of life. No one will be sick, old, infirm, handicapped, blind or deformed. We will be perfect in appearance inside and out!

There are many levels in Paradise, one above the other. The higher the level, the more reward and delight you will receive. Beyond the highest level and the ceiling of Paradise, is the throne of Allah🙵 and the most incredible things of all. When believers enter Paradise, they will be asked to recite as much of the revelations of Allah🙵 as they learned in life. Those who followed Allah's🙵 last revelation, the Qur'an, will be asked to recite from the Qur'an according to how much they learned.

Miraculously, you will begin to ascend upwards as you recite and will pass through higher degrees of the heavens. You will stop in your ascent when you reach the end of what you know of the book. That will be your final destination or home in Paradise. You will know your relatives and family members who made it into Jannah, and you will be reunited in a joyous reunion. (13:23) No one will ever die again, and there will never be any painful separations. Mothers who lost babies in this life will see them as if they were birds fluttering about in delight. Children will find parents, and no one will be lonely, regardless of how many relatives were allowed entry. (52:21)

The angels will present to you your home (your mansion in Paradise), which will be surrounded by gardens, rivers and colorful lights. (39:20) It will neither be too hot, nor too cold, and there will never be any bad weather at your final home. (76:13) There will be creatures whose only purpose is to serve and please you. They will cater to your every need and whim and will never tire in serving you. Every wonderful kind of food you like will be available to you. (52:22-23) There will be crystal and silver dishes and comfortable cushions to recline on. (76:13-16) You will never tire of the varieties; anything you desire, you will have and more! (36:55-58)

And round about them will (serve) boys of everlasting youth. If you see them, you would think them scattered pearls. Surat Al 'Insaan (The Man) 76:19

﴿وَيَطُوفُ عَلَيْهِمْ وِلْدَٰنٌ مُّخَلَّدُونَ إِذَا رَأَيْتَهُمْ حَسِبْتَهُمْ لُؤْلُؤًا مَّنثُورًا﴾ سُورَةُ الإنسان 76:19

They will have in it whatever they wish, and with Us there are things even more than that.
Surat Q'aaf (The letter Q'aaf) 50:35

﴿لَهُم مَّا يَشَاءُونَ فِيهَا وَلَدَيْنَا مَزِيدٌ﴾ سُورَةُ ق 50:35

In Paradise, even wine will be allowable. But it will not be the wine of Earth, with which Shaytan used to trick people. This wine will taste good and will never make you intoxicated or sick. (37:47) It's a reward for us because we stayed away from the harmful wine of the world, (76:21-22) We will wear whatever clothes we like and will be given rich garments of green silk, brocade and jewelry. We will radiate light from before us and from behind us and will never tire of our splendor. (57:12, 76:21)

We will walk the streets and always be amazed and entertained with new delights and scenes. We will go to the markets and meet everyone there and see, smell and hear delights we never knew could exist. No one will ever have any pride, arrogance or hurt feelings, and there will be no bad words used or insults given. (7:43, 88:8-16)

The most honored treasures of Allah🙵 will be opened to us, such as the Fountain of **Salsabil** سَلْسَبِيل, literally, **Seek the Way**, and those who sought the way by doing good deeds will be the ones who drink from it. (76:17-18) The stream of **Kawthar** كَوْثَر **Abundance** is also one of the supreme delights of all in Paradise. Those who drink from it are given unimaginable pleasure. One fountain is reserved for the best people of all. Those closest to Allah will drink from the Fountain of Tasneem, made of the purest wine! (76:5-10, 83:27-28) Being near Allah🙵, the Creator of all things, is the mightiest and most awe-inspiring feature of Paradise. To be near Allah🙵, the Sustainer of the entire Universe, is a feeling none of us could ever understand or imagine. (56:10-26)

Finally, Paradise is forever. It never ends, and we never have to leave; in fact, we will never want to leave. Boredom does not exist there, and we never grow tired of the pleasures and delights within it. (35:35) You will go with only your emaan and the record of your actions, which the angels recorded faithfully. Always be ready for the journey and, insha'Allah, you will never have any need to feel grief or worry when you stand for your Judgement.

Certainly, (Paradise) is the supreme achievement! For this, let everyone work hard who wishes to work hard. Surat As-Saaffat (Those Set in Ranks) 37:60-61

﴿إِنَّ هَٰذَا لَهُوَ الْفَوْزُ الْعَظِيمُ﴾ ﴿لِمِثْلِ هَٰذَا فَلْيَعْمَلِ الْعَامِلُونَ﴾ سُورَةُ الصافات 37:60-61

The Lowest of the Low

Allah said in the Holy Qur'an that if He were to punish people according to what they deserved, there wouldn't be a single living thing left on the Earth. (35:45) That may sound extreme, but when you think of all the wrong-doing committed by people since the beginning of time, it's not so unreasonable.

How many murders, rapes, thefts, wars, beatings and abuses have occurred? A child is tortured to death in front of his parents, or a person starves an animal. A man hurts his wife, or a woman kills her baby. A man slaughters another person, or a man is left to die when he could have been saved. Indeed, when a crime is committed against someone, or when an oppressed soul cries out for mercy, then the severity of the evil deeds are intensified.

They (the humans) go out of bounds arrogantly in the Earth against all right! Oh, humanity! Your transgression is against your own souls. It's merely an enjoyment of the life of the present. In the end, to Us is your return. We will show you the truth of all that you did. Surat Yunus (Jonah) 10:23

﴿فَلَمَّآ أَنجَىٰهُمْ إِذَا هُمْ يَبْغُونَ فِى ٱلْأَرْضِ بِغَيْرِ ٱلْحَقِّ ۗ يَـٰٓأَيُّهَا ٱلنَّاسُ إِنَّمَا بَغْيُكُمْ عَلَىٰٓ أَنفُسِكُم ۖ مَّتَـٰعَ ٱلْحَيَوٰةِ ٱلدُّنْيَا ۖ ثُمَّ إِلَيْنَا مَرْجِعُكُمْ فَنُنَبِّئُكُم بِمَا كُنتُمْ تَعْمَلُونَ﴾

سُورَةُ يُونُس 23:10

Allah tells us that we have the capacity for evil, when we let our low, animalistic desires and pride rule our hearts. If you'll remember from a previous chapter, the angels expressed alarm when Allah announced He was going to create humans. They thought humans would surely cause chaos. (2:30) But Allah declared that He knew what they didn't. When Allah created humans, He proved to the angels that we were better. But Iblis, the wily jinn, refused to believe that humans were the best that Allah created and became determined to corrupt as many of us as possible. (38:82-85)

So while we have the best abilities, faculties and potential, we can also fall prey to our base desires and do the most horrible things imaginable. Thus, the struggle between good and evil began here on Earth. Allah promised to reward those who sided with good, even as He vowed to punish those who moved to the dark side. (65:8-10)

Allah's guidance helped us set up systems of justice on our planet. Legal codes all over the world are likely based on moral principles derived from religious teachings. Some countries have a more professional legal system than others. Some are more fair than others. But the basic principles are usually similar.

The Punishment Fits the Crime

What if someone commits an evil act and never gets punished in this life? What if we never bring the guilty to justice? Or what if the government of a country is committing injustice itself? Who will punish the evildoers?

Throughout history, we have witnessed heinous crimes committed by individuals who were never fully held accountable for their deeds. For example, Hitler killed 11 million people; Ivan the Terrible burnt countless villages to the ground, and Josef Stalin starved 30 million of his own people to death. Where is the justice for all of these individuals?

What of the man or woman who inflicts suffering on the innocent within their reach? What about liars, cheats, hypocrites and adulterers? Where is the justice if all they have to do is die to escape their just retribution? (104:1-9)

We build the tools of our own destruction!

Thankfully, crime and oppression will not go unpunished. As much as we should be rewarded for our emaan and struggles, so too we are punished for our disbelief and evil actions. That is why Allah made **Jahannam** جَهَنَّم Hellfire. (7:40-42)

Shall we treat those who believe and do good deeds the same as those who cause chaos on earth? Shall we treat those who avoid bad deeds the same as those who turn away from good? *Surat Saad (The Letter Saad) 38: 28*

﴿أَمْ نَجْعَلُ ٱلَّذِينَ ءَامَنُوا۟ وَعَمِلُوا۟ ٱلصَّـٰلِحَـٰتِ كَٱلْمُفْسِدِينَ فِي ٱلْأَرْضِ أَمْ نَجْعَلُ ٱلْمُتَّقِينَ كَٱلْفُجَّارِ﴾ سُورَةُ ص 38:28

Indeed, one of the most important principles in Islam is Justice. You get what you deserve. (103:1-3)

By the soul and the order within it, and its knowledge of right and wrong: Truly he succeeds who purifies it, while he who corrupts it, fails. *Surat Ash-Shams (The Sun) 91:7-10*

﴿وَنَفْسٍ وَمَا سَوَّىٰهَا﴾ ﴿فَأَلْهَمَهَا فُجُورَهَا وَتَقْوَىٰهَا﴾ ﴿قَدْ أَفْلَحَ مَن زَكَّىٰهَا﴾ ﴿وَقَدْ خَابَ مَن دَسَّىٰهَا﴾ سُورَةُ الشَّمْس 91:7-10

The highest court of all is Allah's court which will be in session on the Day of Judgement. (21:47) There, everyone will be brought forward, alone and quite helpless. (6:94) Their record will be read, and their desires, motivations and intentions will be made known. (40:10-12) Then they will see for themselves what they really did. (101:1-11)

Committing a sin is like burning down your own home! It will ruin you.

The Reward for Your Actions Goes Both Ways

Those who looked to live a life of goodness and faith will be rewarded with Jannah, while those who sought rebellion against the will of Allah will find themselves in a very bad situation. (45:33) Hellfire awaits them. (38:55-56) They will cry out and say that their wrong-doing was not their fault. (6:148) They will blame Shaytan, who will deny having anything to do with them. (59:16-17) After all, Shaytan will explain, he doesn't have the power to make anyone do anything.

Then, the person will point the finger at someone else, maybe his leader or an idol. (38:59-64) But all those things will deny the accusation and repeat what Shaytan explained. (41:48) Then they will turn to the people who have good emaan and deeds, as shown by the light on their faces. They will beg for some light, but Allah will make a wall in between them and close them off from the good believers. (57:12-15)

The worst people of all, whom Allah has said He will never forgive, will be dragged on their faces and thrown into the pit of Hell: a lake of burning fire that is 70 times hotter than the hottest flames here on Earth. As they are thrown through the seven gates of Jahannam, the angels will scold them, and they will wail in misery. (15:44, 41:19-25)

When they will be thrown in it, they will hear a terrible sound from it, and it will be boiling, seeming as if it will burst out of fury. Whenever a group is thrown into it, its keepers will say to them, "Had no warner come to you?" They will say, "Yes, a warner had come to us, but We had rejected, and said, 'Allah has not revealed anything. You are only in great error.'" And they will say, "Had we been listening or understanding, we would not have been among the people of the Hell." *Surat Al Mulk (The Dominion) 67: 7-10*

﴿إِذَآ أُلْقُوا۟ فِيهَا سَمِعُوا۟ لَهَا شَهِيقًا وَهِيَ تَفُورُ﴾ ﴿تَكَادُ تَمَيَّزُ مِنَ ٱلْغَيْظِ كُلَّمَآ أُلْقِيَ فِيهَا فَوْجٌ سَأَلَهُمْ خَزَنَتُهَآ أَلَمْ يَأْتِكُمْ نَذِيرٌ﴾ ﴿قَالُوا۟ بَلَىٰ قَدْ جَآءَنَا نَذِيرٌ فَكَذَّبْنَا وَقُلْنَا مَا نَزَّلَ ٱللَّهُ مِن شَىْءٍ إِنْ أَنتُمْ إِلَّا فِي ضَلَـٰلٍ كَبِيرٍ﴾ ﴿وَقَالُوا۟ لَوْ كُنَّا نَسْمَعُ أَوْ نَعْقِلُ مَا كُنَّا فِىٓ أَصْحَـٰبِ ٱلسَّعِيرِ﴾ سُورَةُ المُلْك 67:7-10

Those who have sinned will be made to go across the Sirat, where they will be cut and bloodied until they trip over a snag and fall headlong in the abyss. Guarding over it are 19 angels who push back anyone who tries to escape. (32:20) The roar of the blaze will echo within and burst with fury, sending out sparks as big as logs. (77:32) Waves of fire will rush over the punished, and walls of fire will stretch in every direction. **Naar** نَار **Hellfire** is so hot, it's pitch black! There will be no place to run, and no place to rest. (39:16)

The Pit of Hell

Allah will order the wrong-doers to be taken to Hell, and He will finally ask the raging pit, "Is there any more room?" To which Hell will reply, "Are there any more to come?" Truly, the capacity of Hell is endless. (50:30) Different crimes deserve different levels of punishment, and likewise, Hell will have a variety of punishments to offer. (46:18-20) The worst people will be in the very pit of the fire where their flesh will burn off their body in an instant. But then new flesh and skin will appear so they can feel the roasting again and again. (4:56)

An-Nu'man bin Bashir said, "I heard the Prophet ﷺ, 'The least punished person of the (Hell) Fire people on the Day of Resurrection will be a man under whose arch of the feet two smoldering embers will be placed, because of which his brain will boil just like Al-Mirjal (copper vessel) or a Qum-qum (narrow-necked vessel) is boiling with water.'" (Al Bukhari)

عَنِ النُّعْمَانِ بْنِ بَشِيرٍ، قَالَ سَمِعْتُ النَّبِيَّ ﷺ يَقُولُ: «إِنَّ أَهْوَنَ أَهْلِ النَّارِ عَذَابًا يَوْمَ الْقِيَامَةِ رَجُلٌ عَلَى أَخْمَصِ قَدَمَيْهِ جَمْرَتَانِ يَغْلِي مِنْهُمَا دِمَاغُهُ، كَمَا يَغْلِي الْمِرْجَلُ وَالْقُمْقُمُ». رَوَاهُ الْبُخَارِيُّ

Wrong-doers will be punished in quite unique and fitting ways throughout the different levels. Hellfire is even more terrible than words can describe! The people entering into it will beg for mercy but will be told they had their chance for mercy when they were alive in the world. (40:49-50) Their punishment will not end, and some will be left there for ages, while others will remain there forever. In it they will neither die nor live.

Those whom Allah has determined do not belong in the fire forever will be taken out when the term of their punishment ends Their soul has been purged of evil. Indeed, the evil was burned off to a cinder! The angels will pour the Water of Life over them, and they will then be restored whole and admitted to Paradise.

Anas bin Malik said, Verily the Apostle ﷺ said, "He who professed: There is no God but Allah, would be brought out of the Fire even though he has in his heart virtue equal to the weight of a barley grain. Then he who professed: There is no God but Allah, would come out of the Fire, even though he has in his heart virtue equal to the weight of a wheat grain. He would then bring out from the Fire he who professed: There is no God but Allah, even though he has in his heart virtue equal to the weight of an atom." (Muslim)

عَنْ أَنَسِ بْنِ مَالِكٍ، أَنَّ النَّبِيَّ ﷺ قَالَ: «يَخْرُجُ مِنَ النَّارِ مَنْ قَالَ لَا إِلَهَ إِلَّا اللهُ وَكَانَ فِي قَلْبِهِ مِنَ الْخَيْرِ مَا يَزِنُ شَعِيرَةً ثُمَّ يَخْرُجُ مِنَ النَّارِ مَنْ قَالَ لَا إِلَهَ إِلَّا اللهُ وَكَانَ فِي قَلْبِهِ مِنَ الْخَيْرِ مَا يَزِنُ بُرَّةً ثُمَّ يَخْرُجُ مِنَ النَّارِ مَنْ قَالَ لَا إِلَهَ إِلَّا اللهُ وَكَانَ فِي قَلْبِهِ مِنَ الْخَيْرِ مَا يَزِنُ ذَرَّةً». رَوَاهُ مُسْلِمٌ

Hellfire is forever only for the worst criminals and wicked souls. Some will eventually get out, but not others. (35:36-37) The Blessed Prophet ﷺ taught us many dua' to say in which we ask Allah to protect us from ever entering such a horrible place. If you remember why you're alive and avoid what is wrong, then you can, by the grace and mercy of Allah, avoid the punishment that all wrong-doers deserve. (90:4-20) So, no matter what injustice or terrible suffering humans may commit in this life and seem to get away with, we can have the satisfaction that Allah will punish them in the end. For He is the best Judge and the Avenger of Evil. (43:74-77)

Allah's ﷻ justice is **perfect!**

Chapter 7
Prayer

Islam Is a Way of Life

Islam is not only a religion but a lifestyle. Living as a Muslim is unlike practicing any other system or ideology known to the world. What sets a lifestyle apart from mere religion? The word 'religion' comes from the Latin term religio, which means a set of beliefs or practices that bind a community to the same standards. In other words, a religion is whatever makes people behave the same way, whether good or bad, true or untrue.

Islam, on the other hand, is not limited to only establishing a set of common standards. It goes beyond this to actually creating guidelines for every aspect of one's spiritual and social life.

To be a Muslim, one must not only believe in Allah﷾ but also serve Him﷾ in their daily life. **'Ibadah عِبَادَة Worshipping Allah** is part of the deal He extends to us. If we claim to believe in our Creator but then refuse to follow the ways He asks of us, aren't we then behaving like hypocrites?

O you who believe, shall I tell you about a trade that saves you from a painful punishment? That you believe in Allah and His Messenger and carry out Jihad in His way with your riches and your lives. That is much better for you, if you but know. If you do this, He will forgive your sins, and will admit you to gardens beneath which rivers flow, and to pleasant dwellings in gardens of eternity. That is the great achievement. And (He will give you) another thing, which you love: Help from Allah, and victory, near at hand. Surat As-Saff (The Row) 61:10-13

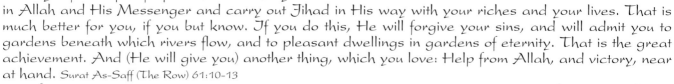

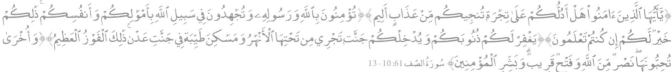

The Islamic way of life assumes that people need reminding of their duties to Allah﷾. This is only natural because we are prone to forget. At times, our low, earthly desires overwhelm us, while other times, Shaytan whispers temptations. With all that we need to accomplish in a day, it is possible, on occasion that we simply get too buried in mundane concerns to remember our Lord.

Thus, Allah﷾ has introduced in the Qur'an and the Sunnah ways to help us maintain and increase our service to Him﷾. From prayers, to fasting, to kind words, and even dua' that can be made at any time, the Islamic way of life allows Muslims to constantly remember their Lord and live according to Islamic teachings. Previous prophets all taught methods of 'ibadah, such as prayer or fasting, but because later generations lost or corrupted those teachings, these rituals became practices that no longer carried the same spiritual significance as they did originally.

The Islamic Lifestyle

The Islamic lifestyle is upheld through five major practices that every Muslim must make a part of his or her life. These rituals, known as the pillars of Islam, act as a wake-up call for our heart and mind. They help us continually refresh our understanding of life and why we are here.

There are Five Pillars, or sacred practices. These are the Shahadah, Salah, Zakah, Siyam and Hajj, which roughly mean Declaration, Prayer, Charity, Fasting and Pilgrimage. Some are performed daily; others, once a year, and one of them is done at least once in your life.

On the authority of 'Abdallah, the son of 'Umar bin Al Khattab﷜, who said, I heard the Messenger of Allahﷺ say, "Islam has been built on five (pillars): testifying that there is no deity worthy of worship except Allah and that Muhammad is the Messenger of Allah, establishing the Salah (prayer), paying the Zakah (obligatory charity), making the Hajj (pilgrimage) to the House, and fasting in Ramadan." (Al Bukhari & Muslim)

عَنْ أَبِي عَبْدِ الرَّحْمَنِ عَبْدِ اللهِ بْنِ عُمَرَ بْنِ الْخَطَّابِ ﷺ قَالَ: سَمِعْتُ رَسُولَ اللهِ ﷺ يَقُولُ: «بُنِيَ الْإِسْلَامُ عَلَى خَمْسٍ: شَهَادَةِ أَنْ لَا إِلَهَ إِلَّا اللهُ وَأَنَّ مُحَمَّدًا رَسُولُ اللهِ، وَإِقَامِ الصَّلَاةِ، وَإِيتَاءِ الزَّكَاةِ، وَحَجِّ الْبَيْتِ، وَصَوْمِ رَمَضَانَ». رَوَاهُ الْبُخَارِيُّ وَمُسْلِمٌ

The **Shahadah** شَهَادَة **Declaration** is the First Pillar. It is the phrase spoken when a person surrenders to Allah ﷻ and becomes a Muslim. No one is a Muslim unless this phrase is said with sincerity, even if the person was born into a Muslim family!

Positive and Negative

The Shahadah consists of two parts: one, a negation and the other, an affirmation. It reads as follows:

أَشْهَدُ أَنْ لَا إِلَهَ إِلَّا اللهِ، وَأَشْهَدُ أَنَّ مُحَمَّدًا رَسُولُ اللهِ

"Ash hadu an Laa ilaha illa Allah wa ash hadu anna Muhammadar Rasul Allah."

I declare that there is no God but Allah. And I declare that Muhammad is the Messenger of Allah.

In the first part, a person declares that they reject everything as their master except Allah ﷻ. No philosophy, religion, leader, cult, idea, idol or custom has any hold over them any longer. They surrender entirely to the will of Allah ﷻ. We know His will by what He told us in the Qur'an. This book becomes our guidebook. (64:13)

In the second part of the Shahadah, a person declares that he or she recognizes that Prophet Muhammad ﷺ was Allah's ﷻ last Messenger to the world and that his example and life practices are the best to follow. He taught people the Qur'an directly and was a role model for its teachings. (33:21)

Obey Allah, and obey the Messenger. But if you turn away, then Our Messenger has only to convey the message clearly. Surat At-Taghabun (The Mutual Disillusion) 64:12

﴿وَأَطِيعُوا اللَّهَ وَأَطِيعُوا الرَّسُولَ فَإِن تَوَلَّيْتُمْ فَإِنَّمَا عَلَىٰ رَسُولِنَا الْبَلَاغُ الْمُبِينُ﴾ سُورَةُ التَّغَابُنِ 64:12

The Shahadah is so important that we say it many times throughout the day in our daily prayers. It is the one phrase that the Prophet ﷺ recommended should be our last words before we die, and it is the one declaration that can lead a person to Paradise.

Abu Hurayrah ﷺ said that the Prophet ﷺ once said, "People, always refresh your faith." When the Companions asked, "Messenger of Allah, how do we do that?" "He replied, "By saying the testament 'La ilaha illa Allah' much and often." (Ahmad)

قَالَ رَسُولُ اللهِ ﷺ: «جَدِّدُوا إِيمَانَكُمْ». قَالُوا: يَا رَسُولَ اللهِ، وَكَيْفَ نُجَدِّدُ إِيمَانَنَا؟ قَالَ: أَكْثِرُوا مِنْ قَوْلِ لَا إِلَهَ إِلَّا اللهُ». رَوَاهُ أَحْمَدُ

The way to enter Islam is to say the Shahadah with full sincerity. This phrase is what distinguishes a Muslim from a non-Muslim. By saying it for the first time, a person enters Islam and gets the added bonus of having all his prior sins forgiven. He or she starts with a clean record with Allah ﷻ like a newborn child.

The next step is to adopt the beliefs and practices that make our faith translate into a way of life that is acceptable to our Creator. Even a person who was born as a Muslim still needs to make a conscious choice of following Islam. (49:14-15) It is our job, for those of us who have accepted Allah's ﷻ deen, to bring the message to as many people as we can so that their minds can be opened to the truth of their Lord. Nobody can be forced to believe. They may be convinced by a Muslim's good example and their own mind. (2:256) Allah ﷻ sent His last Prophet ﷺ with a mission to bring the truth and proclaim it over all other revealed and man-made religions.

He is the One who has sent His Messenger with guidance and the religion of truth, so that He makes it prevail over all religions, even though the mushriks (those who ascribe partners to Allah) dislike (it). Surat As-Saff (The Row) 61:9

﴿هُوَ الَّذِي أَرْسَلَ رَسُولَهُ بِالْهُدَىٰ وَدِينِ الْحَقِّ لِيُظْهِرَهُ عَلَى الدِّينِ كُلِّهِ وَلَوْ كَرِهَ الْمُشْرِكُونَ﴾ سُورَةُ الصَّفِّ 61:9

What Is Salah?

The first and foremost duty in Islam, after faith has been planted in the heart, is the **Salah** صَلاة **Prayer** (or Salat صَلاة). It is the most special act of 'ibadah that a Muslim can do for Allah. The word 'Salah' literally means 'connection.' Thus, the act of Salah is our way of making a connection with our sovereign Lord, Allah.

There are many verses of the Qur'an and sayings of the Blessed Prophet ﷺ that call us to this important act. It has been described as the foundation of the faith. In fact, the Prophet ﷺ once remarked that you can't get any closer to Allah than when you're bowing to Him.

Salah should be offered with a sincere heart and proper devotion, for it has the power to clean the heart and change one's life. It cultivates an inner sense of peace, certainty and discipline in the individual. It generates love, spirituality and truth and promotes awareness of Allah. (13:28) It even raises our morals and values and makes us better human beings. Therefore, Islam has placed more emphasis on Salah than on any other ritual duty.

Recite (O Prophet) what is revealed to you of the Book and establish Salah. Surely Salah restrains one from shameful and evil acts. Indeed remembrance of Allah is the greatest of all things. Allah knows what you do. Surat Al 'Ankabut (The Spider) 29:45

﴿ٱتْلُ مَآ أُوحِيَ إِلَيْكَ مِنَ ٱلْكِتَٰبِ وَأَقِمِ ٱلصَّلَوٰةَ إِنَّ ٱلصَّلَوٰةَ تَنْهَىٰ عَنِ ٱلْفَحْشَآءِ وَٱلْمُنكَرِ وَلَذِكْرُ ٱللَّهِ أَكْبَرُ وَٱللَّهُ يَعْلَمُ مَا تَصْنَعُونَ﴾ سُورَةُ العَنكَبوت 29:45

Whenever anyone went to the Blessed Prophet ﷺ to accept Islam, the first promise that he took from them, after the Shahadah, was that he or she would offer the Salah everyday, five times a day. (32:15-16) We know from the hadith, or sayings of the Prophet ﷺ, that the Blessed Prophet ﷺ considered the neglect of Salah as an act of disbelief.

The Messenger of Allah ﷺ said, "The covenant that stands between us and them is the Salah; whoever abandons it, he has committed disbelief." (At-Tirmidhi)

قَالَ رَسُولُ اللهِ ﷺ: «إِنَّ الْعَهْدَ الَّذِي بَيْنَنَا وَبَيْنَهُمُ الصَّلَاةُ فَمَنْ تَرَكَهَا فَقَدْ كَفَرَ». رَوَاهُ التِّرْمَذِيُّ

This hadith clearly warns that if a Muslim gives up his or her Salah, then his or her conduct will be the conduct of an unbeliever. Finally, the following hadith helps us understand the honor and virtue of Salah as we should. (4:142)

The Prophet ﷺ said, "Angel Jibreel delivered a message from Allah to me, saying, 'I (Allah) ordained five prayers on your community. Whoever fulfills them properly, without any shortcoming, he will have a deal with Me (Allah) that I (Allah) will admit him into Paradise. Whoever does not do them, he will have no deal with Me (Allah), and if I (Allah) will, I may punish him and, if I will, I (Allah) may forgive him.'" (At-Tayalisi)

قَالَ رَسُولُ اللهِ ﷺ: «أَتَانِي جِبْرِيلُ مِنْ عِنْدِ اللهِ تَبَارَكَ وَتَعَالَى، فَقَالَ: إِنَّ اللهَ عَزَّ وَجَلَّ، يَقُولُ: إِنِّي قَدْ فَرَضْتُ عَلَى أُمَّتِكَ خَمْسَ صَلَوَاتٍ، مَنْ وَافَى بِهِنَّ عَلَى وُضُوئِهِنَّ وَمَوَاقِيتِهِنَّ وَرُكُوعِهِنَّ وَسُجُودِهِنَّ فَإِنَّ لَهُ عِنْدِي أَنْ أُدْخِلَهُ بِهِنَّ الْجَنَّةَ، وَمَنْ لَقِيَنِي قَدِ انْتَقَصَ مِنْ ذَلِكَ شَيْئًا، أَوْ كَلِمَةً شِبْهَهَا، فَلَيْسَ لَهُ عِنْدِي عَهْدٌ، إِنْ شِئْتُ عَذَّبْتُهُ، وَإِنْ شِئْتُ رَحِمْتُهُ». رواه الطيالسي

The Blessed Prophet ﷺ said, "Whoever offers their Salah regularly and properly will find that it will be a light for him on the Last Day, a proof for his faith and a means whereby he will be saved. But whoever does not offer Salah regularly and carefully will find that it won't be a light for him, it won't be a proof of faith, nor a way to be saved. The end of such a person will be the same as Qarun, Pharaoh, Haman and Ubai bin Khalaf." [7] (Ahmad)

ذَكَرَ رَسُولُ اللهِ ﷺ، فَقَالَ: «مَنْ حَافَظَ عَلَيْهَا كَانَتْ لَهُ نُورًا وَبُرْهَانًا، وَمَنْ لَمْ يُحَافِظْ عَلَيْهَا لَمْ يَكُنْ لَهُ نُورٌ وَلَا بُرْهَانٌ، وَكَانَ مَعَ فِرْعَوْنَ وَهَامَانَ وَأُبَيِّ بْنِ خَلَفٍ». رَوَاهُ أَحْمَدُ

---

[7] Qarun was a Hebrew who disobeyed Prophet Musa ﷺ. Pharaoh was the evil leader of the Egyptians at the time of Prophet Musa ﷺ. Haman was Pharaoh's prime minister, and Ubai bin al Khalaf was a bitter enemy of the early Muslim community. They all met violent ends and were promised Hellfire.

Regularity Is the Key

Let us imagine what will happen to us if we neglect our prayers. Not only will we be missing out on something that can bring us more peace and stability, we will also be risking the same fate as those who will be in the fire. (19:59) The Blessed Prophet ﷺ once described the five daily prayers as a way to make sins fall away from you like leaves from a tree. It's not hard to imagine this given that the five daily prayers are spaced strategically throughout the day; we are always coming from or needing to make our Salah!

Establish Salah and give in charity and obey the Messenger so that you will receive mercy.
Surat An-Noor (The Light) 24:56

﴿وَأَقِيمُوا ٱلصَّلَوٰةَ وَءَاتُوا ٱلزَّكَوٰةَ وَأَطِيعُوا ٱلرَّسُولَ لَعَلَّكُمْ تُرْحَمُونَ﴾ سُورَةُ النُّور 24:56

Salah is the one act that allows us to build a base of support for the entire structure of our emaan. If there is no base, how can there be anything else? Your Salah strengthens your Muslim identity.

On the authority of Abu Hurayrah ؓ from the Prophet ﷺ, who said, "I have come to know that the prayer is the first action of a person that will be examined. Once it is accepted, the rest of his or her actions will be examined as well. But if it is not accepted, none of the other actions will be examined." (At-Tirmidhi)

عَنْ أَبِي هُرَيْرَةَ قَالَ: قَالَ رَسُولُ اللهِ ﷺ: «إِنَّ أَوَّلَ مَا يُحَاسَبُ بِهِ الْعَبْدُ يَوْمَ الْقِيَامَةِ مِنْ عَمَلِهِ صَلَاتُهُ. فَإِنْ صَلُحَتْ فَقَدْ أَفْلَحَ وَأَنْجَحَ، وَإِنْ فَسَدَتْ فَقَدْ خَابَ وَخَسِرَ». رَوَاهُ التِّرْمَذِي

The Effects of Salah

When a person stands before Allah ﷻ five times a day, head bowed a little, and declares his or her surrender to the Power behind all things—when that person kneels and touches the ground with his or her forehead and makes heartfelt supplications, or dua', he or she becomes worthy of Allah's ﷻ love and generosity. The sins and bad deeds he or she did during the day are erased with the performance of Salah.

The heart begins to strengthen and life becomes purer. The Blessed Prophet ﷺ once told a parable to illustrate this point: Abu Hurayrah ؓ said that the Prophet ﷺ said, "Tell me, if a stream flowed in front of your door and you dipped your body in it five times a day, would any dirt remain on you?" The Companions replied in the negative. The Prophet then continued, 'It is exactly the same with the five daily prayers. Allah erases sins and bad deeds (because of the Salah).'" (Muslim)

عَنْ أَبِي هُرَيْرَةَ، أَنَّ رَسُولَ اللهِ ﷺ قَالَ: «أَرَأَيْتُمْ لَوْ أَنَّ نَهْرًا بِبَابِ أَحَدِكُمْ يَغْتَسِلُ مِنْهُ كُلَّ يَوْمٍ خَمْسَ مَرَّاتٍ هَلْ يَبْقَى مِنْ دَرَنِهِ شَيْءٌ». قَالُوا: لَا يَبْقَى مِنْ دَرَنِهِ شَيْءٌ. قَالَ: فَذَلِكَ مَثَلُ الصَّلَوَاتِ الْخَمْسِ يَمْحُو اللهُ بِهِنَّ الْخَطَايَا». رَوَاهُ مُسْلِم

It is also clear from the sayings of the Blessed Prophet ﷺ that Salah is best done in **Jama'ah** جَمَاعَة **Group** prayer with other Muslims. The Blessed Prophet ﷺ was very insistent about this. He once said that he would almost like to burn down the houses of the lazy people—those who could go to the **Masjid** مَسْجِد **Place of Prayer** for the morning prayer but don't. This is a strongly-worded statement so that everyone can understand how important Salah is for us as a community. The plural of masjid is masaajid. In English, the word for masjid is mosque. Some Muslims prefer to use the word masjid, because it means a place of prayer.

The Blessed Prophet ﷺ stated, "The reward of making the Salah in a group is 27 times more than performing it alone." (Al Bukhari)

عَنْ رَسُولِ اللهِ ﷺ: «صَلَاةُ الْجَمَاعَةِ تَفْضُلُ صَلَاةَ الْفَذِّ بِسَبْعٍ وَعِشْرِينَ دَرَجَةً». رَوَاهُ الْبُخَارِي

Besides the rewards from Allah ﷻ that we get from praying together, there are many other hidden advantages. For instance, if a person makes sure to get to the masjid on time for the Salah, he or she learns the lesson of punctuality.

Additionally, when Muslim brothers and sisters see each other coming to the masjid for this important duty, it reinforces the notion that Islam is built on a united community of believers.

Another of the many advantages is that Salah is both an individual and a group activity. No one feels left out because everyone is actively engaged in asking for guidance from Allah. When he or she is in the group, each one becomes a part of the whole body of believers. Together, those who are performing their Salah look towards Allah, Who created all things and guides those who seek to know more.

Now, imagine the rich rewards and blessings we deny ourselves if we avoid going to the masjid. We deliberately cut ourselves off from the grace of Allah and choose to sit at home. Salah is not a gift to be wasted, and performing Salah in a group contains numerous lessons that we all can learn from! When we offer our Salah to Allah, we should do it with a humble heart, not with pride. We must know that Allah is the most powerful Being whose knowledge is present everywhere.

The Heart of a Believer

Our hearts must be softened with **Taqwa تَقْوى Awareness of Allah** Our soul must feel the thoughts of His magnificence, as if we were a criminal standing before the mightiest judge. When a person stands for Salah, he or she must visualize standing before the Almighty, out of pure love and reverence for Him. When we bow our heads or kneel down, we must keep in mind that we are bowing before Allah, the One Who created life throughout the Universe in ways that scientists are only just beginning to understand.

Even more importantly, whatever we say in the Salah, whether standing or sitting or bowing, must be said with an intelligent appreciation of its meaning. It is not difficult to learn the translation of what is said in the prayers. Only then can the real joy and beauty of Salah be experienced and savored.

The Blessed Prophet ﷺ once remarked that one scholar is harder on the Shaytan than a thousand ignorant worshippers. On another occasion, he explained that you will only be rewarded according to how much you understand what you are doing. The devotion of the heart, and the feelings of awe and humbleness are indeed the very soul of the Salah. The ultimate success and deliverance of the believing women and men is guaranteed if they follow this simple truth.

The believers must eventually succeed, those who humble themselves in their prayers. Surat Al Mu'minun (The Believers) 23: 1-2

﴿قَدْ أَفْلَحَ الْمُؤْمِنُونَ﴾ ﴿الَّذِينَ هُمْ فِي صَلَاتِهِمْ خَاشِعُونَ﴾ سُورَةُالمُؤمِنون 23:1-2

A Story about Sincerity

Ibrahim bin Adham, who was a famous Muslim scholar of long ago, was once asked an interesting question. A group of people came to him, and one of them quoted an ayah from the Qur'an that says, *And your Lord declares, "Call on Me and I will answer your prayer."* Surat Ghafir (The Forgiver) 40:60

﴿وَقَالَ رَبُّكُمُ ادْعُونِي أَسْتَجِبْ لَكُمْ﴾ سُورَةُ غافِر 40:60

Then the person asked the Muslim scholar, "We pray to Allah, but why are we not answered?"
The scholar replied,

You know about Allah, yet you don't obey Him.
You read the Qur'an, yet you don't act according to it.
You know how bad Shaytan is, yet you have joined with him.
You say that you love the Messenger of Allah, yet you abandon his Sunnah.
You declare that you love Paradise, yet you don't do anything to obtain it.
You declare you're afraid of the fire, yet you don't keep yourselves from committing sins.
You agree that we will all die, yet you are not prepared for it.
You're busy finding faults with others, yet you don't look at your own faults.
You eat the food Allah provided for you, yet you don't thank Him,
and you bury your dead, yet you don't take any lesson from it.

The Requirements for Salah

It is important to note that Salah is not some petty activity that can be done inconsiderately. As you have learned in the previous lesson, Salah is the way to elevate one's self both spiritually as well as mentally. It is also the primary tool to exercise our emaan and taqwa on a daily basis.

Establish prayer for My remembrance. Surat Ta-Ha 20:14

﴿وَأَقِمِ ٱلصَّلَوٰةَ لِذِكْرِيٓ﴾ سُورَةُ طه 20:14

The model for how to pray was the Blessed Prophet Muhammad ﷺ. He brought the Qur'an to us and put its teachings into practice. The Qur'an and his Sunnah are a symbiotic connection. They cannot be separated, as the Qur'an itself declares over and over: *Obey Allah and obey the Messenger.* Surat An-Nisa' (The Women) 4: 59

﴿أَطِيعُوا ٱللَّهَ وَأَطِيعُوا ٱلرَّسُولَ﴾ سُورَةُ النِّساء 4:59

Malik ﷺ *narrated that the Messenger of Allah* ﷺ *told us, "Pray as you have seen me praying."* (Al Bukhari)

حَدَّثَنَا مَالِكٌ ﷺ، عَنْ رَسُولِ اللهِ ﷺ قَالَ: «صَلُّوا كَمَا رَأَيْتُمُونِي أُصَلِّي». رَوَاهُ الْبُخَارِيُّ

Therefore, the first Muslims made it a point to note every feature of Salah and every method of how to perform it. Later scholars grouped the preconditions of Salah into six major categories. If all six of these conditions are met, then Salah is to be offered at once. The six requirements are:

1. Correct Time
2. Clean Body
3. Clean Clothes
4. Covered Body
5. Clean Place
6. Facing the Ka'bah

We shall deal with a few of these requirements in this lesson, including Salah times, prayer place, body preparation and **Qiblah** قِبْلَة **Direction of Prayer**.

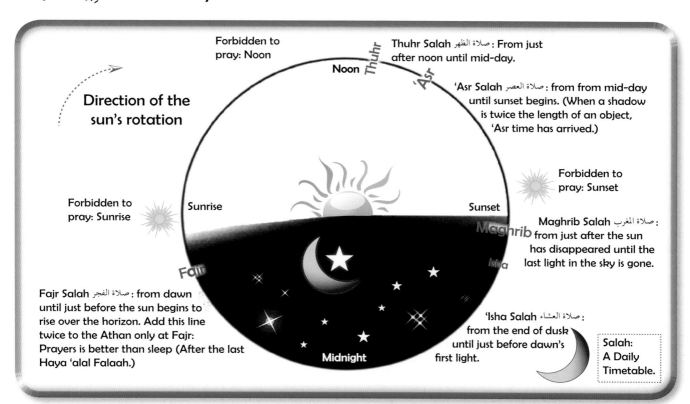

Forbidden to pray: Noon

Thuhr Salah صلاة الظهر : From just after noon until mid-day.

'Asr Salah صلاة العصر : from from mid-day until sunset begins. (When a shadow is twice the length of an object, 'Asr time has arrived.)

Direction of the sun's rotation

Forbidden to pray: Sunset

Forbidden to pray: Sunrise

Sunrise

Sunset

Maghrib Salah صلاة المغرب : from just after the sun has disappeared until the last light in the sky is gone.

Fajr Salah صلاة الفجر : from dawn until just before the sun begins to rise over the horizon. Add this line twice to the Athan only at Fajr: Prayers is better than sleep (After the last Haya 'alal Falaah.)

Midnight

'Isha Salah صلاة العشاء : from the end of dusk until just before dawn's first light.

Salah: A Daily Timetable.

The Timing of Salah

There are five times during the day when Salah is mandatory upon every sane person past the age of puberty. The names of the five prayers are: Fajr, Thuhr, 'Asr, Maghrib and 'Isha. The following chart details the time of day for each of these prayers. These five prayers are the minimum requirement for a Muslim. There are also extra prayers that may be performed that add to a person's record and increases their rewards and spiritual satisfaction.

In any case, no prayer may be offered before its proper time. If we accidentally miss a Salah because we were sleeping or just forgot, then the Prophet advised us to pray the missing Salah right away. Any missed prayer that is done outside the acceptable window of opportunity is considered **Qada'** قَضاء.

Indeed, Salah is a prescribed duty that has to be performed at the appointed times by the believers.
Surat An-Nisa' (The Women) 4: 103

﴿إِنَّ ٱلصَّلَوٰةَ كَانَتْ عَلَى ٱلْمُؤْمِنِينَ كِتَابًا مَوْقُوتًا﴾ سُورَةُ النِّسَاء: 103:4

Take due care of all the prayers and the middle prayer and stand before Allah in total devotion. *Surat Al Baqarah (The Cow) 2:238*

﴿حَافِظُوا عَلَى ٱلصَّلَوَاتِ وَٱلصَّلَوٰةِ ٱلْوُسْطَىٰ وَقُومُوا لِلَّهِ قَانِتِينَ﴾ سُورَةُ البَقَرَة: 238:2

When the time for Salah has arrived, it is the practice of the Muslim community to announce from the masjid that the prayer time has come. This melodic and enchanting call is the **Athan** أذَان **Call to Prayer**, made by a man called a **Mu'athin** مُؤَذِّن. He faces the Qiblah, the direction of Makkah. Putting his hands over his ears, he chants loudly and clearly the following phrases:

اللهُ أَكْبَر . اللهُ أَكْبَر
Allahu Akbar, Allahu Akbar.
Allah is The Greatest. Allah is The Greatest.

اللهُ أَكْبَر . اللهُ أَكْبَر
Allahu Akbar, Allahu Akbar.
Allah is The Greatest. Allah is The Greatest.

أَشْهَدُ أَنْ لا إِلَهَ إلاَّ الله . أَشْهَدُ أَنْ لا إِلَهَ إلاَّ الله
Ashahadu an la ilaha ill Allah. Ashahadu an la ilaha ill Allah.
I bear witness that there is no God except Allah.
I bear witness that there is no God except Allah.

أَشْهَدُ أَنَّ مُحَمَّدًا رَسُولُ الله . أَشْهَدُ أَنَّ مُحَمَّدًا رَسُولُ الله
Ashahadu anna Muhammadar Rasul Allah. Ashahadu anna Muhammadar Rasul Allah.
I bear witness that Muhammad is the Messenger of Allah.
I bear witness that Muhammad is the Messenger of Allah.

حَيَّ عَلى الصَّلاة . حَيَّ عَلى الصَّلاة
Haya 'alas Salah. Haya 'alas Salah.
Hurry to the Prayer. Hurry to the Prayer.

حَيَّ عَلى الفَلاح . حَيَّ عَلى الفَلاح
Haya 'alal Falah, Haya 'alal Falah.
Hurry to Success. Hurry to Success.

اللهُ أَكْبَر . اللهُ أَكْبَر
Allahu Akbar. Allahu Akbar.
Allah is The Greatest. Allah is The Greatest.

لا إِلَهَ إلاَّ الله
La ilaha ill Allah.
There is no God except Allah.

The athan is the same for each prayer, except Salat Al Fajr. This prayer has an extra line: *Prayer is better than sleep* الصَّلاةُ خَيْرٌ مِنَ النَّوْمِ.

اللَّهُمَّ رَبَّ هَذِهِ الدَّعْوَةِ التَّامَّةِ و الصَّلاةِ القَائِمَةِ، آتِ مُحَمَّدًا الوَسِيلَةَ و الفَضِيلَةَ، وابْعَثْهُ مَقَامًا مَحْمُودًا الَّذِي وَعَدْتَهُ، إِنَّكَ لا تُخْلِفُ المِيعاد.

Allaahumma Rabba haathihid-da 'watit-taammati wassalaatil-qaa'imati, 'aati Muhammadanil-waseelata walfadheelata, wab 'ath-hu maqaamam-mahmoodanil-lathee wa'adtahu, 'innaka laa tukhliful-mee'aad.

"Oh Allah, Lord of this perfect call and the Salah which is being established, give Muhammad the right of intercession and honor, and raise him to the praiseworthy position You promised him, and give him intercession for us on the Day of Judgement. Indeed, You never go back on Your word."

Place and Body Preparation

After this public announcement has been given, people begin to ready themselves for prayer. If they are busy, then they wrap things up for their Salah break. Many people go to the masjid to pray, while others pray at home. However, prayer in the masjid is 27 times better, according to many reports from the Blessed Prophet ﷺ.

The place of prayer must be clean and without anything offensive such as idols or dirt. Any place is suitable for prayer as long as it's clean. Muslims usually like to pray on prayer rugs or mats, but you can also pray on grass, cement, wood floors or any surface that is clean. The Blessed Prophet ﷺ once remarked that the whole Earth is a masjid for us. This is a beautiful statement, for Allah's ﷻ entire Universe is reflecting His creative will. How wonderful that we pray within it!

The Prophet ﷺ once said, "Your Lord delights at a shepherd who, on the peak of a mountain top, gives the athan and then offers prayer. Then Allah says, 'Look at this servant of Mine. He gives the athan and performs the prayers. He is in awe of Me. I have forgiven My servant and will admit him to Paradise.'" (An-Nasa'i)

قَالَ رَسُولُ الله ﷺ : « يَعْجَبُ رَبُّكَ مِنْ رَاعِي غَنَمٍ، فِي رَأْسِ شَظِيَّةِ الْجَبَلِ، يُؤَذِّنُ بِالصَّلاةِ وَ يُصَلِّي، فَيَقُولُ اللهُ عَزَّ وَ جَلَّ: انْظُرُوا إِلَى عَبْدِي هَذَا، يُؤَذِّنُ وَ يُقِيمُ الصَّلاةَ، يَخَافُ مِنِّي، قَدْ غَفَرْتُ لِعَبْدِي، وَ أَدْخَلْتُهُ الْجَنَّةَ ». رَوَاهُ النَّسَائِيّ

Head cover

A person also must be properly dressed for Salah. Our clothes must be clean and nice. (74:4) Shorts, muscle shirts or dirty clothes are hardly appropriate when you are about to offer yourself humbly before the Creator of everything.

Children of Adam! Wear your beautiful clothes at every prayer and place of prayer. Eat and drink but do not waste things because Allah does not love people who waste. Surat Al A'raaf (The Heights) 7:31

﴿ يَٰبَنِي ءَادَمَ خُذُوا زِينَتَكُمْ عِندَ كُلِّ مَسْجِدٍ وَكُلُوا وَٱشْرَبُوا وَلَا تُسْرِفُوا إِنَّهُ لَا يُحِبُّ ٱلْمُسْرِفِينَ ﴾ سُورَةُ الأَعْرَافِ 7:31

Clothes must cover specific areas of our bodies for the sake of modesty. For men, the area from the navel to the knees must be covered. For women, the area to be covered is defined as everything except the face and hands. Although some Muslim women also choose to cover their faces outside the home, the face should not be covered during the Salah. Clothes for both men and women should be loose and not transparent. Any color and style is fine as long as the basic requirements are met.

Even Christian and Jewish women are instructed in their religious books to cover their hair, particularly when in prayer. In the not too distant past, women entering churches and synagogues would wear a scarf, a hat or some type of head cover out of modesty and respect. The Bible reads, ...*every woman that prays or prophesies with her head uncovered dishonors her head...If the woman be not covered, let her (hair) also be shorn (shaved off)*. (I Corinthians 11:5-7)

The Blessed Prophet ﷺ once warned that Allah ﷻ will not accept the prayer of a woman with her head uncovered. To cover is an important symbolic gesture on the part of the woman. Although other people judge her by her looks and her beauty, Allah ﷻ only considers her heart and actions. She is coming to Allah ﷻ without her physical charms instead bringing her soul alone.

The Prophet ﷺ said, "Allah does not consider your looks or your wealth. He considers your taqwa and your actions." (Muslim)

قال رسول الله ﷺ : «إِنَّ اللَّهَ لَا يَنْظُرُ إِلَى صُوَرِكُمْ وَأَمْوَالِكُمْ وَلَكِنْ يَنْظُرُ إِلَى قُلُوبِكُمْ وَأَعْمَالِكُمْ». رَوَاهُ مُسْلِمٌ

Having worn the proper clothing and responded to the call of the mu'athin, the person proceeds to the place of prayer. The signal for the start of Salat Al Jama'ah is given when the **Iqamah** إقامة **Second Call to Prayer** is made. The 'iqamah is similar to the athan, but is said a little differently and not as loudly or rhythmically. The 'iqamah can be said three different ways. One of the most common ways is as follows:

اللهُ أَكْبَرُ . اللهُ أَكْبَرُ

Allahu Akbar, Allahu Akbar.
Allah is The Greatest. Allah is The Greatest.

أَشْهَدُ أَنْ لا إلَه إلاَّ الله

Ash hadu an la ilaha ill Allah.
I bear witness that there is no God except Allah.

أَشْهَدُ أَنَّ مُحَمَّدًا رَسُولُ الله

Ash hadu anna Muhammadar Rasul Allah.
I bear witness that Muhammad is the Messenger of Allah.

حَيَّ عَلَى الصَّلاة

Haya 'alas Salah.
Hurry to the Prayer.

حَيَّ عَلَى الفَلاح

Haya 'alal Falah.
Hurry to Success.

قَدْ قَامَتِ الصَّلاة . قَدْ قَامَتِ الصَّلاة

Qadi qamatis Salatu. Qadi qamatis Salah.
Stand for prayer. Stand for prayer.

اللهُ أَكْبَرُ . اللهُ أَكْبَرُ

Allahu Akbar. Allahu Akbar.
Allah is The Greatest. Allah is The Greatest.

لا إلَه إلاَّ الله

La ilaha ill Allah.
There is no God except Allah.

Finally, whether at home, in a group or in a masjid, you stand facing the direction of Makkah to offer your prayers. We face toward the Ka'bah, the cube-shaped building in Makkah, that was established as a place of worship by Prophet Ibrahim ﷺ thousands of years ago. (2:125) By doing this, Muslims unite in worship all over the world, proclaiming that the Message of Allah is one that transcends time and unites the hearts of all believers.

The Qiblah is one of the most fascinating aspects of prayer. We, as a community, have a spiritual center that is not based on a person's birthplace, grave site, mystical temple or magical force. Although the Ka'bah has spiritual significance, it is only a stone building. It is not the place where Allah ﷻ lives or where the Prophet ﷺ is buried. It is the symbol of something greater. Our uniform prayer in the direction of the Ka'bah symbolizes unity and obedience to Allah ﷻ, our Lord and Master.

Wherever you start from, turn your face towards the Sacred Masjid. And wherever you are, turn your face there. Surat Al Baqarah (The Cow) 2:150

﴿وَمِنْ حَيْثُ خَرَجْتَ فَوَلِّ وَجْهَكَ شَطْرَ الْمَسْجِدِ الْحَرَامِ وَحَيْثُ مَا كُنتُمْ فَوَلُّوا وُجُوهَكُمْ شَطْرَهُ﴾ سُورَةُ البَقَرَة 2:150

What Is the Ritual Meaning of Clean and Dirty?

There is a unique requirement in Islam that we must be in a state of **Taharah** طَهَارَة **Ritual Cleanliness** before we offer ourselves in devotion to our Lord. This cleanliness is more than just whether or not you have dirt on your hands. It refers to the unity between your physical condition and your state of mind. Specifically, to be ready for Salah, one must be free from all **Najasa** نَجَاسَة **Ritual Impurity** that makes one unfit to perform a ritual act such as prayer. The causes of impurity are described below.

What Causes Impurity of the Ritual State?

To achieve taharah, it is important to know what causes ritual impurity. If someone becomes impure, then they must become ritually clean again before the Salah can be performed.

Minor Impurities:
1. Passing of urine.
2. Defecation of any kind.
3. Passing gas.
4. Sleeping.
5. Losing consciousness.
6. Touching the private parts directly.
7. Emission of blood or pus from the body. (According to some fiqh schools.)
8. Vomiting. (According to some fiqh schools.)

Major Impurities:
1. Menstrual flow.
2. Emission of certain fluids from the private parts.
3. Intercourse.
4. After-birth bleeding.

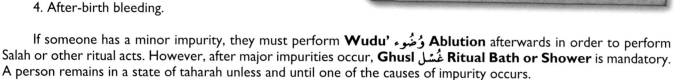

Make Your Wudu' For Salah!

If someone has a minor impurity, they must perform **Wudu'** وُضُوء **Ablution** afterwards in order to perform Salah or other ritual acts. However, after major impurities occur, **Ghusl** غُسْل **Ritual Bath or Shower** is mandatory. A person remains in a state of taharah unless and until one of the causes of impurity occurs.

How Do I Make Wudu'?

"Water makes everything pure."
So said Prophet Muhammad ﷺ. (Dawud)

Making wudu' is easy. All you need is clean water! Before you begin, it is a good idea to make your **Niyyah** نِيَّة **Intention**. This means that you are going to establish in your mind what you're doing before you begin. You can say silently to yourself, "Nuwaytul wudu'," نَوَيْتُ الْوُضُوء, which means, I intend to make wudu'.

This is important because the Blessed Prophet Muhammad ﷺ said,"Actions will be judged by your intentions." (Bukhari)

عَنْ رَسُولِ اللهِ ﷺ : «إِنَّمَا الأَعْمَالُ بِالنِّيَّاتِ». رَوَاهُ الْبُخَارِيُّ

So your wudu' will count if you intended to make it. What if you were watching television and while the show was going on, you ran to make your wudu', but the whole time you were still thinking of the action on TV? You never settled in your mind what you were doing and thus might have even made mistakes. Therefore, make the proper niyyah, or intention for everything you do. To continue with your wudu' procedure say the Basmala, بِسْمِ اللهِ الرَّحْمَنِ الرَّحِيمِ, which means, "In the name of Allah, Most Gracious and Merciful." The Prophet ﷺ advised us to start all things by saying this.

Believers! When you are about to offer your prayers, wash your faces and hands up to the elbows and wipe your heads and feet up to the ankles. *Surat Al Ma'ida (The Table) 5:6*

﴿يَٰٓأَيُّهَا ٱلَّذِينَ ءَامَنُوٓاْ إِذَا قُمْتُمْ إِلَى ٱلصَّلَوٰةِ فَٱغْسِلُواْ وُجُوهَكُمْ وَأَيْدِيَكُمْ إِلَى ٱلْمَرَافِقِ وَٱمْسَحُواْ بِرُءُوسِكُمْ وَأَرْجُلَكُمْ إِلَى ٱلْكَعْبَيْنِ﴾ سُورَةُ المَائِدَة 5:6

Wudu' Procedure:

1. After making niyyah and saying the Basmala, begin by washing the right hand three times to the wrist. Then wash the left hand three times to the wrist.

2. Take water into the mouth with the right hand three times. Each time swish the water around and ensure you rinse your mouth thoroughly. Use your right index finger to rub the teeth and gums.

3. Sniff water in and blow out of the nose three times with the right hand.

4. Take water into both hands and gently wash it over the entire face. Try not to splash all over the place. The Prophet ﷺ once warned us against wasting water even if making wudu' near a river. Every part of the face must be wet from under the chin to the forehead.

5. Next, wash the right arm up to the elbow three times and then the left arm three times.

6. Wet the palms with water and wipe them from the forehead to the back of the head. Then run your hands back up to the front of your head.

7. Use your index fingers and thumbs to rub the ears clean.

8. Wash both feet with the left hand up to the ankle three times. Start with the right foot.

9. Say this phrase:

أَشْهَدُ أَنْ لَا إِلَهَ إِلَّا اللهُ وَحْدَهُ لَا شَرِيكَ لَهُ، وأَشْهَدُ أَنَّ مُحَمَّدًا عَبْدُهُ وَرَسُولُهُ.

"Ash hadu an laa ilaha ill Allah, wahdahu la sharika lahu, wa ash hadu anna Muhamadan 'abduhu wa rasuluhu."

I declare that there is no God but Allah; One, with no partners, and I declare that Muhammad is His servant and Messenger.

10. Say this dua':

اللَّهُمَّ اجْعَلْني مِنَ التَّوَّابِينَ، واجْعَلْني مِنَ المُتَطَهِّرِينَ.

"Allahumma aja'alnee min at tawwabin wa aja'alnee min al mutatahireen."

Allah, make me among the repentant and make me among the clean.

Now you're ready to offer your Salah!

What Is the Way to Perform Ghusl?

The procedure for ghusl is also simple. It can be combined with the wudu' to maximize ritual purity. There are many authentic methods for making the ghusl. Outlined below is one common method:

1. Begin with clean water in either a shower or bathtub.
2. Make the niyyah for ghusl.
3. Wash the right hand and then the left three times each.
4. Wash the private parts with the left hand.
5. Repeat step number 3.
6. Do all the steps from the **Wudu' Procedure**, outlined in numbers 5-10.
7. Pour water over the head three times, then over the right and left side of the body, washing thoroughly. (A woman with a tight braid may leave it tied as long as the water reaches to the roots of her hair.)
8. The entire body should become wet, leaving nothing dry.
9. Wash the feet as in the Wudu' Procedure and then towel dry.
10. Say the same ending dua' as after performing wudu'. (**Steps 9 & 10 in Wudu' Procedure**).

What Is Tayammum?

Islam is a way of life adaptable to all circumstances. When water is scarce, or medically dangerous to use, tayammum can be performed. (5:6)

1. Make the intention to perform tayammum: نَوَيْتُ التَّيَمُّم "Nuwaytul Tayammum." *"I intend to make tayammum."*
2. Say: بِسْمِ اللهِ الرَّحْمَنِ الرَّحِيمِ, *"Bismi Allahi Ar-Rahmani Ar-Rahim." "In the Name of Allah, The Most Gracious, The Most Merciful."*
3. Gently pat the open palms of your hands on clean sand or gravel.
4. Blow off any dust and wipe your hands lightly over your face.
5. Pat the sand or gravel gently again and blow off the dust.
6. Wipe the right hand and arm up to the elbow using your left hand (both the top side and bottom side of the arm), and then wipe the left hand and arm up to the elbow using your right hand.
7. Repeat the Shahadah and dua' from steps 9 and 10 in the Wudu' Procedure on the previous page.

If ritual purity has been achieved, and the other requirements have been met, then you are ready to perform your Salah.

What Is Maseh of the Socks?

If you perform your wudu' and then put on socks, you don't have to wash your feet the next time you make wudu'. Instead, perform wudu' as you normally would, and simply use your right hand to wipe the top of your right and left feet. This is called **Maseh مَسْح Wiping** of the socks.

When performing maseh, you don't wipe the sides or bottoms of your socks. Additionally, if there is a small hole in your sock somewhere, the wiping is still valid. Be sure to use enough water to leave wet lines tracing your fingers where they passed over the sock. The Prophet ﷺ used maseh over leather socks. The thick cloth socks of today are similar to the leather ones from long ago. Either of these materials is valid for us to perform maseh.

Maseh can be done for 24 hours only, from the time the wudu' is first made. If you take off your socks and become ritually impure during that time, then you need to make wudu', before you can put your socks on again for the purpose of wiping over them.

A traveler can wipe over his or her socks for three days. This is a mercy for those who undergo the inconvenience of long distance traveling by road or plane. Again, make sure there are no large holes in the socks, and that you don't take them off if your wudu' is broken. If there is a large hole, or you take your socks off, then you'll need to perform your entire wudu' before putting your socks on again if you want to be able to do maseh for a later prayer.

When Is Prayer Not Due?

There are certain situations when prayer is not due because of reasons beyond our control. A specific time for women is during their menses. During this time, women are not required to make Salah, as a mercy from Allah ﷻ. Women do not have to make up the missed prayers from this time. When menses ends, women must then make ghusl right away and begin offering Salah at the next scheduled prayer.

"Allah make me among the repentant and make me among the clean."

اَللّٰهُمَّ اجْعَلْنِي مِنَ التَّوَّابِينَ، وَ اجْعَلْنِي مِنَ الْمُتَطَهِّرِينَ

What Is the Difference Between Dua' and Salah?

There are two types of prayers in Islam. The first type is known as Salah. It is the standardized set of rituals performed five times a day in which we remind ourselves spiritually and mentally about our ultimate purpose in this life.

The second type of prayer is known as **Dua' دُعاء Supplication**. This is an informal prayer activity where we ask Allahﷻ for guidance, forgiveness, help or anything else. We can make dua' throughout the day in any manner we choose and in whatever words and language we prefer. You will soon learn that there are many beautiful dua' from the Qur'an and hadith. The Salah Procedure is a set of movements and phrases performed in a set method. The Salah consists of standing, bowing, prostrating, sitting, and also involves reciting certain praises and Qur'anic verses. Each complete cycle of these activities makes what is known as a **Rak'ah رَكْعَة Unit of Salah**. The plural of rak'ah in Arabic is rak'aat.

The Unit of Salah

If the six preconditions for Salah are met, as explained in the previous two lessons, then the Salah Procedure can begin. Each prayer throughout the day has its own set number of rak'aat. For example, the pre-dawn prayer, or Fajr, has two rak'aat, while the night prayer, or 'Isha, has four. The chart on this page details the number of rak'aat in each of the daily prayers.

The Blessed Prophet ﷺ taught us how to pray by his example in which he always performed a standard number of rak'aat for each prayer. However, the Blessed Prophet ﷺ showed us that there are variations that are allowed within each physical act of prayer. This is a mercy for Muslims, as it enables us to customize their own unique expression in the Salah.

To illustrate this point, we know that Salah must follow the set pattern of physical movements taught by the Holy Prophet ﷺ. However, some of the phrases said within the Salah can be recited in different ways. Also, some minor hand movements and dua' can vary. The basic rule is that as long as the variation is traceable to the Blessed Prophet ﷺ, it is permissible to use.[8]

Name of Salah	Number of Required Rak'ah
Fajr الفَجْر (Pre-dawn)	2
Thuhr الظُّهر (Afternoon)	4
'Asr العَصر (Late Afternoon)	4
Maghrib المَغرِب (Sunset)	3
'Isha العِشاء (Night)	4

What follows is a description of the basic Salah procedure, complete with phrases and movements. This explanation adheres to the most common method used by most Muslims in the West. Keep in mind that there are variations that are allowed, and you can consult any reputable manual of Salah for them. The Salah must be said in Arabic, and the Blessed Prophet ﷺ always used to teach the non-Arab Muslims to do so. It's another way to unify us and keep us connected to the original language of the Qur'an.

The Salah Procedure

After the conditions for the Salah have been met, and wudu' has been performed, we should ready ourselves mentally and emotionally. (20:14) We should remember that:
1. We are submitting ourselves completely to our Creator. He is our Master, and we are His servants.
2. We all make mistakes and are therefore imperfect.
3. We cannot hide anything from Allahﷻ.
4. Allahﷻ knows all about us and will show us on the Day of Judgement how we fared in life.
5. Allahﷻ is the Most Merciful; even if we make mistakes in our daily life, we should hope for His Mercy and Forgiveness by performing our prayer sincerely.
6. Pray as though it is the last and most important prayer you will ever do.

And be steadfast in Salah (prayer) and give Zakah. Whatever good you send forth for yourselves, you will find it with Allah. Certainly, Allah is watchful of what you do. Surat Al Baqarah (The Cow) 2:110

﴿وَأَقِيمُوا۟ ٱلصَّلَوٰةَ وَءَاتُوا۟ ٱلزَّكَوٰةَ وَمَا تُقَدِّمُوا۟ لِأَنفُسِكُم مِّنْ خَيْرٍ تَجِدُوهُ عِندَ ٱللَّهِ إِنَّ ٱللَّهَ بِمَا تَعْمَلُونَ بَصِيرٌ﴾ سُورَةُ البَقَرَة 2:110

Once we are in the right mental and spiritual frame of mind, we can proceed with the physical aspects of performing our Salah.

---

8 Some minor variations in the procedure are allowed, and one will find that the schools of thought (madhahib) differ in some minor aspects.

Steps of the Salah

Just like with wudu' and anything else important, we begin our Salah with niyyah, or intention. This way we make it clear to ourselves what we're doing before we begin. While facing the Qiblah, properly dressed and in a state of wudu', we say silently to ourselves,

نَوَيْتُ صَلاةَ الـ (اسْمُ الصَّلاة)

"Nuwaytus Salat ul (name of the particular Salah here.)"
"I intend to pray (name of the Salah here)."
What we say in the last space is the name of the prayer we are performing.

Raise hands up and say, "Allahu Akbar." Females may raise their hands up to the side of their head, or may raise their hands just up to the shoulder level. Men stand with their feet shoulder-width apart, and women keep their feet together. Men raise hands to the side of the head; women, up to the shoulders only. After performing this beginning motion of the Salah, a person must consider themselves as cut off from the outside world until they are finished. While we are standing in that position, **Qiyam** قيام **Standing Up**, we must take care not to look around or move our bodies. From the moment we say Allahu Akbar, the prayer starts and we shouldn't do anything except what is allowed in the prayer until we finish. If we laugh, start to talk or walk around, then that Salah is broken and we have to start all over again.

Then we fold our hands over our lower chest.[9] Females put both of their hands on each other and place them on their upper chests. The right hand goes over the left. Then say the **Thana'** ثَناء **Opening Glorification** dua',

سُبْحانَكَ اللَّهُمَّ وبِحَمْدِكَ، وتَبارَكَ اسْمُكَ، وتَعالى جَدُّكَ، ولا إلَهَ غَيْرُك

"Subahanak-allahumma wa bihamdika, wa tabaraka ismuka, wa ta'ala jedduka, wa laa ilaha ghairuka."
"Glory to You, Allah, and praise to You. Blessed is Your Name, great is Your Highness and there is no God except You."[10]

---

9 Some Muslims like to pray with their hands hanging loosely from their sides. This is allowed also, but it is better to fold your hands in front of you, right over left, based on an abundance of hadith about it.

10 There are other opening prayer formulas. This one is the most common. Focus on the place on the floor where you will bow.

11 In Fajr, Maghrib and 'Isha, Surat al Fatihah and follow-up suwar are said aloud in the first two rak'aat. In all remaining rak'aat, and in the Thuhr and 'Asr Salah, everything is said silently. Surat al Fatihah is recited in every rak'ah, while no additional suwar are recited in rak'ah three or four.

134

The very next thing we should say is what Allah referred to as the Greatest Surah, or chapter, of the Holy Qur'an. It is the one surah that Allah gave us which contains everything for us in just seven little verses, or ayaat. It is such an important surah that if we forget to say it in our Salah, then the whole Salah doesn't count. Here is the Arabic text of that surah, which is called Al Fatihah, or the Opening, along with the English meaning. In the Salah, we say it in Arabic only. **II** Before reciting Al Fatihah we say,

أَعوذُ بِاللهِ مِنَ الشَّيْطانِ الرَّجيم

"A'udhu billahi min ash-shaytaan ar-rajeem."
"I ask Allah to protect me from the rejected Shaytan."

Surat Al Fatihah is said in Arabic this way:

﴿بِسْمِ ٱللَّهِ ٱلرَّحْمَٰنِ ٱلرَّحِيمِ﴾ ﴿ٱلْحَمْدُ لِلَّهِ رَبِّ ٱلْعَٰلَمِينَ﴾ ﴿ٱلرَّحْمَٰنِ ٱلرَّحِيمِ﴾ ﴿مَٰلِكِ يَوْمِ ٱلدِّينِ﴾ ﴿إِيَّاكَ نَعْبُدُ وَإِيَّاكَ نَسْتَعِينُ﴾ ﴿ٱهْدِنَا ٱلصِّرَٰطَ ٱلْمُسْتَقِيمَ﴾ ﴿صِرَٰطَ ٱلَّذِينَ أَنْعَمْتَ عَلَيْهِمْ غَيْرِ ٱلْمَغْضُوبِ عَلَيْهِمْ وَلَا ٱلضَّآلِّينَ﴾ سُورَةُ الفَاتِحَة 1:1-7

This means:

In the Name of Allah, the Most Caring and the Most Kind. Praise be to Allah, the Lord of the Universe; the Most Caring and the Most Kind. Master of the Day of Judgment. We serve only You and only turn to You for help. Guide us on the straight path. The path of those whom You are happy with, not the path of those whom You are angry with and not the path of those whom have gone astray. *Surat Al Fatihah (The Opening) 1:1-7*

"Bismi Allahi Ar-Rahmani Ar-Rahim, Alhamdu lillahi rabbi al 'alameen, Ar-Rahmani ar-Rahim, Maliki yawmi addeen, Iyyaka na'budu wa-iyyaka nasta'een, Ihdina assirata almustaqeem, Sirata allatheena an'amta 'alayhim, ghayri almaghdoobi 'alayhim wala addalleen." (1:1-7)

Say: "Ameen," after Surat al Fatihah has been recited. After saying Surat Al Fatihah, we say another portion of the Qur'an. It can be as little as three ayaat long or even a whole long surah! In a third and fourth rak'ah of a prayer, only Surat Al Fatihah is said before bowing. In addition, it is preferred for suwar to be recited in a chronological order throughout the Salah. For example, if a person recites *Surat Al Mulk (The Dominion) (67)* in the first rak'ah, then in the second rak'ah a surat should be read that comes after that in the order of the Qur'an. We chose Surat Al Ikhlas here, but you can choose any one you want.

Surat Al Ikhlas is said in Arabic this way:

﴿قُلْ هُوَ ٱللَّهُ أَحَدٌ﴾ ﴿ٱللَّهُ ٱلصَّمَدُ﴾ ﴿لَمْ يَلِدْ وَلَمْ يُولَدْ﴾ ﴿وَلَمْ يَكُن لَّهُۥ كُفُوًا أَحَدٌۢ﴾ سُورَةُ الإِخْلاص 112:1-4

This means:

Say (O Muhammad): He is Allah the One. Allah is always forever. He doesn't have any children and He was never born and there is nothing the same as Him. *Surat Al Ikhlas (The Purity) 112:1-4*

"Qul huwa Allahu ahad, Allahu assamad, Lam yalid walam yoolad, Walam yakun lahu kufuwan ahad." (112:1-4)

When the recitation has been completed, and with the thought of the majesty of our Lord embedded in our hearts, we should say firmly, "Allahu Akbar" (Allah is greater than everything else).

Then you bend forward at the waist and put your hands on your knees. This is called **Ruku'** رُكوع **Bowing**. Men should take care to keep their back level and their head straight in line with their back. We are bowing to our Creator and therefore must not slouch in a casual manner. According to the Prophet ﷺ, we should have our back so straight that we can balance a glass of water on it. Women can bow a little less rigidly. While in this position of reverence, we humbly express our heart-felt understanding of Allah's power over us by saying silently three times,

سُبْحانَ رَبِّيَ العَظيم
"Soobhaana rabbee Al 'atheem."
"Glory to my great Lord."

Then we raise ourselves back up to the standing position (arms at our sides) and declare three times:

سَمِعَ اللهُ لِمَنْ حَمِدَه

"Sami' Allahu liman hamida."
"Allah hears the person who praises Him."

In response to this statement, it is customary to reply:

رَبَّنا ولَكَ الحَمْد

"Rabbana wa lakal hamd."
"Our Lord, praise is Yours."

Then we say, اللهُ أَكْبَر, and lower ourselves to our knees and make **Sujood** سُجُود **Prostration**. Our elbows must stay up in the air and our feet must be raised up so that the bottom of our toes are on the ground. Place your hands on the floor on each side of your head. Your nose and forehead should touch the ground. Say silently three times, [12]

سُبْحانَ رَبِّيَ الأَعلى

"Soobhana rabbee al 'ala."
"Glory to my Lord, the Most High."

To make our sajdah complete, we must pay particular attention to the way we prostrate.

Ibn 'Abbas narrated that the Prophet said, "We have been ordered to prostrates on seven bones and not to tuck up the clothes or hair." (Al Bukhari)

عَنِ ابْنِ عَبَّاسٍ عَنِ النَّبِيِّ قَالَ: «أُمِرْنَا أَنْ نَسْجُدَ عَلَى سَبْعَةِ أَعْظُمٍ وَلاَ نَكُفَّ ثَوْبًا وَلاَ شَعَرًا» رَوَاهُ الْبُخَارِيُّ

These seven points of contact with the floor are as follows:
1. Face (forehead & nose) (1)
2. Hands (2)
3. Knees (2)
4. Feet upright (2)

Our elbows must be off the ground, and our hands should be placed on either side of the head. In this position, we must imagine inwardly that Allah can see us. We place our faces on the floor in the purest and most expressive act of our surrender, to the only force that matters in the Universe. (96:19)

Think about it: is there any better way for a person to show obedience than to worship with the body, as well as with the heart and mind? Humans are complex because of the connection between our bodies and our souls. How can we surrender our souls and leave the body behind? The two must go hand-in-hand, as Allah taught us to worship Him in the most advanced form of prayer He ever revealed to any messenger.

Indeed, according to the Qur'an, Allah is closer to us than our jugular vein. This is a clear reference to the fact that our life depends solely upon His pleasure. If that one vein were cut, then the person would die. This is an important concept to remember during sajdah.

Abu Hurayrah reported, The Messenger of Allahs said, "The closest one of you comes to his Lord is while he is prostrating." (Muslim)

عَنْ أَبِي هُرَيْرَةَ، أَنَّ رَسُولَ اللهِ قَالَ: «أَقْرَبُ مَا يَكُونُ الْعَبْدُ مِنْ رَبِّهِ وَهُوَ سَاجِدٌ» رَوَاهُ مُسْلِمٌ

---

12 According to the Blessed Prophet, Allah loves odd numbers. The reasoning is that anytime one is added to an even number, it becomes odd, and Allah is One. Even numbers always imply pairs of numbers. Odd has one left out of the pair.

With our senses filled with the love for Allah, we repeat the phrase Allahu Akbar and rise up to a sitting position placing our hands on our knees, pausing for a moment to ask Allah's forgiveness,

أَسْتَغْفِرُ الله

"Astaghfirullah."
I seek Allah's Forgiveness.

Men keep their right heel upright while sitting. Women sit a little to the left side.

Then we say, اللهُ أَكْبَر "Allah is the Greatest" and bow a second time in sajdah, repeating the same phrase three or more times that we said previously. And do one more sujud and say three times,

سُبْحَانَ رَبِّيَ الأَعلى

"Soobhana rabbee al 'ala."
Glory to my Lord, the Most High.

This simple plea, directed towards the Creator of all life and matter, should melt the hearts of the people who are fooled by the illusions of this life. How better can we express the feeling that has lived in the minds and hearts of people for a hundred thousand years? When we recognize that we are not great, and that our existence is pitifully short, we raise ourselves above the physical world of temptation into a higher realm. This is what our sajdah must mean.

Then say,

"Allahu Akbar."

Return to a standing position with your hands folded in front of you. That was one rak'ah, or cycle of prayer.

Repeat steps 3-8

Now imagine that we were praying Fajr Salah, which has two rak'aat. We still have to complete another rak'ah. That is easy. All you have to do is repeat steps 3-8. But after saying Surat Al Fatihah, choose a different surah to recite than what you said in the first rak'ah.

So, for example, if we said *Surat Al Ikhlas* in the first rak'ah, in our second rak'ah, after Surat Al Fatihah, we'll say *Surat An Naas*, or whichever one we choose! After the end of the second sajdah, instead of standing up after saying, الله أَكْبَر, we will return to a sitting position and stay there.

(Note: If you were doing a 3 or 4 rak'aat Salah, all Qur'an reciting will be said quietly to one's self.)

In this posture, we recite the **At-Tahiyyat** التَّحِيّات Greetings, a supplication of praise and blessings for Allah, His Prophet ﷺ and all those praying. The most common method is as follows:

التَّحِيّاتُ لِلهِ وَالصَّلَوَاتُ وَالطَّيِّبَات،
السَّلامُ عَلَيْكَ أَيُّهَا النَّبِيُّ وَرَحْمَةُ اللهِ وَبَرَكاتُه،
السَّلامُ عَلَيْنَا وَعَلَى عِبَادِ اللهِ الصَّالِحين

"Atay hiyatu lillahee wa salawatu wa tayyibatu.
As-salam 'alayka ayyuhan nabeeyu wa rahma tullahee wa barakatuhu,
Assalamu 'alayna wa 'ala 'ibad ilahis sawliheen."
"All purity, prayer and goodness belong to Allah.
Peace be upon you Prophet, and Allah's mercy and blessings.
Peace be upon all righteous servants of Allah."

Then you raise the index finger while saying the next phrase:
أَشْهَدُ أَنْ لا إِلَهَ إِلاَّ الله، وَأَشْهَدُ أَنَّ مُحَمَّدًا عَبْدُهُ وَرَسُولُه

"Ash hadu an laa ilaha ill Allah, wa ash hadu anna Muhammadan 'abduhu wa rasooluhu."
I declare that there is nothing worthy of my allegiance except Allah, He is One with no partners, and I declare that Muhammad is His servant and Messenger.' [13]

If you are in the last required rak'ah of your Salah, you then proceed to end the prayer. For example, if you were praying Fajr Salah, then after the At-Tashahud you would say the ending supplication, known as As-Salat Al Ibrahimiyya, and end your prayer.

But if your prayer required more than two rak'aat, you would say, "Allah is the Greatest," after finishing the At-Tahiyyat and rise back to the standing position to complete the next rak'aat. Then, in the final jalsa, you would say the At-Tahiyyat again and then proceed to end the Salah, as explained below.

Then you say the prayer called **As-Salat Al Ibrahimiyya** الصَّلاةُ الإِبْراهيميّة which is meant to ask Allah to bless the Prophet ﷺ. The words of الصلاة الابراهيمية are as follows:

اللَّهُمَّ صَلِّ عَلَى مُحَمَّدٍ وَعَلَى آلِ مُحَمَّد، كَما صَلَّيْتَ عَلَى إِبْراهيمَ وَعَلَى آلِ إِبْراهيم، إِنَّكَ حَميدٌ مَجيد.
اللَّهُمَّ بارِكْ عَلَى مُحَمَّدٍ وَعَلَى آلِ مُحَمَّد، كَما بارَكْتَ عَلَى إِبْراهيمَ وَعَلَى آلِ إِبْراهيم، إِنَّكَ حَميدٌ مَجيد.

"Allahumma sallee 'ala Muhammadin wa 'ala aalee Muhammadin. Kama sallayta 'ala Ibrahima wa 'ala aalee Ibrahima. Innaka hameedun Majeed. Allahumma barik 'ala Muhammadin wa 'ala aalee Muhammadin. Kama barakta 'ala Ibrahima wa 'ala aalee Ibrahima fil 'alameen. Innaka hameedun majeed."
"Allah send grace upon Muhammad and on the family of Muhammad, just like You sent grace upon Ibrahim and on the family of Ibrahim. You are worthy of all praise, the Majestic. Allah bless Muhammad and the family of Muhammad, just like you blessed Ibrahim and the family of Ibrahim in the world. You are worthy of all praise, the Majestic."

Through As-Salat al Ibrahimiyya, the reward and blessing of our Lord are invoked upon the Blessed Prophet ﷺ, his family and upon all those who bear a special association with him. After doing this, we can ask something for ourselves or for our own benefit. One such supplication is:

اللَّهُمَّ إِنِّي ظَلَمْتُ نَفْسِي ظُلْمًا كَثيرًا، وَلا يَغْفِرُ الذُّنُوبَ إِلاَّ أَنْت؛ فَاغْفِرْ لي مَغْفِرَةً مِنْ عِنْدِك، وَارْحَمْني إِنَّكَ أَنْتَ الغَفُورُ الرَّحيم

"Allahumma innee thzalamtu nafsee thzulman katheeran, wa laa yaghfir udhunooba illa ant. Faghfirlee maghfiratan min 'indika war hamnee. Innaka antal ghafoor ul raheem."
"Allah, I have done wrong to myself! No one can forgive sins except You, so grant me forgiveness from Yourself and have mercy on me. You are the Forgiving, the Merciful."

---

13 The right index finger should be raised up from the knee slightly at this point, to signify the oneness of Allah, and then it is lowered after the completion of this phrase. The thumb and middle finger can be joined together in a circle while the index finger is pointing. You can also move the pointed index finger up and down or side-to-side slightly.

Then you turn your face completely to the right and say,

السَّلامُ عَلَيْكُم ورَحْمَةُ الله

"Assalamu Alaykum warahmatu Allah."

Peace be upon you and the mercy of Allah.

Then you turn your face completely to the left and say,

السَّلامُ عَلَيْكُم ورَحْمَةُ الله

"Assalamu Alaykum warahmatu Allah."

Your prayer is now finished and you can rise and go about your business. It is recommended to stay seated, however, and recite a few brief phrases to remember Allah. Personal requests to Allah for forgiveness or guidance can then be made. This is called thikr and then dua'. Through this prayer, we make an open confession of our sins and bad deeds. We ask Allah for His mercy and His forgiveness. It is best for us to realize that we make mistakes sometimes. This understanding helps us open our hearts and make us aware of our faults. By doing this, we are placing all our hopes in Allah's compassion and love. While we may do our best to fulfill our religious duties, such as Salah, we should recognize that as humans we can never praise Allah as He deserves since He is so Perfect. Thus, we should be humble about our actions and always ask Him to accept our prayer and forgive our sins.

All Movements for a Two-Rak'aat Salah

First Rak'ah

Second Rak'ah

Other Levels of 'Ibadah

In addition to the required five Salah, there are other types of Salah that are performed at other occasions and times. These other forms of prayer are essentially similar to the basic Salah procedure outlined in the previous lesson. Some forms have added features, which will be discussed in this lesson.

Fard	*Required*
Wajib	*Strongly Urged*
Sunnah	*Recommended*
Nafl	*Extra Merit*

The five daily prayers, which must be performed by every sane Muslim past the age of puberty, are known as **Fard** فَرْض **Mandatory** prayers. These are the minimum requirements to which a Muslim must adhere. However, because our minds may wander, or we may lose our concentration, our Salah usually is not as good as it could be.

Islam offers a solution to this problem by allowing us to offer extra prayers to make up for any mistakes in our fard Salah. **Sunnah** سُنَّة or **Nafl** نَفْل prayers can also be performed, as it was the example of the Blessed Prophet ﷺ to make extra prayers to earn the great reward in them. The Blessed Prophet ﷺ taught us when to do them and what the preferred number of rak'ah are in each prayer. These extra prayers are offered either before or after the fard Salah (see the Salah Chart below) and are done in the standard way, as outlined in the previous lesson.

Salah	Sunnah (Recommended) Rak'aat Before	Fard (Mandatory) Rak'aat	Sunnah (Recommended) Rak'aat After	Wajib (Strongly Urged) Rak'aat
Fajr	2	2	0	
Thuhr	4	4	2	
'Asr	0	4	0	
Maghrib	0	3	2	
'Isha	0	4	2	2 Shaf' & 1 Witr

Salat Al Witr

Notice on the Salah Chart, after 'Isha, it says '2' and then '2 Shaf' & 1 Witr' (3 rak'aat). The first sunnah prayer of two-rak'aat is to be said in the normal way, and then completed. The three-rak'aat prayer that follows is a slightly different type of prayer called the **Salat Al Witr** صَلاةُالوتر **Prayer of Al Witr**. This Salah is sometimes referred to as a **Wajib** واجِب **Strongly Encouraged** and very important to do because the Prophet ﷺ never missed it. Witr Salah is the last prayer of the day before going to bed, and consists of an odd number of rak'aat. It can be lengthened to include any amount of odd-numbered rak'aat.

The procedure is quite simple: The first two rak'aat are done in the normal way, and are said in a low voice to one's self. After jalsa, a person merely stands and recites Surat al Fatihah again. Unlike other prayers however, an additional surat is read after Surat al Fatihah in the third rak'ah. Just as the Salah procedure explained in an earlier lesson, the suwar read in the prayers should be said in the same chronological order as they are found in the Qur'an.

When the extra Qur'anic selection is finished, say, "Allahu Akbar." Then make ruku', come back up and say the following supplication, called Dua' Al Qunut, before saying takbeer and making sajdah. Another way to perform this is to say the Dua' Al Qunut before making ruku', saying takbeer and then making ruku'. Both methods are valid. There are different ways of saying Dua' Al Qunut; here is one:

اللّهُمَّ إِنَّا نَسْتَعِينُكَ وَنَسْتَهْدِيكَ وَنَسْتَغْفِرُكَ وَنَتُوبُ إِلَيْكَ، وَنُؤْمِنُ بِكَ وَنَتَوَكَّلُ عَلَيْكَ، وَنُثْنِي عَلَيْكَ الخَيْرَ كُلَّهُ، نَشْكُرُكَ وَلَا نَكْفُرُكَ، وَنَخْلَعُ وَنَتْرُكُ مَنْ

يَفْجُرُكَ، اللّهُمَّ إِيَّاكَ نَعْبُدُ وَلَكَ نُصَلِّي وَنَسْجُدُ وَإِلَيْكَ نَسْعى وَنَحْفِدُ، نَرْجُو رَحْمَتَكَ وَنَخْشى عَذابَكَ، إِنَّ عَذابَكَ الجِدَّ بِالكُفَّار مُلْحِقٌ

"O Allah! We seek Your help, Your guidance and ask Your forgiveness, and we repent to You, believe in You and trust in You. We praise You in the best way, and we thank You, and we are not ungrateful, and we avoid and leave whoever disobeys You. O Allah, You alone we serve and to You we pray and bow down before You. To You we turn quickly and hope for Your Mercy and fear Your punishment. Certainly Your punishment overtakes the unbelievers.'"

If this supplication has not been memorized yet, then a shorter one may be substituted until the longer one is committed to memory. The shorter one is as follows:

Our Lord! Give us the best in this life and the best in the next and protect us from the punishment of the fire. Surat Al Baqarah (The Cow) 2:201

﴿رَبَّنَآ ءَاتِنَا فِى ٱلدُّنْيَا حَسَنَةً وَفِى ٱلْأَخِرَةِ حَسَنَةً وَقِنَا عَذَابَ ٱلنَّارِ﴾ سُورَةُ ٱلْبَقَرَةِ 2:201

After the dua' has been said, say, Allahu Akbar again and go into sujood. Complete the prayer in the same manner you would complete the Maghrib Prayer.

The Blessed Prophet ﷺ said, "O you people of the Qur'an, perform the Witr prayer, for Allah is One and He Loves the Witr." (Agreed upon)

قَالَ رَسُولُ اللهِ ﷺ: «إِنَّ اللهَ وِتْرٌ يُحِبُّ الْوِتْرَ فَأَوْتِرُوا يَا أَهْلَ الْقُرْآنِ». مُتَّفَقٌ عَلَيْهِ

Salat Al Jumu'ah

Islam is a way of life that emphasizes the importance of the community. Therefore, one day out of every week, Muslims congregate for prayer and to hear a **Khutbah** خُطْبَة **Sermon** in which they are reminded of their duty to Allah ﷻ and to each other. This communal prayer, **Salat Al Jumu'ah** صَلَاةُ الْجُمُعَة **Friday Prayer**, occurs every Friday, replacing Thuhr Prayer, and is often held in a masjid.

Allah ﷻ says in the Qur'an, *O you who believe! When the call for Al Jumu'ah prayer is proclaimed, move quickly to the remembrance of Allah and leave off your business. This is best for you if you only knew. Then, when the prayer is finished, you may disperse throughout the land and seek the bounty of Allah. Celebrate the praise of Allah often so you will (really) prosper. Surat Al Jumu'ah (Friday) 62:9-10*

﴿يَٰٓأَيُّهَا ٱلَّذِينَ ءَامَنُوٓا۟ إِذَا نُودِيَ لِلصَّلَوٰةِ مِن يَوْمِ ٱلْجُمُعَةِ فَٱسْعَوْا۟ إِلَىٰ ذِكْرِ ٱللَّهِ وَذَرُوا۟ ٱلْبَيْعَ ذَٰلِكُمْ خَيْرٌ لَّكُمْ إِن كُنتُمْ تَعْلَمُونَ﴾ ﴿فَإِذَا قُضِيَتِ ٱلصَّلَوٰةُ فَٱنتَشِرُوا۟ فِى ٱلْأَرْضِ وَٱبْتَغُوا۟ مِن فَضْلِ ٱللَّهِ وَٱذْكُرُوا۟ ٱللَّهَ كَثِيرًا لَّعَلَّكُمْ تُفْلِحُونَ﴾ سُورَةُ ٱلْجُمُعَةِ 62:9-10

Attending Salat Al Jumu'ah is a duty upon all males over the age of puberty. It must be established in any location where there are at least three adult Muslim males. If any male does not offer this required Salah without a valid reason, it is counted as a sin against him. Only emergencies or extraordinary occurrences count as acceptable excuses.

The Blessed Prophet ﷺ warned that hypocrisy would start to enter the heart if one missed three Al Jumu'ah Prayers in a row. Even if the Muslim male has a job or business during the time of Al Jumu'ah, it is important to make one's employer or teacher aware of the importance of attending the prayer. If it is impossible to obtain permission to leave a job for Al Jumu'ah Prayer, then it may be advisable to find another job that would give you more flexibility and enable you to obey Allah ﷻ by attending this important prayer.

Women are strongly urged to attend Al Jumu'ah Prayer, as well. However, it is not fard upon them as women often have obligations at home. This is a mercy for them. Those women who cannot attend Al Jumu'ah Prayer can pray the normal Thuhr Prayer at home. Travelers, the mentally challenged and children are also exempt.

Because of some cultural traditions that are not Islamic, some Muslims think women should not pray in the masjid or participate in the greater Muslim community. It must be strongly noted that this attitude is incorrect.

Ibn 'Umar reported the Messenger of Allah ﷺ once remarked, "Do not prevent the female servants of Allah from coming to the masjid." (Agreed upon)

عَنِ ابْنِ عُمَرَ، قَالَ قَالَ رَسُولُ اللهِ ﷺ: «لَا تَمْنَعُوا إِمَاءَ اللهِ مَسَاجِدَ اللهِ». مُتَّفَقٌ عَلَيْهِ

Women must take part in the masjid. As evidenced by numerous reports during the time of the Prophet ﷺ, women were as active and as welcome as the men were. The women were so eager to learn and be involved in Muslim affairs that they petitioned the Blessed Prophet Muhammad ﷺ to set aside time for him to teach them exclusively.

The Prophet ﷺ agreed to this request, and set aside one day of the week for the exclusive education of the women, as quoted in the hadith collection of Al Bukhari. In addition, Muslim women were teachers, doctors and business owners as well as equals in political affairs, as evidenced by the fact that women and men both swore allegiance to the Prophet ﷺ.

Therefore, we can see that it is a duty upon all those who build and manage masaajid to fully accommodate for women in all levels of activity and leadership. It is interesting to note that there was no wall or partition separating men and women in the Prophet's ﷺ Masjid, as stated in numerous authentic reports. As men and women become better educated in Islam, they will mold their lives according to the authentic and true practices of the Blessed Messenger ﷺ, insha'Allah. Salat Al Jumu'ah consists of a set procedure. It is held at the time of Thuhr and is done in place of the Thuhr Prayer.

Those planning to attending Al Jumu'ah Prayer should make ghusl in the morning and wear clean clothes, cologne and/or fragrant oils. After the athan has been called, the congregation gathers in the masjid. Upon entering the masjid, it is recommended to say:

اللَّهُمَّ افتحْ لي أبوابَ رَحْمَتِك

"Allahumma aftahle abwaba rahmatika."
"O Allah, open the doors to me of Your Mercy."

Then, a normal two-rak'aat nafl prayer, called the Tahiyyat Al Masjid, can be offered. Afterwards, one quietly sits down and either reads Qur'an or makes thikr. After the first athan for Al Jumu'ah Prayer, a two- or four-rak'aat sunnah prayer can be performed.

The contract between the masjid and the male and female believers should be built on equality—just like the Prophet's ﷺ Masjid was.

When Salat Al Jumu'ah is about to begin, the **Khatib** خَطِيب **Speaker** will go to the front of the masjid and sit at the **Minbar** مِنبَر **Pulpit**, facing the people. He will give the greeting of peace, and the mu'athin will call the athan a second time. From the time the khatib sits at the minbar, no one should speak. To do so during the khutbah will cause the loss of the reward of entire Salah, as if you had never prayed it.

The khatib stands and delivers a short sermon on a topic of interest to the community. Within that sermon, he will remind the believers about their duty to Allah ﷻ and will enlighten them on some aspect of Islam or another related subject. The khutbah consists of two parts. The first usually lasts about twenty minutes or so. After the khatib has finished his first part, he sits down for a moment and quietly asks Allah ﷻ to forgive him. Then the khatib stands again to deliver a second, shorter speech of about 10 minutes. The second khutbah usually ends with dua' to Allah ﷻ. Then the khatib will ask the congregation to rise for prayer by saying:

أقِمِ الصَّلاة

"Ooqeemus Salah"
"Stand up for the prayer"

Everyone will arrange themselves in even and straight rows behind the **Imam** إِمَام **Prayer Leader**. The person who gives the khutbah most often acts as the imam as well. What follows is a normal two-rak'aat prayer in which the imam leads the congregation through the Salah. Surat Al Fatihah and other suwar are read aloud by the imam, with all others listening and following along silently. After the imam finishes the last ayah of Surat Al Fatihah in each rak'ah, everyone responds in one strong voice with **Ameen** آمِـــين.

Abu Hurayrah ﷺ said that the Prophet ﷺ said, "When the Imam says: 'Ghair-il-Maghdubi 'Alaihim Walad-Dallin (not the path of those who earn Your Anger, nor the path of those who went astray [1.7]), then you must say, 'Ameen,' for if one's utterance of 'Ameen' coincides with that of the angels, then his past sins will be forgiven." (Agreed upon)

عَنْ أَبِي هُرَيْرَةَ ﷺ أَنَّ رَسُولَ الله ﷺ قَالَ: «إِذَا أَمَّنَ الإِمَامُ فَأَمِّنُوا، فَإِنَّهُ مَنْ وَافَقَ تَأْمِينُهُ تَأْمِينَ الْمَلَائِكَةِ: غُفِرَ لَهُ مَا تَقَدَّمَ مِنْ ذَنْبِهِ». مُتَّفَقٌ عَلَيْهِ

Prayers in the masjid are worth more than a normal prayer at home. Therefore, it is strongly urged for every male Muslim to go to the masjid for as many group prayers as he can.

'Abdallah bin 'Umar ﷺ said, the Messenger of Allah ﷺ said, "Prayer in a congregation is worth more than twenty-seven prayers performed alone." (Agreed upon)

عَنْ عَبْدِ الله بْنِ عُمَرَ ﷺ: أَنَّ رَسُولَ الله ﷺ قَالَ: «صَلَاةُ الْجَمَاعَةِ أَفْضَلُ مِنْ صَلَاةِ الفَذِّ بِسَبْعٍ وَعِشْرِينَ دَرَجَةً». مُتَّفَقٌ عَلَيْهِ

When the Salah is finished, the people pray two or four rak'aat of sunnah prayer on their own and then go back to their homes or jobs. When leaving the masjid, it is recommended to say:

اللَّهُمَّ إِنِّي أَسْأَلُكَ مِنْ فَضْلِكَ

"Allahuma innee as-aluka min fadlika."
"O Allah, I seek your bounty."

The value and meaning of attending Al Jumu'ah Prayer cannot be overstated. If a person compromises prioritizes staying at work rather than attending the obligatory Al Jumu'ah Prayer, they have forgotten their duties as a Muslim. We are here to surrender our wills to Allah ﷻ, above all else.

Salat At-Tahajjud

From the earliest days of revelation, Allah﷾ instructed His Last Prophet ﷺ to pray at night as much as he could. Allah﷾ praised those people who left their warm and cozy beds to stand in devotion to their Lord. (32:16) He even gave the reason why prayer at night was good by saying that it is the best time to have clear thoughts and no distractions.

Truly, rising by night is most powerful for controlling (the soul), and most suitable for the words (of prayer). Certainly, you have, during the day, busy concerns to deal with. Surat Al Muzzammil (The Enshrouded One) 73:6-7

﴿إِنَّ نَاشِئَةَ ٱلَّيْلِ هِيَ أَشَدُّ وَطْئًا وَأَقْوَمُ قِيلًا﴾ ﴿إِنَّ لَكَ فِي ٱلنَّهَارِ سَبْحًا طَوِيلًا﴾ سُورَةُ الْمُزَّمِّل 6-7:73

Indeed, at night, the rest of the world is asleep and the darkness makes our home look like an unfamiliar place. The world does indeed appear different when it is veiled in faint moonlight. The prayers we make at this time also make us realize that our lives will end, and our souls will cross over into an other-world, a world quite unlike our own.

At-Tahajjud Prayer صَلَاةُ التَّهَجُّد **Night Prayer** is a sunnah for those who have the discipline to do them. It can be done at anytime during the midnight hours (from midnight until the time of Fajr) and does not have any set time requirements on the length of recitation or number of rak'aat.

It is performed as a series of two-rak'aat prayers done in the normal way. For example, a person can pray a two-rak'aat prayer, and then when it is completed, pray another two-rak'aat prayer, and so on, for as long as one wishes. Twelve rak'aat are the maximum number. The Blessed Prophet ﷺ often made eight rak'aat. It is recommended to sleep for part of the night before getting up to pray Tahajjud and then to sleep again afterwards until the time of Fajr.

The righteous are described as follows: *They were in the habit of sleeping only a little at night, and in the early hours of dawn they were found praying for forgiveness.* Surat At-Thaariyaat (The Winds that Scatter) 51:17-18

﴿كَانُوا قَلِيلًا مِّنَ ٱلَّيْلِ مَا يَهْجَعُونَ﴾ ﴿وَبِٱلْأَسْحَارِ هُمْ يَسْتَغْفِرُونَ﴾ سُورَةُ الذاريات 17-18:51

There is one recommendation about Tahajjud to take note of: it is better to make it a regular habit, not an occasional one. Consistency is the key if we want to draw the benefits of this practice.

Salat Al 'Eid

There are two holidays in the Islamic year. Each one of them is named the **'Eid** عيد **Festival**. The first 'Eid comes at the end of Ramadan, or the Month of Fasting, and the second comes at the end of Hajj, or the Pilgrimage. You will be learning more about these two great events in the coming chapters. 'Eid is a time of great joy and celebration. On the first day of 'Eid, Muslims gather for the special prayer known as Salat Al 'Eid.

There is no athan or iqamah for this prayer. Everyone should attend the 'Eid Prayer, which is held a half hour after sunrise (or later), wearing their best clothes and having made ghusl. Men are encouraged to wear a fragrance or cologne. Everyone should follow the Islamic guidelines of modesty, which means men should refrain from wearing any silk or gold, and women should cover themselves appropriately.

Everyone gathers at the appointed time and lines up for the Salah. The Prophet ﷺ urged everyone in the community to come to the place of the 'Eid celebration, regardless of whether or not they could participate in the prayer. That is so that they can share in the joyous occasion after the others have finished the Salah.

The 'Eid Prayer is performed just like a normal two-rak'aat prayer, except that there are several extra **Takbeer** تَكْبِير **Chants of "Allah is The Greatest"** in the first rak'ah and several extra takbeer in the second rak'ah. Most commonly, there are seven and five takbeer total in the first and second rak'aat, respectively.

After the prayer is finished, the people listen to a short two-part khutbah. When the khutbah concludes, everyone rises to greet and hug each other, wishing each other **'Eid Mubarak** عِيدٌ مُبَارَك **Blessed Holiday!** Then people disperse to family gatherings, parties, fairs, carnivals and other celebratory gatherings. Exchanging gifts among families and friends is also common. 'Eid is altogether the happiest time of year for Muslims!

Salat Al Janazah

When a child is born, it is recommended to gently recite the athan in its ear. This is a baby's welcome into the world. Similarly, when any Muslim dies, Islam has a method of bidding them farewell. This special ritual is known as **Salat Al Janazah** صَلاةُالجَنازَة **Funeral Prayer**.

It is a means whereby the living can remind themselves that the loss of a loved one is inevitable. More importantly, it is a reminder for Muslims that the deceased has crossed over into the next life and that we will follow one day.

After the body of the deceased has been ritually washed and wrapped in white cloth, the mourners gather for prayer. There is no athan or iqamah. Nor is there bowing or prostrating in this prayer. It is performed completely while standing. Everyone lines up in rows behind the imam who will lead the Salat Al Janazah. The niyyah should be said to one's self:

نَوَيْتُ صَلاةَ الجَنازَة

"Nuwaytus Salatul Janazah"

"I intend to pray Funeral Prayer."

The procedure for this prayer is simple. The imam says, **Allah is The Greatest** اللهُأَكْبَر, and everyone does the same. The hands are folded over the chest as normal. Then people recite to themselves Surat al Fatihah. Then the imam says, **Allah is The Greatest** اللهُأَكْبَر again, and everyone recites As-Salat al Ibrahimiyya to themselves. The imam says, **Allah is The Greatest** اللهُأَكْبَر a third time, and then everyone recites a small prayer for the deceased. The following prayer is recited for,

اللهُمَّ اغْفِرْ لِحَيِّنا وَمَيِّتِنا، وشاهِدِنا وغائِبِنا، وصَغيرِنا و كَبيرِنا، وذَكَرِنا وأَنْثانا

"Allahumma aghfir leehayyina wa mayyitana,

wa shahidina wa gha'ibina, wa saghirina wa kabirina, wa dhakarina wa unthana."

"O Allah! Forgive our living and our dead: those among us who are present and those who are absent, our young and our old, our males and our females."

Then the next part is said,

اللهُمَّ مَنْ أَحْيَيْتَهُ مِنّا فَأَحْيِهِ عَلى الإسْلام، ومَنْ تَوَفَّيْتَهُ مِنّا فَتَوَفَّهُ عَلى الإيمان

"Allahumma man ahyaitahu minna fa ah yihi 'alal Islam,

wa man tawaffaitahu minna fa tawaffahu 'alal Iman."

"O Allah! Those among us whom You keep alive, keep them alive in Islam. Those among us whom you cause to die, let them die in a state of faith."

Then the imam says, **Allah is The Greatest** اللهُأَكْبَر one last time and then turns his face to the right and says, **Peace and blessings and the Mercy of Allah be upon you** السَّلامُ عَلَيْكُم ورَحْمَةُاللهِ وبَرَكاتُه "Assalamu 'alaykum wa Rahmatullah wa Barakato." Then he turns his face to the left and says the same, completing Salat Al Janazah. Everyone follows the imam. It is customary to visit the families of the deceased and offer words of condolence and support. Loud or excessive crying is forbidden because we should strive to be patient during these difficult times. Death is a part of life as much as for the families of the deceased as for us. We must mourn Islamically and with dignity.

The Prayer of the Traveler

A person traveling on a journey may combine some prayers and shorten them as well. The simple rule is that, while traveling, every four-rak'aat Salah is shortened to two rak'aat only. *(Qasr, see 4:101)* In addition, the Thuhr and 'Asr Salah can be combined either at Thuhr or 'Asr time, depending on your traveling schedule. The same applies for the 'Isha and Maghrib Salah. You can also offer Salah if you're sitting on a plane, riding a horse or in a car while traveling. Just make the movements as you sit. If your vehicle turns away from the Qiblah while you're praying, the prayer is still valid, as you cannot always control the direction of your transportation.

When you travel on the earth, there is no sin on you in shortening your Salah, 49 if you fear that the disbelievers would put you in trouble. Surely, the disbelievers are an open enemy for you. Surat An-Nisa' (The Women) 4: 101

﴿وَإِذَا ضَرَبْتُمْ فِي الْأَرْضِ فَلَيْسَ عَلَيْكُمْ جُنَاحٌ أَن تَقْصُرُوا مِنَ الصَّلَوٰةِ إِنْ خِفْتُمْ أَن يَفْتِنَكُمُ الَّذِينَ كَفَرُوا إِنَّ الْكَافِرِينَ كَانُوا لَكُمْ عَدُوًّا مُّبِينًا﴾ سُورَة

النِّساء 4: 101

Introduction

To round out your knowledge of Salah, it is necessary to detail some essential parts of knowing how to pray. The topics that will be discussed in this lesson are: how to make up for mistakes in your prayer while still in the act of prayer, how to line up in a group prayer, what breaks your Salah and how to join a group prayer that has already started.

Sajdat As-Sahu

We are only human. Even though we did our wudu' and stood up for Salah, it doesn't mean that we are freed from making mistakes. Though we have sunnah Salah to give us a cushion in our prayer record, it is still possible to make mistakes within our regular Salah that can make the entire Salah void. For example, what if you stand up immediately after the second sajdah in the second rak'ah, when you should have sat in jalsa for a moment and recited the At-Tahiyyat? What if you forgot which rak'ah you were in and couldn't remember if it was the third or fourth? What if you forgot that no surat is recited after Al Fatihah in the third and fourth rak'ah? How do we salvage our Salah and fix our errors?

There is an easy and useful technique called **Sajdat As-Sahu** سَجْدَةُ السَّهْو **Prostration of Forgetfulness** that is a way for us to correct the shortcomings in our prayer that occur when our minds wander and we make mistakes. The way Sajdat As-Sahu is performed is simple. It consists of two sajdah. When you think you are in the last rak'ah of your prayer, you might realize you made some kind of serious mistake, such as one of those mentioned in the previous paragraphs. After finishing the prayer and saying, "Assalamu 'alaykum wa Rahmatullah wa Barakato" to each side. Merely say, "Allah is The Greatest" and proceed with the two sajdah.

Lining Up for Salah

Salah is an individual as well as a group experience. If one prays alone, at home or anywhere else, you only have to worry about yourself. When people gather for a **Jama'ah** جَمَاعَة **Congregational** prayer, there are specific steps which must be followed to ensure that it is organized and runs smoothly.

Whenever Salah is performed in jama'ah, one person will act as the imam. This person is responsible for the proper performance of the Salah of the group. There is a great reward for him because of the great responsibility.

The Blessed Prophet Muhammad ﷺ personally taught us how to line up properly. In numerous reports, the Sahaba have said that he would spend a considerable amount of time making sure that everyone was lined up properly. Let's explore the methodology he taught us. In a typical Salah, the

Your mind may wander to something else besides your Salah.

people will make even rows parallel to the Qiblah. The imam will stand in a row by himself in front of the first row of people.

It was narrated that Abu Hurayrah ﷺ said that the Messenger of Allah ﷺ said, *"The best rows for men are in the first rows and the worst rows for men are in the last rows. The best rows for women are in the last rows and the worst rows for women are in the first rows."* (Al Bukhari)

عَنْ أَبِي هُرَيْرَةَ ﷺ أَنَّ رَسُولَ الله ﷺ قَالَ: «خَيْرُ صُفُوفِ الرِّجَالِ أَوَّلُهَا وَشَرُّهَا آخِرُهَا وَخَيْرُ صُفُوفِ النِّسَاءِ آخِرُهَا وَشَرُّهَا أَوَّلُهَا». رَوَاهُ الْبُخَارِيُّ

Men and women are separated during prayer in order to aid concentration and maintain modesty. The normal desire in all of us is to look at the opposite sex, thereby losing focus on Allah ﷻ. This desire easily increases if the genders are mixed together.

The proper order of congregation is as follows: The imam is in the first row alone. The men line up in the rows after him until you have a row with the young boys who are entering puberty. Small children fill the next rows, boys then girls, and finally the women make up the back rows. Everyone earns the same reward, and there is no discrimination in the sight of Allah ﷻ either for men in the first row or women in the last row. They are both the best rows for those who seek the pleasure of Allah ﷻ.

If a congregation is made up entirely of women, then one of the women will act as the imam. She will stand in the middle of the first row of women, with the younger women and then the children lined up behind them. She will lead the women through the movements of the Salah just like a male imam. The same responsibility for the proper performance of Salah is upon both men and women imams. Refer to the diagrams to clearly see how to line up properly.

One final note: if there are not enough people to fill up a row, the people in the short row should center their row in relation to the imam. When a space opens up in a row ahead of you, someone should step forward and fill it. There should be no gaps in any rows, as the Blessed Prophet ﷺ once warned that Shaytan creeps in between the gaps in the rows. That's a figure of speech, reminding us of importance of standing together in unity and support.

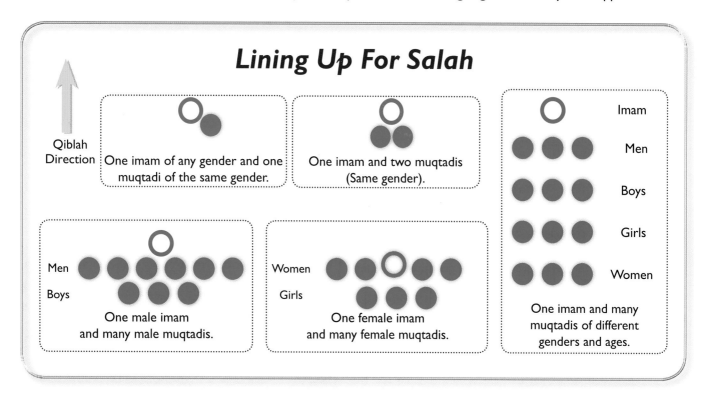

Lining Up For Salah

Qiblah Direction

One imam of any gender and one muqtadi of the same gender.

One imam and two muqtadis (Same gender).

Imam
Men
Boys
Girls
Women

One male imam and many male muqtadis.

One female imam and many female muqtadis.

One imam and many muqtadis of different genders and ages.

What Nullifies Salah?

There are ways to make up for mistakes made in performing your Salah, either through sunnah prayer or Sajdat As-Sahu. Sunnah prayer makes up the errors we don't know about and Sajdat As-Sahu makes up the errors we know about. Refer to those previous sections for the particulars. There are some actions that are so serious that they render your Salah void. In such a case, the entire Salah will have to be re-done. The factors which nullify Salah are:

Forgetting to make your niyyah. If you made no intention for prayer, how can what you're doing be counted for anything?

1. Forgetting to say, "Allahu Akbar" when you begin.
2. Forgetting to recite Surat Al Fatihah in any rak'ah. The Prophet ﷺ said, There is no prayer without Al Fatihah. (Agreed upon)
3. Forgetting to make a required ruku' or sajdah.
4. Turning your body (the shoulders) away from the direction of the Qiblah.
5. Breaking your wudu'.
6. Talking.
7. Laughing.
8. Eating or drinking.
9. Forgetting saying the second Tashahud.
10. Doing anything or acting in any way outside of the prescribed actions of Salah.

If any of the above occur while making Salah, then the Salah is considered broken and will not count for you. Making Sajdat As-Sahu is not sufficient to correct these mistakes. You will have to offer your prayer completely again.

How Do I Join a Group Prayer Late?

We should all take care to arrive on time for any event. It is a practice, or sunnah, in Islam to be very punctual. But what if you happen to accidentally arrive late and the congregation has already begun the prayer? How do you join the group, and what do you have to do when the Salah is over? Joining a group late is not wrong and not difficult. Walk (don't run!) to take a place in the row. Stand facing the Qiblah, make your niyyah for that Salah, raise your hands up normally, and recite the, Takbeerat Al Ihram الله أكبر Allah is The Greatest quietly. Then assume the position the group is in and follow along as if you started with them from the beginning.

For example, if you came in and saw that group in sajdah, you say, "Allah is The Greatest الله أكبر" and make sajdah as well. Yet, the issue of performing a complete rak'ah then enters into the equation. If you joined the jama'ah after they had already completed one or more rak'ah, then you must make-up those rak'aat in the end. Here is how it is done:

If you joined in the second rak'ah of a four-rak'aat prayer, you assume it is your first rak'ah, even though you have to follow along with everyone else until they have finished. When the imam finishes saying, "Peace and blessings and the mercy of Allah - Assalamu 'alaykum wa Rahmatullah wa Barakato," to his right, you don't follow him; instead, continue looking forward. When he says the salaam to the left, you merely say, "Allah is The Greatest الله أكبر" to yourself, then stand and make up for the rak'aat that you missed.

The same procedure works no matter how many rak'ah you missed. What is the cut-off point for whether you missed a rak'ah or not? It is the rising of the back after ruku'. In other words, if you joined a prayer late and everyone was still in ruku', then you do not have to make up that particular rak'ah.

If you join a prayer late in the last rak'ah and the back was already raised, then you follow along until the end. You will then have to repeat all the rak'aat that you missed, as if you are starting the prayer from the beginning. All the normal Salah requirements apply from your personal starting point, whether it be in ruku', jalsa or sajdah.

Making up Missed Rak'aat: An Example with Salat At-Thuhr.

A group performed these rak'aat.

...1st Rak'ah...|...2nd Rak'ah...||..Jalsa..||...3rd Rak'ah...|...4th Rak'ah...||..Jalsa..||... End

You missed the first rak'ah and joined in the second.

...1st Rak'ah...||..Jalsa..||...2nd Rak'ah...|...3rd Rak'ah.....||..Jalsa..||......Stand...|...4th Rak'ah...|...||..Jalsa..||... End

For you   Pause while
              In Jalsa

> **Remember:** Whatever rak'ah you join in is your first rak'ah. So when the group prayer is over, you still have to make up the missing number of rak'aat that are required to complete that prayer.

Why Should I Praise Allah?

Islam teaches us that one of the best things we can ever do is to praise Allah. The word **Tasbeeh** تَسْبِيح **Praise** means to say wonderful things about someone or something to show how excellent they are. Praising Allah keeps us humble and reminds us that only Allah is Great.

Allah says in the Qur'an that every creature in the world praises Him in its own way. If you remember, all the plants and animals follow their instincts in their daily life. By living the way they are supposed to, these creatures are actually praising Allah. All the birds, squirrels, fish, bugs and trees always praise Allah. They are all perfect Muslims and have already surrendered to Allah.

Allah gave us Salah as a way to remember Him. It is also a way to have some of our bad deeds forgiven. In addition to Salah, there is another level of activity that can bring us closer to Allah. If we really love Allah and want to express our affection, then we should also say words to glorify our Creator. The word 'glorify' also means the same thing as praise.

All that is in the heaven and on earth praise Allah.

Abu Hurairah reported the Messenger of Allah said, "Allah says, 'I am near My servant when he thinks of Me and I am with him when he remembers Me. If he remembers Me to himself, then I remember him to Myself. If he remembers me in a gathering, then I remember him in a better gathering than his. If he comes an arm's length closer to Me, I come a yard's length closer to him. If he comes to Me walking, I go to him in a rush.'" (Bukhari)

عَنْ أَبِي هُرَيْرَةَ أنه قال: قال رَسُولَ اللهِ : «يَقُولُ اللهُ تَعَالَى: أَنَا عِنْدَ ظَنِّ عَبْدِي بِي وَأَنَا مَعَهُ حِينَ يَذْكُرُنِي، فَإِنْ ذَكَرَنِي فِي نَفْسِهِ ذَكَرْتُهُ فِي نَفْسِي، وَإِنْ ذَكَرَنِي فِي مَلَإٍ ذَكَرْتُهُ فِي مَلَإٍ خَيْرٍ مِنْهُمْ، وَإِنِ اقْتَرَبَ إِلَيَّ شِبْرًا اقْتَرَبْتُ مِنْهُ ذِرَاعاً، وَإِنِ اقْتَرَبَ إِلَيَّ ذِرَاعاً اقْتَرَبْتُ إِلَيْهِ بَاعاً، وَإِنْ أَتَانِي يَمْشِي أَتَيْتُهُ هَرْوَلَةً». رواه البخاري

So when we remember Allah, He will remember us. The Blessed Prophet Muhammad taught us many beautiful phrases we can say to praise Allah. We can say them after our Salah is finished, or in the morning, on a bus or anywhere we want to. We don't need wudu' and we can even use our own words if we want to. Many Muslims like to say words of praise that the Prophet taught because he said them in such a beautiful way. Let's learn a few of these words of **Thikr** ذِكْر **Remembering Allah** and how they can help us.

Phrases of Thikr

Abu Hurairah reported the Messenger of Allah said, "Whoever says, 'Glory to Allah and His is all Praise,' one hundred times will get all his or her sins forgiven even if they were as much as the foam in the sea." (Muslim)

عَنْ أَبِي هُرَيْرَةَ أنه قال: قال رَسُولَ اللهِ : «مَنْ قَالَ: سُبْحَانَ اللهِ وَبِحَمْدِهِ فِي يَوْمٍ مِائَةَ مَرَّةٍ حُطَّتْ خَطَايَاهُ وَإِنْ كَانَتْ مِثْلَ زَبَدِ الْبَحْرِ». رواه مسلم

Abu Musa Ash'ari reported that Allah's Messenger said to him: "'Abdallah, should I point out to you a treasure from the treasures of Paradise?' 'Abdallah replied, 'Yes, Messenger of Allah. Please tell me.' The Prophet answered, 'Say this phrase, There is no might or power except with Allah.'" (Bukhari)

عَنْ أَبِي مُوسَى الْأَشْعَرِيِّ قَالَ: قَالَ رَسُولُ اللهِ : «يَا عَبْدَ اللهِ بْنَ قَيْسٍ، أَلَا أَدُلُّكَ عَلَى كَنْزٍ مِنْ كُنُوزِ الْجَنَّةِ فَقُلْتُ: بَلَى يَا رَسُولَ اللهِ قَالَ: قُلْ لَا حَوْلَ وَلَا قُوَّةَ إِلَّا بِاللهِ». رواه البخاري

Samurah bin Jundub narrated that the Messenger of Allah said, "Here are some sentences that Allah likes the most. They are SubhanAllah (Glory to Allah), Al hamdulillah (Praise be to Allah),

La ilaha ill Allah (There is no God but Allah) and Allahu Akbar (Allah is Great). You can say them in any order you want." (Muslim)

عَنْ سَمُرَةَ بْنِ جُنْدُبٍ ﷺ قَالَ :قَالَ رَسُولُ اللهِ ﷺ :«أَحَبُّ الْكَلَامِ إِلَى اللهِ أَرْبَعٌ: سُبْحَانَ اللهِ، وَالْحَمْدُ لِلهِ، وَلَا إِلَهَ إِلَّا اللهُ، وَاللهُ أَكْبَرُ. لَا يَضُرُّكَ بِأَيِّهِنَّ بَدَأْتَ». رَوَاهُ مُسْلِمٌ

"SubhanAllah,
Al hamdulillah,
Allahu Akbar."

There is a phrase that is light on the tongue, the Prophet ﷺ said, "Two words are light on the tongue, heavy in the balance, beloved to the Merciful: 'Glory be to Allah and by His praise. Glory be to Allah, the Immense.'" (Bukhari)

عَنْ أَبِي هُرَيْرَةَ ﷺ أَنَّهُ قَالَ: قَالَ رَسُولُ اللهِ ﷺ : «كَلِمَتَانِ خَفِيفَتَانِ عَلَى اللِّسَانِ ثَقِيلَتَانِ فِي الْمِيزَانِ حَبِيبَتَانِ إِلَى الرَّحْمَنِ: سُبْحَانَ اللهِ، وَبِحَمْدِهِ سُبْحَانَ اللهِ الْعَظِيمِ» رَوَاهُ الْبُخَارِيُّ

Praising and remembering Allah ﷻ, or thikr, is so important that the Prophet ﷺ once said, "When a group of people sits together and makes thikr, the angels surround them, peace comes over them, Allah's mercy covers them and Allah speaks to the angels that are near Him (about the group)." (Muslim)

عَنْ أَبِي هُرَيْرَةَ وَأَبِي سَعِيدٍ الْخُدْرِيِّ ﷺ أَنَّهُمَا شَهِدَا عَلَى النَّبِيِّ ﷺ أَنَّهُ قَالَ: «لَا يَقْعُدُ قَوْمٌ يَذْكُرُونَ اللهَ عَزَّ وَجَلَّ إِلَّا حَفَّتْهُمُ الْمَلَائِكَةُ وَغَشِيَتْهُمُ الرَّحْمَةُ وَنَزَلَتْ عَلَيْهِمُ السَّكِينَةُ وَذَكَرَهُمُ اللهُ فِيمَنْ عِنْدَهُ». رَوَاهُ مُسْلِمٌ

Many Muslims remember Allah ﷻ in large gatherings and make thikr in a group. Other people praise Allah ﷻ alone or silently. Whichever way you like to do it, always remember Allah ﷻ everyday with special words of praise. Let's make it our goal to think about Allah ﷻ often and when we do, to say some words that praise and glorify Him.

Remember Me and I will remember you. Be grateful to Me and reject not Faith. Surat Al Baqarah (The Cow) 2:152

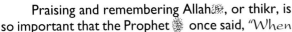

﴿فَاذْكُرُونِي أَذْكُرْكُمْ وَاشْكُرُوا لِي وَلَا تَكْفُرُونِ﴾ سُورَةُ الْبَقَرَةِ 152:2

What Is Dua'?

So far, we have learned about Salah and thikr. There is one more way to make our connection to Allah ﷻ strong and meaningful in our lives. This is making **Dua' دعاء to Call on Someone**. Allah ﷻ said in the Qur'an, When My servants ask about Me, I am indeed close. I listen to the request of every person when he or she calls on Me. So let people listen to My call also and believe in Me, so they can be rightly guided. Surat Al Baqarah (The Cow) 2:186

﴿وَإِذَا سَأَلَكَ عِبَادِي عَنِّي فَإِنِّي قَرِيبٌ أُجِيبُ دَعْوَةَ الدَّاعِ إِذَا دَعَانِ فَلْيَسْتَجِيبُوا لِي وَلْيُؤْمِنُوا بِي لَعَلَّهُمْ يَرْشُدُونَ﴾ سُورَةُ الْبَقَرَةِ 186:2

How do we make dua'? How do we call on Allah ﷻ? This is also an easy thing to do and it doesn't require wudu' either. All you need to do is raise your hands in front of you like you were going to receive something from someone and then ask Allah ﷻ for whatever you like. You can ask Allah ﷻ in any language, not just in Arabic, and you can use your own words or some of the beautiful dua' that Allah ﷻ taught us in the Qur'an. What should we ask Allah ﷻ for?

You can always make dua' for personal reasons. For example, if your mother is sick, you can ask Allah ﷻ to make her healthy again. Or you can ask Allah ﷻ to help you do well in your school. In addition, we can ask for Allah's ﷻ forgiveness for our bad deeds and sins. We can ask for Allah's ﷻ help in a tough time or before we perform a difficult task. We can thank Allah ﷻ for something good that happened and ask Allah ﷻ to help us get through a bad time. We can even just talk to Allah ﷻ about our feelings if we like to because He said, He hears every dua' we say and that He is near.

Don't shy away from Allah ﷻ. As long as what you are asking for is not forbidden or evil, He will listen to you. Of course, Allah ﷻ knows best and sometimes what you think is bad for you might actually be better for you. So even if you don't get what you want, don't ever get discouraged about seeking Allah's help in anything else.

Here are some of the beautiful dua' that Allah taught us in the Qur'an. Try to learn them in Arabic, English or both, and recite them any time you would like. We need Allah, so let's not neglect the One Who can help us more than anyone else in the world. The following three dua' are taken from the Holy Qur'an,

Our Lord, give us the best in this life and the best in the next and protect us from the punishment of the fire. Surat Al Baqarah (The Cow) 2:201

﴿رَبَّنَآ ءَاتِنَا فِي ٱلدُّنْيَا حَسَنَةً وَفِي ٱلْآخِرَةِ حَسَنَةً وَقِنَا عَذَابَ ٱلنَّارِ﴾ سُورَةُ الْبَقَرَةِ 2:201

Our Lord, don't let our hearts go wrong after You've guided us. Give us mercy from You because You are the One Who gives endlessly. Surat Al 'Imran (Family of 'Imran) 3:8

﴿رَبَّنَا لَا تُزِغْ قُلُوبَنَا بَعْدَ إِذْ هَدَيْتَنَا وَهَبْ لَنَا مِن لَّدُنكَ رَحْمَةً إِنَّكَ أَنتَ ٱلْوَهَّابُ﴾ سُورَةُ آلِ عِمْرَان 3:8

Our Lord, we believe, so forgive us our sins and save us from the punishment of the fire. Surat Al 'Imran (Family of 'Imran) 3:16

﴿ٱلَّذِينَ يَقُولُونَ رَبَّنَآ إِنَّنَآ ءَامَنَّا فَٱغْفِرْ لَنَا ذُنُوبَنَا وَقِنَا عَذَابَ ٱلنَّارِ﴾ سُورَةُ آلِ عِمْرَان 3:16

There is another dua' from the Qur'an that is very long, but it is also very beautiful. You can find it in Surah 3, ayaat 26-27 and 29-30. Look them up and read them aloud and remember your Lord as much as you can!

How Is Dua' Answered?

Allah has promised to hear our dua'. How are they answered? Allah has said in the Qur'an that He will help us if we are sincere. If we say our dua' with no sincerity, how can we expect to be helped?

When trouble touches a person, he cries to Us (Allah) lying down, sitting or standing. But when We have solved his problem, he passes on his way, as if he never called on Us while in trouble! Surat Yunus (Jonah) 10:12

﴿وَإِذَا مَسَّ ٱلْإِنسَـٰنَ ٱلضُّرُّ دَعَانَا لِجَنۢبِهِۦٓ أَوْ قَاعِدًا أَوْ قَآئِمًا فَلَمَّا كَشَفْنَا عَنْهُ ضُرَّهُۥ مَرَّ كَأَن لَّمْ يَدْعُنَآ إِلَىٰ ضُرٍّ مَّسَّهُۥ كَذَٰلِكَ زُيِّنَ لِلْمُسْرِفِينَ مَا كَانُوا۟ يَعْمَلُونَ﴾ سُورَةُ يُونُس 10:12

Tell people, If you love Allah, then follow me (the Prophet). Allah will love you and forgive you your sins because Allah is the Forgiving and the Kind. Then tell them, Obey Allah and His Messenger.' But if (people) turn away, then know that Allah doesn't love those who cover up (the truth). Surat Al 'Imran (Family of 'Imran) 3:31-32

﴿قُلْ إِن كُنتُمْ تُحِبُّونَ ٱللَّهَ فَٱتَّبِعُونِي يُحْبِبْكُمُ ٱللَّهُ وَيَغْفِرْ لَكُمْ ذُنُوبَكُمْ وَٱللَّهُ غَفُورٌ رَّحِيمٌ﴾ ﴿قُلْ أَطِيعُوا۟ ٱللَّهَ وَٱلرَّسُولَ فَإِن تَوَلَّوْا۟ فَإِنَّ ٱللَّهَ لَا يُحِبُّ ٱلْكَـٰفِرِينَ﴾ سُورَةُ آلِ عِمْرَان 3:31-32

If we are sincere and call on Allah in both good times and bad, then we become more deserving of Allah's special favors. Everything happens for a reason and only Allah knows the reason. Allah has said He will answer the call of the sincere, but how is the answer given to us?

"Allahumma...."

Man does not weary of asking for good (things), but if ill touches him, he gives up all hope (and) is lost in despair. When we give him a taste of some Mercy from ourselves, after some adversity has touched him, he is sure to say, "This is due to my (merit): I think not that the Hour (of Judgment) will (ever) be established; but if I am brought back to my Lord, I have (much) good (stored) in His sight!" But We will show the Unbelievers the truth of all that they did and We shall give them the taste of a severe Penalty. When We bestow favors on man, he turns away and gets himself remote on his side (instead of coming to Us); and when evil seizes him, (he comes) full of prolonged prayer! Say: See if the (Revelation) is (really) from Allah and yet you reject it? Who is more astray than one who is in a schism far (from any purpose)? Surat Fussilat (Explained in Detail) 41:49-52

﴿لَا يَسْـَٔمُ ٱلْإِنسَـٰنُ مِن دُعَآءِ ٱلْخَيْرِ وَإِن مَّسَّهُ ٱلشَّرُّ فَيَـُٔوسٌ قَنُوطٌ۞ وَلَئِنْ أَذَقْنَـٰهُ رَحْمَةً مِّنَّا مِنۢ بَعْدِ ضَرَّآءَ مَسَّتْهُ لَيَقُولَنَّ هَـٰذَا لِى وَمَآ أَظُنُّ ٱلسَّاعَةَ قَآئِمَةً وَلَئِن رُّجِعْتُ إِلَىٰ رَبِّىٓ إِنَّ لِى عِندَهُۥ لَلْحُسْنَىٰ فَلَنُنَبِّئَنَّ ٱلَّذِينَ كَفَرُواْ بِمَا عَمِلُواْ وَلَنُذِيقَنَّهُم مِّنْ عَذَابٍ غَلِيظٍ۞ وَإِذَآ أَنْعَمْنَا عَلَى ٱلْإِنسَـٰنِ أَعْرَضَ وَنَـَٔا بِجَانِبِهِۦ وَإِذَا مَسَّهُ ٱلشَّرُّ فَذُو دُعَآءٍ عَرِيضٍ۞ قُلْ أَرَءَيْتُمْ إِن كَانَ مِنْ عِندِ ٱللَّهِ ثُمَّ كَفَرْتُم بِهِۦ مَنْ أَضَلُّ مِمَّنْ هُوَ فِى شِقَاقٍۭ بَعِيدٍ﴾ سُورَةُفُصِّلَت 52-49:41

     Allah said that He will help us in ways we won't even expect. This means that He will answer our sincere dua' but that we don't always see how this is done. Perhaps most of our dua' will be answered without our ever knowing it. Remember to always call on Allah; He answers your prayers.

You don't know that maybe Allah might bring out a new situation. Surat Al Talaq (The Divorce) 65:1

﴿لَا تَدْرِى لَعَلَّ ٱللَّهَ يُحْدِثُ بَعْدَ ذَٰلِكَ أَمْرًا﴾ سُورَةُالطَّلَاق 1:65

For those who fear Allah, He always prepares a way out. Surat Al Talaq (The Divorce) 65:2

﴿وَمَن يَتَّقِ ٱللَّهَ يَجْعَل لَّهُۥ مَخْرَجًا﴾ سُورَةُالطَّلَاق 2:65

O men! Call to mind the grace of Allah unto you! Is there a creator, other than Allah, to give you sustenance from heaven or earth? There is no God but He: how then are you deluded away from the Truth? Surat Al Faatir (The Originator) 35:2-3

﴿مَّا يَفْتَحِ ٱللَّهُ لِلنَّاسِ مِن رَّحْمَةٍ فَلَا مُمْسِكَ لَهَا وَمَا يُمْسِكْ فَلَا مُرْسِلَ لَهُۥ مِنۢ بَعْدِهِۦ وَهُوَ ٱلْعَزِيزُ ٱلْحَكِيمُ۞ يَـٰٓأَيُّهَا ٱلنَّاسُ ٱذْكُرُواْ نِعْمَتَ ٱللَّهِ عَلَيْكُمْ هَلْ مِنْ خَـٰلِقٍ غَيْرُ ٱللَّهِ يَرْزُقُكُم مِّنَ ٱلسَّمَآءِ وَٱلْأَرْضِ لَآ إِلَـٰهَ إِلَّا هُوَ فَأَنَّىٰ تُؤْفَكُونَ﴾ سُورَةُفاطِر 3-2:35

Abu Hurairah reported the Messenger of Allah said, "Your prayers will be answered unless you are in a hurry or have no patience." (Bukhari)

عَنْ أَبِي هُرَيْرَةَ أَنَّ رَسُولَ اللهِ قَالَ:
«يُسْتَجَابُ لِأَحَدِكُمْ مَا لَمْ يَعْجَلْ يَقُولُ دَعَوْتُ فَلَمْ يُسْتَجَبْ لِي». رَوَاهُ الْبُخَارِيُّ

Some people asked what it meant to be in a hurry. The Prophet explained that those who are in a hurry are the people who always complain that their prayers are not being answered. Remember that Allah promised to answer the prayers of the sincere. Sometimes prayers are answered and we don't even know it. Other times, what we ask for may not be the best for us in the long run.

Chapter 8
Other Practices and Duties

What Is Zakah?

Among the most important teachings of Islam is the practice of Zakah. It is second in importance only to Salah, and is the Third Pillar of Islam. In many places in the Qur'an, Zakah is mentioned within the same ayah as Salah.

And establish prayer, and give Zakah, and bow down with those who bow down. Surat Al Baqarah 2:43

﴿وَأَقِيمُوا۟ ٱلصَّلَوٰةَ وَءَاتُوا۟ ٱلزَّكَوٰةَ وَٱرْكَعُوا۟ مَعَ ٱلرَّٰكِعِينَ﴾ سُورَةُ البَقَرَة 2:43

The word **Zakah** زَكاة is usually translated as 'charity,' but the word literally means "to make pure." How is this connected with the idea of charity? Quite simply, the world and everything in it has the potential to distract us from our primary mission: to surrender ourselves to Allah. (3:92) Therefore, when we are required to let go of some of our worldly possessions, we are able to refocus on Allah. (2:274)

You who believe! Don't let your riches or your children divert you from the remembrance of Allah. If anyone does that, then the loss is their own. Surat Al Munaafiqoon (The Hypocrites) 63:9

﴿يَـٰٓأَيُّهَا ٱلَّذِينَ ءَامَنُوا۟ لَا تُلْهِكُمْ أَمْوَٰلُكُمْ وَلَآ أَوْلَـٰدُكُمْ عَن ذِكْرِ ٱللَّهِ وَمَن يَفْعَلْ ذَٰلِكَ فَأُو۟لَـٰٓئِكَ هُمُ ٱلْخَـٰسِرُونَ﴾ سُورَةُ المُنَافِقُون 63:9

By giving some of our wealth, we cleanse, or purify, our soul. (92:18) The forces of greed are put in check. The spirit of Islam is at its best when we learn to give freely for Allah's sake. In the Qur'an, Zakah sometimes is called **Sadaqah** صَدَقَة; its general meaning indicates voluntary charity. Zakah is a required duty upon us, while sadaqah is a praiseworthy activity that will gain us extra merit in our records.

The believers, men and women, are protectors of each other. They call to the good and forbid the wrong. They establish Salah, pay the Zakah, and obey Allah and His Messenger. Allah will pour His mercy on them for Allah is Powerful and Wise. Surat At-Tawbah (The Repentance) 9:71

﴿وَٱلْمُؤْمِنُونَ وَٱلْمُؤْمِنَـٰتُ بَعْضُهُمْ أَوْلِيَآءُ بَعْضٍ يَأْمُرُونَ بِٱلْمَعْرُوفِ وَيَنْهَوْنَ عَنِ ٱلْمُنكَرِ وَيُقِيمُونَ ٱلصَّلَوٰةَ وَيُؤْتُونَ ٱلزَّكَوٰةَ وَيُطِيعُونَ ٱللَّهَ وَرَسُولَهُۥٓ أُو۟لَـٰٓئِكَ سَيَرْحَمُهُمُ ٱللَّهُ إِنَّ ٱللَّهَ عَزِيزٌ حَكِيمٌ﴾ سُورَةُ التَّوبَة 9:71

Who Must Pay Zakah?

Those who meet the following criteria are required to give 2.5% of his or her wealth as Zakah:
1. Muslim.
2. Sane.
3. Past the age of maturity.
4. Owns **Nisaab** نِصاب **Minimum Amount of Wealth** (a value equal to about three ounces of gold).
5. Has nisaab for an entire year.
6. Has met his or her expenses.
7. Free of debt.

Zakah should be paid to the Islamic government for distribution to those who deserve it. In the absence of an Islamic government, it is better to give the Zakah to Islamic institutions such as masaajid or charitable organizations to distribute it. Examples of those who should receive Zakah are:
1. The poor.
2. The needy.
3. Those whose hearts are to be reconciled to Islam.
4. People in debt.

5. Stranded travelers.
6. Freed slaves.
7. People who collect Zakah funds.
8. Those who strive in the path of Allah.

The Sadaqat (prescribed alms) are (meant) only to be given to the poor, the needy, to those employed to collect them, to those whose hearts are to be won, in the cause of the slaves and those encumbered with debt, in the way of Allah and to a wayfarer. This is an obligation prescribed by Allah. Allah is All-Knowing, Wise.
Surat At-Tawbah (The Repentance) 9:60

﴿إِنَّمَا ٱلصَّدَقَٰتُ لِلۡفُقَرَآءِ وَٱلۡمَسَٰكِينِ وَٱلۡعَٰمِلِينَ عَلَيۡهَا وَٱلۡمُؤَلَّفَةِ قُلُوبُهُمۡ وَفِي ٱلرِّقَابِ وَٱلۡغَٰرِمِينَ وَفِي سَبِيلِ ٱللَّهِ وَٱبۡنِ ٱلسَّبِيلِۖ فَرِيضَةً مِّنَ ٱللَّهِۗ وَٱللَّهُ عَلِيمٌ حَكِيمٌ﴾ سُورَةُ التَّوۡبَة ٩:٦٠

As a rule, Zakah money should be spent in the local area first, where the donating community lives, and should be collected by local Muslims appointed for that task. Zakah, when it is distributed, should never be done in a way that makes the recipients feel humiliated, for as Allah says, *Kind words are better than charity that humiliates. Allah is All-Independent, Forbearing.* Surat Al Baqarah (The Cow) 2:263

﴿قَوۡلٌ مَّعۡرُوفٌ وَمَغۡفِرَةٌ خَيۡرٌ مِّن صَدَقَةٍ يَتۡبَعُهَآ أَذًىۗ وَٱللَّهُ غَنِيٌّ حَلِيمٌ﴾ سُورَةُ البَقَرَة ٢:٢٦٣

What Are the Benefits of Zakah?

Whatever we have, be it property or money, is a gift that Allah has allowed us to acquire. Allah has full control over our possessions, just as He has full control over our lives. (34:24) If He commanded us to give up everything we have, it would be our duty to do so. But Allah is merciful and promised never to burden us beyond what we can bear. In fact, He asks us to give only 2.5% after expenses each year!

Declare: if your fathers, sons, brothers, wives, relatives, wealth, the business affairs you worry about or your homes that you enjoy are dearer to you than Allah or His Messenger or striving in His cause, then just wait until Allah makes His decision. Allah does not guide the rebellious. Surat At-Tawbah (The Repentance) 9:24

﴿قُلۡ إِن كَانَ ءَابَآؤُكُمۡ وَأَبۡنَآؤُكُمۡ وَإِخۡوَٰنُكُمۡ وَأَزۡوَٰجُكُمۡ وَعَشِيرَتُكُمۡ وَأَمۡوَٰلٌ ٱقۡتَرَفۡتُمُوهَا وَتِجَٰرَةٌ تَخۡشَوۡنَ كَسَادَهَا وَمَسَٰكِنُ تَرۡضَوۡنَهَآ أَحَبَّ إِلَيۡكُم مِّنَ ٱللَّهِ وَرَسُولِهِ وَجِهَادٍ فِي سَبِيلِهِ فَتَرَبَّصُوا۟ حَتَّىٰ يَأۡتِيَ ٱللَّهُ بِأَمۡرِهِۦۗ وَٱللَّهُ لَا يَهۡدِي ٱلۡقَوۡمَ ٱلۡفَٰسِقِينَ﴾ سُورَةُ التَّوۡبَة ٩:٢٤

Another extraordinary favor from Allah is that He gives enormous rewards to those who give Zakah and other charity even though all real property really belongs to Him. It would be perfectly reasonable for Allah to say we should receive no reward for giving, because it is our duty to Him. But Allah loves to forgive, and He loves to reward those who are obedient to Him even though they can't see Him. (30:45) If Allah is pleased with what we have done, the reward from Him is only due to the love and kindness that are among His qualities.

Allah makes three promises to people who pay Zakah. First, Allah will pay them back a hundred or more times for what they give, either in this life or in the hereafter. Second, they will earn great rewards in the next life, and third, they will not be afraid or sad on the Day of Judgement.

The Companions of the Blessed Prophet had the fullest certainty of these promises. When the ayaat extolling the spiritual virtues of spending in Allah's cause were revealed, the men and women who heard them were deeply moved—so much so that even the poor Muslims, who deserved the Zakah, rushed out to find extra jobs so that they could have something to give in Allah's cause. Imagine how strong their faith must have been in order to be willing to do extra work to gain great rewards.

The Blessed Prophet once said, "He who performs three things will have the taste of the faith. (They

The example of the people who spend their wealth in the cause of Allah is like a kernel of corn: It grows seven years, and each ear has a hundred kernels. Allah gives abundant increase to whoever He wants to, for Allah cares for all and knows all things. Those people who spend their wealth in the cause of Allah, and who do not follow their gifts with reminders of how generous they were, nor with hurtful humiliation, they shall have their reward with Allah, and they will not be afraid nor will they be sad. Surat Al Baqarah (The Cow) 2:261-262

﴿مَّثَلُ ٱلَّذِينَ يُنفِقُونَ أَمْوَالَهُمْ فِى سَبِيلِ ٱللَّهِ كَمَثَلِ حَبَّةٍ أَنۢبَتَتْ سَبْعَ سَنَابِلَ فِى كُلِّ سُنۢبُلَةٍ مِّا۟ئَةُ حَبَّةٍ وَٱللَّهُ يُضَاعِفُ لِمَن يَشَآءُ وَٱللَّهُ وَاسِعٌ عَلِيمٌ﴾ ﴿ٱلَّذِينَ يُنفِقُونَ أَمْوَالَهُمْ فِى سَبِيلِ ٱللَّهِ ثُمَّ لَا يُتْبِعُونَ مَآ أَنفَقُوا۟ مَنًّا وَلَآ أَذًى لَّهُمْ أَجْرُهُمْ عِندَ رَبِّهِمْ وَلَا خَوْفٌ عَلَيْهِمْ وَلَا هُمْ يَحْزَنُونَ﴾ سُورَةُ الْبَقَرَةِ 261 - 262

are:) One who worships Allah alone and one believes that there is no god but Allah; and one who pays the Zakah on his property agreeably every year. One should not give an aged animal, nor one suffering from itch or ailing, and one most condemned, but one should give animals of medium quality, for Allah did not demand from you the best of your animals, nor did He command you to give the animals of worst quality." (Abu Dawud)

عَنِ النَّبِيِّ ﷺ قَالَ: «ثَلَاثٌ مَنْ فَعَلَهُنَّ فَقَدْ طَعِمَ طَعْمَ الْإِيمَانِ مَنْ عَبَدَ اللهَ وَحْدَهُ وَأَنَّهُ لَا إِلَهَ إِلَّا اللهُ وَأَعْطَى زَكَاةَ مَالِهِ طَيِّبَةً بِهَا نَفْسُهُ رَافِدَةً عَلَيْهِ كُلَّ عَامٍ وَلَا يُعْطِى الْهَرِمَةَ وَلَا الدَّرِنَةَ وَلَا الْمَرِيضَةَ وَلَا الشَّرَطَ اللَّئِيمَةَ وَلَكِنْ مِنْ وَسَطِ أَمْوَالِكُمْ فَإِنَّ اللهَ لَمْ يَسْأَلْكُمْ خَيْرَهُ وَلَمْ يَأْمُرْكُمْ بِشَرِّهِ». رَوَاهُ أَبُو دَاوُدَ

Apart from the reward in the next life, there are many benefits we can experience now from practicing Zakah and other forms of charity. For example, a Muslim who fulfills his duty properly will experience a special feeling of satisfaction and tranquillity in their heart. As a direct result of the charity given, barriers between the rich and poor will be broken and relationships between people will strengthen. Additionally, Allah promises to grant the one who gives charity greater prosperity and to multiply his wealth more and more!

On the authority of Abu Hurayrah from the Prophet, who said, "Allah said, Spend (on charity), O son of Adam, and I shall spend on you." (Al Bukhari & Muslim)

عَنْ أَبِي هُرَيْرَةَ ﷺ، أَنَّ رَسُولَ اللهِ ﷺ قَالَ: «قَالَ اللهُ: أَنْفِقْ يَا ابْنَ آدَمَ، أُنْفِقْ عَلَيْكَ». رَوَاهُ الْبُخَارِيُّ وَمُسْلِم

Another saying of the Blessed Prophet stated, "There are three things for which I swear. He said, The slave's (of Allah) wealth shall not be decreased by charity, no slave (of Allah) suffers injustice and is patient with it except that Allah adds to his honor; no slave (of Allah) opens up a door to begging except that Allah opens a door for him to poverty." (At-Tirmidhi)

عَنْ رَسُولِ اللهِ ﷺ يَقُولُ: «ثَلَاثَةٌ أُقْسِمُ عَلَيْهِنَّ وَأُحَدِّثُكُمْ حَدِيثًا فَاحْفَظُوهُ. قَالَ مَا نَقَصَ مَالُ عَبْدٍ مِنْ صَدَقَةٍ وَلَا ظُلِمَ عَبْدٌ مَظْلِمَةً فَصَبَرَ عَلَيْهَا إِلَّا زَادَهُ اللهُ عِزًّا وَلَا فَتَحَ عَبْدٌ بَابَ مَسْأَلَةٍ إِلَّا فَتَحَ اللهُ عَلَيْهِ بَابَ فَقْرٍ». رَوَاهُ التِّرْمَذِي

Most people pay their Zakah during the holy month of Ramadan. For in this month, all good deeds are multiplied in merit and reward in our records. In whatever month Zakah is given, the most important aspect is that it is paid once every year. Zakah is the Islamic contribution to social justice. Zakah is given by those who have wealth so that those who don't have any can share in the benefits of their neighbor's prosperity. Muslims have the perfect system for erasing envy and greed, and one that purifies the soul in the process. This is the institution of Zakah. (2:271)

The Danger of Avoiding Zakah

According to the Qur'an, neglecting Salah and Zakah are not the qualities of a Muslim. Rather, they are the signs of the disbelievers, or people who deny Allah in favor of something else, whether that something else is an idol, a false idea or even their own whims and desires. Allah comments on this by saying:

The fate that awaits people who fail to pay their Zakah is a frightening one. The mere thought of the dreadful punishment is enough to make one's hair stand on end. (63:10)

And there are people who hide gold and silver to keep it and not spend it in Allah's cause. Tell them about a painful punishment. On the day when the fire of Hell will be heated with the wealth they hid, they will be burned on their forehead with a branding iron, and on their sides and back. They will be told, "This is the treasure which you hid for yourselves. Now taste the (worth) of what you hid!" *Surat At-Tawbah (The Repentance) 9:34-35*

﴿وَٱلَّذِينَ يَكْنِزُونَ ٱلذَّهَبَ وَٱلْفِضَّةَ وَلَا يُنفِقُونَهَا فِي سَبِيلِ ٱللَّهِ فَبَشِّرْهُم بِعَذَابٍ أَلِيمٍ﴾ ﴿يَوْمَ يُحْمَىٰ عَلَيْهَا فِي نَارِ جَهَنَّمَ فَتُكْوَىٰ بِهَا جِبَاهُهُمْ وَجُنُوبُهُمْ وَظُهُورُهُمْ هَـٰذَا مَا كَنَزْتُمْ لِأَنفُسِكُمْ فَذُوقُوا مَا كُنتُمْ تَكْنِزُونَ﴾ سُورَةُ التَّوْبَةِ 9:34-35

A hadith of the Blessed Prophet ﷺ explains what this ayah means: Abu Hurayrah ◉ reported Allah's Messenger ﷺ as saying, "Whoever has gold or silver (money) but does not fulfill their responsibilities of that ownership (by paying the Zakah), then plates of fire will be made for him or her on the Day of Judgement. These plates will be heated (to scorching) in the fire, and then they will be put on the forehead, sides and back of the guilty person. These plates will be heated up again and again to scorch him or her, and this will continue throughout the Day of Judgement , which will be equal to 50 thousand years of this world." (Muslim)

You can't take it with you, so use it wisely here!

أَبَا هُرَيْرَةَ ◉، يَقُولُ قَالَ رَسُولُ اللهِ ﷺ: «مَا مِنْ صَاحِبِ ذَهَبٍ وَلَا فِضَّةٍ لَا يُؤَدِّي مِنْهَا حَقَّهَا إِلَّا إِذَا كَانَ يَوْمُ الْقِيَامَةِ صُفِّحَتْ لَهُ صَفَائِحُ مِنْ نَارٍ فَأُحْمِيَ عَلَيْهَا فِي نَارِ جَهَنَّمَ فَيُكْوَى بِهَا جَنْبُهُ وَجَبِينُهُ وَظَهْرُهُ كُلَّمَا بَرَدَتْ أُعِيدَتْ لَهُ فِي يَوْمٍ كَانَ مِقْدَارُهُ خَمْسِينَ أَلْفَ سَنَةٍ حَتَّى يُقْضَى بَيْنَ الْعِبَادِ فَيُرَى سَبِيلُهُ إِمَّا إِلَى الْجَنَّةِ وَإِمَّا إِلَى النَّارِ». رَوَاهُ مُسْلِمٌ

People who have been blessed by Allah ◉ with money and prosperity are ungrateful if they don't want to pay the Zakah. Indeed, Zakah is reasonable, fair and for the benefit of the needy. If we try to avoid Zakah, we are committing a crime against the needy and are denying them their rights. Those who deny even this small responsibility to their fellow men deserve the punishment that awaits them. (63:5-7)

Zakah Table

Asset Type	Minimum Amount Required for Zakah (Nisaab)	Rate of Zakah
Agricultural produce	5 Awsuq (653 kg) per harvest	5% for irrigated land, 10% for rain fed land
Gold, silver, ornaments of gold and silver	85 grams of gold or 595 grams of silver	2.5% of value
Cash	Value of 595 grams of silver	2.5% of amount
Trading goods	Value of 595 grams of silver	2.5% of goods
Cows and buffaloes	30 animals	For every 30, one 1-year-old; for every 40, one 2-year-old
Goats and sheep	40 animals	One for first 40; two for 120; three for 300; one more for every 100
Material extracted from mines	Any quantity	20% of material's value

Sample Zakah
Calculation Sheet

1. Ending yearly bank balance + Cash on hand: $ _____

2. Total current value of stocks, shares: $ _____

3. Income from real estate, other sources: $ _____

4. Current value of gold and silver bullion: $ _____

5.
   a. Total weight of gold jewelry (in ounces): _____.
   b. Current price of an ounce of gold: $ _____
   c. Total eligible gold (multiply 5a and 5b): $ _____

6.
   a. Total weight of silver jewelry (in ounces): _____.
   b. Current price of an ounce of silver: $ _____
   c. Total eligible silver (multiply 5a and 5b): $ _____

7. Total value of yearly wealth (add lines 1, 2, 3, 4, 5c, 6c):
                 $ _____

8. Multiply line 7 by 0.025:
                 $ _____

9. Amount of Zakah to pay:
                 $ _____

Literature Selection

The Three Heroes Who Failed

From *Sahih Muslim*

On the authority of Abu Hurayrah☺, who said, "I heard the Messenger of Allah☺ say, 'Surely, the first person who will be judged on the Day of Resurrection will be a shaheed (a martyr). He will be brought before Allah who will then list the favors that were bestowed upon him (in the world), and the shaheed will recognize them. Then (Allah) will ask, "What did you do with them?" He will reply, "I fought in Your cause and died a shaheed."

But Allah will say, "You're lying. You only fought so people would call you brave, and so they said it." Then the command will be issued, and he will be dragged on his face and thrown in Hellfire. Then a person who acquired and taught knowledge and recited the Qur'an will be brought before Allah who will then remind the person of the blessings (he received), and he will recognize them. Then Allah will ask, "What did you do with them?" He will reply, "I acquired and taught knowledge and recited the Qur'an for Your sake." But (Allah) will say, "You're lying. You acquired knowledge only so people would call you a scholar, and you recited the Qur'an only so they would call you a reciter, and so you were called those things." Then the command will be issued, and he will be dragged on his face and thrown into Hellfire. Then a person whom Allah made influential and who was given riches would be brought forward and informed about the favors he received, and he will recognize them. Then Allah will ask, "What did you do with them?" He will reply, "I donated in every cause You would have wanted me to." Allah will say, "You're lying. You only donated so that people would call you generous, and so they said it." Then the command will be issued, and he will be dragged on his face and thrown in Hell.'"

عَنْ أَبِي هُرَيْرَةَ ☺، قَالَ: سَمِعْتُ رَسُولَ اللهِ ☺ يَقُولُ: «إِنَّ أَوَّلَ النَّاسِ يُقْضَى يَوْمَ الْقِيَامَةِ عَلَيْهِ رَجُلٌ اسْتُشْهِدَ فَأُتِيَ بِهِ فَعَرَّفَهُ نِعَمَهُ فَعَرَفَهَا، قَالَ: فَمَا عَمِلْتَ فِيهَا؟ قَالَ قَاتَلْتُ فِيكَ حَتَّى اسْتُشْهِدْتُ، قَالَ: كَذَبْتَ، وَلَكِنَّكَ قَاتَلْتَ لِأَنْ يُقَالَ: جَرِيءٌ، فَقَدْ قِيلَ، ثُمَّ أُمِرَ بِهِ فَسُحِبَ عَلَى وَجْهِهِ حَتَّى أُلْقِيَ فِي النَّارِ. وَرَجُلٌ تَعَلَّمَ الْعِلْمَ وَعَلَّمَهُ وَقَرَأَ الْقُرْآنَ، فَأُتِيَ بِهِ، فَعَرَّفَهُ نِعَمَهُ فَعَرَفَهَا، قَالَ: فَمَا عَمِلْتَ فِيهَا؟ قَالَ: تَعَلَّمْتُ الْعِلْمَ وَعَلَّمْتُهُ، وَقَرَأْتُ فِيكَ الْقُرْآنَ، قَالَ: كَذَبْتَ، وَلَكِنَّكَ تَعَلَّمْتَ الْعِلْمَ لِيُقَالَ: عَالِمٌ، وَقَرَأْتَ الْقُرْآنَ لِيُقَالَ: هُوَ قَارِئٌ، فَقَدْ قِيلَ، ثُمَّ أُمِرَ بِهِ، فَسُحِبَ عَلَى وَجْهِهِ حَتَّى أُلْقِيَ فِي النَّارِ. وَرَجُلٌ وَسَّعَ اللهُ عَلَيْهِ، وَأَعْطَاهُ مِنْ أَصْنَافِ الْمَالِ كُلِّهِ، فَأُتِيَ بِهِ، فَعَرَّفَهُ نِعَمَهُ فَعَرَفَهَا، قَالَ: فَمَا عَمِلْتَ فِيهَا؟ قَالَ: مَا تَرَكْتُ مِنْ سَبِيلٍ تُحِبُّ أَنْ يُنْفَقَ فِيهَا إِلَّا أَنْفَقْتُ فِيهَا لَكَ، قَالَ: كَذَبْتَ، وَلَكِنَّكَ فَعَلْتَ لِيُقَالَ: هُوَ جَوَادٌ، فَقَدْ قِيلَ، ثُمَّ أُمِرَ بِهِ فَسُحِبَ عَلَى وَجْهِهِ، ثُمَّ أُلْقِيَ فِي النَّارِ».

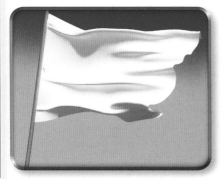

What Is Fasting?

The Fourth Pillar of Islam is known as **Siyam** صَوْم **Fasting**. During the month of **Ramadan** رَمَضان, the ninth month of the Islamic lunar calendar, Muslims are required to fast from dawn until dusk.

Throughout human history, the institution of fasting has been both a personal and a shared experience. From the very beginning of time, humans have been involved in the great struggle to master their desires and emotions. The need to eat is one of the most powerful urges all must face. Many fail by eating too much and/or eating unhealthy foods.

Anyone who has ever sought to come closer to their spiritual self has had to overcome their body's desire for satisfaction. Hence, the practice of fasting is known throughout human history. Previous prophets have enjoined fasting upon their peoples, and untold numbers of wise men and women have made self-denial a part of their lives.

When we deny something that our body craves, we elevate our minds; reason and will become stronger than our animal urges and passions. In this way, our thinking becomes clearer, and we learn that we are, indeed, not governed by our lower self. We gain greater awareness of ourselves and, hence, are able to bring ourselves closer to Allah.

We have created man in the best composition. Surat At-Tin (The Fig) 95:4

﴿لَقَدْ خَلَقْنَا الْإِنسَٰنَ فِي أَحْسَنِ تَقْوِيمٍ﴾ سُورَةُ التِّينِ 95:4

When we rise above the flesh, we recognize the force of our spirit, our very human will. As Allah declared, *You who believe! Fasting is prescribed for you as it was prescribed for those before you so you can gain more awareness.* Surat Al Baqarah (The Cow) 2:183

﴿يَٰٓأَيُّهَا الَّذِينَ ءَامَنُوا كُتِبَ عَلَيْكُمُ الصِّيَامُ كَمَا كُتِبَ عَلَى الَّذِينَ مِن قَبْلِكُمْ لَعَلَّكُمْ تَتَّقُونَ﴾ سُورَةُ البَقَرَةِ 2:183

Imagine waking up, long before the first light of the sun has risen over the darkened sky, and having your **Sahoor** سُحُور **Pre-Dawn Meal**. When the hint of light approaches, the meal is finished, and you pray the morning prayer with great clarity of mind and thought. You make your intention to fast that day for Allah's sake and then either return to bed for a few hours to sleep or stay awake and read Allah's words in the Qur'an. Then you prepare to face the day.

نَوَيْتُ صَوْمَ اليَوْمِ عَنْ أَدَاءِ شَهْرِ رَمَضَان
"I intend to fast today for the month of Ramadan."

During the daylight hours, a fasting person abstains from all food, liquids, inhaled substances, sexual activity and nutritional supplements or any non-essential oral medicine. In addition, all normally undesirable behavior is especially frowned upon. No fighting, cursing, arguing, lying or other sins are to be indulged in. Of course, a Muslim must naturally avoid such sins anyway, but sometimes people fall into error. Abstaining from these for a month is the corrective action.

Ramadan: The Month of Training

The month of Ramadan provides us with a spiritual and moral boot camp. We know that fasting in Ramadan is a duty we owe Allah. Any sins may spoil our record with Allah, so we take great pains to be on our best behavior. This intense modification of our habits is designed to help train us to avoid such sins throughout the rest of the year.

The Blessed Prophet once remarked, *"Whoever doesn't give up lying and acting on lies during fasting, then Allah has no need of him giving up food and drink."* (Al Bukhari)

قَالَ رَسُولُ اللهِ: «مَنْ لَمْ يَدَعْ قَوْلَ الزُّورِ وَالْعَمَلَ بِهِ, وَالْجَهْلَ, فَلَيْسَ لِلهِ حَاجَةٌ فِي أَنْ يَدَعَ طَعَامَهُ وَشَرَابَهُ». رَوَاهُ الْبُخَارِيُّ

On another occasion, he ﷺ warned, "There are people who fast and get nothing from their fast except hunger, and there are those who pray and get nothing from their prayer but a sleepless night." (Ibn Majah)

قَالَ رَسُولُ اللهِ ﷺ : «رُبَّ صَائِمٍ لَيْسَ لَهُ مِنْ صِيَامِهِ إِلَّا الْجُوعُ وَرُبَّ قَائِمٍ لَيْسَ لَهُ مِنْ قِيَامِهِ إِلَّا السَّهَرُ». رَوَاهُ ابْنُ مَاجَه

Clearly, moral behavior is as important as the physical aspects of fasting.

The Blessed Prophet ﷺ also said, "Fasting is a shield. So, the person observing fasting should avoid sexual relation with his or her mate and should not behave foolishly and impudently, and if somebody fights with him or abuses him, he should tell him twice, 'I am fasting.'" (Al Bukhari)

قَالَ رَسُولُ اللهِ ﷺ : «الصِّيَامُ جُنَّةٌ، فَلَا يَرْفُثْ وَلَا يَجْهَلْ، وَإِنِ امْرُؤٌ قَاتَلَهُ أَوْ شَاتَمَهُ فَلْيَقُلْ إِنِّي صَائِمٌ». رَوَاهُ الْبُخَارِيُّ

Abu Hurayrah ﷺ narrated that Allah's Messenger ﷺ said, "Allah said, 'All the deeds of Adam's sons (people) are for them, except fasting which is for Me, and I will give the reward for it.' Fasting is a shield or protection from the fire and from committing sins. If one of you is fasting, he should avoid sexual relation with his wife and quarreling, and if somebody should fight or quarrel with him, he should say, 'I am fasting.' By Him in Whose Hands my soul is, the unpleasant smell coming out from the mouth of a fasting person is better in the sight of Allah than the smell of musk. There are two pleasures for the fasting person, one at the time of breaking his fast, and the other at the time when he will meet his Lord; then he will be pleased because of his fasting." (Al Bukhari)

عَنْ أَبَا هُرَيْرَةَ عَنِ النَّبِيِّ ﷺ قَالَ: «قَالَ اللهُ كُلُّ عَمَلِ ابْنِ آدَمَ لَهُ إِلَّا الصِّيَامَ، فَإِنَّهُ لِي، وَأَنَا أَجْزِي بِهِ. وَالصِّيَامُ جُنَّةٌ. وَإِذَا كَانَ يَوْمُ صَوْمِ أَحَدِكُمْ، فَلَا يَرْفُثْ وَلَا يَصْخَبْ، فَإِنْ سَابَّهُ أَحَدٌ، أَوْ قَاتَلَهُ فَلْيَقُلْ إِنِّي امْرُؤٌ صَائِمٌ. وَالَّذِي نَفْسُ مُحَمَّدٍ بِيَدِهِ لَخُلُوفُ فَمِ الصَّائِمِ أَطْيَبُ عِنْدَ اللهِ مِنْ رِيحِ الْمِسْكِ، لِلصَّائِمِ فَرْحَتَانِ يَفْرَحُهُمَا إِذَا أَفْطَرَ فَرِحَ، وَإِذَا لَقِيَ رَبَّهُ فَرِحَ بِصَوْمِهِ». رَوَاهُ الْبُخَارِيُّ

Ramadan has such a wondrous impact on our morals and behavior that it has been described as the month of forgiveness. The Blessed Prophet ﷺ once declared, "During the month of Ramadan, the gates of Paradise are open, the gates of Hellfire are closed and the devils are chained." (Al Bukhari & Muslim)

قَالَ رَسُولُ اللهِ ﷺ : «إِذَا دَخَلَ شَهْرُ رَمَضَانَ فُتِّحَتْ أَبْوَابُ السَّمَاءِ، وَغُلِّقَتْ أَبْوَابُ جَهَنَّمَ، وَسُلْسِلَتِ الشَّيَاطِينُ». رَوَاهُ الْبُخَارِيُّ وَمُسْلِم

At another time, the Blessed Prophet ﷺ said, "All the previous sins of a person are forgiven if they fast in the month of Ramadan with full faith and with the desire of fulfilling their duty to Allah and earning His reward." (Al Bukhari)

قَالَ رَسُولُ اللهِ ﷺ : «مَنْ صَامَ رَمَضَانَ إِيمَانًا وَاحْتِسَابًا غُفِرَ لَهُ مَا تَقَدَّمَ مِنْ ذَنْبِهِ». رَوَاهُ الْبُخَارِيُّ

Ramadan is a blessed month for another reason. It marks the beginning of Allah's ﷻ first revelation of His Message to the Blessed Prophet Muhammad ﷺ. Allah ﷻ announced, Ramadan is the (month) in which the Qur'an was sent down as a guide to humanity and (to provide) clear signs for guidance and judgement. So every one of you who is present during that month should spend it in fasting. Surat Al Baqarah (The Cow) 2:185

﴿شَهْرُ رَمَضَانَ الَّذِي أُنزِلَ فِيهِ الْقُرْآنُ هُدًى لِّلنَّاسِ وَبَيِّنَاتٍ مِّنَ الْهُدَىٰ وَالْفُرْقَانِ فَمَن شَهِدَ مِنكُمُ الشَّهْرَ فَلْيَصُمْهُ﴾ سُورَةُ الْبَقَرَةِ 2:185

Who Fasts?

Who must fast? Every sane, healthy Muslim past the age of puberty must observe Ramadan. Those who are exempt are the very young (below the age of puberty), the permanently sick, the elderly who are too weak and the mentally challenged. A person who can no longer fast due to old age or permanent sickness can still share in the rewards by contributing money towards feeding two needy people per day. This is called giving **Fidya** فِدْيَة **Compensation**.

The Blessed Prophet ﷺ said, "Whoever provides food for the breaking of the fast for another person earns the same merit as the one who was fasting, without lowering in any way the reward of the person who fasted." (At-Tirmidhi)

قَالَ رَسُولُ اللهِ ﷺ : «مَنْ فَطَّرَ صَائِمًا كَانَ لَهُ مِثْلُ أَجْرِهِ غَيْرَ أَنَّهُ لَا يَنْقُصُ مِنْ أَجْرِ الصَّائِمِ شَيْئًا». رَوَاهُ التِّرْمَذِيّ

There is a another category of people who are temporarily exempted from fasting during Ramadan. They have to make up the missed days at a later date. If a person is traveling or ill, they may skip fasting days and make them up later. (2:185) Women who are on their monthly cycle or who recently gave birth are exempted from the fast. However, they must make up the days they missed at a later time when they are able, preferably before the next Ramadan.

Pregnant and breastfeeding women have special permission not to fast during Ramadan if they feel that they or their babies will be harmed by it, but they are not prohibited from fasting if they feel they can definitely handle it. According to many scholars they do not have to make up the days they missed at a later time when they are able and it is sufficient to give fidya.

If a person accidentally or unintentionally swallows something while fasting, their fast is not broken. The Blessed Prophet ﷺ explained that we should continue to fast, and we should simply consider the sip of liquid or bite of food as from Allah's ﷻ mercy.

Abu Hurayrah ﷺ narrated that the Prophet ﷺ said, "If somebody eats or drinks forgetfully then he should complete his fast, for what he has eaten or drunk has been given to him by Allah." (Al Bukhari)

عَنْ أَبِي هُرَيْرَةَ ﷺ عَنِ النَّبِيِّ ﷺ قَالَ: «إِذَا نَسِيَ فَأَكَلَ وَ شَرِبَ فَلْيُتِمَّ صَوْمَهُ، فَإِنَّمَا أَطْعَمَهُ اللهُ وَ سَقَاهُ». رَوَاهُ الْبُخَارِيُّ

Wudu' must still be performed while one is fasting, but it should be done carefully. Teeth can be brushed normally. The rule is not to let anything pass into the throat.

If a person breaks their fast intentionally, before it's time to stop fasting, then they have committed a grave sin and must try to make up for it right away. Some scholars say in order to make up for this sin, we must either free a slave, fast for 60 days straight, feed 60 people two meals or feed one person two meals for 60 days. The penalty is harsh, but it fits the crime. Breaking the fast for no reason means we temporarily put our desires above Allah's ﷻ command. Such a severe penalty reminds us how hateful to Allah the crime is.

When the sun has declined completely past the horizon at the end of the day, then the period of fasting is over. Muslims then have an **Iftar** إفطار literally **Break Fast**, which is the first meal after a day of fasting, eaten before going to pray Salat Al Maghrib. According to the sunnah, the best things for breaking the fast are dates, milk or water because they are easier on a stomach that has been empty all day. Before eating we make the following dua':

اللهُمَّ لَكَ صُمْتُ، وَبِكَ آمَنْتُ، وَعليكَ توكَّلتُ، وَعَلى رِزْقِكَ أفْطَرْتُ

Allahumma laka sumtu wa bika amantu wa alayka tawakkaltu wa ala rizqika aftartu

"Oh Allah I've fasted for You, and I've believed in You, and with what You provided for me I break my fast."

The Lessons of Fasting

The lessons learned during Ramadan are many. We learn what it means to be hungry, so we feel more compassion for the poor. We understand how close we are to leaving this world at any moment and how much we depend on food and drink. We learn to control our urges and clear our minds and thoughts for the serious remembrance of Allah ﷻ. We restrain our anger and train our habits towards prayer, forgiveness, self-sacrifice and good behavior.

With all these benefits coming from the observance of this blessed month, is it any wonder it is the best time of the year for every Muslim? Most Muslims prefer to perform their prayers in the masjid during Ramadan, as Allah's ﷻ rewards are increased for any good action done in this month.

Following the prayer, Muslims eat dinner and then prepare for spiritual renewal by reading the Qur'an, making dua' to Allah ﷻ and spending time with family. Allah ﷻ declared, *When My servants ask you about Me, I am indeed close. I listen to the call of every supplicant when they call on Me. Let them, whoever will, listen to My call and believe in Me so they can walk in the right way.* Surat Al Baqarah (The Cow) 2:186

﴿وَإِذَا سَأَلَكَ عِبَادِي عَنِّي فَإِنِّي قَرِيبٌ أُجِيبُ دَعْوَةَ الدَّاعِ إِذَا دَعَانِ فَلْيَسْتَجِيبُوا لِي وَلْيُؤْمِنُوا بِي لَعَلَّهُمْ يَرْشُدُونَ﴾ سُورَةُ البَقَرَةِ 2:186

In the later part of the evening, Muslims gather together in the masjid for **Salat At-Tarawih** صَلاةُ التَّراوِيح **Resting Prayer**, a special type of prayer held only during the month of Ramadan. It consists of a series of two-rak'aat prayers behind an imam. Salat At-Tarawih is performed after 'Isha Prayer and is a strongly recommended practice of the Blessed Prophet ﷺ and the righteous Companions.

'Abdur Rahman bin 'Abdul Qari said, "I went out in the company of 'Umar bin Al Khattab one night in Ramadan to the mosque and found the people praying in different groups. A man praying alone or a man praying with a little group behind him. So, 'Umar said, 'In my opinion I would better collect these (people) under the leadership of one Qari (Reciter)' (i.e. let them pray in congregation). So, he made up his mind to congregate them behind Ubai bin Ka'b. Then on another night, I went again in his company and the people were praying behind their reciter. On that, 'Umar remarked, 'What an excellent Bid'a (innovation in religion) this is; but the prayer which they do not perform, but sleep at its time is better than the one they are offering.' He meant the prayer in the last part of the night. (In those days) people used to pray in the early part of the night."

One particular night of Ramadan has extra special significance. It is the night when the first ayaat of the Qur'an were revealed. It is known as **Laylat Al Qadr** لَيْلَةُ القَدْر **the Night of Power** (Night of Measurement). According to the hadith of the Blessed Prophet ﷺ, it falls on one of the odd-numbered nights in the last 10 days of Ramadan. Many Muslims stay up all night seeking their Lord's forgiveness and guidance. Allah﷾ described Laylat Al Qadr this way:

Behold, We (began) this revelation on the Night of Power! And how is this night different from the rest? The Night of Power is greater than a thousand months; for in it, hosts of angels descend and the Spirit (Angel Jibreel), by their Lord's leave, to accomplish every task. Peace prevails 'till the break of dawn!
Surat Al Qadr (The Night of Decree) 97: 1-5

﴿إِنَّا أَنزَلْنَاهُ فِي لَيْلَةِ الْقَدْرِ﴾ ﴿وَمَا أَدْرَاكَ مَا لَيْلَةُ الْقَدْرِ﴾ ﴿لَيْلَةُ الْقَدْرِ خَيْرٌ مِّنْ أَلْفِ شَهْرٍ﴾ ﴿تَنَزَّلُ الْمَلَائِكَةُ وَالرُّوحُ فِيهَا بِإِذْنِ رَبِّهِم مِّن كُلِّ أَمْرٍ﴾ ﴿سَلَامٌ هِيَ حَتَّىٰ مَطْلَعِ الْفَجْرِ﴾ سُورَةُ الْقَدْر 97:1-5

During the last 10 days of Ramadan, some Muslims perform what is known as **I'tikaf** اعْتِكاف **Retreat**. Muslims spend entire days in the masjid, or the last 10 days, focusing exclusively on prayer and worship. They only venture out for showers and similarly legitimate needs. They spend their time in prayer, reading, study circles and making dua'. (2:187) The Blessed Prophet ﷺ used to practice this form of 'ibadah (service to Allah﷾). The minimum duration of i'tikaf is one day, one night or even one moment.

Joy at the End of Ramadan

The end of Ramadan occurs when the next crescent moon has been sighted, 29 or 30 days after fasting began. Following the sighting, Muslims celebrate one of the two most important holidays in the Islamic year: **'Eid Al Fitr** عِيدُ الفِطْر **Festival of Breaking the Fast**.

Muslims have to give a certain portion of food or money to the needy people, called **Sadaqat Al Fitr** صَدَقَةُ الفِطْر **Charity of the Fast Breaking**, allowing everyone to partake of the joys of 'Eid. It is an obligation upon every Muslim household. Parents must consider their children when calculating the total to give. It is the equivalent of the cost of one meal per person in the house.

The holiday begins with Salat Al 'Eid and khutbah on the morning after the end of Ramadan and lasts two days afterward with dinner parties, family outings, fairs, carnivals and joyous celebrations. Fasting is not allowed on the actual 'Eid day, as everyone should participate in the festivities.

Fasting on Other Occasions

There are other fasts encouraged throughout the year, but they are not required. They are performed for extra merit and reward from Allah﷾.

Abu Aiyub Al Ansari﷜ narrated that The Messenger of Allah ﷺ said, "Whoever observes the fast of Ramadan and then follows it up with six days of fasting in (the month of) Shawwal, it will be as if he fasted his whole lifetime." (Muslim)

عَنْ أَبِي أَيُّوبَ الْأَنْصَارِيِّ ﷜ أَنَّ رَسُولَ اللَّهِ ﷺ قَالَ: «مَنْ صَامَ رَمَضَانَ، ثُمَّ أَتْبَعَهُ سِتًّا مِنْ شَوَّالٍ كَانَ كَصِيَامِ الدَّهْرِ». رَوَاهُ مُسْلِمٌ

The fast of six days in the month of Shawwal usually begins on the second day of the month and lasts until the seventh. The days can also be separated and fasted at random, provided they are all completed during the month of Shawwal. Voluntary and recommended fasting can also be done on the ninth and tenth of the month of Muharram. This commemorates a fast in honor of Prophet Musa☮. The actual day is known as 'Ashura (the tenth) and is the main focus. Fasting on the ninth day of the month of Hajj is also praiseworthy.

Many Muslims like to fast in the month of Sha'ban. The Blessed Prophet ﷺ once explained that it is a neglected month for 'ibadah. His wife 'Aishah☮ reported that he fasted frequently during this month.

The Prophet ﷺ also used to fast on Mondays and Thursdays. He explained that those are the days when our deeds are presented to Allah☮, and he preferred to fast on those days. In addition, fasting is a way to make up for some types of mistakes and sins. If you break a promise or an oath, you can either feed 10 poor people, buy 10 poor people clothes, free a slave or at the very least, fast for three days. (5:89)

The Salat Al 'Eid Thikr

Muslims who gather prior to the start of the special 'Eid khutbah join together and chant the following thikr of Allah☮:

Allah is The Greatest, Allah is The Greatest, Allah is The Greatest	اللهُ أَكْبَرَ، اللهُ أَكْبَرَ، اللهُ أَكْبَرَ.
There is no God, but Allah	لا إِلَهَ إِلّا الله.
Allah is The Greatest, Allah is The Greatest, Allah is The Greatest	اللهُ أَكْبَرَ، اللهُ أَكْبَرَ، وللهِ الْحَمْدُ.
To Him belongs all Praise	
Allah is the Greatest	اللهُ أَكْبَرُ كَبِيرًا، وَالْحَمْدُ للهِ كَثِيرًا.
And all Praise is due to Him	وَسُبْحانَ اللهِ بُكْرَةً وَأَصِيلا.
And Glory to Allah	
Eventide and in the morning	لا إِلَهَ إِلّا اللهُ وَحْدَه.
There is no God, but Allah the Unique	صَدَقَ وَعْدَه، وَنَصَرَ عَبْدَه،
He has fulfilled His Promise	وَأَعَزَّ جُنْدَهُ وَهَزَمَ الْأَحْزابَ وَحْدَه.
And made Victorious His servant	
And made Mighty His soldiers	
And defeated the confederates	لا إِلَهَ إِلّا الله، وَلا نَعْبُدُ إِلّا إِيّاه.
There is no God, But Allah	مُخْلِصِينَ لَهُ الدِّين، وَلَوْ كَرِهَ الْكافِرُون.
He alone we worship	اللهُمَّ صَلِّ عَلى سَيِّدِنا مُحَمَّد.
With sincere and exclusive devotion	
Even though the idolaters hate it	وَعَلى آلِ سَيِّدِنا مُحَمَّد
O Allah, have Mercy on our Prophet Muhammad	وَعَلى أَصْحابِ سَيِّدِنا مُحَمَّد
And on the family of our Prophet Muhammad	وَعَلى أَنْصارِ سَيِّدِنا مُحَمَّد
And on the companions of our Prophet Muhammad	وَعَلى أَزْواجِ سَيِّدِنا مُحَمَّد
And on the helpers of our Prophet Muhammad	
And on the wives of our Prophet Muhammad	وَعَلى ذُرِّيَةِ سَيِّدِنا مُحَمَّدٍ. وَسَلِّمْ تَسْلِيمًا كَثِيرًا.
And on the progeny of our Prophet Muhammad	
And Bestow upon them much peace.	

Hadith of the Blessed Prophet Muhammad ﷺ about Ramadan

Salman ؓ reports that on the last day of Sha'ban, the Messenger of Allah ﷺ addressed us and said, "O people, there comes upon you now a great month, a most blessed month, in which lies a night greater in worth than one thousand months. It is a month in which Allah has made it compulsory that fasting should be observed by day; and He has made the taraweeh by night a Sunnah. Whosoever tries drawing nearer to Allah by performing any non-obligatory deed in this month, for him shall be such a reward as if he had performed a fard (obligatory observance) in any other time of the year. And Whosoever performs a fard, for him shall be the reward of seventy fard in any other time of the year. This is indeed the month of patience, and the reward for true patience is Jannah (Paradise). It is the month of sympathy for one's fellowmen; it is the month wherein a true believer's rizq (provisions) is increased. Whosoever feeds a fasting person in order to break the fast (at sunset), for him there shall be forgiveness of his sins and emancipation from the fire of jahannam (Hellfire), and for him shall be the same reward as for him (whom he fed), without that person's reward being diminished in the least." Thereupon we said, "O Messenger of Allah, not all of us possess the means whereby we can provide enough for a fasting person to break his fast." The Messenger of Allah replied, "Allah grants this same reward to him who gives a fasting person a single date or a drink of water or a sip of milk to break the fast. This is a month, the first part of which brings Allah's Mercy, the middle of which brings His forgiveness and the last part of which brings emancipation from the fire of jahannam (Hell). Whosoever lessens the burden of his servants (bondsmen) in this month, Allah will forgive him and free him from the fire of jahannam. And in this month, four things you should endeavour to perform in great number, two of which shall be to please your Lord, while the other two shall be those without which you cannot make do. Those which shall be to please your Lord, are that you should in great quantity recite the 'Kalimah Tayyibah': La ilaha illa Allah and make much istighfaar (beg Allah's forgiveness with Astaghfirullah). And as for those two without which you cannot make do, you should beg Allah for entry into Paradise and seek refuge with Him from the fire of hell. And whosoever gave a person, who fasted, water to drink Allah shall grant him a drink from my fountain such a drink, where after he shall never again feel thirsty until he enters Jannah." (Ibn Khuzaimah)

عَنْ سَلْمَانَ ؓ، قَالَ: خَطَبَنَا رَسُولُ اللهِ ﷺ في آخِرِ يَوْمٍ مِنْ شَعْبَانَ، فَقَالَ: «أَيُّهَا النَّاسُ، قَدْ أَظَلَّكُمْ شَهْرٌ عَظِيمٌ، شَهْرٌ مُبَارَكٌ، شَهْرٌ فِيهِ لَيْلَةٌ خَيْرٌ مِنْ أَلْفِ شَهْرٍ، شَهْرٌ جَعَلَ اللهُ صِيَامَهُ فَرِيضَةً، وَقِيَامَ لَيْلِهِ تَطَوُّعًا، مَنْ تَقَرَّبَ فِيهِ بِخَصْلَةٍ مِنْ خِصَالِ الْخَيْرِ، كَانَ كَمَنْ أَدَّى فَرِيضَةً فِيمَا سِوَاهُ، وَمَنْ أَدَّى فِيهِ فَرِيضَةً، كَانَ كَمَنْ أَدَّى سَبْعِينَ فَرِيضَةً فِيمَا سِوَاهُ، وَهُوَ شَهْرُ الصَّبْرِ، وَالصَّبْرُ ثَوَابُهُ الْجَنَّةُ، وَشَهْرُ الْمُوَاسَاةِ، وَشَهْرٌ يُزَادُ فِي رِزْقِ الْمُؤْمِنِ فِيهِ، مَنْ فَطَّرَ فِيهِ صَائِمًا كَانَ مَغْفِرَةً لِذُنُوبِهِ، وَعِتْقَ رَقَبَتِهِ مِنَ النَّارِ، وَكَانَ لَهُ مِثْلُ أَجْرِهِ، مِنْ غَيْرِ أَنْ يَنْقُصَ مِنْ أَجْرِهِ شَيْءٌ، قَالُوا: يَا رَسُولَ اللهِ: لَيْسَ كُلُّنَا يَجِدُ مَا يُفَطِّرُ الصَّائِمَ، قَالَ رَسُولُ اللهِ صَلَّى اللهُ عَلَيْهِ وَسَلَّمَ: يُعْطِي اللهُ هَذَا الثَّوَابَ مَنْ فَطَّرَ صَائِمًا عَلَى مَذْقَةِ لَبَنٍ، أَوْ تَمْرَةٍ، أَوْ شَرْبَةٍ مِنْ مَاءٍ، وَمَنْ أَشْبَعَ صَائِمًا سَقَاهُ اللهُ مِنْ حَوْضِي شَرْبَةً لَا يَظْمَأُ حَتَّى يَدْخُلَ الْجَنَّةَ، وَهُوَ شَهْرٌ أَوَّلُهُ رَحْمَةٌ، وَأَوْسَطُهُ مَغْفِرَةٌ، وَآخِرُهُ عِتْقٌ مِنَ النَّارِ، وَمَنْ خَفَّفَ فِيهِ عَنْ مَمْلُوكِهِ غَفَرَ اللهُ لَهُ وَأَعْتَقَهُ مِنَ النَّارِ، اسْتَكْثِرُوا فِيهِ مِنْ أَرْبَعِ خِصَالٍ، خَصْلَتَانِ تُرْضُونَ بِهِمَا رَبَّكُمْ تَعَالَى، وَخَصْلَتَانِ لَا غِنَى بِكُمْ عَنْهُمَا، فَأَمَّا الْخَصْلَتَانِ اللَّتَانِ تُرْضُونَ بِهِمَا رَبَّكُمْ: فَشَهَادَةُ أَنْ لَا إِلَهَ إِلَّا اللهُ، وَتَسْتَغْفِرُونَهُ، وَأَمَّا اللَّتِي لَا غِنَى بِكُمْ عَنْهُمَا: فَتَسْأَلُونَ اللهَ الْجَنَّةَ، وَتَعُوذُونَ بِهِ مِنَ النَّارِ، وَمَنْ أَشْبَعَ فِيهِ صَائِمًا سَقَاهُ اللهُ مِنْ حَوْضِي شَرْبَةً لَا يَظْمَأُ حَتَّى يَدْخُلَ الْجَنَّةَ». رَوَاهُ ابْنُ خُزَيْمَةَ

The Story of the Ka'bah

The main feature in the city of Makkah is the **Ka'bah** كَعْبَة, a Cube-Shaped Building, in the center of town. It is a shrine, or holy place, that has existed for thousands of years. Four thousand years ago, the valley of Makkah, then called Bakkah, was a dry and uninhabited place. All that changed, however, when one special man brought his wife and young son to the area and told them that this was their new home.

The man was Prophet Ibrahim. He was instructed by Allah to bring his second wife Hajar and their young child Isma'il to Arabia from Palestine. Allah instructed Prophet Ibrahim to leave them there, and he did so, with some supplies of food and water. The supplies quickly ran out though, and within a few days mother and son began to suffer the effects of dehydration and hunger.

In desperation, Hajar ran up and down the two hills of **As-Safa and Al Marwa** الصَّفَا وَالمَرْوَة trying to spot any help in the distance, but there was none. Finally, she collapsed next to her son Isma'il and prayed to Allah for help. The frustrated little boy struck his foot on the ground, causing water to gush forth from the earth. The water was cool and sweet. Hajar and Isma'il were saved. With the water supply secure, they were able to trade water with wandering nomads for food and other needs.

In time, Prophet Ibrahim returned from Palestine to see to his family in Bakkah and was amazed to see them the masters of a very profitable well. His son Isma'il was also developing a strong sense of wisdom and justice. Prophet Ibrahim received revelation from Allah to build a shrine dedicated to Him alone. (3:96) Ibrahim and Isma'il obeyed without question and constructed a small stone structure which was to be the gathering place for all who wished to strengthen their faith in Allah. (2:125)

Remember that Ibrahim and Isma'il built the foundations of the House (and prayed), "Our Lord! Accept this from us because You are the Hearing and Knowing. Our Lord! Make us Muslims who bow to You. And of our descendants, make them Muslims bowing to You also. Show us where to perform our rituals and turn to us because You are the One who accepts repentance and is merciful."
Surat Al Baqarah (The Cow) 2:127-128

﴿وَإِذْ يَرْفَعُ إِبْرَاهِيمُ ٱلْقَوَاعِدَ مِنَ ٱلْبَيْتِ وَإِسْمَاعِيلُ رَبَّنَا تَقَبَّلْ مِنَّا إِنَّكَ أَنتَ ٱلسَّمِيعُ ٱلْعَلِيمُ﴾ ﴿رَبَّنَا وَٱجْعَلْنَا مُسْلِمَيْنِ لَكَ وَمِن ذُرِّيَّتِنَا أُمَّةً مُّسْلِمَةً لَّكَ وَأَرِنَا مَنَاسِكَنَا وَتُبْ عَلَيْنَا إِنَّكَ أَنتَ ٱلتَّوَّابُ ٱلرَّحِيمُ﴾ سُورَةُ البَقَرَة 2:127-128

As the years passed, Isma'il was blessed with prophethood, and he called the nomads of the desert to surrender to Allah's will. (19:54-55) Eventually, people began settling in the valley of Bakkah, and the name was later changed to Makkah. After many centuries, Makkah became a vibrant city. This was due to its reliable water source, the well of Zamzam, as it came to be called. But gradually, people began to develop false ideas, such as the existence of spirits and many gods. Eventually, the Ka'bah was turned into a house for storing idols and statues that people worshipped in addition to Allah. It would be many thousands of years before Allah would send another prophet to eradicate those false ideas and restore the Ka'bah to the worship of the One True God. That prophet, a descendant of Prophet Ibrahim and Isma'il, was Muhammad. (2:129)

The Pilgrimage

The Fifth Pillar of Islam is **Hajj** حَج **Pilgrimage**. It occurs in the month of Dhul Hijjah, the twelfth month of the Islamic lunar calendar. It is a journey that every sane adult Muslim must undertake at least once in their lives, if they can afford it and are physically able. (3:97)

Once a year, Muslims of every ethnic group, race, social status and culture gather together in Makkah and stand before the Ka'bah, praising Allah with one harmonious voice. This ritual dates back to the time of Prophet Ibrahim and is designed to promote the bonds of Islamic brotherhood, demonstrating that all people are equal before their Lord.

The **Hujjaj** حُجَّاج **Pilgrims** dress in ihram, which is both a physical and spiritual state. (A male who completes Hajj is called **Hajj** حَاج or **Hajji** حَجِّي and a female, **Hajjah** حَاجَّة. The plural is **Hujjaj** حُجَّاج or **Hajeej** حَجِيج.) Ihram is required of the pilgrims when they come near the place where the pilgrimage begins. Here they make their intention to immediately perform Hajj. Pilgrims spend five to six days together performing acts of 'ibadah, affirming their emaan and renewing their sense of purpose in their lives.

During the occasion of Hajj, Muslims all over the world celebrate a holiday known as 'Eid Al Adha, the Festival of the Sacrifice. Together we commemorate the ultimate act of obedience when Prophet Ibrahim was commanded to sacrifice his beloved son, Isma'il. Ibrahim proved he was willing to give up the one thing he truly loved, for Allah's sake. Because of the strength of Ibrahim's ﷺ emaan, Allah ﷻ instead provided him with a ram for sacrifice. (37:101-111)

Makkah is a place that non-Muslims are forbidden from entering. It is the direction towards which Muslims pray and the one place where our hearts long to go.

Performing Hajj

The main feature of Makkah is the Ka'bah.

Every year, millions of eager Muslims from around the world anticipate making Hajj. Once they reach Makkah, there are two different types of rituals to be performed while in the city. There is **'Umrah** عُمْرَة **Short Pilgrimage** and the main pilgrimage, or Hajj.

'Umrah is different than the once-in-a-lifetime Hajj. It is an extra service on your part to Allah ﷻ. It is not fard. (2:158,196) Although some of the rituals of Hajj are performed in this mini pilgrimage, they are fewer and shortened. 'Umrah can be made at any time during the year. If it is done in Ramadan, the Blessed Prophet ﷺ remarked that you will receive the reward of Hajj! However it does not replace the duty to complete this important pillar of Islam.

Many pilgrims who are performing the Hajj during its season arrive a few days before the actual start and perform 'umrah first. Then when Hajj begins, they perform this also. This gives you the benefit of two blessed rituals in one visit. Combining 'umrah with Hajj is called Hajj At-Tamattu. There are two other ways of making Hajj, known as Ifrad and Qiran. These are similar, but they either exclude 'umrah, or add a few practices. Regardless of the method of Hajj one chooses, there are certain restrictions placed upon pilgrims while they are in a state of ihram.
The Hajji may not:

1. Engage in intimate relations.
2. Wear clothes with stitching (Applies only to men; a woman can wear her normal clothes.)
3. Shave the hair or cut the nails.
4. Put on cologne or scented oils.
5. Kill living things or hunt.
6. Fight, argue or bother any living thing.
7. A woman should not cover her face.
8. Use perfumed soap when bathing.
9. Be married while in ihram.

The Blessed Prophet Muhammad ﷺ said, "Whoever performs the pilgrimage for Allah's sake and avoids intimate relations (while in Ihram) and does not fight with anyone nor abuses anyone, he or she will return home (free from sins) like on the day his or her mother gave birth to him." (Agreed)

قَالَ رَسُولُ الله ﷺ: «مَنْ حَجَّ لِلهِ فَلَمْ يَرْفُثْ وَلَمْ يَفْسُقْ رَجَعَ كَيَوْمِ وَلَدَتْهُ أُمُّهُ». مُتَّفَقٌ عَلَيْه

What Is the Talbiyah Dua'?

During Hajj, there is a special dua' that we make to Allah ﷻ. It should be said often and with an earnest heart, and is learned by every pilgrim. It is as follows:

لَبَّيْكَ اللهُمَّ لَبَّيْكَ، لَبَّيْكَ لا شَرِيكَ لَكَ لَبَّيْكَ،
إنَّ الحَمْدَ والنَّعْمَةَ لَكَ والمُلْكَ، لا شَرِيكَ لَك.

Labbaik Allahuma Labbaik,
Labbaika La Sharika Laka Labbaik,
In-nal-hamda, Wan-ni'mata, Laka Wal-mulk,
La Sharika Lak

"Here I am at Your service.
Oh Allah, here I am at Your service.
You have no partner.
Here I am at your service.
All praise and blessings belong to You.
All dominion is Yours, and You have no partner.'"

This is a beautiful way of presenting ourselves on this journey before our Lord—perhaps the most difficult undertaking of our lives. Hajj is the yearly gathering whereby Muslims affirm their unity and humility before their Lord.

There is no other gathering in the entire world that compares to Hajj. Everyone is treated as equals, regardless of color, status, education, economic level or gender. Everyone stands together shoulder-to-shoulder, and no one should receive preferential treatment. Everyone who performs Hajj returns home changed by the experience.

The Blessed Prophet ﷺ once advised, "Hurry to go on your Hajj journey if it is due on you, for none among you knows what will happen to him (tomorrow)." (Ahmad)

قَالَ رَسُولُ اللهِ ﷺ : «تَعَجَّلُوا إِلَى الْحَجِّ يَعْنِي الْفَرِيضَةَ فَإِنَّ أَحَدَكُمْ لَا يَدْرِي مَا يَعْرِضُ لَهُ». رَوَاهُ أَحْمَد

It is true, our life span may be measured as long or short. We want to make the most of the time we have in this life. By performing Hajj perfectly and as soon as possible, we can hope for Paradise—a beautiful reward. Hajj is so important that the Blessed Prophet ﷺ once mentioned that if a woman performs Hajj, it will be counted for her as if she made jihad in Allah's ﷻ cause. However, because of illness, poverty or political strife, Hajj will be impossible for some people. They are not punished for failing to perform it, as Allah ﷻ is ever-aware of everyone's circumstances and intentions.

Hajj is our chance to purify our soul with the greatest cleaning agent and to bring ourselves closer to our true nature and purpose in this life. Even before we take any vacation or trip anywhere in the world, the Blessed Prophet ﷺ advised us to make Hajj first or to visit Al Madinah or Masjid al Aqsa in Jerusalem. Make your intention to perform Hajj, and when the chance comes, do so without delay!

Common 'Umrah & Hajj Rites

1. Arrive at a fixed point outside Makkah called the 'Miqat,' or entry station to Hajj. You bathe, put on ihram, pray two rak'aat, make the intention for 'Umrah and begin reciting the talbiyah.

2. Arrive at Masjid Al Haram, touch, point to or kiss the Black Stone. Then walk around the Ka'bah seven times repeating dua' and prayers. This is called the **Tawaf طَواف**. Offer a two-rak'aat Salah. Afterwards, drink Zamzam water.

3. Proceed to the walkway between the hills of As-Safa and Al Marwa. Walk back and forth between them seven times called, **Sa'i سَعي**. Men's heads are cut or shaved, while women merely cut a lock of hair. This completes the 'Umrah portion of the Hajj rituals. At this point a break can be made from some of the ihram restrictions.

4. Make your intention for Hajj on the 8th of the month of Dhul Hijjah and bathe. Then put on the ihram garments again. After visiting the Ka'bah and performing tawaf, travel to a place called Mina and remain there from Thuhr until Fajr Salah the next morning.

5. Travel to the valley of 'Arafat. Remain there in the open terrain praising Allah ﷻ and remember the intensity of Judgement Day. Combine Thuhr and 'Asr Salah. It is optional to pray at the foot of the Mount of Mercy.

6. After sunset, travel to Muzdalifah. Combine Maghrib and 'Isha Salah and remain there at night. Gather a set number of small stones for later use. Stand by the Sacred Monument at dawn and glorify Allah ﷻ.

7. Travel back to Mina to throw the stones at the pillars, which represent the Shaytan. Performing this is called **Stoning of the Jamarat رَمي الجَمَرات**. Then an **Udhiya أُضْحِيَة Animal Sacrifice** should be made. (22:37) Men's heads are cut or shaved, while women merely cut a lock of hair. Prepare to celebrate 'Eid Al Adha and exchange ihram for normal clothes.

8. Return to Makkah on the 10th of the month; make tawaf and optional sa'i. Drink Zamzam water. Return to Mina for 3-4 days, stoning the pillars each day. Finally, after the 12th day of Dhul Hijjah, make a **Farewell Tawaf طَواف الوَداع** in Masjid Al Haram (the Ka'bah area), asking Allah's ﷻ forgiveness and making dua'. This completes the Hajj ritual.

Many people then go to Madinah to visit the Prophet's ﷺ Masjid. This is optional. Some may go to Jerusalem afterwards to visit Al Quds and Masjid Al Aqsa.

Mount 'Arafat.

Stoning of the Jamarat

Mina at night.

Masjid Al Mashaar Al Haram, Muzdalifah.

Miqat مِيقات

Route of Hajj

Al Masjid Al Haram
المَسْجِدُ الحَرام

Mina مِنى

What Are the Three Duties?

Islam teaches that there are duties upon every Muslim with regards to the society around them. How can we talk about surrendering our wills to Allah﷽ but forget the fact that we are part of a society that also needs to be guided to the right path?

For example, there was once a story told about a city that was full of evil people. Allah﷽ sent Angel Jibreel﷽ to destroy it, but when he arrived, he was stunned to find a very pious man among them—one who worshipped Allah﷽ often. The Angel rushed back to Allah﷽ and said that he was about to destroy the city of the evil people but stopped when he found that there was a man who prayed living there. Allah﷽ merely commanded, "Start with that one."

Why would the pious man be the first to be destroyed? Perhaps it is symbolic of the fact that worship and prayer are not our only duties as Muslims. We must also try to influence others to do right. Since this pious man never carried his knowledge to others, he was not deemed worthy of preferential treatment by Allah﷽.

How many peoples have We destroyed that gave themselves to wrongdoing? They fell from their roofs! And how many wells lie idle and neglected and castles, high and strong also? Don't they travel through the land so that their hearts may learn the wisdom (in all this) and that their ears may learn to hear? Truly it's not their eyes that are blind, but the hearts within their chests! Surat Al Hajj (The Pilgrimage) 22:45-46

Abu Bakr As-Siddiq﷜ narrated: "O you people! You recite this Ayah: Take care of yourselves! If you follow the guidance no harm shall come to you from those who are astray (5:105). I indeed heard the Messenger of Allah ﷺ saying: 'When the people see the wrongdoer, and they do not stop him (from doing wrong), then it is soon that Allah shall envelope you in a punishment from Him.'" (Abu Dawud)

﴿فَكَأَيِّن مِّن قَرْيَةٍ أَهْلَكْنَٰهَا وَهِيَ ظَالِمَةٌ فَهِيَ خَاوِيَةٌ عَلَىٰ عُرُوشِهَا وَبِئْرٍ مُّعَطَّلَةٍ وَقَصْرٍ مَّشِيدٍ ۝ أَفَلَمْ يَسِيرُوا۟ فِى ٱلْأَرْضِ فَتَكُونَ لَهُمْ قُلُوبٌ يَعْقِلُونَ بِهَآ أَوْ ءَاذَانٌ يَسْمَعُونَ بِهَا فَإِنَّهَا لَا تَعْمَى ٱلْأَبْصَٰرُ وَلَٰكِن تَعْمَى ٱلْقُلُوبُ ٱلَّتِى فِى ٱلصُّدُورِ﴾

سُورَةُ ٱلْحَجّ 22: 45 - 46

عَنْ أَبِي بَكْرٍ الصِّدِّيقِ أَنَّهُ قَالَ يَا أَيُّهَا النَّاسُ إِنَّكُمْ تَقْرَءُونَ هَذِهِ الْآيَةَ ﴿يَٰأَيُّهَا ٱلَّذِينَ ءَامَنُوا۟ عَلَيْكُمْ أَنفُسَكُمْ لَا يَضُرُّكُم مَّن ضَلَّ إِذَا ٱهْتَدَيْتُمْ﴾ 5: 105 وَإِنِّي سَمِعْتُ رَسُولَ اللهِ ﷺ يَقُولُ: «إِنَّ النَّاسَ إِذَا رَأَوْا ظَالِمًا فَلَمْ يَأْخُذُوا عَلَى يَدَيْهِ أَوْشَكَ أَنْ يَعُمَّهُمُ اللهُ بِعِقَابٍ مِنْهُ». رَوَاهُ أَبُو دَاوُدَ

In Islamic teachings, there are several duties that a Muslim has to do, based on the commandments of Allah﷽ in the Qur'an. Three of those duties positively impact the society around them. You don't have to do them every day, nor is there any set time or place in which they must be performed. The simple rule is, if the situation presents itself to do one of these three duties, then you should do them. The three duties are:

1. Inviting others to Islam,
2. Striving in the way of Allah and
3. Encouraging the good while forbidding the evil. We shall explore each of these separately.

What Is Da'wah?

Call people to the path of your Lord with wisdom and inspiring speech. Reason with them in a superior and respectful manner. Certainly, your Lord knows best who strays from His path and who is guided. Surat An-Nahl (The Bees) 16:125

﴿ٱدْعُ إِلَىٰ سَبِيلِ رَبِّكَ بِٱلْحِكْمَةِ وَٱلْمَوْعِظَةِ ٱلْحَسَنَةِ وَجَٰدِلْهُم بِٱلَّتِى هِيَ أَحْسَنُ إِنَّ رَبَّكَ هُوَ أَعْلَمُ بِمَن ضَلَّ عَن سَبِيلِهِ وَهُوَ أَعْلَمُ بِٱلْمُهْتَدِينَ﴾ سُورَةُ ٱلنَّحْل 16:125

Ideally, the duty of anyone who believes strongly in something is to bring what he or she knows to others. What good is something if it's not shared? In Islam, the way to salvation in this life and the next is to share knowledge of Islam with others.

The term here is **Da'wah** دَعْوَة **Calling Others**. A person who is giving da'wah, or telling others about Islam, is termed a **Da'i** دَاعِي **Caller**.

There are two levels of da'wah. First, there is the organized effort to promote Islam, done by people who band together for such a purpose. They get together and plan strategies for how best to tell others about Allah's deen. In fact, it was the practice of the Blessed Prophet ﷺ to send people far and wide to teach people about Allah, Islam and their duty to their Creator. The words spoken in promotion of the truth are the best of all. They are following the command of Allah when He said, *Whose word is better than one who calls people to Allah, works righteousness and declares, "I bow in peaceful surrender (to Allah)?"* Surat Fussilat (Explained in Detail) 41: 33

﴿وَمَنْ أَحْسَنُ قَوْلاً مِّمَّن دَعَا إِلَى اللَّهِ وَعَمِلَ صَلِحًا وَقَالَ إِنَّنِي مِنَ الْمُسْلِمِينَ﴾ سُورَةُ فُصِّلَت 33:41

The second level is the personal level. Everyday we come into contact with lots of Muslims and non-Muslims. They all need to be reminded of their purpose in life. But this doesn't mean you talk about religious issues all day long with everyone you meet. If you see someone who could use some good spiritual advice, you should not hesitate to give it. If the opportunity arises to talk about some aspect of Islam, take it. Don't be afraid or shy, for you are sharing the truth. Others need to know before it's too late.

The Blessed Prophet ﷺ once remarked, "Convey this Message even if only one sentence (ayah)." (Al Bukhari)

قَالَ رَسُولَ اللهِ ﷺ : «بَلِّغُوا عَنِّي وَلَوْ آيَةً». رَوَاهُ الْبُخَارِيُّ

The Blessed Prophet ﷺ said, "Learn the required duties of Islam and the Qur'an then teach them to others, for I will not live forever." (At-Tirmidhi)

عَنْ أَبِي هُرَيْرَةَ ﷺ قَالَ، قَالَ رَسُولُ اللهِ ﷺ : «تَعَلَّمُوا الْقُرْآنَ وَالْفَرَائِضَ وَعَلِّمُوا النَّاسَ فَإِنِّي مَقْبُوضٌ». رَوَاهُ التِّرْمِذِي

So you can see that not only must we bring ourselves closer to the One Who created us, but we must also share that knowledge with others. If we don't, others may accuse us on the Day of Judgement of neglecting to tell them about the one thing that would have saved them from Hellfire.

What Is Jihad?

The word **Jihad** جِهَاد, literally means to work for something with determination. It does not mean only 'holy war.' The Arabic word for war is **harb** حَرْب and the word for fighting is **qitaal** قِتَال. This is important to know because making jihad is any action that is done to further the cause of Allah. Even giving da'wah in a difficult situation, traveling for the sake of gaining knowledge or donating money when it's a hardship can be a type of jihad.

However, the word jihad is most often associated with the act of physically confronting evil and wrong-doing. Hence, it can be applied to the act of fighting as well. But the goal of a physical jihad is not to wage war, gain riches or kill people; it is to further the cause of Allah, Islam, and to ensure justice on Earth. (5:8) Then, when the evil is removed or the opposing side seeks peace, we are to make peace as well. (8:61)

Abu Musa ﷺ narrated, "The Messenger of Allah was asked about a man who fights out of bravery, one who fights out of protection (for himself or others), and one who fought to be seen. Which of them is in the cause of Allah? He said, 'Whoever fought so that the Word of Allah is supreme, then he is in Allah's cause.'" (Agreed upon)

عَنْ أَبِي مُوسَى ﷺ، قَالَ: «سُئِلَ رَسُولُ اللهِ ﷺ عَنِ الرَّجُلِ يُقَاتِلُ شَجَاعَةً وَ يُقَاتِلُ حَمِيَّةً وَ يُقَاتِلُ رِيَاءً فَأَيُّ ذَلِكَ فِي سَبِيلِ اللهِ؟ قَالَ: مَنْ قَاتَلَ لِتَكُونَ كَلِمَةُ اللهِ هِيَ الْعُلْيَا فَهُوَ فِي سَبِيلِ اللهِ». مُتَّفَقٌ عَلَيْهِ

Physical jihad may only be initiated for three reasons:
1. To defend the Muslim community against aggression.
2. To eliminate an evil force that is oppressing people.
3. To remove any barrier to the free flow of Islamic da'wah. (8:39)

The first two are easy to understand. The third would be necessary if, for example, there was a country which forbade the practice of Islam or its preaching. It's interesting to note that the Prophet ﷺ once said, "The Mujahid is one who strives against his own soul." (At-Tirmidhi)

قَالَ رَسُولَ اللهِ ﷺ : «الْمُجَاهِدُ مَنْ جَاهَدَ نَفْسَهُ». رَوَاهُ التِّرْمِذِيّ

The Prophet's ﷺ statement referred to the struggle against your own soul and the temptations that affect it as a kind of Jihad. If Muslims are being oppressed or victimized, then they must fight back. (42:41-42) If anyone dies in jihad, they are promised Paradise. A **Shaheed** شَهِيد **Martyr** is described this way by Allah ﷻ, *Don't think that those who were killed in Allah's Cause are dead. No, they are alive, finding their bounty in the presence of their Lord.*
Surat Al 'Imran (The Family of 'Imran) 3:169

﴿ وَلَا تَحْسَبَنَّ الَّذِينَ قُتِلُوا فِي سَبِيلِ اللَّهِ أَمْوَاتًا بَلْ أَحْيَاءٌ عِندَ رَبِّهِمْ يُرْزَقُونَ ﴾ سُورَةُ آلِ عِمْرَان 3:169

A Mujahid مُجَاهِد **is Someone who Engages in jihad.** Allah ﷻ also explained for us the reasons why fighting is sometimes a part of jihad. Allah ﷻ said, *Let those fight in the Cause of Allah who sell the life of this world for the next life. To the one who fights in the Cause of Allah, whether he is killed or achieves victory, We shall soon give him a great reward. And why shouldn't you fight in the Cause of Allah and of those who, being weak, are mistreated, the men, women and children whose only cry is: Our Lord! Save us from this land whose people are oppressors and bring to us from You someone who will protect us, and bring to us from You someone who will help. Those who believe fight in the Cause of Allah, and those who reject faith fight in the cause of evil. So fight against the friends of Shaytan. Weak is the plan of Shaytan.* Surat An-Nisa' (The Women) 4: 74-76

﴿ فَلْيُقَاتِلْ فِي سَبِيلِ اللَّهِ الَّذِينَ يَشْرُونَ الْحَيَاةَ الدُّنْيَا بِالْآخِرَةِ وَمَن يُقَاتِلْ فِي سَبِيلِ اللَّهِ فَيُقْتَلْ أَوْ يَغْلِبْ فَسَوْفَ نُؤْتِيهِ أَجْرًا عَظِيمًا ﴾ ﴿ وَمَا لَكُمْ لَا تُقَاتِلُونَ فِي سَبِيلِ اللَّهِ وَالْمُسْتَضْعَفِينَ مِنَ الرِّجَالِ وَالنِّسَاءِ وَالْوِلْدَانِ الَّذِينَ يَقُولُونَ رَبَّنَا أَخْرِجْنَا مِنْ هَذِهِ الْقَرْيَةِ الظَّالِمِ أَهْلُهَا وَاجْعَل لَّنَا مِن لَّدُنكَ وَلِيًّا وَاجْعَل لَّنَا مِن لَّدُنكَ نَصِيرًا ﴾ ﴿ الَّذِينَ آمَنُوا يُقَاتِلُونَ فِي سَبِيلِ اللَّهِ وَالَّذِينَ كَفَرُوا يُقَاتِلُونَ فِي سَبِيلِ الطَّاغُوتِ فَقَاتِلُوا أَوْلِيَاءَ الشَّيْطَانِ إِنَّ كَيْدَ الشَّيْطَانِ كَانَ ضَعِيفًا ﴾ سُورَةُ النِّسَاء 4:74-76

In principle, the Muslim Ummah can declare jihad to defend themselves, or struggle against an evil oppressor. (8:65-66) But commanding the Ummah or a Muslim nation to engage in jihad can only be done by the **Amir** أمِير **Leader of the Ummah** or the Muslim country. (4:59)

As there is no Muslim amir or khalifa for the Muslim ummah, legitimate claims to call for jihad can be made by the leaders of Muslim nations. Muslims have settled throughout the world and live quite comfortably in non-Muslim lands. Now, although there are many Muslim countries, due to this very issue of their disunity, they are unable to unite together to elect a khalifa or one leader for the whole ummah. When the Muslim ummah is able to elect a leader, then it is his responsibility to look after the affairs of the ummah including declaring jihad, if necessary. If jihad is declared, Muslims must obey and follow the rules of engagement laid out in the Qur'an and hadith. (9:38-41)

According to Islamic teachings, a Muslim army should only fight against those who are fighting us. (22:39-40) We are not allowed to hurt women, children, the elderly or the sick, nor are we allowed to harm plants, homes, property or animals. Anyone who declares jihad but doesn't follow these rules is a wrong-doer and must be stopped. If we are called upon to participate in jihad, as declared by our chosen leader, then we must give our all in the effort. Allah ﷻ has promised that those who struggle with their strength, property and lives will be rewarded with the highest rank near to Him. (9:20, 3:195 & 49:15)

Intentionally taking one's own life, even in warfare, is forbidden in Islam. The Blessed Prophet Muhammad ﷺ once said, "A person who kills himself with a weapon will have that weapon in his hand and will kill himself forever in the fire of Hell." (Al Bukhari)

قَالَ رَسُولُ اللهِ ﷺ : «وَمَنْ قَتَلَ نَفْسَهُ بِحَدِيدَةٍ، فَحَدِيدَتُهُ فِي يَدِهِ، يَجَأُ بِهَا فِي بَطْنِهِ فِي نَارِ جَهَنَّمَ خَالِدًا مُخَلَّدًا فِيهَا أَبَدًا». رَوَاهُ الْبُخَارِيُّ

The earliest Muslims, though they fought the enemy with bravery and courage, never ever threw themselves on the enemy's swords and spears; they, including the Sahaba, fought with full faith that they might live to fight again another day. In the pursuit of jihad, it is necessary for us to correctly understand the Islamic teachings by studying them, directly from the Qur'an and the Sunnah. Only then can the duty of jihad be properly carried out, and can the Muslims take a stand for justice and fairness on Earth.

As for those who strive hard in Us (Our Cause), We will surely guide them to Our Paths. And verily, Allah is with the good doers. Surat Al-Ankaboot 29:69

﴿وَلَا تَحْسَبَنَّ الَّذِينَ قُتِلُوا فِي سَبِيلِ اللَّهِ أَمْوَاتًا بَلْ أَحْيَاءٌ عِنْدَ رَبِّهِمْ يُرْزَقُونَ﴾ سُورَةُ العَنْكَبوت 69:29

The Blessed Prophet ﷺ once said, "Allah grants time to the oppressor, but when He finally seizes him, He doesn't let him escape." (Al Bukhari, Muslim)

قَالَ رَسُولُ اللهِ ﷺ : «إِنَّ اللهَ لَيُمْلِي لِلظَّالِمِ حَتَّى إِذَا أَخَذَهُ لَمْ يُفْلِتْهُ». رَوَاهُ الْبُخَارِيُّ وَمُسْلِمٌ

The Blessed Prophet ﷺ once said, and beware of going to extremes in religious matters, for those who came before you were destroyed because of going to extremes in religious matters. (An-Nasa'i)

قَالَ رَسُولُ اللهِ ﷺ : «إِيَّاكُمْ وَالْغُلُوَّ فِي الدِّينِ فَإِنَّمَا أَهْلَكَ مَنْ كَانَ قَبْلَكُمُ الْغُلُوُّ فِي الدِّينِ». رَوَاهُ النَّسَائِيُّ

Encouraging the Good and Forbidding the Evil

An important part of our daily life is not compromising our morals and beliefs. If a friend starts drinking alcohol or watching unacceptable programs on television, should we join him, ignore him or encourage healthy habits and entertainment?

Many people stand by and do nothing when others do or say the wrong things. Yet, what happens when people stand by and do nothing while sinful things are occurring that harm others and the society? The world is built by people who care, and caring people take action to make the world a better place for all. Read what Allah ﷻ said, You who believe, stand up firmly for justice as witnesses before Allah, and even (be a fair witness) against yourselves or your parents or your relatives also. And whether it's (against) the rich or poor, too, because Allah can protect both sides the best. Don't follow the lusts (of your hearts) lest you swerve and if you distort (the truth) or decline to do justice, Allah is indeed aware of everything you do. Surat An-Nisa' (The Women) 4:135

﴿يَا أَيُّهَا الَّذِينَ آمَنُوا كُونُوا قَوَّامِينَ بِالْقِسْطِ شُهَدَاءَ لِلَّهِ وَلَوْ عَلَى أَنْفُسِكُمْ أَوِ الْوَالِدَيْنِ وَالْأَقْرَبِينَ إِنْ يَكُنْ غَنِيًّا أَوْ فَقِيرًا فَاللَّهُ أَوْلَى بِهِمَا فَلَا تَتَّبِعُوا الْهَوَى أَنْ تَعْدِلُوا وَإِنْ تَلْوُوا أَوْ تُعْرِضُوا فَإِنَّ اللَّهَ كَانَ بِمَا تَعْمَلُونَ خَبِيرًا﴾ سُورَةُ النِّسَاء 135:4

In the same way, if you saw members of a charitable organization giving food to the poor, what would you do? Should you just ignore them, saying, "It's not my problem," or "They have enough assistance?" Or would you offer help in distributing the food or, at the very least, give the workers some kind words of encouragement? (14:24)

Whoever recommends and helps a good cause becomes a partner in it. And whoever recommends and helps an evil cause shares in its burdens, and Allah has power over all things. (4:85)

﴿مَّن يَشْفَعْ شَفَاعَةً حَسَنَةً يَكُن لَّهُ نَصِيبٌ مِّنْهَا وَمَن يَشْفَعْ شَفَاعَةً سَيِّئَةً يَكُن لَّهُ كِفْلٌ مِّنْهَا وَكَانَ اللَّهُ عَلَى كُلِّ شَيْءٍ مُّقِيتًا﴾ سُورَةُ النِّسَاء 4:85

Abu Sa'id Al Khudri narrated, I heard the Messenger of Allah saying, "He who amongst you sees something abominable should modify it with the help of his hand; and if he has not strength enough to do it, then he should do it with his tongue, and if he has not strength enough to do it, (even) then he should (abhor it) from his heart, and that is the least of faith." (Muslim)

عَنْ أَبِي سَعِيدٍ الْخُدْرِيِّ سَمِعْتُ رَسُولَ اللهِ يَقُولُ: «مَنْ رَأَى مِنكُمْ مُنْكَرًا فَلْيُغَيِّرْهُ بِيَدِهِ فَإِنْ لَمْ يَسْتَطِعْ فَبِلِسَانِهِ فَإِنْ لَمْ يَسْتَطِعْ فَبِقَلْبِهِ وَذَلِكَ أَضْعَفُ الْإِيمَانِ». رَوَاهُ مُسْلِمٌ.

Islam is a proactive way of life, meaning, we are highly encouraged to get involved and take action in the defense and promotion of the truth. Why are Muslims asked to get involved in bettering the welfare of the society and uplifting those around them? Quite simply, because Allah says, You are the best community brought out of humanity. You encourage what is right and forbid what is wrong, and you believe in Allah. Surat Al 'Imran (The Family of 'Imran) 3:110

﴿كُنتُمْ خَيْرَ أُمَّةٍ أُخْرِجَتْ لِلنَّاسِ تَأْمُرُونَ بِالْمَعْرُوفِ وَتَنْهَوْنَ عَنِ الْمُنكَرِ وَتُؤْمِنُونَ بِاللَّهِ وَلَوْ ءَامَنَ أَهْلُ الْكِتَابِ لَكَانَ خَيْرًا لَّهُم مِّنْهُمُ الْمُؤْمِنُونَ وَأَكْثَرُهُمُ الْفَاسِقُونَ﴾

سُورَةُ آلِ عِمْرَان 3:110

Islam teaches that it is our nature to incline toward good and to right wrongs. When we see misconduct, it is our nature to want to stop it because it is displeasing to our senses.

In Arabic, these two actions are called **Encouraging the Good** الأَمْرُ بِالْمَعْرُوف and **Forbidding the Bad** النَّهْيُ عَنِ الْمُنْكَر. When we try to make our societies better by opposing evil, we make a safer and more orderly world for all to live in. Peace and security are the basic goals of a civilization. Islam gives us the definitive prescription for achieving that condition and making it a reality.

What sorts of things should we try to encourage in our societies? Free medical care, aid to the poor and orphans, better schools, accountability in government, clean water and air, humane treatment of animals and assistance for the elderly and handicapped are good things to start with.

What evils should we strenuously oppose and work against? Pornography, bars and pubs, smoking, sexually suggestive images on TV and in advertisements, corruption in government, waste and pollution and inhumane treatment of all creatures. (30:41) These issues need many concerned people to make a change. (3:178-179)

This world is not perfect, but we can employ our hands, words and feelings toward providing justice, fairness, equality and making the world a better place. This is the purpose of encouraging the right and forbidding the wrong.

The Prophet said, "The metaphor of a person who complies with Allah's orders and prohibitions in comparison to those who violate them is like the metaphor of some people who drew lots for their seats in a boat. Some of them were given seats on the upper deck, and the others, on the lower deck. When those on the lower deck needed water, they would have had to go up to fetch the water, so they said, "Let us make a hole in our part of the ship and save those who are above us from our troubling them." If the people on the upper deck let the others do what they suggested, all the people in the boat would be destroyed, but if they prevented them, both groups would be safe." (Al Bukhari)

عَنِ النَّبِيِّ : «مَثَلُ الْقَائِمِ عَلَى حُدُودِ اللهِ وَالْوَاقِعِ فِيهَا كَمَثَلِ قَوْمٍ اسْتَهَمُوا عَلَى سَفِينَةٍ، فَأَصَابَ بَعْضُهُمْ أَعْلَاهَا وَبَعْضُهُمْ أَسْفَلَهَا، فَكَانَ الَّذِينَ فِي أَسْفَلِهَا إِذَا اسْتَقَوْا مِنَ الْمَاءِ مَرُّوا عَلَى مَنْ فَوْقَهُمْ فَقَالُوا لَوْ أَنَّا خَرَقْنَا فِي نَصِيبِنَا خَرْقًا، وَلَمْ نُؤْذِ مَنْ فَوْقَنَا. فَإِنْ يَتْرُكُوهُمْ وَمَا أَرَادُوا هَلَكُوا جَمِيعًا، وَإِنْ أَخَذُوا عَلَى أَيْدِيهِمْ نَجَوْا وَنَجَوْا جَمِيعًا». رَوَاهُ الْبُخَارِيُّ.

This example illustrates the way in which everyone benefits when one enjoins the good on others and the ways in which we can suffer if we do not stop others from doing harm.

Jihad in the News

I turned on the evening news to see what was happening in the world. The first report was about a terrorist group, the Islamic Jihad Brigade, which was planting bombs on planes. The second report was about <u>Muslim extremist</u> groups declaring a jihad against America. The final report was about <u>Islamic terrorism</u> in the West.

Whew, talk about some issues! It seems that whenever some trouble happens in the Middle East, or elsewhere, non-Muslims somehow try to connect it with Islam or Muslims. Even worse, many times, so-called Muslim people will talk about **Jihad جهاد Struggling in Allah's Cause** when they're not even good Muslims to begin with.

Just what is jihad and why do the non-Muslim media make it look like all Muslims are bomb-throwers and radicals? This is an issue that Muslims feel strongly about because it affects us inside as well as outside the Ummah, or community.

After the United States federal building in Oklahoma City, Oklahoma, was bombed in 1995, several masaajid were burnt down; Muslim homes were vandalized, and the FBI and the news media were fingering Muslims as the responsible party. They made all Muslims seem as if they were somehow guilty!

Then, when the nation found out that it was a white Christian man who did the bombing, did the media apologize to us? Did churches get burnt down or was Jesus made fun of? Did they talk about <u>Christian terrorism</u>? Of course not! In this case, they recognized that a religion could not be blamed for what this man did, no matter what the culprit said.

The situation became even worse after the September 11, 2001, attack on the World Trade Center in New York City. Even though Muslims condemned the act and suffered hundreds of losses of their own in the Twin Towers, the media and some politicians still convinced the American public to immediately jump to the wrong conclusions. Instead of blaming a radical fringe element from the Middle East that wanted to make a political statement. For the next several months, the news was filled with discussions about the very religion of Islam itself and its alleged "acceptance of violence."

Even though multitudes of Muslim leaders pointed out that suicide bombing and killing innocent civilians are against the teachings (and practice) of the Prophet ﷺ, all the false stereotypes and prejudices against Islam came out, with no checks or balances. The resulting wars in Afghanistan, Iraq, and elsewhere, gave many Muslims the impression that one small Western minority was effectively using the West to further its own interests in the Middle East. Other nations soon followed and used the War on Terror to crush the Muslim movements in their lands, movements that only wanted to gain freedom and fairness and to get out from under military occupation.

It is interesting to note that Islam is the only spiritual tradition that seems to be mentioned by name in connection with terrorism. This is the fault of the often-biased media that sees Islam as a strange and exotic thing. You will never hear reporting about a Christian terrorist or a Jewish terrorist, for example, even if people from those groups do terrible things in the name of their beliefs. Even the Nazis of Germany, the KKK, the IRA, the Aryan Nation and others are all Christians acting on behalf of their religion, but you will never hear their religion being mentioned.

So just what is the position of Islam on war and conflict? Allah﷾ has said in the Qur'an that He does not love those who create trouble in the Earth. (16:90) He also said that people who do wrong will be punished. This does not mean that Islam prohibits fighting or self-defense. Allah﷾ said, *And those who, when they are oppressed wrongly, help and defend themselves.* Ash-Shura (The Consultations) 42:39

﴿وَ ٱلَّذِينَ إِذَآ أَصَابَهُمُ ٱلْبَغْيُ هُمْ يَنتَصِرُونَ﴾ سُورَةُالشُّورى 39:42

Islam stands against random violence and senseless killing. According to the Qur'an, *whoever kills a person not in retaliation for a person killed, nor (as a punishment) for spreading disorder on the earth, is as if he has killed the whole of humankind, and whoever saves the life of a person is as if he has saved the life of the whole of humankind.* (The Table) 5: 32

﴿أَنَّهُ مَن قَتَلَ نَفْسَا بِغَيْرِ نَفْسٍ أَوْ فَسَادٍ فِي ٱلْأَرْضِ فَكَأَنَّمَا قَتَلَ ٱلنَّاسَ جَمِيعًا وَمَنْ أَحْيَاهَا فَكَأَنَّمَآ أَحْيَا ٱلنَّاسَ جَمِيعًا﴾ سُورَةُالمَائِدَة 32:5

Of course, the life in question is of an innocent person. *(See 2:190, 2:229 and 16:90, for example.)*

Chapter 9
Tales of Ancient Days

The First Humans

You have already learned that Allah offered the responsibility of free will to the rest of the Universe and that all animate and inanimate things declined, knowing what a huge burden it would be.

Then Allah offered this trust to the unformed human soul, and the soul accepted. Therefore, Allah announced that He was going to create a khalifa. When the angels realized what choices and actions would be available to humans, they worriedly asked Allah if it would be good for Earth. Will you place there a creature who will create disorder and shed blood?" they asked. Surat Al Baqarah (The Cow) 2:30

Allah, ever well aware, told them that He knew what they did not. He even added that they will soon be ordered to bow down to humans. (38:71-72) Then He caused humans to form. When **Adam** آدَم and **Hawwa** حَوَّاء awakened to a fully conscious mind, Allah gave them the awareness and understanding of their environment and the world around them.

Then Allah commanded the angels to explain the significance of the earthly environment, but they could not. So Allah proved to the angels that Adam was capable of understanding his environment in ways the angels could not. The angels were amazed and bowed in respect to Adam when Allah ordered them to. (2:31-34)

Another race of beings, which Allah had created before humans, was the jinn. One of these jinn, by the name of Iblis, was watching the angels bow. He stood stiffly as they bowed. (18:50) Allah questioned him, "O Iblis, why didn't you bow along with the angels?" Surat Al Hijr (The Rocky Tract) 15:32

Iblis was full of vanity and pride; he exclaimed, "You made me from fire and him from dirt." Surat Al A'raf (The Heights) 7:12

Iblis thought he was too good to bow to a creature made from dirt (water, carbon and other elements of the earth). Allah commanded Iblis to go away, but Iblis foolishly challenged Allah by saying, "O my Lord! Because you misled me, I shall indeed adorn the path of error for them (mankind) on the earth, and I shall mislead them all." Surat Al Hijr (The Rocky Tract) 15:39

Allah responded with His own challenge, saying Iblis could remain alive until the Day of Judgement and could try to carry out his sinister pledge. Then Allah said, "Over My servants you will have no authority, except with the ones who put themselves in the wrong and follow you." Surat Al Hijr (The Rocky Tract) 15:42

Iblis arrogantly declared that he would create false desires in humans to lead them away from the truth. (4:119) So Allah warned Iblis that if any humans chose to believe in him, then they would enter Hellfire along with all the evil jinn who dared to defy Allah. (4:121) Iblis left to carry out his plans, confident of his victory. But Allah had equipped humans with defenses that Iblis, also known as Shaytan, never knew they had: intellect and the ability to reason.

Meanwhile, Adam continued to live in the Garden with his wife, Hawwa, whom Allah had also created. They lived a wonderful life of rest, enjoyment and satisfaction. Allah gave them only one rule to follow: stay away from one particular tree, while warning them of the dangers of Shaytan. Allah said, "This is an enemy to you and your mate." Surat Ta-Ha 20:117

Some time later, Shaytan came into the Garden and began to whisper to the couple. He approached Adam and Hawwa and started tempting them with his lies. (4:120) He told them that if they ate from the forbidden tree, they would be powerful and live forever. He said, "Oh Adam, shall I lead you to the tree of Eternity and to a kingdom that never decays?" Surat Ta-Ha 20:120

After some time, their desires got the better of them, and they ate from the forbidden tree. As soon as they ate, they realized their mistake and tried to hide. They began to feel embarrassed by one another's bodies and tried to cover themselves with leaves. (20:121)

Allah's Forgiveness

Allah knew what they had done, as He is All Seeing and All Knowing. He expelled Adam and Hawwa from the Garden and ordered them to live out their lives on Earth. But Allah is Merciful and soon taught them how to repent and ask for forgiveness for their deeds.

They said, "Our Lord, we have wronged ourselves, and if you don't forgive us and have mercy on us, we will surely be lost." *Surat Al A'raf (The Heights) 7:23*

Adam and Hawwa earnestly asked for Allah's forgiveness, and He granted them their request. (3:135) Then Allah assured them, "If, and it will happen, there comes to you guidance from Me, whoever follows My guidance will not lose his way, nor fall into despair. But whoever turns away from My guidance, certainly he will have a life narrowed down and We will raise him up blind on the Day of Judgement." *Surat Ta-Ha 20:123-124*

Adam and Hawwa took this simple instruction and lived out their lives according to Allah's command. In time, they had two sons, **Habeel هابيل Abel** and **Qabeel قابيل Cain**. Allah made Adam His first prophet, or guide for humanity. It was Adam's duty to teach his children to fear Allah and to obey His commands out of love for Him. His wife and children were his first followers.

Adam's two oldest sons decided that they wanted to present an offering to Allah to show their devotion. One day, they went out and each set up a small stone altar, or platform, upon which to offer their gift to Allah. Both Qabeel and Habeel presented their offerings, but Qabeel looked over at his brother's altar in jealousy and envy. Finally, he felt convinced that Allah accepted only his brother Habeel's offering.

In a jealous rage, Qabeel threatened to kill his younger brother. Habeel merely protested that Allah only accepts the offerings of those who are good. (5:27) Habeel then tried to admonish his brother by saying, "If you raise your hand against me, it is not for me to stretch my hand against you to kill you, for I fear Allah, the Lord of the Worlds. As for me, I want you to take my sin on yourself as well as your sins, for you will be a dweller of the fire. The only reward for people who do evil." *Surat Al Ma'idah (The Table) 5:28-29*

Qabeel's rage exploded in a blind fury! He attacked his younger brother and murdered him mercilessly. He was the world's first murderer. After realizing what he had done, Qabeel was filled with regret. He had let his passion and envy rule his mind and had forgotten his reason, instead listening to the whisperings of Shaytan. He even tried to hide the body as he didn't know what to do with it.

While thinking about what to do, he saw a black raven scratching at the ground as if digging for something. As Qabeel watched the raven dig, he cried out, "Woe is me! If only I could be like this raven and hide the shame of my (murdered) brother." *Surat Al Ma'idah (The Table) 5:31*

He realized he could bury his brother's body. He dug a hole in the earth and covered his dead brother with dirt. Thus, the prophecy of Allah found its fulfillment. Allah said that humans could be enemies to each other on earth. In time, after Prophet Adam passed away, his descendants split up into groups and went in different directions.

All the people were no more than a single community; later, they differed. But for a word from your Lord that had already come to pass, a decisive judgement would have been made about their mutual differences. *Surat Yunus (Jonah) 10:19*

﴿وَمَا كَانَ ٱلنَّاسُ إِلَّا أُمَّةً وَٰحِدَةً فَٱخْتَلَفُوا ۚ وَلَوْلَا كَلِمَةٌ سَبَقَتْ مِن رَّبِّكَ لَقُضِيَ بَيْنَهُمْ فِيمَا فِيهِ يَخْتَلِفُونَ﴾ سُورَةُ يُونُس 10:19

The story of Prophet Adam is ancient, but the lessons continue to play out to this very day. Allah sent many guides to the children of Adam in the generations to come. Some prophets and messengers were followed by their people, and some were not. All of those who lived before us are awaiting judgement. We must follow the guidance of Allah as left to us by His last Messenger or lose in this life and the next.

Salasilah Nabi/Rasul

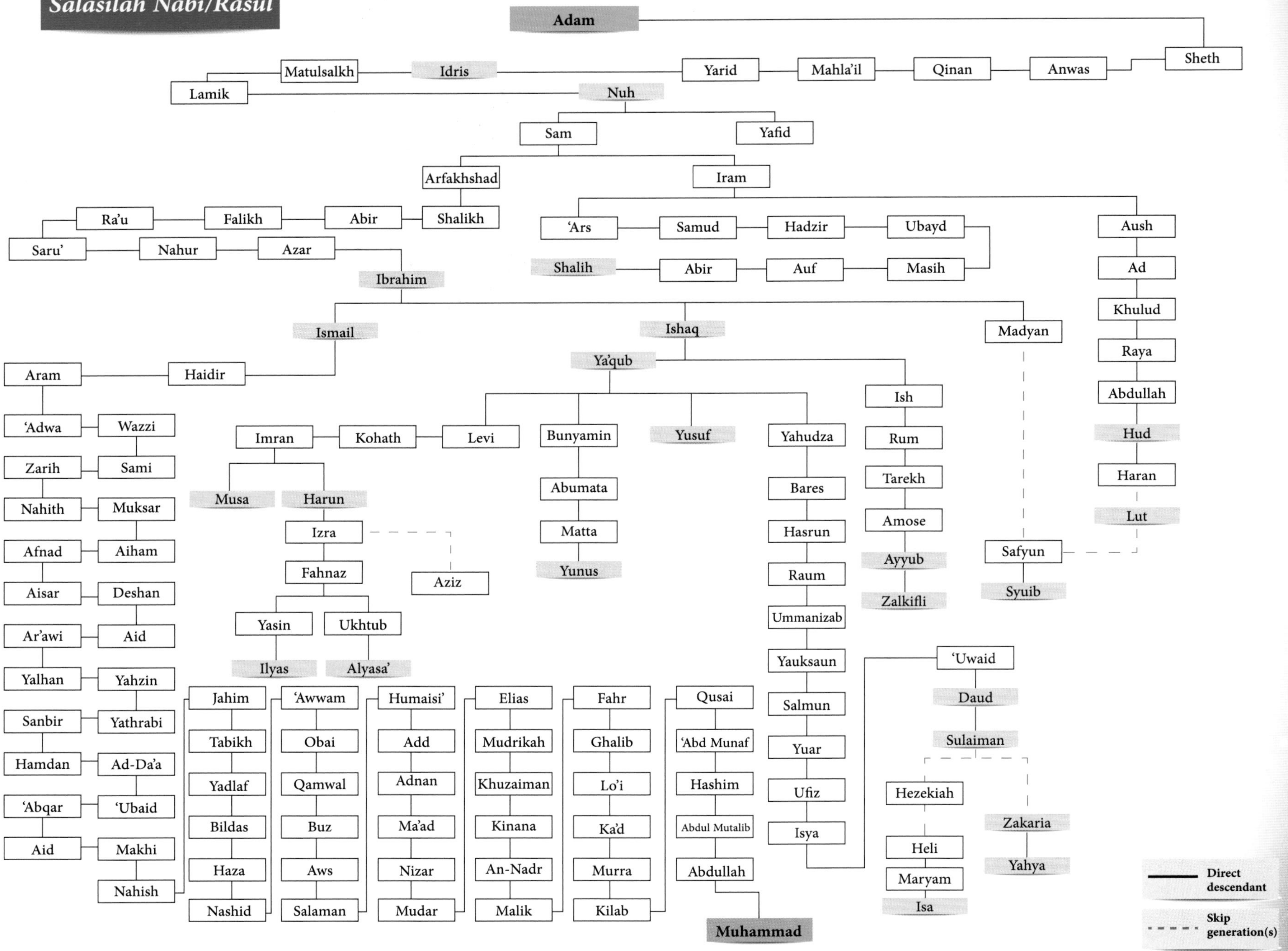

Legend:
— Direct descendant
----- Skip generation(s)

Adam

Sheth — Anwas — Qinan — Mahlā'il — Yarid — Idris — Matulsalkh — Lamik — Nuh

Nuh — Yafid, Sam, Ham

Sam — Iram, Arfakhshad
Iram — 'Ars, Abir, Auf, Masih, Ubayd, Hadzir, Samud, Shalih
'Ars — Shalih
Samud

Aush — Ad — Khulud — Raya — Abdullah — Hud — Haran — Lut

Madyan ----- Safyun — Syuib

Arfakhshad — Shalikh — Abir — Falikh — Ra'u — Saru' — Nahur — Azar — Ibrahim

Ibrahim — Ismail, Ishaq, Haidir

Ishaq — Ish, Ya'qub
Ish — Rum — Tarekh — Amose — Ayyub — Zalkifli

Ya'qub — Yahudza, Yusuf, Bunyamin, Levi
Yahudza — Bares — Hasrun — Raum — Ummanizab — Yauksaun — Salmun — Yuar — Ufiz — Isya
Bunyamin — Abumata — Matta — Yunus
Levi — Kohath — Imran — Harun, Musa
Harun — Izra — Fahnaz — Yasin — Ilyas, Alyasa'
Izra ----- Aziz
Ukhtub — Alyasa'

'Uwaid — Daud — Sulaiman
Daud — Hezekiah — Heli — Maryam — Isa
Sulaiman ----- Zakaria — Yahya

Ismail — Haidir
Haidir — Nabit ... — Aram, 'Adwa, Wazzi, Sami, Muksar, Aiham, Deshan, Aid, Ar'awi, Yalhan, Sanbir, Yathrabi, Ad-Da'a, Hamdan, 'Ubaid, Makhi, Aid, Nahish

'Abqar — 'Ubaid — Hamdan — Ad-Da'a — Yathrabi — Sanbir — Yalhan — Ar'awi — Aid — Deshan — Aisar — Afnad — Aiham — Muksar — Nahith — Sami — Zarih — Wazzi — 'Adwa — Aram

Nahish — Makhi — Aid — 'Abqar — Yahzin — Haza — Bildas — Yadlaf — Qamwal — Obai — Jahim
Jahim — Tabikh — Yadlaf — Bildas — Haza — Nashid
'Awwam — Obai — Qamwal — Buz — Aws — Salaman
Humaisi' — Add — Adnan — Ma'ad — Nizar — Mudar
Elias — Mudrikah — Khuzaiman — Kinana — An-Nadr — Malik
Fahr — Ghalib — Lo'i — Ka'b — Murra — Kilab
Qusai — 'Abd Munaf — Hashim — Abdul Mutalib — Abdullah

Muhammad

The Human Saga

We have learned in previous lessons that the descendants of Adam ﷺ spread out in all directions across the globe. Some groups, or tribes, migrated to Europe, while others migrated to Asia, South America and even as far as Australia. By exploring caves, archeologists have discovered evidence of human habitation on every continent. They have found rock paintings, tools and burial sites. Ancient campfires, dating back tens of thousands of years, have also been unearthed. As Allah ﷻ tells us, *Many were the ways of life that have passed away before you. Travel over the Earth and see what was the end of those who rejected.* Surat Al 'Imran (The Family of 'Imran) 3:137

﴿قَدْ خَلَتْ مِن قَبْلِكُمْ سُنَنٌ فَسِيرُوا۟ فِى ٱلْأَرْضِ فَٱنظُرُوا۟ كَيْفَ كَانَ عَٰقِبَةُ ٱلْمُكَذِّبِينَ﴾ سُورَةُ آلِ عِمْرَان 137:3

There is so much we will never know about ancient humans and their ways—so many names, and deeds of valor and of cowardice. How many great men and women arose and put their lives on the line, bettering humanity? And how many evil people, who rebelled against all goodness, worked their plots and schemes?

We will never know the names of the countless prophets that Allah ﷻ sent to the various peoples. Nevertheless, Allah ﷻ has revealed some of their stories to us in the Qur'an to illustrate the eternal struggle between good and evil that began between Prophet Adam ﷺ and Iblis the Shaytan.

One of these stories from prehistoric times is that of Prophet **Nuh** ﷺ نُوح **Noah** and his efforts to bring his people out of darkness and ignorance. We are uncertain of how many years passed between the time of Prophet Adam ﷺ and the time of Prophet Nuh ﷺ. Perhaps as many as 100,000 years may have elapsed, for we know that Nuh's ﷺ people were sophisticated enough to live in villages and were skilled in farming.

We can, perhaps, assign a rounded figure of his era to between 5,000 and 10,000 years ago. The geographic location seems to be somewhere in ancient Mesopotamia, where, indeed, some of the world's oldest farming villages have been discovered.

How Did Idol-worship Develop Among Nuh's ﷺ People?

Idol-worship was a well-established tradition when Nuh ﷺ was born into his small farming village. The crude statues may have been prominently displayed in the center of the village, framed by the rising mountains all around the large, fertile valley. The Blessed Prophet Muhammad ﷺ explained how the worship of idols was adopted by Nuh's ﷺ ancestors. In a hadith, he explained that there were five famous people who lived in the remote past. They each had many followers and exerted a great influence in their villages.

Their names were Wud, Suwa,' Yaghuth, Ya'uq and Nasra. They each lived at different times and were known for different qualities. After they passed away, legends and stories developed around them. These stories were passed on by village storytellers from generation to generation.

Some people went so far as to build statues to honor and remember famous individuals. As generations passed, Shaytan introduced the idea to them that their forefathers actually worshipped these images. Slowly, people began to believe that these idols were real gods who made the rains fall that nourished their crops. In time, rituals and prayers were introduced, and people virtually forgot about the Supreme Being, Allah ﷻ.

It was during this time that Allah ﷻ chose a righteous man named Nuh ﷺ to spread His guidance and message. A simple villager was chosen to proclaim Allah's ﷻ message to a network of farming villages steeped in ignorance. We record his story directly from the Qur'an.

The Mission Begins

Allah sent Nuh to his people with this mission: Warn your people before there comes to them a terrible Penalty. So Nuh announced, "My People! I am a clear Warner sent to you with the message that you should serve Allah, fear Him, and obey me. And Allah will forgive you your sins, and will respite you to an appointed term. Indeed when Allah's term comes, it is not deferred, if you only know!" Surat Nuh (Noah) 71:1-4

Then Nuh went from village to village with his message, *Surely We sent Nuh to his people. So he said, "My people! Serve Allah! You have no other god but Him. I fear for you the punishment of an awful day!" The chiefs of his people said, "Indeed we see you in an obvious error." He said, "O my people, there is no error in me, but I am a messenger from the Lord of all the worlds. I am only carrying out the duties of My Lord's mission. My advice is sincere to you, and I know things from Allah that you don't. Don't you ever consider that there is coming to you a message from your Lord through a man of your own people? You are warned so you may fear Allah and receive His mercy." Surat Al A'raf (The Heights) (7:59-63)*

So the chiefs of his people who disbelieved replied, *"We don't see you as anything more than a man like us. The only people who seem to be listening to your message are the poor and foolish. We don't see anything in you that is any better than us. We think you are a liar!" Surat Hud 11:27*

Nuh replied, *"My people! Consider if I have a sign from my Lord and that He sent mercy to me from Himself. But the mercy is hidden from your eyes. Should we force you to accept it if you hate it? My people! I'm not asking for any money in return. My reward is from none but Allah. And I won't drive away anyone who believes for they will surely meet their Lord, and I think you are the ignorant ones!" "My people! Who would help me against Allah if I drove the (poor) away? Won't you listen? I'm not telling you that I have the treasures of Allah, nor do I know what is hidden, and I'm not an angel. And I don't say that the people you consider poor will be denied good from Allah. Allah knows best what is in their souls. If I (turned the poor believers away) then I would be a wrong-doer." Surat Hud 11:28-31*

They said, *"Nuh! You have argued with us and lengthened our dispute too long. We dare you to bring on us what you threaten us with, if you are truthful." Nuh replied, "Truly Allah will bring it on you if He wills, and then you won't be able to stop it. My words to you will not help you, as much as I like to give you good advice. If Allah wills to let you stray, He is your Lord, and you will return to Him." Surat Hud 11:32-34*

Nuh's Despair

Nuh, in his despair, prayed to Allah. He said, *"But my call added only to their flight (from the truth). Whenever I called them, so that You might forgive them, they put their fingers into their ears, and wrapped their clothes around themselves, and grew obstinate, and waxed proud in extreme arrogance." Surat Nuh (Noah) 71:6-7*

Nuh continued his plea to Allah, *"So I have called to them aloud. Further, I have spoken to them in public and secretly in private saying, 'Ask forgiveness from your Lord, for He is Forgiving. He will send rain to you in abundance; give you increase in wealth and sons, and bestow on you gardens and rivers (of flowing water). What's the matter with you that you don't place your hope for kindness and perseverance in Allah, seeing that He is the One Who created you in (the womb) in stages?'"*
"Don't you see how Allah created the seven skies, one above the other, and made the moon a light in their midst and made the sun as a lamp? Allah has produced you from the Earth, growing (gradually), and, in the end, He will return you into the (Earth) and raise you forth (again at the Resurrection). Allah has made the Earth for you as a carpet (spread out) that you may go about on spacious plains." Surat Nuh (Noah) 71:8-20

Nuh said, *"My Lord! They have disobeyed me and they follow (men) whose wealth and children give them nothing but loss. And they have planned a tremendous plot, and they have said (to each other), 'Don't abandon your gods; don't abandon Wud or Suwa nor Yaghuth, Ya'uq or Nasr.' They have already misled many, and You grant no increase to the wrongdoers except in straying (from their goal)." Surat Nuh (Noah) 71:21-24*

And it was revealed to Nuh, *"None of your people will believe except those who have already believed. So don't worry over their actions any longer. Build a ship under Our sight and Our direction and don't call on Me anymore about those who are in sin, for they are going to be overwhelmed." Surat Hud 11:36-37*

He started making the Ark. Whenever the leaders of his people passed by him, they mocked at him. He said, "If you ridicule us now, we will look down on and ridicule you also. Soon you will know who will have a punishment that will cover them in shame, on whom will be an ever-lasting punishment!" *Surat Hud 11:38-39*

At last, when Our command came and the oven overflowed, We said, "Take into the Ark a pair of two from every species, along with your family, except those against whom the Word has already been pronounced and (also take into it) those who have believed." And there were only a few who had believed with him. He (Nuh) said, "Embark it. With the name of Allah it sails and anchors. Surely, my Lord is Most Forgiving, Very Merciful." *Surat Hud 11:40-41*

And Nuh said, "My Lord! Don't leave any unbelievers in the land! For, if You do leave (any of) them, they will mislead Your servants and will breed none but wicked, ungrateful people. My Lord, forgive me, my parents, and all who enter my house in faith, and (all) believing men and believing women. To the wrongdoers, grant no increase but in punishment!" *Surat Nuh (Noah) 71:26-28*

And it was sailing with them amidst the waves like mountains. And Nuh called out to his son, who was at an isolated place, "O my child, come on board with us, and do not be in the company of the disbelievers." He said, "I shall take shelter on a mountain which will save me from the water." He said, "There is no saver today from the command of Allah, except the one to whom He shows mercy." And the waves rose high between the two, and he was among those who were drowned. *Surat Hud 11:42-43*

It was said (by Allah), "O earth, suck in your water, and O heaven, stop." And water subsided, and the matter was over. It (the Ark) came to rest on the Judi, and it was said, "Away with the wrongdoers." Nuh called unto his Lord and said, "My Lord, my son is a part of my family, and surely Your promise is true, and You are the greatest of all judges." He said, "O Nuh, in fact, he is not a part of your family. Indeed, he is (a man of) bad deeds. So do not ask Me something of which you have no knowledge. I exhort you not to be among the ignorant." He said, "My Lord, I seek refuge with You that I should ask You something of which I have no knowledge. If You do not forgive me and do not show mercy to me, I shall be among the losers." It was said, "O Nuh, disembark in peace from Us and with blessings upon you and upon the peoples (springing) from those with you. And there are peoples whom We shall give some enjoyment, then a painful punishment from Us will visit them." *Surat Hud 11:44-48*

The Conclusion

The story of Prophet Nuh is one of the most dramatic and intense stories in the Holy Qur'an. For hundreds of years, he tried in every way he could think of, to convince his people to give up sin and idol-worship. But time and time again, they arrogantly refused him and those who believed with him.

Prophet Nuh even lost of one of his sons and his wife because they refused to enter the safety of the ship when the valley was about to be flooded. In the end, Allah informed Prophet Nuh that if a family member is a disbeliever, you no longer have any ties to him or her. (9:23)

Researchers have been searching for the ship, or 'Ark,' of Nuh, for generations. The ship is most likely located on a mountain near northern Iraq or southeastern Turkey. The ancient name of this unknown mountain is Mount Judi. (54:15) There are numerous lessons to learn from Nuh's story and many points to ponder. Ultimately, we understand that the penalty will come, and those who are steeped in sin and ignorance will suddenly find their time is up.

The Ancient Prophets

Allah﷾ sent a prophet or messenger to every community. He did this so that everyone would have a fair chance to hear His message and then decide freely whether to accept it or not. Even though later generations often corrupted or changed the message of a particular prophet, the true spirit of the message remained in one form or another. If the message was completely lost, then Allah﷾ would send another prophet to confront the falsehood and re-establish the truth.

Not all the stories of the prophets are recorded or clear in history after the time of Nuhﷺ. Allah﷾ only includes the stories of some of the prophets in the Qur'an to illustrate lessons and points He wishes to explain to us. Because the invention of writing was still unknown at the time of Nuhﷺ, and for thousands of years afterwards, we must rely on what Allah﷾ and our historians tell us about that age of humanity. We will next explore the story of Prophet **Hud**ﷺ هُود as he tried to bring truth to his community.

Ruins of the People of 'Aad in Oman.

The Lost City of Iram

The archeologist removed his hat and poured a cup full of sand out of it. The last sandstorm was terrible, and the men were still digging the trucks out from under the piles of yellow, granulated sand. The band of archeologists came to the trackless Arabian desert to uncover something captured by a satellite photo, what appeared to be an ancient road leading to the Empty Quarter region of southeastern Arabia.

It was so hot and dry there that very little lived within a hundred miles of where they stood. Few trees, shrubs or even lizards could survive here for very long. A few moments later, the archeologist climbed over a sand dune to get his bearings. When he cleared the top of the rise, he nearly dropped his canteen in astonishment! There before him, like a dead giant, lay the blackened ruins of a long-dead city made of stone.

What used to stand as a fantastic city six thousand years ago now was cracked and crumbled. "My God," he must have muttered. "No one could have survived that!" What the archeologist was referring to was the obvious devastation that had struck the city. The towers were beaten and broken, the walls were buried in sand. The surrounding terrain for hundreds of miles was barren and dry.

The lost city of Iram, also known as Ubar, was finally uncovered in 1992 after lying buried under the sand for over 5,000 years. What makes this find even more exciting is that the Qur'an gives the story of this city and its inhabitants, the 'Aad people. The Qur'an even described the mighty towers which ringed the city.

Of Iram , the men of tall pillars, likes of whom were never created in the lands. Surat Al Fajr (The Dawn) 89:7-8

﴿إِرَمَ ذَاتِ ٱلْعِمَادِ﴾ ﴿ٱلَّتِى لَمْ يُخْلَقْ مِثْلُهَا فِى ٱلْبِلَـٰدِ﴾ سُورَةُالفَجْر 89:7-8

Who Were the 'Aad?

The 'Aad people ruled over a mighty trading city whose main products were frankincense and myrrh, two valuable fragrances. Their city was also an important stop along the trade route from the coast near the Indian Ocean to Palestine and beyond. The ancient Greek geographer, Claudius Ptolemy, heard the legends of this lost city and correctly guessed that it lay somewhere in the southern Arabian peninsula. But already by his time, the city had laid in ruins for thousands of years.

Allah﷾ describes the 'Aad people thus, *(Remember) the 'Aad and the Thamud. Clearly, will their (fate) appear to you from the traces of their buildings. The Shaytan made their deeds pleasing to them and kept them back from the way, though **they** were gifted with intelligence and skill. Surat Al 'Ankabut (The Spider) 29:38*

﴿وَعَادًا وَثَمُودَا وَقَد تَّبَيَّنَ لَكُم مِّن مَّسَـٰكِنِهِمْ وَزَيَّنَ لَهُمُ ٱلشَّيْطَـٰنُ أَعْمَـٰلَهُمْ فَصَدَّهُمْ عَنِ ٱلسَّبِيلِ وَكَانُوا مُسْتَبْصِرِينَ﴾ سُورَةُالعَنكَبوت 29:38

The 'Aad people took their mighty wealth and power to be a sign of their unmatched strength. All travelers had to pass through their city and pay homage to their idols. The countryside was full of fields, farms and springs of water. The weather was always pleasant and mild. They lived a very good life indeed.

The 'Aad behaved arrogantly in the land, against all right. They boasted, "Who is superior to us in power?" But didn't they see that Allah, who created them, was superior to them in strength? But they continued to reject our signs. Surat Al Fussilat 41:15

﴿فَأَمَّا عَادٌ فَاسْتَكْبَرُوا فِي الْأَرْضِ بِغَيْرِ الْحَقِّ وَقَالُوا مَنْ أَشَدُّ مِنَّا قُوَّةً ۖ أَوَلَمْ يَرَوْا أَنَّ اللَّهَ الَّذِي خَلَقَهُمْ هُوَ أَشَدُّ مِنْهُمْ قُوَّةً ۖ وَكَانُوا بِآيَاتِنَا يَجْحَدُونَ﴾ سُورَةُ فُصِّلَت 41:15

It was indeed a powerful city-state. With their wealth, they were able to construct tall buildings and guard towers of sizes that were unheard of at the time. But their wealth was not obtained by completely honest means. They oppressed the surrounding villages and tribes and raised high taxes on those they controlled. They were tyrants and many who fell under their influence suffered from terrible injustice.

It was in this place that Allah chose a man by the name of Hud to be His prophet. Hud was born either within the city itself or in the countryside. We know nothing of his childhood or what events shaped and molded his character. We do know that he was honest, upright, and strong. He had to be for all the opposition he received. When he began his mission, he tried to shock his people by exposing the truth of which they were unaware.

The Mission Begins

When their brother Hud said to them, "Won't you have awareness of Allah? I am a Messenger to you that you can trust. So be aware of Allah and obey me. I'm not asking for any reward from you. My reward is only from the Lord of the Universe." Surat Ash-Shura (The Consultations) 26:124-127

Then he pointed out to the people their mighty city and asked the question, "Do you build a monument on every high place to amuse yourselves? Are you making your fine buildings in the hope of living there (forever)? And when you apply your strong hand, do you enforce it like you had absolute power? Now be aware of Allah and obey me." Surat Ash-Shura (The Consultations) 26:128-131

Then, after mentioning the rewards they would earn from Allah for following His will, Hud waited for their answer. The people began to shout and raise their fists. Finally, the leaders of the city announced, "It's all the same whether you advise us or not! You're only talking in the same way the ancient people did, and we're not about to be punished." Surat Ash-Shura (The Consultations) 26:136-138

Hud was not to be outdone so easily. On another occasion, he announced in public, "My people! Serve Allah! You have no other god but Him. (Your other gods) are nothing but made up things. My people! I'm asking for no reward from you. My reward is from the One Who made me. Won't you understand? My People! Ask forgiveness from your Lord and turn to Him. He will send you rain and add strength to your strength, so don't go back into sin!" Surat Hud 11:50-52

They said, "Hud! You haven't brought us any proof, and we won't desert our gods just on your word. We refuse to believe you!" Surat Hud 11:53

Then the leaders insulted Prophet Hud and made the people laugh at him. They said, "We think some of our gods must have made you crazy!" He replied," I call Allah to witness, and you see also that I am free from the sin of making partners with Him. So plan your worst against me, and give me no chance. I put my trust in Allah, my Lord and your Lord! Nothing moves without Him having a hold on its forelock. Indeed, my Lord is on the straight track." Surat Hud 11:54-56

Then Hud issued this warning, "If you turn away, at least I gave you the message that I was sent with. My Lord will make another nation succeed you, and you won't harm Him in the least, for my Lord is a guardian over all things." Surat Hud 11:57

Said the chiefs of his people who disbelieved, "We think you're crazy and a liar!" He said, "My people! I'm not crazy, but I'm a Messenger from the Lord of the Universe." Surat Al A'raf (The Heights) 7:66-67

Then Prophet Hud✥ tried one last time to reason with them. He announced, "Aren't you amazed that there has come to you a message from your Lord through a man of your own people, to warn you? Remember that He made you successors after the people of Nuh and gave you power among the nations. Remember the benefits from Allah so you can prosper." *Surat Al A'raf (The Heights) 7:69*

They said, "Do you come to us and tell us to serve only Allah and to give up the religion of our fathers? Bring on us what you threaten us with if you are telling the truth!" *Surat Al A'raf (The Heights) 7:70*

He said, "The punishment and anger are already coming upon you from your Lord. Don't argue with me about the names (of idols) you invented. You and your ancestors had no authority from Allah (to make them up.) Then wait and see. I am also waiting with you." *Surat Al A'raf (The Heights) 7:71*

The End of the 'Aad

With their own tongues, the majority of the 'Aad chose to reject Allah✦ and embrace destruction. They dared Allah✦ to bring the punishment on them in this life. They sat smug and secure in their mighty fortress and thought Hud✥ was crazy and a nuisance. But while the 'Aad were sitting comfortably in their homes, Allah✦ sent the message to Prophet Hud✥ to gather his followers and leave the city, never to return.

Soon, without warning, a terrible wind arose in the moonlit countryside, tearing trees from their roots and raising the dirt and sand high in the sky. As the huge storm swelled and loomed over the city, the people must have thought it was nothing more than a mid-season disturbance.

So, when they saw it as a cloud proceeding towards their valleys, they said, "This is a cloud that will bring us rain." No, it is the very thing you asked to hasten up—a wind in which there is a painful punishment that will destroy every thing with the command of its Lord! So they became such that nothing remained to be seen except their dwelling places. This is how We punish the guilty people. *Surat Al Ahqaf 46:24-25*

The sky turned darker, and the people in the streets looked up nervously as the black cloud raised itself over the horizon. The leaders in their luxurious rooms must have looked around at each other, thinking it would pass. People shuttered their windows, and the horses and camels began to cry and stamp. The violent storm tore whole caravans out of its path, and finally descended upon the city, perhaps with more force than a tornado! The sand covered the streets, and windows and doors were knocked off their hinges. The people were buffeted with flying rocks and debris, running about in the streets in panic.

Sounds of choking, pelting, screaming and cursing could be heard as the people trampled each other and scattered in all directions. The fierce storm raged for seven nights and eight days as the earth rumbled. In the end, nothing living was left, and all the wells, streams and farmlands were covered over with a thick layer of sand.

With the city destroyed, and mountains of sand covering hundreds of miles, the traders' traditional routes were abandoned. As the centuries passed, people remembered the city in legend only. Such was the end of the People of 'Aad.

And as for 'Aad, they were destroyed by a violent windstorm, that He imposed on them for seven nights and eight consecutive days; so you could see them thrown on the ground, as if they were trunks of hollow palm-trees. Now, do you see any remnant of them? *Surat Al Haaqqa (The Reality) 69:6-8*

Who Were the Thamud?

Much of Northern Arabia is arid land and desert. There is very little rainfall in most of the region and life is hard for the people who live there. The only places where many people can live together are the small patches of fertile land surrounding the scattered water wells.

Over 3,000 years ago, **Thamud** ثَمُود, a mighty group of people, controlled Northern Arabia. Their soldiers guarded every well and kept all the other people away from the water. If they let some people bring their herds of animals to drink from the well, they charged them a lot of money for the service.

The leaders of Thamud grew very wealthy from this. No matter how hot the weather was or how much the common people, passing caravans and shepherds needed water, they only gave any if they were paid hefty sums. To protect their wealth and power, Thamud built many castles and kept an army of soldiers all over the city. They thought they were the strongest people anywhere.

The Hopeful Son

Among the Thamud, a special boy named Salih was born. He would later have a mission that would change his people's way of life forever. We can well imagine that he had an easy life growing up. His family members were part of the ruling tribe and he never went without food or water

or whatever else he needed. He probably received a good education and many people thought he would make a fine leader one day.

But then, something happened. Allah doesn't tell us in the Qur'an how Salih came to be interested in the truth. Perhaps he saw the misery and sadness of the poor people who were not allowed to water their animals on hot days. Or maybe he didn't believe in the idols his people were worshipping and decided to look for the real power behind everything in the world, just like the young Ibrahim did. However he found the truth, Allah chose him and made him a prophet with a mission to stop the evil ways of the Thamud.

Salih, who was by now a strong young man, began his mission right away. He had to convince his people to give up idols and let others use the wells. He started by going around his city and telling people about his beliefs.

And to (the people of) Thamud (We sent) their brother, Salih. He said, "O my people, worship Allah. You have no god other than Him. He has created you from earth and made you settle therein. So, seek His forgiveness, then turn to Him in repentance. Surely, my Lord is near, responsive to the prayers." Surat Hud 11:61

Clearly, his people were amazed! Salih was from among them. He had an easy life because of the Thamud. How was this young man speaking out against the very way of life that made them wealthy?

They said, "You were one of us! Our hopes (for the future) were on you, up until now. Are you telling us not to worship what our own fathers worshipped? We have doubts about what you are calling us to." Surat Hud 11:62

He said, "O my people! Tell me, if I have a clear proof from my Lord and there has come to me a Mercy (prophethood) from Him, who then can help me against Allah, if I were to disobey Him? Then you increase me not but in loss." Surat Hud 11:63

The Great Debate

Prophet Salih☼ continued his mission, even though the powerful leaders of Thamud said they didn't believe him. In fact, everyone started talking about Salih☼, whether for good or bad. Some people, mostly the poor, accepted the message of Salih☼, while the arrogant and wealthy rejected him.

Then said the chiefs of his nation who were disbelievers and who denied facing the Hereafter and whom We made affluent in the worldly life, "This (man) is nothing but a human being. He eats from what you eat from and drinks from what you drink. If you obey a human like yourselves, then you will be absolute losers. Does he promise you that, when you die and are turned into dust and bones, you are to be brought forth? Far too improbable is what you are being promised. There is nothing but our worldly life. We die and we live and we are not to be raised again." Surat Al Mu'minun (The Believers) 23:33-37

Prophet Salih☼ didn't give up, because he wanted to confront the main crime of the Thamud: their total and selfish control of the wells. He told his people, *"I am your messenger who you can trust! So be aware of Allah and obey me! I'm not asking for any reward from you. My reward is only from the Lord of the Universe." Surat Al Shu'araa' (The Poets) 26:143-145*

"Will you be left secure in whatever is here, In gardens and springs, And in farms and date-palms, the spathes of which are interwoven? You hew out houses from the hills with pride. So fear Allah and obey me, And do not obey the order of the transgressors Who make mischief on the land and who do not set things right." They said, "You are merely one of those bewitched. You are nothing but a human like us. So, bring a sign if you are one of the truthful." Surat Al Shu'araa' (The Poets) 26:146-154

So Salih☼ brought a camel to the people one day and announced, *"This camel has a right to go to the well for water. You also have a right to use the wells, but on set days in turns. Don't hurt her, or the punishment of a mighty day will come over you." Surat Al Shu'araa' (The Poets) 26:155-156*

The Terrible Crime

Salih's☼ plan was simple. He called people to Allah☼ and gained many followers. At the same time, he exposed the great wrong of Thamud and ordered them to give everyone the right to use the water wells. When they challenged him for a sign, he brought out a special camel and told them to take turns with the camel for water. That would be their test. The leaders, however, had plans of their own. They went to the poor people who believed in Salih☼ and tried to put doubt and fear in their minds.

The leaders of the arrogant party among his people said to those who were reckoned powerless - those among them who believed: "know ye indeed that Salih is an apostle from his Lord?" They said, "We do indeed believe in the revelation which hath been sent through him." The Arrogant party said, "For our part, we reject what ye believe in." Surat Al 'Araaf (The Heights) 7:75-76

The camel was a test. The Thamud were ordered to let the camel have its turn to drink. Then they would learn that everyone should have a fair share.

The leaders of Thamud also had a plan for dealing with Salih's☼ special camel. They said, *"We see a bad sign in you and in your followers." Salih answered them, "Your 'bad sign' is with Allah and you are a people being tested." Surat An Naml (The Ant) 27: 47*

The leaders of Thamud could not take it any longer! They shouted and cursed in anger and one of them took out a long sword and ran at the special camel standing nearby. Before anyone knew what was happening, the evil man killed the camel.

But they called to their companion and he took a sword in hand and hamstrung (her). Surat Al Qamar (The Moon) 54:29

Prophet Salih and his followers were horrified by this cruelty. The leaders of Thamud just laughed and congratulated the man who did it. They went away cheering and announcing what they had done. Then they dared Salih's Lord to punish them. Prophet Salih stood up and called to the Thamud, *"Go and enjoy yourselves in your homes for three days and then the promise (of punishment) will be fulfilled!"* Surat Hud 11:65

For the moment, however, they seemed to go unpunished. There were no lightning bolts from the sky and no angry angels coming after them. They laughed and called Salih a liar.

The Nine Evil Brothers

Prophet Salih became the victim of a cruel whisper campaign. The leaders of Thamud sent their people everywhere to tell people that the message of Salih was false and that the test of camel was a joke. Salih heard about all the talk and cried out, *"My Lord! Help me. They're accusing me of being a liar."* Allah sent him the message, *"In just a little while they will be very sorry."* Surat Al Mu'minun (The Believers) 23:39-40

In the same city, there lived a family of nine brothers. Every one of them was a troublemaker. One day, after hearing everything that went on between Salih and their leaders, they got together and said to each other, *"Let's make a promise by god that we will attack Salih and his family at night. Then we'll say in the morning that none of us were anywhere near (Salih's) house and that we don't lie."*
Surat Al Naml (The Ant) 27: 49

They wanted to kill Salih to get rid of him and his whole family once and for all. But Allah wasn't going to let that happen. He sent a message to Prophet Salih that he should gather all his followers and leave the city. So Salih did as he was commanded and left the city with the few believers.

It was the third day after the camel had been attacked, and the Thamud must have thought that now Salih would really be proven a liar. Everyone was going along with their normal routine: the soldiers were keeping people away from the wells and charging a lot of money to use them, the priests kept praying to idols and the Thamud and their leaders were busy eating, drinking and having fun with their money made from ill-gotten gains.

Then a strange tremor shook the land and the cliff walls into which their cities were carved. After it passed, without any real damage, the people went about their daily lives. But then suddenly, out of nowhere, a massive earthquake struck.

The force of the quake sent people to the floor like piles of sticks. Rocks were falling everywhere. The people of Thamud panicked and screamed in horror. When it was all over, many of the dead lay buried under tons of rock and rubble. The wreckage was extensive, and the leaders were all dead. With their cities destroyed, the few survivors scattered and fled in the morning. This was the end of the arrogant Thamud.

Allah describes this event: *The mighty blast overtook the evil people and they lay on their faces in their homes before the morning as if they had never lived and prospered there. The Thamud rejected their Lord and so the Thamud were removed!* Surat Hud 11:67-68

The land of Al Hijr is now a dry wasteland. A few ruins of stone buildings carved into the cliffs is all that remains of the mighty Thamud.

Thousands of years later, when Prophet Muhammad was traveling through the area where Thamud used to live, now called Al Hijr, he noticed that his Companions had taken some water from an ancient well and were using it to drink and make bread. When he saw them doing this, he ordered them to pour the water on the ground and to feed the bread to the camels. He pointed to another well, the well that Salih's camel drank from and said that they should drink from there. All other wells in the land were bad, he told them.

Claimed by Three, Followed by One

There is one ancient prophet who is revered in the world today by the followers of three distinct spiritual traditions. The Jews hold him as their forefather; the Christians respect him as a prophet, and the Muslims love him as one of the greatest of Allah's﷾ chosen guides to humanity.

The name of this prophet is **Ibrahim** عليه السلام إِبْرَاهِيم, also known as **Abraham** in the English-speaking world. He lived in ancient Mesopotamia around 1,900 BCE. But who can claim his legacy? Who can say that they are following in the footsteps of Prophet Ibrahim عليه السلام? As you follow his story in this lesson, you will begin to see that, although he is claimed by three groups, one follows his example and lives by his example more closely than the others.

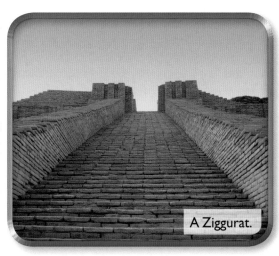

A Ziggurat.

An Idol for Sale

"Idols! Get your idols here!" the young man cried as he hoisted a small stone carving over his head. "Only five silver pieces! Get your idols here!" He had been walking around the splendid city of Ur all morning, trying to sell the small idols his father, Azar the idol-maker, sent with him. He had only one left to sell and knew that he couldn't return home until they were all sold.

He wasn't having much success getting rid of the last one, though. The streets were busy with traders, shoppers, incoming caravans and any number of other colorful sights. The young man, whose name was Ibrahim عليه السلام, looked up at the hot sun in the sky and felt a sudden flash of heat.

He decided to go down to the banks of the Euphrates River to cool off. As he passed through the city gates, he must have been awe-struck to see the endless fields of barley and wheat. If he turned around and looked back at the city, he might have seen the mighty Ziggurats, or 'step-temples,' of the gods. But he continued forward since he was focused on a different goal.

When he reached the cool water, he put the idol on the ground and waded into the refreshing river. After he cooled off, he returned to shore and got ready to leave. He picked up the idol and was about to go when a strange thought entered his mind. If that idol his father made was really a god, what power did it have? What could it do? Everyone prays to them and worships them, but what power could they wield?

Almost without thinking, Ibrahim عليه السلام swung the idol over his head and threw it in the river. "If you have power," he must have thought, "then save yourself." But the idol merely hit the water with a splash and sank quickly in the shallow waters. Ibrahim عليه السلام was scared for a moment. He thought for sure that a thunderbolt would strike him or something. He waited tensely and watched. Nothing happened.

Finally, he waded out in the river and fished the idol off the bottom. He held it up and looked at it. It still had the same expression on its face as before—only this time, it was all wet. "Hmm," he thought. "You can't even save yourself." At that moment, Ibrahim عليه السلام knew the idols were a lie.

Ibrahim's عليه السلام Search for Truth

Ibrahim عليه السلام spent the next few days in restless thought. He no longer felt good about selling the idols that his father made. When he began to avoid his shop, his father thought he was going through a stage that would soon pass.

Finally, Ibrahim عليه السلام could stand it no longer. He confronted his father and said, *"Do you take idols for gods? I see you and your people making a big mistake."* Surat Al An'aam (The Cattle) 6:74

After that, Ibrahim عليه السلام began to spend much of his time out in the fields, alone. He wanted to know what his life meant. What was it all for? He looked around for something more powerful than an idol.

He began to stare at the night sky. Then he saw a bright star. He declared, "This is my lord." But when it set, he lamented, "I don't love those who set." When he saw the moon rising in splendor, he said, "This is my lord." But when it set, too, he said, "Unless I'm guided by the True Lord, I will probably be lost." When he saw the sun rising up, he said, "This is my lord. This is greater." But when it set, he said, "O my people! I am indeed free from all that you join as partners." "For me, I have set my face firmly towards the One who created the skies and the Earth. I will never make partners with Allah." *Surat Al An'aam (The Cattle) 6:76-79*

Azar, the Idol-maker

Ibrahim返 returned to his home and said to his father, "Father! Why do you serve what can't hear or see or do any good for you? My father! I have gained some knowledge that you don't have, so follow me. I will guide you to a way that is right. My father! Don't serve Shaytan, for he is a rebel against the Merciful God. My father! I'm afraid that a punishment might strike you from the Merciful God because you've become a friend to Shaytan."

His father replied, "Do you hate my gods, Ibrahim? If you don't stop this, I'll stone you to death. Now get away from me for a good long time!"

(Before leaving), Ibrahim told him, "Peace be to you. I will pray to my Lord for your forgiveness. He is good to me. And I will turn away from you and those you call upon besides Allah. I will call on my Lord, and maybe by my prayers I won't be left without blessings." *Surat Maryam (Mary) 19:42-48*

The Public Battle

Ibrahim asked his father and his people, "What are these images you worship so much?" They replied, "Our ancestors worshipped them also." Ibrahim replied, "Then you're making a big mistake, and your ancestors did also." The people answered, "Have you brought us the truth, or are you only joking?" He replied, "No! Your Lord is the Lord of the skies and the Earth. He created them, and I testify to it. By Allah! I have a plan for your idols when you're not looking." *Surat Al Anbiya' (The Prophets) 21:52-57*

But his people did not listen to him and teased him harshly.

Then he glanced up at the stars and cried, "I'm hurt (in my heart)." So they turned away from him and left him alone. He approached their idols and addressed them, "Why don't you eat the offerings placed before you? Why don't you speak?" *Surat As-Saaffat (Those Set in Ranks) 37:88-92*

Then, when the day of a great festival came, the people left the city and ventured out in the fields for their celebrations. With the temple unguarded, the time came for Ibrahim返 to act. He fell upon the idols and broke them to pieces, all except the biggest one , so that they may come back to it. *Surat Al Anbiya' (The Prophets) 21:58*

When the people returned and saw what had happened, they were enraged and tried to find out who did it. They asked, "Who has done this to our gods? He must be an evil man." Some people said, "We heard of a boy who talked about them. His name is Ibrahim." (The priests) said, "Then bring him before the eyes of the people so they can see him." (When he was brought) They asked, "Are you the one who did this to our gods, Ibrahim?" He answered, "Their biggest idol must have done it! Ask them (the broken idols), if they can speak." Then the people turned to themselves and said, "We're certainly foolish." Then

Ibrahim's返 curiosity and thirst for knowledge is best illustrated by the following incident.

Once Ibrahim said to Allah, "My Lord! Show me how You give life to the dead." Allah answered him, "Don't you believe?"

"I do," Ibrahim answered. "I only want to satisfy my own curiosity."

Allah replied, "Take four birds and train them to obey you. Then put one of them on each hill and call them to you. They will come to you quickly. By this know that Allah is the Powerful and Wise." *Surat Al Baqarah (The Cow) 2:260*

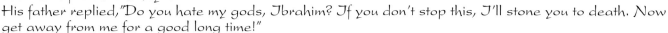

191

they were filled with shame. They said, "You know full well the idols can't speak."
Ibrahim then declared, "So why do you serve, besides Allah, things that can do you no good or bad? To heck with you and the things you worship besides Allah. Don't you have any sense?" Surat Al Anbiya' (The Prophets) 21:58-67

They said, "Build a fire and throw him in the burning flames!" Surat As-Saaffat (Those who set the Ranks) 37::97

They said, "Burn him and protect your gods if you can!" We (Allah) ordered, "Oh fire! Be cool and a safe place for Ibrahim." When they saw the miracle, they were wonder-struck. Then they thought about another plan (to get rid of him), but We (Allah) made them the ones who lost the most. Surat Al Anbiya' (The Prophets) 21:68-70

The Showdown with Namrud

Meanwhile, Ibrahim was receiving revelation from Allah, which he began to write on scrolls of leather. This book is called the **Suhuf صُحُف Scrolls** of Ibrahim. He continued his mission of teaching and calling people away from the idols. With the grace of Allah, he managed to convince quite a few people, including some of his own family members. His nephew Lut became a firm supporter.

But Ibrahim's enemies launched a dangerous plot. They informed the city authorities that idol-worship was being subverted, and eventually news reached the King of Ur, Namrud. He was briefed about this man who rejected the gods. Namrud ordered Ibrahim to be brought before him. When the young man was taken to the palace, he was thrown in a great room. There before him, surrounded on both sides with his nobles and soldiers, was the great King Namrud. Ibrahim neither bowed nor uttered any words of worship to the self-proclaimed god-king. Namrud must have felt insulted.

Do you not know the one who argued with Ibrahim about his Lord, because Allah had given him kingship? When Ibrahim said, "My Lord is the One Who gives life and brings death," he said, "I give life and I bring death." Said Ibrahim, "Allah brings the sun out from the East; now, you bring it out from the West." Here, baffled was the one who disbelieved, and Allah does not bring the wrongdoers to the right path. Surat Al Baqarah (The Cow) 2:258

Namrud knew he could not answer the challenge, and he was silent. But instead of realizing the limitation of his power, he ordered Ibrahim removed from his court. Ibrahim knew he was no longer welcome in Mesopotamia, the land between the two rivers. Not even his own father was on his side. So when Allah gave the command to leave, Ibrahim gathered his followers and left. He secretly headed West towards a land that Allah promised would be blessed for all nations. (21:71)

Just before setting out, however, he asked Allah to forgive his father, just like he promised his father he would, because Ibrahim was very tender-hearted. But Allah will not forgive those who choose to do wrong. (9:114)

Two Men Who Parted

Ibrahim traveled for weeks towards his new home, but along the way, he found that there were too many people in his group. Some people were close to Lut and quarreled with Ibrahim's close companions. After discussing the situation, it was decided that the two groups would separate. Lut took his people and headed for the Cities of the Plain, while Ibrahim continued on into Palestine.

Ibrahim settled on a decent patch of land and organized his followers into a tight-knit community. He married a woman named Sarah and watched over his people. He received Allah's messages and established a viable spiritual life and tradition in the people.

Isma'il and Ishaq

For many years Ibrahim lived with Sarah, but she bore him no children. She seemed to be barren. Because it was important for Ibrahim to have heirs to teach his knowledge to, he married Hajar, Sarah's maid servant, as a second wife. Ibrahim and Hajar were blessed with a boy they named Isma'il. (37:101)

A short time later, Allah sent His angels, disguised as men, to visit Ibrahim's home. They greeted him with the words of peace, and he, thinking they were travelers, prepared a tray of meat for them. When they didn't eat, he felt uneasy about them. But they told him not to fear.

They declared, "We have been sent against the people of Lut." Surat Hud 11:70

Detail of winged human-headed lion from kingdom of Namrud - British Museum.

Lut had parted ways with Ibrahim and went to the Cities of the Plain. There, he became a prophet to the people. However, many refused to listen to him, including members of his own family. Now was the time Allah would deal with those wrong-doers. Then the angels told Ibrahim that he was going to have a son with his first wife, Sarah. Sarah was standing in the door and laughed when she heard what the angels said. She was old and never thought she would have a child.

She said, "Oh me? How can I have a child, given that I'm an old woman and my husband here is an old man? That would be a miracle!" The angels replied, "Are you amazed at Allah's command? The grace of Allah and His blessings are upon you, people of this house. For He is indeed praiseworthy and full of glory!." Surat Hud 11:71-73

Before leaving, Ibrahim begged the angels to spare Lut and his people. The angels told him not to appeal against Allah's command, and then they left. (11:77-83) In time, Sarah bore a son named Ishaq. She loved him greatly. Later, Allah instructed him to settle Hajar and her son Isma'il in another land that needed a prophet: a role that Isma'il would later fulfill.

The Valley of Bakka

Ibrahim journeyed south for about two weeks into the Arabian peninsula, until he found a barren valley. It was here that he was told to leave Hajar and Isma'il. He gave them a few supplies and then returned north to Palestine.

Hajar and Isma'il soon ran out of water and were nearly overcome in the heat. Allah gave them a well known as Zamzam, which enabled them to survive. The water source also gave them a valuable commodity they could trade with passing nomads. A few desert tribes began to move into the valley as it now had a water supply. When Ibrahim returned for a visit, he was amazed at how things had developed. He knew Allah's plan was the right one.

In time, Isma'il grew into a fine young man and brought great pleasure to his parents. Ibrahim loved his son dearly, and that would be his next test. Ibrahim saw in a dream that he was sacrificing his son. When he told him of it, the boy said, "My father! Do what you have been commanded to do. I will be, if Allah wills, patient." So when they both surrendered their wills (to Allah), and he had lain him on his forehead, We called out to him, "Ibrahim! You have fulfilled the (requirements) of the vision already." This is how We reward those who do right. For this was clearly a great test for him. Surat As-Saaffat (Those who set the Ranks) 37:102-106

They found an animal nearby, a ram perhaps, and sacrificed it instead. Ibrahim showed that he was ready to give up everything he loved in this life for the sake of Allah. Ibrahim and Isma'il built the foundations of the building we would later call the Ka'bah. Ibrahim, sensing that this town would eventually become a center for prayer to Allah, made the following dua':

"My Lord, make this city peaceful, and keep me and my children away from worshiping idols. My Lord, they have misled many a people. So, the one who follows me does surely belong to me. As for the one who disobeys me, then You are Most-Forgiving, Very-Merciful. Our Lord, I have settled some of my children in a valley of no vegetation, close to Your sanctified House, so that, Our Lord, they may establish Salah. So, make hearts of people yearn towards them, and provide them with fruits, so that they may be grateful." Surat Ibrahim 14:35-37

Then Ibrahim thanked Allah for his children and prayed that his plea would be accepted. In time, Allah made Isma'il a prophet, and he led the first community in the valley of Bakka, later renamed Makkah. (19:54-55)

Who Follows Ibrahim's Example?

Jews, Christians and Muslims all revere Prophet Ibrahim. But while everyone loves him, who has remained faithful to his example? The Holy Qur'an declares: *The same way of life has been established for you (Muslims) that was established for Nuh. It is the same inspiration to you that We (Allah) gave to Ibrahim, Musa and 'Isa, that you should stick strongly to your way of life and make no divisions in it.* Surat Ash-Shura 42:13

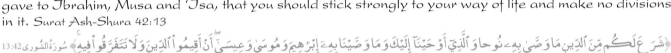

Prophet Ibrahim was given the same inspiration as the later prophets. He rejected idol-worship, stood up for justice, called people to the truth and obeyed Allah's commands. Allah declares: *Ibrahim was neither a Jew nor a Christian. But he was upright, a Muslim and was not one of those who associate partners with Allah. The closest of people to Ibrahim are those who followed him, this prophet and those who believe, and Allah is the Guardian of all believers.* Surat Al 'Imran (The Family of 'Imran) 3:67-68

Prophet Ibrahim called all people to Allah's way of life. This is unlike some followers of Judaism, who believe that they alone are God's chosen people, to the exclusion of all others. (4:49-50) Additionally, Ibrahim always preached the Oneness of Allah, in contrast to the concept of the Trinity that most Christians believe in today. Some Christians go even further and erect statues or make paintings of their god, which is a practice forbidden by their 10 Commandments.

If Prophet Ibrahim were to come back in the world today, who do you think he would choose to be among? Who would seem faithful to his way?

Say, Allah has told the truth. So, follow the Faith of Ibrahim, the upright one. He was not one of those who ascribe partners to Allah. Surat Al 'Imran (The Family of 'Imran) 3:95

Who follows Prophet Ibrahim?

194

What Is Sabr?

Life may seem unfair at times. Sometimes, bad things happen to good people. Other times, people who commit evil appear to have an easy life, even though we may think they don't deserve it.

Allah🕊 made this world as a testing ground. As you learned before, Allah🕊 wants us to choose to love and obey Him. Shaytan wants us to forget Allah🕊 and do wrong. Our lives are constantly influenced by our surroundings and we can either let ourselves go towards the good or bad.

Even things like being rich or poor, or happy or sad are part of the test. None of us knows what will happen tomorrow. Every sunrise brings a new day full of possibilities and challenges.

No matter what happens, the sun still rises over the world every day.

If ye have received a blow, the (disbelieving) people have received a blow the like thereof. These are (only) the vicissitudes which We cause to follow one another for mankind, to the end that Allah may know those who believe and may choose witnesses from among you, and Allah loveth not wrong-doers. Surat Al 'Imran 3:140

﴿إِن يَمْسَسْكُمْ قَرْحٌ فَقَدْ مَسَّ ٱلْقَوْمَ قَرْحٌ مِّثْلُهُ وَتِلْكَ ٱلْأَيَّامُ نُدَاوِلُهَا بَيْنَ ٱلنَّاسِ وَلِيَعْلَمَ ٱللَّهُ ٱلَّذِينَ ءَامَنُوا۟ وَيَتَّخِذَ مِنكُمْ شُهَدَآءَ وَٱللَّهُ لَا يُحِبُّ ٱلظَّٰلِمِينَ﴾ سُورَةُ آلِ عِمْرَانَ 3:140

What is important is not what happens to you, but what you do about it. The Blessed Prophet Muhammad ﷺ once said, *It's amazing that there's good in everything that happens to a believer (in Allah) and it's only that way for a believer. If something nice happens to him, he's thankful. If something bad happens to him, he has sabr and that's best for him.* (Muslim)

قَالَ رَسُولُ اللهِ ﷺ : «عَجَبًا لِأَمْرِ المُؤْمِنِ إِنَّ أَمْرَهُ كُلَّهُ خَيْرٌ وَلَيْسَ ذلِكَ لِأَحَدٍ إِلَّا لِلمُؤْمِنِ إِنْ أَصَابَتْهُ سَرَّاءُ شَكَرَ فَكَانَتْ خَيْرًا لَهُ وَإِنْ أَصَابَتْهُ ضَرَّاءُ صَبَرَ فَكَانَ خَيْرًا لَهُ». رَوَاهُ مُسْلِمٌ

The word **Sabr** صَبْر means patience. We can't control what happens to us most of the time and we understand that life may not always go our way. But Allah🕊 mentioned in the Qur'an that He will not give someone a test that is more than they can bear.

On no soul do We place a burden greater than it can bear: before Us is a record which clearly shows the truth: they will never be wronged. Surat Al Mu'minun (The Believers) 23: 62

﴿وَلَا نُكَلِّفُ نَفْسًا إِلَّا وُسْعَهَا وَلَدَيْنَا كِتَٰبٌ يَنطِقُ بِٱلْحَقِّ وَهُمْ لَا يُظْلَمُونَ﴾ سُورَةُ المُؤْمِنُونَ 23:62

If we are tested, we can handle it—if we want to. We can also give up, get upset at Allah🕊 and feel hopeless. But with piety and faith, we would understand that the life of this world is finite. We would then step up to the challenge and come closer to Allah🕊 in our hearts, asking for His help and strength. Remember that challenges are opportunities for learning and improving. That is the proper use of sabr. Allah🕊 has promised a wonderful reward in Heaven, Jannah, for those who have sabr in this life.

O you who believe! Seek help with patient perseverance and prayer; Indeed Allah is with the people who have sabr. Surat Al Baqarah (The Cow) 2:153

﴿يَٰٓأَيُّهَا ٱلَّذِينَ ءَامَنُوا۟ ٱسْتَعِينُوا۟ بِٱلصَّبْرِ وَٱلصَّلَوٰةِ إِنَّ ٱللَّهَ مَعَ ٱلصَّٰبِرِينَ﴾ سُورَةُ البَقَرَةِ 2:153

Aisha🕊 narrated: The Blessed Prophet ﷺ said, "No believer is pricked by a thorn or more, except that Allah will raise him thereby one degree in status, or will thereby erase a sin." (Muslim)

عَنْ عَائِشَةَ ۗ، قَالَتْ قَالَ رَسُولُ اللهِ ۗ: «مَا يُصِيبُ الْمُؤْمِنَ مِنْ شَوْكَةٍ فَمَا فَوْقَهَا إِلاَّ رَفَعَهُ اللهُ بِهَا دَرَجَةً أَوْ حَطَّ عَنْهُ بِهَا خَطِيئَةً». رَوَاهُمُسْلِمٌ

The Blessed Prophet Muhammad ۗ once said, "If a bad situation comes over you, never say, 'What if I would have done something else; would something different have happened?' Instead you should say, 'Allah has planned and Allah has carried out His plan.'" (Muslim)

قَالَ رَسُولُ اللهِ ۗ: «وَإِنْ أَصَابَكَ شَيْءٌ فَلَا تَقُلْ لَوْ أَنِّي فَعَلْتُ كَانَ كَذَا وَكَذَا وَلَكِنْ قُلْ قَدَرُ اللهِ وَمَا شَاءَ فَعَلَ». رَوَاهُمُسْلِمٌ

Prophet Ayyoub ۗ had everything: a farm, animals, a big family and prosperity.

The prophet you will be learning about next endured unimaginable tests. So many unfortunate things happened and so many heartaches afflicted him. Shaytan worked very hard to get this prophet to give up on Allah ۗ. In the following section, we will learn a beautiful lesson on sabr through Prophet Ayyoub ۗ, who exercised sabr no matter how terrible things became.

The Contented Prophet

Prophet Ayyoub ۗ lived a long time ago in a village somewhere in northern Arabia, near Palestine. He was respected among his people and had a nice home and family. He wasn't wealthy, but he had an easy life and was very happy. Prophet Ayyoub ۗ would convey Allah's ۗ guidance to his people and some would heed it, while others would not. But they never troubled the older man and his life was not too difficult. He was a contented prophet.

As we learned before, life can change in an instant. As Allah ۗ said, *Verily the knowledge of the Hour is with Allah (alone). It is He Who sends down rain and He Who knows what is in the wombs. No person knows what will happen to them tomorrow Nor does any one know in what land he is to die. Verily with Allah is full knowledge and He is acquainted (with all things).* Surat Luqman 31:34

﴿إِنَّ اللَّهَ عِنْدَهُ عِلْمُ السَّاعَةِ وَيُنَزِّلُ الْغَيْثَ وَيَعْلَمُ مَا فِي الْأَرْحَامِ وَمَا تَدْرِي نَفْسٌ مَاذَا تَكْسِبُ غَدًا وَمَا تَدْرِي نَفْسٌ بِأَيِّ أَرْضٍ تَمُوتُ إِنَّ اللَّهَ عَلِيمٌ خَبِيرٌ﴾ سُورَةُ

لُقْمَان 31:34

Allah ۗ was going to test Ayyoub ۗ. Prophet Muhammad ۗ once said that when Allah ۗ loves a person, He tests him. For those with a special status with Allah ۗ, He sometimes sends them special or more difficult tests. Why is this so?

Do you think you can say, I believe and not be tested in your emaan? We tested those before you and Allah will certainly show who is true and who is false. Surat Al 'Ankabut (The Spider) 29:2-3

﴿أَحَسِبَ النَّاسُ أَنْ يُتْرَكُوا أَنْ يَقُولُوا آمَنَّا وَهُمْ لَا يُفْتَنُونَ﴾ ﴿وَلَقَدْ فَتَنَّا الَّذِينَ مِنْ قَبْلِهِمْ فَلَيَعْلَمَنَّ اللَّهُ الَّذِينَ صَدَقُوا وَلَيَعْلَمَنَّ الْكَاذِبِينَ﴾ سُورَةُالعَنْكَبُوت 29: 2-3

The purpose of the test is to prove whether or not we truly believe in Allah ۗ. If we get mad and feel hopeless after a hard test, it means we don't perceive anything beyond our own short life in this world. It means we are not putting our trust in Allah ۗ and reminding ourselves that true and everlasting happiness is only in the hereafter.

Think about it: if you love Allah ۗ and don't let the matters of this world bother you too much, whether good or bad, don't you deserve to get the greatest reward for not following your desires and the Shaytan? Of course you do. Let's see what happened to Prophet Ayyoub ۗ and how he handled his situation.

Disaster Strikes!

Prophet Ayyoub's ۗ test began when he awoke one day to find that his animals started to get sick and die, one after the other. The rain also ceased to fall from that day on, so his crops soon withered and died. In the past, people used animals for food and farming, and a person's crops were their sustenance. Therefore, when all of his animals and crops died, Prophet Ayyoub ۗ lost all his income. Imagine how bad he must have felt. He had a family to feed and people who depended on him.

And if that wasn't bad enough, his children also began to get sick and die. Prophet Ayyoub☷ suffered horribly from all of this immense loss. He watched as his crops, animals and family passed away before his eyes, and he could do nothing to save them. To make matters even worse, his house and land were also destroyed.

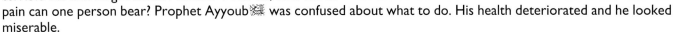

Imagine him standing there, alone, with no house, no family and no income. No one, not even his neighbors, came to his aid. Just a year earlier, Prophet Ayyoub☷ seemed to have it all and now he had lost everything.

Then, Shaytan began telling Prophet Ayyoub☷ horrible things, planting seeds of doubt about Allah☷. Perhaps he whispered words like this to the prophet, "See what Allah☷ did to you. See how much Allah's☷ love is worth!"

Shaytan caught Ayyoub☷ when he was weak from sadness and disaster. Wouldn't many people listen to those terrible lies and forget about Allah☷? After all, how much pain can one person bear? Prophet Ayyoub☷ was confused about what to do. His health deteriorated and he looked miserable.

But do you remember what Allah☷ affirmed? He said He won't test or burden someone with a test that is more difficult than they can handle. The choice is up to us to decide if we want to rise up to the challenge and remain firm in our emaan or give up. Prophet Ayyoub☷ understood this and decided to stand firm with his emaan.

And (remember) Ayyoub, he prayed to Allah, Sadness and misery have caught hold of me, but You are the Most Merciful of the Merciful! Surat Al Anbiya' (The Prophets) 21:83

Ayyoub☷ was tested with the worst situation any of us could ever imagine. He could have let himself go crazy or become an unbeliever, but instead, he strengthened his emaan and learned the lesson from his suffering that this world is only temporary and that the real life is yet to come. He turned to Allah☷.

After Difficulty There Is Relief

Shaytan realized he was powerless against this true Muslim. Prophet Ayyoub☷ completely surrendered to Allah☷. The Holy Qur'an mentions tests and how hard they can be. At the same time, no test lasts forever. Eventually, as Allah☷ says, *There is ease after a difficult time.* Surat As-Sharh (The Relief) 94:5

And Prophet Ayyoub☷ was going to reach his time of ease. Allah☷ revealed to him, *Kick the ground. A spring will be appear where you can bathe and drink.* Surat Saad (The Letter "Saad") 38:42

The cool water felt like a life-saver to him. It was a sign that his life was going to become good again. Prophet Ayyoub☷ picked himself up and started all over again with more faith than ever before. He went to his people and told them about the wonderful lessons of sabr that he learned. Eventually, he rebuilt his whole life, including his home and farm. Prophet Ayyoub☷ also got his wife back and had many children. But he never took for granted what he had and was always thankful to Allah☷, aware of the fact that this life is more temporary than most people even realize.

Allah☷ told him, *Take some grass in your hand and slap it. Then don't break (your promise.) Indeed, We found him full of sabr. He was excellent in Our service and he always turned to Us!* Surat Saad 38:44

Allah☷ tells us to consider Prophet Ayyoub's☷ example and to learn from it. The next time something good happens, remember Allah☷ and be thankful. Don't just remember Allah☷ in your hard times. When something bad happens, no matter how horrible it is, remember that life is a test. Always try to come closer to Allah☷ in your heart and call out to Him with all your worries and fears. He has promised that He heeds every cry.

Have sabr, because the promise of Allah is true. Ask forgiveness for your sins and glorify Allah at night and in the morning. Surat Al Ghaafir (The Forgiver) 40:55

The Great City of Sin

Almost 3,000 years ago, there was a beautiful city called Nineveh located on the banks of the Tigris River in Mesopotamia. Although Prophet Ibrahim﷽ was also from Mesopotamia, Nineveh was a different city than Prophet Ibrahim's﷽ home town. In addition, this story occurred 1,000 years later.

Nineveh was a huge, bustling metropolis of over 100,000 people. It was surrounded by farms and towns and had contacts with cities all over the region. This city was ruled by kings and had a very powerful army. Idol-worship was the religion most people followed, and sinfulness was rampant. Most people cheated others, stole, committed murder, gambled, or got drunk.

The kings and rulers used their power to amass great wealth. They wasted money on building huge palaces for themselves and throwing endless parties and ceremonies. On the other han d, the government neglected the poor leaving them in misery and neglect. Although it was a great and powerful city, it was also ruled by fear and oppression.

Nineveh is located in the Fertile Crescent.

The Prophet Who Left His People

As we have seen before, Allah﷽ always gives people a chance to hear the Message of Truth so they could become good, moral people. He would never destroy a city or end a civilization without sending them His warnings. If people listened and gave up their hurtful and evil ways, then Allah﷽ would let their community and culture continue.

The prophet Allah﷽ chose for Nineveh was named Yunusﷺ, the son of Matta. He entered the city and began to preach to the people about giving up idols, serving only Allah﷽ and living a good and clean life. Yet, most of the people ignored him. He must have felt like he was talking to a brick wall! Everywhere he went—in the markets, restaurants and homes of people—nobody cared about what he was saying.

After trying to convince them of the truth for some time, Prophet Yunusﷺ warned them that if they didn't believe in Allah﷽, His wrath would come on them. He did not wait for Allah﷽ to tell him to leave the city. Instead of completing his mission, he left the city and made his way south to the coast where the Tigris River emptied, between the present day countries of Iran and the Arabic Gulf countries.

He didn't know where he was going and he didn't know what he was going to do. He thought that he had fulfilled his mission and was not required to spend more time or effort with his people. In addition, he didn't want to go back to Nineveh. He thought that the people of Nineveh did not respond to his message from Allah﷽, and therefore they deserved the punishment of Allah﷽. But Allah﷽ is more merciful than that and wanted to make sure that everyone heard the message before taking any action. Allah﷽ would soon show him what he had to do.

And remember Zun-nun (Yunus), when he departed in anger, when he walked away in anger and thought that We would never put him to trouble.! (The Prophets) 21:87

The Great Whale

Prophet Yunusﷺ booked passage on a ship. He watched as boxes and baskets full of trade goods were loaded, until it seemed that the boat would burst from all the cargo. After a little while, the ship's captain ordered the boat to set sail into the sea. After a few hours of sailing, however, the sky started to fill with dark storm clouds. In those days, ships were not as big as they are today and a big storm could sink a boat—especially one full of cargo.

Everyone on board became afraid of the ominous sky. After a little while, the winds grew and the waves rose higher and higher. Water began spilling onto the deck and the storm became more and more violent. The sky was dark, the sea was raging, and the wind was beating into the faces of the sailors.

At that time, many people were superstitious. They believed that a storm occurred because someone on board was bad luck. To find out who brought the bad luck with them, everyone would have to cast lots, or do a random drawing. Whoever came up with the unlucky marker was then thrown overboard so that the angry sea would become calm again. Imagine the fear in everyone's mind as the sailors and people held the drawing. As fate would have it, Yunus ﷺ drew the bad marker. Little did he know what was going to happen next.

A Cry from the Darkness

As the storm whipped up ever higher waves, the sailors grabbed Yunus ﷺ and took him to the edge of the deck. The dark, gray-green waves were crashing as far as the eye could see. Suddenly the sailors threw him overboard into the sea and watched as he struggled against the swirling waters. After a few minutes, the wind began to die down and the storm ended. Everyone on the boat was happy and relieved. The captain ordered people to start bailing out the water from the bottom of the boat so they could be on their way.

Meanwhile, Prophet Yunus ﷺ struggled to keep his head above water. He saw the ship sailing away and thought he was done for. But Allah ﷻ had other plans for him. From out of the deep, dark depths of the sea something moved. A shadow on the face of the empty sea came closer to the near drowning man. Before he knew what was happening, a whale came up from under him, taking him into its mouth and down into its belly. Prophet Yunus ﷺ was swallowed whole.

Imagine the shock of being inside the stomach of a whale. Even though he was now in an animal that lived under water, Prophet Yunus ﷺ didn't drown. There was a small pocket of air in the stomach of the whale, and Yunus ﷺ struggled to keep his head in it so he could breathe. He spent a long time there, losing all sense of place and direction. He thought for sure he was going to die. But after suffering for a while, he realized that there was only One who could save him—the One Lord that he had disobeyed and ran away from. He knew he was being punished for his shortcomings and taught a lesson.

Then, he called (Us) in the depths of darkness saying, "There is no god but You. Pure are You. Indeed I was among the wrongdoers." Surat Al Anbiyaa' (The Prophets) 21:87

The Messenger of Allah ﷺ said, "The supplication of Thun-Nun (Prophet Yunus) when he supplicated, while in the belly of the whale was: 'There is none worthy of worship except You, Glory to You, Indeed, I have been of the transgressors.' So indeed, no Muslim man supplicated with it for anything, ever, except Allah responds to him." (Tirmidhi)

قَالَ ﷺ: «دَعْوَةُ ذِي النُّونِ إِذْ دَعَاهُ وَهُوَ فِي بَطْنِ الْحُوتِ: لَا إِلَهَ إِلَّا أَنْتَ سُبْحَانَكَ إِنِّي كُنْتُ مِنَ الظَّالِمِينَ، فَإِنَّهُ لَمْ يَدْعُ بِهَا رَجُلٌ مُسْلِمٌ فِي شَيْءٍ قَطُّ، إِلَّا اسْتَجَابَ اللهُ لَهُ». رَوَاهُ التِّرْمَذِيُّ

So We listened to him and delivered him from distress, and so do We deliver those who have faith. Surat Al Anbiyaa' (The Prophets) 21:88

Allah ﷻ heard his cries for forgiveness and forgave him. Allah ﷻ has promised to forgive our sins if we just ask for His forgiveness sincerely. So Allah ﷻ ordered the whale to release Prophet Yunus ﷺ from inside its body. The mighty creature swam as fast as it could towards the sea shore and in one mighty heave, it spit the helpless man out of its belly and into shallow water. Prophet Yunus ﷺ must have been amazed as he struggled to stand up in the low water.

As he crawled up onto the beach, we can imagine him looking back at the sea and seeing the whale heading back towards deeper waters. He was so thankful to Allah. But his difficult experience caused him to be sick. As he lay on the hot sand, he felt weak and tired.

Allah knew he needed help until he recovered. Out of the ground, Allah caused a gourd to grow bigger and bigger until its leaves completely covered him in shade. Perhaps the fruit of this plant also provided food for him. Prophet Yunus knew he would live and he knew what he had to do.

But We cast him forth on the barren shore in a state of sickness. And We caused to grow over him a spreading gourd plant. And We sent him (on a mission) to a hundred thousand (men) or more. Surat As Saaffat (Those Set in Ranks) 37:145-147

A City Is Saved

When he finally felt well enough to return to his city, Yunus was very motivated. He was more humble and more kind than before. People saw the change in him and were attracted to such a wonderful man. Many people listened to him and were won over by his teachings. Because so many people decided to give up idol-worship, Allah did not destroy the city. Instead, He allowed their civilization to continue on for a long time after.

And they believed, so We permitted them to enjoy (their life) for a while. Surat As Saaffat (Those Set in Ranks) 37:148

Prophet Yunus achieved his mission and never forgot the great lesson he learned about Who he really depended on for his life. He always remained thankful to Allah, never failing to help people or do good for the rest of his days.

The reconstructed Mashki Gate of Nineveh.

The Three Unknown Prophets

The Prophets to the World

Islam teaches that Allah sent prophets and messengers to every nation. The last of these was Prophet Muhammad whose message was meant for the whole world and would be protected.

So when we study any world religion, which was founded before the mission of Prophet Muhammad, we must investigate whether it was started by an authentic prophet or not.

Any religion started after the time of Allah's last Messenger is completely a false invention, as the Blessed Prophet said that after him there would be no more revelations from Allah to the world.

We are interested in researching the history of ancient societies to identify the names and teachings of whatever spiritual guides were in existence long ago. But sometimes we will never be able to discover the names of those prophets. Most of the prophets, in fact, will always remain anonymous with their true identity never to be known. (40:78)

Biblical city ruins in Jordan.

The Three Unknown Prophets

In the Qur'an, Allah gives us the story of the Three Prophets He sent to the same city, at the same time. No names are given, and the city's location and identity also remain a mystery. What makes this story all the more intriguing is that an ordinary person takes up the cause of the Three Prophets and tries to convince his people to follow them, with surprising results.

Was the city an ancient Mayan or African town? Was it in Asia or North America? Perhaps it was Cahokia, near the Mississippi River, or Meroe, along the Nile. We will possibly never know in this life. But the important thing is the lesson taught by the preaching of the man who obeyed the call of Allah. Let's look at their story.

The Companions of the City

Cite to them the example of the People of the Town, when the messengers came to it. When We sent to them two (apostles), and they rejected both of them, so We confirmed them with a third one. So they said, "We are sent to you."

They (the people of the Town) said, "You are no more than human beings like us, and the Rahman (the All-Merciful Allah) has not sent down anything. You are but telling a lie."

They (the messengers) said, "Our Lord knows that we are undoubtedly sent to you. Our obligation is no more than to convey the message clearly."

They (the People of the Town) said, "We take you as a bad omen for us. If you do not desist, we will certainly stone you, and you will be afflicted by a painful punishment from us."

They said, "Your bad omen is with yourselves. (Do you take it as bad omen) if you are given good counsel? Rather, you are a people who cross all limits."

And there came a man rushing from the farthest part of the city. He said, "O my people, follow the messengers. Follow those who do not claim any reward from you and who are on the right path. What excuse do I have if I do not worship the One who has created me and to whom you will be returned? Shall I adopt those gods besides Him whose intercession, if Rahman (the All-Merciful Allah) intends to do harm to me, cannot help me in the least, nor can they come to my rescue? In that case, I will be in open error indeed. Undoubtedly I have believed in your Lord so listen to me." (Thereafter, when his people killed him) it was said to him, "Enter the Paradise." He said, "Would that my people knew how my Lord has forgiven me and placed me among the honored ones!" Surat Ya-sin 36:13-27

The ruins of Old Ma'rib.

The End of the City

The wicked people of the city were no doubt rejoicing in driving away Allah's Messengers and all those who dared to believe. Now they felt that they could return to their old ways, oppressing their neighbors and cheating and stealing from them. But Allah decreed the end of that civilization, and they lost their chance to save themselves from the punishment of the Next Life.

As Allah said, *"We didn't send against his people any forces from the sky, nor did We need to do so. It took no more than a huge explosion, and they lay still." Surat Ya-sin 36:28-29*

In conclusion, Allah gives us a telling statement about the state of most people on Earth. He announces, *"Alas for the servants! When a Messenger comes to them, they mock him. Don't they see how many generations before them We destroyed? None of them will return. Each one will be brought before Us (for judgement)." Surat Ya-sin 36:30-32*

We will never know the identity of the Three Messengers, the Advocate or their city. But we do know who the real winners were in the end—not the people who enjoyed their sinful way of life for a few moments more but the ones who surrendered their wills to Allah and held true to their faith. Let us follow the lesson of those who always surrender to Allah.

Who was Yusuf عليه السلام?

Allah سبحانه وتعالى describes the saga of Prophet Yusuf عليه السلام as the most beautiful of all stories. Indeed, anyone who has read it comes away with a feeling of excitement and wonder. The most amazing adventures befell one young man who lived around 1600 BCE, and these adventures tested his faith to the limits. But who is Yusuf عليه السلام, and where did he come from?

Ibrahim's عليه السلام son Ishaq عليه السلام, who remained in Palestine, had a child named **Ya'qub يَعْقوب Jacob**. In turn, Ya'qub عليه السلام had 12 sons and many daughters. One of these sons was named Yusuf عليه السلام. He and his baby brother Benjamin were both from the same mother. The 10 other brothers were from a different mother. To tell the story of Yusuf عليه السلام in words other than Allah's سبحانه وتعالى would be a great injustice. We will relate the story of Yusuf عليه السلام directly from the verses in Surat Yusuf (Joseph). Prepare yourselves for a most beautiful story!

The Strange Dream

We are now going to tell you the most beautiful of all stories in Our revealing this portion of the Qur'an. You did not know this story before. Surat Yusuf (Joseph) 12:3

Yusuf told his father, "Father! I saw (in a dream) 11 stars and the sun and the moon all bowing themselves to me!" My son, his father replied, "Don't tell this dream to your brothers because they might plan against you (out of jealousy). Shaytan is the enemy of people! I believe your Lord will choose you and teach you how to understand dreams. He will complete His blessing upon you and upon the descendants of me, Ya'qub, even as He completed it to your fore-fathers, Ibrahim and Ishaq , before! Allah has all knowledge and wisdom."
Certainly, in the example of Yusuf and his brothers are lessons for people who look for truth. Surat Yusuf (Joseph) 12:4-7

One day Yusuf's عليه السلام older brothers complained amongst themselves, "Our father loves Yusuf and his younger brother (Benjamin) more than us, even though we are just as good! Our father is obviously out of his mind!" Surat Yusuf (Joseph) 12:8

Then one of the brothers suggested, "So let's kill Yusuf or send him away to some far off land. Then our father will give us all his attention. There will be plenty of time to be good later!" Surat Yusuf (Joseph) 12:9

But one of the other brothers (who was not as bad) said, "Don't kill him! Instead, why don't we throw him down into the dried-up old well?" Then some passing caravan will find him and take him away. Surat Yusuf (Joseph) 12:10

After they agreed to this plan, the brothers went to their father and asked permission to take Yusuf عليه السلام out for a day of fun. When their father hesitated, they complained, "Father! Why don't you trust Yusuf with us? We really love him. Send him with us tomorrow to enjoy himself and play. We'll take good care of him." Their father replied, "It worries me, that you want to take him out. I'm afraid that a wolf might eat him while you're not looking." They answered, "If a wolf were to eat him while we are so large a group, then we would have to be eaten first!" So, they took Yusuf out with them. But secretly they had all decided to throw him down the dried-up well. When they seized Yusuf and threw him into the dark hole, We (Allah), told him in his heart, "One day you will bring out the truth about this plan of their's when they won't even know you." Surat Yusuf (Joseph) 12:11-15

The brothers returned home in the early part of the night crying, "Oh father! We went racing with each other and left Yusuf alone to watch our things. Then a huge wolf came and ate him. But you'll probably never believe us even though we're telling the truth." Then they pulled out his shirt, which they had secretly stained with false blood. "No!" Ya'qub said. "You must have made up a story to use. I can only wait patiently against what you claim. It is Allah whose help is sought against what you describe." Surat Yusuf (Joseph) 12:16-18

The Journey to Egypt

Later that day, a caravan of travelers was passing by and decided to send their water-boy to the well for water. When he let down his bucket into the well. He shouted, "Hey! Look! Good news! Here is a fine young boy!" Then they hid him like merchandise! But Allah knows what they were doing! They sold him (in Egypt) for the miserable price of a few counted silver coins. They considered him of little value. Surat Yusuf (Joseph) 12:19-20

The man who bought him, **'Aziz Misr عَزِيزُ مِصْر Minister in Egypt**, took the boy home and said to his wife, "Treat him well because he might bring us some good, or we could even adopt him as a son." In this way, We settled Yusuf in a new land so We could teach him how to interpret dreams. Allah has full power and control over His plans, but most people don't realize it. Surat Yusuf (Joseph) 12:21

When Yusuf (grew to be a young man,) We gave him strength and knowledge. This is how We reward those who do right. But (Wife of 'Aziz Misr) was attracted to him and wanted to seduce him and change his nature. One day she bolted the doors and said to him, "Now come to me!"
"Allah forbid!" cried Yusuf. "Your husband is my master! He's the one who made my life here bearable! Nothing good comes to people who do wrong!" But she desired him greatly, and he would have desired her, but he remembered the signs of his Lord. We turned him away from (all) shameful deeds. He was one of Our sincere servants. Surat Yusuf (Joseph) 12:22-24

So, they both raced each other to the door, and she tore his shirt from behind. (When Yusuf flung the door open) there, in front of them, stood her husband. Wife of 'Aziz Misr thought quickly and said, "What other punishment can there be for a man trying to seduce your wife but prison or a painful beating!" "But she's the one who tried to seduce me away from my own self!" cried Yusuf.

'Aziz Misr couldn't make up his mind because he was fond of both Yusuf and his wife, so a witness from her family observed that if his shirt was ripped from the front, then she is truthful and he is a liar! But if his shirt is torn from the back, then she is the liar and he is telling the truth! Surat Yusuf (Joseph) 12:25-27
When he saw that Yusuf's shirt was indeed torn from the back, he said, "This is certainly your trickery, O woman. Great is the trickery of you women indeed. O Yusuf ignore this matter, and you (O woman), seek forgiveness for your sin, for you were guilty in fact. Surat Yusuf (Joseph) 12:28-29

Wife of 'Aziz Takes Revenge

When the details of what happened reached other people, the women of the city began to gossip, The wife of the great minister was trying to seduce her own slave from himself. He must have inspired her with violent love. She's clearly going out of her mind! Soon (Wife of 'Aziz Misr) heard of their malicious talk. She decided to invite the (gossiping) women to visit her, and she prepared a banquet for them. She had a knife placed at each of their seats (and while they were cutting their food); she called out to Yusuf, "Come here before us." When the ladies saw him, they were amazed by his handsome features. In their amazement, they cut right through (their fruit) to their hands. They exclaimed, "Allah save us! He is no mortal! This is none other than a noble angel!" Surat Yusuf (Joseph) 12:30-31

Wife of 'Aziz Misr announced triumphantly, "There, before you, is the man you teased me about! I tried to seduce him from his nature, but he got away from me and is still innocent! But now if he doesn't do what I say, he will be thrown into prison with the worst criminals!" Surat Yusuf (Joseph) 12:32

"My Lord!" He cried out. "Prison is better than what they are calling me towards. Unless you turn their trap away from me, I might become attracted to them and act like an ignorant fool."
So his Lord heard (his prayer) and turned their trap away from him. Certainly, He hears and knows (all things). Then it occurred to the husbands of the women, after they heard what their wives wanted Yusuf for, that it would be best to put him in prison for a while. Surat Yusuf (Joseph) 12:33-35

The Prisoners' Dreams

Along with Yusuf were two other men in prison. The first one said, "I see myself (in a dream) pressing wine." The second one said, "I see myself (in a dream) carrying bread on my head with a swarm of birds eating from it." So they asked Yusuf, "Tell us the meaning of these (strange dreams) because we can tell that you're a good person." Surat Yusuf (Joseph) 12:36

Yusuf answered, "Before your next meal comes, I will reveal to you the meaning of (your dreams) prior to the events actually happening. This is part of what my Lord has taught me. I've given up the ways of people who disbelieve in Allah and who even deny the next life. I follow the ways of my fathers: Ibrahim, Ishaq and Ya'qub. We never made any partners with Allah. This comes from the grace of Allah upon us and to other people though most people are not thankful." Surat Yusuf (Joseph) 12:37-38

Then he said, "My two fellow companions of the prison! I ask you, 'Are many gods arguing among themselves better or Allah the One, Supreme?' If you don't serve Him, then you serve nothing but names which you and your fathers made up. Allah gave no permission for anyone to do that. The right to command is for none but Allah. And He has commanded that you serve nothing but Him. That is the straight way of life, but most people don't understand" Surat Yusuf (Joseph) 12:39-40

"My two fellow companions of the prison! As for the first one of you, he will again pour out the wine for his master to drink. As for the other, he will be hung from a stake and the birds will eat off his head. The matter you two asked me about has been decided." Yusuf quietly whispered to the one he knew was going to be released, "Mention me to your master." But Shaytan made the man forget about it. So Yusuf lingered in prison a few more years. Surat Yusuf (Joseph) 12:41-42

The King of Egypt

One day, the king of Egypt [14] called to his ministers, "I saw (in a dream) seven fat cows being eaten by seven skinny ones, and seven green ears of corn and seven others withered. Ministers, tell me what my vision means if you can understand dreams."

---

14 The ruler of Egypt during this story is always called a king مَلِك and not Pharaoh. But in the story of Prophet Musa ﷺ, the ruler of Egypt is called Pharaoh فِرْعَون and not a king. This is because during Yusuf's ﷺ stay in Egypt, the northern half of the country was being ruled by foreign invaders from the Middle East called 'Hyksos,' who ruled there between 1652 BCE and 1544 BCE. They were able to overpower Egyptian armies due to their superior weapons and tactics. Their chieftains were kings who at first rejected the worship of most of the Egyptian idols and required tribute from the real Egyptian Pharaohs, who were confined to the remote south of the country. When the native Egyptians, led by Prince Kamose of Thebes, finally threw the Hyksos out, they started their native, Pharaoh-based system again and at the same time made the Jews slaves. Thus, when Prophet Musa ﷺ was there, many hundreds of years later, the ruler would be called Pharaoh. Allah's ﷻ book is accurate even to the smallest details!

They replied, "It's a confused bunch of symbols. We are not skilled in figuring out the meaning of dreams." But the king's wine-pourer, who had been released (from prison), and who now remembered (Yusuf) after so long said, "I will tell you what it means. Send me (to the one who can solve this riddle)." *Surat Yusuf (Joseph) 12:43-45*

When the man arrived at the prison, he went to Yusuf's cell and said, "Yusuf! Man of truth! Tell us the meaning of seven fat cows being eaten by seven skinny ones, and of seven green ears of corn followed by seven withered ones. Tell me, so I can return to the people, and they will understand."

Yusuf answered, "For seven years you will diligently grow crops like you always do, but when you harvest them, leave all the grains on the stalk except the little that you must eat. Then, after this will come seven dreadful years (of bad harvests) in which you will live off of what you stored in advance, saving only small, guarded supplies. Then, after that period, a year will come in which the people will have abundant water, and they will press (juice and oil)." *Surat Yusuf (Joseph) 12:46-49*

When the wine-pourer returned with the meaning of the dream, the king said, "Bring that young man to me." The messengers went to the prison to release Yusuf, but he refused to leave his cell, saying, "Go back to your master and ask him, 'What are the ladies who cut their hands up to?' My Lord is aware of their trap." *Surat Yusuf (Joseph) 12:50*

The king then ordered the ladies who were involved to be gathered before him and asked, "What were your intentions when you tried to seduce Yusuf from his own self?" The ladies answered, "God save us! We don't know anything bad about him!" Then (Wife of 'Aziz Misr) said, "The truth is now clear to all. It was I who tried to seduce him from his nature. He is indeed true and virtuous."

Yusuf said, "I wanted this (public hearing) so that (the minister, 'Aziz Misr,) would know that I did not betray him in his absence and that Allah will never guide the plan of betrayers. Nor do I absolve myself (of all blame); the human soul is certainly prone to evil unless my Lord gives His Mercy. Certainly, my Lord is Forgiving and Most Merciful." *Surat Yusuf (Joseph) 12:51-53*

Then the king commanded, "Bring him to me; I will take him to be my special servant." When Yusuf was brought, the king reassured him, "Be certain that today you are before me and that your position is firmly set with your honesty fully proved!" Yusuf said, "Put me in charge of all the storehouses in the land. I will guard them like one who knows their importance." *Surat Yusuf (Joseph) 12:54-55*

Thus, We put Yusuf in the position where he could take anything in the land he pleased. We give Our Mercy to whom We please, and We never let be lost the reward of those who do good. Certainly, the reward of the next life is the best for those who believe and are constant in doing good. *Surat Yusuf (Joseph) 12:56-57*

The Brothers Come Forth

The foretold famine struck, forcing people far and wide to go to Egypt to buy food. Among these came Yusuf's brothers.

When they came before his (court) to buy things, they didn't recognize him, although Yusuf instantly knew who they were. After he had given them the supplies, they needed, he told them, "Bring to me the youngest brother you have from the same father as yourselves. Don't you see that I give generously and that I provide the best hospitality? Now, if you don't bring him to me you will not get any more (grain) from me, nor shall you ever come near me again." Surat Yusuf (Joseph) 12:58-60

They answered, "We will certainly get our way from his father. Indeed we will do it." Then (Yusuf) said to his boys, "Put their goods in their camel-packs. Perhaps they will recognize it when they go back to their family; perhaps they will come again." Surat Yusuf (Joseph) 12:61-62

When the brothers returned to their father, they said, "Father! We won't get any more grain unless we take our youngest brother with us next time. So send (Benjamin) with us so we can get our supplies. We will take good care of him." "Shall I trust you with him when I had already trusted you with his brother (Yusuf) so long ago?" he replied. "But Allah is the best to take care of things, and He is the Most Merciful of all." Surat Yusuf (Joseph) 12:63-64

When they opened their baggage, they found their goods given back to them. They said, "Our father, what else should we want? Here are our goods given back to us, and we shall bring food to our family, protect our brother and add the measure of one camel more. That is an easy measure." Surat Yusuf (Joseph) 12:65

Ya'qub said, "I'll never send him with you unless you swear a special promise to me, in Allah's name, that you will be sure to bring him back unless you yourselves are trapped." After they had sworn their special promise he said, "Allah, be the Witness and Guardian over all that we say!"
Then he instructed his sons, "Don't enter the city all from the same road, but rather, each of you pick a different gate. Not that I can help you against Allah's plan with my advice. No one can command except Allah. In Him do I put my trust, and let everyone who trusts put their trust in Him." Surat Yusuf (Joseph) 12:66-67

And when they entered the city in the way their father had told them to, it did not help them in the least against (the plan of) Allah. It was just something Ya'qub felt he had to say. For he was, by Our teaching, very experienced. But most people don't know that. And when they came to Yusuf, he lodged his brother (Benjamin) with himself. He said, "Look, I am your brother! So do not grieve for what they have been doing." Surat Yusuf (Joseph) 12:68-69

Yusuf's Plan

When Yusuf had given them the supplies they needed, he (had his servant) put the drinking cup of the king into the youngest brother's saddlebag. Then, when the caravan was setting out for the return journey, he had a guard shout out after them, "Hey! You in the Caravan! Stop, you are thieves!" Surat Yusuf (Joseph) 12:70

The brothers halted their caravan and shouted back, "What are you missing?" The guards surrounded them and the leader replied, "We are missing the great cup of the king. Whoever finds it will get the reward of a load of valuables. I will do my duty and find it!" Surat Yusuf (Joseph) 12:71-72

The brothers said, "By God! You know we didn't come to make trouble in this country, and we're not thieves!" The guards answered, "What should be the punishment of this crime if we prove you're lying?" They replied, "The penalty should be that the owner of the saddle bag in which you find the item should be held as a slave to pay for the crime. This is how we punish criminals in our country." Surat Yusuf (Joseph) 12:73-75

(The guards called their master, Yusuf, over to the caravan) and he began to search the brothers' baggage. Then, when he opened the bag of (Benjamin), there was the missing cup of the king! This is how We (Allah) planned it for Yusuf. He couldn't hold his brother, according to the law of the king, except that Allah willed it (so). We increase (in wisdom) whoever We want to, but over all intelligent people is the All-Knowing. Surat Yusuf (Joseph) 12:76

The brothers cried out, "If he stole something, then you should know he had another brother who used to steal also."(Upon hearing their lies, Yusuf became angry) but he kept his feelings locked in his heart so as not to give away the secret to them. He simply said, "You are in the worst position, and Allah knows best the truth of what you claim!" They begged, "Great one! Listen to us! He has an old and respected father (who will grieve for him), so keep one of us in his place. We see that you are gracious in doing good." But Yusuf replied, "God forbid that we take anyone except the one who had our property. If we did so, we would be acting wrongly." Surat Yusuf (Joseph) 12:77-79

When they saw no hope of changing his mind, they held a meeting in private. The eldest among them said, "Don't you remember that we made a promise with our father, in Allah's name, and how before this we failed in our duty with Yusuf? As for me, I won't leave this land until my father allows me or Allah commands me, and He is the best to command. Go back to father and say, 'Father! Your son stole something. We say only what we know, and we could not guard against what we didn't expect! Ask at the town we passed through and in the caravan in which we returned, and (you will find) we are telling the truth.'" Surat Yusuf (Joseph)12:80-82

When Ya'qub was informed, he cried out, "No! You just made up a story good enough to cover you! All I can do is be patient. Maybe Allah will bring them all back to me (in the end), for He is indeed full of knowledge and wisdom." Then he turned away from them and cried, "How great is my sadness for Yusuf." And his eyes became white and blinded with sorrow, and he fell into a silent daze. Surat Yusuf (Joseph) 12:83-84

The brothers said, "By Allah! Won't you ever stop remembering Yusuf, even until you reach the last moments of illness or until you die?" Ya'qub answered them, "I only complain about my problems and sorrow to Allah, and I know things from Allah that you don't. My sons! Go back to Egypt, ask about Yusuf and his brother and never give up hope of Allah's Mercy. Truly, no one despairs of Allah's Mercy except those who have no faith." Surat Yusuf (Joseph) 12:85-87

The Truth Is Out!

When the brothers returned to Egypt and entered Yusuf's presence, they said, "Great one! Grief has come upon us and our family. We have only a little money, so give us full supplies, we beg you, and treat it as charity for us. Allah rewards the charitable." Yusuf answered, "Do you remember how you dealt with Yusuf and his youngest brother in your ignorance?" Surat Yusuf (Joseph) 12:88-89

(When they realized who Yusuf was) they asked, "Are you really Yusuf?"
"I am Yusuf, and this is my brother!" He replied (pointing to Benjamin), "Allah has been gracious to us. Whoever is righteous and patient, Allah will never let their reward be lost, because they did right."
Surat Yusuf (Joseph) 12:90

(The brothers began weeping) and cried out, "By Allah! Indeed Allah has preferred you above us! We are guilty of sin!" "There will be no shame put on you today," Yusuf replied. "Allah will forgive you, and He is the

Most Merciful of all. Go and take my shirt, and put it over the face of my father. He will come to see clearly again. Then bring him and all your family back to me here." *Surat Yusuf (Joseph) 12:91-93*

After the caravan had left Egypt and was on its way home, Ya'qub exclaimed to the people around him, "I feel the presence of Yusuf. And don't think I'm senile." They said, "By Allah! You have an old wandering mind." But when the bringer of the good news came and put the shirt over Ya'qub's face, he immediately regained clear sight. Then he said, "Didn't I tell you that I know from Allah things you don't?" *Surat Yusuf (Joseph) 12:94-96*

Then the brothers begged, "Father! Ask forgiveness for our sins for we were truly at fault." "I will ask my Lord to forgive you," he replied. "For He is the Forgiving and Merciful." Then, (after they all traveled to Egypt) and came before Yusuf, he provided a home for his parents with himself and declared, "Enter Egypt in safety, if it please Allah." He raised his parents high (in respect) and they all (his two parents and eleven brothers) fell down in prostration before him. He announced before them, "My Father! This is the fulfillment of the vision I had so long ago. Allah has made it come true! He was indeed good to me when He took me out of prison and brought you all here out of the desert even after Shaytan had caused jealousy between me and my brothers. Surely, my Lord understands better the mysteries of all He plans to do, for certainly He is full of knowledge and wisdom." *Surat Yusuf (Joseph) 12:97-100*

Yusuf continued saying, "My Lord! You have indeed given me some power and taught me how to understand visions. Creator of the skies and the Earth! You are my Protector in this world and in the next. Take my soul as one surrendering to Your Will. Join me with the righteous!" *Surat Yusuf (Joseph) 12:101*

This is one of the hidden stories, which We (Allah) reveal by inspiration to you. You were not there with them when they put the details together in weaving their plots. Yet most people will not believe, no matter how strongly you want them to. *Surat Yusuf (Joseph) 12:102-103*

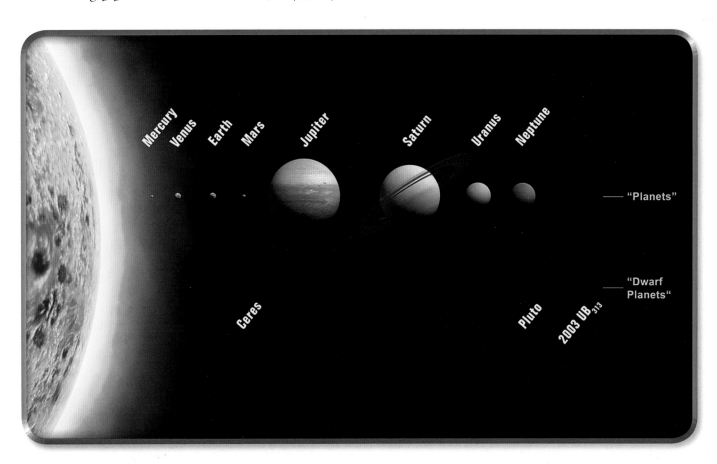

Chapter 10
Bani Isra'il

The Enslavement of the Hebrews

The family and tribe of Prophet Yusuf, who were called **Banu Isra'il بَنو إِسْرائيل, the Descendants of Prophet Jacob**, had all immigrated to Egypt in search of a better life. They were initially welcomed in the land by the rulers of Egypt, who were from the tribe called Hyksos. The Hyksos were invaders who only ruled Egypt for a short time.

When the Egyptians overthrew the invaders, they reinstituted their own people as Pharaohs and mistreated the Hebrew immigrants. Hebrew means literally people from the other side, as their forefather Ibrahim had crossed from the other side of the Euphrates River and into Palestine long before this time.

Many Egyptians were resentful of the Hebrews. Over the course of many centuries, the descendants of Yusuf and his people lost more and more rights. Finally, by about 1500 BCE, they were reduced to the status of forced laborers, or slaves of the state. The Hebrews were in a miserable situation. However, it was far worse that they had forgotten most of what their forefathers had known about Allah. The Hebrews mostly followed Egyptian customs. Many even worshipped Egyptian idols, and they knew little of the good and moral way of life.

But no matter how much the Hebrews assimilated, the Egyptians still did not like these outsiders. In about the year 1200 BCE, the Egyptians saw that the Hebrew population was increasing at an alarming rate and sent forth a decree from the house of Pharaoh: all Hebrew baby boys must be killed. The Egyptians then proceeded to carry out this evil scheme, and although the Hebrews tried their best to resist, they were powerless in the face of the soldiers who went house-to-house obeying their master's wishes.

And when Musa said to his people, "Remember Allah's blessing upon you when He delivered you from Pharaoh's people who had been inflicting a grievous torment on you, slaughtering your sons and leaving your women alive. In that there was a great trial from your Lord." Surat Ibrahim (Abraham) 14:6

The Baby in a Basket

Allah had a plan to deal with the evil pharaoh. He sent a revelation to a certain Hebrew mother, which included some very unusual instructions.

We inspired the mother of Musa saying, "Suckle him (Musa). Then once you fear about him, cast him in the river, and do not fear, and do not grieve. Surely We are going to bring him back to you and appoint him one of (Our) messengers." Surat Al Qasas (The Stories) 28:7

Later, when the soldiers were coming to her part of town, the woman took a basket of reeds and put her baby boy into it. She went down to the river and set the basket in the water. Perhaps with a bitter tear, she pushed the tiny craft out into the current and watched it float away. Allah then revealed to her that he would, indeed, be safe. (20:39) As Allah would have it, the river brought the basket to one of Pharaoh's river-side palaces. Asyah, Pharaoh's wife, was amazed to see the basket and ordered it brought to her.

So the family of Pharaoh picked him up, so that he becomes for them an enemy and a (cause of) grief. Indeed Pharaoh, Haman and their armies were mistaken. And the wife of Pharaoh said, (to Pharaoh about Musa), "He may be a delight of eye for me and you. Do not kill him. It is hoped that he will be of benefit to us, or we will adopt him as a son." And they were not aware (of what was going to happen). Surat Al Qasas (The Stories) 28: 8-9

The mother of Musa (which is what Asyah named the infant) felt heartsick for her baby. She found out that a baby was brought into Pharaoh's household from the river, and that there were many stories told about it. Her pain at losing her son almost made her go to Pharaoh and ask for him back. But Allah strengthened her heart so her belief could remain true. (28:10) Musa's mother asked her daughter to go near the palace and try to keep an eye on what was happening with the baby as best she could.

211

Meanwhile, inside the palace, the baby refused to take milk from anyone. He was crying and hungry and in danger of dying unless someone could feed him. The servants of the palace looked frantically for anyone who could feed the baby.

Perhaps Musa's ﷺ older sister heard someone talking as they were going out from the palace. She quickly thought to present herself saying, *"I know of a family that can feed and raise him for you with great concern for his welfare."* Surat Al Qasas (The Stories) 28: 12

Thus, Allah ﷻ fulfilled his promise to Musa's ﷺ mother and returned her child to her. However, she had to pretend that the baby was not hers, as the house of Pharaoh had a claim on him now. But at least she knew he was safe and that she would be able to be near him.

The Big Brawl

Musa ﷺ grew strong, and in time became a handsome and powerful young man. He was privileged to be a part of Pharaoh's household, and Asyah, his adopted mother, must have been very gracious to him. It may have been hidden from Musa ﷺ for a time that he was a Hebrew and not an Egyptian, but it didn't matter, as he had the protection of Asyah behind him. He could go and do as he pleased.

But he was not arrogant or vain, nor did he go to the other Hebrews and act like he was better than them. His real mother had raised him with good values in her home, with his older sister and his brother Harun ﷺ. Perhaps she even revealed to him his true identity.

And when he reached his maturity and became perfect, We gave him wisdom and knowledge. This is how We reward those who are good in their deeds. Surat Al Qasas (The Stories) 28:14

One day, while Musa ﷺ was out walking in the city, he found two men fighting in a hidden area with no one else around. One was a Hebrew and the other, an Egyptian. The Hebrew man called out to Musa ﷺ for help, and Musa ﷺ tried to intervene. During the scuffle Musa ﷺ hit the Egyptian, unintentionally killing him. Musa ﷺ felt terrible and asked Allah ﷻ for forgiveness and mercy. Thanks to his mother's influence, Musa ﷺ believed in the oneness of God and rejected the Egyptian idols. Allah ﷻ forgave Musa ﷺ and settled his heart.

He (Musa) said, "O my Lord! As You have favored me, I will never be a supporter of the sinners." Surat Al Qasas (The Stories) 28:17

The next day, Musa ﷺ went out in the city again and saw the same Hebrew man he saved earlier. The man was fighting with another Egyptian. When the Hebrew asked for help again, Musa ﷺ shouted at him, "You're clearly a brawler!" Musa ﷺ thought he would try to break up the fight, and when he came near the struggling men, the Egyptian said, *"Hey Musa! Are you going to kill me like you killed that man yesterday? You only want to be a tyrant in the land and not a peace-maker!"* Surat Al Qasas (The Stories) 28:19

Someone had found out about the dead man! Musa ﷺ knew he was in trouble. Then someone came running to Musa ﷺ and said, *"Hey Musa! The leaders are having a meeting about you, to order your execution. You have to get out of here. Take my advice! I mean it!"* Surat Al Qasas (The Stories) 28:20

Then Musa ﷺ grabbed whatever supplies he could and escaped from Egypt. He headed east across the Sinai desert.

So, he went out of it (the city), looking around in a state of fear. He said, "O my Lord, save me from the cruel people." Surat Al Qasas (The Stories) 28:21

The Daughters of Madyan

Musa ﷺ traveled on until he reached Madyan, a land located in the northern tip of the Arabian peninsula. Upon arriving out of the trackless wilderness.

I hope my Lord shows me an easy road. And when he arrived at the waters of Madyan, he found a large number of people watering (their animals) and found, aloof from them, two women keeping (their animals) back. He said, "What is the matter with you?" They said, "We cannot water (our animals) until these shepherds take (their animals) back after watering them, and our father is a very old man." Musa took the water buckets and watered the whole flock for the women. When he had finished, he returned to a shady spot and said, "My Lord! I am in need of any good You send me." Afterwards, one of the women came back to him, walking shyly, and said, "My father has invited you to a dinner so he can reward you for watering (our animals) for us." So when he (Musa) came to him (the father of the women) and narrated to him the whole story, the latter said, "Do not fear; you have escaped from the wrongdoing people." *Surat Al Qasas (The Stories) 28:22-25*

So Musa﷽ went to the camp of the old leader—who was actually Prophet Shu'ayb﷽—and was invited inside. During the course of the dinner, Musa﷽ told the old man all that had happened to him.

One of his (daughters) suggested, "Dearest Father, hire him for wages. The best man to employ is one who is strong and honest." The father announced to Musa, "I want to marry you to one of my daughters. My condition is that you work for me for eight years, but if you stay for 10 years, it will be a mercy from you (to me). But I don't want to put too big a burden on you. You will see that, as Allah wills, I am one of the righteous." Musa said, "Let that be the (deal) between me and you. Whichever length of time I work, don't have any ill feelings towards me. Let Allah be the witness to what we say." *Surat Al Qasas (The Stories) 28:26-28*

The Burning Bush

Musa﷽ married one of his daughters and worked for her father for the required number of years. When his obligation was over, he decided to strike out on his own. He packed up his belongings and headed for the Sinai Peninsula with his wife. One evening, Musa﷽ was looking out from his camp, and he thought he saw a light on a nearby mountain. The mountain, known as Mount Tur, loomed over him like a monolith. He had to find out who was there.

He told his wife to remain in camp while he went to get some information from the one who started the fire. At the very least, he thought that he could bring a burning branch to start their own campfire. Musa﷽ climbed the mountain until he reached a small valley within it. There he saw a small tree, or bush, that was on fire.

So when he came to it, he was called by a voice coming from a side of the right valley in the blessed ground, from the tree, saying, "O Musa, I am Allah, the Lord of the worlds." *Surat Al Qasas (The Stories) 28:30*

Musa﷽ was then commanded to remove his shoes because he was on holy ground. Allah﷽ gave Musa﷽ two secret miracles that would prevent Pharaoh or his people from harming him, "Throw down your stick." So when he saw it moving as if it were a snake, he turned back in retreat and did not look back. (Allah said to him), "O Musa come forward and do not fear; you are one of those in peace. Insert your hand into your bosom, and it will come out white without any evil (disease), and press your arm to your side for (removing) fear. Thus these are two proofs from your Lord (sent) to Pharaoh and his chiefs. Indeed they are transgressing people." *Surat Al Qasas (The Stories) 28:31-32*

Mount Tur, where Allah﷽ spoke with Musa﷽.

Allah﷽ bestowed the gift of Prophethood on him. Allah﷽ informs us, Remember when your Lord called Musa saying, "Go to the transgressing people, The people of Pharaoh. Do they not fear Allah?" He (Musa) said, "My Lord, I fear that they will reject me. My heart gets straitened, and my tongue is not fluent; so send for Harun. Moreover, they have (leveled) a charge of offence against me, and I fear they will kill me." *Surat Ash-Shuaraa (The Poets) 26:10-14*

Musa﷽ knew for certain what he had to do. He instructed his family to return to Madyan and remain there while he secretly traveled back to Egypt to meet up with his brother Harun﷽. Then he would have to face the pharaoh of Egypt. But would he listen? Time would tell.

The Showdown with Pharaoh

Musa returned to Egypt in about the year 1225 BCE, almost 10 years after he had barely escaped with his life. He met up with his brother, Harun, to whom Allah had also granted Prophethood in order to help Musa. (19:53)

It didn't take long for Pharaoh to find out that Musa had returned. He ordered his men to bring Musa and his brother to him. His palace was a huge stone mansion filled with statues, Hieroglyphics writings, soldiers and priests. When Musa was brought in front of Pharaoh, Asyah must have felt pained at the thought of what her husband might do to him.

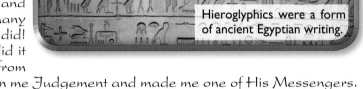

Hieroglyphics were a form of ancient Egyptian writing.

The Pharaoh said, "Musa, didn't we love you and care for you as a child, and didn't you live many years with us? But then you did the crime you did! You're a thankless man!" Musa answered, "I did it back then, and I was wrong. So I ran away from you and feared you. But my Lord has since given me Judgement and made me one of His Messengers. And you say it was a favor, what you did for me, but you enslaved the Children of Isra'il!"
Surat As-Shuaraa (The Poets) 26:18-22

Musa then announced, "Pharaoh! I am a Messenger from the Lord of the Worlds! I say nothing but the truth about Allah. I have come to you from your Lord with a clear sign, so let the Children of Isra'il leave with me!" Surat Al A'raaf (The Heights) 7:104-105

Pharaoh asked, "Who is this Lord of the Worlds?" Musa answered, "He is the Lord of the skies, the Earth, and all in between if you want to know." Pharaoh said to those around him, "Do you hear that!" Musa continued, "He is your Lord and the Lord of your ancestors, from the very beginning." Pharaoh said "This Messenger sent to you (Hebrews) is insane!" Musa said, "He is the Lord of the East and the West and all in between, if you only had sense!" Pharaoh declared, "If anyone makes any god other than me, I will imprison him!" Musa called out, "Even if I showed you clear proof? " Surat Ash-Shuaraa (The Poets) 26:23-30

The Pharaoh replied, "If you have really come with a sign, then show it if you're telling the truth." So Musa threw his staff down and then it became a real serpent. Then he pulled out his hand, and it glowed white (to everyone's eyes!) The Pharaoh's advisers whispered to their master, "He is a skilled sorcerer. His plan is to drive you from your kingdom." Then they asked each other, "What should we do?" One advisor said, "Delay him and his brother in suspense. Then send men to all the different cities to gather all our finest sorcerers." Surat Al A'raaf (The Heights) 7:106-112

The day's meeting was adjourned, and Musa and Harun were probably allowed to go back among the Hebrews until the next meeting. Perhaps they spread the word that Allah's Messenger was among them and that they were about to be delivered from their difficulties.

The Sorcerers Speak

Whatever happened in the time after the first meeting, it was short, for when the Pharaoh of Egypt called the people to him, they had to move quickly. Then Musa and Harun were summoned to the court of Pharaoh once more. On one side of the chamber stood Pharaoh's finest sorcerers and workers of magic.

The sorcerers came to Pharaoh. They said, "Of course we will be rewarded if we win?" The Pharaoh answered, "Yes, and of course, you will be among the closer ones (to me)." The sorcerers said, "Musa, will you go first or shall we?" He said, "You throw." So when they threw, they bewitched the eyes of the people, and made them frightened, and produced great sorcery. Surat Al A'raaf (The Heights) 7:113-116

The sorcerers threw their sticks and ropes and chanted strange words, causing everyone to think that the sticks had become snakes.

So, when they had cast, Musa said, "All that you have brought is magic. Allah will certainly bring it to naught. Be assured that Allah does not set right the work of the mischief-makers." *Surat Yunus (Jonah) 10:81*

We revealed to Musa, "Throw your staff." Then all of a sudden, it began to swallow all that they had concocted. Thus the truth prevailed, and what they were doing became a nullity. So, they were overcome then and there and turned humiliated. The sorcerers fell to their knees and bowed. They cried, "We believe in the Lord of the Universe—the Lord of Musa and Harun!" *Surat Al A'raaf (The Heights) 7:117-122*

Pharaoh was enraged! He shouted at them, "Do you believe in him without my permission? This must be a trick which you all planned in the city to make the people run away. Soon you will know (your fate). I will have your hands and feet cut off on opposite sides, and I'll have you killed on a stake." They replied, "For us, we will only be returned to our Lord. You only want to take revenge on us because we believe in the signs of our Lord that have come to us!" Then they prayed to Allah, "O our Lord, pour out patience upon us, and cause us to die as Muslims."
Surat Al A'raaf (The Heights) 7: 123-126

The meeting was again adjourned and Musa and Harun went back among their people. Meanwhile, the nobles of the court asked the Pharaoh, "Are you going to let Musa and his people cause chaos in the land and abandon your gods?" The Pharaoh ordered, "We will kill their male children (again) and keep their females alive. We have total power over them!" *Surat Al A'raaf (The Heights) 7: 127*

When the threat was announced in the Hebrew areas of the city, Musa said to his people, "Seek help from Allah and be patient. Surely, the land belongs to Allah. He lets whomsoever He wills inherit it from among His servants; and the end-result is in favor of the God-fearing." But then his people started complaining against him, "We've had trouble both before and after you came to us!" Musa replied, "Maybe your Lord will destroy your enemy and make you survive in the Earth. Then He might test you by your actions." *Surat Al A'raaf (The Heights) 7: 127-129*

The Arrogance of Pharaoh

And We seized the people of Pharaoh with years of famine and poor production of fruits so that they may learn a lesson. When good times came to them, they said, "This is our right." And if an evil touched them, they took it as an ill omen of Musa and those with him. Listen, their ill omen lies with Allah only, but most of them do not know. *Surat Al A'raaf (The Heights) 7: 130-131*

The truth of Prophet Musa's teachings reached even to Egyptians, and some of Pharaoh's own people began to believe. One Egyptian man even challenged the Pharaoh and told him to listen to Musa's message. (40:28-35) Pharaoh became more arrogant and ordered **Haman** هَامَان, his second-in-command, to build a huge tower. The Pharaoh said, Build me a huge palace so I can climb to the sky and touch the God of Musa, for I think Musa is a liar! *Surat Al Qasas (The Stories) 28:38*

But the Egyptian man, who now believed in Allah, told the Pharaoh that even if he built up all the treasures in the world, it wouldn't matter, since everything in this life passes away. Although the Pharaoh tried to have the man killed for his insolence, Allah helped the man to escape. (40:38-45)

Meanwhile, Musa and Harun kept spreading the message of Allah's truth among Banu Isra'il; few truly believed, however. (10:83) Then Allah instructed Prophet Musa and Harun to turn their homes into places of worship of Allah and to establish times of prayer. (10:87) This they did, and many more people began to learn about Allah and their duty to Him. Before the next meeting with Pharaoh, Musa said, "Our Lord, You have given Pharaoh and his group glamour and riches in the worldly life, so that, our Lord, they mislead (people) from Your path. Our Lord, obliterate their riches and harden their hearts, so that they may not come to believe until they witness the painful punishment." Allah said, "The prayer of the two of you has been granted so stand firm, and never follow the way of the ignorant." *Surat Yunus (Jonah) 10:88-89*

Pharaoh boasted to Musa⸭, "Whatever signs you bring against us from your magic, we will never believe you." Surat Al A'raaf (The Heights) 7: 132

So Allah⸭ sent terrible plagues against the land, which caused many deaths. Locusts descended on the fields, devouring the crops; lice infected the city; frogs filtered into the city from the swamps; and, a mysterious blood-red color seeped out into the water. Pharaoh rejected the call, even after all this. (7:133) After each plague, Pharaoh would beg Prophet Musa⸭ to stop and would promise that he would believe in him. But whenever the plague was removed, the Pharaoh would break his promise. (7:134-135)

The Woman Who Defied Pharaoh

After hearing all the exchanges between Musa⸭ and her husband, Asyah, the wife of Pharaoh, decided to take a stand of her own. She couldn't sit by silently any longer. She came to believe that Musa⸭ was a true prophet and that her husband was wrong. She said something that would make her husband very angry with her.

And Allah has cited for the believers the example of the wife of Fir'aun (Pharaoh), when she said, "My Lord! Build for me, in nearness to You, a palace in Paradise. Save me from the Pharaoh and his actions and save me from evil people." Surat At-Tahrim 66:11

Pharaoh was livid and ordered Asyah, his own wife, to be tortured until she broke. According to Salman Al Faresi, Allah⸭ sent invisible angels to spread their wings over her, shielding her from the pain and suffering of the torture. When she died, she became a **Shaheed** شَهِيد **Martyr**, someone who dies for the sake of Allah⸭.

The Great Escape!

The arrogance of Pharaoh grew to the breaking point. He was surely going to order his soldiers to exterminate Musa⸭ and his people. So Allah⸭ sent the inspiration to Musa⸭ to organize his people for the great escape. (26:52) Everyone was told to prepare to leave when the signal was given. As soon as the time came, all the Hebrews and the Egyptians who believed in Musa's⸭ message silently poured forth from their homes one night. They carried with them whatever they could and moved as quietly as possible.

By the time the dawn rose over the Egyptian countryside, Musa's⸭ entire people had evacuated and were heading towards Palestine. There were perhaps thousands of men, women and children. Few had any horses or mules, and many were weak or elderly and needed extra help in their journey. When the Egyptians found out that they were gone, they informed Pharaoh. Allah⸭ mentioned, *So Pharaoh sent into the cities (his) men to muster (people) saying, "These are a small band, and indeed they are enraging us. And we are a host, well-armed."* Surat As-Shuaraa (The Poets) 26:53-56

Then Pharaoh arranged his army of spearmen, archers, charioteers, horsemen and foot soldiers and marched forth out of the city in pursuit of the fleeing Hebrews. After several days of hard traveling, Musa⸭ led his people to an area of small, shallow lakes, just north of the Gulf of Suez. Perhaps they planned to thread their way through the narrow land corridors and enter Palestine secretly, but their plan was thwarted by Pharaoh's expert trackers. In the distance, the Hebrews saw the huge dust cloud of an approaching army. Many panicked, and others cowered in fear, as their only escape route was blocked by water.

When Pharaoh and his army came upon the parted sea and saw the fleeing people, his arrogance pushed him to order his army in after them. He led the charge down into the corridor between the water, in full battle array. With the help of Allah⸭, Musa⸭ saved his people and brought the message of truth back to them. Along the way, he managed to convince quite a few Egyptians of Allah's⸭ truth as well. But now that the period of slavery was over, the real struggle was about to begin.

So they (the people of Pharaoh) pursued them (the people of Musa) at the time of sunrise. And when the two hosts saw each other, the companions of Musa said, "Surely we are overtaken." He said, "Never! Indeed with me is my Lord. He will guide me." My Lord is with me and He will give me guidance! Then Allah inspired Musa to hit the sea in front of them with his staff, and by a miracle of Allah, the waters parted, leaving a clear path across the bottom to the other side. Musa and Harun called to the people to run for their lives to the far shore, and they all did so. After the last of Musa's people were safely on the other side, Allah sent the waves crashing down upon Pharaoh and his army, resulting in their death. Surat As-Shuaraa (The Poets) 26:60-67

Banu Isra'il and Musa ﷺ

The Hebrews, or Banu Isra'il, were out of Egypt and safe from the hands of its rulers. Now what would they do? Prophet Musa ﷺ was inspired by Allah ﷻ to lead his people towards Mount Tur (also known in the West as Sinai) where he had received revelation the first time. Along the way, problems were beginning to mount. As they passed near the lands of a small nation in the southern Sinai peninsula, Banu Isra'il noticed that idols were a part of the culture there.

We made the children of Isra'il cross the sea, then they came across a people sitting in devotion before their idols. They (the Israelites) said, "O Musa, make a god for us like they have gods." He said, "You are really an ignorant people. What these people are engaged in is sure to be destroyed and false is what they are doing." He said, "Shall I seek any one other than Allah as God for you, while He has given you excellence over the (people of all the) worlds." Surat Al A'raaf (The Heights) 7:138-140

Within a few days, the huge group of people reached Mount Tur and began to settle themselves there. Prophet Musa ﷺ put his brother Harun ﷺ in charge and then went up the mountain with a few supplies to await the command of his Lord. (7:142) When Musa ﷺ reached the sacred valley, called Tuwa, he made a small encampment and remained there for 40 days. After arriving, Musa ﷺ asked of Allah ﷻ a strange request.

When Musa came at Our appointed time and his Lord spoke to him, he said, "My Lord, show (Yourself) to me that I may look at You." He said, "You shall never see Me. But look at the mount. If it stays at its place, you will see Me." So when his Lord appeared to the mount, He made it smashed, and Musa fell down unconscious. When he recovered, he said, "Pure are You. I repent to You, and I am the first to believe (that no one can see You in this world)." He said, "Musa, I have chosen you above all men for my messages and for My speaking (to you). So, take what I have given to you, and be among the grateful." Surat Al A'raaf (The Heights) 7:143-144

Then Allah ﷻ explained to Musa ﷺ how he must lead the nation and instruct them. He also revealed laws to Musa ﷺ that he then carved onto thin stone slabs. Finally Allah ﷻ revealed to him, *"Hold to these firmly, and order your people to follow as best they can these teachings. I will soon show you the final destination of the wicked."* Surat Al A'raaf (The Heights) 7:145

After receiving the laws of Allah ﷻ, Prophet Musa ﷺ gathered the small stone slabs and descended to where his people were camped. Allah's ﷻ last words to Musa ﷺ were that his people were being tested by Samiri, a man from the tribe of Banu Isra'il.

He (Allah) said, "We have then put your people to test after you (left them) and Samiri has misguided them." So, Musa went back to his people, angry and sad. He said, "O my people, did your Lord not promise you a good promise? Did then the time become too long for you, or did you wish that wrath from your Lord befalls you, and hence you broke your promise to me?" Surat Ta-Ha 20:85-86

Prophet Musa ﷺ went up Mount Tur to await the command of his Lord.

The Golden Calf

When Prophet Musa ﷺ returned to his people, Allah's ﷻ warning was confirmed: Samiri had suggested to the people to make an idol of their own. The people donated whatever jewelry, gold plates and serving vessels they had. They melted them in a fire and shaped it into the image of a small calf. Then they began to worship it. Only a few people realized it was a shameful thing to do. (7:148-149) When Musa ﷺ came back into the camp and saw what was going on, he put the stone tablets down and then grabbed his brother Harun ﷺ by the hair.

When Musa returned to his people, angry and sad, he said, "How bad is the thing you have done in my absence! How did you act in haste against the command of your Lord?" He dropped down the tablets and grabbed the head of his brother, pulling him towards himself. He (Harun) said, "My mother's son, the people took me as weak and were about to kill me. So do not let the enemies laugh at me, and do not count me with the wrong-doers." *Surat Al A'raaf (The Heights) 7:150*

Prophet Musa addressed the people, saying, "My People! Didn't your Lord make a great promise to you? Did the promise seem far off, or did you wish for the wrath of your Lord to be upon you, and so you broke your promise to me?" They replied, "We didn't break our promise to you as far as we could hold it. We were made to carry the ornaments of the people and throw them in the fire. This is what the Samiri told us to do. Then he made the image of a calf that seemed so crude. Then (he and his followers) said, 'This is your god and the god of Musa, but Musa has forgotten.'" *Surat Ta-Ha 20:86-89*

Musa asked Samiri why he did it, to which Samiri replied that his inner-self suggested that he do this. Musa ordered him banished from the camp. Then he melted the calf-idol down into small bits and sent people to throw the remnants of it into the sea. (20:95-97)

Musa immediately began to pray for Allah's forgiveness for himself and his brother. (7:151) Afterwards, he took up the tablets again and began to teach the people the laws that Allah made for them. (7:154) Prophet Musa then chose 70 representatives from Banu Isra'il, and they gathered on Mount Tur to ask Allah's forgiveness for the rest of the people. The mountain quaked and Musa begged for forgiveness. Finally, Allah granted it after explaining that His mercy is stronger than His anger. (7:155-156 & 2:54)

The Rebellion against Prophet Musa

Prophet Musa then led the people away in the direction of Palestine. However, along the way, the people began to grumble and complain about the hardships of traveling. (2:61) Prophet Musa had divided up the people into 12 tribes so that they could be better organized. When the leaders of the 12 tribes complained about the lack of water, Allah inspired Prophet Musa to hit a large rock with his staff, and 12 springs gushed out. (7:160)

When Allah commanded them to sacrifice a cow to show obedience to Him, they were so reluctant that it was clear they weren't genuine believers yet. (2:67-71) Also along the way, Banu Isra'il entered several towns and disobeyed Prophet Musa's instructions about how to behave. (2:58-59) They broke the rules whenever Prophet Musa ordered them to obey Allah, and they made his task of leadership a difficult one. (7:161-166)

The mountain quaked when Banu Isra'il gathered on Mount Tur to ask Allah's forgiveness.

Musa and Khidr[15]

Prophet Musa, though an honored prophet, made mistakes. Once, after the leaders of Banu Isra'il had given him a particularly hard time, he stood up among them and said, "Who is the smartest man among the people? I am the smartest!" Because Musa didn't say that Allah was the most knowledgeable of all, Allah led him on a quest to learn wisdom. Allah told him to go to the coast of the Red Sea where it meets the Gulf of Aqaba and the Gulf of Suez and look for a person there who was more learned than even he.

Prophet Musa asked Allah, How can I find him? Allah instructed, take a fish in a basket, and you will find him where you lose that fish. So Musa set out with his servant-boy Yusha' on the mysterious journey to find the wisest man in the world.

15 In this story, hadith from the Al Bukhari collection and the story from Surat Al Kahf (The Cave), number 18 in the Qur'an are combined as the two complement each other.

Musa said to his servant, "I won't give up (my search for the wise man) until I reach the meeting of the two seas, or until I've traveled for years!"

And when they reached the place where the two seas met, the servant forgot about the fish (they brought for lunch). It (miraculously) shot straight into the water (and got away).

After they traveled on further, Musa said to his servant, "Bring us our meal, for we have been traveling hard."

But the servant answered, "Didn't you see what happened when we rested on the rocks (by the sea)? I forgot to tell you about the fish. Only Shaytan could have made me forget to tell you. The fish jumped into the sea in a miraculous way!" Musa cried, "That was the (sign) we were seeking." Then they retraced their path back (to where they were before). There, they found one of Our servants on whom We (Allah) placed mercy from Us, and who received much knowledge from Us. Surat Al Kahf (The Cave) 18:60-65

Musa said to him, "Let me follow you so that you can teach me something about the truth you have learned." The man **(whose name was Khidr)** replied, "You certainly won't be able to have patience with me! And how can you have patience with things you don't fully understand?" He (Musa) said, "You will see, if Allah wills, that I will be patient. I won't disobey you at all." He (Khidr) replied, "If you want to follow me, then ask me no questions about anything until I myself tell you about it." Surat Al Kahf (The Cave) 18:66-70

So, they both moved ahead, until when they boarded a boat, he sliced it (by removing one of its planks). He (Musa) said, "Did you damage it in order to drown everyone on board? This is a strange thing you have done!"

He (Khidr) replied, "Didn't I tell you that you wouldn't have patience with me?"

He (Musa) said, "Don't scold me for forgetting, and don't give me a hassle over this, please." Then they traveled on land until they met a young boy. But he (Khidr) killed him right away. He (Musa) cried, "Have you killed an innocent person who has killed no one? What a horrible thing you've done!" He (Khidr) answered, "Didn't I tell you that you wouldn't have any patience with me?" He (Musa) replied, "If I ever ask you about anything again, don't let me follow you anymore, and you would have full right to leave me." Surat Al Kahf (The Cave) 18:71-76

Then they traveled until they came to a small town. When they asked the townspeople for food, they refused to give them any. (Khidr and Musa) then saw an old wall that was crumbled and falling down. But he (Khidr) went and fixed it.

He (Musa) commented, "If you wanted to, you could have asked the people here for payment for doing that work."

He (Khidr) answered, "This is where we separate. Now I'll tell you the meaning of all those things you couldn't be patient about. As for the boat, it belonged to some poor men who made their living by the sea. I only wanted to make it defective because there was a certain king coming their way who seized every boat by force.

As for the young man, his parents were believers (in Allah), and we were afraid that he would sadden them with his rebellious and bad behavior. So we wanted their Lord to give them a better child in exchange who was more pure and loving. As for the wall, it belonged to two orphans in the town. Under it was a buried treasure that was meant for them. Their father was a good man, so your Lord wanted them to grow up and find their treasure, as a Mercy from your Lord. I didn't do it for me. This is the meaning of what you had no patience with." *Surat Al Kahf (The Cave) 18:77-82*

Prophet Musa's Legacy

The Blessed Prophet Musa led his people to the threshold of Palestine. There he commanded them to attack a mighty city of idol-worshippers whom Allah had decided to punish. Allah reminded them that he had sent them prophets in the past and that they were now living like kings since they were no longer slaves. Then he commanded them to enter the Holy Land promised to the descendants of Prophet Ibrahim.

But Banu Isra'il were afraid to fight, and they told him they would never go into battle unless the evil people left. Musa sent two scouts to look for weaknesses in the city's walls. Soon enough, they returned with news of a weak gate that would be easy to attack and lead to an easy victory.

They said, "O Musa, we shall never enter it, in any case, so long as they are there. So go, you and your Lord, and fight. As for us, we are sitting right here." He said, "O my Lord, I have no control except over myself and my brother. So, make a distinction between us and the sinning people." He (Allah) said, "This (land) is prohibited to them for forty years. They shall be wandering around the earth. So, do not grieve for the sinning people." *Surat Al Ma'idah (The Table Spread) 5:24-25)*

Allah then declared that Banu Isra'il would be forbidden to enter the Holy Land of Palestine for 40 years. Prophet Musa then led his people back into the desert. For 40 years, he bore the brunt of their rebelliousness. But given their spiritual condition, they fell below Allah's standards of being true servants. Wandering in the desert functioned as a training camp for them and as a crash course in obedience to the Truth.

Prophet Musa recorded the **Tawrah** تَوْرَاة, which consisted of Allah's rules for them and for any prophets who would come later. By the time Prophet Musa passed away, the leaders of Banu Isra'il were mature enough to call themselves an organized nation. They entered Palestine in about 1200 BCE and dwelled in a civilized fashion.

The mission of Banu Isra'il was to call surrounding nations to the worship of Allah and to be an example to others. (5:12) Unfortunately, Banu Isra'il did not fulfill this responsibility. (2:75-77, 5:44-45) Not only did they fail to fulfill their mission, but Banu Isra'il also rejected and killed other prophets sent to them from Allah (5:70). They even started to write their own books and said that they were revelations from Allah. (2:87-90) Their own tribal history, collected in the Bible, witnesses their wrong doing. *(See in the Bible: Jeremiah 7:6-7 or Mathew 23:13-39, for example)*

By about the year 900 BCE, Banu Isra'il began calling themselves 'Jews,' after one of their kingdoms, called Judah. Today, many Jews claim to follow the legacy of Prophet Musa, but many of them fall far short of his example. (2:83-85) Many even claim that they are God's chosen people, and so they shy away from calling others to the Truth. (2:94-96) They also believe that God will not punish them in the afterlife. (7:169)

Little of Prophet Musa's original message survives today. Only a few of the descendants of Banu Isra'il have remained pure and followed the truth. (2:121) Those who are fortunate discover Islam and study it with an open heart. Then they become our Muslim brothers and sisters. Only then do they truly follow in the footsteps of the Blessed Prophet Musa. (42:13, 4:153-155)

People of the Book! (Jews and Christians). Now there has come to you Our Messenger (Muhammad), who is revealing to you a lot that you used to hide in the book (you had before) and passing over a lot (of things that are now unnecessary). There has come to you from Allah a (new) light and a clear book. *Surat Al Ma'idah (The Table) 5:15*

﴿يَٰأَهْلَ ٱلْكِتَٰبِ قَدْ جَآءَكُمْ رَسُولُنَا يُبَيِّنُ لَكُمْ كَثِيرًا مِّمَّا كُنتُمْ تُخْفُونَ مِنَ ٱلْكِتَٰبِ وَيَعْفُوا۟ عَن كَثِيرٍ قَدْ جَآءَكُم مِّنَ ٱللَّهِ نُورٌ وَكِتَٰبٌ مُّبِينٌ﴾

سُورَةُ المَائِدَة 5:15

The Kingdom of Isra'il

Allah granted the descendants of Prophet Musa and Banu Isra'il a country of their own in ancient Palestine, which was then called Canaan. (10:93) They named it 'Isra'il.' Allah took the pledge of Banu Isra'il that they would obey His laws and be a light and guide to other nations, calling them to the truth.

In order to make their own nation, Banu Isra'il had to fight off many others. Allah sent them prophets to guide them, but they gave as much trouble to those prophets as their forefathers had given to Prophet Musa. (16:124) Finally, in about the year 1020 BCE, a local prophet chose **Talut** طالُوت, a poor young man, to be their king. It was not that Allah wanted them to have a king, rather they themselves demanded to have one because all the other surrounding nations had one too. (2:246) So Allah granted them one as a test.

When their prophet announced that Talut was to be king, they grumbled more, as he was poor and not influential. They agreed to follow him, however, after much argument. (2:247-248) Talut proved to be an able leader and a military genius. He defeated the Canaanites in many battles and forged a powerful, though small, army. In one decisive battle, the Canaanites brought out a man named **Jalut** جالُوت who was tall, strong and fearless. (2:249-250) He was able to easily defeat many soldiers from Banu Isra'il and caused Talut's army lose hope.

Finally, Allah inspired **Dawud** داود, a brave young man, to come forward and face the menacing warrior. With a slingshot, Dawud knocked the giant warrior to the ground and then killed him with a sword. The army of Talut then defeated the enemy and carved out a secure country. (2:251) After Talut passed away, Dawud was made king. In addition, Allah granted him the Zabur and made him a prophet. He proved to be fair and just and a brilliant general who drove his enemies further away. (21:80)

One interesting episode illustrates the wisdom of Dawud and his young son, Sulayman. Once, a man came and complained that his neighbor's sheep had come into his field and ruined some of the crops. At first, Dawud ordered that the man could keep the sheep that wandered onto his land as compensation for the damages. But Sulayman, who, as the son of a ruler, usually attended the public forums, offered a solution that was more equitable. He suggested that the man keep the sheep only until he was compensated for his loss. So, after taking wool, milk, and baby lambs equal to his loss in crops, he would then return the original sheep to his neighbor. This way, both sides received their fair shares.

And (remember) Dawud (David) and Sulayman (Solomon), when they were adjudicating about the tillage in which the goats of other people wandered at night (and trampled it), and We were witness to their Judgement. So, We enabled Sulayman to understand it. And to each one of them We gave wisdom and knowledge. And with Dawud We subjugated the mountains that pronounced tasbeeh (Allah's purity) and the birds as well. And We were the One who did (it). Surat Al Anbiya' (The Prophets) 21:78-79

Who Was Sulayman?

After Prophet Dawud passed away in 961 BCE, his son, Sulayman, became king. He was to be the last righteous ruler of Banu Isra'il. Because of his piety and wisdom, Allah was to make him a prophet as well. During his reign, the nation of Banu Isra'il grew strong and powerful. Sulayman called his people to obey Allah and he sent messages to other nations inviting them to the service of the One God.

After the end of his rule, at about 922 BCE, Banu Isra'il quickly fell into dispute and made divisions among themselves. They failed to keep their pledge to Allah, and sought worldly power over the rewards of the next life. Within years, Banu Isra'il divided their nation into two different countries: Judah in the south, and Isra'il in the north. Their division made it easier for foreign enemies to attack them.

In 721 BCE, the Assyrians conquered Isra'il, and in 587 BCE, Judah fell to the Babylonians. Banu Isra'il lost their nation and their ways, and their set of beliefs evolved into what is modern-day Judaism. (4:51-55) The Judaism of today has lost much of the real message that was given to the ancient prophets. One of the most powerful was Prophet Sulayman because of the gifts that Allah gave him.

The Power of Prophet Sulayman

Prophet Sulayman was given many special abilities from Allah. He was granted the power to understand the signals, or 'speech,' of birds and other animals, and he could even control the spirit-creatures known as jinn.

And Sulayman inherited (the traits of) Dawud and said, "O people we have been taught the speech of birds, and all sorts of things are given to us. Indeed, this is the evident grace (of Allah)." And mustered for Sulayman were his forces from among the jinn and the humans and the birds. So all of them were kept under (his) control. *Surat An-Naml (The Ants) 27:16-17*

Once, while his army was marching, he passed through a valley with many ant-hills. Allah✦ tells us that the ants warned each other to get in their holes so they wouldn't be stepped on by Prophet Sulayman's✦ army! (27:18)

Sulayman✦ heard the ants and laughed. Then he prayed to Allah✦, and thanked him for the power He gave him. He said, "My Lord! Direct me so that I may be thankful for Your favors, which You have given me and my parents, and that I may do the good things that please You. Admit me, by Your grace, to the ranks of Your righteous servants." *Surat An-Naml (The Ants) (27:19)*

Prophet Sulayman✦ could understand the language of animals, including ants.

The Hoopoe Bird Speaks

One day, Prophet Sulayman✦ was inspecting his birds when he noticed one of them was missing. He asked for it and declared that the bird would be punished if it didn't offer a good excuse. (27:20-21)

The bird, called **Hudhud** هُدْهُد **Hoopoe**, eventually arrived with interesting news. It had found a country far to the south that was unknown to Sulayman✦, called **Saba'** سَبَأ. The land was ruled by a woman with a magnificent throne. The location of the Saba' kingdom is believed to have been in Ethiopia and Yemen.

The Hoopoe continued saying, "I found her and her people worshipping the sun besides Allah. Shaytan has made their deeds seem pleasing in their eyes, and has kept them away from the Path. Thus, they haven't received the guidance that they should serve only Allah. Who brings to light what is hidden in space and the Earth, and knows what you hide and what you reveal. Allah! There is no god but He! Lord of the Throne Supreme!" Prophet Sulayman said, "We shall see if you are telling the truth or a lie. You go with this letter of mine to them. Then wait for their reply." *Surat An-Naml (The Ants) 27:22-28*

The Queen of Saba'

The letter was tied to the bird's leg, and it flew south over the Arabian desert until it landed several days later in the palace of Queen Balqees, ruler of Saba'. She opened the letter and had someone translate it for her. When she heard its message, she immediately called for her advisors to be brought.

She announced to them, "My nobles! Here is a letter delivered to me that is worthy of considering. It is from Sulayman and says, 'In the Name of Allah, The Most Gracious, The Most Merciful. Don't be too proud towards me, but come to me in surrender (to Allah only).'"
Then she asked her advisors, "Nobles! Give me advice in this decision of mine. I never decide anything except in your presence."
They said, "We are a mighty nation and can wage terrible war. But the orders come from you, so think about what to command."
She said, "When kings enter a country, they ruin it and make the best of its people the worst. That's how they behave. But I'm going to send him a present, and then I'll wait and see what my ambassadors have to say when they return." *Surat An-Naml (The Ants) 27:29-35*

The Jinn and the Righteous Servant

Queen Balqees's ambassadors traveled north until they reached Jerusalem, the capital of Isra'il. When they approached Sulayman✦ in his audience chamber, they laid gold and treasures at his feet.

But Sulayman✦ was a Prophet of Allah✦, one not to be swayed by jewels or bought off with fancy rings. He told them, "Are you going to bring me a pile of wealth? What Allah already gave me is better than what He gave you. You are the ones who are happy with your gift." *Surat An-Naml (The Ants) 27:36*

Sulayman, thinking that those people were trying to buy him off, declared, "Go back to (your leaders), and be sure we will come to them with powerful forces they will never be able to match. We will expel them in disgrace, and they will feel humbled." *Surat An-Naml (The Ants) 27:37*

The ambassadors left in a hurry, and returned home with the news. When she received Sulayman's message, Queen Balqees knew drastic action was needed to save her land. She decided to go personally to Jerusalem and meet with Sulayman and try to make a peace treaty with him. Perhaps, she realized, the biggest difference between herself and him was in spiritual beliefs. He worshipped Allah, while she worshipped the sun. She would meet him face-to-face. When Sulayman was informed that the Queen of Saba' was coming herself for a visit, he knew he had to move carefully. He wanted her and her people to give up idol worship, so he needed some demonstration of the power of Allah.

Then he remembered something the Hoopoe told him. In his court, Sulayman called out, "O chieftains, which one of you will bring her throne to me before they come to me submissively?" A stalwart of the jinn said, "I will bring it to you before you rise up from your place, and for this (task) I am powerful, reliable." Said the one who had the knowledge of the book, "I will bring it to you before your glance returns to you." So when he saw it (the throne) well placed before him, he said, "This is by the grace of my Lord, so that He may test me whether I am grateful or ungrateful. Whoever is grateful is grateful for his own benefit, and whoever is ungrateful, then my Lord is Need-Free, Bountiful." *Surat An-Naml (The Ants) 27:38-40*

The Meeting with Balqees

The throne was brought to Prophet Sulayman, all the way from Yemen, so quickly that it seemed like magic. The Queen knew nothing about it, as she was already on her journey northward. Sulayman ordered his people to alter the throne and disguise it so it didn't look like her chair. He remarked that this would be her test to see if she could receive guidance.

A few weeks later, Queen Balqees arrived in Jerusalem with her caravan. She was brought to the audience chamber of Sulayman, and he asked her, "Is this your throne?" She looked at it for a moment and said, "It was just like this!" Then she realized the power of Sulayman as Allah's prophet, and declared her submission to Allah. She was given the great honor of entering the main palace of the city. When Sulayman brought her to the front gates and opened them up, Queen Balqees thought there was a shallow lake inside, for the floor was translucent and shimmered.

She tucked up her skirt in her hand, uncovering her legs, and was about to step in, when Sulayman told her, "This palace is paved with smooth glass." At that moment, she fully realized the lesson of her disguised throne; namely, that things are not always as they seem. Her people saw the powerful sun in the sky and thought it was a god; she saw glass and thought it was water. In both cases, it was an error. She declared, "My Lord! I have wronged my soul. I surrender (to You) with Sulayman, to the Lord of the Universe." *Surat An-Naml (The Ants) 27:42-44*

The Legend of Sulayman

Prophet Sulayman was powerful and wise. He had great armies and extended his influence over many nations. He could ask Allah to calm stormy weather for him and it would be done. (21:81) He built huge temples and palaces and other fortifications in his kingdom. He had the power to command the jinn to work for him, and they helped in the construction of arches, pillars, basins and giant cauldrons.

The Blessed Prophet Sulayman passed away while he was sitting on his throne, before the work was completed. But his body still sat upright and was balanced on his staff. The jinn thought he was still alive and completed their work. If they would have known that he had passed away, they would have stopped and fled, for they considered working for humans humiliating. What signalled to them his death was that a small worm had gnawed into his staff and unbalanced his body, causing it to topple over. (34:14) By this time, the work was already finished. The jinn did indeed feel humiliated and fled away.

One legend tells of a very mischievous jinn that Prophet Sulayman imprisoned in a lamp and set adrift in the ocean. From this legend comes the story of Aladdin and the Magic Lamp. Another legend tells of secret treasure caves in East Africa where Sulayman hid piles of gold and silver. Many explorers have risked their lives searching for the lost mines of Sulayman. Despite all the legends, one thing remains clear: Prophet Sulayman was one of the mightiest rulers the world has ever seen. Yet, people must look past his glory and treasures into the most valuable message of all: obtaining the pleasure of Allah. Submitting to His will is the only real treasure worth possessing.

Who Was Dhul Qarnayn?

The Holy Qur'an mentions the story of a very interesting ruler named **Dhul Qarnayn** ذُو الْقَرْنَيْن **Master of the Two Horns,** who is given as an example of a wise ruler. This title refers to the fact that his empire consisted of two great areas of territory that arched outwards in the shape of two horns.

Muslim scholars have long guessed at his true identity but no firm agreement has yet been made. Some say he was Alexander the Great, who lived from 356 BCE to 323 BCE. But that is highly unlikely, since Alexander was not a known believer.

This ruler, as he is mentioned in the Qur'an, is described as righteous and aware of Allah. The only clues we have to his identity are that he controlled two large areas of land that formed the shape of a horn and that he built a wall to stop invading barbarian tribes.

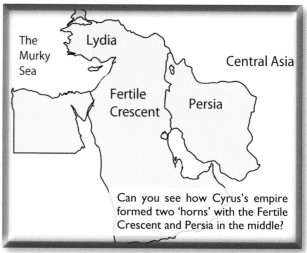

Can you see how Cyrus's empire formed two 'horns' with the Fertile Crescent and Persia in the middle?

Most scholars today are of the opinion that this mighty ruler was Cyrus the Great of Persia who ruled around 549 BCE. His first conquest was over the Lydians. Lydia was located in modern-day Turkey. Next, he defeated the Chaldeans in the Fertile Crescent and allowed all captive peoples, including the Jews, to return to their homelands.

Finally, he conquered vast swaths of territory in Central Asia. Thus his empire formed the shape of two large 'horns.' Cyrus was killed in battle in 529 BCE by a fierce nomadic tribe in the east. During his reign, he proved to be a just man. In his story are lessons about how to fear Allah and to deal with power and its responsibilities.

The Tests of Dhul Qarnayn

The Jews of Al Madinah often tried to trap the Blessed Prophet Muhammad. In order to embarrass him, they would ask him about things that they felt he didn't know the answer to so that they could prove he was not a real Prophet of Allah. But Allah protected His Prophet and revealed the stories that the Jews asked about. One of these stories is about Dhul Qarnayn.

(The Jews) ask you, (Muhammad) about Dhul Qarnayn. Tell them, "I will narrate to you something of his story." We (Allah) established his power on Earth and gave him the ability and knowledge to travel. He followed one direction (with his army) until he reached the setting of the sun. He found that it set behind a sea of murky water. Surat Al Kahf (The Cave) 18:83-86

The scholars have identified this dark sea as being most probably off the coast of Turkey, where the water is indeed colored with a dark hue. Another possible dark sea is a large lake named Ochrida in Asia Minor, which is fed by springs. The water is dark and murky in this 170 square mile lake. Dhul Qarnayn saw the sun falling behind the western horizon of the dark water and made camp.

Near it, he found a community of people. We said, Dhul Qarnayn! (You can either) punish them or treat them with kindness. He decreed, "Whoever does wrong shall be punished. Then he will be sent back to his Lord; and He will punish him with a terrible punishment. But whoever believes and works righteousness, he shall have a goodly reward, and his work will be easy as we order it by our command." Surat Al Kahf (The Cave) 18: 86-88

Dhul Qarnayn's first test was in how he would treat these people who had no real laws. These were, perhaps, the Lydians. He decided to give them laws and to fairly rule them by this code.

Then he followed (another) road, until he came to the rising of the sun. He found it rising on a people for whom We had provided no covering protection against the sun. (He left them) as they were. We completely understood what was before him. Surat Al Kahf (The Cave) 18:89-91

From Asia Minor (Turkey), he journeyed deep into Central Asia to the East, in the direction of the rising sun. So his second test related to the treatment of people who were not educated or well civilized. They lived perhaps in the northern reaches of the Fertile Crescent, and because they did not know how to make shelters, they slept under trees and possibly in caves. Dhul Qarnayn could have easily enslaved them, but instead he chose to leave them alone.

The Yajuj and Majuj

Then he followed (another) way (north into Central Asia) until he reached (a valley) between two mountains. There he found beneath them a people who scarcely understood a word (of his own language). They (managed to get their message across) saying, "Dhul Qarnayn! The Yajuj and Majuj (people) cause chaos in the land. Can we pay you tribute in order that you might build a wall between us and them?" He said, "(The power) which my Lord has established me in is better (than tribute). Just help me with your strength (and labor). I will build a strong wall between you and them. Bring me blocks of iron." After a while passed, his men finished filling up the narrow pass between the two steep mountain-sides. Then he commanded, "Blow (with your bellows and melt the iron)." When it (became as red) as fire, he ordered, "Bring me molten lead so I can pour it over top." Surat Al Kahf (The Cave) 18:92-96

The people in the valley were afraid of two barbarian tribes, the **Yajuj** يَأْجُوج and **Majuj** مَأْجُوج, who periodically invaded and plundered the land. They convinced Dhul Qarnayn to build a wall to keep the invaders out. The wall was soon finished.

You can imagine the terror of the people when they saw the dust clouds of the approaching armies in the distance. Would Dhul Qarnayn's wall hold? After repeated attacks, the barbarians were unsuccessful. Because this was the only pass through the mountains for many miles, the invaders were effectively sealed on the other side for good.

Thus the (Yajuj and Majuj invaders) were made powerless to scale it or to dig through it. Dhul Qarnayn said, "This is a mercy from my Lord. But when the promise of my Lord comes to pass, He will make it into dust, and the promise of My Lord is true." On that Day, We (Allah) will leave them (the barbarians) to surge like waves, one over another. The trumpet will be blown, and We shall collect all (humans) together. And We shall present Hell that Day for Unbelievers to see, all spread out. (Unbelievers) whose eyes had been under a veil from Remembrance of Me and who had been unable even to hear. Surat Al Kahf (The Cave) 18:97-101

The Sign of the Last Day

This famous wall does exist, and its ruins are located in northern Central Asia. There are many different walls there, strung throughout the Caucasus mountains, and any one of them could be the iron wall in question. One such wall, whose ruins lie in a valley about 150 miles southeast of the city of Bukhara, has long since lost much of its iron due to rust.

The seventh century Chinese traveler Hiouen Tsiang reports seeing this huge iron wall with a gate near a place called Derbend. The Muslim Khalifa Wathiq, who ruled from 842-846 CE, sent a team to Central Asia to report on this wall mentioned in the Qur'an. The explorers found it in a valley that was about 150 yards wide. It was supported by two huge jambs and was made of iron bricks welded together with lead. Two huge gates of iron were placed in the middle of the wall. This was reported in the year 985 CE by the famous Muslim geographer Muqaddasi.

One prophecy that Dhul Qarnayn made was that the wall would only last for so long, and then it would be gone. (18:98) When the barrier is no longer there, the invaders from the other side will surge over the land and cause great destruction. Some scholars are of the opinion that the Russians and Chinese are the Yajuj and Majuj. This cannot be proven, but it does make for interesting discussion.

In any case, Dhul Qarnayn passed his third test by helping a people in need of protection against a terrible and cruel enemy. He didn't ask for any money from them except that they also help in the construction of the defensive wall. With his example, we can see that a ruler must establish justice, not be a tyrant over weaker people and help those in need without forcing them to pay anything in gold and riches. How many of the rulers in our modern world could pass these tests?

Travel through the Earth and see how Allah began the creation. So, too, will Allah produce creation again because Allah has power over all things. Surat Al 'Ankabut (The Spider) 29:20

﴿قُلْ سِيرُوا۟ فِى ٱلْأَرْضِ فَٱنظُرُوا۟ كَيْفَ بَدَأَ ٱلْخَلْقَ ثُمَّ ٱللَّهُ يُنشِئُ ٱلنَّشْأَةَ ٱلْءَاخِرَةَ ۚ إِنَّ ٱللَّهَ عَلَىٰ كُلِّ شَىْءٍ قَدِيرٌ﴾ سُورَةُ ٱلْعَنكَبُوت 20:29

Chapter 11
The Legacy of Prophet 'Isa عليه السلام

The Power of Rome

The year was 20 BCE in the Western calendar. One empire ruled supreme over all others in the Mediterranean region: Rome. At the height of its power, the Roman Empire controlled all of Egypt, North Africa, Western Europe and the Middle East up to Mesopotamia. Each of the areas controlled by Rome was divided into provinces that were controlled by local governors who answered only to the Roman emperor, Augustus Caesar.

At that time, Palestine was a mosaic of different peoples and ethnic groups. There were Arabs, Jews, Syrians, Phoenicians, Romans and many other ethnicities. The Jews returned to Palestine in 540 BCE after Cyrus the Great, a Persian king, conquered Mesopotamia. He permitted them to leave Babylon, where they had been held prisoner for generations.

Although the Jews had lost their religious writings when their nations of Judah and Isra'il were crushed, a priest by the name of **Uzayr** عُزَيْر **Ezra** tried to recapture the original writings. He called this book the "Tawrah," which was the same name that Allah﷽ had given to the book of Prophet Musa﷽. (3:78)

Of course, it wasn't an accurate book, nor was it the real Tawrah, for it contained only scattered fragments of the original writings. But Uzayr, who had the authority of the Persian kings behind him, ordered all Jews to follow it, which they did. (9:30)

The Jews governed themselves for the next few centuries, giving nominal allegiance to the Persian Empire. In about 200 BCE, however, the Jews fought Syrian invaders in a battle called the Revolt of the Maccabees. The Jews were brutal but successful and continued as a semi-independent nation.

But the invasion of the mighty Romans after 100 BCE was too much for any small nation to repel. Although the Jews tried to fight off the Roman invaders in several different battles, most notably at a hill-top fortress named Masada, they were eventually crushed and had to live as just another conquered people in the Roman empire.

In 70 BCE, as a punishment to the rebellious Jews, the Romans burned Jerusalem to the ground and destroyed the temple that was built by Prophet Sulayman﷽ so many years before.

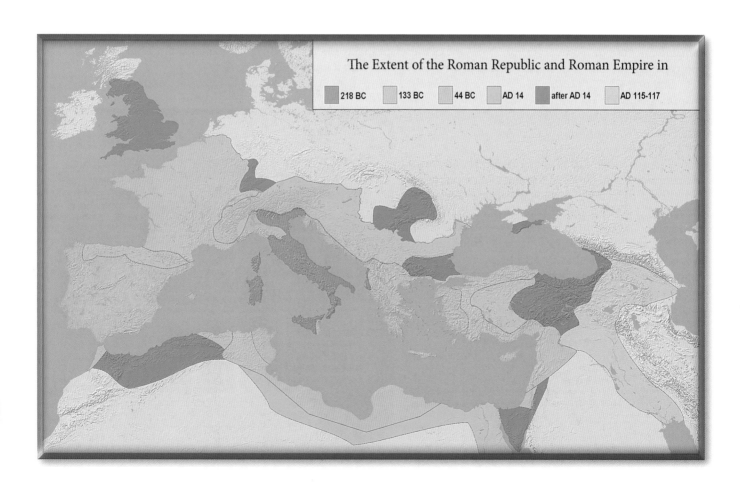

The Extent of the Roman Republic and Roman Empire in

218 BC | 133 BC | 44 BC | AD 14 | after AD 14 | AD 115-117

The Importance of the Priesthood

Without the benefit of a temple to unite the Jews, the rabbis assumed the local spiritual leadership. But the Jews disputed how to perform their religious duties. After all, they didn't even have their original revelations any longer, so it was easy to fall into disagreements. (3:19-20)

The two main groups who opposed each other were the Sadducees and the Pharisees. Each group had its own understanding and interpretation of the religion. But regardless of the differences, the priesthood became the most important institution in the life of the scattered Jewish communities. (62:5-6) Synagogues were set up as a gathering place for men to read their religious writings and to chant prayers. Because women were considered unclean, they were rarely ever allowed to go to the synagogue or even to touch religious scrolls.

The priests held such power over their people that they could make whatever laws they deemed fit. (5:78-79) As Allah declared, *They have taken their rabbis and their monks as gods beside Allah, and also (they have taken) Masih the son of Maryam (as god). And they were not commanded but to worship only One God. There is no god but He. Pure is He from what they associate with Him. Surat At-Tawbah (The Repentance) 9:31*

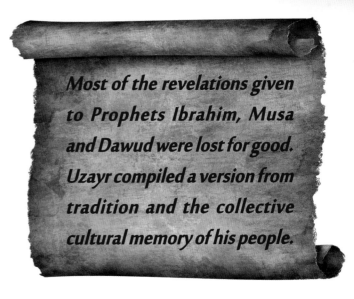

Most of the revelations given to Prophets Ibrahim, Musa and Dawud were lost for good. Uzayr compiled a version from tradition and the collective cultural memory of his people.

﴿ٱتَّخَذُوٓاْ أَحْبَارَهُمْ وَرُهْبَٰنَهُمْ أَرْبَابًا مِّن دُونِ ٱللَّهِ وَٱلْمَسِيحَ ٱبْنَ مَرْيَمَ وَمَآ أُمِرُوٓاْ إِلَّا لِيَعْبُدُوٓاْ إِلَٰهًا وَٰحِدًا لَّآ إِلَٰهَ إِلَّا هُوَ سُبْحَٰنَهُ عَمَّا يُشْرِكُونَ﴾ سُورَةُ التَّوْبَةِ ٩:٣١

A Mother's Prayer

Although many Jews had diverted from the straight path, the Qur'an clearly states that there were some who remained sincere to God. (2:250-251; 5:69) One of these spiritually sincere Jews was an expectant mother whose husband had recently passed away. In secret, she prayed to Allah with a very unique request.

She prayed: *"O my Lord, I have vowed that what is in my womb will be devoted exclusively for You. So, accept (it) from me. You, certainly You, are the All-Hearing, the All-Knowing." Surat Al 'Imran (The Family of 'Imran) 3:35*

She was a member of a very important household of the priestly class. Some of the most influential priests came from this family, including a high priest named **'Imran** عِمْرَان, a descendant of prophet Harun. (3:33-34) So naturally, this pious woman asked Allah to help make her child a priest as well. Females could never be rabbis in Judaism, as that position was only reserved for men, so you can imagine her disappointment when she gave birth to a baby girl.

So, when she delivered her, she said, "O my Lord, I have delivered her, a female child." And Allah knew better what she had delivered, and the male was not like the female, "I have named her Maryam, and I place her and her progeny under Your shelter against Satan, the rejected." Surat Al 'Imran (The Family of 'Imran) 3:36

228

The Guardian

Because the new mother was a widow, a male relative had to, by custom, be appointed to provide her and the baby with financial support. Accordingly, the older men were assembled and they drew lots to see who would have to support the mother and baby, though none of them wanted the extra expense. (3:44) The draw fell on Zakariyya☆, and thus, upon his shoulders came this responsibility. Yet, he was no ordinary relative. Zakariyya☆ was a prophet of Allah☆—what better person to help raise the baby Maryam☆?

As time passed and Maryam☆ grew older, she would spend more and more time in Zakariyya's☆ home. He was tutoring her, giving her religious lessons that no one else would. Even though she was a girl, and was forbidden by Jewish custom to study such topics, Zakariyya☆ was a true follower of Allah☆ and didn't succumb to discrimination.

Zakariyya☆ was old and had no children, but he was very poor. He didn't always have enough extra money to buy food for his wife and Maryam☆. Then a miraculous thing began to happen. Zakariyya☆ would visit Maryam☆ in her study chamber, and he would find that there was already food there!

Mihrab, Umayyad Masjid - Damascus.

So, her Lord accepted her, a good acceptance, and made her grow, a good growth, and made Zakariyya her guardian. Whenever Zakariyya visited her at the place of worship, he found food with her. He said, "Maryam, from where did you have this?" She said, "It is from Allah. Surely, Allah gives to whom He wills without measure." Surat Al 'Imran (The Family of 'Imran) 3:37

Zakariyya☆ saw what a good and wholesome young girl Maryam☆ was, and he began to long for a child of his own. What also pained him was the lack of faith of his relatives in Allah's☆ teachings and commandments.

Yahya☆ Is Born

Zakariyya prayed to Allah in secret. "My Lord!" he said, "My bones are weak and my hair is gray, but I am always blessed in my prayer to You. My Lord, now I'm afraid of what my relatives will do after me. But my wife is barren, so grant me an heir from Yourself. One that will truly represent me and the legacy of Ya'qub. Make him, My Lord, someone You will be pleased with." Surat Maryam (Mary) 19:3-6

While he was standing in prayer in the room, an angel from Allah☆ came and announced to him, *"Allah gives you the good news of Yahya. He will witness about the truth of a word from Allah, and (he will be) noble, chaste, and a Prophet among the company of the righteous."* Surat Al 'Imran (The Family of 'Imran) 3: 38-39

Zakariyya☆ replied, *"My Lord! How can I have a son when I am old and my wife is barren?"* The angel replied, *"So it will be that Allah does what He wishes."* He begged, *"My Lord! Give me a sign."* The angel replied, *"Your sign will be that you won't be able to speak to anyone for three days, except through hand motions."* So celebrate the praises of your Lord over and over, and glorify Him at night and in the morning. Surat Al 'Imran (The Family of 'Imran) 3: 40-41

Then Zakariyya☆ came out of his chamber and told the people, by hand gestures, to praise Allah☆ in the night and in the morning. (19:11) To everyone's astonishment, Zakariyya's wife soon gave birth to a healthy baby boy. He was named 'Yahya☆,' or 'life' because he was a life granted by Allah☆. The boy grew up in wisdom and knowledge, under the careful guidance of his father Zakariyya☆. Later, when the young man began to receive revelation, Allah told him, *Yahya! Take hold of the book (Allah's revelations) firmly!* Surat Maryam (Mary) 19:12

As Allah☆ tells us, He gave Yahya☆ wisdom, even as a boy, and made him feel kindness towards all living things. He was pure, devout, kind to his parents and not arrogant. (19:13-14) But the roads of Maryam☆ and Yahya☆ would not end there. Both would grow up as true believers and play a large role in the coming of the next major messenger from Allah☆.

Maryam's Quest

Maryam grew to be a very spiritual young woman. She knew her duty to Allah, and always tried to be sincere. When her guardian, Prophet Zakariyya, passed away, Maryam was left on her own.

Although Prophet Zakariyya had secretly taught her spiritual knowledge, she could never hope to be a priest or teacher, because she was a woman. In the corrupted religion that her people practiced, women were not allowed to even touch the holy books. Additionally, the people around her knew very little of the truth and instead practiced all kinds of superstitions and cultural practices. (2:102)

Seeing all the lies and hypocrisy from those around her, Maryam must have been in despair. The good teachings of Prophet Musa were being hopelessly twisted, and the priests were fighting over meaningless issues. Many of them didn't live like good examples themselves. (5:63-66)

As Allah tells us, Maryam was a pure woman who avoided sin and bad behavior. (66:12) She left the area to worship Allah by herself. Her cousin, Yahya, had already left and was trying to understand the purpose of his life. She, too, felt obliged to do the same.

And when the angels said, "O Maryam, Allah has chosen you and purified you and chosen you over the women of all the worlds. O Maryam, stand in devotion to your Lord and prostrate yourself and bow down in ruku' with those who bow." Surat Al 'Imran (The Family of 'Imran) 3:42-43

The Journey of Faith

Relate in the book (the story of) Maryam when she left her people and traveled to a place in the East. She built a lean-to (a half-tent) to screen herself from passing (people). Then, We (Allah) sent Our Angel to her, and he seemed to her like a man in all respects. She cried out, "I ask the protection of the Merciful from you. (Stay away) if you fear Allah." Surat Maryam (Mary) 19: 16-18

Maryam was alone, trying to meditate, when all of a sudden she saw a man approaching her tent. She called on Allah's name to ward the stranger off. Little did she know, the stranger was sent from Allah himself.

Remember the time when the angels said, "O Maryam, Allah gives you the good news of a Word from Him whose name is Masih 'Isa, the son of Maryam a man of status in this world and in the Hereafter, and one of those who are near (to Allah). He shall speak to people while (he is still) in the cradle, and also later, when he is of mature age, and he shall be one of the righteous." She said, "O

I found one upright man among a thousand, but not one upright woman among them all. (Ecclesiastes 7:1)

A woman should learn in quietness and full submission. I do not permit a woman to teach or to assume authority over a man; she must be quiet. For Adam was formed first, then Eve. And Adam was not the one deceived; it was the woman who was deceived and became a sinner. (I Timothy 2:11-14)

To the woman he said, "I will greatly increase your pains in childbearing; with pain you will give birth to children. Your desire will be for your husband, and he will rule over you." (Genesis 3:16)

Then the angel who was speaking to me came forward and said to me, "Look up and see what is appearing."
I asked, "What is it?"
He replied, "It is a basket." And he added, "This is the iniquity of the people throughout the land."
Then the cover of lead was raised, and there in the basket sat a woman! He said, "This is wickedness," and he pushed her back into the basket and pushed its lead cover down on it. (Zechariah 5:7)

Most people practiced or believed in magic and superstition. (4:51-55)

my Lord, how shall I have a son while no human has ever touched me?" Said He, "That is how Allah creates what He wills. When He decides a matter, He simply says to it 'Be,' and it comes to be." *Surat Al 'Imran (The Family of 'Imran) 3:45-47*

Imagine Maryam's 👑 surprise at this momentous news. Allah👑 chose her to have a son who would be a sign from Allah👑! Before departing, the angel informed her that her son's mission would be to call Bani Isra'il back to true faith. (3:49) The very thing she had hoped for and dreamed of.

The Birth of 'Isa👑

The angel "breathed" into her a **Ruh** روح **Spirit**, from Allah👑, and soon she began to show signs of pregnancy. Before anyone could question her about it, she packed up her few belongings and retreated into a more remote and secluded place. (19:22 and 23:50)

And the pains of childbirth drove her to the trunk of a palm tree. She cried out (in her anguish), "Oh! If only I died before this! If only I was no more—gone!" But (a voice) cried out to her from beneath her, "Don't panic, for your Lord has provided a trickle of water below you. Shake the trunk of the palm tree and fresh dates will fall on you. Eat and drink and cool your eyes. If you see any person, tell them, "I have promised a fast to the Merciful and won't talk to anyone today." *Surat Maryam (Mary) 19: 23-26*

Maryam 👑 gave birth to a healthy baby boy. She named him **'Isa** عيسى **Jesus**, just as the angel had told her before. He was to be the **Masih** مَسيح, the anointed one. After resting and nursing the baby for a time, she realized that she couldn't raise him on her own. He had to grow up in a community and learn the knowledge of his faith and people. She decided to return home, after being gone for nearly two years. But how would she be welcomed? How could she explain what had happened to her? Her relatives were decent people and members of the priestly class. Surely they would understand—after all, she grew up among them, and they knew her honesty well.

When she brought the baby to her people, carrying him, they shouted at her, "Maryam! What a strange thing you have brought! Sister of Harun! Your father wasn't a bad man, nor was your mother a loose woman." *Surat Maryam (Mary) 19: 27-28*

Her relatives were shocked, and immediately started to accuse her of committing a sin. They even reminded her that she was a descendant of the house of Harun and that she brought shame on the whole family. Maryam 👑 stood mute. She was overwhelmed that they would turn on her, after she went through the most holy and wonderful experience. She was shocked and stunned. (4:156) She couldn't open her mouth to speak in the face of their accusations and insults.

So, she pointed towards him (the baby). They said, "How shall we speak to someone who is still a child in the cradle?" *Surat Maryam (Mary) 19:29*

Then something wondrous happened—the baby began to speak.

The infant 'Isa said loudly, "I am a servant of Allah! He has given me revelation and made me a prophet. He has made me blessed wherever I am, and has made prayer and charity my duty as long as I live. He has made me kind to my mother, and not defiant. Peace is on me the day I was born, the day that I die, and the day I will be raised to life again." *Surat Maryam (Mary) 19:30-33*

The people around Maryam 👑 were speechless. No one would question Maryam 👑 again, and no one would bother her. Allah👑 eased her transition back home.

The Early Years of 'Isa

When 'Isa was a child, he grew up under the care of his mother, Maryam. He was good to her and always obeyed her wishes. He had a good teacher in his mother as she had been trained by Prophet Zakariyya when she was young.

Christian tradition teaches that Maryam married a man named Joseph before the baby was born and that 'Isa grew up learning the carpentry trade. Yet this story is not supported by any Qur'anic or written historical evidence, so Muslims don't share the same version of 'Isa's life.

We do know, from the Qur'an, that Prophet Yahya was traveling throughout Palestine and announcing to people that a new messenger from Allah was about to come. This unusual news made the Jewish king, Herod, suspicious. His power lay in keeping his Roman overlords pleased by maintaining order. Prophet 'Isa had barely begun his mission when Herod ordered Yahya to be arrested and killed.

Grave of Prophet Yahya, also known as John the Baptist, inside Omayyad Masjid.

The Message Begins

Allah began sending revelations to Prophet 'Isa when he was nearly 30 years old, instructing him to call the spiritually lost Jews back to a more godly way of life. (3:46) Prophet 'Isa then began to travel from village to village, teaching his message of love, justice and true sincerity to God. Because many of the people he met disbelieved in his call, Allah granted him many miracles to impress them.

And (shall make him) a messenger to the Children of Isra'il (who will say to them), "I come to you with a sign from your Lord, that is, I create for you from clay something in the shape of a bird; then I blow in it, and it becomes a living bird by the will of Allah, and I cure the born-blind and the leper, and I cause the dead to become alive by the will of Allah, and I inform you of what you eat and what you store in your homes." Surat Al 'Imran (The Family of 'Imran) 3:49

He took some clay and shaped it into the form of a bird. Miraculously, the clay bird became real and flew away. (5:110) Later, he was granted the ability to heal sick people and those who suffered from blindness. 'Isa was even able to revive people who were thought to have just died. You would think that as he traveled performing these miracles that everyone would believe.

Quite the contrary occurred, though. Most people dismissed 'Isa as nothing more than a magician. (5:110) Here is an example of one of his public statements: *"I have come to you to confirm the Tawrah, which came before me, and to make allowed some things that were forbidden to you before. I have come to you with a sign from your Lord, so fear Allah and obey me. It is Allah Who is my Lord and your Lord, so serve Him! This is the straight way." Surat Al 'Imran (The Family of 'Imran) 3:50-51*

Everywhere he went, he preached using either sermons or parables, which were revealed to him through revelation. His message, which is called the **Injeel الإنجِيل Gospel** (A Proclamation of Good News), was meant for Bani Isra'il to listen to and accept. (5:46)

The Disciples of Prophet 'Isa

Soon it became very difficult for 'Isa to carry on his mission alone. He went from place to place, preaching. It was hard for him to handle the crowds of people who came to either learn from him or curse at him.

He prayed to Allah to send him help, because most people did not believe him or his teachings. Thereafter, he began to recruit people who would serve as his close **Disciples حَوارِيّون** those who would help him in his mission.

'Isa looked for disciples who would commit to spreading the truth about Allah among the people. When he had recruited a good number of them, he took their oath of service.

So, when 'Isa sensed disbelief in them, he said, "Who are my helpers in the way of Allah?" The disciples said, "We are helpers of Allah. We believe in Allah so be our witness that we are Muslims." Our Lord, we have believed in what You have revealed, and we have followed the messenger. So, record us with those who bear witness (to the Truth)." Surat Al 'Imran (The Family of 'Imran) 3:52-53

With the added help, Prophet 'Isa was able to organize better. He spread his disciples among crowds to answer everyone's questions. In time, many more people were won over to the persuasive message and truly surrendered their wills to their Lord. Once, when the spiritual strength of the disciples was weak, they asked Prophet 'Isa for a special miracle.

When the disciples said, " 'Isa, son of Maryam! Can your Lord send to us a table spread (with food) from Paradise?" 'Isa replied, "Be aware of Allah if you are believers." They said, "We only want to eat from it and satisfy our hearts and to know that you have indeed told us the truth, and so that we may witness the miracles ourselves. So 'Isa, the son of Maryam, prayed, "Oh Allah our Lord! Send to us from Paradise a table spread (with food) so that there will be enough for all of us. A sign from You. Provide for us and You are the best of Providers." Surat Al Ma'idah (The Table) 5:112-114

We can well imagine that perhaps the disciples were tired from their traveling, and maybe had a lack of faith for a moment. But Allah revealed to 'Isa, *I will send it to you, but if any of them reject (faith) after this, I will punish him with a penalty like I have never inflicted on anyone in the Universe. Surat Al Ma'idah (The Table) 5:115*

The Plot Against Prophet 'Isa

Some of the leaders of the Jews were angry with Prophet 'Isa for teaching people that their religion had been corrupted. The rabbis held complete authority over their people in local matters. As long as they kept the peace and paid their taxes to the Roman governor, they could do as they wished. The enemies of 'Isa met in Jerusalem to discuss the matter, and they decided to get rid of him. The Christians say that one of 'Isa's own disciples betrayed him for 30 pieces of silver, but we don't know for sure.

The involved rabbis brought 'Isa before the court and subjected him to intense questioning and torture. 'Abdallah bin Mas'ud narrated *"As if I saw the Prophet talking about one of the prophets whose nation had beaten him and caused him to bleed, while he was cleaning the blood off his face and saying, 'O Allah! Forgive my nation, for they have no knowledge.'"* This hadith is most likely referring to Prophet 'Isa.

عَنْ عَبْدُاللهِ بِنِ مَسْعُودٍ قَالَ: « كَأَنِّي أَنْظُرُ إِلَى النَّبِيِّ يَحْكِي نَبِيًّا مِنَ الأَنْبِيَاءِ ضَرَبَهُ قَوْمُهُ فَأَدْمَوْهُ وَهُوَ يَمْسَحُ الدَّمَ عَنْ وَجْهِهِ، وَيَقُولُ: اللَّهُمَّ اغْفِرْ لِقَوْمِي فَإِنَّهُمْ لَا يَعْلَمُونَ» . رَوَاهُ الْبُخَارِيُّ

The rabbis would have killed 'Isa themselves if they could have, but because they had to obey Roman laws, they were not allowed to execute anyone without the Roman governor's permission. They arranged a meeting with Pontius Pilate, the Roman governor for the province of Judea, and tried to convince him that Prophet 'Isa was planning a rebellion against Rome. The exact details of this informal trial are unknown to us, but we know that the rabbis successfully convinced Pontius Pilate and got an order for 'Isa's execution.

Prophet 'Isa prayed to Allah for protection, and later a wondrous thing happened. As the Roman soldiers were marching 'Isa through a crowd to be executed, some sort of confusion occurred, and the guards lost their grip on 'Isa. Muslim scholars say that the guards might have then grabbed the man who betrayed 'Isa instead, because they looked almost alike, and then went forward and executed this other man, thinking it was 'Isa. The Qur'an states that the Jews did not kill 'Isa, nor did they have him nailed to a wooden cross. Allah states, however, that the Jews thought they did it.

And for their saying (The Jews), "We have certainly killed the Masih 'Isa the son of Maryam, the Messenger of Allah," while in fact they did neither kill him nor crucify him, but they were deluded by resemblance. Those who disputed in this matter are certainly in doubt about it. They have no knowledge of it, but they follow whims. It is absolutely certain that they did not kill him.
Surat An-Nisa' (The Women) 4:157

The nickname 'Christ-killer' has haunted Jews throughout Europe, and many massacres of Jews have taken place because of it. Muslims have never blamed Jews for this crime, because Islam doesn't acknowledge a crime to have occurred in the first place. Additionally, it is forbidden in Islam to blame an entire people for a crime because of the acts of only one person. So what happened to Prophet 'Isa? The Qur'an states, *But Allah lifted him towards Himself. Allah is All-Mighty, All-Wise. Surat An-Nisa' (The Women) 4: 158*

Most scholars believe that Prophet 'Isa was brought into Paradise, where he will remain until the end of times. (4:159) According to the sayings of Prophet Muhammad , 'Isa will return one day to fight an evil ruler called the Dajjal and will then die a natural death on Earth.

The Legacy of Prophet 'Isa

Within a few years of Prophet 'Isa's disappearance, his disciples fell into disputes among themselves. Some wanted to remain faithful to the message they were given, while others wanted to make it easier for non-Jews to enter the new way of life. The second group became more powerful, and were strengthened even more when a Jewish leader named Paul entered the conflict on their side. Paul had never met 'Isa and had previously persecuted his followers.

Paul claimed a vision of 'Isa appeared to him compelling him to travel into the desert for a while to think. When he returned to Palestine, he introduced people to his new ideas. Many followed him, and those who wanted to remain faithful to 'Isa's original teachings were ostracized.

Paul slowly began to change the original message of 'Isa. For example, he taught that the laws given to previous prophets were no longer applicable. By about the year 60 CE, these new teachings became dominant. Paul also traveled all throughout the Roman world teaching his theories, refining his doctrines and winning many more converts from the Greeks and Romans.

A Roman governor began to notice this new movement. He called it Christianity. (The Greek word for 'Masih' is 'Christos.') Paul and his followers accepted this name and began to use it. But, even more shocking is that Paul began writing letters to other groups of Christians, those who had beliefs that were different from his teachings. He started telling them that Prophet 'Isa was the real and only son of God.

Later, he would teach that God comprised three different entities and that 'Isa was one of them. This theory, called the Trinity, officially stated that 'Isa was the son of Allah and was also Allah at the same time. To further please the Greeks and Romans and attract them to his ideas, Paul emphasized that no one needed to follow traditional Jewish religious rituals, despite the fact that Prophet 'Isa never said this himself.

He also taught that everyone was doomed to Hellfire due to the first or 'original' sin of Adam and his wife from long ago. The only way to be rid of this sin, Paul explained, was to believe that 'Isa died to take the punishment for us. In other words, Paul taught that only by killing Himself could God forgive our sins. Anyone who disagreed with Paul was called a disbeliever. Paul's version of Christianity appealed to many in the Roman empire. Some even began worshipping Maryam, the mother of 'Isa. To this day, many Christians still call upon her for guidance and favors.

The Truth Is Known!

What does Allah say about the doctrines that Christianity teaches?

The likeness of 'Isa (Jesus) is the same as that of Adam: He (Allah) created him from dust and said, "Be" and he was. Surat Al 'Imran (The Family of 'Imran) 3:59

People of the Book! Don't go to extremes in your religion, nor say anything about Allah but the truth. 'Isa, the Masih, the son of Maryam, was a Messenger from Allah and His word bestowed on Maryam and a spirit from Him. So believe in Allah and His Messengers. Don't say, "Trinity." Don't do it! It will be better for you because Allah is One God. Glory be to Him. He is far above having a child. *Surat An-Nisa' (The Women) 4:171*

Certainly, infidels are those who say, "God is the Masih, son of Maryam (Jesus son of Mary)." Say, "Who then has the power to do anything against Allah, if He wills to eliminate the Masih son of Maryam and his mother and all those on earth?" Unto Allah belongs the kingdom of the heavens and the earth and what lies between them. He creates what He wills. Allah is powerful over everything. *Surat Al Ma'idah (The Table) 5:17*

They reject (faith) who say that Allah is the Masih, son of Maryam. The Masih, himself said, "Children of Isra'il! Serve Allah, my Lord and your Lord." *Surat Al Ma'idah (The Table) 5:72*

Travel by ship enabled Paul to spread his version of Christianity faster than any other preachers.

On the Day of Judgement, Allah will ask 'Isa if he ever taught people to worship him and his mother instead of Allah. Imagine the stunned look on the faces of most of the Christians when he replies, "Glory to You! I could never say what I had no right to say! If I said such a thing, You would have indeed known about it...I never said anything to them except what You commanded me to. Namely: To serve Allah, Who is my Lord and your Lord..." *Surat Al Ma'idah (The Table) 5:116-117*

'Isa's message, the Injeel, was never written down in his lifetime. His later followers wrote what they remembered or heard from others, but there was no way to check for accuracy. When the Christians finally did compile their holy book, they gathered together many different writings from many different sources, and voted on should be included in their book, or 'Bible.' A council was held in the year 325 CE (325 years after 'Isa left Earth). The place was a small Greek city called Nicea.

Why was the book made? A Roman leader, Emperor Constantine, wanted the Christians in his empire to stop fighting over their differing beliefs. They were divided into many groups, each accusing the other in misunderstanding the true teachings of 'Isa.

Paul's teachings eventually came to dominate the Bible. (2:79) The men who were closer to the real teachings of 'Isa and against those of Paul were in the minority at that meeting. (3:113) Over the past 2,000 years, several other additions have been made to the religion, and there has been an increase in the divisions and groups.

The Jews say, " 'Uzair (Ezra) is the Son of Allah" and the Christians say, "Masih (the Christ) is the Son of Allah." That is their oral statement. They imitate the saying of the earlier disbelievers. May Allah ruin them, how far they are turned back from the truth! They have taken their rabbis and their monks as gods beside Allah, 11 and also (they have taken) Masih the son of Maryam (as god). And they were not commanded but to worship only One God. There is no god but He. Pure is He from what they associate with Him. *Surat At-Tawbah 9: 30-31*

Say, "Do you worship, besides Allah, what has no power to do you harm or bring you benefit?" Allah is the All-Hearing, the All-Knowing. Say, O people of the Book, be not excessive in your religion unjustly, 44 and do not follow the desires of a people who have already gone astray, misled many and lost the right path. *Surat Al Ma'idah (The Table) 5:76-77*

Do not be like those who became divided and fell into disputes after the clear signs had come to them. Those are the ones for whom there is a grave punishment. *Surat Al 'Imran (The Family of 'Imran) 3:105*

Literature Selection

The Boy and the King

From *Sahih Muslim*

Suhaib reports that the Messenger of Allah said, "There once lived a king who had a sorcerer. When the sorcerer started to grow very old, he told the king, 'I'm getting old now. So please send me a young man to whom I can teach my magic.'

The king granted the request and arranged for a young man to be the sorcerer's apprentice. On his way to the sorcerer, the young man came across a monk sitting by the road. He stopped to speak with the monk and was impressed with his knowledge. It became his habit that whenever he went to the sorcerer, he would visit with the monk first.

Sometimes the visit to the monk would cause him to be late. As a punishment for being late, the sorcerer would beat the young man. One day, while he was sitting with the monk, the young man complained about this.

So the monk told him, 'When you're afraid of the magician, tell him, 'My family kept me.' And when you're afraid of your family tell them, 'The sorcerer delayed me.'

This pattern went on unchanged. Then one day the young man saw a great beast blocking the road. As he was dangerous to go near, the people couldn't go around it. The young man thought to himself, 'Now here is a way I can find out whether the knowledge of the sorcerer is better than the knowledge of the monk.'

So he grabbed a stone, and said, 'My Lord, if the way of the monk is more to Your liking than the way of the magician, then cause the death of this beast so people can pass again!' He then threw the rock at the beast's head, killing it immediately, and the people were able to travel freely once more.

When the young man told the monk about this, he replied, 'My son, today you have become better than me, but now I think you've come to a point where you might be tested. Should that happen, don't reveal my location.'

In time, the young man began to cure people from blindness, leprosy and all manner of diseases. News of his abilities finally reached a royal official who had become blind. So, he went to the young man with expensive gifts, and said, 'All this will be yours if you heal me.'

The young man replied, 'I, myself, do not heal anyone. It is Allah Who gives healing. If you will have faith in Allah, I will pray for you, and He may heal you.' The royal official put total faith in

Allah and Allah cured him of his blindness.

When he returned to the king, and sat with him as he always did, the surprised king asked him, 'Who has returned your sight?'

He answered, 'My Lord has.'

Then the king demanded, 'Do you have a lord besides me?!'

The official replied, 'Allah is your Lord and mine.'

The enraged king ordered him arrested, and he was tortured until he spoke about the young man. The young man was promptly summoned to the court, where the king asked him, 'My son, have you become so skilled in magic that you can heal the blind, and the lepers and all manner of ailments?'

'I don't heal anyone,' he replied. 'It's only Allah Who heals.'

Then he was arrested and tortured until he disclosed the location of the monk, who, in turn was summoned. The king ordered him, 'Give up your belief.' When the monk refused, the king commanded a saw to be placed in the center of his head, and the monk was cut in half. Then the royal minister was sent for and commanded to give up his belief. He also refused and was cut as well.

Finally, the young apprentice was brought and ordered to give up his belief. When he also declined, the king handed him over to a company of his soldiers and told them, 'Take him to a high mountain, and when you get to the top, if he still refuses to give up his faith, throw him off.'

So they took him to the mountain and were bringing him to the highest point. Then he prayed, 'Oh Lord, deliver me from them in whatever way You will.'

Then the mountain shook and crumbled down. The young man then walked back into the presence of the king, who asked, 'What happened to the rest of your group?'

He answered, 'Allah has saved me from them.'

He was then handed over to another group with orders to take him out to sea in a small boat. If he still persisted in his faith, he was to be thrown overboard. As they rowed out to sea, the young man prayed, 'Oh Lord, deliver me from them in whatever way You will.'

Then a wave overturned the boat and the men drowned, though the young man was able to swim to shore.

He then went back to the king, who asked, 'What happened to the rest of your group?'

He answered, 'Allah has saved me from them.' Then the young man continued, 'You will never be able to kill me unless you follow my instructions.'

So the king asked, 'What are your instructions?'

The young man replied, 'Gather your people in an open place. Next, tie me to the trunk of a tree. Then, take an arrow from my quiver, and while placing it in the middle of a bow, you must declare, 'In the name of Allah, the Lord of this young man,' then shoot the arrow at me. If you do this then you can kill me.'

So the king made the necessary arrangements. The people were gathered in an open place, the young man was tied to the trunk of a tree, and the king placed one of the young man's arrows in the middle of a bow. He then declared, 'In the name of Allah, the Lord of this young man!' and shot the arrow. It struck the young man on the side of his head. He raised his hand to the wound as he died.

Upon seeing this, all the people began to cry out, 'We believe in the Lord of this young man!' Someone whispered to the king, 'Do you see? What you feared is now happening: the people are starting to believe in Allah.' Then, the king ordered great pits to be dug along the roads, and he had huge fires built. Whoever refused to give up their faith would be thrown in the fire or be made to jump in it. And so the believing people were brought to the pit. Then a woman came along with a small boy. She winced and hesitated to be thrown in the fire. Her son encouraged her saying, 'Be steady mother. You are in the right.' So she threw herself in the ditch along with her child, to be with the martyrs in Paradise."

Cursed were the People of the Trench, the (people of the) fire that was rich with fuel. When they were sitting by it and were watching what they were doing with the believers. They punished them for nothing but that they believed in Allah, the All-Mighty, the Worthy of All Praise, the One to whom belongs the Kingdom of the heavens and the earth. And Allah is witness over every thing. Surat Al Burooj (The Mansions of the Stars) 85:4-9

﴿قُتِلَ أَصْحَٰبُ ٱلْأُخْدُودِ ﴾﴿ ٱلنَّارِ ذَاتِ ٱلْوَقُودِ ﴾﴿ إِذْ هُمْ عَلَيْهَا قُعُودٌ ﴾﴿ وَهُمْ عَلَىٰ مَا يَفْعَلُونَ بِٱلْمُؤْمِنِينَ شُهُودٌ ﴾﴿ وَمَا نَقَمُوا مِنْهُمْ إِلَّا أَن يُؤْمِنُوا بِٱللَّهِ ٱلْعَزِيزِ ٱلْحَمِيدِ ﴾﴿ ٱلَّذِي لَهُ مُلْكُ ٱلسَّمَٰوَٰتِ وَٱلْأَرْضِ وَٱللَّهُ عَلَىٰ كُلِّ شَيْءٍ شَهِيدٌ ﴾ سُورَةُ الْبُرُوج 85:4-9

The Christian World at a Glance

During Prophet 'Isa's ﷺ life on Earth, the Jews of Palestine were against his message and teachings. They were afraid of losing their power, and many of them wanted to keep a steady hold on their religious traditions.

After 'Isa ﷺ left the world, his followers spread his message far and wide. Some followers, like Barnabas and Thomas, who both left written records of 'Isa's ﷺ life, wanted to maintain the message just as they had received it.

But some new converts, like Paul and Luke, sought to modify, or change, the message to make it easier for non-Jews to accept. They didn't consider that they had no right to make up their own teachings or to alter those of Prophet 'Isa ﷺ.

From the years 40 CE to 150 CE, numerous new groups of Christians were formed in the many areas of the Roman world. Some followed Paul's teachings, while others followed different ones. For example, the Christians who were most likely to follow the teachings of the Trinity, that of God having a son, were those who lived in lands influenced by the Greeks or in Italy. In these countries, there were well-established traditions of man-gods and sons of gods. If you have read of Zeus, Jupiter or Hercules, whose stories comprise Greek mythology, you'll understand why one more concept of 'son of God' could easily be accepted. Christians who uphold this belief are called Trinitarians. Those Christians who held closer to the true teachings of 'Isa ﷺ and his faithful disciples were concentrated in North Africa, Palestine and Syria. These are known as Unitarians.

The Romans Lay a Heavy Hand

At first, the Romans were not interested in Christianity of any variety, as they ruled an empire with a thousand different kinds of religions. But as Christianity spread, in all its different versions, the rulers in Rome began to take note.

One of the problems that the Roman government faced with the new faith was that it taught people to worship an 'unseen god,' and not the very visible Roman emperor. One of the foundations of Roman society was based on the premise that the emperor was a 'god on Earth,' and all people had to worship him. As long as they continued to worship the emperor, then they could keep their own local religion as well.

The Christians, whether Unitarian or Trinitarian, refused to give offerings or bow to the statues of the emperors. This was a serious crime in the Roman world. Paul himself was arrested while in Rome, and he was brought for questioning before Caesar. He was later released.

In time, the Roman government started a campaign against the Christian religion. They began to persecute those who claimed to be Christians. Churches were closed, Christian leaders were arrested and property was seized. By the year 250 CE, Christians were being burned alive, and they were even fed to savage lions for the bizarre entertainment of the citizens of Rome in the arenas. But due to the determined efforts of many underground Christian leaders, the movement kept spreading. Christian teachings appealed to many, particularly its emphasis on compassion, mercy and love.

The Hunt Begins

During the reign of Emperor Hadrian, who ruled from 117 CE to 138 CE, the order went out to all provinces in the empire to further persecute the Christians. In addition, local governors were charged with stamping out Christianity in their districts.

In the city of Ephesus, which is located in modern-day Turkey, a group of young converts to Christianity gathered secretly to plan their escape. The Roman governor was rounding up Christians in the city, and executing them if they refused to renounce, or give up, their faith.

These young converts publicly declared, ."*Our Lord is the Lord of the heavens and the earth. We shall never invoke any god other than Him; otherwise we would be saying something far from the truth.*" *Surat Al Kahf (The Cave) 18:14*

The Christian Martyrs' Last Prayer, painting by Jean-Léon Gérôme.

When they found out that they were the next to be arrested, they ran, barely escaping the guards who came after them. They met at their secret place in the hills, knowing that they could never go home. They talked among themselves, saying, *"Our people here have taken to serving gods other than Him. Why don't they bring clear authority for what they do? Who does more wrong than one who invents a lie against Allah? When you turn away from them and the things they worship besides Allah, get to the cave. Your Lord will shower His mercy on you and take care of your problem."* Surat Al Kahf (The Cave) 18:15-16

One of them knew about a cave they could use as a hideout, so, they went there and set up a temporary base. One night they sat around their fire together and prayed to Allah, *"Our Lord! Grant us mercy from You, and resolve our problem for us in a rightly guided way."* Surat Al Kahf (The Cave) 18:10

Then, as they lay down to sleep for the night, a miraculous thing occurred. Allah says, *We drew (an unconscious state) over them for a number of years in the cave.* Surat Al Kahf (The Cave) 18:11

Allah put them in a state of hibernation, and they literally slept for decades! Allah describes them in the cave like this, *You would see the sun when it rose, declining to the right from the cave, and when it set, turning away from them to the left, while they lay in the open space in the middle of the cave. You would (if you saw them) think they were awake, while they were asleep. We turned them on their right side and on their left. Their dog would stretch his legs at the entrance. If you would have come upon them, you would have run away in fright!* Surat Al Kahf (The Cave) 18:17-18

The Sleepers Awaken

Then We awakened them in order to test which of their two groups would be best at figuring out how many years they were there. Surat Al Kahf (The Cave) 18:12

If anyone stumbled upon the Sleepers in the Cave, they would have been filled with terror and run away.

They probably were amazed to find spider webs all over the place, and leaves and debris covering the entrance to their cave. When they awoke, they started asking each other a series of questions. The young people knew they couldn't stay there forever. They also realized that something strange had happened, given the condition of their cave. But they were all right, and their dog Qitmir was also fine. They decided to send one of them back to the city to see what was going on.

In this way We raised them up until they asked each other. One of them said, "How long did you tarry?" They said, "A day or part of a day." They said, "Your Lord knows best how long you tarried." So, send one of you with this silver (coin) of yours to the city and let him look around which of the eatables are the purest and let him bring you some food from there. And he must act in polite manner and must not let anyone know about you. If they (the habitants of the city) will know about you, they will stone you or force you to revert to their faith, and in that case, you will never find success." Surat Al Kahf (The Cave) 18:19-20

So one of them went out to enter the city secretly. However, as soon as he entered the city, he found everyone staring at him. He was confused. What was wrong with him? What he didn't realize was that he and his companions had awakened during the reign of Emperor Theodosious II, who ruled from the years 408 CE to 450 CE.

The young man's clothes were in a style that had not been worn for centuries. To those around him, he appeared as if he just stepped out of a time machine. When he asked people for directions, because the city looked completely changed to him, he used old words and grammar from a time long past.

The young man must have attracted quite a crowd of curious people right away and realized he had failed miserably as a spy. He resolved to buy his food and get back to his friends as fast as he could. So he went to a food market and quickly picked out some breads and vegetables.

As he went to pay for his food, everyone watched in amazement as he pulled out his money from his bag. On the table he placed some coins that were minted in the reign of Emperor Hadrian, over 300 years before.

The people were struck with amazement. The local authorities were summoned, and the youths were brought from the cave for questioning. Everyone was stunned by their story. But none more so than the youths themselves. When they entered the cave, they had been following a religion that would only result in their persecution. They had literally run for their lives because of their beliefs. But now, in this time, Christianity had become the official religion of Rome. They were safe now and could live by their convictions.

In time, the local government was flooded with requests by the people to build a memorial, or monument, over the cave where they had slept. (18:21) Instead, they built a religious center to commemorate this miracle of Allah. The story of the Sleepers of the Cave is recorded in the history books of the Roman empire. The historian, James of Sarug, wrote down their story a few years after the last of the Sleepers had passed away. In the year 474 CE, he told the tale in his book entitled *Sermons*.

Because there were many stories and legends about the Sleepers, in time, people began to vary the stories about them. As Allah narrates, some people said the young people of the cave numbered four, five or as many as seven. But then Allah states that only He knows how many there were. (18:22) On another issue, Allah recounts how people differ over the number of years they spent in the cave. He says, *(Some say) they stayed in the cave for three hundred years, (others) add nine more. Declare to them, "Allah knows best how long they stayed. With Him are the secrets of space and the Earth. He sees clearly and hears perfectly."* Surat Al Kahf (The Cave) 18:25-26

So only Allah knows for certain how long they remained there. The main lessons of the story, however, are important to know:
1. Never give in to falsehood, even if you have to escape from it to remain true.
2. Never despair of Allah's help.
3. Work together as a group and follow the plan that was agreed upon.
4. Things always change, and the future may be radically different from what you are experiencing now.

This last lesson was the most important one for the early Muslims of Makkah to hear. Allah revealed this story to the believers at a time when the idol-worshippers were persecuting Prophet Muhammad and those who believed with him. The story gave them hope that despite their current suffering, their beliefs could become the dominant force in society if they held firm. And so it came to be. But the believers didn't have to wait hundreds of years. In fact, the victory of Islam over idol-worship would happen in less than 30 years.

Monument to the Seven Sleepers - Ephesus, Turkey.

Chapter 12
The Final Prophet

The Two Warring Giants

By 570 CE, small empires had spread throughout the world, and power was held by only a small group of rulers. In Europe, North Africa and Asia Minor, the Byzantine Roman Empire had grown into a world power after most of the western Roman Empire collapsed under barbarian attacks. In the Middle East, the Persian Empire extended from Mesopotamia and Palestine, to the borders of India and up into Central Asia.

Meanwhile, India was divided into a variety of warring states, and China had only recently been reunified after a devastating period of disunity and war that had all but ruined traditional society. Due to their proximity, the greatest large-scale armed conflict occurred between the Byzantine and Persian empires. The Byzantines were Christians, while the Persians were Zoroastrians, followers of Zoroaster.

Periodically, they would go to war with each other and attempt to grab strategic land. The major battleground was in Syria, Armenia and Palestine. For hundreds of years, these two giant empires sent massive armies to do battle in those lands. Sometimes one side would win; other times it would lose. The impact on the cities and people of the Middle East, however, was disastrous.

Learning Stagnates

With the resources of most empires and states devoted to war, there was little money left over for supporting schools, artistry or learning. The average person in the world could not read or write, and books were considered a luxury. Few went to school, except the children of the nobility, and what they were taught amounted to little more than memorizing religious texts or poetry. Education for girls and women was nearly nonexistent, as they were only expected to acquire habits related to family life.

The development of most new inventions was connected in some way to warfare. New siege equipment or steel-making techniques would be far more useful to a general or king than any new discovery in math or city planning. Learning was stagnant and the future looked very bleak. Because human rights were not important, most cities lacked law and order. Bandits ruled the countryside, and high taxes were levied arbitrarily by local leaders.

The State of Christianity

Christianity was the dominant religion in Europe and Asia Minor. But it was not the teachings of Prophet 'Isa ﷺ that were followed in most places. The Roman Empire created a religious organization called the Catholic Church.

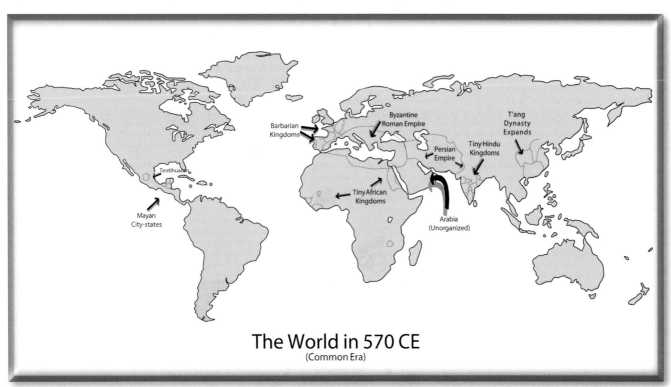

The World in 570 CE
(Common Era)

This institution came into being some three centuries after Prophet 'Isa. Catholicism supported the teachings of Paul, the self-proclaimed "Teacher of the Gospel." Thus, the Catholic Church taught the concept of the Trinity.

This church also taught that a person could only enter heaven if they were a member of the official Church, and if they obeyed the Pope. The Pope, meaning 'father,' was the leader of the Church. The Pope was considered to be infallible, incapable of making a mistake or sin, and in direct contact with God. They believed that a Pope had the power to assist someone to enter heaven or hell. In addition, priests were given the authority to forgive people's sins.

The only people who were able to read the various assorted teachings of 'Isa, which had now been collected in a book called the Bible and written in Latin (the scholarly language of the time), were people who were trained in the doctrines of the Church. Most people were not allowed to read it because it was only to be interpreted by priests.

You can well imagine how much power the Church had over people's lives. In time, this absolute power led to corruption. The Church collected huge taxes and built large cathedrals and mansions for their leaders to live in. If anyone was thought to disobey the Church's teachings, they would be labeled a 'heretic' or 'unbeliever,' and would be tortured or even killed. This was an important tool to prevent the masses from leaving Catholicism, given that there were still many different kinds of Christianity in competition with the Catholics.

In Egypt and Syria, for example, there were many groups of Unitarian Christians, particularly the Nestorian Christians. They opposed the Trinitarian ideas and had their own versions of the Bible. Indeed, unity among the Christians was scarce.

The Zoroastrians

The people of Persia followed the teachings of an ancient teacher by the name of Zoroaster, who is believed to have lived some time between 1500 and 1000 BCE. Zoroaster may have been an authentic prophet though some historians question whether he was a real or mythical person. There is a lack of information on Zoroaster and the religion because the religious writings have been lost. The rituals, beliefs and cultural practices have also changed over time.

By the sixth century, this religion promoted that there was one transcendent god, named Ahura Mazda, who was the source of all good. However, it also said that there was a rival to Mazda, named Angra Mainyu and considered to be the source of all evil. While the evil Mainyu opposed Mazda, the religion taught that good would eventually prevail.

The original teachings of Zoroaster may have been true revelations from Allah, as the Blessed Prophet Muhammad didn't have a problem in entering into a solemn peace treaty with a community of Zoroastrians living on the eastern side of the Arabian peninsula. However, the belief that God has a rival, in the form of Angra Mainyu, is clearly against the teachings of Islam.

Other obvious idol-worshipping practices have been mixed together in the rituals of Zoroastrians. Fire plays a prominent role in several religious ceremonies. Huge temples were built all over the Persian Empire, in which fires were kept aflame as a part of their worship. A plant, called 'haoma,' would be brought to the fires and pounded with hammers until the juice ran out of the stalks. Zoroastrians would then drink this liquid and say it was the drink of immortality.

The Zoroastrians did not believe in burying their dead and would instead place the bodies of the dead on mountain tops and rock pillars so the wind and vultures could do away with them. Clearly, this was not what Allah would reveal to any nation. As illustrated in the examples of these two religions, both major world powers were following traditions that were influenced by superstition and were far from the straight path.

Where Is Arabia?

The Arabian peninsula lays to the south of two of the world's great empires. It is a very large peninsula that juts out into the sea and is midway between Africa and India. Because of its strategic location, the peninsula has had many important trade routes running through its vast expanse of open land.

The terrain and climate vary greatly from region to region. In the southern portion is the land of Yemen, where there is sufficient rainfall for farming and cultivation. In ancient days the name of this region was Saba', and it was from here that Queen Balqees ruled.

In most of central Arabia, there are large, arid deserts that are so hot that no one can live there. A few scattered springs dot the land where people could live, but these oases were often too small to support much population. Northern Arabia is generally dry but does get enough rainfall for limited cultivation. There are small cities and towns, and many of the people intermix with those in Palestine and Syria. The western edge of Arabia is called the Hijaz. It is an arid region that receives some rainfall. What is most noteworthy is that the holy cities of Makkah and Al Madinah are there.

In 570 CE, both cities supported large populations numbering in the several thousands. Makkah was famous for its cube-shaped structure, the **Ka'bah** كَعْبَة. It was built by the Blessed Prophet Ibrahim ﷺ in ancient times and later became the center of Arab idol-worshipping rituals. It was the religious capital of Arabia.

Al Madinah, on the other hand, was a city built along a string of valleys and had abundant water. Wheat, barley and dates were grown in abundance in Al Madinah, which was then called Yathrib, and the city was a major food supplier for the surrounding Arab peoples.

Who Were the Ancient Arabs?

In ancient days, most of the Arabs, or inhabitants of Arabia, were Bedouin, nomadic people who moved from place-to-place periodically in order to graze their animals. They were a poor people, but most of them had at least some camels, horses or goats. As time passed, some of these Bedouin settled into valleys and made small towns, which eventually grew into cities. The Arab cities became major stops along the trade routes from India to Palestine and then into Europe. The Arabs became very skilled in business and trade, developing profitable trade markets of their own. The Arabs were divided into many different religions. Some, mostly in the north, were Christians. Others, mainly in Al Madinah, were Jews.

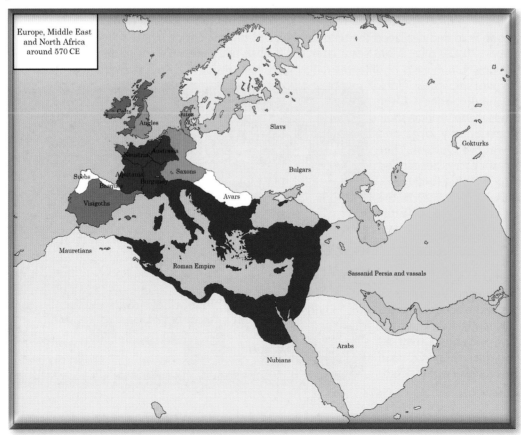

Arabia did not have a unified government of any kind. There was no king or emperor who could claim to rule over all the peninsula. Instead, the Arabs grouped themselves by their tribes. Each tribe had a **Shaykh** شَيْخ **Chief**. The word of the shaykh was law in the tribe. Each tribe held on to a distinct identity, and outsiders were considered foreigners. Loyalty to one's tribe was strong. If one member of the tribe was in trouble, the others would help him, even if he was in the wrong.

Because of this code of loyalty, revenge was also a strong element of tribal life. If a person from one tribe killed someone from another, the victim's tribe would try its best to take revenge. Sometimes this would lead to year-long disputes that would cost many people's lives. Bravery was also highly respected in the Arab culture of the time. However, this bravery was often sought through immoral means. For example, people would try to steal from other tribes to show their own people how brave they were. Their "heroism" would be captured in tributes that poets recited in their honor.

Other problems in this society included alcoholism, prostitution, gambling and raiding. Enemies were tortured, and baby girls were often buried alive. The society at large did not value women; thus, they had very few rights. For example, in much of Arabia, women were considered to be a man's property. A son could inherit the wife of his deceased father, even his own mother. A man could use and abuse women as he pleased, and there was no limit to the number of wives a man could have. However, Arabs were known for their code of honor, and the guest or traveler was given high regard. Guests were warmly welcomed in a person's home and treated like family for the duration of their stay.

Who Were the Quraysh?

The roots of the Quraysh go back to Prophet Ibrahim. Hajar, the wife of Prophet Ibrahim ﷺ, settled in the barren valley of Bakkah around 1900 BCE. There was no visible water source, and she and her son, Isma'il, were in danger of dying from dehydration. Then Allah ﷻ caused a spring to bubble up through the dry desert, which we know today as the well of Zamzam. Bedouin tribes passing by were drawn to the water, and soon Hajar and Isma'il ﷺ presided over a small encampment. When Prophet Ibrahim ﷺ returned a few years later, he found his wife and grown son had become the masters of a very profitable oasis.

To give thanks to Allah ﷻ, Prophet Ibrahim ﷺ and his son Isma'il ﷺ, built the Ka'bah as a holy shrine. Isma'il ﷺ was later granted prophethood, and he taught the revelations of Allah ﷻ to the people who came to stay at the oasis in the valley of Bakkah. He had many children, who in turn had children of their own. After many centuries passed, Bakkah became a thriving town. The people later started calling the town 'Makkah,' and the Ka'bah remained integral to the local culture.

The Ka'bah was the center of religion for the people who settled there, and for a time, they and their descendants worshipped Allah ﷻ alone. But as the years passed, and more and more people came to dwell in the town, the idea of idol-worship took hold and displaced the true teachings of the ancient prophets. (8:35)

By the year 570 CE, over 2,000 years later, the Ka'bah had become a shrine dedicated to idol-worship. Statues and idols belonging to hundreds of different tribes were kept inside the Ka'bah. Every year, these tribes would travel to Makkah to worship their idols, conduct trade and do business. Over time, many tribes made Makkah their home. One particularly large and wealthy tribe was the Quraysh. They claimed their ancestry descended from the time of Prophet Ibrahim ﷺ.

Part of their power lay in the fact that they controlled the water supply of the city. The well of Zamzam was under their control, and most other wells outside the city were also owned by members of their tribe. Due to their influence, the Quraysh were the heads of the council of tribal leaders who ruled Makkah. Their will and reputation extended over all aspects of life in the city. The Quraysh were the power brokers of Makkah.

Makkah is the holiest city on Earth to Muslims.

The Dream and the Sacrifice

Many years before the birth of Muhammad ﷺ, there lived a man by the name of 'Abdel Muttalib. He was a member of the Quraysh tribe, yet very poor. The Banu Hashim, his particular family clan, had the job of bringing water into the city for the traders and caravans passing through.

The scarcity of water in the area made the job very difficult. The well of Zamzam had been lost for centuries, perhaps covered with sand after wars or fierce sandstorms. Any water supplies had to come through wells located some distance outside the city center of Makkah.

'Abdel Muttalib had trouble bringing water from so far, so he made it his mission to rediscover the lost well. He had heard stories that the well was located somewhere in Makkah. With the help of his son Al-Mughirah, he had dug all around the city, with no luck.

A mouth piece of the well of Zamzam with its ring and lid dating back to 1299 H.

Finally, one night, he dreamed that the lost well was located in between two large idols that stood near the Ka'bah. He roused his son and rushed to the spot to dig. Miraculously, 'Abdel Muttalib's shovel struck into the earth, releasing a spout of fresh water. The lost well of Zamzam had been found! Eventually, he realized that his family was too small to manage the well. With the well of Zamzam under his control, he would need many strong sons to defend their claim. He declared that if Allah would bless him with 10 sons, he would sacrifice one of them at the Ka'bah as thanks.

Even though the Arabs worshipped idols, they still knew of the name Allah. However, they imagined that God was too remote and far-removed from human concerns and that the idols would bring them favors and luck instead. It was rare for a person to call on Allah for anything.

Remember, Allah alone deserves the exclusive submission. As for those who have adopted guardians other than Him (saying), "We worship them for no other reason but because they would bring us near to Allah closely," Allah will judge between them in the matters in which they are differing. Surely, Allah does not guide anyone who is a liar, highly infidel. Surat Az-Zumar (The Groups) 39:3

﴿أَلَا لِلَّهِ ٱلدِّينُ ٱلْخَالِصُ وَٱلَّذِينَ ٱتَّخَذُوا۟ مِن دُونِهِۦٓ أَوْلِيَآءَ مَا نَعْبُدُهُمْ إِلَّا لِيُقَرِّبُونَآ إِلَى ٱللَّهِ زُلْفَىٰٓ إِنَّ ٱللَّهَ يَحْكُمُ بَيْنَهُمْ فِى مَا هُمْ فِيهِ يَخْتَلِفُونَ إِنَّ ٱللَّهَ لَا يَهْدِى مَنْ هُوَ كَٰذِبٌ كَفَّارٌ﴾ سُورَةُ ٱلزُّمَرِ 3:39

In the following years, 'Abdel Muttalib was blessed with a total of 10 sons. He knew he had to keep his public pledge, as people expected him to, but which of his 10 sons should he sacrifice? They were all grown, and none of them would volunteer for such a thing. So he put each of their names in a drawing to pick one by chance. He drew three times in a row, and each time the same name was drawn: 'Abdallah, his youngest and most beloved son.

Because 'Abdel Muttalib was a man of his word, he made preparations for the sacrifice. But many people liked 'Abdallah because he was well-mannered and intelligent. Some people approached 'Abdel Muttalib and convinced him to seek the advice of a local shaman woman.

She informed him that he must put 10 camels on one side and 'Abdallah on the other. Then he should draw lots and add 10 more camels every time 'Abdallah's name was drawn. 'Abdel Muttalib drew nine times, and each time the draw was for 'Abdallah. 'Abdel Muttalib continued to add 10 more camels until there were 100 camels in all.

Finally the draw came up on the camel's side, so 'Abdel Muttalib sacrificed 100 camels to compensate for the life of his son. Thereafter it became the custom in Arabia to pay 100 camels to the family of someone who was killed.

'Abdallah and Aminah

'Abdel Muttalib was so happy that his son was saved that he decided to make a real celebration. He searched Makkah to find a noble wife for 'Abdallah and chose Aminah, a woman from the Banu Zahra tribe of Makkah. 'Abdallah was a little over the age of 20 when he married Aminah, and the young couple lived together happily for two weeks. Soon, however, it was 'Abdallah's turn to go on a business trip to Syria.

The young wife cried out to her maid-servant, an African teenager named Barakah, "How strange! How can my husband go on a trading journey to Syria while I'm still a new bride, and the traces of henna-dye are still on my hands?" She was heartbroken when he set off with the other men on the long trip northward. In her sorrow, Aminah fainted.

Two months passed with no word of the caravan. One morning, Aminah called Barakah at dawn and seemed full of joy. She said to her, "Barakah! I've seen a strange dream!"

"I hope it was something good, my lady." she replied.

"I saw lights coming from my womb, lighting up the mountains, the hills and the valleys all around Makkah!" Aminah recounted excitedly.

Barakah asked Aminah if she felt pregnant, and she replied that she did but felt no pain. Barakah then answered, "You will give birth to a blessed child who will bring goodness."

A few months later, a ruler of Yemen, named Abraha, was marching his army to attack Makkah. He wanted to destroy the Ka'bah to force the Arabs to make their pilgrimages to the great church he had built in his own country instead of to Makkah.

'Abdel Muttalib, whom Aminah trusted more than anyone, told her she had to join everyone else and run for the hills. Aminah strongly refused to go and replied that Allah would not let Abraha destroy the Ka'bah.

Abraha's army, which included several elephants, appeared on the outskirts of Makkah soon enough. But as the army rested, an epidemic of small-pox, carried by winged creatures, raced through the soldiers in just a few days, causing the men to rapidly die. Abraha fled with his few remaining men, and died before returning to Yemen. Thus, Makkah was saved.

Have you not seen how your Lord dealt with the People of the Elephant? Has He not turned their plan into nullity? And He sent upon them flying birds in flocks, throwing upon them stones of baked clay, and thus He turned them into an eaten-up chaff. Surat Al-Fil (The Elephant) 105:1-5

﴿أَلَمْ تَرَ كَيْفَ فَعَلَ رَبُّكَ بِأَصْحَابِ ٱلْفِيلِ﴾ ﴿أَلَمْ يَجْعَلْ كَيْدَهُمْ فِي تَضْلِيلٍ﴾ ﴿وَأَرْسَلَ عَلَيْهِمْ طَيْرًا أَبَابِيلَ﴾ ﴿تَرْمِيهِم بِحِجَارَةٍ مِّن سِجِّيلٍ﴾ ﴿فَجَعَلَهُمْ كَعَصْفٍ مَّأْكُولٍ﴾ سُورَةُ الفِيل 105:1-5

A few months later, while he was returning from his first business venture, 'Abdallah and his friends stopped over in Yathrib to rest. There he became sick and soon passed away. When the news reached Aminah, she cried and wept for days. Barakah stayed by her side and nursed her and comforted her. 'Abdallah's father, 'Abdel Muttalib, tried to make her feel better by telling her that the baby growing within her would be like a young 'Abdallah to them. But he too was filled with sorrow at the loss of his favorite son.

One night, while sleeping, Aminah had a dream in which she was told to name her child 'Muhammad,' meaning 'highly praised,' Although it was an unusual name among the Arabs, when the baby was born in the year 570 CE, 'Abdel Muttalib proclaimed the baby's name in the courtyard of the Ka'bah. Aminah and 'Abdel Muttalib were happy at the birth. Baby Muhammad ﷺ was such a beautiful child. Even though Aminah was a widow and had no one to support her, 'Abdel Muttalib told her not to worry; he would be her financial support.

The Banu Sa'd

After some time, nurse-maids from the desert came to Makkah to find children to foster. It was a custom in those days for city mothers to send their young children to be raised by women in the desert who would teach them to be strong and resilient. None of the foster mothers went to Aminah's house, because they thought she was a poor widow. Likewise, one foster mother, named Halima, could not find anyone willing to let her take a baby, as she appeared frail and weak.

'Abdel Muttalib brought the two women together. Aminah was happy her child would experience desert living, and Halima was happy she would not go back empty handed. As long as Muhammad ﷺ stayed with Halima, good fortune came to her family. Baby Muhammad ﷺ remained with Halima's tribe, the Banu Sa'd, for five years, with only a few visits to his mother in Makkah. When he was finally returned to the care of the anxious Aminah, she saw how strong and well-mannered her son had become and felt a great warmth inside. The years apart had been hard, but now they were together again.

When Muhammad ﷺ turned six years old, Aminah decided to visit the grave of her dear 'Abdallah in Yathrib. Together, Aminah, Barakah and the young Muhammad ﷺ set off as part of a caravan going in that direction. They reached Yathrib in 10 days, and for the next month, Aminah left her son with relatives while she wept by 'Abdallah's grave.

But it was to be a short-lived reunion. While on the road back to Makkah, Muhammad's ﷺ mother fell sick with fever. On a pitch black night, she called out to Barakah and whispered in her ear, "Barakah, I shall leave this world shortly. I give my son, Muhammad, to your care. He lost his father while he was in my womb. Here he is now, losing his mother right before his very eyes. Be a mother to him, Barakah, and don't ever leave him."

Barakah began to weep, and the little Muhammad ﷺ awoke and began crying as well. He threw himself into his mother's arms and held on tightly. The final moments passed like a heartbeat stopped in time, and then the lady Aminah breathed her last. Barakah and Muhammad ﷺ cried long into the night. In the morning, Barakah dug a grave with her own hands in the hard, sun-baked earth and laid the noble woman to rest. Then she took the boy and returned to Makkah.

His grandfather received the young boy, now an orphan, and with tears in his eyes, promised to care for him. Barakah moved into 'Abdel Muttalib's home to be Muhammad's ﷺ caretaker and kept her promise to Aminah. But the sorrow of losing both his parents was going to have a lasting effect on the boy, who would one day grow to be a very important man.

Muhammad's ﷺ Childhood

Muhammad ﷺ was an orphan, having neither a living father nor mother. In Arabian society, where people were valued according to their family tribe, he would have been considered worthless. But Muhammad's ﷺ grandfather loved the boy dearly.

'Abdel Muttalib used to allow Muhammad ﷺ to sit on his own carpet in the courtyard pavilion of the Ka'bah where the leaders used to meet. Whenever someone tried to discourage him, his grandfather would say, "Leave him there. Don't disturb my son, Muhammad."

But 'Abdel Muttalib was very old, and had few days remaining in his life. Nearing the end when he was weak, he made his son Abu Talib promise to care for the young Muhammad ﷺ. Soon enough, his grandfather passed away. Muhammad ﷺ, at nearly 10 years of age, once again lost someone close to him. Muhammad ﷺ, along with Barakah, went to live under the care of Abu Talib.

Muhammad ﷺ with His Uncle

Abu Talib was true to his promise and warmly invited Muhammad ﷺ into his household. He soon became impressed with the boy's manners and discipline. At meal times, a large spread of food would be placed on a sheet on the floor, and everyone would sit around it and eat. All the other children used to jump up and down and grab at the food. But, as Abu Talib's maid narrates, Muhammad ﷺ used to sit still and take whatever food was given to him. From a young age he displayed good manners and spoke clearly and politely.

When Muhammad ﷺ was 12 years old, Abu Talib planned to make a business trip to Syria. In those days, merchants would load camels and horses with goods and travel from city-to-city to buy, sell and trade in the markets. The route from Makkah to Syria was always very profitable.

Abu Talib had no intention of taking the young Muhammad ﷺ along with him. It would be a hard journey, and there would be no time to deal with a young boy. But after Muhammad's ﷺ repeated requests, Abu Talib gave in and agreed to let him come along on the condition that Muhammad's ﷺ job would be to tend to the animals.

The caravan set out a few weeks later, and began the long journey northward to **Ash-Sham** الشّام **Syria**. After weeks of hard traveling, the caravan and its attendants arrived in a region called Busra. There they decided to rest and make some business deals.

Just ahead on the road was a Christian monastery, where there lived a monk by the name of Bahira, a Christian who devoted his time to religious studies. That morning, Bahira had watched the caravan pulling into the area and was startled to see that a cloud seemed to follow them, shielding them from the sun.

He had read that clouds make constant shade over a prophet, so he felt sure that someone special had arrived. He sent an invitation to the men of the caravan to come to the monastery for dinner, making sure to insist that everyone should come.

When all the merchants arrived, the monk asked if everyone was present. They answered that everyone was there except a boy who was left behind to watch the animals. Bahira requested that he be invited as well, and so someone left to fetch the young Muhammad ﷺ.

Once he arrived and joined the dinner party, Bahira watched the boy carefully and noted his behavior. He asked Muhammad ﷺ questions and was amazed at the wisdom of his answers. After a little while, Bahira took Abu Talib and his nephew aside and said, "This is the Last Prophet." When Abu Talib asked him how he knew this, the monk replied, "The signs of the Last Prophet are written in our books, and clouds only cast shade over a prophet. When you were approaching, I saw a cloud shading your caravan, and I had no doubt that the Last Prophet foreseen in our holy books was with you. For this reason I invited you in order that I might meet him."

Bahira was informed about Muhammad's ﷺ family situation, which further convinced him of Muhammad's ﷺ special status. Then, he asked Muhammad ﷺ to lift his shirt, and the monk found a special birthmark on his back, just between the shoulders.

Bahira looked at the spot, which was about the size of a small egg, and declared, "Now I am most certain that this is the last Prophet for whom the Jews and Christians await." He then instructed Abu Talib to take special care of him and to keep him safe. (7:157) Abu Talib quickly finished his business in Syria and returned home with his caravan. After this, Abu Talib kept a closer eye on his nephew.

Muhammad ﷺ as a Teenager

Excitement entered Muhammad's ﷺ life when he was 15. A war broke out between the Quraysh and Hawazin tribes over an issue of revenge. It was called the Al Fijar War. A few battles broke out, with both sides raining arrows down on the other.

However, Muhammad ﷺ didn't actually participate in any of the hand-to-hand fighting, nor did he charge the enemy himself. As a teenage boy, it was his job to find all the arrows that he could gather from the battlefield for re-use by the archers on his side.

It was a dangerous job, and, undoubtedly, a few other boys were struck by arrows or captured by the enemy. But Muhammad ﷺ came through unscathed and saw his first taste of action. Neither side won any battle outright, and the war lasted a total of about four years.

A short time later, a group of concerned citizens in Makkah wanted to form a charitable institution to help take care of all the poor people who wandered the streets of Makkah. On one night, several people gathered together and took a pledge to." ..help the poor and the needy, assist the oppressed, protect the weak, secure their rights from tyrants and establish peace and harmony among the people."

Muhammad ﷺ participated in this meeting and took the oath. In later years, after Muhammad ﷺ became a prophet, he said, "What I witnessed, in the house of 'Abdallah bin Jad'an, was such a good pact that if now in Islam I were summoned unto it, I would gladly respond." (Al Baihaqi)

قَالَ النَّبِيُّ ﷺ : «لَقَدْ شَهِدْتُ فِي دَارِ عَبْدِ اللهِ بنِ جَدعانَ حِلْفًا، لَوْ دُعِيتُ بِهِ فِي الإِسْلَامِ لَأَجَبْتُ». رَوَاهُ الْبَيْهَقِي

Muhammad ﷺ became known to the people as an honest boy who could be trusted in everything he said and did. He was given the nickname of **As-Sadeq** الصَّادِق **The Truthful One**.

Muhammad's ﷺ Early Adulthood

As a young man of 20, Muhammad ﷺ displayed the character of good upbringing. Other young men spent their time dancing, drinking wine and consorting with lowly women. Muhammad ﷺ, on the other hand, had no desire to participate in such immoral activities. He never attended wild parties, nor did he ever try to taste wine, seeing what the intoxication of alcohol could do to a respectable person.

Instead, Muhammad ﷺ spent his time working for his uncle in the pastures outside Makkah. Abu Talib was not a rich man, so he needed all the extra help he could get. For years now, Muhammad ﷺ worked as a shepherd for his uncle's sheep. It was a quiet job that gave a young man a lot of time to think.

Abu Hurayrah ﷺ reported that the Messenger of Allah ﷺ said, "Every Prophet has tended sheep." He was asked: "And did you?" He replied, "Yes, I tended them for a few carats for the Makkans." (Al Bukhari)

عَنْ أَبِي هُرَيْرَةَ ﷺ عَنِ النَّبِيِّ ﷺ قَالَ: «مَا بَعَثَ اللهُ نَبِيًّا إِلاَّ رَعَى الْغَنَمَ. فَقَالَ أَصْحَابُهُ وَأَنْتَ فَقَالَ نَعَمْ كُنْتُ أَرْعَاهَا عَلَى قَرَارِيطَ لأَهْلِ مَكَّةَ». رَوَاهُ الْبُخَارِيُّ

Muhammad ﷺ had no formal schooling or education. There were no academies in Makkah, nor could Abu Talib afford to send his nephew to a tutor for writing lessons. But this did not stop Muhammad ﷺ from observing and learning everything he could.

He often liked to join the meetings of the leaders of Makkah and watch the proceedings. He would also listen to the orators and poets who came every year for the annual gathering in the Ka'bah to honor their idols.

As related before, the tradition of making a pilgrimage to Makkah began with Prophets Ibrahim ﷺ and Isma'il ﷺ many thousands of years earlier. The tradition remained, but the focus was now the idols and not Allah ﷺ.

Muhammad ﷺ never liked idol-worship, and never bowed to any statues. When he was a boy among the Banu Sa'd, he lived a Bedouin lifestyle, which had little time for formal rituals or fancy idols. Therefore, from his earliest days, he never developed the taste for believing in gods of wood or stone.

His years as a shepherd also taught him that the world was a wide and mysterious place, one that could never be created by an idol. Indeed an idol was only a thing made by a man's own hands. Imagine how many evenings Muhammad ﷺ must have looked out over the endless horizon and watched as the afterglow of sunset disappeared in a haze of brilliant reds, yellows and oranges. Then, it would all be replaced by a dark blue curtain of night dotted with twinkling stars and the bright face of the moon. No, Muhammad ﷺ knew that idols were not real.

In his spare time, Muhammad ﷺ tried his hand at trade and business. He would take some extra goods that his uncle gave him and enter the marketplace to make deals. He was fair and honest in his dealings with others and always displayed good manners. People gave him another nickname **Al Ameen** الأَمِين **The Trustworthy**. This experience was soon to pay off in a big way. For as we will see, if a person is kind, fair and well-mannered, it is more valuable than any amount of gold or silver.

Marriage to Khadijah ﴿

Abu Talib heard that a lady by the name of Khadijah ﴿ was looking to hire someone to take a caravan of merchandise to Syria. Khadijah ﴿ was a wealthy widow who came from a very good family background. She had been married twice before to rich men who left her all their money when they died.

Many of the leading citizens of Makkah had asked for her hand in marriage, but she refused them all, thinking that they were only after her money. Thus, she decided to spend her time in the trading business, and was very successful.

Abu Talib, who wanted to help Muhammad earn more money in supplementing his meager wages as a shepherd, went to Khadijah ﴿ and told her that he knew of a good person who would make a fine leader for her caravan.

Khadijah ﴿, who had also heard of the honest young man, agreed to put Muhammad ﷺ in charge. Thus, when the caravan was ready, Muhammad ﷺ guided it out of Makkah

The tools of business in the Middle East: merchandise and an abacus.

in the direction of Syria. Khadijah ﴿ sent her servant, Maysara, along to secretly watch how Muhammad ﷺ behaved and conducted himself. While in Syria, Muhammad ﷺ transacted many very good deals, bringing in huge profits and then returned to Makkah.

Maysara came to love and respect Muhammad ﷺ for his fairness, kindness and good manners. When the caravan was only a few hours from Makkah, Maysara suggested that Muhammad ﷺ ride ahead and be the first to tell Khadijah ﴿ all about the successful trip. Muhammad ﷺ agreed, and arrived on horseback in front of Khadijah's ﴿ house at about noon. Khadijah ﴿ saw him arrive and came down from her terrace to meet him.

She listened carefully as Muhammad ﷺ told her all the details of the trip. He was soft-spoken and gentle in his speech, and Khadijah ﴿ was pleased with his dealings. After he finished, Muhammad ﷺ returned home to his uncle's house. Maysara arrived with the caravan a short time later and told Khadijah ﴿ all that he had seen. He spoke of Muhammad's ﷺ honesty, humility, and good morals. Maysara concluded, "Among all the young men of Makkah whom I know well, there are none comparable to Muhammad."

For some days after, Khadijah ﴿ began to consider Muhammad ﷺ as more than a businessman. She was 40 years old, yet had consistently refused to marry any of the nobles of Makkah. Now she began to consider marriage to Muhammad. Although he was much younger than she, his words, manners and honesty had captured her, heart and mind.

Khadijah ﴿ spoke to her close friend, Nafisa, about her dilemma. Nafisa told her not to worry, and that she, herself, would take care of the matter. The next day, she went to Abu Talib's house and asked to see Muhammad ﷺ. When he arrived, she asked him why he was not married yet. Muhammad ﷺ replied that he couldn't afford to get married at this time. Nafisa then asked him, "What if money didn't matter and you were invited to marry a woman of beauty, nobility and wealth? What would you say?"

Muhammad ﷺ was puzzled, and asked, "Who is she?"
Nafisa replied, "Khadijah." Muhammad ﷺ said, "But how can I marry Khadijah?"
"I will take care of the matter." Nafisa smiled.
Muhammad ﷺ replied, "Then I accept."

It is clear from this conversation that Muhammad ﷺ, who was only 25, had already developed a measure of warmth and respect for Khadijah ﴿. Therefore, the marriage was not delayed. Within three months of his return from Syria, Muhammad ﷺ and Khadijah ﴿ were married.

Muhammad ﷺ Averts a War

Not too long after Muhammad's ﷺ marriage, there was a bad storm and flood that damaged many buildings in Makkah. One of the damaged structures was the Ka'bah itself. It became clear to all that repairs had to be made to the shrine, or it would collapse and need to be rebuilt from scratch.

After collecting supplies from a shipwrecked Roman boat on the Red Sea coast and enlisting the aid of an Egyptian carpenter, the work began. To give honor to each of the tribes of Makkah, the labor was divided up into equal shares. Young men from each tribe worked in shifts during their allotted hours, and the work proceeded smoothly.

When the rebuilt walls were nearly complete, an issue arose when it became time to replace the fabled **Al Hajar Al Aswad** الْحَجَرُ الْأَسْوَد **Black Stone**. It was a pitch-colored stone from the original shrine built by Ibrahim so long ago. Its presence in the Ka'bah wall made people feel connected to the legendary prophets of old even though they worshipped idols in place of God.

Every clan of the Quraysh wanted the honor of placing the Black Stone back in its proper place, and the leaders argued about who should do it. Some men vowed to start a war if their clan wasn't given the honor, and they dipped their fingers in a bowl of blood to show their resolve.

One of the wise Makkans, Abu Umayah, shouted to get everyone's attention saying, "Let the first one who enters the gate Al Safa decide the matter for us." The crowd agreed to this proposal and then sat down and waited to see who would come through the gate to the courtyard of the Ka'bah.

Very soon, a young man walked through the gate on his way to the Ka'bah, and when everyone saw who it was, they cried out, "It is Al Ameen! We will abide by his decision." Everyone put down their weapons and told Muhammad the story of what had happened. With anger still visible on the faces of many, they asked Muhammad to decide the matter of who should have the honor of replacing the Black Stone.

Muhammad thought for a minute, and then said, "Bring me a big sheet of cloth." When it was brought, he spread it on the ground and placed the Black Stone in the center with his own hands. Then he asked the chiefs of every clan to take a hold of the cloth and lift it up. After they were all holding an edge of the cloth, Muhammad

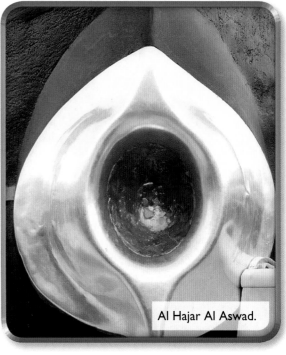

Al Hajar Al Aswad.

asked them to follow him to the Ka'bah wall. When he reached the right place, he stood up on a stone and asked the leaders to lift the sheet up high next to the wall.

Then Muhammad took the stone with his own hands and placed it into its rightful position. Everyone was amazed at his wise decision, and the people dispersed, feeling satisfied. A war was narrowly averted because of Muhammad's wisdom.

The Light of Revelation

Muhammad and Khadijah lived happily together. Barakah, Muhammad's caretaker from childhood, lived in another house owned by Khadijah. One day, when Barakah was visiting Muhammad's home, Muhammad asked her, "Oh mother. Now I'm a married man, and you are still unmarried. What would you say if someone wanted to marry you?" Barakah looked at Muhammad and replied, "I shall never leave you. Does a mother abandon her son?"

Muhammad smiled and kissed her forehead. He looked at his wife Khadijah and said, "This is Barakah. This is my mother after my own mother. She is the rest of my family." Khadijah said to Barakah, "You have sacrificed your youth for the sake of Muhammad. Now he wants to pay back some of his obligations to you. For my sake and his, agree to be married before old age overtakes you."

Barakah finally agreed to their request, and a match was found with a man from Yathrib, named Ubayd. Barakah and Ubayd had one son that they named Ayman, but her husband soon passed away. Barakah returned back to Makkah to live with Muhammad and Khadijah once more.

By then, Muhammad had been married to Khadijah for 15 years. They had four daughters: Zaynab, Ruqaiyyah, Umm Kulthum and Fatimah. They also had one son, Qasim, who passed away as an infant. Much later, yet another son, 'Abdallah, would also not survive infancy.

Muhammad and Khadijah's marriage and life together was happy and filled with love. Muhammad always treated his wife with respect and was never harsh towards her. As he grew older, however, Muhammad began to grow restless. He had been an orphan, had known loss and had seen the lack of compassion that his society had towards the less fortunate.

He also was a man with a searching heart. Ever since he was a young boy, he had disliked the worship of idols. Perhaps his time as a shepherd reinforced his convictions that the Creator was not a piece of wood kept in the Ka'bah. How many nights had he spent on the plains, looking up at the stars and the endless horizon? Surely, he thought, Allah is greater than what his fellow Arabs were saying about Him!

The Arabs knew that Allah, the Supreme Ruler of the Universe, existed. But they thought Allah was far away and no longer paying attention to the people. They believed other gods were necessary to help them in their daily lives. So the Arabs made gods out of sticks, stones, bones and other things. Muhammad knew these ideas were foolish and ignorant.

Once, while he was walking in town, Muhammad saw some poor people and he felt very sorry for them. Nobody was helping them. When he came home, Khadijah asked him why he was sad. When he told her what he saw, he added that he couldn't help them, since he didn't have much money himself.

Khadijah thought of a way to heal his noble heart and called the leaders of Makkah together. She declared to everyone that she was giving Muhammad control over all her wealth. This generous decision enabled Muhammad to help the poor whenever he wished. He never abused or squandered the wealth Khadijah gave him.

But something was still missing in his heart; it still felt empty inside. Muhammad remembered the solitude he experienced in the open fields while tending his uncle's sheep. At the age of forty, the work of a shepherd was no longer possible. So he looked for another setting where he could be alone to think about the meaning of life.

He knew the cave of Hira, a small cave high in a nearby mountain, and thought immediately to go there. He found that it suited his purpose, and he made it a regular habit of hiking up the mountain, sitting long hours pondering over why he was alive, what was his purpose in life and how to help his society.

Then, on an evening in the year 610 CE, during one of his extended stays on the mountain, an hour came where his thinking and meditating became more urgent than ever before. An energy entered his mind, and a flushed feeling pierced his heart.

Although the cave was dim and cold, heat and warmth seemed to fill the space around him, illuminating him. Suddenly, without warning, a blazing light filled the cave and dazzled his eyes. Out of nowhere, and yet everywhere at once, a voice called to him saying, "READ."

Muhammad was taken aback and quite startled. All he could think of saying was, "I can't read." For it was true, he did not know how to read or write.

Suddenly, he felt a pressure squeezing on his chest, until he thought his lungs would collapse. Again the voice commanded, "READ."

Muhammad, now frantic, desperately pleaded, "But I can't read."

The squeezing occurred again, and Muhammad thought for sure he was going to faint. The voice boomed out louder, "READ."

In order to save himself from more pain, he blurted out, "What should I read?"

This time there was no painful squeezing. No pressure on his lungs. The voice merely continued, *Read with the name of your Lord who created (everything), He created man from a clot of blood. Read, and your Lord is the most gracious, Who imparted knowledge by means of the pen. He taught man what he did not know.* Surat Al 'Alaq 96:1-5

﴿ اقْرَأْ بِاسْمِ رَبِّكَ الَّذِي خَلَقَ ﴾ ﴿ خَلَقَ الْإِنسَٰنَ مِنْ عَلَقٍ ﴾ ﴿ اقْرَأْ وَرَبُّكَ الْأَكْرَمُ ﴾ ﴿ الَّذِي عَلَّمَ بِالْقَلَمِ ﴾ ﴿ عَلَّمَ الْإِنسَٰنَ مَا لَمْ يَعْلَمْ ﴾ سُورَةُ الْعَلَقِ 96:1-5

Muhammad repeated those words, and then all was still. The light was gone, and everything was quiet. He didn't know what happened to him. He became scared. He rushed from the cave and stumbled in the dark down the trail that led back to town.

Suddenly, he heard that voice again, coming from above, from the skies, from all around. He looked up and saw a vision of a perfect man, filling the space between the earth and sky. He was saying, "Muhammad, you are the Messenger of Allah, and I am Jibreel."

A moment later, the vision disappeared, and Muhammad ran straight home to his wife, Khadijah. He burst through the door crying, "Cover me! Cover me!" She held him long into the night. Her heart ached for him, and she didn't know what to do as he lay trembling in her arms.

Chapter 13
The Struggle Begins

The Meeting with Waraqah

Muhammad ﷺ said, "Cover me, cover me," huddled under the blanket, shivering. He cried out to his wife, "Khadijah, what happened to me?" Khadijah responded, "Be glad, son of my uncle, and have a light heart. By Allah! Allah will never disgrace you, because, by Allah, you keep good relations with relatives, speak the truth, help the poor and the needy, treat guests well, and help those who are in trouble." (Al Bukhari)

قَالَ النَّبِيُّ ﷺ: «زَمِّلُونِي زَمِّلُونِي، فَزَمَّلُوهُ، فَلَمَّا سُرِّيَ عَنْهُ، قَالَ: يَا خَدِيجَةُ، لَقَدْ أَشْفَقْتُ عَلَى نَفْسِي بَلَاءٌ، لَقَدْ أَشْفَقْتُ عَلَى نَفْسِي بَلَاءٌ. قَالَتْ خَدِيجَةُ: أَبْشِرْ، فَوَ اللهِ لَا يُخْزِيكَ اللهُ أَبَدًا، إِنَّكَ لَتَصْدُقُ الحَدِيثَ، وَتَصِلُ الرَّحِمَ، وَتَحْمِلُ الكَلَّ، وَتُقْرِي الضَّيْفَ، وَتُعِينُ عَلَى نَوَائِبِ الحَقِّ». رَوَاهُ البُخَارِيُّ

Muhammad ﷺ drifted off to sleep in his wife's loving arms and lay feverishly in his bed the whole night. Khadijah ﷺ didn't know who to turn to for help, so she ran to her cousin Waraqah bin Nawfal. He was an elderly blind man. He considered himself a Christian and would study religious writings before he lost his sight. He also detested idol-worship and hoped that spiritual reform would come some-day to the immoral and hard land.

When she told him of everything that happened, Waraqah was filled with joy and proclaimed loudly, "Holy! Holy! By the One Who controls my soul! Khadijah, if your news is true, it must have been the great spirit that spoke to Musa! Muhammad must be the prophet of this nation. Tell him to be firm."

Khadijah ﷺ returned home to find Muhammad ﷺ still in bed. She watched him in his sleep. Then she noticed he was starting to sweat on his forehead. A moment later, he opened his eyes and she heard him muttering some strange words. He began to recite what sounded like poetry:

You, who are wrapped up, arise and warn! Glorify your Lord, and keep your clothes pure! Avoid the idols. Don't give (in charity) with the expectation of receiving anything back. For your Lord's sake, be patient.
Surat Al Muddaththir (The One Enveloped) 74:1-7

﴿يَا أَيُّهَا الْمُدَّثِّرُ﴾ ﴿قُمْ فَأَنْذِرْ﴾ ﴿وَرَبَّكَ فَكَبِّرْ﴾ ﴿وَثِيَابَكَ فَطَهِّرْ﴾ ﴿وَالرُّجْزَ فَاهْجُرْ﴾ ﴿وَلَا تَمْنُنْ تَسْتَكْثِرُ﴾ ﴿وَلِرَبِّكَ فَاصْبِرْ﴾ سُورَةُ الْمُدَّثِّر 74:1-7

Khadijah ﷺ was worried, and asked Muhammad ﷺ to rest a little longer. But he replied, "Khadijah, the time for resting is over. Jibreel has asked me to warn people and to call them to Allah and to His service. But who shall I call? Who will listen to me?"

Khadijah ﷺ thought for a moment, and then smiled. She told her husband what Waraqah had told her. Then she said that she would be the first to accept the invitation. She would accept the call of Allah ﷻ. Thus, Khadijah ﷺ became the first person to accept Islam.

A few days later, Khadijah ﷺ took Muhammad ﷺ to meet Waraqah. Muhammad ﷺ approached the blind man respectfully. Waraqah immediately asked him to tell him everything that happened. After Muhammad ﷺ finished, Waraqah called out in his weak voice, "By the power that holds my life! If what you say is true, I swear that you are the prophet of this land. That same spirit that came to Musa has come to you. They will disbelieve you! They will persecute you! You will be abused and chased. If I ever live to see that day, I will surely help the cause of Allah. Allah knows I will."

Then Waraqah lamented that he was no longer young and would not be able to see the events that would soon unfold. He kissed Muhammad ﷺ on his forehead and then left silently as Muhammad ﷺ returned home. Waraqah passed away a few months later.

Soon thereafter, a new revelation came to Prophet Muhammad ﷺ commanding him thus: *You who are covered in a cloak! Stand in prayer by night, but not all of it, half of it or a little less or more. Recite the Qur'an in slow and measured tones. Soon We will send you a heavy Message. Indeed the rising by night is the most powerful for controlling (the soul), and the best for forming words (of praise). Indeed, you are busy in the day with ordinary duties. But remember the name of your Lord, and devote yourself to Him completely. He is the Lord of the East and the West. There is no god but Him. Take Him, then, as the One to take care of your affairs.* Surat Al Muzzammil (The Enshrouded One) 73:1-9

﴿يَـٰٓأَيُّهَا ٱلْمُزَّمِّلُ﴾ ﴿قُمِ ٱلَّيْلَ إِلَّا قَلِيلًا﴾ ﴿نِّصْفَهُۥٓ أَوِ ٱنقُصْ مِنْهُ قَلِيلًا﴾ ﴿أَوْ زِدْ عَلَيْهِ وَرَتِّلِ ٱلْقُرْءَانَ تَرْتِيلًا﴾ ﴿إِنَّا سَنُلْقِى عَلَيْكَ قَوْلًا ثَقِيلًا﴾ ﴿إِنَّ نَاشِئَةَ ٱلَّيْلِ هِىَ أَشَدُّ وَطْـًٔا وَأَقْوَمُ قِيلًا﴾ ﴿إِنَّ لَكَ فِى ٱلنَّهَارِ سَبْحًا طَوِيلًا﴾ ﴿وَٱذْكُرِ ٱسْمَ رَبِّكَ وَتَبَتَّلْ إِلَيْهِ تَبْتِيلًا﴾ ﴿رَّبُّ ٱلْمَشْرِقِ وَٱلْمَغْرِبِ لَآ إِلَٰهَ إِلَّا هُوَ فَٱتَّخِذْهُ وَكِيلًا﴾ سُورَةُ الْمُزَّمِّل 1:37-9

The Pause in Revelation

For a lengthy period of time, Prophet Muhammad ﷺ did not receive any more revelations, which caused him to think that perhaps Allah ﷻ was angry with him. In despair, Prophet Muhammad ﷺ even thought about throwing himself off a nearby mountain, but Angel Jibreel ﷺ, who brought the first revelation, came to confirm, "Oh Muhammad! You are indeed Allah's Apostle in truth." But when would the messages come again? When would he know more?

Then, after six months passed, out of nowhere, Muhammad ﷺ saw the same Angel he had seen before. He revealed this Qur'anic surat: *By the brilliance of daybreak and the still of the night, your Lord is with you (Muhammad) and is not displeased. Indeed, your future is brighter than your past, because your Lord will grant you (what you want) and you will be pleased. Didn't He find you an orphan and care for you? Didn't He find you lost and show you the way? And didn't He find you poor and provide for you? Therefore, be kind to the orphan, gentle to the poor, and declare the (mercy) and blessings of your Lord.* Surat Ad Duha (The Morning Bright) 93:1-11

﴿وَٱلضُّحَىٰ﴾ ﴿وَٱلَّيْلِ إِذَا سَجَىٰ﴾ ﴿مَا وَدَّعَكَ رَبُّكَ وَمَا قَلَىٰ﴾ ﴿وَلَلْـَٔاخِرَةُ خَيْرٌ لَّكَ مِنَ ٱلْأُولَىٰ﴾ ﴿وَلَسَوْفَ يُعْطِيكَ رَبُّكَ فَتَرْضَىٰٓ﴾ ﴿أَلَمْ يَجِدْكَ يَتِيمًا فَـَٔاوَىٰ﴾ ﴿وَوَجَدَكَ ضَآلًّا فَهَدَىٰ﴾ ﴿وَوَجَدَكَ عَآئِلًا فَأَغْنَىٰ﴾ ﴿فَأَمَّا ٱلْيَتِيمَ فَلَا تَقْهَرْ﴾ ﴿وَأَمَّا ٱلسَّآئِلَ فَلَا تَنْهَرْ﴾ ﴿وَأَمَّا بِنِعْمَةِ رَبِّكَ فَحَدِّثْ﴾ سُورَةُ الضُّحَىٰ 1:93-11

Who Were the Next to Respond to the Call?

Angel Jibreel ﷺ came several more times to the Blessed Prophet ﷺ during the coming weeks. He taught him how to make the Salah and wudu' and revealed the first and most important surat of the Qur'an, Al Fatihah:
In the name of Allah, the Beneficent, the Merciful. Praise belongs to Allah, the Lord of All the Worlds. The All-Merciful, the Very-Merciful. The Master of the Day of Requital. You alone do we worship, and from You alone do we seek help. Take us on the straight path. The path of those on whom You have bestowed Your Grace; Not of those who have incurred Your wrath nor of those who have gone astray. Surat Al Fatihah (The Opener) 1:1-7

﴿بِسْمِ ٱللَّهِ ٱلرَّحْمَٰنِ ٱلرَّحِيمِ﴾ ﴿ٱلْحَمْدُ لِلَّهِ رَبِّ ٱلْعَٰلَمِينَ﴾ ﴿ٱلرَّحْمَٰنِ ٱلرَّحِيمِ﴾ ﴿مَٰلِكِ يَوْمِ ٱلدِّينِ﴾ ﴿إِيَّاكَ نَعْبُدُ وَإِيَّاكَ نَسْتَعِينُ﴾ ﴿ٱهْدِنَا ٱلصِّرَٰطَ ٱلْمُسْتَقِيمَ﴾ ﴿صِرَٰطَ ٱلَّذِينَ أَنْعَمْتَ عَلَيْهِمْ غَيْرِ ٱلْمَغْضُوبِ عَلَيْهِمْ وَلَا ٱلضَّآلِّينَ﴾ سُورَةُ الْفَاتِحَة 1:1-7

Muhammad ﷺ did not know it then, but it would take 23 years for the entire Qur'an to be revealed to him. Nor did he imagine all the struggles and adventures that were soon to come. All he knew was that he was commissioned as Allah's ﷻ last Messenger and that his people, the Arabs, were the first he must convince of the truth.

Zayd bin Harithah ﷺ, the adopted son and freed servant of Muhammad ﷺ, also accepted the call of Islam and became a Muslim. Zayd was brought to Makkah as a slave when just a small boy. One of Khadijah's ﷺ relatives had purchased him and had given him to Khadijah ﷺ as a present.

When Khadijah ﷺ offered to give him to Muhammad ﷺ as his servant, Muhammad ﷺ set him free. But Zayd didn't want to leave. He came to love Muhammad ﷺ so much that he stayed on in the household, even when Zayd's real father, who had been searching for his lost son for years, came to Makkah and found him.

When Zayd was given the choice to stay with Muhammad ﷺ or return with his real father, Zayd answered, "I shall never leave this man. He has treated me nobly, as a father would treat his son. I never felt for a single day that I was a servant. He looked after me well. He is kind towards me and is concerned about my happiness. He is the most noble of men and the greatest person in the world. How can I leave him and go with you, father? I shall never leave him." Zayd knew Muhammad ﷺ well and was certain of the truth of what Muhammad declared. Barakah also accepted Islam as soon as it was offered to her.

One day, while Muhammad ﷺ and his wife were both bowing in prayer, Muhammad's ﷺ 10-year-old cousin, 'Ali ﷺ, walked into the room. He was surprised at what they were doing and stood and watched until they finished.

Then he asked the Prophet ﷺ, "Who were you bowing to?"

The Blessed Prophet ﷺ answered, "We were bowing to Allah, Who has made me a prophet and Who commanded me to call people to Him." Then the Prophet ﷺ invited 'Ali ﷺ to join him in the new way of life and to give up the ignorant culture of Makkah.

When the verses of the Qur'an were recited to 'Ali ﷺ, he was overcome with joy at the beauty of what he heard. He asked to have time to ask his father's permission to accept the new teachings and he rushed away. 'Ali ﷺ spent the night in bed, tossing and turning, but he never spoke to his dad. Instead, he went back to Muhammad ﷺ and Khadijah ﷺ in the morning and declared, "Allah created me without asking my father, Abu Talib. So why should I ask my father now to serve Allah?"

Next, Muhammad ﷺ approached his good friend, Abu Bakr bin Abi Quhafa ﷺ, a local businessman. Though at the time Abu Bakr ﷺ was only 38 years old, he was wealthy and was the head of his clan. When the Blessed Prophet Muhammad ﷺ approached him with the teachings of Islam, Abu Bakr ﷺ listened carefully to them. Idols were false, the Prophet ﷺ proclaimed, and Allah ﷻ is one. Goodness is the way to live our lives, and the time of the last revelation to the world had come. Abu Bakr ﷺ had known Muhammad ﷺ for years and trusted him completely. He accepted Islam gladly and without hesitation.

So the first Muslims were Khadijah ﷺ, Barakah, Zayd, 'Ali and Abu Bakr ﷺ. For the next three years, Muhammad ﷺ preached to his close friends and relatives privately. All of his daughters also accepted Islam as well as a few of his other friends and their friends. The time was not right to go public yet. So Muhammad ﷺ concentrated on gathering a strong base of believers from amongst his closest friends and family members. For now, the Prophet ﷺ would devote his time to teaching the new Muslims the basic teachings of the faith: the oneness of Allah ﷻ, justice, brotherhood, compassion to all and how to acquire peace within one's self.

Indeed, the rising by night is the most powerful for controlling (the soul), and the best for forming words (of praise). Surat Al Muzzammil (The Enshrouded One) 73:6

﴿إِنَّ نَاشِئَةَ ٱلَّيْلِ هِيَ أَشَدُّ وَطْـًٔا وَأَقْوَمُ قِيلًا﴾ سُورَةُ الْمُزَّمِّل 73:6

The Preaching

The Blessed Prophet ﷺ began to teach Islam to small groups of people. At first only the poor and common people wanted to listen. One day, a group of Makkan nobles came to the courtyard of the Ka'bah where Muhammad ﷺ was teaching. They saw all the common people and didn't want to associate with such lowly people. In the Makkan society of that time, everyone was status-conscious.

They asked Muhammad ﷺ to send the common people away so the nobles could listen to his message. They were curious about it. Muhammad ﷺ was about to send the poor people away when these verses were revealed, *Do not expel those who call out to their Lord morning and evening seeking His pleasure. You are not responsible for anything in their account, and they are not responsible for anything in your account, that you should expel them and thus become one of the unjust.* Surat Al An'aam (The Cattle) 6:52

﴿وَلَا تَطْرُدِ الَّذِينَ يَدْعُونَ رَبَّهُم بِالْغَدَوٰةِ وَالْعَشِيِّ يُرِيدُونَ وَجْهَهُ مَا عَلَيْكَ مِنْ حِسَابِهِم مِّن شَيْءٍ وَمَا مِنْ حِسَابِكَ عَلَيْهِم مِّن شَيْءٍ فَتَطْرُدَهُمْ فَتَكُونَ مِنَ الظَّالِمِينَ﴾ سُورَةُ الأنعام 6:52

After Muhammad ﷺ recited the revelation, the shocked nobles left. "How could Islam teach that the poor were equal to the rich?" they thought. Muhammad ﷺ understood at this point that status meant nothing in Islam and that faith in Allah ﷻ was the only way to judge a person's worth.

After three years, Muhammad ﷺ had gained some 30 converts to Islam. They would meet in the home of a man named Al Arqam. The believers were both males and females, young and old, rich and poor. Increasingly, ayaat were revealed explaining the teachings of Islam in greater detail. The Qur'an was beginning to take shape in a concrete way.

The Makkans began to hear more about Muhammad ﷺ and his new ideas, but many felt it was a new cult that would eventually die out. Few Makkans wanted to become Muslim after they found out that joining the believers would mean freeing slaves, treating women equally, supporting orphans, breaking idols, helping the poor, praying everyday and being absolutely honest.

In addition, Islam taught that religion was to be taken seriously. In contrast, the spiritual life of idol-worshippers was comprised of rituals and sacrifices that were not given as much consideration. Islam also taught that humans would be resurrected after death and they would be judged according to their faith and actions. These two concepts were virtually unknown in Arabia at that time.

The Major Public Call

One day, the Blessed Prophet ﷺ received the revelation telling him to, *Proclaim what you have been ordered, and turn away from the idol-worshippers.* Surat Al Hijr (The Rocky Tract) 15:94

﴿فَاصْدَعْ بِمَا تُؤْمَرُ وَأَعْرِضْ عَنِ الْمُشْرِكِينَ﴾ سُورَةُ الحِجْر 15:94

This would mark the next level in the Islamic movement: making a public call for the people to accept Islam. The Blessed Prophet ﷺ first arranged a large dinner and invited all his distant relatives whom he had not yet approached about Islam. After the meal, the Blessed Prophet ﷺ stood and declared the message of Islam, asking people to accept it.

None of the elders were convinced, and they started to leave. But 'Ali ﷺ stood and declared that he would follow Muhammad ﷺ and help him in the cause. Imagine the courage of the young boy to declare publicly that he was a Muslim. The people just laughed, however, and went home. This gave the Makkans a new excuse to publicly insult the Prophet ﷺ and his followers.

Ibn 'Abbas ﷺ narrated that one day the Prophet ﷺ ascended Safa mountain and said, "Oh Sabah!" All the Quraysh gathered round him and said, "What is the matter?" He said, "Look, if I told you that an enemy is going to attack you in the morning or in the evening, would you not believe me?" They said, "Yes, we will believe you." He said, "I am a Warner to you in face of a terrible punishment." On that Abu Lahab said, "May you perish! Is it for this thing that you have gathered us?" So Allah revealed: "Perish the hands of Abu Lahab!" (111.1) (Al Bukhari)

عَنِ ابْنِ عَبَّاسٍ ﷺ قَالَ صَعِدَ النَّبِيُّ ﷺ الصَّفَا ذَاتَ يَوْمٍ فَقَالَ: يَا صَبَاحَاهُ! فَاجْتَمَعَتْ إِلَيْهِ قُرَيْشٌ قَالُوا مَا لَكَ قَالَ: أَرَأَيْتُمْ لَوْ أَخْبَرْتُكُمْ أَنَّ الْعَدُوَّ يُصَبِّحُكُمْ أَوْ يُمَسِّيكُمْ أَمَا كُنْتُمْ تُصَدِّقُونِي؟ قَالُوا بَلَى. قَالَ: فَإِنِّي نَذِيرٌ لَكُمْ بَيْنَ يَدَيْ عَذَابٍ شَدِيدٍ. فَقَالَ أَبُو لَهَبٍ: تَبًّا لَكَ أَلِهَذَا جَمَعْتَنَا فَأَنْزَلَ اللهُ ﴿تَبَّتْ يَدَا أَبِي لَهَبٍ وَتَبَّ﴾ سُورَةُالْمَسَد:111:1. رَوَاهُالْبُخَارِيُّ

As-Safa mountain today.

Muhammad ﷺ was shocked. But then Allah ﷻ revealed the following surat to him, The hands of Abu Lahab will perish! He will perish. Neither his wealth nor possessions will save him, for he will be surrounded by a fierce blaze. And his contemptuous wife, (whose slander) made (tempers) rise, shall join him, shackled in fibrous chains. Surat Al Masad (The Palm Rope) 111:1-5

﴿تَبَّتْ يَدَا أَبِي لَهَبٍ وَتَبَّ﴾﴿مَا أَغْنَى عَنْهُ مَالُهُ وَمَا كَسَبَ﴾﴿سَيَصْلَى نَارًا ذَاتَ لَهَبٍ﴾﴿وَامْرَأَتُهُ حَمَّالَةَ الْحَطَبِ﴾﴿فِي جِيدِهَا حَبْلٌ مِنْ مَسَدٍ﴾ سُورَةُالْمَسَد:111:1-5

The Hostility Peaks

After the Blessed Prophet ﷺ and the believers started to preach Islam openly around the city, the leaders of the idol-worshippers became very hostile. Some of them sincerely believed in the power of the idols. Others were afraid of angering the surrounding tribes, who housed their idols in the Ka'bah and made yearly pilgrimages to the city in their honor. Still others, whose business opportunities were profitable as the keepers of the idols, felt they would suffer if they got rid of the idols.

Whatever the reasons, the leaders and the people of their tribes began to view the Muslims as a real threat that must be opposed. Muhammad ﷺ was sometimes pelted with rocks as he walked. He was also bothered and insulted whenever he went to pray near the Ka'bah. They accused him of being a soothsayer, one who talks to evil spirits.

And this (Qur'an) is not brought down by devils. It neither suits them, nor are they able to (do this). In fact, they are kept far away from hearing (it at the time of revelation). Surat As-Shuaraa (The Poets) 26: 210-212

﴿وَمَا تَنَزَّلَتْ بِهِ الشَّيَاطِينُ﴾﴿وَمَا يَنْبَغِي لَهُمْ وَمَا يَسْتَطِيعُونَ﴾﴿إِنَّهُمْ عَنِ السَّمْعِ لَمَعْزُولُونَ﴾ سُورَةُالشُّعَرَاء،26:210-212

Other people said he was possessed by a jinn. Yet others said he was crazy. No one could explain why an illiterate man, never having recited anything before, nor who knew anything about poetry, was now reciting messages that were unlike anything they had ever heard.

But Prophet Muhammad ﷺ was reciting more than mere poetry. He was proclaiming a message that taught that people were equal, regardless of color, that women had equal status with men, that the powerful must respect the rights of the weak and that idols were the inventions of their own hands. For these teachings, the people ridiculed and harassed the Prophet ﷺ and the believers.

The Makkan leaders asked Abu Talib to talk some sense into Muhammad ﷺ. So one day, he went to Muhammad ﷺ and asked him to stop preaching his message. Muhammad ﷺ merely replied, "My uncle, by Allah, if they put the sun in my right hand and the moon in my left, and asked me to give up my mission, I would not do it until either Allah made this deen victorious or I died (in the struggle)." Abu Talib was satisfied with Muhammad's ﷺ sincerity and told his nephew to preach whatever he wished.

Sometimes the Blessed Prophet ﷺ felt depressed that more people weren't accepting Islam. He couldn't believe that so many people, including his own relatives, would fight against something that was good for them. He would have never imagined that his own people would throw rocks and insult him on the streets. Allah ﷻ comforted him by acknowledging his frustrations. He revealed this ayah: You would almost kill yourself with grief, following them around because they don't believe in these words. Surat Al Kahf (The Cave) 18:6

Many other Muslims were also being harassed, but Muslims who had higher social status only suffered taunts, insults, and fist-fights. Those who had no family connections, or were of a lower status, were beaten, kidnapped, tortured or even killed.

A slave of African heritage, named Bilal bin Rabaah ﷺ, accepted Islam. When his master found out, he beat Bilal ﷺ mercilessly. He often tied him down in the hot desert sand, forcing him to wear metal body armor under the bright sun. One time, huge rocks were placed over Bilal's ﷺ chest while he laid in the hot sun. His master thought that this would push Bilal ﷺ to give up his new faith. Yet, Bilal ﷺ never broke, and he endured the suffering.

When Abu Bakr ﷺ heard of this torture, he rushed to offer to buy Bilal ﷺ from the cruel man. Bilal's ﷺ master reluctantly agreed, and Abu Bakr ﷺ took him to safety and freed him from slavery.

Another Muslim, a woman named Sumaiyah ﷺ, was arrested by the Makkan leaders and tortured so badly by Abu Jahl that she died. Other Muslims also lost their lives at the hands of angry mobs.

One woman became so enraged when she found out her slave, Khabbab bin al Aratt, had become a Muslim that she beat him and placed hot coals on his head! The Prophet, passing by and seeing the torture, was powerless to stop it. Allah had not yet ordered him and his followers to defend themselves with physical force. Yet he cried out, "My Lord, save him, give him patience." A few months later, the cruel woman was bitten by a dog and got sick. The only cure doctors prescribed in those days for this type of sickness was to put hot, burning iron on the top of the head. As a result, she suffered very horribly.

This period of persecution and torture of the believers went on for some time. Due to the hostility, the Muslims kept their prayers and meetings secret, often meeting in the home of Al Arqam. When the unbelievers discovered the Muslims' meeting place, they plotted secretly to trap the Muslims after they left Al Arqam's house. They set up ambushes on the main road and waited. Khadijah ﷺ found out about this plan and wanted to send a secret message to her husband, so she asked Barakah and Zayd to find a way around the ambushes. The pair walked carefully around the alleyways and finally reached the safety of Al Arqam's house. It was a risky mission, and they could have been seriously harmed if they were captured.

Barakah then left and made her way back to Khadijah's ﷺ home safely. Zayd ﷺ remained behind in the house of Al Arqam. The Prophet ﷺ said to the men with him, "If one of you wanted to marry a woman from the people of Paradise, let him marry the mother of Ayman."

No one said a word. Barakah was not attractive and was now in her forties. But a moment later, Zayd ﷺ stood up and said, "Messenger of Allah, I will marry the mother of Ayman. By Allah, she is better than women who have grace and beauty." A few days later, the couple were married, and in time were blessed with a son whom they named Usamah bin Zayd. The Prophet ﷺ loved the little baby so much that he would often feed him with his own hands.

But the persecution of the Muslims went on, and the idol-worshippers wanted to take away even the simplest joys from the followers of Prophet Muhammad ﷺ. Once, when Muhammad ﷺ was praying in the courtyard of the Ka'bah, some idol-worshippers threw garbage on him. Fatimah ﷺ, Muhammad's ﷺ beloved daughter, was nearby when she saw it and came running to her father, crying and cursing the idol-worshippers who stood nearby. She removed the garbage from her father's back, sat and wept. The Prophet ﷺ prayed to Allah ﷺ to punish the idol-worshippers and displayed his great patience. The time for self-defense still had not yet arrived.

The Cunning Offer

'Utbah bin Rabi'ah, a leader of the Quraysh, thought of a clever way to end the divisions happening in the city. Although Muslims were suffering under the hands of the Quraysh, many men and women continued to embrace Islam. 'Utbah went to the Prophet ﷺ and gave him this offer, "If you want money, we will pool our wealth together so you will be the richest man among us. If you want status, we will make you our leader, so that no one can decide anything without your consent. If you want power, we will make you our king. Finally, if you are unable to cure yourself of the visions that you have been seeing, we will find the best cure until your health is perfect again."

But the Blessed Prophet Muhammad ﷺ refused these tempting offers and instead recited Surat 41 (Fussilat - Explained in Detail) of the Holy Qur'an. 'Utbah listened to the fascinating words and then returned to the other Quraysh leaders in a state of wonder. He told them that they should leave Muhammad ﷺ alone. That if he succeeded in his mission, all of Makkah would benefit. The idol-worshippers were not happy at all with 'Utbah's words, and resolved to make life even more difficult for the Muslims.

The Attacks Intensify

The poets of Makkah were unleashed against the Muslims in a new propaganda war. They would taunt Muhammad ﷺ in the streets and ask why Allah ﷻ wasn't giving him news of the market prices, or why Allah ﷻ didn't show Himself to the people.

Allah ﷻ revealed the following ayaat in answer to their taunts, *If We (Allah) sent to you (Muhammad) a (message) written on paper that they could touch with their hands, the unbelievers would be sure to say, "This is obviously only magic." Then they say, "Why isn't an angel sent down to him?" If We did send an angel, then the question would be settled at once, and they would have no chance then. If We did send an angel, We would send him (disguised) like a man, and We would have then caused them to be confused about an issue they were already confused about. The Messengers before you (Muhammad) were mocked, but their insulters were trapped by what they mocked.* Surat Al An'aam (Cattle) 6:7-10

﴿وَلَوْ نَزَّلْنَا عَلَيْكَ كِتَابًا فِي قِرْطَاسٍ فَلَمَسُوهُ بِأَيْدِيهِمْ لَقَالَ ٱلَّذِينَ كَفَرُوٓاْ إِنْ هَٰذَآ إِلَّا سِحْرٌ مُّبِينٌ﴾﴿وَقَالُواْ لَوْلَآ أُنزِلَ عَلَيْهِ مَلَكٌ وَلَوْ أَنزَلْنَا مَلَكًا لَّقُضِيَ ٱلْأَمْرُ ثُمَّ لَا يُنظَرُونَ﴾﴿وَلَوْ جَعَلْنَٰهُ مَلَكًا لَّجَعَلْنَٰهُ رَجُلًا وَلَلَبَسْنَا عَلَيْهِم مَّا يَلْبِسُونَ﴾﴿وَلَقَدِ ٱسْتُهْزِئَ بِرُسُلٍ مِّن قَبْلِكَ فَحَاقَ بِٱلَّذِينَ سَخِرُواْ مِنْهُم مَّا كَانُواْ بِهِۦ يَسْتَهْزِءُونَ﴾ سُورَةُ الأنعام ٦:٧-١٠

It was Muhammad's ﷺ habit to go out and greet incoming caravans and invite the people to Islam. The Quraysh leaders then also arranged for people to go out who would shout that Muhammad ﷺ was crazy and not to listen to him. Allah ﷻ revealed these ayaat to comfort him in his trials, *The unbelievers say, "Don't listen to this Qur'an, but talk loudly when it's being read so you can gain the upper hand." But We will give the unbelievers the taste of a severe penalty and pay them back for the worst of their deeds.* Surat Fussilat (Explained in Detail) 41:26-27

﴿وَقَالَ ٱلَّذِينَ كَفَرُواْ لَا تَسْمَعُواْ لِهَٰذَا ٱلْقُرْءَانِ وَٱلْغَوْاْ فِيهِ لَعَلَّكُمْ تَغْلِبُونَ﴾﴿فَلَنُذِيقَنَّ ٱلَّذِينَ كَفَرُواْ عَذَابًا شَدِيدًا وَلَنَجْزِيَنَّهُمْ أَسْوَأَ ٱلَّذِي كَانُواْ يَعْمَلُونَ﴾ سُورَةُ فُصِّلَت ٤١:٢٦-٢٧

The Muslims then received unexpected support that would strengthen them and Muhammad ﷺ. This support was Hamza ﷺ, the Lion-Hunter, an uncle of Prophet Muhammad ﷺ. He would spend long periods of time in the open desert, and was known for his courage, strength and martial prowess. One day, Abu Jahl pursued Muhammad ﷺ through the streets, insulting him and his beliefs. Hamza ﷺ, who had just returned from a lion hunt, heard of what was happening and, without greeting anyone, went straight to the courtyard of the Ka'bah. When he saw Abu Jahl, he hit him hard with his bow. Abu Jahl backed down and left the scene. Then Hamza ﷺ declared his acceptance of Islam and took the oath of allegiance to Muhammad ﷺ. The Muslims felt heartened, while the idol-worshippers nearby were shocked.

The Great Escape

The idol-worshippers intensified their persecution of the Muslims. More people were arrested and tortured. Whenever the Makkan nobles found out that someone accepted Islam, they would go to that person and threaten them saying, "We will destroy all your hope and ruin your reputation." Abu Sufyan, the leader of the council of Makkah, thought of ways to do away with Islam forever. He and the other idol-worshippers thought that if they harassed the Muslims enough, they would abandon their faith.

Prophet Muhammad ﷺ knew he had to take action to protect the Muslims, particularly those who were more vulnerable, such as those with weak family connections and a lower social status. He hated to see his fellow believers suffering, and was himself powerless to do anything about it. (6:33-36)

Then one day, the Prophet ﷺ received guidance that the most vulnerable Muslims should escape Makkah and go to Abyssinia, an African country across the Red Sea. An-Najashi, the king of Abyssinia, was a fair Christian ruler.

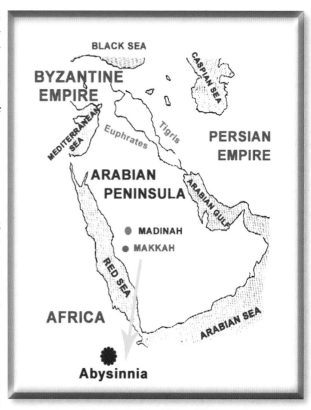

Accordingly, the Muslims made secret plans to send out small groups to the coast where they could buy passage on a ship to Africa. The first group of Muslims, eleven men and four women, left the city by night and journeyed to Abyssinia.

Abu Bakr ﷺ was with this group when they reached a small city near the coast of the Red Sea. There, a local tribal chief named Ibn Ad-Daghina promised to protect Abu Bakr ﷺ, so he returned with him to Makkah. The chief announced to the Makkan nobles that they must allow Abu Bakr ﷺ to live in peace. The Makkan leaders agreed, and they left Abu Bakr ﷺ alone for a while.

Meanwhile, the Muslims who arrived safely in Abyssinia lived there in peace for some time. Later, they received false reports that the idol-worshippers were no longer persecuting the Muslims, so they hurriedly returned to Makkah. Of course, the persecution had not stopped, and people were being beaten and harassed as much as ever. In turn, the Prophet ﷺ organized an even larger group of nearly 80 men and numerous women and children to escape to safety.

They set out secretly for Abyssinia and were gone before the idol-worshippers knew what had happened. A few days later, the Makkans realized that their favorite and easiest targets were gone. They were filled with rage, and vowed to bring them back by any means necessary.

Muslims in the King's Court

The Makkan leaders had some trade agreements with the king of Abyssinia, and thought that they could use this to their advantage. They sent two of their most persuasive speakers, 'Amr bin Al 'As and 'Abdallah bin Abu Rabi'ah, to meet with the king, bearing expensive gifts.

After arriving in Abyssinia, the pair gained an audience with the king. They explained to him that there were people from Makkah who had taken refuge in Abyssinia who had forsaken the religion of their forefathers, but who were also not Christians. They asked the king's permission to seize them and return them to Arabia.

As he was curious to know their side of the story, the king decided to hear the case of these people who left their ancestors' religion. He thus ordered the Muslim delegation to his court for a hearing. When they arrived, the king asked the leader of the Muslim group, Ja'far bin Abi Talib ﷺ, "What is this new religion which made you separate from your people; a religion which is different from mine as well as from any other known religions?"

Ja'far ﷺ stepped forward and declared, "Oh King! We were in a state of ignorance and immorality. We worshipped stones and idols, ate dead animals, committed all sorts of injustices, broke family ties and treated our neighbors badly. The strong among us would exploit the weak as well.

"Then Allah sent us a prophet, one of our own people, whose family history, truthfulness, trustworthiness and honesty were well known to us. He called us to serve one God alone and to reject the stones and idols that we and our fathers used to worship.

"He commanded us to speak the truth, to honor our promises, to help our relatives, to be good to our neighbors, to stop killing and to avoid fornication. He commanded us to stop lying and not to take the property of orphans or to falsely accuse a married woman. He ordered us not to associate anyone with Allah.

"He commanded us to establish prayer, to fast and to spend in charity. We believed in him and what he brought to us from Allah, and we follow him in what he asks us to do and in what he tells us not to do.

"So our own people have attacked us, treated us badly, and tried to take us back to the old bad ways and worship of idols. They made life unbearable for us in Makkah, so we have come to your country to seek safety and to live in justice and peace."

After hearing this beautiful speech, the king was inclined favorably toward the Muslims. He then asked to hear some of the verses of the Qur'an. Ja'far ﷺ, a very wise caller to Islam, chose the ayaat carefully. He recited verses from Surat Maryam, which spoke of Maryam and the birth of Prophet 'Isa ﷺ.

And mention in the Book (the story of) Maryam, when she secluded herself from her people to a place towards the East. Then she used a barrier to hide herself from them. Then, We sent to her Our Spirit, (Jibreel) and he took before her the form of a perfect human being. She said, "I seek refuge with the All-Merciful (Allah), against you, if you are God-fearing." He said, "I am but a message-bearer of your Lord (sent) to give you a boy, purified." She said, "How shall I have a boy while no human has ever touched me, nor have I ever been unchaste?" He said, "So it is; your Lord said, 'It is easy for Me, and (We will do this) so that We make it a sign for people and a mercy from Us, and this is a matter already destined.'" So she conceived him, and went in seclusion with him to a remote place. Then the labor pains brought her to the trunk of a palm tree. She said "O that I would have died before this, and would have been something gone, forgotten." Then he called her from beneath her, 'Do not grieve; your Lord has placed a stream beneath you. Shake the trunk of the palm tree towards yourself, and it will drop upon you ripe, fresh dates. So eat, drink and cool your eyes. Then if you see any human being, say (to him), 'I have vowed a fast (of silence) for the All-Merciful (Allah) and therefore, I shall never speak to any human today.'" Then she came to her people carrying him (the baby). They said, "O Maryam you have committed something grave indeed. O sister of Harun, neither your father was a man of evil, nor was your mother unchaste." So, she pointed towards him (the baby). They said, "How shall we speak to someone who is still a child in the cradle?" Spoke he (the baby), "Verily, I am the servant of Allah. He has given me the Book and made me a prophet. And He has made me a blessed one wherever I be and has enjoined Salah and Zakah upon me as long as I am alive. And (He has made me) good to my mother, and he did not make me oppressive (or) ill-fated. And peace is upon me the day I was born, the day I shall die, and the day I shall be raised alive again." Surat Maryam (Mary) 19:16-33

After reciting, the king turned to the ambassadors and proclaimed that he would never return the Muslims to them. The next day, 'Amr bin Al 'As returned for another meeting to try a different approach. He told the king that Muslims deny that 'Isa ﷺ is the son of God and that he is only a revered prophet to them.

The king had Ja'far ﷺ brought to him again and asked him about this. Ja'far ﷺ replied that Islam teaches that 'Isa ﷺ was Allah's ﷻ prophet, a spirit and command from Him, and that he was born of a virgin named Maryam. The king drew a line on the floor with his staff, declaring that the difference between Christianity and Islam was no thicker than a line drawn in the dust. The Makkans were left to return to Arabia empty-handed.

The Boycott and Year of Sorrow

Soon, the Blessed Prophet's ﷺ teachings were being discussed in other cities and towns. The Christian community of Najran sent 20 men to Makkah to meet Muhammad ﷺ and discover what he was teaching. After listening to the Prophet ﷺ, all 20 men decided to accept the new faith. They were convinced it was a continuation of the true message of Prophet 'Isa ﷺ.

The Makkan leaders were so angry when the news reached them that they rushed to the scene and said to the group, "May God humiliate you, you shameful delegation! Your people have sent you to bring them news of this man, but no sooner did you sit with him than you left your religion and believed in him!"

Such was the power of the message of the Qur'an that people were drawn to it, despite their will. One night, each of the four worst Makkan nobles, Abu Sufyan, Abu Jahl, 'Amr and Al Akhnas, left their homes to sit outside the windows of Muhammad's ﷺ house to listen to him read the Qur'an long into the night.

None of the four knew of the others that were also hiding and were most embarrassed when they discovered each other. Two more nights passed with each man coming back to listen more. Finally, they swore an oath that none of them would return, so that others would not be encouraged to enter Islam.

The Makkan leaders, most of whom were from the tribe of Quraysh, decided on a new strategy to punish the Muslims. They agreed to form a total boycott against the clans of Banu Hashim and Banu Muttalib, to which many Muslims belonged. The idol-worshippers wrote on paper that no Arab tribe should have any dealings with these two clans, nor should they sell them any food nor offer a contract in marriage.

They hung this paper in the Ka'bah, which was the custom for official announcements. Then they sent armed men to force all the boycotted people out of town and into a small valley outside Makkah called the Shi'b Abi Talib. The Muslims spent three years in this desolate valley suffering tremendous hardships. Revelations from Allah came to strengthen the hearts of the people, and a food-sharing system was worked out so that everyone got a fair share.

Food supplies were always low. Some kindhearted people felt sorry for the Muslims and smuggled goods into the camp, but it was never enough. Visiting Arab tribes from the surrounding areas, coming to Makkah for the pilgrimage months, often complained to the Makkan leaders about their cruelty and advised that the boycott should be lifted.

During an argument among the leaders about the boycott, Abu Jahl declared that the boycott was a sacred law and could not be abandoned. Others around him, however, wanted the pact removed. All went to the Ka'bah only to discover that the boycott decree had been eaten away by mites—all except for the heading which read, "In Your Name, Lord." Their "sacred law" was gone. The boycott was lifted, and the clans of Banu Hashim and Banu Muttalib were allowed to return to their homes. Prophet Muhammad ﷺ immediately resumed preaching Islam to the Quraysh, and the Muslims worked to regain their strength.

But tragedy was soon to follow this positive turn of events. Muhammad's ﷺ uncle, Abu Talib, who had provided some measure of protection for him, passed away of old age. Even more tragic was the death of his beloved wife, Khadijah. She had been his wife for nearly 25 years. She was the mother of his children and his support and source of strength. She was the first to accept Islam and the first to comfort him when Prophethood was bestowed upon him.

What helped Muhammad ﷺ through these tough times was the fact that he had dealt with horrible loss before in his life. He lost his father, mother and grandfather in years past. But his grief was still great, and he called this year the Year of Sorrow.

The Mission Continues

The Blessed Prophet ﷺ continued his mission now, but without help or support from any powerful tribal leader. The Qur'an continued to be revealed to give further shape to the teachings of Islam, and people were still embracing the religion in a steady stream.

Previously, Ibn Ad-Daghina had made a deal with the Quraysh leaders. It was that Abu Bakr would be spared from harassment if he practiced Islam within the confinement of his own home. So Abu Bakr decided to build a small, one-room building in front of his house to use as a masjid. He would pray in it everyday. Many times, he would cry when reciting the beautiful verses of the Qur'an.

Soon, many curious women and children started to gather and watch Abu Bakr through the open window, affected by the beauty of the Qur'an. The Makkan leaders became outraged when they found out, and they sent a message to Ibn Ad-Daghina to come at once.

When he arrived, they convinced him to give up his protection of Abu Bakr. They feared their own women and children would become attracted to Islam as well. The chief went to Abu Bakr and asked to be released from protecting him. Abu Bakr said, "I release you from your promise to protect me, and I'm happy with the protection of Allah."

One joyous highlight that occurred during this sad time was when the Prophet ﷺ became engaged to Abu Bakr's daughter 'Aishah. The marriage would be delayed another three years until she was of marriage age. In the meantime, the Companions asked the Prophet ﷺ to marry a widowed Muslim woman named Sawda, as she had no family support. The Prophet ﷺ agreed, and the Muslims celebrated this strengthening of the community.

Literature Selection

Isra' and Mi'raj:
The Night Journey and Ascension

From Sahih Al Bukhari

In the year 621 CE, a wonderful event occurred in the life of the Blessed Prophet ﷺ. He was honored by Allah﷽ with a trip in which he saw Paradise and Hellfire for himself. This trip was called the **Isra' and Mi'raj** الإِسْرَاءُوالمِعْراج. This undoubtedly increased his strength and his resolve and helped him in his mission to bring people to Allah's﷽ deen.

While staying in the house of his cousin Hind bint Abi Talib (Um Hani﷽), she related that, "The Messenger of Allah spent the night in my house. He said his night prayers and went to sleep. Just before dawn, the Messenger of Allah woke us up, and we all prayed the Fajr prayer together. When the prayer was finished, he said, 'Um Hani, I prayed with you the night prayer in this place. Then I went to (Jerusalem) and prayed there, and as you see, I have just finished praying the dawn prayer with you.' I answered, 'Messenger of Allah, don't tell people about this because they will tease you and hurt you.' He replied, 'By Allah I shall tell them.'"

For this literature selection, we will be combining several different ahadith (plural of hadith), which are found in the collection compiled by Imam Al Bukhari. While reading this selection, keep in mind the tremendous honor that Allah﷽ bestowed upon His Prophet ﷺ by allowing him to see the "other side" in his lifetime.

Anas bin Malik narrated that the night Allah's Messenger ﷺ was taken for a journey from the sacred mosque (of Mecca) Al-Ka'ba: "Three persons came to him and carried him and placed him beside the well of Zamzam. From among them Gabriel took charge of him. Gabriel cut open (the part of his body) between his throat and the middle of his chest (heart) and took all the material out of his chest and `abdomen and then washed it with Zamzam water with his own hands till he cleansed the inside of his body, and then a gold tray containing a gold bowl full of belief and wisdom was brought and then Gabriel stuffed his chest and throat blood vessels with it and then closed it (the chest)."

Anas☀ reported that the Messenger of Allah☀ said, "Then a creature, all in white, smaller than a mule, but bigger than a donkey (called the 'Buraq') was brought to me. The creature's stride was so wide that it reached the farthest point of its eyesight in one step. I was carried on it."

~*~*~*~*~*~

Angel Jibreel☀ then took Muhammad☀ to Jerusalem, where he tethered the Buraq. Then the spirits of other Prophets of old were brought. The Blessed Prophet Muhammad☀ led them in prayer before beginning the fantastic tour of the next life. In Al Quds (Jerusalem), the journey to Heaven began.

~*~*~*~*~*~

Jibreel then took my hand and ascended with me to the nearest heaven. When I reached the nearest heaven, Jibreel said to the gatekeeper of the first heaven, "Open (the gate)."
The gatekeeper asked, "Who is it?"
"Jibreel."
"Is there anyone with you?" The gatekeeper asked.
"Yes, Muhammad is with me."
"Has he been called?" "Yes," Jibreel replied.
So the gate was opened, and we passed through the nearest heaven. There we saw a man sitting with some people on his right and some others on his left. When he looked towards his right, he laughed, but when he looked towards his left, he wept. He then said to me, "Welcome! Righteous Prophet and righteous son."
I asked Jibreel, "Who is that?"
"He is Adam, and the people on his right and left are the souls of his offspring. Those on his right are the People of Paradise, and those on his left are the People of Hell, and when he looks towards his right, he laughs, and when he looks towards his left, he weeps."
Then he ascended with me until we reached the second heaven, and he (Jibreel) said to its gatekeeper, "Open (the gate)." The gatekeeper said the same thing that the gatekeeper of the first heaven had said, and then he opened the gate.

~*~*~*~*~*~

Muhammad met Prophets Yahya and 'Isa in the second heaven, Yusuf in the third, Idris in the fourth, Harun in the fifth and Musa in the sixth. He greeted them all and was greeted in return with the words,"Welcome! Righteous Prophet and righteous brother."
Then I went into the seventh heaven. There I passed by Ibrahim (who was resting against the side of the Baytul Ma'moor, the Ka'bah of the angels) and he said, "Welcome! Righteous Prophet and righteous son."
I asked Jibreel, "Who is that?"
"He is Ibrahim," Jibreel answered.
Then Jibreel showed Muhammad his true form, with 600 wings of such magnitude that one flap of his green wings completely covered the horizon.
Then he took me until we reached the Sidrat-il-Muntaha (the Tree of the Furthest Boundary), which was shrouded in colors I can hardly describe. Then (I was brought close) to the Baytul Ma'moor (in which 70,000 angels visit everyday), and three containers were offered to me. One contained wine; the other, milk and the third honey. I took the milk. Jibreel said, "This is the Islamic way of life, which you and your followers are following."

~*~*~*~*~*~

Then Jibreel led Muhammad into the place where the souls of those who lived on Earth were receiving their rewards and delights. He found it filled with walls of pearl, gardens and mansions, mountains of amber and fountains all around. Then he was brought near the power of Allah Himself. There he was plunged into the highest reality of all and saw the structure and essence of all existence. He could not fully describe in words what he saw of this part of his journey.

~*~*~*~*~*~

Then Jibreel ascended with me to a place where I heard the writing of the pens (recording the words of Allah's commands). There Allah commanded that my followers should pray 50 times a day. When I was returning (towards Earth) with this order of Allah, I passed by Musa, who asked me, "What has Allah commanded of your followers?"

I replied, "He commanded them to pray 50 prayers a day."

Musa said, "Go back to your Lord (and appeal for a reduction), because your followers won't be able to bear it. By Allah! I tested people before you, and I tried my best with Bani Isra'il (without success)."

(So I went back to Allah and requested a reduction) and He reduced it to half. When I passed by Musa again and informed him about it, he said, "Go back to your Lord, because your followers won't be able to bear it."

So I returned to Allah and requested a further reduction, and half of it was reduced. I again passed by Musa, and he said to me, "Return to your Lord, for your followers won't be able to bear it."

So I returned to Allah and He said, "These are five prayers, and they are all (equal to) 50 (in reward), for My Word does not change."

I returned to Musa, and he told me to go back once again. I replied, "Now I feel too shy to ask my Lord any further. I will just accept this and submit to Him." As I left, I heard a voice saying, "You have submitted to My command, and I have reduced the burden for My servants."

Muhammad was brought back to Makkah just before dawn.

~*~*~*~*~*~

In many other ahadith, the Blessed Prophet ﷺ recounted some of the wonderful things he saw in Paradise. Quite a few of these features of Paradise can be read about in the lesson entitled "What is Paradise." It's no wonder that the Companions, in later years, would describe the Prophet ﷺ speaking about the next life as if he were seeing it in front of him!

After the Blessed Prophet ﷺ announced in public what had happened to him, many of the idol-worshippers ridiculed him. They said he must have gone crazy, and some of the Muslims began to feel weak in their emaan. Everyone agreed that no one could travel to Jerusalem and back in a single night. Some of the weak-minded Muslims even gave up their faith altogether.

People went to Abu Bakr ﷺ and told him what was happening. He declared in front of everyone, "By Allah! If Muhammad himself has said it, then it is true. He tells us that the word of Allah comes to him directly from Heaven to Earth, at any hour of night or day, and we believe him. Isn't this a greater miracle than what we are doubting here today?"

Then Abu Bakr ﷺ, followed by many of the Muslims, went to the Prophet ﷺ and listened to his story directly. When the Prophet ﷺ finished describing Jerusalem and its streets and buildings, everyone who had ever been there knew that the description was accurate. It was also well known that Muhammad ﷺ had never been to Jerusalem.

Abu Bakr ﷺ, who had visited Jerusalem, many times, declared happily, "You speak the truth, Messenger of Allah." Then the Prophet ﷺ told of a caravan he saw on the road leading into Makkah. Sure enough, a few hours later, a caravan entered Makkah from the north, and when the travellers were questioned, the leaders described how they were led by a stranger to their lost animal in the desert. It was also found that one of their camels was carrying a water jar on its back that had a broken seal, further confirming Muhammad's ﷺ story. The Muslims were overjoyed, and their sense of wonder was heightened, leaving the idol-worshippers to mutter in disbelief among themselves.

The Day of Ta'if

After realizing that they couldn't break the spirit of the Muslims, the idol-worshippers began to show more boldness. It was bad enough that many of the Muslims had suffered beatings, insults and even death for their belief, but now the idol-worshippers were starting to make life unbearable for even those who had stronger family ties.

The Blessed Prophet ﷺ himself barely escaped when someone tried to strangle him while he was praying near the Ka'bah one afternoon. With the situation deteriorating, he knew that a place of safety was needed, or Muslims might be murdered in large numbers by the Makkans.

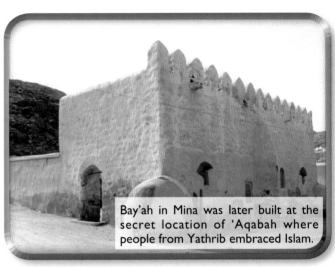

Bay'ah in Mina was later built at the secret location of 'Aqabah where people from Yathrib embraced Islam.

The Blessed Prophet ﷺ, accompanied by his adopted son Zayd bin Harithah ﷺ, traveled to the hilltop city **Ta'if** طائف, which was to the southwest of Makkah. There they met with some of the leaders of the local Thaqif tribe and asked them to consider accepting Islam. They refused to listen and ordered Muhammad ﷺ and Zayd to leave. Then they unleashed their unruly children upon the pair, inciting them to pelt them with stones as they left the city.

The Prophet ﷺ and Zayd ﷺ ran out of town, under a shower of rocks and debris. Just outside of the city, they found a small enclosed garden where they were able to rest. The owner of the garden felt so sorry for Muhammad ﷺ that he sent him a gift of some grapes.

The Prophet Muhammad ﷺ said, "O Allah! I complain to You of my weakness, my scarcity of resources and my humiliation before the people. O Most Merciful of those who are merciful. O Lord of the weak and my Lord too. To whom have you entrusted me? To a distant person who receives me with hostility? Or to an enemy to whom you have granted authority over my affair? So long as You are not angry with me, I do not care. Your favour is of more abundance to me. I seek refuge in the light of Your Face by which all darkness is dispelled and every affair of this world and the next is set right, lest Your anger or your displeasure descend upon me. I desire your pleasure and satisfaction until you are pleased. There is no power and no might except by You." (At-Tabarani)

قَالَ رَسُولُ اللهِ ﷺ : «"اللَّهُمَّ إِنِّي أَشْكُو إِلَيْكَ ضَعْفَ قُوَّتِي، وَقِلَّةَ حِيلَتِي وَهَوَانِي عَلَى النَّاسِ، يَا أَرْحَمَ الرَّاحِمِينَ، أَنْتَ رَبُّ الْمُسْتَضْعَفِينَ وَأَنْتَ رَبِّي، إِلَى مَنْ تَكِلُنِي؟ إِلَى بَعِيدٍ يَتَجَهَّمُنِي، أَمْ إِلَى عَدُوٍّ مَلَّكْتَهُ أَمْرِى؟ إِنْ لَمْ يَكُنْ بِكَ غَضَبٌ عَلَيَّ فَلَا أُبَالِي، وَلَكِنْ عَافِيَتَكَ أَوْسَعُ لِي مِنْ ذُنُوبِي، أَعُوذُ بِنُورِ وَجْهِكَ الَّذِي أَشْرَقَتْ لَهُ الظُّلُمَاتُ وَصَلُحَ عَلَيْهِ حَالُ الدُّنْيَا وَالآخِرَةِ، مِنْ أَنْ يَنْزِلَ عَلَيَّ غَضَبُكَ أَوْ يَحِلَّ بِي سَخَطُكَ، لَكَ الْعُتْبَى حَتَّى تَرْضَى، وَلَا حَوْلَ وَلَا قُوَّةَ إِلَّا بِكَ». رواه الطبراني

Angel Jibreel ﷺ came to the Prophet ﷺ and said he would destroy the entire city if he wanted him to. The Holy Prophet ﷺ declined the offer, explaining that he was sent as a guide and a mercy to people.

And We have not sent you but as mercy for all the worlds. Surat Al Anbiya' (The Prophets) 21:107

﴿وَمَآ أَرْسَلْنَٰكَ إِلَّا رَحْمَةً لِّلْعَٰلَمِينَ﴾ سُورَةُ الأَنْبِيَاء 21:107

Thereafter, the Blessed Prophet ﷺ prayed to Allah ﷻ and then returned home to Makkah from what he later termed "the most difficult day of my life."

A Light from the North

The situation was getting worse for the Prophet ﷺ. The idol-worshippers began attacking him personally and directing much of their anger at him. Once, while he was walking, one of the Makkans threw dirt on his head and insulted him. When the Prophet ﷺ returned home, his daughter Fatimah ﷺ began crying as she cleaned her father's hair and clothes. The Prophet ﷺ said, "Don't cry, Fatimah. Your father has Allah for a protector." Fatimah's ﷺ two older sisters,

Ruqaiyyah ﷛ and Um Kulthum ﷛, were now living at home again because their husbands were made to divorce them at the command of Abu Lahab. Her third sister, Zaynab ﷛, had a slightly better husband. He resisted the pressure to divorce his wife, an act that was encouraged to insult the family of the Prophet ﷺ.

For the next several months, the Blessed Prophet ﷺ traveled from tribe-to-tribe outside of Makkah, offering the teachings of Islam to them. A few people converted to Islam, but the tribes did not commit to anything.

One evening, Muhammad ﷺ learned of a small group of people who were visiting from Yathrib, a city far to the north of Makkah. When he learned the whereabouts of their camp, he waited until nightfall and headed quietly out of the city in that direction. When he reached their camp a few moments later, he approached the small group and began explaining the beliefs of Islam to them. The six people, who were all from Al Khazraj tribe, embraced Islam joyfully.

When the group returned to Yathrib, they spread the news about Islam. Yathrib was a cosmopolitan city with Jews, idol-worshipping Arabs and a few Christians, so the people were already exposed to many different ideas and were curious to know more.

The First Pledge of 'Aqaba

The following year, 12 people from Yathrib came to Makkah for the pilgrimage season. But they weren't there to worship the idols; they were there to see Muhammad ﷺ. In a secret location called 'Aqaba, the same 12 people embraced Islam and promised to obey the following six rules. They agreed to:
1. Not join partners with Allah ﷻ.
2. Not commit adultery.
3. Not steal.
4. Not kill their female children.
5. Not bring false charges.
6. Obey the Messenger of Allah, Muhammad ﷺ, in all that is good.

This was later known as the pledge of 'Aqaba. After the group made this promise, Prophet Muhammad ﷺ told them, "Whoever fulfills the pledge will be rewarded by entering Paradise after their death. Whoever neglects any part of it must be prepared to face Allah. He may forgive the person or He may not." (Al Bukhari)

قَالَ رَسُولُ اللهِ ﷺ : «فَمَنْ وَفَى مِنْكُمْ فَأَجْرُهُ عَلَى اللهِ، وَمَنْ أَصَابَ مِنْ ذَلِكَ شَيْئًا فَعُوقِبَ فِي الدُّنْيَا فَهُوَ كَفَّارَةٌ لَهُ، وَمَنْ أَصَابَ مِنْ ذَلِكَ شَيْئًا ثُمَّ سَتَرَهُ اللهُ، فَهُوَ إِلَى اللهِ إِنْ شَاءَ عَفَا عَنْهُ، وَإِنْ شَاءَ عَاقَبَهُ. فَبَايَعْنَاهُ عَلَى ذَلِكَ». رَوَاهُ الْبُخَارِيُّ

The Prophet ﷺ sent one of his trusted Companions, Mus'ab bin Umair ﷛, to Yathrib with the group. He was to teach them Islam and give the call to others in the city. As you will see, Mus'ab ﷛ was very successful.

The Second Pledge of 'Aqaba

The Prophet ﷺ and the Muslims in Makkah weathered the insults inflicted on them by the Makkans for yet another year. Then, in the thirteenth year of his Prophethood, a group representing the tribes of Al Aws and Al Khazraj of Yathrib came to the Prophet ﷺ.

This time 71 men and two women came to meet with the Blessed Prophet ﷺ. Meeting at the same, secret location, 'Aqaba, this large group declared that they were Muslims and asked the Prophet ﷺ to come with them back to Yathrib!

Just before the new Muslims took the oath of service to the Prophet ﷺ, the Prophet's uncle 'Abbas ﷛ told them, "You people of Al Aws and Al Khazraj! As you know, Muhammad has respect and status here due to his lineage. His family and friends have protected him from the idol-worshippers who wish to destroy him. He is one of the most respected among his people. He refuses to join anyone but you. If you think you can carry out what you have promised in inviting him to your city, and if you can defend him against his enemies, then the burden of proof rests in your hands. But if you're going to surrender him and abandon him after you've taken him with you, then you had better leave him here."

All the new Muslims promised to defend the Prophet ﷺ with their lives. This second oath is known as the Second Pledge of 'Aqaba. The people then returned to Yathrib with the instructions to be ready to act when necessary.

The Muslim Sanctuary

Although the meeting was held in secret, it didn't take long for the Makkan leaders to find out about it. They were angered that Islam was spreading despite all their best efforts to stamp it out. They resolved to increase their persecution of the Muslims. Although many of the less protected Muslims were still safe in Abyssinia, there were new people accepting Islam all the time. Thus, many new targets opened up for the idol-worshippers.

The Blessed Prophet ﷺ called yet another secret meeting in which he ordered his followers to prepare to leave Makkah for Yathrib. The plan was for people to leave in small groups by night, so the Makkans would suspect nothing.

Soon, Muslims were slipping out of Makkah every night and heading towards safety in Yathrib where they were welcomed by the Muslim community there. Islam was spreading rapidly, and there were now hundreds of Muslims in that city.

After most of the Muslims had escaped, only Muhammad ﷺ, Abu Bakr ﷺ, 'Ali ﷺ and a few others remained. When the Makkans discovered what was happening, they were livid. They also feared that Muhammad ﷺ might be able to raise an army in Yathrib to attack them.

The Makkans leaders held a meeting to discuss the situation. One of them proposed killing Muhammad ﷺ and ending the threat Islam posed to them once and for all. They asked that every family send one of its members to help kill Muhammad ﷺ. In this way it would be difficult for the Banu Hashim tribe to avenge his death.

As the Makkans were hatching their fiendish plot, Muhammad ﷺ received permission from Allah ﷻ to emigrate. He asked Abu Bakr ﷺ to have two camels ready for their escape. Later in the day, as he learned of the plot against his life, he hurried to Abu Bakr's ﷺ house and told him the time had come to move. They would leave that night. Muhammad ﷺ asked 'Ali ﷺ to return some money that was entrusted to him to its owners and to prepare to leave for Yathrib as well.

When half the night was over, Muhammad ﷺ left his house to begin his journey. As he came out of the house he threw some sand towards the men who were waiting to kill him and recited the following verse from Surat Ya-sin: *"And We have made before them a barrier and a barrier behind them, then We have covered them over so that they do not see."* (36:9) Allah ﷻ made Muhammad ﷺ invincible to those men and he was able to pass right in front of them!

Then, Muhammad ﷺ, Abu Bakr ﷺ and a Bedouin guide crept out of the city, heading south, in the direction opposite of Yathrib. Knowing of the plot against the Prophet's life, 'Ali ﷺ made a brave decision. He made it look as if Muhammad ﷺ was in his house, then lay on the bed, covered by sheets and the green robe the Prophet ﷺ often wore.

The hours passed and all was quiet. Then the group of young men entered the house secretly. The blades of their spears and swords glinted in the moonlight. They all knew there would be no one to protect Muhammad ﷺ now, and each one was eager to be the first to strike.

They filed into Muhammad's ﷺ bedroom and circled around his bed. One of them wanted to see just how surprised Muhammad ﷺ would be when he saw them in the moment before his death, so he pulled away the covers. Suddenly, all the men gasped in disbelief. There was 'Ali ﷺ, lying in the Prophet's ﷺ bed. It would have been of no use to kill 'Ali ﷺ, and they didn't have the permission of their elders to do so anyway. They stormed out of the house in disgust, sounding the alarm that Muhammad ﷺ had escaped. This was the story of Al Hijrah.

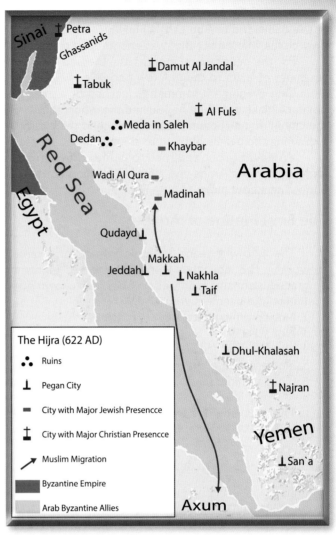

The Hijra (622 AD)

⁘ Ruins

⊥ Pegan City

▬ City with Major Jewish Presencce

⊥ City with Major Christian Presencce

↗ Muslim Migration

■ Byzantine Empire

Arab Byzantine Allies

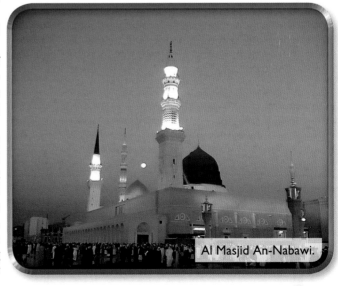

Al Masjid An-Nabawi.

Chapter 14
Islam Becomes a Nation

Al Hijrah and the Cave of Thawr

When the Makkans were alerted to Muhammad's ﷺ escape from death, they gathered together, shouting and cursing. The men who were supposed to kill Muhammad ﷺ the night before went out into the countryside in the hopes of capturing him. Meanwhile, Muhammad ﷺ and Abu Bakr ﷺ began Al Hijrah. They were guided to the cave of Thawr, a small cave south of the city. Although not many people knew about it, Abu Bakr's ﷺ trusty guide, 'Abdallah bin Urayqit, did. He left the pair there and took the camels away for hiding.

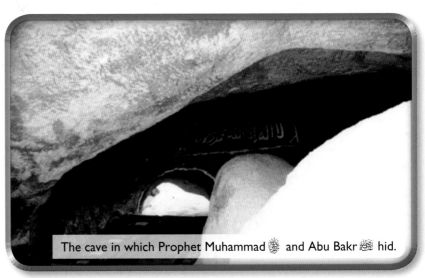
The cave in which Prophet Muhammad ﷺ and Abu Bakr ﷺ hid.

Only Abu Bakr's ﷺ two daughters, 'Aishah ﷺ and Asma' ﷺ, his son, 'Abdallah bin Abu Bakr ﷺ and a servant named Amir knew about the hide-out. During the day, 'Abdallah ﷺ would gather news of the Quraysh, and Asma' ﷺ would bring food to the cave. Amir, a servant, would graze a flock of sheep near the cave to cover up any tracks. Muhammad ﷺ and Abu Bakr ﷺ spent three long days in the cave hiding from the Makkans who were scouring the countryside hoping to redeem their failure. The Prophet ﷺ spent much of his time praying to Allah ﷻ to keep them safe and help them eventually reach Yathrib safely.

One afternoon, a group of Quraysh warriors came upon the cave and asked a shepherd nearby if he had seen anyone. The shepherd boy replied that he had not but that they might try looking in the cave. When he heard the shepherd's answer from his hiding spot, Abu Bakr ﷺ trembled and expected to be found. He retreated into a dark corner and remained motionless. Some of the Quraysh men climbed up the hillside to the cave's entrance but then came right back down the hill.

Their fellow warriors asked them why they didn't enter the cave. The men replied that there was an unbroken spider's web and a pigeon's nest in the entrance. No one could have entered the cave without having broken the web or causing the pigeons to fly away in fear.

Anas bin Malik reported that Abu Bakr Siddiq reported him thus: "I saw the feet of the polytheists very close to us as we were in the cave. I said, 'Allah's Messenger, if one amongst them were to see at his feet he would have surely seen us.' Thereupon he said, 'Abu Bakr, what can befall two who have Allah as the third One with them.'" (Al Bukhari)

حَدَّثَنَا أَنَسُ بْنُ مَالِكٍ: «أَنَّ أَبَا بَكْرٍ الصِّدِّيقَ، حَدَّثَهُ قَالَ: نَظَرْتُ إِلَى أَقْدَامِ الْمُشْرِكِينَ عَلَى رُءُوسِنَا وَنَحْنُ فِي الْغَارِ فَقُلْتُ يَا رَسُولَ اللهِ لَوْ أَنَّ أَحَدَهُمْ نَظَرَ إِلَى قَدَمَيْهِ أَبْصَرَنَا تَحْتَ قَدَمَيْهِ فَقَالَ: يَا أَبَا بَكْرٍ مَا ظَنُّكَ بِاثْنَيْنِ اللهُ ثَالِثُهُمَا». رَوَاهُ الْبُخَارِيُّ

The Prophet's ﷺ statement reminded Abu Bakr ﷺ that Allah ﷻ was with them as their Protector and that they should therefore not be afraid of others. The Makkans decided to head in another direction and left. Abu Bakr ﷺ exclaimed, "Al hamdulillah. Allahu Akbar."

The Journey to Yathrib

After the third day had passed with no success, the Makkans began to tire of their search. When 'Abdallah informed his father and the Prophet ﷺ about this, they decided to continue their journey. Abu Bakr's ﷺ servant brought three camels to the cave, and Asma' ﷺ came along with some bags of supplies.

There were no ropes for them to tie the bags together over the camels' backs, so Asma' ﷺ, thinking quickly, ripped the extra cloth of her dress-belt and twisted that into a temporary rope. After this, she was often called by the nickname **The Lady of The Two Belts** ذَاتُ النِّطَاقَيْنِ.

The guide led them through unknown tracks, heading toward the direction of Yathrib. He had to be careful because the Makkans leaders had now announced a reward of one hundred camels for anyone who would capture

Muhammad ﷺ. Given the value of camels in that society and time period, the reward was a very attractive opportunity for anyone with a sword.

A Makkan warrior by the name of Suraqa had heard reports about three people being seen in the southern hills. Suraqa figured the three people were Muhammad ﷺ and his Companions. In order to secure their capture, he told others that he knew those three, and therefore Muhammad ﷺ was not among them. Thus, he secretly set out a little while later in full battle gear, heading in the direction of the reported sighting.

Sure enough, after several hours of hard riding, he came within sight of the Prophet ﷺ and his group. Suraqa urged his horse faster, but it stumbled and fell, throwing him on his head. When he regained his mount and charged forward again, the horse stumbled once more, throwing him on his head again!

Suraqa was thrown much like this rodeo rider.

When he managed to get back into his saddle, he let loose a battle cry, and charged headlong at the three. But his horse stumbled a third time, throwing him on his head. Suraqa began to feel that there was an otherworldly force preventing him from charging, so he asked permission to approach Muhammad ﷺ. Suraqa introduced himself and promised that he would not tell anyone that he had found them. When Suraqa returned to Makkah, he kept his word and said he didn't find Muhammad ﷺ anywhere.

The Celebration in Quba

The Muslims in Yathrib were eagerly awaiting the news of Muhammad's ﷺ arrival. They heard the reports from Makkah about the unsuccessful plot to kill him and of the chase and the reward for his capture. The Prophet ﷺ was their teacher, friend and brother. If anything happened to him, they would be heart-broken. Everyone waited in anticipation.

A few days later, under the harsh summer sun, the three arrived at Quba, a small town just a few miles from Yathrib. The people of Quba were overjoyed at the arrival of the Prophet ﷺ and came out cheering and waving. A group of girls came singing a welcome song, "We are the girls of Banu Najjar, Oh what a wonderful neighbor is Holy Muhammad."

The Prophet ﷺ stayed in the town and rested for four days. The Muslims quickly dedicated the place for the first masjid there. During the Prophet's ﷺ stay, 'Ali ﷺ came walking in from the desert. He had returned all the money to its rightful owners as the Prophet ﷺ had directed him and then traveled on foot all the way from Makkah. The trip took about two weeks. 'Ali's ﷺ feet were bruised and bleeding, and the Prophet ﷺ used his own hands to care for him.

The Triumphant Entry Into Yathrib

After his rest in Quba, the Prophet ﷺ was ready to enter the city of Yathrib. The city also was eager to welcome him. It was a divided city that had known much war. The two largest groups, Al Aws and Al Khazraj tribes, had fought many wars in the past and were tired of warfare.

The Jews of the city were divided into three clans. They lived just outside of the city center, often competing with the idol-worshippers for power and status in local politics. The few foreigners, Persians, Christians and others, looked on with worry at the disunity and instability of the city's people. Everyone saw in Muhammad ﷺ a solution for the trouble.

Quba Masjid مَسْجِدُقِباء is the oldest mosque in the world.

As also We have sent in your midst a messenger from among you who recites to you Our verses and purifies you, and teaches you the Book and the wisdom, and teaches you what you did not know. *Surat Al Baqarah (The Cow) 2:151*

﴿كَمَآ أَرْسَلْنَا فِيكُمْ رَسُولًا مِّنكُمْ يَتْلُواْ عَلَيْكُمْ ءَايَٰتِنَا وَيُزَكِّيكُمْ وَيُعَلِّمُكُمُ ٱلْكِتَٰبَ وَٱلْحِكْمَةَ وَيُعَلِّمُكُم مَّا لَمْ تَكُونُواْ تَعْلَمُونَ﴾ سُورَةُ البَقَرَة 2:151

The day the Prophet ﷺ entered into the city was a day of celebration. Everyone came out and lined the streets to see the man they had heard so much about. The Muslims, both the recent Makkan immigrants and those of Yathrib, thanked Allah ﷻ and came to greet their trusted friend and guide.

The Prophet is closer to the believers than their own selves, and his wives are their mothers and those having mutual kinship are closer to one another (for the purpose of inheritance) than (other) believers and emigrants, according to the Book of Allah, unless you do some good to your friends (by making a will in their favor). This had been written in the Book (the Preserved Tablet). *Surat Al Ahzab (The Confederates) 33:6*

﴿ٱلنَّبِيُّ أَوْلَىٰ بِٱلْمُؤْمِنِينَ مِنْ أَنفُسِهِمْ وَأَزْوَٰجُهُۥٓ أُمَّهَٰتُهُمْ وَأُوْلُواْ ٱلْأَرْحَامِ بَعْضُهُمْ أَوْلَىٰ بِبَعْضٍ فِي كِتَٰبِ ٱللَّهِ مِنَ ٱلْمُؤْمِنِينَ وَٱلْمُهَٰجِرِينَ إِلَّآ أَن تَفْعَلُوٓاْ إِلَىٰٓ أَوْلِيَآئِكُم مَّعْرُوفًا كَانَ ذَٰلِكَ فِي ٱلْكِتَٰبِ مَسْطُورًا﴾ سُورَةُ الأحزاب 33:6

As the Prophet's ﷺ camel made its way through the crowds, the girls of Yathrib, not to be outdone by the girls of Quba, came out with a song of their own. From that day onward, the city was renamed **Madinat An-Nabi** مَدِينَةُ النَّبِيِّ the **City of the Prophet** ﷺ. It is now called only Al Madinah.

When he entered the city, everyone wanted the Prophet ﷺ to stay in their house as their honored guest. People started to argue and beg the Prophet ﷺ to stay with them. The leaders of the Bani Salem clan actually took hold of the reins of his camel and declared, "Messenger of Allah ﷺ! Come with us! We are the most numerous, best supplied and strongest."

The Blessed Prophet ﷺ, whose wisdom in similar circumstances was displayed so long ago in the dispute about the Black Stone, announced, "Let go of the camel. She is under Allah's command!" People came to understand that he was letting his camel choose where he would stay.

Everyone agreed with that wise solution, and the camel was let loose. It then started walking. After a few minutes, it sat down on a vacant lot owned by two orphans. Then, suddenly, the camel stood up again and walked in a circle. It passed in front of a nearby house, and then sat back down again in the vacant lot.

The orphans, Suhail and Sahl, who owned the land, came running and eagerly wanted to donate their land for the Prophet ﷺ. However, seeing that the pair were poor, the Prophet ﷺ insisted on paying them a fair price for the land. After the price was agreed upon, the community joined hands to build the masjid of the Prophet ﷺ. While the construction began, the Prophet ﷺ stayed in the house of Abu Ayyoub al Ansari ﷺ, as the camel had also hesitated by his door before moving on to the empty lot.

Abu Ayyoub's ﷺ home had two floors, and the bedroom was on the upper floor. Abu Ayyoub ﷺ insisted that the Prophet ﷺ sleep on the second floor, but the Prophet ﷺ only wanted to sleep somewhere on the first floor, making it easier to meet with people. Accordingly, Abu Ayyoub ﷺ cleared out a space.

طَلَعَ البَدْرُ عَلَيْنَا
The Full Moon Rose Over Us

طَلَعَ البَدْرُ عَلَيْنَا
Oh the Full Moon rose over us

مِنْ ثَنِيَّاتِ الوَدَاع
From the Valley of Al-Wada'

وَجَبَ الشُّكْرُ عَلَيْنَا
And we owe it to show gratefulness

مَا دَعَا لِلَّهِ دَاع
Where the call is to Allah

أَيُّهَا المَبْعُوثُ فِينَا
Oh you who were raised among us

جِئْتَ بِالأَمْرِ المُطَاع
Coming with a word to be obeyed

جِئْتَ شَرَّفْتَ المَدِينَة
You have brought to this city nobleness

مَرْحَبًا يَا خَيْرَ دَاع
Welcome best caller to God's way

That night, Abu Ayyoub and his wife were so worried that they couldn't get to sleep. They felt bad about sleeping above the Prophet ﷺ, and were afraid of coming between him and any wahi or revelation that might come down upon him. The next morning they told the Prophet ﷺ their fears, and begged him to sleep on the second floor. They explained that they would never want to sleep above the Messenger of Allah ﷺ. The Prophet ﷺ told them not to worry and that he preferred the first floor.

Then one night, Abu Ayyoub accidentally broke a jar full of water and it spilled all over the floor. He and his wife mopped up the water as fast as they could. They were afraid that some of it would leak through the floor, onto the Blessed Prophet ﷺ who was sleeping downstairs. The next morning they asked him if he had felt any dripping water in the night, and the Blessed Prophet ﷺ laughed and assured them he had not. Abu Ayyoub then again insisted that he wouldn't feel better unless they switched floors.

Finally, the Blessed Prophet ﷺ agreed to sleep on the second floor, and Abu Ayyoub and his wife were overjoyed. In later years, Abu Ayyoub said he never had a better and more pleasant sleep than when he was sleeping on the first floor, under the Messenger of Allah ﷺ.

The Prophet's ﷺ Masjid

The construction of the masjid took about seven months. It was a simple structure made of mud bricks, wooden poles and a roof made of palm leaves. It was large enough to accommodate a good-sized crowd. The Prophet's ﷺ new quarters were in a separate building, through which a doorway opened up into the main masjid area.

The Muslims of Al Madinah were made up of two groups: those who escaped Makkah, **Al Muhajirun** المُهاجِرون **The Immigrants**, and the native Muslims of the city, **Al Ansar** الأنصار **The Helpers**. Al Muhajirun were poor, given that they had escaped Makkah with little more than the clothes on their backs.

Abu Hurayrah reported that, "Allah's Messenger went out (of his house) one day or one night, and there he found Abu Bakr and 'Umar also. He said, 'What has brought you out of your houses at this hour?' They said, 'Allah's Messenger, it is hunger.' Thereupon he said, 'By Him in Whose Hand is my life, what has brought you out has brought me out too; get up.' They got up along with him and (all of them) came to the house of an Ansari, but he was not at home. When his wife saw him she said, 'Most welcome,' and Allah's Messenger said to her: 'Where is so and so?' She said, 'He has gone to get some fresh water for us.' When the Ansari came and he saw Allah's Messenger and his two Companions, he said, 'Praise be to Allah, no one has more honourable guests today than I (have).' He then went out and brought them a bunch of ripe dates, dry dates and fresh dates, and said, 'Eat some of them.' He then took hold of his long knife (for slaughtering a goat or a sheep). Allah's Messenger said to him: 'Beware of killing a milch animal.' He slaughtered a sheep for them and after they had eaten of it and of the bunch and drank, and when they had taken their fill and had been fully satisfied with the drink, Allah's Messenger said to Abu Bakr and Umar: 'By Him in Whose Hand is my life, you will certainly be questioned about this bounty on the Day of Judgement. Hunger brought you out of your house, then you did not return until this bounty came to you.'" (Muslim)

عَنْ أَبِي هُرَيْرَةَ، قَالَ: «خَرَجَ رَسُولُ اللهِ ذَاتَ يَوْمٍ أَوْ لَيْلَةٍ فَإِذَا هُوَ بِأَبِي بَكْرٍ وَعُمَرَ فَقَالَ: مَا أَخْرَجَكُمَا مِنْ بُيُوتِكُمَا هَذِهِ السَّاعَةَ. قَالَا: الْجُوعُ يَا رَسُولَ اللهِ. قَالَ: وَأَنَا وَالَّذِي نَفْسِي بِيَدِهِ لَأَخْرَجَنِي الَّذِي أَخْرَجَكُمَا. قُومُوا. فَقَامُوا مَعَهُ فَأَتَى رَجُلًا مِنَ الْأَنْصَارِ فَإِذَا هُوَ لَيْسَ فِي بَيْتِهِ فَلَمَّا رَأَتْهُ الْمَرْأَةُ قَالَتْ: مَرْحَبًا وَأَهْلًا. فَقَالَ لَهَا رَسُولُ اللهِ: أَيْنَ فُلَانٌ؟ قَالَتْ: ذَهَبَ يَسْتَعْذِبُ لَنَا مِنَ الْمَاءِ. إِذْ جَاءَ الْأَنْصَارِيُّ فَنَظَرَ إِلَى رَسُولِ اللهِ وَصَاحِبَيْهِ ثُمَّ قَالَ: الْحَمْدُ لِلهِ مَا أَحَدٌ الْيَوْمَ أَكْرَمَ أَضْيَافًا مِنِّي - قَالَ - فَانْطَلَقَ فَجَاءَهُمْ بِعِذْقٍ فِيهِ بُسْرٌ وَتَمْرٌ وَرُطَبٌ فَقَالَ: كُلُوا مِنْ هَذِهِ. وَأَخَذَ الْمُدْيَةَ فَقَالَ لَهُ رَسُولُ اللهِ: إِيَّاكَ وَالْحَلُوبَ. فَذَبَحَ لَهُمْ فَأَكَلُوا مِنَ الشَّاةِ وَمِنْ ذَلِكَ الْعِذْقِ وَشَرِبُوا فَلَمَّا أَنْ شَبِعُوا وَرَوُوا قَالَ رَسُولُ اللهِ لِأَبِي بَكْرٍ وَعُمَرَ: وَالَّذِي نَفْسِي بِيَدِهِ لَتُسْأَلُنَّ عَنْ هَذَا النَّعِيمِ يَوْمَ الْقِيَامَةِ أَخْرَجَكُمْ مِنْ بُيُوتِكُمُ الْجُوعُ ثُمَّ لَمْ تَرْجِعُوا حَتَّى أَصَابَكُمْ هَذَا النَّعِيمُ». رَوَاهُ مُسْلِمٌ

The condition of Al Muhajirun was very difficult. To ease their suffering, the Blessed Prophet ﷺ gathered the Muslims together and announced that the two parties would be joined together in brotherhood. Every **Ansar** أنصار (singular of Al Ansar) would adopt a **Muhajir** مُهاجِر (singular of Al Muhajirun) and share half their possessions with him or her. Al Ansar happily responded to the call, and soon every poor Muslim from Makkah was given the means to earn a livelihood. This built a strong bond of brotherhood in the hearts of the people and helped to alleviate the suffering of the poor.

Because housing was still in short supply, there was an area of the masjid reserved for the poorest Muslims. They could sleep there at night and rest for as long as they needed. The masjid was lit at night by burning torches. It was the special center where the community gathered to pray, talk, rest and meet.

The Prophet ﷺ as a Leader

Everyone agreed that the Prophet ﷺ was going to be the new leader of the city. Because the people of Al Madinah had trouble getting along, it was clear that the Blessed Prophet ﷺ represented the highest authority in the city. As the Muslim community grew, it became increasingly easier for the Muslims to organize themselves. In Al Madinah, Islam had found a home.

One of the first things the Prophet ﷺ did upon entering the city was to make a treaty of peace and friendship between the Muslims and the Jewish tribes. The Jews had welcomed the arrival of the Prophet ﷺ, as had everyone else, and had hopes he would join their religion.

The treaty spelled out the rights and responsibilities of both sides and was agreed to by both sides. The main points of the treaty were as follows:

1. Whoever either rebels or promotes disorder will be considered a common enemy to be fought by all.
2. Muslims and Jews must help defend each other against outside attackers.
3. Non-Muslims who live in Al Madinah will have rights of life and property.
4. Jews and Muslims will respect each other's rights and way of life.
5. No group can declare war against an outside enemy without the permission of the Prophet ﷺ.
6. In case of a war with outsiders, both Jews and Muslims will share the expenses of the battles.
7. No one will have the right to make any deals or treaties with the Makkans or their allies.

As you can see, the main points of the treaty were in the best interests of everyone in Al Madinah. In addition, the treaty also contained several explanations of the rights everyone would enjoy. Historians identify this treaty as effectively establishing the first Islamic state. The treaty has 63 articles.

The Prophet ﷺ also made a treaty with the Christians of Najran, a land in southern Arabia near the borders of Yemen. The treaty contained, among other things, the following main points:

1. Christians have rights to safe and secure property, and those rights will be respected by Muslims.
2. No churches will be harmed, nor will any monasteries be closed or priests bothered, nor will their religious symbols be harmed.
3. The Christians will not have to provide any supplies for the Muslim troops if there is a war with an enemy,
4. No Muslim will interfere in the practice of the Christians and their religion.

Finally, the Prophet ﷺ made a peace treaty with the Zoroastrians, who maintained a temple in eastern Arabia. The main points were that:

1. Zoroastrians will have their rights of life and property respected.
2. They can use whatever wells and pastures they choose.
3. Their temples will not be closed or bothered, and they have the right to practice their religion.
4. They will be defended in case of war and can continue the cultural practices that are part of their religion.

From these treaties, it is clear that one of the fundamental teachings of Islam is that people, both Muslims and non-Muslims, are entitled to many rights, a concept that the modern world has only recently acknowledged.

The truth of Allah ﷻ is clear to anyone who has eyes to see. If a person is not yet ready to listen to their heart and accept Islam, you can't force them to be a Muslim. Allah ﷻ declared in the Qur'an, *There is no compulsion in Faith. The correct way has become distinct from the erroneous. Now, whoever rejects the Taghut (the Rebel, the Satan) and believes in Allah has a firm grasp on the strongest ring that never breaks. Allah is All-Hearing, All-Knowing. Allah is the Protector of those who believe. He brings them out of the depths of darkness into the light. As for those who disbelieve, their friends are the Rebels. They bring them out from the light into the depths of darkness. Those are people of the Fire. There they will remain forever.*
Surat Al Baqarah (The Cow) 2:256-257

﴿لَآ إِكْرَاهَ فِى ٱلدِّينِ قَد تَّبَيَّنَ ٱلرُّشْدُ مِنَ ٱلْغَىِّ فَمَن يَكْفُرْ بِٱلطَّٰغُوتِ وَيُؤْمِنۢ بِٱللَّهِ فَقَدِ ٱسْتَمْسَكَ بِٱلْعُرْوَةِ ٱلْوُثْقَىٰ لَا ٱنفِصَامَ لَهَا وَٱللَّهُ سَمِيعٌ عَلِيمٌ﴾﴿ٱللَّهُ وَلِىُّ ٱلَّذِينَ
ءَامَنُوا۟ يُخْرِجُهُم مِّنَ ٱلظُّلُمَٰتِ إِلَى ٱلنُّورِ وَٱلَّذِينَ كَفَرُوٓا۟ أَوْلِيَآؤُهُمُ ٱلطَّٰغُوتُ يُخْرِجُونَهُم مِّنَ ٱلنُّورِ إِلَى ٱلظُّلُمَٰتِ أُو۟لَٰٓئِكَ أَصْحَٰبُ ٱلنَّارِ هُمْ فِيهَا خَٰلِدُونَ﴾ سُورَةُ ٱلْبَقَرَةِ

257-256:2

Islam Abolished Racism

Like almost every other aspect of Islam, its teachings concerning equality of all people were new to Arabia, and the world. Prior to Islam, racism was normal.

Arabs thought they were superior to non-Arabs, and light-skinned people looked down upon those who were dark. In addition, the Arabs believed that a person's importance descended from the lineage of their ancestors. For example, if a person belonged to a certain family, they considered themselves better than others.

Of course, it wasn't just a problem in Arabia. The entire world was covered in a cloud of racism. In China, people from the plains were considered subhuman. In India, there were four castes, or social groups, and the caste of priests, called "Brahmins," oppressed those below them. The problem also was pervasive in Europe and in North and South America. The Greeks called non-Greeks 'barbarians,' while the Aztecs thought that non-Aztecs were fit only for sacrifices to their gods. In the face of all this ignorance, the message of Islam stood out.

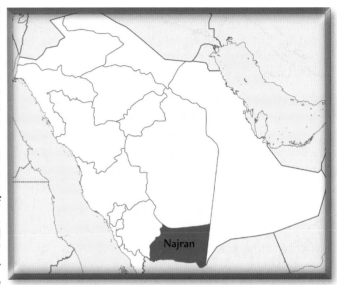

Najran

The Prophet ﷺ said, "You are all the children of Adam, and Adam was created from dust." (At-Tirmidhi)

قَالَ رَسُولُ الله ﷺ :«النَّاسُ بَنُو آدَمَ وَ آدَمُ مِنْ تُرَابٍ». رَوَاهُ التِّرْمِذِيّ

The Qur'an taught that the only real superiority of one person over another was in their taqwa (awareness of Allah ﷻ) and actions. Is the person a good person? Does he have good manners? Does he serve Allah ﷻ and perform good deeds? As Allah ﷻ declared, Oh Humanity! We created you from a single pair of a male and a female and made you into nations and groups so you can come to know each other. The noblest among you in the sight of Allah is the one with the most taqwa. Surely Allah is All-Knowing, All-Aware. Al Hujurat (The Dwellings) 49:13

﴿يَٰٓأَيُّهَا ٱلنَّاسُ إِنَّا خَلَقْنَٰكُم مِّن ذَكَرٍ وَأُنثَىٰ وَجَعَلْنَٰكُمْ شُعُوبًا وَقَبَآئِلَ لِتَعَارَفُوٓا۟ إِنَّ أَكْرَمَكُمْ عِندَ ٱللَّهِ أَتْقَىٰكُمْ إِنَّ ٱللَّهَ عَلِيمٌ خَبِيرٌ﴾ سُورَةُ ٱلْحُجُرَاتِ 49:13

The Blessed Prophet ﷺ put these teachings into practice from the earliest stages of his mission, embracing people of every color, race, and social status.

The Blessed Prophet ﷺ said, "There is no superiority of an Arab over a non-Arab or a non-Arab over an Arab. And there is no superiority of a white over a black or a black over a white, except with God-consciousness." (Ahmad)

قَالَ رَسُولُ الله ﷺ :«لَا فَضْلَ لِعَرَبِيٍّ عَلَى عَجَمِيٍّ، وَلَا لِعَجَمِيٍّ عَلَى عَرَبِيٍّ، وَلَا لِأَبْيَضَ عَلَى أَسْوَدَ، وَلَا لِأَسْوَدَ عَلَى أَبْيَضَ: إِلَّا بِالتَّقْوَى». رَوَاهُ أَحْمَد

Some of the non-Muslims were not pleased with these open and fair teachings. The Jews began to feel hostility towards the Muslims; they wanted to believe that Allah ﷻ sent prophets only to them. The idol-worshippers couldn't believe that a black person could be equal to an Arab.

But the Muslim community was living by the tenets of Islam, and therefore, men and women of all colors were living as brothers and sisters. Barakah was an African woman who had helped raise Muhammad ﷺ from birth and could be described as a motherly figure to him. The following story illustrates how the Prophet ﷺ worked to break down the barriers of racism.

The Blessed Prophet ﷺ went to an Arab family who had a daughter of marriage age. He asked them if their daughter would like to marry Bilal, who was of African descent. The family started offering excuses and indicated they would rather not have their daughter marry him.

The Prophet ﷺ then informed them, "Isn't it enough for you that Bilal is a man of Paradise?" When the family heard that, they realized that Allah﷼ doesn't care about color, so they shouldn't as well. They agreed, and the marriage took place soon afterwards.

In later years, there was a poor elderly black lady who used to go to the masjid and sweep it on her own. When she passed away, however, no one told the Prophet ﷺ. As he hadn't seen her in a while, he asked about her one day and was told that she passed away. He scolded the people for not telling him and immediately made supplications to Allah﷼ for her.

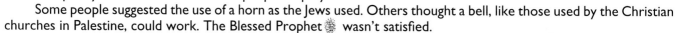

There is no superiority of a white over a black or a black over a white.

The Athan Is Called for the First Time

When the Prophet's masjid was being constructed, the Blessed Prophet ﷺ, who was over 50 years old at the time, helped lay out the bricks. Upon completion, the issue quickly arose of how to call the people to prayer.

Some people suggested the use of a horn as the Jews used. Others thought a bell, like those used by the Christian churches in Palestine, could work. The Blessed Prophet ﷺ wasn't satisfied.

Then Allah﷼ sent a dream to 'Abdallah bin Zayd, one of the Companions of the Prophet ﷺ. In it, he saw a man in a green robe who recited beautiful verses to him.

When he went to the Prophet ﷺ and told him what he had dreamt, the Prophet ﷺ declared that what he saw was a true dream from Allah﷼. The Prophet ﷺ was confident in this declaration, as Islam teaches that some dreams are given by Allah﷼ and accurately foretell the future.

So the Prophet ﷺ asked him to teach the words to Bilal﷼, who had a beautiful and strong voice. When the time came for the Salah, Bilal﷼ stood up on one of the walls of the masjid and called out in a loud and clear voice:

اللهُ أَكْبَرُ . اللهُ أَكْبَرُ

Allah is the Greatest. Allah is the Greatest.

اللهُ أَكْبَرُ . اللهُ أَكْبَرُ

Allah is the Greatest. Allah is the Greatest.

أَشْهَدُ أَنْ لا إِلَه إِلّا الله . أَشْهَدُ أَنْ لا إِلَه إِلّا الله

I bear witness that there is no God except Allah.

I bear witness that there is no God except Allah.

أَشْهَدُ أَنَّ مُحَمَّدًا رَسولُ الله . أَشْهَدُ أَنَّ مُحَمَّدًا رَسولُ الله

I bear witness that Muhammad is the Messenger of Allah

I bear witness that Muhammad is the Messenger of Allah

حَيَّ عَلى الصَّلاة . حَيَّ عَلى الصَّلاة

Hurry to the Prayer.

Hurry to the Prayer.

حَيَّ عَلى الفَلا ح . حَيَّ عَلى الفَلا ح

Hurry to Success.

Hurry to Success.

اللهُ أَكْبَرُ . اللهُ أَكْبَرُ

Allah is the Greatest. Allah is the Greatest.

لا إِلَه إِلّا الله

There is no God except Allah.

Everyone came running to the masjid from all quarters of Al Madinah to find out what was going on. 'Umar bin al Khattab﷼ rushed to the Prophet ﷺ and announced that he heard the exact same words in a dream the night before. From then on, the athan has been the way Muslims call each other to Salah. The Muslim call to prayer rejects the use of an artificial tool such as a horn, bell or drum and instead advocates the pure human voice.

The Community Grows

The Muslims were beginning to enjoy a measure of stable community life in Al Madinah. Islamic social and political teachings were implemented with wonderful results. By the second year of Al Hijrah, the duty of Zakah was announced, and this helped in relieving the needs of the poor.

At the same time, the believers were taught how they should behave in their personal lives. Neighbors should be kind to each other, the young should address the old with respect, and a husband and wife should be honest and faithful to each other.

Drinking intoxicants, such as wine, was soon forbidden, and collecting interest money on loans was outlawed. Other laws that were being revealed in the Qur'an included the rights of women and orphans, and laws related to marriage and divorce.

The Hostility of the Jews

Not everything was peaceful in Al Madinah. The three Jewish clans of **Qaynuqa'** قَيْنُقَا ع, **Quraytha** قُرَيْظَة and **Nadir** نَضِير began to regret inviting Prophet Muhammad ﷺ to the city. At first they thought well of him, but when they realized he was teaching a way of life that was vastly different from theirs, they became angry.

Islam taught that most of the Jews had diverged from the true teachings of the prophets of old. Furthermore, it proclaimed that Prophet 'Isa ﷺ, whom the Jews hated, was a prophet that had actually been sent to them. In addition, some Jews were leaving their religion and becoming Muslim. Even a rabbi, by the name of 'Abdallah bin Salam, accepted Islam, along with his whole family.

Why did the Jews begin to hate the message of Islam, when it was calling them to Allah ﷻ and affirming the truth of the prophets of old? Just as the idol-worshippers refused to give up their familiar customs, the Jews were also reluctant to give up their traditions no matter how false. Soon the leaders of the Jewish tribes began to meet among themselves and plan ways to disrupt the growth of Islam. They decided to send people to the Muslim community who would falsely announce their acceptance of Islam. This way, they would gain access to Muslim circles and sow confusion, raising doubt in people's minds.

The situation became very serious. One day, a Jewish man tried to rekindle the disagreements between Al Aws and Al Khazraj, which had otherwise been forgotten. The Prophet ﷺ rushed to the scene and repeatedly reminded the believers of their new bonds of brotherhood. Allah ﷻ revealed many ayaat during this period that explained to Muslims that they should be aware of this type of treachery. (5:78-82)

The Makkans Plot

The idol-worshippers in Makkah did not forget about the Muslims. They were still interested in doing away with Islam. They used many tricks to try to weaken or scare the Muslims. For example, they would periodically send out small raiding parties to attack the outskirts of Al Madinah.

If they were successful in capturing some Muslims, they would take them back to Makkah, where they would be tortured. In addition, the raiders would set fire to the crops and trees. This would destroy the Muslims' means of livelihood and cause havoc in their land. After a few months, the Prophet ﷺ organized small groups of Muslims to go on patrol and defend against these attacks.

The first battle began rather simply. Abu Sufyan, who was an avowed enemy of Islam, was leading a very large caravan of goods from Syria to Makkah. The caravan was said to have hundreds of camels and valuable goods, and was guarded by 30 or so Makkans.

The approaching caravan was expected to make its way through a city near Al Madinah called Badr. The Prophet ﷺ felt the caravan was a viable target for the Muslims to attack. Through such an attack, they could reclaim some of the losses they suffered when they were forced to leave all their possessions in Makkah to make Al Hijrah to Al Madinah. It would also help make up for the losses due to the raids of the Makkans on Al Madinah. So the Blessed Prophet ﷺ began to organize a group to go and capture the caravan.

Meanwhile, Abu Sufyan, was worried that the Muslims might try to make this attack. He sent a message ahead to Makkah, asking for an army to be raised to go and fight any Muslims in the area. The Makkans joyously agreed and marched out from the city with one thousand fighters, fully equipped and armored.

When the Prophet ﷺ received the news of the approaching Quraysh army, he called a meeting to do **Shura** شُوْرَى **Consultation**. The Prophet ﷺ was confident that his own tribesmen would be in support of the war, but he wanted to make sure Al Ansar, who had newly joined Islam, were also in favor. The response was overwhelmingly favorable, with Al Ansar stating that they would follow Allah's ﷻ Prophet ﷺ wherever he led them, remaining strong in their faith.

Thus, Allah's ﷻ Prophet ﷺ mobilized every fighter he could and left Al Madinah with only 313 men. Most of his army was comprised of Al Ansar. In addition, they had only 100 camels and horses to aid their army. With only one camel or horse for every three men, everyone, including the Prophet ﷺ, took turns riding.

The Prophet ﷺ knew the city called Badr had many wells and was a likely resting point for Abu Sufyan. It was 80 miles from Al Madinah. The Muslims marched there to wait in ambush around the wells. Abu Sufyan, anticipating their plan, took a route that circumvented Badr, and he headed safely to Makkah.

Abu Sufyan sent a message to the Makkans assuring them that his caravan was safe. However, Abu Jahl, another avowed enemy of Islam, urged the army to continue forward. At Abu Jahl's urging, the majority of the Makkans, 1,000 or more, headed for Badr. As they marched, they sang songs of their brave ancestors and the glory of battle.

The Battle of Badr

It has been narrated on the authority of 'Umar bin Al Khattab ﷺ who said, "When it was the day on which the Battle of Badr was fought, the Messenger of Allah ﷺ cast a glance at the infidels, and they were one thousand while his own Companions were three hundred and nineteen. The Holy Prophet turned (his face) towards the Qiblah then he stretched his hands and began his supplication to his Lord: 'O Allah, accomplish for me what Thou hast promised to me. O Allah, bring about what Thou hast promised to me. O Allah, if this small band of Muslims is destroyed. Thou will not be worshipped on this earth.'" (Muslim)

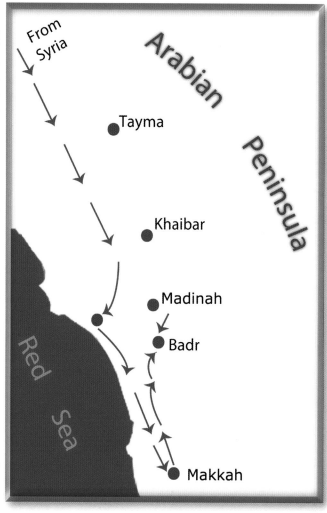

عَنْ عُمَرَ بْنُ الْخَطَّابِ ﷺ قَالَ: «لَمَّا كَانَ يَوْمُ بَدْرٍ نَظَرَ رَسُولُ اللهِ ﷺ إِلَى الْمُشْرِكِينَ وَهُمْ أَلْفٌ وَ أَصْحَابُهُ ثَلَاثُمِائَةٍ وَ تِسْعَةَ عَشَرَ رَجُلاً فَاسْتَقْبَلَ نَبِيُّ اللهِ الْقِبْلَةَ ثُمَّ مَدَّ يَدَيْهِ فَجَعَلَ يَهْتِفُ بِرَبِّهِ اللَّهُمَّ أَنْجِزْ لِي مَا وَعَدْتَنِي اللَّهُمَّ آتِ مَا وَعَدْتَنِي اللَّهُمَّ إِنْ تَهْلِكْ هَذِهِ الْعِصَابَةُ مِنْ أَهْلِ الإِسْلَامِ لاَ تُعْبَدْ فِي الأَرْضِ».

رَوَاهُ مُسْلِم

The Muslims dug a trench, which they would use as a source of protection for their army. They also filled all of the city's wells with sand, except the one closest to Makkah. This would force the Makkan army to engage in a battle with the Muslims, if they wanted to drink. The Muslims went to sleep that night, knowing a fierce fight with the idol-worshippers was awaiting them the next day.

The next morning, the Muslims found that Allah ﷻ had poured rain down from the skies over the night. This filled the trench with water, and offered another source of protection for the Muslims. The rain made the land under the approaching Makkans soft and difficult to tread. A lighter rain fell on the Muslims, which stiffened the sand and made it easier to run on.

A little while later, the Makkans came into sight—all 1,000 of them. As was customary, individual duels were called for by the Quraysh. Hamza, 'Ali, and 'Ubaydah bin al Harith ﷺ—all of whom were the Prophet's own relatives and from his clan, the Banu Hashim—were sent to fight in hand-to-hand combat against three Makkan champions: Shaybah bin Rabi'ah, 'Utbah bin Rabi'ah and Walid bin 'Utbah. In less than a few minutes, under the eyes of both armies, the three Muslims killed two of the three opponents. 'Ubaydah, who suffered an injury to his leg, later died as a result of his wound.

The enraged idol-worshippers rushed forward in a mad charge, and the two armies collided. It was the 17th of

Ramadan, in the year 624 CE, and the Muslims were fasting. They were also greatly outnumbered by the Makkans. But Allah﷾ heard and answered His Messenger's dua' by sending 1,000 angels to the battlefield to strengthen the physical and spiritual prowess of the Muslims.

The Fierce Fight

The fighting erupted all along the battle line. At first the idol-worshippers threatened to push the Muslims back, but the believers charged into battle without fear. They knew that a person who died fighting in the cause of Allah﷾ would be rewarded with Paradise, and so bodily injury mattered little.

Bilal﷜ spotted his old master, Umaya bin Khalaf, who used to torture him and roll heavy stones on his chest. Bilal uttered a fierce battle cry, charged straight towards him and killed him. A Sahaba by the name of Mu'ath bin 'Amr﷜ engaged Abu Jahl in combat and struck him down. Hamza and 'Ali﷜, along with other Muslims, plunged right into the middle of the idol-worshippers—not even noticing that they were outnumbered! The dust rose, and the battle raged as the Quraysh were struck down, one-by-one. The Muslims chanted, "Allah is One! Allah is One!" and pressed forward.

Prophet Muhammadﷺ stood in the middle of the battle, fighting as well. Once, when a large group of idol-worshippers were charging towards him, he took up a handful of dirt and threw it in their faces. Then, the Blessed Prophetﷺ commanded the Sahaba around him to stand their ground.

The Muslims stood firm and beat back the superior Makkan force. Many of the major leaders of the idol-worshippers were killed in the battle, including Abu Jahl. As the Makkans took note of their defeat, where nearly 70 died and another 70 captured, they turned around and began running away. The idol-worshippers were beaten. The survivors were filled with shame, and they returned to Makkah.

The Aftermath

The Muslims remained at Badr for the rest of the day. They buried the dead Makkans there and collected **Al Anfaal الأنفال Spoils of War** for later distribution. The Prophetﷺ distributed it equally amongst his people, which further increased his respect and loyalty among them.

The victorious Muslims returned to Al Madinah, and the people rejoiced. The prisoners that had been captured by the Muslims were ransomed, meaning that their families back in Makkah had to pay money to get them released. Some, who could not afford to pay the ransom fee, were allowed to go free after teaching 10 Muslims to read and write.

(Remember) when you sought help of your Lord, and He answered you (saying), "I will help you with a thousand of the angels, each behind the other (following one another) in succession." Allah made it only as glad tidings, and that your hearts be at rest therewith. And there is no victory except from Allah. Verily, Allah is All-Mighty, All-Wise. (Remember) when He covered you with a slumber as a security from Him, and He caused water (rain) to descend on you from the sky, to clean you thereby and to remove from you the rijz (whispering, evil-suggestions) of Shaytan (Satan), and to strengthen your hearts, and make your feet firm thereby. (Remember) when your Lord revealed to the angels, "Verily, I am with you, so keep firm those who have believed. I will cast terror into the hearts of those who have disbelieved, so strike them over the necks and smite over all their fingers and toes." This is because they defied and disobeyed Allah and His Messenger. And whoever defies and disobeys Allah and His Messenger, then verily, Allah is Severe in punishment. Surat Al Anfaal (The Spoils of War) 8:9-13

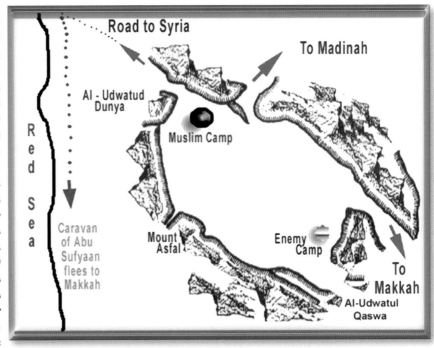

﴾إِذْ تَسْتَغِيثُونَ رَبَّكُمْ فَاسْتَجَابَ لَكُمْ أَنِّي مُمِدُّكُم بِأَلْفٍ مِّنَ الْمَلَـٰٓئِكَةِ مُرْدِفِينَ﴾ ﴿وَمَا جَعَلَهُ اللَّهُ إِلَّا بُشْرَىٰ وَلِتَطْمَئِنَّ بِهِۦ قُلُوبُكُمْ وَمَا النَّصْرُ إِلَّا مِنْ عِندِ اللَّهِ إِنَّ اللَّهَ عَزِيزٌ حَكِيمٌ﴾ ﴿إِذْ يُغَشِّيكُمُ النُّعَاسَ أَمَنَةً مِّنْهُ وَيُنَزِّلُ عَلَيْكُم مِّنَ السَّمَاءِ مَاءً لِّيُطَهِّرَكُم بِهِۦ وَيُذْهِبَ عَنكُمْ رِجْزَ الشَّيْطَـٰنِ وَلِيَرْبِطَ عَلَىٰ قُلُوبِكُمْ وَيُثَبِّتَ بِهِ الْأَقْدَامَ﴾ ﴿إِذْ يُوحِي رَبُّكَ إِلَى الْمَلَـٰٓئِكَةِ أَنِّي مَعَكُمْ فَثَبِّتُوا الَّذِينَ آمَنُوا سَأُلْقِي فِي قُلُوبِ الَّذِينَ كَفَرُوا الرُّعْبَ فَاضْرِبُوا فَوْقَ الْأَعْنَاقِ وَاضْرِبُوا مِنْهُمْ كُلَّ بَنَانٍ﴾ ﴿ذَٰلِكَ بِأَنَّهُمْ شَاقُّوا اللَّهَ وَرَسُولَهُ وَمَن يُشَاقِقِ اللَّهَ وَرَسُولَهُ فَإِنَّ اللَّهَ شَدِيدُ الْعِقَابِ﴾ سُورَةُ الأنفال 13-9:8

In the same year, the order came from Allah﷾ that Muslims should no longer pray towards Jerusalem, as they had been doing, but instead should pray towards the Ka'bah in Makkah. The actual ayaat were revealed during the time of prayer, and as the verses came to him, Prophet Muhammad ﷺ turned from the direction of Jerusalem in the west towards Makkah in the south. The masjid in which they were praying became known as the **Masjid Qiblatain** مَسْجِدُ القِبْلَتَيْن **Masjid of the Two Qiblas**.

We have been seeing you turning your face to the heavens. So, We will certainly assign to you a Qiblah that you would like. Now, turn your face in the direction of the Sacred Mosque (Al-Masjid-ul-Haram), and (O Muslims), wherever you are, turn your faces in its direction. Even those who have been given the Book know well that it is the truth from their Lord, and Allah is not unaware of what they do. Surat Al Baqarah (The Cow) 2:144

﴾قَدْ نَرَىٰ تَقَلُّبَ وَجْهِكَ فِي السَّمَاءِ فَلَنُوَلِّيَنَّكَ قِبْلَةً تَرْضَاهَا فَوَلِّ وَجْهَكَ شَطْرَ الْمَسْجِدِ الْحَرَامِ وَحَيْثُ مَا كُنتُمْ فَوَلُّوا وُجُوهَكُمْ شَطْرَهُ وَإِنَّ الَّذِينَ أُوتُوا الْكِتَابَ لَيَعْلَمُونَ أَنَّهُ الْحَقُّ مِن رَّبِّهِمْ وَمَا اللَّهُ بِغَافِلٍ عَمَّا يَعْمَلُونَ﴾ سُورَةُ البَقَرَة 144:2

This change signaled to the Muslims that their next great focus was to cleanse Makkah and the Ka'bah of all idol-worship. But as you will see, it wasn't going to be easily achieved.

Masjid Qiblatain or Masjid of the Two Qiblas.

Events in Al Madinah

The victory at the Battle of Badr secured the position of the Muslims more than ever. Everyday, people from various backgrounds in Al Madinah were announcing their acceptance of Islam. In addition, the Prophet ﷺ sent out many of his Companions to preach the religion to people wherever they went. More treaties were made with friendly tribes, giving the Muslims more confidence than they ever enjoyed before.

But this didn't mean that they were suddenly going to start living the easy life. They knew the real purpose of their lives and, therefore, didn't devote their time to merely getting rich and living the good life. Many of the new Muslims arriving included those who needed financial support, food or shelter. Other Muslims stepped forward and donated generously, often giving all they had.

Once, a poor woman came to 'Aishah ﷺ with her two hungry children. 'Aishah ﷺ gave only three dates to the mother and watched as the woman gave a date to each of her young ones. The children devoured them quickly but still complained of being hungry. The mother divided her last date in half and gave the pieces to her grateful kids.

Often, the Prophet ﷺ didn't have any food in his house. He would give away whatever he had to those who were in need, with little consideration for himself. His usual meal consisted of dates, barley and milk. He seldom ate meat, bread or other foods that were considered a luxury among the Muslims. He was a man who had looked into Paradise. He knew that the best way to please Allah ﷻ was in giving to others. The bonds of brotherhood grew firm, and the Muslims enjoyed the growth of a vibrant and rewarding community life. At the request of Abu Bakr ﷺ, the Prophet ﷺ married Hafsah ﷺ, the daughter of 'Umar bin al Khattab ﷺ. She was a recent widow—her husband had died in the Battle of Badr.

Sadly, one of the Prophet's ﷺ daughters, Ruqaiyyah ﷺ, passed away from illness. The Prophet ﷺ and 'Uthman bin Affan ﷺ, Ruqaiyyah's ﷺ husband, mourned her loss. Some time later, the Prophet's ﷺ other daughter, Um Kulthum ﷺ, married 'Uthman ﷺ, and his spirit was gladdened. In later years, people would give him the nickname, **The One with the Two Lights** ذُو النُّورَيْن, as he had been married to two of the Holy Prophet's ﷺ daughters.

The Prophet's ﷺ other daughter, Zaynab ﷺ, was still married to an idol-worshipper that had been captured in the Battle of Badr. The Prophet ﷺ eventually freed him upon his daughter's request. His mercy lead Abu Al 'As, Zaynab's ﷺ husband, to publicly declare his acceptance of Islam—right in front of the Quraysh! Once freed, he quickly returned to Al Madinah where he was reunited with Zaynab ﷺ. Life was nearly normal for the Muslims in Al Madinah.

The Showdown with the Banu Qaynuqa'

The Jewish clans were alarmed by the Muslim victory. They thought for sure that the Muslims would lose. They were now fully committed to their campaign opposing the Muslims and plotted against the new community whenever they could. One of the three Jewish tribes that lived within the city was the Banu Qaynuqa'. They had shouted, "Muhammad ﷺ is dead!" at the top of their lungs even while the Muslims were rejoicing at the news of the victory at Badr. They were bitter and hated to see the power of the Muslims growing.

One day, a fight erupted between a Jewish shopkeeper and a Muslim man after the shopkeeper played a trick on a woman by tearing her cover off. The two men were both killed in the fight and a street battle broke out between the Jews and Muslims. When the dust settled, the Prophet ﷺ arrived on the scene and saw the turmoil that had occurred. He appealed to the leaders of the Banu Qaynuqa' to respect the terms of the treaty they signed. They ridiculed him, saying, "Muhammad ﷺ! Don't think you are invincible. The people you fought (at Badr) were not good fighters. We are not the Makkans who ran away. If you were to turn your army against us, you would find us really skilled at war."

After that public challenge, the Muslims had no choice but to fight the Banu Qaynuqa'. The Muslims surrounded the neighborhood and maintained a blockade for 15 days. The Jews of the Banu Qaynuqa' finally had to surrender. Some time later, the Prophet ﷺ decided to forgive their treachery and rebelliousness. He ordered that they could all go free, provided they left Al Madinah. The Banu Qaynuqa' gathered themselves and their property and headed northwards, eventually settling near the border of Syria. One internal enemy was peacefully vanquished, and the Muslims breathed easier.

The Makkans Want Revenge

The Makkans were filled with bitterness at their losses at Badr. Poets recited verses calling for revenge; Jewish leaders from Al Madinah came to comfort the Makkans, and Hind—the daughter of 'Utbah bin Rabi'ah, the sister of Walid bin Utba and the niece of Shaybah bin Rabi'ah, who were all killed at Badr battle—called for a new attack. Her husband, Abu Sufyan, vowed to take revenge. At Badr, 11 of his 14 fellow leaders were killed as he saw to the safe return of the caravan.

He wanted to show that he was a warrior as well. A few months later, Abu Sufyan secretly led 200 armed men to Al Madinah. They attacked a small orchard in the middle of the night, killing two people they found there. When the alarm was raised, the Muslims gave chase, but the Makkans were too far ahead to engage. To help in their speedy escape, the Makkans began dropping their supplies as they galloped. And so, the raid was called the Flour Battle after the bags of flour the enemy dropped.

This raid had the opposite effect of what Abu Sufyan intended. Since the damage was so light, people started saying that the Quraysh were weak and that they ran away in the night. Soon, the Arab tribes that controlled the coastal roads to Syria were won over to the Muslim side and agreed to peace treaties. This loss of their trade routes northward angered the Quraysh even further.

The Makkans resolved to fight the Muslims again and raised money and supplies for months until they were ready. 'Abbas, the uncle of the Prophet ﷺ, still lived in Makkah. He sent a secret note informing the Prophet ﷺ of the Makkans' plans. Thus, the Prophet ﷺ began preparations of his own.

The idol-worshipping Makkans soon formed an alliance of tribes and marched out of Makkah with an army of 3,000 men. Many Makkan women came along as a way to bolster the spirits of the men. The Prophet ﷺ marched out of Al Madinah with an army of 1,000 warriors, and a few Muslim women who would serve as doctors and nurses. The two armies met on the far side of Mount Uhud, to the north of Al Madinah.

The Battle Begins

Before reaching the place designated for the combat, the Prophet ﷺ noticed something strange. Some of his men, who were under the command of a man named 'Abdallah bin Ubayy, didn't look like any Muslims he knew. When he asked, the Prophet ﷺ found out that they were Jewish friends of Ibn Ubayy. The Prophet ﷺ explained that they could only join the fight if they became Muslims. The Jews refused, and so the Prophet ﷺ ordered them to return home. Ibn Ubayy, who was a known **Hypocrite مُنافِق**, decided to take all his men home, just as the Prophet ﷺ began to arrange the men in their battle positions. (6:25)

When he left, he took 300 men with him. The remaining 700 Muslims felt discouraged when they saw the army of 3,000 men marching towards them. (3:173) The Prophet ﷺ ordered 50 archers to stand guard on a hill to watch a narrow pass through which the enemy might try a sneak attack. The archers were ordered not to move under any circumstances. The position of the Muslims was good and the men were ready. The Prophet ﷺ raised his own sword in the air and declared that anyone could have it if they fulfilled one condition. A man named Abu Dujanah came forward and asked what he had to do.

The Prophet ﷺ replied, "Strike the enemy with it until it breaks." Abu Dujanah happily agreed, and tied a red scarf around his head, which was his way of saying he would fight to the death. After he took the sword, he started to dance for joy in between the two rows of the fighters. This was always his custom before entering battle. When the Prophet ﷺ saw him performing his dance, he remarked that "This would be hateful to Allah, except under these circumstances."

The individual duels began between the two armies. The three Muslim champions, Hamza, 'Ali and Abu Dujanah ﷺ, easily beat their Makkan opponents. A mob of enraged idol-worshippers charged forward, as their women threatened to ignore them if they lost. The Makkans crashed upon the Muslim lines like a tidal wave. The Muslims fell back but fought fiercely. The Muslims in the back rows were shooting arrows as fast as they could into the charging warriors but could barely keep up.

Small groups of Makkans charged together at different places to break the Muslim formations but were unsuccessful. Finally, Hamza ﷺ shouted a fierce battle cry, "Die! Die!" and plowed right into the middle of the idol-worshippers. 'Ali ﷺ struck down the Makkans's flag-bearer and the Muslims shouted, "Allahu Akbar!" and advanced forward. Abu Dujanah saw one Makkan fighting a Muslim with his fingernails. As he drew closer to deal with the attacker, he discovered that it was Hind, the wife of Abu Sufyan. He moved away, knowing the Prophet ﷺ would never have approved of shedding the blood of a woman.

Hamza ﷺ, meanwhile, was leading a column of Muslims, and nearly broke through the ranks of the enemy. Then an Abyssinian slave by the name of Wahshi came out of nowhere and struck down Hamza ﷺ with a javelin throw. Hind had promised him his freedom if he slew the man who killed her father.

When the Muslims saw that Hamza had fallen, they fought even harder. A group of Muslims broke through to the enemy's rear, and even the Makkans' idol, brought with them for luck, had fallen off its camel and lay broken in pieces. The Makkans began to retreat and run from the battlefield as the Muslims shouted their battle cries. The panicked idol-worshippers were dropping their swords and running without thought of their goods or camp.

Some of the Muslims halted and, instead of pursuing the idol-worshippers, began grabbing Al Anfaal from the fallen enemies. When the archers, who were stationed on the hill, saw this, they wanted to run down to go and get the loot. (3:149-152)

Although their commander ordered them to stand their ground, all of them left except 10. The Makkan cavalry, under the command of Khalid bin Walid, saw the opportunity and rushed through the pass, attacking the Muslims from behind. The few archers left on the hill were killed. (3:153)

Makkan cavalry seized the high ground once Muslim bowmen left it for the booty on the plains.

The Muslims turned and panicked at the unexpected threat, and the fleeing idol-worshippers turned back and attacked again. The Muslims were caught between two forces! In the confusion, the Prophet was wounded by a strike to the mouth and had to be helped back to Mount Uhud. (3:153, 172)

The idol-worshippers attacked the Prophet and those who stood by him. Um Amarah, a Muslim woman who had come along to nurse the wounded, saw the Prophet under attack and rushed to where he stood, firing arrows at the advancing Makkans. With the last of her arrows gone, she slashed and struck at the attackers with a sword until she herself sustained many wounds. In later years, the Prophet would remark that no one had done any better than what Um Amarah had done that day.

Many of the Muslims panicked when they thought the Prophet had been killed. Many turned and ran for their lives. Other Muslims, who saw the Prophet climbing the mountain under fierce attack by the Makkans, rallied the rest of the Muslims and moved in that direction. The Muslims retreated to the side of Mount Uhud and began climbing higher. Here they were able to make a stand and hold off the Makkans. Fatimah, along with 'Ali, quickly rushed to her father and helped to treat the wound he suffered on his face.

The Aftermath

The Makkans proceeded to comb the battlefield for Muhammad. They wanted him dead and looked for him frantically. In the pause, most of the Muslim soldiers were able to escape up the mountain and join the Muslim defenses there. One Makkan group came forward and called up to the Muslims, "Where is Muhammad?! Death to me if he lives!"

The Prophet grabbed a javelin and threw it at the advancing group. It struck the man who was standing next to the leader. The Makkans made repeated assaults up the hillside, but couldn't break through the Muslim battle line. By noon that day, both sides were so exhausted that the fighting subsided.

Meanwhile, the Makkan women, led by Hind, had rushed onto the battlefield and were starting to mutilate the dead Muslim soldiers. They cut off the ears and noses of the dead, and when Hind found Hamza's body, she cut it open and chewed on his liver. The Muslims returned to Al Madinah, while the Makkans retired to their camp and celebrated. The next morning, the Prophet assembled his army and marched out to meet the idol-worshippers again.

Abu Sufyan learned of the march of the Muslim army and couldn't believe it. He sent a message to the Muslims that he would fight them again. However, he told his fellow leaders and allies that because the Makkans lost more men than the Muslims, it might not be a good idea. The Prophet waited with his army at Uhud for three days and nights, lighting huge bon-fires to let the Makkans know of their position and numbers. Abu Sufyan decided against taking another chance with the Muslims and withdrew to Makkah, claiming his one day of half-victory.

The main lesson of Uhud for the Muslims was the importance of obeying their commander, the Prophet. Although the Muslims didn't lose the battle outright, they did lose the chance for another stunning victory. The Jews and the hypocrites were elated by the setback.

Reactions after Uhud

Allah revealed many ayaat explaining to the Muslims why they did not win an outright victory at Uhud. They had been too concerned with worldly wealth; they disobeyed orders and were shaken when some thought the Prophet was killed. This reawakened the Muslims' sense of duty and many asked Allah for forgiveness.

The hypocrites told the Muslims that no one would have died if they had declined to fight like they had done. But Allah answered them saying: *How is it that, when you suffered a hardship the twice of which you had inflicted upon them, you say, "Where did this come from?" Say, "This is from your own selves. Allah is surely Powerful over everything."* Surat Al 'Imran (The Family of 'Imran) 3:165

﴿أَوَلَمَّآ أَصَـٰبَتْكُم مُّصِيبَةٌ قَدْ أَصَبْتُم مِّثْلَيْهَا قُلْتُمْ أَنَّىٰ هَـٰذَا قُلْ هُوَ مِنْ عِندِ أَنفُسِكُمْ إِنَّ ٱللَّهَ عَلَىٰ كُلِّ شَىْءٍ قَدِيرٌ﴾ سُورَةُ آلِ عِمْرَان 3:165

The ones who said about their killed brethren while they themselves sat (at home), "If only they had listened to us, they would not have been killed." Say, "Avert death from your own selves, if you speak the truth." Think not of those who are killed in the Way of Allah as dead. Nay, they are alive, with their Lord, and they have provision. They rejoice in what Allah has bestowed upon them of His Bounty. Rejoice for the sake of those who have not yet joined them, but are left behind (not yet martyred) that on them no fear shall come, nor shall they grieve. Surat Al 'Imran (The Family of 'Imran) 3:168-170

﴿ٱلَّذِينَ قَالُوا لِإِخْوَٰنِهِمْ وَقَعَدُوا لَوْ أَطَاعُونَا مَا قُتِلُوا قُلْ فَٱدْرَءُوا عَنْ أَنفُسِكُمُ ٱلْمَوْتَ إِن كُنتُمْ صَـٰدِقِينَ﴾ ﴿وَلَا تَحْسَبَنَّ ٱلَّذِينَ قُتِلُوا فِى سَبِيلِ ٱللَّهِ أَمْوَٰتًا بَلْ أَحْيَاءٌ عِندَ رَبِّهِمْ يُرْزَقُونَ﴾ ﴿فَرِحِينَ بِمَآ ءَاتَىٰهُمُ ٱللَّهُ مِن فَضْلِهِ وَيَسْتَبْشِرُونَ بِٱلَّذِينَ لَمْ يَلْحَقُوا بِهِم مِّنْ خَلْفِهِمْ أَلَّا خَوْفٌ عَلَيْهِمْ وَلَا هُمْ يَحْزَنُونَ﴾

سُورَةُ آلِ عِمْرَان 3:168-170

In these and other ayaat, Allah clearly stated that no one can save themselves from death, even if they sit at home. No one will live forever, so if a person goes out and strives in Allah's cause, then he will receive the best reward in the next life.

Dangers Grow

The Arab tribes living in the outer areas felt more confident because the Muslims showed their vulnerability in the battle of Uhud. The chief of the Banu 'Amr tribe, Abu Bur'a, came to Al Madinah and proclaimed that he would allow the preaching of Islam in his lands. Before returning to his people, he asked the Prophet to send some Muslim teachers with him to explain Islam to his tribe.

The Prophet sent 70 of his followers with Abu Bur'a. Upon arriving at a place called Bir Ma'unah, the Muslims were surrounded and killed by tribesmen of the Banu 'Amr. Only one Muslim was able to escape the betrayal by pretending to be dead. He returned to Al Madinah and told the Prophet about the massacre. The Muslims grieved for their lost Companions.

The same thing happened to six teachers who were sent to the Al Kada tribe. Four were killed, and two were sold as slaves to the Makkans. One of these men, Khubeyb, was bought by the family of Harith, a Makkan who had been killed in the Battle of Badr.

The members of the clan gathered around Khubeyb to take their revenge, but just before they executed him, he asked to be allowed to make a two-rak'aat prayer. They allowed him that and when he had finished, he declared, "I am dying as a Muslim. I don't care if my headless body drops to the right or left. Why should I? My death is in the way of Allah. If He wills, He can bless every part of my damaged body."

The second prisoner, a man named Zayd, was on his way to be executed when Abu Sufyan called out to him, "Wouldn't you rather be safe at home, and Muhammad was in our hands instead?" Zayd answered, "What, Abu Sufyan? What are you saying? I would rather die than have the Prophet's foot tread upon a thorn in the streets of Al Madinah."

Abu Sufyan remarked, as he watched the execution, "The gods be my witness. I have never known anyone to show love, as do the Companions towards Muhammad." When the Muslims heard of the executions of Khubeyb and Zayd by the Makkans, they were filled with sadness. A Muslim poet by the name of Hassan bin Thabit composed a poem in their honor and called to the Muslims to remember their brave examples.

The climate for Muslims was becoming dangerously uncertain in some regions. The Makkans were sending messages to other tribes, encouraging them to attack Muslims wherever they found them. For a time, it appeared as if peace was only a far-off dream.

The Conflict with the Banu Nadir

If you will remember, the Banu Qaynuqa' clan of Jews was expelled from Al Madinah after they publicly challenged the Muslims and displayed disloyalty. They failed to honor the letter or spirit of the treaty they signed and instead worked for disunity and chaos in the city. They left Arabia shortly after their expulsion. (5:61-64)

Banu Nadir بَنو نَضِير, one of the two remaining Jewish clans, then took up the cause of fighting against Islam. They were close allies of the hypocrites in Al Madinah, who had become Muslims only because it seemed advantageous for them to do so. They had no faith in Allah or His Prophet , and tried to subtly confuse the Muslims around them. An example was when one of their leaders, Ibn Ubayy, left the battlefield of Uhud with 300 of his men, when the Muslims needed them the most.

The leaders of the Banu Nadir were particularly interested in the fall of Islam, and they began to make plans to kill Prophet Muhammad . But the Muslims learned of this plot. The Prophet sent a message ordering them to leave the area of Al Madinah. This was their punishment for violating the treaty by attempting to kill him and by making secret deals with the enemies of Islam.

The leaders of the Banu Nadir met together to decide what to do. Some wanted to leave, but then a message came from the leader of the hypocrites, Ibn Ubayy. He told them to stay on their land, and that he would come and fight with them, bringing 2,000 fighters. After agreeing not to give up their rich farms, the Banu Nadir decided to stay and fight the Muslims. Ten days later, the battles began throughout Al Madinah. The Banu Nadir barricaded themselves in their section outside of town, and they had plenty of supplies on hand for war. For 20 days, the Muslims and Jews fought street battles even in bad weather conditions.

Finally, the Blessed Prophet ordered that all the date-palms in the orchards outside of Al Madinah should be cut down. Though Islam generally discourages inflicting harm on trees during war, special permission was given in this case because the Jews were fighting in order to keep their rich farmland. (59:1-5)

When they saw their destroyed orchards, the Banu Nadir knew there was nothing left worth fighting for. In addition, the promised help of Ibn Ubayy never came. He backed out of a fight again! The Banu Nadir agreed to surrender to the Muslims on the condition that they would be allowed to leave the city safely.

The Prophet let them leave, allowing each person to take three camel-loads of goods with them. The Banu Nadir left Al Madinah and headed north to Syria. Many, however, went to live in the Jewish fortress city of Khaybar, a three-day journey from Al Madinah. The Banu Quraytha was the last Jewish clan remaining in the city.

The Muslims came into possession of much land, goods and supplies when the Banu Nadir left. The Blessed Prophet distributed Al Anfaal among Al Muhajirun so that they would no longer have to depend on the support of Al Ansar. So yet another enemy of peace was successfully forced to leave Al Madinah. The Muslims rejoiced, and their prestige rose in the eyes of the Arab tribes around them.

The rich lands of the Banu Nadir.

The Makkans Build Their Strength

Abu Sufyan and the other leaders of Makkah were concerned that Muslim power was growing again. After the defeat of the Banu Nadir, and other minor victories with hostile Arab tribes, the Makkans resolved to attack the Muslims again. A delegation consisting of the senior leaders of the Banu Nadir arrived from Khaybar. Most of the Banu Nadir had moved in with the Jews of Khaybar after they were forced to leave Al Madinah. However, they were determined to take revenge against the Muslims. The delegation met with the leaders of Makkah and urged them to attack the Muslims in Al Madinah. The Makkans listened intently, as they were still very much hostile towards Islam.

The idol-worshippers were a little puzzled, however, that the Jews were coming to them, asking them to attack the Muslims. After all, the Jews claimed to believe in One God, the same as the followers of Islam. The Makkans then asked the Jews if they thought that idol-worship, as they practiced it, was better than Islam.

The Jews answered that the idol-worshipping of the Makkans was better than the Muslim's belief in the One God. Thus, they demonstrated their rebelliousness against Allah yet again, by saying idol-worship was better than **Monotheism التَّوحِيد Belief in only One God.** Allah later revealed an ayah condemning the Jews for declaring that idolatry was superior to true faith in God alone.

Have you not seen those who were given a portion of the Scripture, who believe in superstition and false objects of worship and say about the disbelievers, "These are better guided than the believers as to the way?" Those are the ones whom Allah has cursed, and he whom Allah curses never will you find for him a helper. Surat An-Nisa' (The Women) 4: 51-52

﴿أَلَمْ تَرَ إِلَى ٱلَّذِينَ أُوتُوا۟ نَصِيبًا مِّنَ ٱلْكِتَبِ يُؤْمِنُونَ بِٱلْجِبْتِ وَ ٱلطَّغُوتِ وَ يَقُولُونَ لِلَّذِينَ كَفَرُوا۟ هَٰؤُلَآءِ أَهْدَىٰ مِنَ ٱلَّذِينَ ءَامَنُوا۟ سَبِيلًا﴾﴿أُو۟لَٰٓئِكَ ٱلَّذِينَ لَعَنَهُمُ ٱللَّهُ وَمَن يَلْعَنِ ٱللَّهُ فَلَن تَجِدَ لَهُۥ نَصِيرًا﴾ سُورَةُ ٱلنِّسَاء 4:51-52

The plans were made after several more trips to and from Khaybar and Makkah. The Makkans would rally an army drawn from all the surrounding cities and towns, while the Banu Nadir and their allies would be waiting to attack the Muslims from behind. Under the leadership of Huyayy bin Akhtab, the Jews sent messages to hostile Arab tribes in central and northern Arabia, seeking their support against the Muslims. They even made a promise to the large tribe of Ghatafan for a whole year's worth of the harvest from the orchards of Al Madinah, if they defeated the Muslims.

When the time came to march, the idol-worshippers assembled an army of over 10,000 warriors, all fully equipped and armed for battle. This vast force, never seen before in Arabia, marched towards the unsuspecting Muslims.

The Defense Strategy

When word of the huge mobilization of idol-worshippers reached Al Madinah, the Muslims were struck with fear and panic. There had never been an army that large in Arabia before. How could the Muslims hope to win against such an immense number of men, horses and war machinery?

The Prophet called a shura, gathering the Muslim leaders to discuss a strategy. Meeting the approaching army outside of the city was out of the question this time. The available Muslim warriors were ill-equipped and barely numbered 3,000.

One of the Sahaba, a skilled strategist named Salman al Faresi, suggested a unique plan. He was from Persia and knew how wars could be waged between large armies. He suggested that they dig a **Khandaq خَنْدَق Trench**, around the exposed areas of Al Madinah while fortifying the city walls into thick barriers. With mountains encircling a good portion of the city, the main defenses could be directed towards only one side.

The one weak spot was the eastern side of the city, where the Banu Quraytha lived. But they had a fortress that the idol-worshippers were unlikely to attack. They also had a treaty with the Muslims that they still appeared to be honoring. The Prophet agreed with this plan, and work began at once. The Muslims were divided into crews, and everyone participated in the defense construction. Some were given the job of building and joining walls together, while others were positioned in the front of the city, digging the enormous trench.

The Prophet himself was digging with the people. The Muslims sang songs as they worked to keep up their spirits. After many days of hard labor, the Muslims had completed a six-foot deep trench that was nearly eight feet across. The hastily-built trench was dug on the northern edge of the city. When the project was done, the weary Muslims divided into defense units and were stationed around the city and the trench. There they awaited the arrival of a menacing army.

The Attack Begins

The huge idol-worshipping army first arrived at Uhud, hoping to meet the Muslims there. However, when they found the area empty, the leaders of the horde directed their troops toward Al Madinah. Imagine how the Muslims felt, seeing the huge army advancing in the distance. It was so large that it seemed to advance from all directions. Men, horses and camels seemed to pour endlessly into the plain just outside the city.

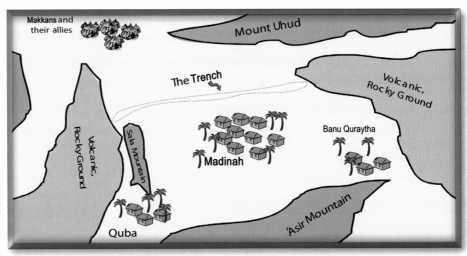

The horde assembled, beating war drums and chanting battle cries. Muslim men and women looked on from their posts and knew the time for war had come. If they lost, they would all be killed or sold into slavery. The tribal leaders were about to order an all out assault on the city when they noticed the huge trench dug around the front of the city's walls. They became confused. They had no idea what this trench meant; it was an unknown strategy in the Arabian peninsula.

As they slowly approached the trench, they realized it was too wide for horses to jump over. Slowly, they came to the realization that the trench was a distraction and a trap. As soon as they backed away, they were attacked by a wave of arrows from the Muslims. They cursed them, and, after a few small assaults, were beaten back by Muslim archers. The idol-worshippers were resigned to make camp and prepare for a long siege.

The Siege of Al Madinah

It was winter, and cold winds blew over the desert at night. The Muslims were safe and warm in Al Madinah, but the idol-worshippers had only flimsy tents to keep out the chill. During the day, the idol-worshippers unsuccessfully tried to charge the trench in groups. Anyone who made it through the trench was met with determined Muslim guards and soon dispatched.

Food supplies were low in Al Madinah, forcing many Muslim soldiers to tie rocks around their waists to press against their empty stomachs. But the defense of the city was holding and the horde of idol-worshippers began to lose their determination. After a few days, the Makkan leaders realized that the siege might have to be prolonged for a long time. The Banu Nadir also began to fear. They had worked very hard to assemble the tribes of Arabia under the Makkans and knew such an accomplishment might never occur again.

The Banu Nadir sent messages to the idol-worshippers, begging them to keep up the attack and not to leave. Huyayy bin Akhtab, the leader of the Banu Nadir, promised to get the Banu Quraytha to attack the Muslims unexpectedly. Then Huyayy secretly went to the leader of the Banu Quraytha and tried to convince him to use his forces to attack the Muslims from behind. At first, the chief of the Banu Quraytha didn't want to join; he wanted to honor the treaty he had with the Muslims. He also knew what happened to the two other Jewish clans who tried to fight the Muslims.

But Huyayy described the size of the Makkan army and the weakness of the Muslims. The leader of the Banu Quraytha, Ka'b bin Asad, agreed to listen to the plans. Huyayy even promised to move all his Banu Nadir fighters into the strong fortress and help defend it, should the Muslims discover their plot and try to counter attack. Finally, Ka'b agreed and became convinced that they could wipe out the Muslims. The Banu Quraytha would attack the Muslims from behind on the same day that the idol-worshippers would make an all-out assault on the trench.

The Betrayal of the Banu Quraytha

The news of the betrayal of the Banu Quraytha reached the Prophet ﷺ and his Companions quickly. They were shocked and dismayed. They had held off the idol-worshippers thus far and depended on the Banu Quraytha to hold the rear of the city safe. A delegation consisting of the chiefs of Al Aws and Al Khazraj tribes went to the Jewish settlement to plead with them to honor the treaty.

When they arrived, the situation was far worse than expected. The Jews were preparing for war and gathering weapons and supplies. The two chiefs tried to convince the Banu Quraytha not to break the treaty. They explained that they might suffer a worse fate than the two other Jewish clans that were forced to leave Al Madinah.

The people of the Banu Quraytha answered by insulting the Prophet ﷺ, declaring the treaty null and void. The two Muslim chiefs hastily left the scene as the anger of the Jews began to boil. The delegates returned to the Prophet ﷺ and informed him of what had happened. The Muslims now feared that the idol-worshippers might circle around to the other side of the city where the Jewish fortresses were and enter through the walls of the Banu Quraytha. The Banu Quraytha, for their part, immediately cut off all food supplies to the Muslims. Within days, the Muslims began to feel hunger; the women and children were fed in preference while the fighters continued to tie stones around waists to reduce their feelings of hunger.

The leaders of the Makkan horde, however, were elated. The news of the betrayal of the Banu Quraytha caused their spirits to soar and they thought victory was in their grasp. The warriors began to dance and sing songs in expectation of the day of the attack. The idol-worshippers planned a three-pronged attack, with Abu Sufyan leading the main body of men over the trench. The Banu Quraytha were to attack from behind.

Recall when they came upon you from above you and from below you, and when the eyes were distracted, and the hearts reached the throats, and you were thinking about Allah all sorts of thoughts. At that occasion, the believers were put to a trial and were shaken with a violent convulsion. Surat Al Ahzab (The Confederates) 33:10-11

﴿إِذْ جَآءُوكُم مِّن فَوْقِكُمْ وَمِنْ أَسْفَلَ مِنكُمْ وَإِذْ زَاغَتِ ٱلْأَبْصَٰرُ وَبَلَغَتِ ٱلْقُلُوبُ ٱلْحَنَاجِرَ وَتَظُنُّونَ بِٱللَّهِ ٱلظُّنُونَا ۝ هُنَالِكَ ٱبْتُلِيَ ٱلْمُؤْمِنُونَ وَزُلْزِلُوا۟ زِلْزَالًا شَدِيدًا﴾ سُورَةُ الأحزاب 33:10-11

The people of Al Madinah became fearful as they watched the idol-worshippers prepare their forces. The hypocrites of the city even convinced some Muslims to run away and abandon their assigned posts. (33:12-20) But the Prophet ﷺ and the strongest Companions remained firm, knowing that even if they died, they would win in the end by entering Paradise. (33:22-24)

The Enemy Is Divided

Some of the Quraysh horsemen were so encouraged by their new fortunes that they attempted an assault on the trench a few days before the main assault was to start. They found a spot where the trench was narrow and attacked it fiercely until they actually gained a position on the other side. 'Ali bin Abi Talib ﷺ, and the other Muslim defenders there, rushed to the scene to engage the enemy in battle. 'Amr bin Wudd, a fearsome warrior, yelled a challenge to the Muslims for a hand-to-hand duel. 'Ali ﷺ came forward and quickly killed him.

The other idol-worshippers, seeing their champion dead, ran back across the trench as fast as they could. But even though the front line was held for the moment, in the rear of the city, the Banu Quraytha's warriors were starting to descend from their fortress and occupy the houses close to the Muslim area of the city.

Many women and children were living in the walled houses, with only a few Muslim soldiers there to protect them. Safiyah bint Abdel Muttalib saw a Jewish scout skulking through the alley inspecting the Muslim defenses there. She asked an old man to go out and kill the spy. The old man refused out of fear. Safiyah then grabbed an iron rod and crept out in the street. Then she came upon the warrior from behind, killing him with one swift strike and sounded the alarm to other women to be alert. Some Muslims stood on their roof tops and shouted, "Allahu Akbar!" all night to frighten the Jews and keep them from attacking.

The Prophet ﷺ, seeing that the Muslims were hemmed in on both sides, had no other choice but to attempt to divide his enemies. He sent a secret message to the leaders of the powerful Ghatafan tribe that if they withdrew, he would give them one third of the harvest of Al Madinah for a year. The Ghatafan were only there to appease their friends among the Banu Nadir and were growing weary of the siege that had lasted over three weeks so far. This caused the tribal leaders to hesitate in their planning with the other tribes and the Makkans.

The Prophet ﷺ also sent a man named Nu'aym to the Banu Quraytha. He was an old friend of the Jews, and they didn't know he had converted to Islam. He pretended he was an unbeliever and convinced the Banu Quraytha that they shouldn't attack unless the Makkans promised to protect the tribe if the Muslims won. Thus, the Banu Quraytha began to hesitate.

Then Nu'aym went to the Quraysh camp and told them that the Banu Quraytha had broken the deal. Lastly, he went to the Ghatafan camp and told the leaders there the same thing. The next day, Abu Sufyan, who believed the words of Nu'aym, sent a messenger to the Banu Quraytha telling them that the attack would begin the very next day. The Jews replied that the next day was Saturday and that they wouldn't work or fight on their holy day.

Abu Sufyan was enraged by their disobedience and sent them the message that if they didn't attack tomorrow then the deal would be over. He added that the Quraysh would attack them as well. The Jews refused again and said they would not make any attacks on any days unless the Quraysh promised to protect them from the Muslims. Abu

Sufyan was completely convinced now that the Banu Quraytha had gone back on their secret deal with him. When Abu Sufyan went to the leaders of the Ghatafan tribe, he found out they also wanted to postpone any attack while they considered Muhammad's ﷺ offer of free harvest for a year. Abu Sufyan was bitter with anger.

The Wrath of Nature

That night, as the confused and divided idol-worshippers slept uneasily in their tents, a wind began blowing over the plain. Within the hour, the wind became a raging storm! Hundreds of exposed tents started to fall down; sand whipped the faces of men and horses, and the idol-worshippers were thrown into confusion.

Some of the leaders met hastily, as the winds howled through the frightened horde, and they suggested a retreat. They saw a bad omen in the storm and thought the Muslims might take the opportunity to attack. Every man grabbed whatever supplies he could pile on his horse and began to move as the storm continued to swirl all about them. By the time the day dawned, the battlefield was empty. The idol-worshippers, both Makkans and their tribal allies, had returned home.

O you who believe, remember Allah's favor to you, when the forces (of the infidels) came upon you, and We sent upon them a wind, and the forces (of angels) you did not see. Allah is watchful of whatever you do. Surat Al Ahzab (The Confederates) 33:9

﴿يَٰٓأَيُّهَا ٱلَّذِينَ ءَامَنُوا۟ ٱذۡكُرُوا۟ نِعۡمَةَ ٱللَّهِ عَلَيۡكُمۡ إِذۡ جَآءَتۡكُمۡ جُنُودٌ فَأَرۡسَلۡنَا عَلَيۡهِمۡ رِيحاً وَجُنُوداً لَّمۡ تَرَوۡهَا وَكَانَ ٱللَّهُ بِمَا تَعۡمَلُونَ بَصِيراً﴾ سُورَةُ الأحزاب 33:9

The Muslims rejoiced at this miracle that saved them, and shouts of "Allahu Akbar!" rang through the streets. The Blessed Prophet ﷺ and the grateful Muslims gathered in the masjid to give thanks to Allah ﷻ.

The Campaign against the Banu Quraytha

There was one issue remaining. The Banu Quraytha had betrayed the Muslims in their greatest hour of need by breaking the treaty they had signed and affirmed. They joined the enemies of the people of Al Madinah and, had they won, would have shown no mercy to the Muslims. The time had come to deal with these traitors. The Prophet ﷺ ordered the mu'athin to proclaim as part of the athan, "No good Muslim will pray the 'Asr prayer except in the neighborhood of the Banu Quraytha!"

The Muslims immediately mobilized and began an assault on the Jewish fortresses. The Banu Quraytha held off the Muslim attacks, which were led by 'Ali ؓ, for 25 days and nights. But inch by inch, the Muslims pressed forward. During one assault, 'Ali ؓ picked up a huge door and used it as a shield while he led a charge of Muslim fighters.

Finally, the Banu Quraytha realized that they could never hope to win and so asked for a negotiated settlement. The Prophet ﷺ refused to negotiate and demanded their surrender. The Banu Quraytha, fearing a harsh judgement, refused. They sent messages to people they knew among the Al Aws tribe, asking them to help so that their punishment would be exile only.

Accordingly, some Aws men went to the Prophet ﷺ and begged that the Prophet ﷺ give the Banu Quraytha a similar arrangement like that of the Banu Qaynuqa' and Banu Nadir. The Prophet ﷺ replied, "Men of Aws, would you be happy if one of your own men decided the issue?" They replied in the affirmative. The Prophet ﷺ thus gave up his right to decide.

When this message was communicated to the Banu Quraytha, they immediately nominated Sa'd bin Mu'ath, the chief of Al Aws tribe, with whom they had a friendship in the past. Sa'd and the chief of Al Khazraj had gone to the Banu Quraytha to plead with them not to break the treaty with the Muslims during the siege of Al Madinah.

First, Sa'd commanded that the Banu Quraytha surrender their weapons, leave their fortresses and let themselves be taken into the custody of the Muslims. Then he gathered the leaders of the Banu Quraytha and asked them what the judgement was for a traitor according to their own holy book. The rebel leaders all bowed their heads in shame, for they knew that the punishment for betrayal in the Tawrah was death.

He has brought those of the people of the Book (the Jews) who had backed them, down from their fortresses and cast awe into their hearts so as to make you kill some of them and take others as captives, and He let you inherit their land and their homes and their wealth and a land you have not trodden (so far). And Allah is Powerful to do any thing.
Surat Al Ahzab (The Confederates) 33:26-27

﴿وَأَنزَلَ ٱلَّذِينَ ظَٰهَرُوهُم مِّنْ أَهْلِ ٱلْكِتَٰبِ مِن صَيَاصِيهِمْ وَقَذَفَ فِي قُلُوبِهِمُ ٱلرُّعْبَ فَرِيقًا تَقْتُلُونَ وَتَأْسِرُونَ فَرِيقًا﴾ ﴿وَأَوْرَثَكُمْ أَرْضَهُمْ وَدِيَٰرَهُمْ وَأَمْوَٰلَهُمْ وَأَرْضًا لَّمْ تَطَـُٔوهَا ۚ وَكَانَ ٱللَّهُ عَلَىٰ كُلِّ شَيْءٍ قَدِيرًا﴾ سُورَةُالأحزاب:33:26-27

Sa'd then decreed that all the leaders should be executed, and the men, women and children be taken as captives of war. (Mothers and children were not separated, and all the people were made into servants.) Thus, the Banu Quraytha were punished according to their own book. The Muslims rejoiced in their good fortune, and now Al Madinah was safe from its internal and external enemies. However, new threats would appear soon enough.

Because of that We ordained for the Children of Israel that if anyone killed a person not in retaliation of murder, or (and) to spread mischief in the land, it would be as if he killed all mankind, and if anyone saved a life, it would be as if he saved the life of all mankind. And indeed, there came to them Our Messengers with clear proofs, evidences and signs, even then after that, many of them continued to exceed the limits (by doing oppression unjustly and exceeding beyond the limits set by Allah by committing the major sins) in the land! The recompense of those who wage war against Allah and His Messenger and do mischief in the land is only that they shall be killed or crucified or their hands and their feet be cut off from the opposite sides or be exiled from the land. That is their disgrace in this world, and a great torment is theirs in the Hereafter. Except for those who (having fled away and then) came back (as Muslims) with repentance before they fall into your power; in that case, know that Allah is Oft-Forgiving, Most Merciful. Surat Al Ma'idah (The Table) 5:32-34

﴿مِنْ أَجْلِ ذَٰلِكَ كَتَبْنَا عَلَىٰ بَنِي إِسْرَٰٓءِيلَ أَنَّهُۥ مَن قَتَلَ نَفْسًۢا بِغَيْرِ نَفْسٍ أَوْ فَسَادٍ فِي ٱلْأَرْضِ فَكَأَنَّمَا قَتَلَ ٱلنَّاسَ جَمِيعًا وَمَنْ أَحْيَاهَا فَكَأَنَّمَآ أَحْيَا ٱلنَّاسَ جَمِيعًا ۚ وَلَقَدْ جَآءَتْهُمْ رُسُلُنَا بِٱلْبَيِّنَٰتِ ثُمَّ إِنَّ كَثِيرًا مِّنْهُم بَعْدَ ذَٰلِكَ فِي ٱلْأَرْضِ لَمُسْرِفُونَ﴾ ﴿إِنَّمَا جَزَٰٓؤُا۟ ٱلَّذِينَ يُحَارِبُونَ ٱللَّهَ وَرَسُولَهُۥ وَيَسْعَوْنَ فِي ٱلْأَرْضِ فَسَادًا أَن يُقَتَّلُوٓا۟ أَوْ يُصَلَّبُوٓا۟ أَوْ تُقَطَّعَ أَيْدِيهِمْ وَأَرْجُلُهُم مِّنْ خِلَٰفٍ أَوْ يُنفَوْا۟ مِنَ ٱلْأَرْضِ ۚ ذَٰلِكَ لَهُمْ خِزْيٌ فِي ٱلدُّنْيَا ۖ وَلَهُمْ فِي ٱلْأَخِرَةِ عَذَابٌ عَظِيمٌ﴾ ﴿إِلَّا ٱلَّذِينَ تَابُوا۟ مِن قَبْلِ أَن تَقْدِرُوا۟ عَلَيْهِمْ ۖ فَٱعْلَمُوٓا۟ أَنَّ ٱللَّهَ غَفُورٌ رَّحِيمٌ﴾ سُورَةُالمائدة:5:32-34

Chapter 15
The Final Victory

The First Islamic Pilgrimage

After the failed siege of Al Madinah, the prestige of the Muslims rose further in the eyes of the surrounding tribes of the region. Hundreds more people were accepting Islam every week, and the Prophet ﷺ sent many s to different towns and villages to teach Islam to the people.

But as Islam progressed in the hearts and minds of the people, another issue remained unresolved. The Ka'bah, the shrine built by Prophet Ibrahim ﷺ so long ago, now was a temple for idols. Furthermore, the Makkans prevented any Muslim from approaching it.

Muslims honor the practices of Prophet Ibrahim ﷺ. The Beloved Prophet Ibrahim ﷺ tried to teach others that there was only One God, and he built the Ka'bah for Muslims to pray there to Allah ﷻ. This teaching of Prophet Ibrahim ﷺ endured, so the Muslims during the time of Prophet Muhammad ﷺ also felt a longing to go and once again make the Ka'bah a pure and sacred place.

One night the Blessed Prophet ﷺ had a dream in which he saw himself, joined by other Muslims, making a pilgrimage to Makkah. The next morning he came out and announced to the community that he was organizing an 'umrah, or short pilgrimage, to Makkah.

After the preparations were made, the Prophet ﷺ set out with 1,400 of his followers who were armed with nothing more than their small travelers' swords. It was the year 628 CE (6 AH, after Hijra). This was the first pilgrimage in Islam that would re-establish the ancient practices of Prophet Ibrahim ﷺ.

The Muslim pilgrims, or Hujjaj, journeyed towards Makkah, praising Allah ﷻ and rejoicing in their new effort for Allah's ﷻ cause. The Prophet ﷺ had no intention of forcing his way into Makkah, as it was the season of pilgrimage in the peninsula, and all tribes observed a general truce and avoided fighting. This was another reason why the Muslims traveled so lightly armed.

The Treaty of Hudaibiyah

When the Makkans learned that Muslim pilgrims were coming to their city, they were shocked. They realized that it wasn't an armed invasion and were confused about what to do. If they attacked the Muslims, all the other people of Arabia would see that the custodians of the Ka'bah, the Quraysh, had violated the months of truce.

The Quraysh decided not to allow the Muslims to enter the city. They sent out a cavalry unit under the command of Khalid bin Walid and 'Ikrima bin Abu Jahl to turn the Muslims back. Khalid was the same military commander at Uhud who had attacked the Muslims from behind when the archers deserted their posts. 'Ikrima was still embittered about his father, who was killed at Badr.

When the Prophet ﷺ learned that the enemy was approaching, he asked his followers if anyone knew of another way into Makkah. One of them did, and he guided the Muslim pilgrims through some narrow passes.

When they arrived at an area called Hudaibiyah, the Prophet's camel halted. When the Makkan cavalry realized that they had lost their target, they searched further away from Makkah. Soon a message was sent to the Muslim camp, proclaiming that no one would be allowed to enter the city. 'Uthman ﷺ went to talk to some of the Makkans about allowing the Muslims in for pilgrimage. Because he was delayed, some Muslims thought he was killed, and for that reason had not returned. They were angry and wanted to fight. The Prophet ﷺ swore that if they killed 'Uthman ﷺ, he would invade the city.

He moved under a tall tree and took a pledge from all the Muslims there that they would fight to the last man if the Makkans had killed 'Uthman ﷺ and violated the holy months of pilgrimage. This is known as the Pledge of Ridwan. A short time later, 'Uthman ﷺ returned, and everyone breathed easier.

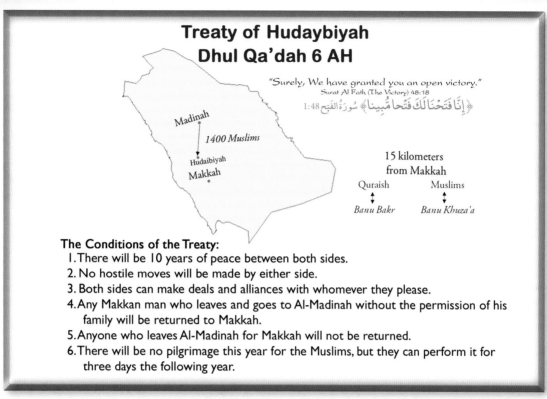

Treaty of Hudaybiyah
Dhul Qa'dah 6 AH

"Surely, We have granted you an open victory."
Surat Al Fath (The Victory) 48:18

﴿ إِنَّا فَتَحْنَا لَكَ فَتْحًا مُّبِينًا ﴾ سُورَةُ الفَتح 1:48

Madinah

1400 Muslims

Hudaibiyah
Makkah

15 kilometers
from Makkah

Quraish   Muslims

Banu Bakr   Banu Khuza'a

The Conditions of the Treaty:
1. There will be 10 years of peace between both sides.
2. No hostile moves will be made by either side.
3. Both sides can make deals and alliances with whomever they please.
4. Any Makkan man who leaves and goes to Al-Madinah without the permission of his family will be returned to Makkah.
5. Anyone who leaves Al-Madinah for Makkah will not be returned.
6. There will be no pilgrimage this year for the Muslims, but they can perform it for three days the following year.

Indeed, Allah was pleased with the believers when they gave the Bay'ah (pledge) to you (O Muhammad) under the tree; He knew what was in their hearts, and He sent down As-Sakinah (calmness and tranquillity) upon them, and He rewarded them with a near victory. Surat Al Fath (The Victory) 48:18

﴿ لَقَدْ رَضِيَ ٱللَّهُ عَنِ ٱلْمُؤْمِنِينَ إِذْ يُبَايِعُونَكَ تَحْتَ ٱلشَّجَرَةِ فَعَلِمَ مَا فِي قُلُوبِهِمْ فَأَنزَلَ ٱلسَّكِينَةَ عَلَيْهِمْ وَأَثَٰبَهُمْ فَتْحًا قَرِيبًا ﴾ سُورَةُ الفَتح 18:48

An official delegation arrived from Makkah to discuss the situation with the Prophet ﷺ. After many meetings and proposals, an agreement was finally reached. A treaty was signed between the Muslims and the idol-worshippers. This pact, called the Treaty of Hudaibiyah, was signed in the year 628 CE (6 AH, after Hijrah).

The main points of the treaty were as follows:
1. There would be 10 years of peace between both sides.
2. No hostile moves would be made by either side.
3. Both sides could make deals and alliances with whomever they pleased.
4. Any Makkan man who left for Al Madinah without the permission of his family would be returned to Makkah.
5. Anyone who left Al Madinah for Makkah would not be returned.
6. There would be no pilgrimage that year for the Muslims, but they could perform it the following year for three days.

The Blessed Prophet ﷺ accepted these conditions although many of the Muslims did not agree with the fifth point. When 'Umar bin al Khattab ﷺ complained about the treaty, the Blessed Prophet ﷺ replied, "I am the servant of Allah, and His messenger. I always obey His commands, and He will never fail me." (48:24-26)

The Blessed Prophet ﷺ declared that the Muslims had fulfilled their 'umrah this year. Then, they began their return journey to Al Madinah with the good news of a 10-year peace treaty. Allah ﷻ revealed Surat Al Fath (The Victory). In one of the ayaat it says, *Certainly, We have granted you a clear victory.* Surat Al Fath (The Victory) 48:1

﴿ إِنَّا فَتَحْنَا لَكَ فَتْحًا مُّبِينًا ﴾ سُورَةُ الفَتح 1:48

The following year, the Muslims were able to enter Makkah on a three-day pilgrimage without trouble from the Makkans. None of the Quraysh wanted to be known as a people who could not abide by their own treaty. When the Prophet ﷺ and the Muslim pilgrims were leaving Makkah to return to Al Madinah, Hamza's ﷺ daughter, who was looking for her chance to escape the idol-worshippers, ran after them and found safety in the Muslim ranks. As you will soon see, the treaty of peace was the best thing that could have happened for the Muslims—and for more reasons than the pilgrimage.

The Regret of the Makkans

Abu Jundal☺, one of the Makkan delegates at Hudaibiyah, accepted Islam shortly after the treaty went into effect. He escaped Makkah and came running after the Muslim caravan of pilgrims; the marks of torture inflicted on him were visible on his body. The Muslims felt sorrow at seeing how he had suffered. When some Makkans came to retrieve him, Abu Jundal☺ begged to stay and be protected. The Blessed Prophet☺, honoring his promises, sadly told him that he had to return.

The Blessed Prophet☺ said, "Abu Jundal, be patient and control yourself. Surely Allah will make some way out for you and for the vulnerable (Muslims in Makkah). We have bound ourselves to make peace between ourselves and the (Makkans), and we have exchanged the pact of Allah, and we will not break that." (Ahmad)

Remains of the original Hudaibiyah Mosque, Makkah Al Mukarramah.

قَالَ رَسُولُ اللهِ ﷺ : «يَا أَبَا جَنْدَل اصْبِرْ وَاحْتَسِبْ فَإِنَّ اللهَ عَزَّ وَجَلَّ جَاعِلٌ لَكَ وَلِمَنْ مَعَكَ مِنَ الْمُسْتَضْعَفِينَ فَرَجًا وَمَخْرَجًا إِنَّا قَدْ عَقَدْنَا بَيْنَنَا وَبَيْنَ الْقَوْمِ صُلْحًا فَأَعْطَيْنَاهُمْ عَلَى ذَلِكَ وَأَعْطَوْنَا عَلَيْهِ عَهْدًا وَإِنَّا لَنْ نَغْدِرَ بِهِمْ». رَوَاهُ أَحْمَد

A few weeks later, a woman who had embraced Islam in Makkah, escaped her family and finally made it to Al Madinah. Sure enough, her relatives arrived a short time later and demanded her return to deal with her. But this time, the Prophet☺ refused to give up a Makkan refugee.

The astonished idol-worshippers reminded the Prophet☺ angrily that they had an agreement, that called for the return of any Makkans to Makkah. The Prophet☺ smiled and pointed out to them that the treaty said, in exact words "any man from Makkah." The woman would not be returned.

The angry idol-worshippers could argue no further and left Al Madinah, thwarted in their plans. The Muslims rejoiced. Thereafter, many women from Makkah who had embraced Islam escaped to Al Madinah, knowing that they would be safe.

O you who believe, when the believing women come to you as emigrants, put them to a test. Allah knows best about their faith. So, if you find them faithful, do not send them back to the disbelievers... Surat Al Mumtahana (The Woman to Be Examined) 60:10

﴿يَا أَيُّهَا الَّذِينَ آمَنُوا إِذَا جَاءَكُمُ الْمُؤْمِنَاتُ مُهَاجِرَاتٍ فَامْتَحِنُوهُنَّ اللَّهُ أَعْلَمُ بِإِيمَانِهِنَّ فَإِنْ عَلِمْتُمُوهُنَّ مُؤْمِنَاتٍ فَلَا تَرْجِعُوهُنَّ إِلَى الْكُفَّارِ ...﴾ سُورَةُ المُمْتَحِنَة 60:10

Not long after, another Muslim, by the name of Abu Basir☺, escaped from Makkah. When the Makkans again came to Al Madinah, the Prophet☺ relinquished him to them. The Blessed Prophet☺ said, "Abu Basir, we have promised them, and in our way of life to break a promise is a sin. Go and Allah will find some way to save you." (Al Baihaqi)

«يَا أَبَا بَصِيرٍ، انْطَلِقْ، فَإِنَّ اللهَ تَعَالَى سَيَجْعَلُ لَكَ وَلِمَنْ مَعَكَ مِنَ الْمُسْتَضْعَفِينَ فَرَجًا وَمَخْرَجًا». رَوَاهُ البَيْهَقِي

Abu Basir☺ obeyed the Prophet☺, and accompanied by two idol-worshippers, he left for Makkah. On the way he managed to escape. But the fugitive didn't return to Al Madinah, knowing he would have to be turned over to the Makkans once again. Instead, he took shelter in a cave near the route used by caravans going to Syria. When he would see a caravan, he would charge down and attack it, damage the goods and disappear back into the hills. Some of the persecuted new Muslims of Makkah heard about this. They also wanted to flee their own persecutors, so they went and joined Abu Basir☺. Little by little, their number reached nearly 70 people.

The number was significant enough to make it difficult for the Makkans to send caravans to Syria. Many merchants and guards paid with their lives. In fact, after some time, there were so many losses suffered by these surprise attacks that the Makkans began to worry. They did the only thing that would quickly save the situation. They sent a delegation to Al Madinah and begged the Prophet☺ to remove the part of the treaty that required Makkans to be returned to Makkah. The Prophet☺ joyfully agreed, and Abu Basir's men were allowed to live in Al Madinah. When the good news arrived at Abu Basir's camp, he was very sick. After he heard the news, he died smiling.

Using the Time of Peace

The Muslims, now freed from the fear of Makkan attacks, made good use of the period of peace. The Prophet ﷺ made numerous treaties with other tribes around Arabia, and thousands of people were accepting Islam at every turn. Even Khalid bin Walid ؓ, the military genius of the Quraysh, became a Muslim.

To eliminate another potential threat to Muslim safety, the Blessed Prophet ﷺ marched an army to the hostile Jewish fortresses of Khaybar, three days to the north. After several battles, the Jews surrendered and agreed to maintain a peace. The Prophet ﷺ allowed them to stay on their lands and even returned some religious scrolls to them that were seized in the fighting.

The Jews agreed to pay one-half of the yearly crops of Khaybar to the Muslim government, and not to make any secret deals with hostile enemies. To cement the new arrangement, the Blessed Prophet ﷺ married a Jewish woman named Safiyah bint Huyayy, who became a firm and committed Muslim for the rest of her life. In addition, the Blessed Prophet ﷺ began the next phase of his mission: to reach out to the people of the world with the message of Islam.

We did not send you (O prophet) but to all of mankind, as a bearer of good news and as a Warner, but most people do not know. Surat Saba' (Sheba) 34:28

﴿وَمَآ أَرْسَلْنَٰكَ إِلَّا كَآفَّةً لِّلنَّاسِ بَشِيرًا وَنَذِيرًا وَلَٰكِنَّ أَكْثَرَ ٱلنَّاسِ لَا يَعْلَمُونَ﴾ سُورَةُ سَبَأٍ ٣٤:٢٨

He sent letters to the leaders of all the known empires, countries and cities, inviting them to consider Islam as their way of life. Copies of some of those letters still exist today, and are found in museums throughout the Muslim world.

A message was sent to Khusroe, the King of Persia, whose borders extended to India. When the letter was translated for him, however, he tore it up in anger out of arrogance and pride. When the Prophet ﷺ heard of the actions of Khusroe, he remarked, "What Khusroe did to our letter, Allah will do to his empire."

An-Najashi of Abyssinia also received a formal invitation to accept Islam. Already impressed with the Muslim way of life after playing host to a Muslim refugee community for so many years, King Najjashi secretly accepted Islam. Heraclius, the Byzantine Roman emperor, who was visiting in Jerusalem, also received a letter.

After reading it, the emperor wanted to know more about Muhammad ﷺ. He asked his servants to find someone in Jerusalem who knew Muhammad ﷺ and bring him. As fate would have it, Abu Sufyan was in the city on a trading mission. He was brought to Heraclius where he was questioned about Muhammad's ﷺ background, teachings, stature and reputation.

Abu Sufyan answered all questions truthfully, as he had no reason to lie. When the questioning was finished, Heraclius remarked, "If all of what you say is true, I'm sure his kingdom will reach the place here where I walk. I was certain that a prophet was coming, but I didn't think he would be born in Arabia."

Heraclius sent a respectful letter in reply to Al Madinah. It is said that Heraclius wanted to accept Islam and announced this to his nobles. But they became alarmed, as they believed in Trinitarian Christianity, and started shouting and arguing. To keep his kingdom, Heraclius quickly told them that he was not serious, and he gave them gifts and money to appease them.

Later, after envoys of the Prophet ﷺ were killed by some allies of the Byzantines in northern Arabia, the Prophet ﷺ sent an army of 3,000 men under the command of Zayd bin Harith ؓ to deal with the hostile enemy. The Byzantines mobilized an army of over 100,000 men to meet the Muslims. At a place called Mu'tah in Syria, the two armies met and fought in the year 629 CE (7 AH).

After a fierce fight, the massive Byzantine army fled from the battlefield the following day, thinking that Muslim reinforcements were on their way. Zayd ؓ died during this battle, however. The Muslim soldiers returned to Al Madinah under the command of Khalid bin Walid ؓ. At first, the people accused the soldiers of running away from a fight, but the Prophet ﷺ declared that they were warriors who would fight again another day.

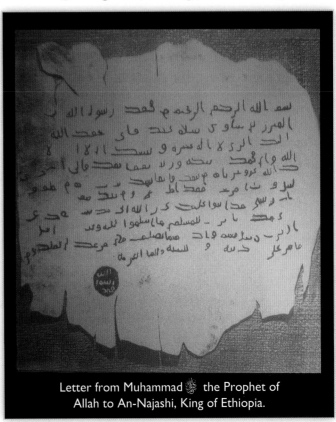

Letter from Muhammad ﷺ the Prophet of Allah to An-Najashi, King of Ethiopia.

The Blessed Prophet ﷺ also sent an invitation to the archbishop of Egypt, who ruled the Christian Copts, that lived there. The Archbishop replied explaining that though he would like to accept Islam, he would refuse as it would mean a loss of all his power.

He sent respectful gifts to the Prophet ﷺ, however, which consisted of money, various Egyptian products and two slave women that were named Mariyah and Sireen. On their journey to Al Madinah, the women were told about Islam, and they accepted it before ever meeting the Prophet ﷺ.

The Prophet ﷺ freed them after they arrived. Hassan bin Thabit ﷺ married Sireen, and Mariyah was married to the Blessed Prophet ﷺ and became one of the "Mothers of the Believers," as his wives were known.

The Makkans' Big Mistake

Two years had passed after the signing of the treaty, and peace still reigned. During this time, the tribe of Banu Khuza'a became allies of the Muslims, while the Banu Bakr became allies of the idol-worshippers in Makkah.

Towards the end of the year 630 CE, the Banu Bakr, supplied with fresh weapons from the Quraysh, attacked the camp of the Banu Khuza'a at night, causing much death and destruction. The Banu Bakr warriors then carried off all the loot to Makkah, where they took shelter.

The chief of the Banu Khuza'a went to Al Madinah. He complained with a loud voice of the injustice done against his people. The Prophet ﷺ came out of the masjid and was told the story of what happened. The Prophet ﷺ, angry at the senseless attack and killing done by the allies of the Makkans, sent a message off to Makkah that stated the following three options:

1. The Banu Bakr must pay compensation for the victims they killed, or
2. The Makkans should break their alliance with the Banu Bakr, or
3. The Makkans should declare the Treaty of Hudaibiyah null and void.

The idol-worshippers, who perhaps saw the victory of the Banu Bakr as a sign of more good fortune in their interrupted war against the Muslims, shouted that the treaty was now over. When the news of the Makkans' response reached Al Madinah, the Prophet ﷺ knew the time had come for final victory.

After a few days, the Makkans realized that they had made a big mistake. Abu Sufyan went to Al Madinah himself and begged for the treaty to remain valid. The Prophet ﷺ refused to see him. Then, Abu Sufyan went to Abu Bakr, 'Umar, Fatimah and others ﷺ and begged for their help. They all refused to speak with him. Abu Sufyan returned to Makkah, bitter and frightened.

The Liberation of Makkah

The Blessed Prophet ﷺ raised an army of 10,000 Muslim men and women and set out for Makkah during the month of Ramadan in the year 630 CE (8 AH). He took great care to keep his army's departure a secret. After a few days of travel, the huge army arrived at the hillsides just outside of Makkah. There, the Prophet ﷺ ordered them to make camp. He asked each small group of soldiers to start a campfire. Looking out upon the endless sea of campfires surrounding them, the Makkans were terrified.

They knew fighting such an army would be impossible. They had few fighters in the city, and all the famous warriors of Arabia had already gone over to the Muslim side. Abu Sufyan had no choice but to go to the Muslim camp and meet with the Blessed Prophet ﷺ.

Abu Sufyan declared his acceptance of Islam, and agreed to surrender Makkah peacefully. The Prophet ﷺ told him that he didn't want any blood to be shed upon entering Makkah and that anyone near the Ka'bah, in their homes or even in Abu Sufyan's own house would be safe from reprisals.

Abu Sufyan ﷺ then returned to Makkah and informed the people that he was surrendering the city, that there was no hope of opposing the huge Muslim forces. He told them about Muhammad's ﷺ promise of safety and that everyone should go and remain in their homes.

Makkah was liberated peacefully.

The next morning, the Prophet ﷺ divided his army into three massive columns and instructed each to enter Makkah from a different direction. The sight of 10,000 Muslims, dressed in white, entering victoriously into the city, that only eight years ago was unthinkable, brought joy to many, especially the Prophet ﷺ.

There was only one incident of bloodshed. Some idol-worshippers attacked a group of Muslim soldiers. However, they were quickly subdued by Khalid bin Walid ﷺ.

The first thing on the Blessed Prophet's ﷺ agenda was to clear the Ka'bah of all the idols. With all the Muslims and Makkans looking on, he approached the sacred shrine and gave thanks to Allah ﷻ for the victory.

The keeper of the key to the Ka'bah door, still an idol-worshipper, was brought forward. When he was asked for the key, he refused. 'Ali ﷺ snatched it away and brought it to the Prophet ﷺ. The Blessed Prophet ﷺ, however, ordered it to be returned to its keeper. The keeper of the key was so amazed that he declared himself a Muslim and willingly gave the key to the Prophet ﷺ with his own hand. The Muslims then entered and threw the idols out of Prophet Ibrahim's ﷺ ancient shrine, exclaiming with excitement, Allahu Akbar! Allahu Akbar!

The Prophet ﷺ recited the following ayah as the work progressed, *And say, Truth has come and falsehood has vanished. Falsehood is surely bound to vanish. Surat Al Isra' (The Journey by Night) 17:81*

﴿وَقُلْ جَآءَ ٱلْحَقُّ وَزَهَقَ ٱلْبَٰطِلُ إِنَّ ٱلْبَٰطِلَ كَانَ زَهُوقًا﴾ سُورَةُ ٱلْإِسْرَاء ١٧:٨١

With that task done, the Blessed Prophet ﷺ addressed the crowd of Makkans who had come to watch, saying, *"There is no god but Allah. No one shares in His power. He has fulfilled His promise. He helped His servant, Muhammad."* (At-Tabarani)

قَالَ رَسُولُ اللهِ ﷺ: «لَا إِلَهَ إِلَّا اللهُ وَحْدَهُ لَا شَرِيكَ لَهُ، صَدَقَ وَعْدَهُ وَنَصَرَ عَبْدَهُ». رَوَاهُ ٱلطَّبَرَانِيُّ

Key for the Ka'ba made in 765 AH / 1364 AD.

"People of Quraysh! Allah has done away with the evils of ignorance. Loyalty to tribalism is gone forever. All human beings are brothers to each other. They are the children of Adam, and Adam was made from dust. From now on, no one should take revenge. People must learn to live in peace." Then the Blessed Prophet recited this ayah from the Qur'an: *Oh Humanity! We have created you from a male and female and made you into nations and ethnic groups so you can come to know each other. The best among you is the one who has the most taqwa.'* (Al Hujurat (The Dwellings) 49:13) He asked all the assembled Makkans, *"People of Makkah! What do you think I am going to do with you?"* They answered, *"Noble Brother, and son of a noble brother, only goodness."*

إِنَّ رَسُولَ اللهِ ﷺ قَامَ عَلَى بَابِ ٱلْكَعْبَةِ، وَقَالَ: «يَا مَعْشَرَ قُرَيْشٍ، إِنَّ اللهَ قَدْ أَذْهَبَ عَنْكُمْ نَخْوَةَ ٱلْجَاهِلِيَّةِ، وَتَعَظُّمَهَا بِٱلْآبَاءِ، ٱلنَّاسُ مِنْ آدَمَ، وَآدَمُ مِنْ تُرَابٍ، ثُمَّ تَلَا هَذِهِ ٱلْآيَةَ: ﴿يَٰٓأَيُّهَا ٱلنَّاسُ إِنَّا خَلَقْنَٰكُم مِّن ذَكَرٍ وَأُنثَىٰ وَجَعَلْنَٰكُمْ شُعُوبًا وَقَبَآئِلَ لِتَعَارَفُوٓا۟ إِنَّ أَكْرَمَكُمْ عِندَ ٱللَّهِ أَتْقَىٰكُمْ إِنَّ ٱللَّهَ عَلِيمٌ خَبِيرٌ﴾ سُورَةُ ٱلْحُجُرَات ٤٩:١٣ ثُمَّ قَالَ: يَا مَعْشَرَ قُرَيْشٍ، مَا تَرَوْنَ أَنِّي فَاعِلٌ فِيكُمْ؟ قَالُوا: خَيْرًا، أَخٌ كَرِيمٌ، وَٱبْنُ أَخٍ كَرِيمٍ».

The Makkans held their breath to hear what their punishment would be. After all, they had tortured, murdered and persecuted their fellow men and women only for believing in one god and for enjoining justice. The Blessed Prophet ﷺ replied in words that are to this day renowned for their nobility and mercy. He announced, *"There is no blame on you this day. Go to your homes, for you are all free."* (Al Baihaq)

قَالَ رَسُولُ اللهِ ﷺ: «لَا تَثْرِيبَ عَلَيْكُمُ ٱلْيَوْمَ. ٱذْهَبُوا فَأَنْتُمُ ٱلطُّلَقَاءُ». رَوَاهُ ٱلْبَيْهَقِيُّ

The Prophet ﷺ then asked Bilal ﷺ to climb to the top of the Ka'bah and give the athan for the noon prayer. Imagine the honor! No one has ever been permitted to call the athan from the Ka'bah's roof since that day in the year 630 CE (8 AH). The Muslims, emotional and with heartfelt prayer, prayed in gratitude to Allah ﷻ. It was a day of victory that would live on in the hearts and minds of Muslims forever.

Organizing in Makkah

The Blessed Prophet ﷺ remained in Makkah for 15 days. During this time, a number of important activities took place. The Ka'bah was cleansed of idols and pagan paintings to be rededicated to the service of Allah ﷻ alone.

Important ayaat about the Hajj and Zakah were revealed as well as ayaat about relations between people. More treaties were signed with peoples, tribes and leaders all over southern Arabia, and the administration of Makkah was organized.

From Yemen in the south to Syria in the north, Islam was expanding. Muslim teachers, who were sent to the various peoples of Arabia, were achieving great success. After seeing how fair and just Muhammad ﷺ was, virtually everyone in Makkah converted to the Muslim religion of their own accord.

The Battle of Hunayn

Do you remember the story of Ta'if? It was one of the first cities that the Prophet ﷺ visited asking to be allowed to preach Islam there. Do you remember the anger of the people and how they chased the Prophet ﷺ away with stones? How would they react to the news that Makkah was now Muslim?

When the news of the fall of Makkah reached the leaders of the Thaqif tribe, who ruled Ta'if, they became enraged and wanted to fight the Muslims. One of their leaders, named Malik bin 'Awf, succeeded in organizing an alliance between his tribe and the Hawazin, Nasr and Jusham tribes.

Then he ordered that every warrior should bring his wives, children and wealth along with them to the battlefield. He explained to the other leaders that this would make the men fight more fiercely, given that they had everything to lose if they were defeated.

Together, this huge force began its slow journey towards Makkah, where they hoped to defeat the Muslims and save idol-worship. They eventually took up positions in a canyon named **Hunayn** حُنَيْن that had a narrow pass leading to it. Malik placed his warriors among the rocks, and commanded them to ambush the Muslims when the signal was given.

Meanwhile back in Makkah, the Prophet ﷺ had received the news of the declaration of war against the Muslims. He raised an army of 12,000 men, including the new converts from the Quraysh, and set out to meet the enemy. They arrived at the pass of Hunayn in the evening and settled down for the night. The next morning, the Muslim force entered the valley where they expected the enemy might be. As the Muslims passed through the canyon of Hunayn, Malik bin 'Awf ordered his army to attack in the darkness, just before dawn. A rain of arrows fell upon the Muslim column, which was then followed by a charge of idol-worshippers coming down the valley walls.

The Muslims panicked and fell into confusion. Some of them ran out of the canyon as fast as they could. Some of the Quraysh leaders were secretly happy to see the Muslims being routed and whispered to each other that the Muslims were going to be defeated.

The Prophet ﷺ, however, stood his ground and refused to run away. He was surrounded by some faithful men of Al Ansar and Al Muhajirun and shouted to the soldiers running away to come back. They were too scared to listen and retreated in a mob. The Thaqif and Hawazin men came pouring into the valley dressed in black and carrying spears. Their leader, Malik, carried a black banner and headed the maddening assault from a red camel.

The Prophet ﷺ tried to charge right into the horde with his few followers behind him, but Abu Sufyan held him back. The Prophet's ﷺ uncle, 'Abbas, who had a loud voice, shouted to the fleeing Muslims, "Men of Al Ansar! Men of Al Muhajirun! Men who pledged their allegiance under the tree! Muhammad ﷺ is alive! Charge forward with him!"

The sound of his powerful voice echoed off the canyon walls. The Muslims heard the call and came back to their senses. They were ashamed at their panic and began to swell back into the valley towards the Prophet ﷺ and those who had stayed with him. The entire camp of the Hawazin and Thaqif were engaged now, and the battle raged in the crisp morning light. The returning Muslims cried out, "At Your service, Allah! At Your service!"

The Battle Turns

The Muslim clans and units reorganized themselves and marched forward, shoulder-to-shoulder. They shouted to one another, "Rally forth to battle!" and moved as if one body. The Prophet ﷺ cried out, "Now the battle has begun! Allah will not fail the Prophet and will fulfill the promise He gave him."

Then he asked 'Abbas to scoop up a handful of stones. The Prophet ﷺ took them and flung them in the faces of the enemy and declared, "Ruin to the enemies of Allah!" Men fell on all sides as the Muslims surged forward realizing that, regardless of achieving victory in this battle or dying as martyrs, it was a win-win situation. The shouts of "Allahu Akbar" began to erode the confidence of the idol-worshippers, and they started to fall back.

By the afternoon, the leaders of the Thaqif and Hawazin realized their cause was hopeless. Most of their warriors were killed, wounded or captured, and they were in danger of total annihilation. They ordered a general retreat, and the remnants of their fighters fled from the battlefield.

They ran right past their wives, children and wealth and never looked back. The advancing Muslim columns captured all the women and children, as well as 22,000 camels, 40,000 goats and 4,000 ounces of silver. The total number of captives came to nearly 6,000.

Allah has surely blessed you with His help on many battlefields, and on the day of Hunayn, when you were proud of your great number, then it did not help you at all, and the earth was straightened for you despite all its vastness then you turned back on your heels. Then Allah sent down His tranquility upon His Messenger and upon the believers and sent down troops that you did not see and punished those who disbelieved. That is the recompense of the disbelievers. Yet Allah relents, after that, to whomsoever He wills. Allah is Most-Forgiving, Very-Merciful. Surat At-Tawbah (The Repentance) 9:25-27

﴿لَقَدْ نَصَرَكُمُ ٱللَّهُ فِي مَوَاطِنَ كَثِيرَةٍ وَيَوْمَ حُنَيْنٍ إِذْ أَعْجَبَتْكُمْ كَثْرَتُكُمْ فَلَمْ تُغْنِ عَنكُمْ شَيْئًا وَضَاقَتْ عَلَيْكُمُ ٱلْأَرْضُ بِمَا رَحُبَتْ ثُمَّ وَلَّيْتُم مُّدْبِرِينَ﴾ ﴿ثُمَّ أَنزَلَ ٱللَّهُ سَكِينَتَهُۥ عَلَىٰ رَسُولِهِۦ وَعَلَى ٱلْمُؤْمِنِينَ وَأَنزَلَ جُنُودًا لَّمْ تَرَوْهَا وَعَذَّبَ ٱلَّذِينَ كَفَرُوا۟ وَذَٰلِكَ جَزَآءُ ٱلْكَٰفِرِينَ﴾ ﴿ثُمَّ يَتُوبُ ٱللَّهُ مِنۢ بَعْدِ ذَٰلِكَ عَلَىٰ مَن يَشَآءُ وَٱللَّهُ غَفُورٌ رَّحِيمٌ﴾ سُورَةُ التَّوْبَةِ 9:25-27

The Muslim soldiers continued their pursuit of the fleeing Thaqif and Hawazin, who eventually made it back to their fortress city of Ta'if. There they barricaded the gates and readied themselves for a last stand.

The Muslims made camp nearby and began the long siege of the city. They built a masjid and prepared their strategy. One of the Muslim soldiers, a man named At-Tufayl, was from a tribe in southern Arabia that had experience in siege warfare. An urgent request was sent for him to bring his tribe and all their war machines to the siege.

Four days later, his tribe, the Banu Daws, arrived. They brought catapults and wooden canopies that could be moved with men hiding inside, much like a tank. This covering would protect the soldiers from arrows that the Thaqif were raining down on any Muslims who came within range.

After several days of trying, the Muslims were still unable to penetrate the massive fortress. The Prophet ﷺ then gave the order to destroy the orchards and vineyards around the city of Ta'if. When they saw from the walls that their land was being decimated, the people of Ta'if sent messages asking that the orchards be spared.

The Prophet ﷺ learned from some Thaqif members who had joined the Muslim side that the city was well prepared for a siege and could hold out for a long time. So, as the holy months of pilgrimage were arriving, the Prophet ﷺ lifted the siege and marched his victorious army back to Makkah. He vowed to resume the siege the following year.

Once back in Makkah, he performed 'umrah and visited the holy places. A few months later, some of the leaders of the Hawazin tribe who had recently embraced Islam went to the Prophet ﷺ and begged that the women and children of their tribe be released.

The Blessed Prophet ﷺ granted this request and the entire Hawazin tribe converted to Islam, thus increasing the strength of the Muslims even further. Thus, as the Prophet ﷺ displayed his great love and mercy for people, more and more people adopted Islam as their way of life.

On a personal level, the Blessed Prophet ﷺ suffered the loss of his beloved daughter Zaynab ﷺ. When she was escaping Makkah to make Al Hijrah, an idol-worshipper named Huwayrith struck her with a blow to the stomach.

At the time she was pregnant, and because of the damage to her body, she lost

Ancient catapults.

the baby, and her physical strength never fully recovered. Soon after the Battle of Hunayn, Zaynab ﷺ passed away. Um Kulthum ﷺ and Ruqaiyyah ﷺ had already preceded her in death. The only surviving child of the Blessed Prophet ﷺ now was Fatimah ﷺ. But soon Mariyah gave birth to a healthy baby boy whom the Blessed Prophet ﷺ named Ibrahim.

The Campaign of Tabuk

In the year 630 CE, the Prophet ﷺ received the news that a large force of Byzantine Roman soldiers, some 100,000, had gathered in Syria. The Roman emperor, Heraclius, was planning to invade Al Madinah. Therefore, swift action was needed on the part of the Muslims. The Blessed Prophet ﷺ sent out a call to arms among the Muslims, but a famine in the Hijaz region of Arabia had severely reduced the availability of food. The Muslim army would not be well supplied.

It was at this time that the real believers came forward and contributed whatever they could. 'Uthman ﷺ donated 1,000 gold coins and 300 camels, 'Umar ﷺ donated half of everything he owned, while Abu Bakr ﷺ donated all his worldly wealth, except the clothes he was wearing!

Muslim women came forward and donated money and jewelry. One poor Muslim worked all night watering someone's garden so he could donate a handful of dates to the cause. The Prophet ﷺ was so pleased with that gift that he ordered the dates to be placed on top of the pile of donated money and goods. At the same time that all the goodwill was being displayed by the believers, many hypocrites came forward and started making excuses about why they should be able to stay behind.

Allah ﷻ revealed the ayah, *They advise against venturing out in the desert heat. Tell them, "The fire of Hell is hotter, if they only knew." They laugh now, but their pleasure is short lived. They shall cry much more, and they will deserve every bit of it. Surat At-Tawbah (The Repentance) 9:81-82*

﴿...وَقَالُوا لَا تَنفِرُوا فِي ٱلْحَرِّ قُلْ نَارُ جَهَنَّمَ أَشَدُّ حَرًّا لَّوْ كَانُوا يَفْقَهُونَ﴾ ﴿فَلْيَضْحَكُوا قَلِيلًا وَلْيَبْكُوا كَثِيرًا جَزَآءً بِمَا كَانُوا يَكْسِبُونَ﴾ سُورَةُ التَّوْبَةِ 9:81-82

When the army finally left for Syria, the Muslim force numbered 30,000 men, including many horses, quite a few camels and some women who would act as doctors. After many days of hard travelling, the Muslims made camp at Al Hijr near the ruins of the ancient Thamud people. Water was scarce, and the desert winds were fierce. The Blessed Prophet ﷺ ordered that no one should go alone into the desert, but two men disobeyed. One of them was carried away and lost, and the other was found buried in the sand.

During the night, a sandstorm descended upon the area and filled the only available water-well. The next morning, some Muslims began to panic. Soon, however, a passing rain cloud came and filled some dry pools with water for the army. The Muslims set off again in the direction of **Tabuk** تَبُوك, a small town in the northern part of Arabia. The Byzantines already knew of the Muslim advance and decided to withdraw their army. It is possible that they did not want to face 30,000 Muslims, when only 3,000 had given them so much trouble before at Mu'tah.

When the Blessed Prophet ﷺ finally reached Tabuk, he found that the Byzantine army had dispersed and withdrawn.

The Blessed Prophet ﷺ took the opportunity to make alliances with the local leaders in Syria, to give da'wah and to strengthen the Muslim position in northern Arabia. One after another, the local governors and chieftains came to the Prophet's ﷺ camp and declared their submission to the government of Al Madinah.

One local ruler named Ukaydir refused to meet with the Muslims. So the Prophet ﷺ sent Khalid bin Walid ﷺ with 500 mounted Muslim warriors to that city. Khalid found that the gates to the city were shut tight. But the Muslims soon learned that Ukaydir was outside the city on a hunting trip. They captured him and forced him to open the city to them.

The Muslims received enormous tribute, which included thousands of animals, coats of armor and loads of grain. After meeting the Prophet ﷺ, Ukaydir accepted Islam. The Muslim army returned to Al Madinah about 50 days later victorious, embarrassing the hypocrites who had stayed home.

The campaign to Tabuk enabled the Blessed Prophet ﷺ to create a buffer zone for the Muslims, all along the northern edge of Arabia. It created more places where Muslims could travel and spread the faith. It also distinguished the true believers, who were willing to sacrifice, from the hypocrites, who wanted to stay safe at home. In all, the campaign was a great success.

Sadly, the Prophet's ﷺ baby, Ibrahim, soon fell ill. He was less than two years old and had been a source of great joy for the Blessed Prophet ﷺ. Everyday after he finished work, the Prophet ﷺ would go and visit Ibrahim and play with him.

When the news reached the Blessed Prophet of Ibrahim's ﷺ illness, he rushed to Mariyah's side. Along the way, however, he suddenly felt weak in the knees and could hardly stand. He asked a Sahabi named 'Abdul Rahman bin 'Awf ﷺ to help him walk there. When he arrived, he stayed by Mariyah's side and watched as the baby slowly slipped away.

It was narrated that Asma' bint Yazid said, "When Ibrahim, the son of the Messenger of Allah ﷺ, died, the Messenger of Allah wept. The one who was consoling him, either Abu Bakr or 'Umar, said to him: 'You are indeed the best of those who glorify Allah with what is due to him.' The Messenger of Allah said, 'The eye weeps and the heart grieves, but we do not say anything that angers the Lord. Were it not that death is something that inevitably comes to all, and that the latter will surely join the former, then we would have been more than we are, verily we grieve for you.'" (Ibn Majah)

عَنْ أَسْمَاءَ بِنْتِ يَزِيدَ، قَالَتْ: «لَمَّا تُوُفِّيَ ابْنُ رَسُولِ اللهِ ﷺ إِبْرَاهِيمُ بَكَى رَسُولُ اللهِ فَقَالَ لَهُ الْمُعَزِّي - إِمَّا أَبُو بَكْرٍ وَ إِمَّا عُمَرُ - أَنْتَ أَحَقُّ مَنْ عَظَّمَ اللهَ حَقَّهُ. قَالَ رَسُولُ اللهِ: تَدْمَعُ الْعَيْنُ وَ يَحْزَنُ الْقَلْبُ وَ لاَ نَقُولُ مَا يُسْخِطُ الرَّبَّ لَوْ لاَ أَنَّهُ وَعْدٌ صَادِقٌ وَ مَوْعُودٌ جَامِعٌ وَ أَنَّ الْآخِرَ تَابِعٌ لِلْأَوَّلِ لَوَجَدْنَا عَلَيْكَ يَا إِبْرَاهِيمُ أَفْضَلَ مِمَّا وَجَدْنَا وَ إِنَّا بِكَ لَمَحْزُونُونَ». رَوَاهُ ابْنُ مَاجَه

Ancient Thamud.

Literature Selection

The Farewell Khutbah of the Blessed Prophet ﷺ

خطبةُ الوداعِ لِرَسُولِ اللهِ ﷺ

(Abridged)

Taken from the sayings of the Blessed Prophet ﷺ

During the last year of the Blessed Prophet's ﷺ life, he made a pilgrimage to Makkah in which he gave a khutbah in the valley of 'Uranah, near the plain of 'Arafat, to over 120,000 Muslims. By the year 632 CE, Islam had become triumphant in all of Arabia and was beginning to take a foothold in Syria, Africa and other lands. The tone of the Prophet's ﷺ speech suggested to many that he was near the end of his mission as well as his life. The basic character of a Muslim is mentioned within the address as well as a very important final instruction for all Muslims until the end of time.

The Farewell Speech of Prophet Muhammad ﷺ

All praise be to Allah. We glorify Him, seek His help and pardon, and turn only to Him. We seek the protection of Allah from the evils of ourselves, and from the bad consequences of our deeds. Whoever Allah guides cannot be led astray by anyone, and whoever Allah leaves to stray, no one can guide.

I declare that there is no God but Allah, He is alone with no partner, and I declare that I, Muhammad, am His servant and Messenger. I advise you, servants of Allah, to be aware of Allah, and I urge you to obey Him. I open this speech with what is good.

All you people, listen to my words, because I don't know if I shall ever be with you again here after this year. Therefore, listen to what I'm saying to you carefully and take these words to those who could not be here today.
All you people your lives, property and honor are sacred for you, until you appear before your Lord; just as you consider this month (of Hajj), this day, and this city (of Makkah) holy. Return the things that are entrusted to you to their rightful owners. You will meet your Lord and be held answerable for your actions. Haven't I conveyed the message? Allah, be my witness!

Be careful: only the person who committed a crime is responsible for it. A son is not responsible for the crime of his father, and a father is not responsible for the crime of his son. Know that every Muslim is a brother to every other Muslim and that Muslims are one brotherhood. Nothing is allowed for a Muslim if it belongs to another Muslim unless it was given freely and willingly. Do not oppress each other. Haven't I conveyed the message? Allah, be my witness!
All practices of idolatry and ignorance are now under my feet. Every right (of revenge) coming from murders in pre-Islamic days is cancelled, and the first of these to be cancelled is from the murder of Rabi'ah bin al Harith... Interest (money on loans) is forbidden; therefore, all interest requirements are canceled. Your original money is yours to keep. Do no wrong, and you will not be wronged. Allah has decreed that there shall be no interest, and so all the interest that is due to 'Abbas, the son of Abdel Muttalib, is canceled.

All you people, be aware of Allah concerning women. Indeed, you've taken them on the security of Allah and made them lawful to you with Allah's words. Indeed, it is true you have certain rights with your women, but they also have rights on you. It is their duty to honor their intimate rights and not to do improper actions, which, if they do, then you will have the right to reprimand them though not harshly. If they respect your rights, then to them belongs the right to be fed and clothed in kindness. Treat your women well and be kind to them, for they are your partners and committed helpers. It is also your right that they don't make friends with a person you don't approve of as well as to never be unfaithful.

Beware of Shaytan for the safety of your way of life. He has lost all hope in leading you astray in this land, but he will be happy if you follow him in small things. Therefore, abstain from obedience to Shaytan.

Indeed, I'm leaving behind me two things, the Book of Allah and my example (Sunnah), and if you follow these you will never go astray. If you were asked about me, what would you say?

All the people replied, "We declare that you have conveyed the message and fulfilled your mission!"

All you people, listen to me closely: serve Allah, say your five daily prayers, fast during the month of Ramadan and give of your wealth in Zakah. Perform the Hajj if you can afford it. Obey whatever I command you, for that is the only way you will get into Paradise.

All you people, indeed your Lord is One and your ancestor is one. All of you belong to the line of Adam, and Adam was created from dust. An Arab is not better than a non-Arab, nor is a white better than a black, or a black better than a white, except in taqwa. The noblest among you (humans) is the one who is the most aware of Allah.

All you people, no prophet will come after me, and no new way of life will be born. Reason well, all you people, and understand the words which I am telling you.

All those who listen to me shall pass on my words to others; and those, to others again; and may the last ones understand my words better than the first. Be my witness, Oh Allah, that I have conveyed Your Message to Your people.

When the prophet ﷺ finished his speech, he received the following revelation from Allah, Today, I have completed for you your way of life and granted you the last of My blessings. I have chosen Islam as your way of life. Surat Al Ma'idah (The Table) 5:3

﴿ٱلۡيَوۡمَ أَكۡمَلۡتُ لَكُمۡ دِينَكُمۡ وَأَتۡمَمۡتُ عَلَيۡكُمۡ نِعۡمَتِي وَرَضِيتُ لَكُمُ ٱلۡإِسۡلَٰمَ دِينًا﴾ سُورَةُ المائِدَة 5:3

As the Prophet ﷺ delivered this speech, one of the Sahaba, Rabi'ah bin Khalaf, repeated it loudly, sentence by sentence, and asked every now and then to make sure everyone was hearing it and repeating it to those yet further away.

The Task Ahead

The Blessed Prophet ﷺ returned to Al Madinah at the conclusion of his pilgrimage to Makkah. He declared that non-Muslims would never be allowed in the holy city again and that those who heard his words should tell them to others. You read his **Khutbat Al Wada'** خُطْبَةُ الوَدَاع **Farewell Sermon** and perhaps noticed a subtle message to the Muslims.

The Blessed Prophet ﷺ succeeded in bringing Islam to his people even as he equipped them to spread it further. The revelation of the Qur'an was complete, and thousands were memorizing it, learning it, living by it and teaching it.

An entire generation of people grew up as Muslims and were firm and committed believers. For example, 'Ali ﷺ and Fatimah's ﷺ two sons, Hassan and Hussain, were born into a believing Muslim family. They spent their childhood in the masjid, climbing on their grandfather's back while he bowed before Allah ﷻ in prayer.

The growth of Islam was reaching an international level. It would never be in danger of destruction again, such as when the idol-worshippers tried to suppress it. At 63 years of age, the Prophet ﷺ was aging. He began to turn his attention to the northern borders of Arabia again, where the armies of Persian and Byzantine empires lurked. The Prophet ﷺ called for the mobilization of an army to go to Palestine and put an end to the Byzantine threat once and for all.

For this task, the Prophet ﷺ chose Usamah bin Zayd ﷺ, a familiar young man, barely 20 years of age, to be the commanding officer. His father was the commander that had been martyred at Mu'tah, and his mother was Barakah. He was given good advice about war tactics from the Prophet ﷺ and then was left to organize his expedition. Shortly thereafter, the Blessed Prophet ﷺ became ill and had to limit his activities. The Muslims became worried about his condition.

The Fight against False Prophets

A few people in the Arabian peninsula saw a quick way to seize power and wealth. They simply declared that they were prophets too, just like Prophet Muhammad ﷺ. Because these individuals lived far from Makkah, they were able to convince their local people to follow them and promised them great riches.

Who is more unjust than the one who fabricates a lie against Allah or says, "Revelation has been sent to me," whereas no revelation has been sent to him, and the one who says, "I would produce the like of what Allah has revealed." If only you could witness when the unjust are in the throes of death, and the angels stretch their hands (and say), "Out with your souls. Today, you shall have your punishment, a punishment of humiliation, because you have been saying about Allah what is not true and have been showing arrogance against His verses." Surat Al An'aam (Cattle) 6:93

﴿وَمَنْ أَظْلَمُ مِمَّنِ افْتَرَىٰ عَلَى اللَّهِ كَذِبًا أَوْ قَالَ أُوحِيَ إِلَيَّ وَلَمْ يُوحَ إِلَيْهِ شَيْءٌ وَمَن قَالَ سَأُنزِلُ مِثْلَ مَا أَنزَلَ اللَّهُ وَلَوْ تَرَىٰ إِذِ الظَّالِمُونَ فِي غَمَرَاتِ الْمَوْتِ وَالْمَلَائِكَةُ بَاسِطُو أَيْدِيهِمْ أَخْرِجُوا أَنفُسَكُمُ الْيَوْمَ تُجْزَوْنَ عَذَابَ الْهُونِ بِمَا كُنتُمْ تَقُولُونَ عَلَى اللَّهِ غَيْرَ الْحَقِّ وَكُنتُمْ عَنْ آيَاتِهِ تَسْتَكْبِرُونَ﴾ سُورَةُ الأنعام:6:93

One of these men was a war leader by the name of Tulayha. He discovered a well in the desert one day and convinced his people that this was the proof of his Prophethood. He was too afraid to contradict Prophet Muhammad ﷺ while he was alive and only rebelled later on.

Khalid bin Walid ﷺ led a force to put down his rebellion; thereafter, Tulayha lived the rest of his life as a practicing Muslim. Another such false prophet was a man named Musaylimah. He sent a message to Prophet Muhammad ﷺ saying, "I, too, am a prophet like you. To us belongs half the Earth, and to the Quraysh belongs the other half, if the Quraysh would just be fair about it."

Obviously, Musaylimah wanted to control half of Arabia as his own property. Prophet Muhammad ﷺ sent a reply stating that "The Earth belongs to no one but Allah, and Allah grants it to whomever He wills among His worthy and righteous servants. Peace belongs to the rightly guided." Musaylimah, who gained the nickname, "The Liar," was later stopped in his tracks during the time of Abu Bakr ﷺ, the first Muslim Khalifa.

The Danger of Al Aswad Al 'Ansi

In the last days of the Blessed Prophet's ﷺ life, unsettling news came in from Yemen. A man by the name of Al Aswad Al 'Ansi began telling people he was a prophet and that everyone in Yemen should obey him and give him their money. Of course, he was no such thing. Al Aswad Al 'Ansi wanted power, money and glory, which he believed he could gain by being seen as a prophet. He knew that Prophet Muhammad ﷺ was ill and therefore felt the time had come to make his move. What he failed to realize was that a true prophet of Allah was not interested in riches. Also, as the Blessed Prophet ﷺ said in his farewell speech, *"There will be no new prophet after me."* (At-Tabarani)

«لَا نَبِيَّ بَعْدِي». رَوَاهُ الطَّبَرَانِيّ

Muhammad is not the father of any of your men. He is the Messenger of Allah and the Seal of the Prophets. Allah has knowledge of all things. Surat Al Ahzab (The Confederates) 33:40

﴿مَّا كَانَ مُحَمَّدٌ أَبَآ أَحَدٍ مِّن رِّجَالِكُمْ وَلَـٰكِن رَّسُولَ ٱللَّهِ وَخَاتَمَ ٱلنَّبِيِّنَ وَكَانَ ٱللَّهُ بِكُلِّ شَىْءٍ عَلِيمًا﴾ سُورَةُ الأَحْزَابِ 40:33

When Al 'Ansi's claims to Prophethood reached Al Madinah, the Muslims became alarmed. It could divide the community, weaken Islam and give a green light to others who might say they were prophets too. Al 'Ansi and his followers began attacking Muslim neighborhoods throughout the region and even captured the town of San'a. They unleashed a reign of terror and banditry from Aden to Ta'if, and everywhere in between.

Prophet Muhammad ﷺ knew something had to be done to protect the future of the Muslim Ummah. But he was ill with fever and was too weak to act against Al Aswad Al 'Ansi. Action was needed, and the Prophet ﷺ called upon some unique and resourceful Yemeni Muslims to help. He sent letters to some trusted Yemeni Companions and ordered them to stop Al 'Ansi in any way possible. (47:7) The man in the forefront of the fight against Al Aswad Al 'Ansi was a brave man by the name of Fayruz Ad Daylami. Below is his story, told in his own words.

The Story of Fayruz Ad Daylami

I, Fayruz, and those who were with me, never doubted the faith of Allah﷾ for a minute. No belief in (Al 'Ansi) entered any of our hearts. Instead, we waited for opportunities to get a hold of Al 'Ansi and eliminate him by any means. When we received the letters from the Messenger of Allah ﷺ, we felt strengthened in our mutual goal, and each one of us was determined to do what he could.

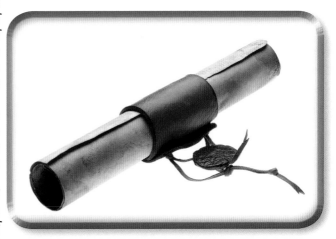

Because of his considerable success, severe arrogance took hold of Al Aswad Al 'Ansi. He bragged to the commander of his army, Qays bin Abd Yaghuth, about how powerful he was. His attitude and relationship towards his commander changed so much that Qays felt that even he wasn't safe from his violence.

My cousin Dadhawayh and I went to Qays. We informed him of what the Prophet ﷺ told us, and we invited him to "make lunch" out of Al 'Ansi before Al 'Ansi could make "dinner" out of him. He was interested in our idea and thought we were a blessing from Allah﷾ for him. He then told us some of Al 'Ansi's secrets.

The three of us vowed to confront the traitor from within his own castle, while our other brothers would confront him outside. We were all of the opinion that our cousin Athad, whom Al 'Ansi had seized after killing her husband, should join us.

We went to Al 'Ansi's castle and met with her in secret. I said to her, "Cousin, you know what harm and evil this man has brought to you and us. He killed your husband and dishonored the women of your tribe. He has slaughtered your menfolk and taken their rights away. This is a letter from the Messenger of Allah, peace be on him. It is to us in particular, and to the people of Yemen in general, in which he asks us to put an end to this trouble. Will you help us in this?"

"How can I help you?" she asked.

"On his removal from the land..." I said.

"Rather on his assassination," she suggested.

"By Allah, I had nothing else in mind." I replied, "but I was afraid to say it to you."

She stood up and said, "By the One Who sent Muhammad with the truth and with good news and warnings, I have not doubted in Islam for a minute. Allah has not created a more disgusting man than that devil, Al 'Ansi. By Allah, from the first time I saw him, I've only known him to be bad and corrupt. He never promotes the truth and does not stop himself from doing every horrible deed."

"How can we go about getting rid of him?" I asked.

Athad answered, "He is well guarded and protected. There is not a place in his castle which isn't surrounded by guards. However," she smiled, "there is one broken-down and ruined room that is slightly open to the outside. In the early evening, go there. You will find weapons and a lantern there. You will find me waiting also."

"But getting through a small crack into a room in a castle such as this is no easy task," I commented. "Someone might walk by and alert the guards and that will be the end of us."

"You may be right. But I have a suggestion."

"What is it?"

"Send a man tomorrow that you trust disguised as one of the maintenance workers. I'll tell him to make an opening in the room from the inside so it will be easier to enter," she said.

"That's a brilliant suggestion!" I exclaimed.

I then left her and told the two others what we had decided, and they agreed on the plan. We left right away to get ourselves prepared. We informed a select group of believers who were willing to help us and gave them the signal they should look for (to attack the castle). The time was to be in the early morning of the next day.

When night fell and the appointed time came, I went with my two Companions to the opening in the castle wall and uncovered it.

We entered the ruined room and took the lantern. We also found the weapons nearby. Then we proceeded to the bedroom of the enemy of Allah.

There, we saw our cousin Athad standing by his door. She pointed out where he was, and we entered. He was asleep and snoring. I plunged the blade in his neck, and he bellowed like a bull being slaughtered. When the guards heard this, they came quickly to his door and shouted, "What's going on?"

Athad answered them through the door. "Don't worry," she called. "The prophet of God is receiving revelation."

The guards said, "Oh," and left.

We hid in the castle until dawn. Then I stood on the wall and shouted, "Allahu Akbar! Allahu Akbar!" and went on with the athan until I reached the part, "Ash hadu anna Muhammadur Rasulullah!" Then I added, "Wa ash hadu anna Al Aswad Al 'Ansi Kadh-dhab (I testify Al Aswad Al 'Ansi is a liar)."

That was the signal. Muslims then rushed towards the castle from every direction. The guards were frightened when they heard the athan and were suddenly faced with crowds of Muslims shouting, "Allahu Akbar!" By sunrise, the mission was accomplished. When it was fully light, we sent a letter to the Messenger of Allah giving him the good news of the death of Allah's enemy.

The Prophet's ﷺ Last Days

The Prophet's ﷺ illness continued to increase, and the Muslims became worried for his health. He was old and didn't have the vigor of his youth anymore although he was always active.

One night the Prophet ﷺ suffered from sleeplessness and decided to take a walk in the midnight air of Al Madinah. Accompanied by his attendant, a young man named Abu Muwayhibah, he headed for the graveyard and stared at the silent graves. He said, "Peace be upon you, people of the graves. You are blessed in your present state which you have come to, which is different from the state of people who still live on earth. Assaults are falling, one after another, like waves of darkness, each worse than the previous one."

After praying for the souls of the dead, the Blessed Prophet told his attendant, "Abu Muwayhibah! I have been given the keys of this world and eternity in it. And now I am being offered Paradise and meeting with Allah. I am asked to choose between them." Abu Muwayhibah cried out, "I would give everything for your sake, sir! Isn't it possible to have both? Please take the keys of this world, eternity in it as well as Paradise." The Prophet answered, "No, by Allah, Abu Muwayhibah. I have chosen Paradise and meeting with my Lord."

When the people were informed of what the Prophet ﷺ said, their fears increased. The army of Usamah, which was nearly ready to march, paused in its preparations, and everyone waited tensely.

The Prophet's ﷺ Cheerful Mood

The next morning, Muhammad ﷺ found 'Aishah ﷺ, one of his wives, complaining about a severe headache. She was holding her head with her hands and muttering, "Oh my aching head!" He ﷺ said, "Rather, I should say, O my head, O 'Aishah!"

The Prophet ﷺ, however, continued with his duties as best as he could. He still met with delegations from tribes that wanted to accept Islam, taught men and women about their deen, pleaded with the believers to live lives based on goodness and led the Salah in the main masjid in Al Madinah.

The Prophet ﷺ began to suffer a severe fever a few days later and found it hard to meet with too many people. When he heard that some of the elder Muslims were grumbling about the appointment of the youthful Usamah to head the army, his headache worsened. The Prophet ﷺ asked his wife Hafsah ﷺ to pour some cold water over his head to reduce the heat in his forehead.

Then he entered the masjid and told the people that the decision of making Usamah bin Zayd commander was final and that the people had no right to second-guess it. He added that people used to complain against Usamah's father, Zayd, who showed his bravery when martyred at Mu'tah. The Prophet ﷺ concluded his speech by saying, "Didn't he make the best choice, who, when given the option of taking this world, the other world or in submitting to whatever is with Allah, chose the last alternative?"

The Muslims realized that the Prophet ﷺ was referring to himself and were filled with remorse. Abu Bakr ﷺ began weeping, and the Muslims fell silent. Usamah was chosen by the Prophet ﷺ and no longer would anyone question the decision. When the Prophet's ﷺ condition worsened, he asked that Abu Bakr ﷺ lead the prayers for him. This signaled to many Muslims that the Prophet ﷺ was tapping Abu Bakr ﷺ to lead the Ummah after him. Even when he felt strong enough to come in the masjid for Salah, he asked Abu Bakr ﷺ to continue leading the Salah while he prayed behind him in the rows.

The Whisper to Fatimah ﷺ

One day, while his daughter Fatimah ﷺ was attending to him, the Prophet ﷺ whispered something in her ear that made her cry. Then he whispered something that made her smile. 'Aishah ﷺ asked her what he said, but Fatimah ﷺ refused to tell what she regarded as a personal secret. The fever continued to burn in Muhammad's ﷺ forehead, and his body shivered with chills. The Prophet ﷺ overheard Fatimah ﷺ lamenting, "Oh, the terrible pain my father is suffering!" The Blessed Prophet ﷺ opened his eyes and said to her, "Your father will suffer no more pain after this day."

The anxious Muslims filed in and out throughout the day, some offering medicines and others praying. Everyone was anxious for the safety of the beloved Prophet ﷺ. In his last hour, as his head was resting on 'Aishah's ◉ lap, the Blessed Prophet ﷺ called out his last words.

As 'Aishah ◉ tells the story, "The Prophet's head was getting heavier in my lap. I looked at his face and found that his eyes were still. I heard him murmur, 'Rather, Allah on High and Paradise.' I said to him, 'By Him Who sent you as a prophet to teach the truth, you have been given the choice and you chose well.' The Prophet of Allah passed away while his head was on my side between my chest and my heart. It was my youth and inexperience that allowed me to let him die in my lap. I then placed his head on the pillow and got up to bemoan my fate and to join the other women in our sadness and sorrow." It was the 12th of Rabi' ul Awwal 11 AH, June 8th in the year 632 CE.

Later, Fatimah ◉ told 'Aishah ◉ what was whispered to her. She said, "The first time he told me that he would not recover from his sickness, so I cried. The second time he told me I would be the first from his family to join him, so I smiled." This prediction would soon come true.

The Muslims Grieve

With the Blessed Prophet ﷺ having left this world, the new Muslim community had to try to make sense out of what his mission meant and how they were to get along without him. When the Prophet ﷺ was alive and with them, there were no doubts or uncertainties. A person had only to ask his guidance, and he would be sure to receive an answer that was both wise and practical. But now he was gone.

When 'Umar ◉ heard the news of the Prophet's ﷺ demise, he came running and drew his sword in anger. He declared that he didn't believe the Prophet ﷺ was gone and that he'd fight anyone who said otherwise. He was overcome with great stress at the thought of losing his beloved friend and guide.

Abu Bakr ◉ arrived, and when he saw how distraught 'Umar ◉ was, he went to his friend and announced in a loud voice, "If anyone worships Muhammad, know that Muhammad has died. But if anyone worships Allah, then know that He is alive and cannot die."

Then Abu Bakr ◉ recited an ayah from the Qur'an to drive the point home. *Muhammad is no more than a Messenger. There were many Messengers who passed away before him. If he died or was killed, would you then turn around and run? If anyone ran away, it wouldn't do any harm to Allah. But Allah will reward quickly those who (serve Him) thankfully.* Surat Al 'Imran (The Family of 'Imran) 3:144

﴿وَمَا مُحَمَّدٌ إِلَّا رَسُولٌ قَدْ خَلَتْ مِن قَبْلِهِ ٱلرُّسُلُ أَفَإِيْن مَّاتَ أَوْ قُتِلَ ٱنقَلَبْتُمْ عَلَىٰٓ أَعْقَٰبِكُمْ وَمَن يَنقَلِبْ عَلَىٰ عَقِبَيْهِ فَلَن يَضُرَّ ٱللَّهَ شَيْئًا وَسَيَجْزِي ٱللَّهُ ٱلشَّٰكِرِينَ﴾

سُورَةُ آلِ عِمْرَان 3:144

'Umar ◉ accepted the wisdom of his friend's speech, and slumped down into the arms of his friend and wept at the devastating loss. A few hours later, when the time for the next Salah had come, Bilal ◉ began giving the athan. When he came to the name "Muhammad" in the athan, he broke down in tears. People in the streets heard him pause and saw him weeping. Everyone else began weeping as well. After a few moments of gentle crying, Bilal ◉ resumed his duty and finished the athan. Then, in his sorrow, he vowed to never say the athan again.

The Blessed Prophet ﷺ had fulfilled his mission. In his Farewell Speech he had declared, *"Be my witness, Oh Allah, that I have conveyed Your Message to Your people."* (Al Bukhari)

قَالَ رَسُولُ اللهِ ﷺ: «اللَّهُمَّ هَلْ بَلَّغْتُ؟ اللَّهُمَّ اشْهَدْ». رَوَاهُ الْبُخَارِيُّ

May Allah ◉ bless Prophet Muhammad ﷺ and give him the best in Jannah and make us among his company in the next life. Ameen.

The First Khalifa

'Ali ◉ was placed in charge of all the funeral arrangements for the Blessed Prophet ﷺ. It was agreed that the Prophet ﷺ would be buried in the exact same place that he died. Then the community mournfully performed the task of laying the Prophet ﷺ to rest in the earth. They buried him on the night of the 13th, in the month of Rabi' ul Awwal, in the year 632 CE (11 AH). The Janazah Prayer was attended by thousands of Muslims.

After the burial of the Blessed Prophet Muhammad ﷺ, it was up to the Muslim community to choose a leader. There was no argument about whether or not the Muslims should do this, for there were many sayings of the Prophet ﷺ about those who would lead the Muslim community after him. The Prophet ﷺ even gave instructions about the qualities of leadership and how Muslims should obey those in authority over them.

The senior members of the Muslim community gathered quickly, and after some discussion, they elected Abu Bakr ﷺ to be the first **Khalifa** خَلِيفَة **the Leader of the Ummah**. The job of the khalifa was to implement the laws of Islam in society, promote Islamic teachings, defend Muslims and establish justice among all people, thereby strengthening the Muslims.

Abu Bakr ﷺ, who was one of the first to believe in the message of Islam, was considered by most to be the logical choice for this new responsibility. He was the best friend of the Prophet ﷺ, and had earned the title **As-Siddeeq** الصِّدِّيق **the Truth-Affirming** for declaring the truth of whatever the Prophet ﷺ taught.

Abu Bakr ﷺ addressed the crowds of Muslims as they gathered after his election. He gave a formal acceptance speech as the Khalifa. His address is considered one of the most noble ever given by any ruler in all of human history.

Reflections on the Life of the Last Prophet of Allah ﷺ

There has never been a more humane and understanding man than the Blessed Prophet Muhammad ﷺ. He ﷺ demonstrated the best virtues of humanity and stood for the truth at a time when the world was filled with darkness and ignorance.

He ﷺ was the best model of a husband, father, leader and friend. He ﷺ was gracious to all and patient even with those who mocked and persecuted him. He ﷺ never laid a hand in anger upon any woman or child and was always compassionate and respectful towards others. When he had the idol-worshippers of Makkah in his grip, instead of taking the revenge that most would say he was entitled to, he forgave them and let them go on their way.

He ﷺ was so concerned with the welfare of others that he even forbade people to abuse animals. He ﷺ loved children and taught people that men and women were equal in the sight of Allah ﷺ. There has never been anyone quite like him. Even when all of Arabia and some of Syria were completely in his control, he did not behave like a king or a tyrant. He ﷺ didn't build palaces or wear fancy clothes or make people bow to him. Instead, he wore regular clothes, lived in a small mud-brick house, ate little and treated all men and women as his brothers and sisters.

Barakah, his nurse-maid from long before who was now about 70 years old, visited his grave everyday and cried softly. Once she replied to a person who asked why she came every day, "By Allah, I knew that the Messenger of Allah would die, but I cry now because the revelation from on high has come to an end for us."

How can any more be said for a man who lived so closely to the way of life that Allah ﷺ made for us? As Muslims, when we hear the name of our beloved Rasulullah (Messenger of Allah), we should ask Allah ﷺ to send peace and blessings upon him.

Surely, Allah and His angels send blessings on the Prophet. O you who believe, do pray to Allah to bless him, and send your salam (prayer for his being in peace) to him in abundance.
Surat Al Ahzab (The Confederates) 33:56

﴿إِنَّ ٱللَّهَ وَمَلَٰٓئِكَتَهُۥ يُصَلُّونَ عَلَى ٱلنَّبِيِّ يَٰٓأَيُّهَا ٱلَّذِينَ ءَامَنُوا۟ صَلُّوا۟ عَلَيْهِ وَسَلِّمُوا۟ تَسْلِيمًا﴾
سُورَةُ الأحزاب 56:33

Chapter 16
Biographies of Companions

The Election of Abu Bakr

It's difficult to imagine the sorrow that swept over the Muslim community after everyone heard about the death of the Beloved Prophet . People were rushing from all over Arabia to Al Madinah because they couldn't believe what they had heard. What would become of the Ummah now? How would Islam survive without its Great Leader?

The day after the Prophet passed away, a decision had to be made about the future of the Muslim community. The Blessed Prophet had left the Qur'an and his Sunnah, and now it was up to his faithful followers to carry on with the mission.

A group of Al Ansar organized a conference to decide what to do. Abu Bakr , 'Umar and leaders from Al Muhajirun quickly joined in the meeting. The issue was, of course, who should lead the community now that the Blessed Prophet was gone.

Some of Al Ansar thought the new leader should be elected from among them because they had provided protection for the Prophet and offered him a place to live. Some of Al Muhajirun argued that only a Makkan should be chosen because Makkans were the first people to respond to the Prophet's call.

As everyone began to debate and argue, Abu Bakr stood up and said, "All the good things Al Ansar said about themselves are true, but the Arabs only recognize the authority of Quraysh. I suggest one of two men; accept one or the other as you like." He then took the hands of 'Umar and Abu 'Ubaydah and held them up for people to come and offer their oath to one of them.

People began to argue further, with no solution in sight. Finally, 'Umar declared, "Abu Bakr , how can anyone else fill the office as long as you're alive? You are the most important of Al Muhajirun. You were with the Messenger of Allah in the cave of Thawr. You led the Salah during his last days. Hold out your hand so that I may give my bay'ah to you."

'Umar took Abu Bakr's hand and promised to be loyal to him as the first Khalifa of the Muslim Ummah. Others immediately agreed and understood that the Prophet himself had given many clues as to his preference for Abu Bakr to succeed him. Suddenly, everyone was surging forward and pledging their bay'ah to him. Abu Bakr was elected as the first Khalifa.

Abu Bakr's Acceptance Speech

The next day, as thousands more Muslims were pouring into Al Madinah to give their bay'ah to Abu Bakr , he stood before the huge crowd and gave his acceptance speech. Abu Bakr's first duty was to lay to rest the Blessed Prophet , his beloved friend. After the Blessed Prophet was washed and wrapped in a burial shroud, he was buried right were he had lain when he passed away. This was on his own instructions. The funeral prayer for the Blessed Prophet was solemn, as all the thousands of people were bidding farewell to the man who had changed their lives forever.

The Emergency Action

Not everyone who had become a Muslim was sincere. Some Arab tribes, especially those far away from the area of Makkah and Al Madinah, accepted Islam only because it seemed to be the trend. This fact became immediately clear when several of these tribes rebelled and declared that they would no longer pay their Zakah or perform other Islamic duties.

Different Bedouin Arabs began raiding Al Madinah and creating all sorts of trouble for the sincere Muslims. To make matters worse, a couple of Bedouin leaders declared themselves new prophets of Allah. This was despite the fact that the Qur'an referred to Prophet Muhammad as the seal of the prophets, which meant that he was the last one. The most powerful of these men was known as Musaylimah the Liar.

Abu Bakr's ﷺ Speech

O People! I have been put in authority over you and I am not the best of you. So if I do the right thing then help me and if I do wrong then put me straight. Truthfulness is a sacred trust and lying is a betrayal. The weak amongst you is strong in my sight. I will surely try to remove his pain and suffering. And the strong amongst you is weak to me I will–Allah ﷻ willing–realize the right from him fully. When obscene things spread among any nation, calamities generally continue to descend upon them. As long as I obey Allah ﷻ and His messenger ﷺ, you should obey me and if I do not obey Allah ﷻ and His messenger ﷺ, then obedience to me is not incumbent upon you. Arise to your prayers, may Allah bless you.

أما بعدُ، أَيُّها النَّاسُ فَإِنِّي قد وُلِّيتُ عليكُم ولستُ بخيرِ كم فإن أَحْسَنْتُ فَأَعِينُونِي وإِن أَسَأْتُ فَقَوِّمُونِي. الصِّدْقُ أمانةٌ والكَذِبُ خِيَانَةٌ. والضَّعيفُ فيكم قويٌّ عندي حتى أرجعَ إليه حقَّه إِن شاءَ اللهُ، والقويُّ فيكم ضعيفٌ عندي حتى آخذَ الحقَّ منه إن شاءَ الله. لا يَدَعُ قومٌ الجهادَ في سبيلِ الله عزّوجلّ إلا خَذَلَهم اللهُ بالذُّلِّ ولا تَشيعُ الفاحشةُ في قومٍ إلا عَمَّهم الـ بالبلاءِ. أَطيعُونِي ما أَطَعْتُ اللَّهَ ورسولَه فإذا عَصَيتُ اللَّهَ ورسولَه فلا طاعةَ لي عليكُم. قُومُوا إلى صلاتكم يَرْحَمْكُمُ الله.

Abu Bakr ﷺ had only a few troops left in Al Madinah since he just sent a large army to Syria to fight against the Byzantines and their allies. That army was under the command of a young man named Usamah bin Zayd ﷺ, whom the Prophet ﷺ had appointed for that task. Abu Bakr ﷺ still managed to gather a small army to defend Al Madinah against the increasing Bedouin attacks.

He ordered his small but tough army to go and stop the rebellions. Before any battle would begin, the Muslim generals would invite the rebels back to Islam. Many tribes gave in without a fight, but a few unruly tribes were hungry for a battle and engaged the Muslims in war.

Yet in battle after battle, the Muslims were victorious over the rebellious Bedouin and made them sign treaties of peace. But the huge battle with Musaylimah the Liar was yet to come.

At a place called Yamama, the Muslim army, with only 13,000 soldiers, met Musaylimah's army of 40,000. After many hard days of battle, the Muslims defeated the enemy and Musaylimah died in battle. The danger of false prophets ended, and all the Bedouin Arabs agreed to remain faithful Muslims loyal to the Islamic government in Al Madinah. The Wars of the Apostasy lasted only a year. Abu Bakr ﷺ demonstrated his excellent leadership qualities during this time.

The Growth of the Islamic Nation

One of the primary duties of Muslims was to deliver the message of Islam to all people and to fight against evil rulers who tried to prevent them from doing that. The Qur'an prohibited forcing anyone to become Muslim. It only called for ridding the land of any evil rulers who would forbid people to hear the message.

The two great empires of the day were the Byzantines and the Persians. The Blessed Prophet ﷺ had sent letters to the rulers of both lands inviting them to Islam. They both refused and were ready to fight against the Muslims. The Persians had even supplied arms and money to the rebellious Bedouin to try and bring about the defeat of Islam. In the interests of self-defense and fighting against evil, the Muslims had to engage in battle.

After the Ridda Wars (Wars of Apostasy) ended, thousands more people converted to Islam every month. This ensured the survival of Islam and increased the numbers of Muslim soldiers, or mujahidun, enormously. Islam started to gain converts in Syria and Palestine as well, thanks to the preaching of Muslim merchants and travelers.

One Muslim leader, who lived near the border of Persian-controlled Iraq, came to Al Madinah to ask for protection for his people from constant Persian threats and attacks. Abu Bakr ﷺ sent an army of 8,000 men, under the command of Khalid bin Walid ﷺ in 633 CE (12 AH), to engage the Persians in battle.

After a series of stunning victories, the outnumbered Muslims captured huge areas of the Persian empire. Within one year, most of the lands of southern Iraq were firmly under Muslim control. Muslim preachers entered every town

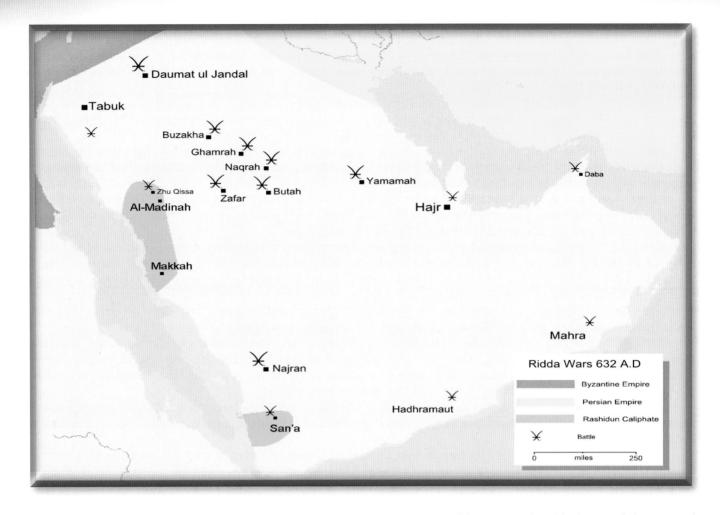

Ridda Wars 632 A.D

and village, teaching Islam to the people. Soon thousands were accepting Islam every day. Muslims in Palestine and Syria were under threat of attack from the Byzantines, so Abu Bakr ordered Khalid bin Walid to move his army to Syria to meet the new threat. After a few important battles, the Muslims drove the Byzantines away and secured the entire northern frontier of Palestine.

In one battle, a group of Muslim women were spotted by the Byzantines and were attacked. The women, led by a sister named Khawlah, picked up their tent poles and used them as spears to fight the raiding enemy soldiers. The women held the enemy away and killed many of them, as the Byzantines only had short swords and were speared whenever they tried to get close. When Khalid's reinforcements arrived, they drove the Byzantines away. Islam was on the move.

The Changing of Leadership

Two years and three months had passed with Abu Bakr as Khalifa, but he was old and fell ill. While on his death bed, he called a council of the important Companions of the Prophet and discussed with them who should lead after him. He suggested that 'Umar bin Al Khattab should lead the Ummah; everyone agreed it was the best choice.

A few days later, after Abu Bakr passed away, 'Umar took the bay'ah of the Muslims, becoming the new Khalifa. He gave the following speech: "My fellow Muslims! Abu Bakr is with us no more. He has been successful in running the affairs of the Ummah for more than two years and completed some of the tasks begun by the Prophet .

"I wish the responsibility of leading the Ummah was given to someone else. I never wanted such a job. However, I promise you I will not run away from this position. I will carry out my duty to the best of my ability.

"I seek guidance from the Qur'an, the teachings of the Messenger of Allah and the example set by Abu Bakr in running the affairs of the government. In this task, I seek your participation and help. If I am right, follow me. If I do wrong, correct me so that we don't go astray."

A Major Defeat for Persia

'Umar ﷺ had no time to rest. Pressure from Persian soldiers on the Iraqi front was increasing and action was needed. A new army was sent from Al Madinah to a place near the Euphrates River called Al Qadisiyyah. The people who lived in the area supported the Muslims and rebelled against the Persians because the Persian rulers had always been so harsh with them.

After a fierce battle, the outnumbered Muslims defeated the Persian army and took control of almost all of southern Iraq. As the message of Islam spread among the people there, thousands of Christians and Persians accepted Islam every day. Muslims would soon be forced to enter Persia itself for the final showdown.

Meanwhile, in the West, the Muslim forces facing the Byzantines in Syria were also winning battle after battle. In almost every case, the Muslim army would only have to surround a city, cut off its supplies and ask the people to surrender with the promise that they would not be harmed.

Nearly every city in Syria fell to the Muslims this way and little actual fighting occurred. The Byzantines were almost racing with each other to surrender to the Muslims! People were also happy with Muslim rule because Muslim governments charged much lower taxes than the Byzantines did.

Once the Muslims controlled the cities, life returned to normal for the people there. Because of the noble behavior of the Muslims, thousands of Christians accepted Islam daily. After the Muslims took the huge city of Damascus, the Byzantine emperor, in faraway Constantinople, decided to organize an army of 250,000 men to fight the Muslims. At a place called Al Yarmuk, in the year 637 CE (16 AH), an army of 40,000 Muslims defeated the Byzantines and forced them to retreat. In that same year, the Muslims gained control of Jerusalem, and 'Umar ﷺ arrived to accept the surrender of the city. Palestine, Syria and Iraq were in Muslim hands for good.

'Umar ﷺ helped to further organize the national Muslim government. The expanding Muslim world was organized into eight provinces and each was ruled by a governor appointed by the Khalifa. He also reorganized the government system of tax collection, and the treasury kept detailed accounts of everything in writing. This would help them raise the funds needed to face the growing threat of further attacks from the east.

Indeed, the Persians tried to launch more assaults against the Muslims in Iraq, but the Muslim armies were so successful in defeating these attacks that they followed the retreating Persians right into Persia. Soon almost all of Persia would be in Muslim hands!

'Umar ﷺ ruled as Khalifa for 10 years. In that time, the borders of the Islamic nation were doubled, and the numbers of believing Muslims were in the millions. Sadly, 'Umar ﷺ was killed by Fayrouz, a Persian rebel who had come to Al Madinah to assassinate him..

As he lay on his death bed suffering from a knife wound, he appointed a committee of important Muslims to choose a new khalifa within three days of his death. After a few days of debate, they chose 'Uthman bin Affan ﷺ, a trusted Companion of the Prophet ﷺ. But as we shall see, the problems he inherited caused him a lot of difficulty.

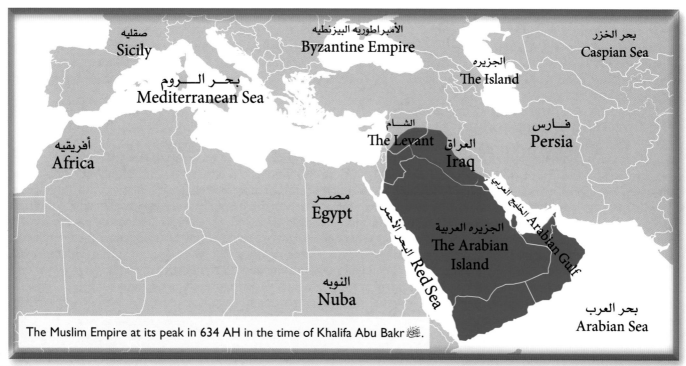

The Muslim Empire at its peak in 634 AH in the time of Khalifa Abu Bakr ﷺ.

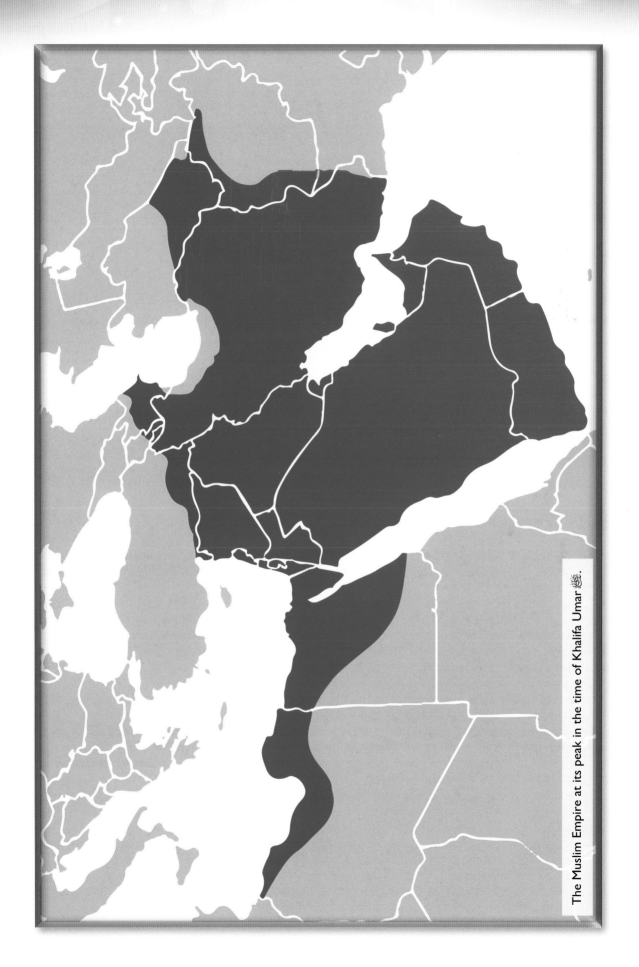

The Muslim Empire at its peak in the time of Khalifa Umar ﷺ.

The Great Challenges

'Uthman ﷺ became the leader at a time when Muslims were making great strides on all fronts. To continue this progress, 'Uthman ﷺ ordered the building of the first Muslim navy. He also ensured that an official copy of the mus-haf was available in every major Muslim city.

Everything seemed to be going well for the Muslims — even new lands were added to the Islamic empire. But some new problems began to arise. 'Uthman ﷺ was not as strict as 'Umar ﷺ and was shy about confronting people who did wrong. People loved the gentle character of 'Uthman ﷺ. However, when it became known that some of the Muslim governors in the provinces weren't behaving according to Islamic practices, people began to complain that 'Uthman ﷺ wasn't taking strong enough action against them.

Part of the problem was that the Muslim administrators in the new territories relied heavily on the system of the local government of the Persians and Byzantines. The Muslims were still not skilled at governing large cities and lands, so they often retained the same city workers and tax collectors that were there before Islamic rule.

At the same time, some Muslim governors were misusing the money that was supposed to go to the people. They used the money to build lavish palaces and to buy themselves expensive clothes. 'Uthman ﷺ removed some of the corrupt governors. However, in places like Syria and Egypt, the governors had become so powerful that they sometimes ignored the Khalifa's written messages.

A third problem was that many of the powerful governors were from the same family as 'Uthman ﷺ and many people accused him of favoritism. Although this was untrue, some Muslims in Al Madinah persisted in their belief. Thus, opposition to 'Uthman ﷺ spread.

On one occasion, a group of people came from the different provinces to complain about their governors. Khalifa 'Uthman ﷺ listened to them and promised that he would take action. The people began their journey back home, satisfied that justice would be served. On the way, an enemy of Islam named 'Abdallah bin Saba planted a fake letter on a man travelling with the group. The letter ordered all the people, who complained about their governors, to be killed when they returned home. He signed the letter from " 'Uthman."

When the people in the caravan found this false letter, they believed that 'Uthman ⬥ intended to murder them. Accordingly, they returned to Al Madinah, surrounded 'Uthman's ⬥ house and demanded he come out. When they showed him the letter they had found, 'Uthman ⬥ said the letter was a fake and that he didn't have anything to do with it.

The small mob of angry people refused to believe him, and killed him on June 20th, 656 CE (18th Thul Hijjah 35 AH). 'Uthman ⬥ was 79 years old. To make matters worse, they refused to run away. Instead, they stayed in the city to press their case. The Muslims in Al Madinah were shocked and in grief. 'Uthman ⬥ was loved by all for his gentleness and kindness, and now he had been cruelly murdered.

The Election of 'Ali ⬥

'Ali ⬥ was voted the next Khalifa by the people in the great masjid. Soon, Muslims from all over Arabia came to give him their bay'ah. But the immediate problem that faced him was the same one that had faced 'Uthman ⬥: what to do about the governors in Iraq, Egypt and Syria? In addition, a large number of Muslims began demanding immediate punishment for the killers of 'Uthman ⬥.

'Ali ⬥ was in a difficult situation. He decided to delay his investigation into the murder until the situation could be better understood and addressed. This was in keeping with 'Ali's ⬥ intellectual mind. He was always opposed to hasty or impulsive decisions..

But some people took this delay the wrong way and thought that 'Ali ⬥ was refusing to bring the killers to justice. When 'Aishah ⬥, the widow of the Prophet ﷺ, heard about this, she joined with a group of people who decided to fight against the Khalifa to force him to punish the killers.

Meanwhile, 'Ali ⬥ was taking action to address the other problems before him. He sent written messages to certain governors, asking them to step down from their posts. Some of the governors went voluntarily, but a few of them, most importantly, Mu'awiyah of Syria, refused to even read the letter. Trouble would soon come from Syria, but 'Ali ⬥ had other matters to attend to first.

The Battle of the Camel

A group of very famous Sahaba including Az-Zubayr bin Al 'Awwam ⬥, Talha bin 'Ubaidullah ⬥ and 'Aishah ⬥ traveled with a group of like-minded people to Al Basrah to seek support to confront 'Ali. They found some of the killers of 'Uthman ⬥ in the city and executed them. Then, they defeated 'Ali's ⬥ supporters there. They soon gathered a huge army to force the Khalifa to listen to their demands.

When news of this reached 'Ali ⬥, he organized an army of his own and marched to Al Basrah to stop Az-Zubayr ⬥ and his supporters. He didn't want them, or anyone else, to take the law into their own hands. 'Abdallah bin Saba was in 'Ali's ⬥ army with many of his supporters. When 'Ali ⬥ asked him and his men to leave, knowing that they were suspicious characters, they devised a disastrous plan.

The two armies met outside of Al Basrah in the year 656 CE (36 AH). 'Ali ⬥ and Az-Zubayr ⬥ met face to face and negotiated a peace agreement. After they returned to their camps, 'Abdallah bin Saba, the same man who plotted the murder of 'Uthman ⬥, made his move.

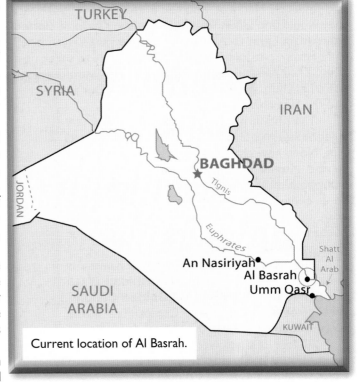

Current location of Al Basrah.

Before anyone could stop them, a few of his men charged and swung their swords as if the battle had begun. They had been hiding behind both armies waiting to strike. In the confusion, the men of both armies rushed to fight each other. Each thought that they had been ordered to do so.

Thousands of Muslims were engaged in battle against each other. Upon seeing the fighting, 'Aishah ⬥ became alarmed and tried to stop it. She mounted her camel and rode out into the battle trying to tell the people to stop. But, her own army thought she had come to encourage them to fight more, so the battle went on.

When 'Ali ﷺ saw that 'Aishah's ﷺ presence was inciting the fight, he ordered some of his soldiers to cut down her camel so that no one would see her any more. After that, 'Ali's ﷺ men reached her, cut down her camel and escorted her off the battlefield. 'Ali's ﷺ army defeated the rebels and peace was restored. The affair was known as the Battle of the Camel, after 'Aishah's ﷺ ride into the battle on her camel.

The Battle of Siffin

To save Al Madinah from any more political trouble, 'Ali ﷺ moved the capital of the Islamic empire to the new Muslim city of Kufah, near the border with Iraq. With the immediate problem solved, 'Ali ﷺ turned his attention to the rebellious governors.

He decided to replace every governor ever appointed by 'Uthman ﷺ, because he felt that they were weak and untrustworthy. Mu'awiyah of Syria again refused to step down and instead gathered an army to defend his position.

'Ali ﷺ marched his own army from Kufah to a place in Syria called Siffin. There he found Mu'awiyah's army ready to face him. 'Ali ﷺ tried to start peace talks with Mu'awiyah. But Mu'awiyah refused saying that he would never negotiate until the issue of 'Uthman's ﷺ killers was settled once and for all.

A three-day battle began, and 'Ali's ﷺ army made steady progress against Mu'awiyah's forces. When it looked as if he was going to lose, Mu'awiyah ordered his soldiers to hang pages from the Qur'an on the end of their spears so 'Ali ﷺ would pause. The trick worked; Mu'awiyah and 'Ali ﷺ began negotiations.

A group of Muslims in 'Ali's ﷺ army, were angry that their leader didn't go for a total victory, and they rebelled against 'Ali ﷺ. They became known as Khawarij. They left the battlefield and returned to Kufah to prepare an army to attack 'Ali's ﷺ forces.

'Ali and Mu'awiyah ﷺ pulled back their armies and returned to their own lands while the negotiations went on. 'Ali ﷺ put down the revolt of the Khawarij fighters when he returned and then worked to strengthen his position in Kufah. After several months of sending messages and proposals back and forth, 'Ali and Mu'awiyah ﷺ finally agreed that 'Ali ﷺ would step down and have an election for a new Khalifa.

But Mu'awiyah's ﷺ tricked 'Ali ﷺ. In a big public gathering, after 'Ali's ﷺ representative declared 'Ali ﷺ would step down as Khalifa, one of Mu'awiyah's ﷺ friends stood up and said that Mu'awiyah ﷺ would now be the new Khalifa.

This double-cross astonished everyone. The most angry people of all were the few rebel Khawarij fighters that had gone into hiding or who had pretended to make peace. They decided to kill both Mu'awiyah ﷺ and 'Ali ﷺ. Then they would find a new khalifa. While the Khawarij plotted, Mu'awiyah and 'Ali's ﷺ armies made moves against each other from Egypt to Al Madinah. Mu'awiyah ﷺ even briefly attacked and occupied Makkah and Al Madinah.

Finally, one lone Khawarij man was able to sneak up on 'Ali ﷺ and stab him. 'Ali bin Abu Talib ﷺ died in the year 661 CE (40 AH), just after Fajr prayer. The last of the true Khulafa' who lived totally by the Qur'an and the Sunnah was gone.

The Khawarij agent sent to kill Mu'awiyah ﷺ failed to assassinate his target though he did wound him. Now, new challenges presented themselves to the Muslim community, which was divided along political lines and badly divided. Unity would soon come, and a new line of khulafa' would arise, but it would not be completely according to the Sunnah. In fact, it would cause even greater challenges in the future.

The period of rule of the first four Khulafa' is known as the **Al Khilafah Ar-Rashidah الخلافة الرَّاشِدَة Period of the Rightly Guided Caliphs**. All four of these men were Companions of the Blessed Prophet ﷺ from the earliest days of Islam.

All four of them were given the good news by the Prophet ﷺ that they were guaranteed Paradise, and all four lived simple and moral lives based completely on the Qur'an and the Sunnah.

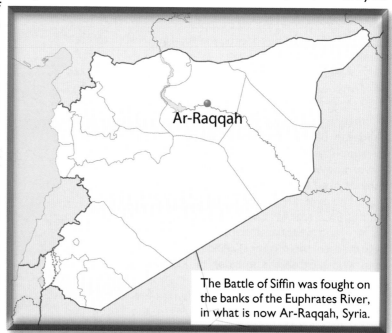

Ar-Raqqah

The Battle of Siffin was fought on the banks of the Euphrates River, in what is now Ar-Raqqah, Syria.

Who Was Um Salamah ?

One of the most interesting stories of the **Sahabiyyat** صَحابِيَّات **Female Companions** of Prophet Muhammad comes to us from the eventful life of Hind. She was also known as Um Salamah .

She and her husband, 'Abdallah bin 'Abdul Asad, were among the first to accept Islam in Makkah. When the leaders of the Quraysh heard about her and her husband's conversion, they began to antagonize and ridicule them. The Quraysh incited people to insult them in the streets. But the young couple remained firm in their faith.

Um Salamah, her husband and her son were among the people whom the Prophet sent seeking refuge in Abyssinia at the peak of the Makkans' persecution. Um Salamah left behind her nice home, relatives and her life of comfort. But she loved Allah more and was willing to sacrifice in any way for His cause.

A short time later, false reports reached the Muslims in Abyssinia. They claimed that, due to the increased numbers of Muslims in Makkah, the Quraysh were not as confrontational with the believers as before. Wishing to return home and to be near the Prophet again, Um Salamah and her family joined a group of Muslims that were making preparations to return.

No sooner had they arrived in Makkah, however, than they found out that the Makkans had started a new phase of vicious persecution and torture against the Muslim community. When the Prophet ordered the Muslims to secretly immigrate to Al Madinah, Um Salamah was among the first to try to leave. It would be a hard and difficult journey. We will see what happened next, as she recounts in her own words, the most interesting part of her tale.

Um Salamah - My Journey

When Abu Salamah (my husband) decided to leave for Al Madinah, he prepared a camel for me, helped me mount it, and placed our son, Salamah, up on my lap. My husband took the lead and began moving without waiting for anything else. Before we were out of the city of Makkah, however, some people from my own clan stopped us and told my husband:

"Although you can do what you like with yourself, you have no authority over your wife. She is one of our daughters. Do you expect us to let you take her away from here?"

Then they overwhelmed him and carried me away. When my husband's clan, the Banu 'Abdul Asad, saw my clan taking both me and my child, they became angry.

"No! By God!" they shouted. "We will not abandon the child. He is our son and we have the first claim on him."

They grabbed him by the hand and pulled him away from me. Suddenly, I found myself alone and desperate. My husband had to head for Al Madinah by himself, and his clan had taken my son away from me. My own clan overpowered me and forced me to remain with them.

From that very moment, the day when my husband and son were separated from me, I made it my habit to go out at noon every day to that valley and sit in the very same spot where this tragedy occurred. I would recall those terrible moments and weep until night fell.

I continued doing this for a year or so, until one day, a man from the Banu Umayah passed by and saw my condition. He went back to my clan and said, "Why don't you free this poor woman? You caused her husband and her son to be separated from her." He continued to try and influence them by softening their hearts. Finally, they told me, "Go and join your husband if you want."

But how could I go to my husband in Al Madinah and leave my son, a piece of my own flesh, in Makkah among the Banu 'Abdul Asad? How could I be free from sorrow, and my eyes free from tears, if I went to the place of al hijrah not knowing anything more about my son, who I would be leaving behind in Makkah?

A few people realized what I was going through, and their sympathies went out to me. They asked the Banu 'Abdul Asad on my behalf and succeeded in convincing them to return my son. I didn't want to stay in Makkah waiting until I could find someone to travel with, because I was afraid that something else might happen that would delay or stop me from reaching my husband. So, I quickly got my camel ready, placed my son on my lap and left in the direction of Al Madinah. I had just reached Tanim (a point three miles out from Makkah) when I met a man named 'Uthman bin Talha.

"Where are you going, Daughter of Zad?" He asked.

"I am going to my husband in Al Madinah."

"And there's no one with you?"

"No, by Allah, except Allah and my son."

"By Allah, I won't abandon you until you reach Al Madinah," he promised.

He then took the harness of my camel and led us forward. I have, by Allah﷾, never met an Arab more generous and noble than he. When we stopped to rest, he would make my camel kneel down, wait until I dismounted, lead the camel to a tree and tie it. He would then go to the shade of another tree. When we were rested, he would get the camel ready and lead us forward again.

He did this every day until we reached the outskirts of Al Madinah. When we arrived at a village near Quba belonging to the clan of Banu 'Amr bin 'Awf, he said, "Your husband is in this village. Enter it with the blessings of Allah." Then he turned back and headed for Makkah.

Tragedy and Good Fortune

The couple's paths finally came together after a long separation. Um Salamah﷞ was happy to see her husband, and he was delighted to see his wife and child. Important events soon followed in succession. First, there was the Battle of Badr in which 'Abdallah fought. Then the Battle of Uhud followed, in which the Muslims were severely tested. 'Abdallah came out of that battle wounded very badly.

He appeared at first to respond well to treatment, but his wounds never healed completely, and he remained confined to his bed. One day, while Um Salamah﷞ was attending to him, he said to her, "I heard the Messenger of Allah says, 'Whenever a hardship afflicts anyone, he should say, Surely from Allah we come and to Him we will certainly return.' "

Then 'Abdallah prayed, "My Lord, give me in return something good from this which only You, the Exalted and Mighty, can give." 'Abdallah remained sick in bed for several more days. His condition worsened. One morning the Prophet ﷺ came to see him. While the Prophet ﷺ was still at his bedside, 'Abdallah passed away. With his blessed hands, the Prophet ﷺ closed the eyes of his dead Companion.

The Blessed Prophet ﷺ said, "My Lord, grant forgiveness to Abu Salamah. Elevate him among those who are near to You. Take charge of his family at all times. Forgive us and him, Oh Lord of the Universe. Widen his grave and enlighten it for him." (Muslim)

قَالَ ﷺ : «اللَّهُمَّ اغْفِرْ لِأَبِي سَلَمَةَ وَارْفَعْ دَرَجَتَهُ فِي الْمَهْدِيِّينَ وَاخْلُفْهُ فِي عَقِبِهِ فِي الْغَابِرِينَ وَاغْفِرْ لَنَا وَلَهُ يَا رَبَّ الْعَالَمِينَ وَافْسَحْ لَهُ فِي قَبْرِهِ. وَنَوِّرْ لَهُ فِيهِ» رَوَاهُ مُسْلِم

Um Salamah﷞ remembered the prayer her husband had quoted on his deathbed and began repeating it, "My Lord give me something good out of this." The Muslims were greatly saddened by the plight of Um Salamah﷞. She became known as 'The Widow.' She had no one in Al Madinah of her own except her small children. She was alone and had no source of income.

Both Al Muhajirun and Al Ansar felt they had a duty to Um Salamah﷞. When she had completed the **'Iddah** عِدَّة **Waiting Period** before re-marriage is allowed (a total of four months and 10 days), Abu Bakr﷠ proposed marriage to her, but she refused. Then 'Umar﷠ asked to marry her, but she also declined the proposal.

The Blessed Prophet ﷺ then approached her with a proposal of his own, and she replied with a very interesting answer. She said, "Messenger of Allah, I have three characteristics. I am a woman who is extremely jealous, and I'm afraid that you'll see in me something that will anger you and cause Allah to punish me. Second, I am a woman who is already a bit old, and third, I am a woman who has a young family."

The Prophet ﷺ replied with an interesting answer of his own. He ﷺ said, "Regarding the jealousy you mentioned, I pray to Allah, the Almighty, to let it go away from you. Regarding the question of age you have mentioned, I am afflicted with the same problem as you. Regarding the dependent family you have mentioned, your family is like my family."

They were then married, and in this way, Allah﷾ answered her prayer of replacing a tragedy with something better. From that day on, Um Salamah﷞ became one of the **Umuhat al Mu'mineen** أَمَّهَاتُ الْمُؤْمِنِين **Mothers of Believers**, as the wives of the Prophet ﷺ were known. She would soon became an important teacher and narrator of hadith, helping the early Muslims—in particular women—in understanding Islam. May Allah﷾ bless Um Salamah﷞ with Jannah. Ameen!

Who Was Mu'ath bin Jabal ﷺ?

Mu'ath bin Jabal ﷺ was a young man in Yathrib (Al Madinah) who accepted Islam at the hands of Mu'sab bin Umayr ﷺ. If you will remember, Mu'sab ﷺ was the person that the Blessed Prophet ﷺ sent to Yathrib to help guide the new Muslims there.

Mu'ath ﷺ was one of the over 70 men and women who traveled to Makkah as part of the Second Pledge of 'Aqaba. In this pledge, the new believers promised to defend and follow Allah's Messenger ﷺ. After he returned to Yathrib, he joined a group of Muslims who campaigned against idols in the city. They would go from house-to-house, trying to convince the people to smash their idols.

After the Prophet ﷺ made Al Hijrah to Al Madinah, Mu'ath ﷺ spent as much time as he could in his company. He memorized the entire Qur'an and learned all the teachings of Islam in great detail.

Once the Prophet ﷺ said of him, Out of my entire Ummah, Mu'ath bin Jabal ﷺ is the most knowledgeable regarding permissible and prohibited things. (Ahmad)

قَالَ رَسُولُ اللهِ ﷺ : «أَعْلَمُ أُمَّتِي بِالْحَلَالِ وَالْحَرَامِ مُعَاذُ بْنُ جَبَلٍ». رَوَاهُ أَحْمَد.

After the liberation of Makkah, the Blessed Prophet ﷺ asked Mu'ath ﷺ to stay there and help instruct the Makkans in the knowledge of the Qur'an and in the teachings of the Islamic way of life.

The Mission to Yemen

Sometime after the Prophet ﷺ had returned to Al Madinah, delegates came from the land of Yemen announcing that many of the people there had accepted Islam. They asked for teachers who could come and instruct their nation in the ways of Islam.

The Blessed Prophet ﷺ organized a group of Sahaba to be sent and placed Mu'ath bin Jabal ﷺ in charge as their **Amir أمير Leader**.

Some companions of Mu'ath bin Jabal ﷺ said, "When the Messenger of Allah ﷺ intended to send Mu'ath bin Jabal to the Yemen, he asked, 'How will you judge when the occasion of deciding a case arises?' He replied, 'I shall judge in accordance with Allah's Book.' He asked, '(What will you do) if you do not find any guidance in Allah's Book?' He replied, '(I shall act) in accordance with the Sunnah of the Messenger of Allah.' He asked, '(What will you do) if you do not find any guidance in the Sunnah of the Messenger of Allah and in Allah's Book?' He replied, 'I shall do my best to form an opinion and I shall spare no effort.'
The Messenger of Allah then patted him on the breast and said, 'Praise be to Allah Who has helped the messenger of the Messenger of Allah to find something which pleases the Messenger of Allah.' (Ahmad)

عَنْ أَصْحَابِ مُعَاذِ بْنِ جَبَلٍ ﷺ أَنَّ رَسُولَ اللهِ ﷺ لَمَّا أَرَادَ أَنْ يَبْعَثَ مُعَاذًا إِلَى الْيَمَنِ قَالَ: كَيْفَ تَقْضِي إِذَا عَرَضَ لَكَ قَضَاءٌ. قَالَ أَقْضِي بِكِتَابِ اللهِ. قَالَ: فَإِنْ لَمْ تَجِدْ فِي كِتَابِ اللهِ. قَالَ فَبِسُنَّةِ رَسُولِ اللهِ. قَالَ: فَإِنْ لَمْ تَجِدْ فِي سُنَّةِ رَسُولِ اللهِ وَلَا فِي كِتَابِ اللهِ. قَالَ أَجْتَهِدُ رَأْيِي وَلَا آلُو. فَضَرَبَ رَسُولُ اللهِ صَدْرَهُ وَقَالَ: الْحَمْدُ لِلهِ الَّذِي وَفَّقَ رَسُولَ رَسُولِ اللهِ لِمَا يُرْضِي رَسُولَ اللهِ. رَوَاهُ أَحْمَد.

When it came time to bid farewell, the Prophet ﷺ said to Mu'ath ﷺ, "'O Mu'ath, perhaps you shall not meet me again after this year. Perhaps when you return you shall see only my mosque and my grave.' Mu'ath wept upon hearing this as he knew in his heart that he was never to meet the Prophet in this world again. A feeling of sadness and desolation overtook him as he parted from the Prophet. The Prophet's premonition was correct, the eyes of Mu'ath never beheld the Prophet after that moment. The Prophet died before Mu'ath returned from Yemen." (Ahmad)

عَنْ مُعَاذِ بْنِ جَبَلٍ ﷺ لَمَّا بَعَثَهُ النَّبِيُّ ﷺ إِلَى الْيَمَنِ خَرَجَ مَعَهُ رَسُولُ اللهِ ﷺ يُوصِيهِ وَمُعَاذٌ رَاكِبٌ وَرَسُولُ اللهِ يَمْشِي تَحْتَ رَاحِلَتِهِ فَلَمَّا فَرَغَ قَالَ يَا مُعَاذُ إِنَّكَ عَسَى أَنْ لَا تَلْقَانِي بَعْدَ عَامِي هَذَا أَوْ لَعَلَّكَ أَنْ تَمُرَّ بِمَسْجِدِي هَذَا أَوْ قَبْرِي فَبَكَى مُعَاذٌ جَشَعًا لِفِرَاقِ رَسُولِ اللهِ ثُمَّ الْتَفَتَ فَأَقْبَلَ بِوَجْهِهِ نَحْوَ الْمَدِينَةِ فَقَالَ: إِنَّ أَوْلَى النَّاسِ بِي الْمُتَّقُونَ مَنْ كَانُوا وَحَيْثُ كَانُوا. رَوَاهُ أَحْمَد.

When Mu'ath ﷺ returned a few years later, the Blessed Messenger of Allah ﷺ had indeed passed away. Mu'ath ﷺ was surely overcome with grief when he visited his grave. However, Mu'ath ﷺ found relief in remembering the sayings of the Prophet ﷺ and in hoping to meet him one day in the next life. Mu'ath bin Jabal ﷺ loved the Prophet ﷺ dearly.

Later Life in the Service of Islam

Mu'ath once said to his son, "My son, when you pray, do so as one who is bidding farewell to this world, and don't assume you will have another chance to pray again. My son, know that a believer dies in between two deeds: one he offers for today wherein he will attain immediate blessings, and the second in what he offers towards the Day of Resurrection, and in that he will gain the ultimate benefits."

In later years, a man named Al Khawlani entered the masjid in the city of Homs, Syria. He wrote, "I saw 30 elderly men who were Companions of the Blessed Prophet . A slightly younger man with bright eyes and long, dark eyelashes sat among them. Whenever the elders needed an explanation about something, they went and asked him, and did so with great love and reverence. I asked someone who was sitting next to me, 'Who is that man?' He replied, 'That is Mu'ath bin Jabal, may Allah be pleased with him.' Instantly, I felt a sudden intense love and admiration for him. I stayed near their circle and listened closely to their discussion until they dispersed."

One Friday, Mu'ath bin Jabal was giving a khutbah in which he said, "Coming your way are awful trials where money will be plentiful, and the Qur'an will be read by a believer, as well as a hypocrite. The young, old, strong and weak from all nations will read the Qur'an. But a person will read the Qur'an in public and will be amazed and bewildered as he says to himself, 'How is it that I am reading the revealed Qur'an, and people seem neither to listen, nor do they follow its warnings?'"

During the rule of Khalifa 'Umar bin al Khattab, Mu'ath was sent to Palestine to teach new Muslims the Qur'an. Mu'ath was old by then, and it wasn't long before he became ill. When he was near his last days, he prayed, "Welcome death, welcome. A visitor has come after a long absence. Oh Lord, You know I did not desire the world or to lengthen my time in it. Oh Lord, accept my soul with goodness as You would accept a believing soul." He then passed away as a life-long da'i, as well as a wise and intelligent servant of Islam.

What Is a Sahaba?

Once the Blessed Prophet ﷺ remarked, "'I wish that I had seen our brothers!' The people with him said, 'Messenger of Allah! Are we not your brothers?' 'No,' he said, 'You are my companions. Our brothers are those who have not yet come. And I will precede them to the Hawd.' (The Hawd: the watering place of the Prophet, may Allah bless him and grant him peace, from which he will give to the people of his community on the day of rising.) They asked him, 'Messenger of Allah! How will you recognize those of your community who come after you?' He said, 'Doesn't a man who has horses with white legs and white blazes on their foreheads among totally black horses recognize which ones are his own?' They said, 'Of course, Messenger of Allah.' He went on, 'Even so will they come on the day of rising with white marks on their foreheads, hands and feet from wudu', and I will precede them to the Hawd.'" (Malek)

قالَ رسولُ اللهِ ﷺ : «وَدِدْتُ أنَا قَدْ رَأَيْنَا إخْوانَنا. قالوا أوَ لَسْنا إخْوانَكَ يا رَسولَ الله؟ قالَ أَنْتُمْ أصْحابي وَ إخْوانُنا الذينَ لَمْ يَأتوا بَعْد. فقالوا كيفَ تَعْرِفُ مَنْ لَمْ يَأتِ بَعْدُ مِنْ أُمَّتِكَ يا رَسولَ الله؟ فقالَ: أرأيْتَ لَوْ أنَّ رَجُلاً لَهُ خَيْلٌ غُرٌّ مُحَجَّلَةٌ بَيْنَ ظَهْرَي خَيْلٍ دُهْمٍ بُهْمٍ، ألاّ يَعْرِفُ خَيْلَهُ؟ قالوا: بَلى يا رَسولَ اللهِ. قالَ: فإنَّهُم يَأتونَ غُرًّا مُحَجَّلينَ مِنَ الوُضوءِ وَ أنا فَرَطُهُم عَلى الحوضِ». رَواهُ مالِكٌ

A Sahaba, or Companion, of the Blessed Prophet ﷺ is anyone who heard, knew or spent time with him. These are the people who learned directly from him and passed their knowledge of Islam directly to their descendants. They were blessed in a way we can never be.

There were tens of thousands of Sahaba, each with their own unique story. Most were converts to Islam who had left idol-worship, Judaism or Christianity. A few were born into Muslim families whose parents were convert men and women. Bilal, Anas, Abu Bakr, Um 'Amaarah, 'Uthman, Fatimah, Hussain, 'Aishah and 'Umar ﷺ are great examples for us even to this day. May Allah ﷻ help us learn from them.

Who Was Abu Hurayrah ﷺ?

One of the most well-known of all the Prophet's ﷺ Companions was a man named Abu Hurayrah ﷺ. He belonged to the Banu Daws Tribe, which lived along the coast of the Red Sea. If you will remember, the Banu Daws were the ones who came to help the Muslims at the siege of Ta'if.

After the chief of the tribe, Al Tufayl bin 'Amr, had accepted Islam, Abu Hurayrah was curious about the religion. When he heard what Islam was all about from his chief, Abu Hurayrah ﷺ accepted Islam as well. He was eager to meet the Prophet ﷺ and asked to accompany his chief on his next trip to Makkah. Thus, on his next journey, Al Tufayl took the young man along with him to see the Blessed Prophet ﷺ. When Abu Hurayrah ﷺ came to Makkah, the Prophet ﷺ met with him and asked him his name. "'Abdush-Shamms (Servant of the Sun)," he replied.

The Blessed Prophet ﷺ exclaimed, "Instead, let your name be 'Abdur Rahman, Servant of the Merciful." He immediately accepted the new name. A few weeks passed, and then one day, the Prophet ﷺ noticed that he liked to play with cats and kittens. The Blessed Prophet ﷺ called out to him, Abu Hurayrah, which means the Kitten Man, or literally, Father of the Kitten. The nickname remained and that's what everyone called him from then on.

After learning more about Islam from the Blessed Prophet ﷺ, Abu Hurayrah ﷺ returned to his village for a number of years to teach the religion to others. A few years after Al Hijrah to Al Madinah, however, he and some other Muslims from his clan also went to live in Al Madinah. Because he was poor and unmarried, he went to live in a room in the masjid called Bayt as-Saff with the other very poor Muslims.

The Mother of Abu Hurayrah ﷺ

Abu Hurayrah's ﷺ widowed mother had also come to Al Madinah although she was still an idol-worshipper. Her son always felt sad because she never accepted Islam even though he kept trying to convince her of the truth. One time, when he tried to explain Islam to her again, she started yelling and saying terrible things against the Blessed Prophet ﷺ. Abu Hurayrah ﷺ came to the Prophet ﷺ with tears in his eyes. Upon seeing his sorrow, the Holy Prophet ﷺ asked him what happened. Abu Hurayrah ﷺ replied, "I've never given up on inviting my mother to Islam, but she's always refused me. Today, I invited her again, and she said some words I couldn't stand. Please, make dua' to Allah﷽ that my mother's heart will be moved towards Islam." The Prophet ﷺ immediately prayed to Allah﷽ for Abu Hurayrah's mother.

Later, he went home and found his door closed. He heard some water being splashed, and when he tried to enter the house, his mother said, "Stay out there, Abu Hurayrah." Then she got dressed and finally said, "Come in!" As soon as he entered and saw his mother, she announced smiling, "I declare that there is no God but Allah and that Muhammad is His servant and messenger." Abu Hurayrah ﷺ hugged his mother joyfully, and then ran back to the Prophet ﷺ, crying tears of happiness. He announced, "I bring good news, Rasulullah. Allah has answered your prayer and guided my mother to Islam!"

The Long Memory

Abu Hurayrah ﷺ loved the Prophet ﷺ and wished to learn as much as he could. Once, when he was sitting in the masjid, the Prophet ﷺ heard him pray, "O Lord...I ask you for knowledge which will not be forgotten." The Prophet ﷺ himself said, "Ameen." From then on, he spent a lot of time with the Blessed Prophet ﷺ. He memorized the entire Qur'an and many sayings of the Prophet ﷺ. He learned so many hadith that everyone became amazed with his knowledge. Abu Hurayrah ﷺ later married Busrah bint Ghazwan and had many children of his own. He was also appointed the governor of Al Madinah, and later, of Bahrain.

But he never forgot his roots. He would often say, "I grew up as an orphan, and I immigrated as a poor person. I used to be given food by Busrah bint Ghazwan. I served people when they returned from journeys and led their camels when they set out. Then Allah caused me to marry Busrah. So praise be to Allah who strengthened his way of life and made Abu Hurayrah a leader."

Indeed, he became a leader in more ways than one. After the Prophet ﷺ had passed away, Abu Hurayrah ﷺ dedicated his life to spreading his knowledge of the Prophet's ﷺ sayings to all. A Muslim leader named Marwan bin al Hakim wanted to test Abu Hurayrah's ﷺ memory of hadith one day. He invited Abu Hurayrah ﷺ, who was then very old, to sit with him and tell him what the Prophet ﷺ had said. Secretly, Marwan had a scribe behind a curtain who was told to write down whatever Abu Hurayrah ﷺ narrated. After many hours of speaking, he left. Marwan read the sheets of hadith. After a year had passed, Marwan invited Abu Hurayrah ﷺ again. He asked Abu Hurayrah ﷺ to repeat the traditions he knew, and Marwan found that Abu Hurayrah ﷺ had not forgotten a single word. Truly, Allah﷽ answered his prayer, and gave him knowledge that would not be forgotten.

The Daughter of the Prophet

Fatimah was the fifth child of Muhammad and Khadijah. She was born in the year 606 CE, during the time before prophethood was bestowed on her father. While she was still an infant, Muhammad started the habit of going to the mountains around Makkah to meditate and think.

Her younger brother died soon after his birth, so she never knew him, and her three older sisters, Zaynab, Ruqaiyyah, and Umm Kulthum, were soon married and left home. This left Fatimah, along with Barakah, Zayd bin Harith (the adopted son of Muhammad), 'Ali (the Prophet's cousin) and Khadijah, as part of the main household of the Prophet.

When Fatimah turned five years old, she learned that her father had been chosen by Allah to be His Prophet. Her mother, Khadijah, who was the first to believe in the message, explained to her daughter what her father had to do now. Fatimah spent a lot of time with her father, and often went with him on his walks through the streets of Makkah. She even attended many of the secret gatherings that were held by the early Muslims when they were a persecuted minority.

One day, Fatimah was with her father when a group of idol-worshippers came and threw garbage on his back in the courtyard of the Ka'bah. With tears in her eyes, she cleaned the garbage off and yelled at the men. When the Prophet finished his prayer, he made a dua' that Allah would punish those idol-worshippers. Later, at the Battle of Badr, those men would pay with their lives for what they had done to the Prophet.

The families into which Fatimah's three older sisters married all started persecuting them to retaliate against the Prophet for speaking out against idol-worship. Ruqaiyyah and Umm Kulthum moved back into the Prophet's house after their husbands divorced them. Everyone was happy that they were now out of those bad families.

A short time later, the Makkans forced all the Muslims from their homes and made them live in a dusty, enclosed valley where there were only limited supplies of food. Fatimah was just 12 years old when she patiently endured the three long years of the boycott.

Even when it was finally over, Fatimah continued to face more trials and hardships. Her loving mother, Khadijah, passed away. Her death meant the loss of the one woman that everyone looked to for compassion. The Prophet's beloved uncle, Abu Talib, also passed away that year. Due to these events, this year came to be known as the Year of Sorrow.

A Loving Daughter

Fatimah soon realized that she had to give more comfort and support to her father. With great love and devotion, she dedicated herself to looking after him. She was so concerned with his health and welfare that she gained the nickname, the Mother of Her Father.

The Blessed Prophet had a special love for his daughter on account of her sincerity and good heart. Fatimah earned the title, **Az-Zahra'** الزَّهْرَاء, which means **The Shining Person**. That was because her beaming face seemed to radiate light. She preferred spending her time studying the Qur'an and serving Allah over such trivial things as gossiping and passing time in useless games.

Fatimah also had a close physical resemblance to her father. Once, 'Aishah remarked, "I've never seen anyone in Allah's creation resemble the Messenger of Allah more in speech, conversation and manners than Fatimah. When the Prophet saw her approaching, he would welcome her, stand up, kiss her, take her by the hand and then set her down in the same place he had been."

After Fatimah made Al Hijrah from Makkah to Al Madinah, she stayed at first with her stepmother, Sawda, until her own home was ready. Soon, she started to receive marriage proposals which she promptly turned down. Then the young man 'Ali bin Abi Talib gained the courage to go to the Prophet and ask for Fatimah's hand in marriage.

When he approached the Prophet to ask, however, he became nervous and tongue-tied. He stared at the ground and said nothing. The Blessed Prophet then asked, "Why have you come? Do you need something?"

'Ali still couldn't bring himself to say what he wanted.

The Prophet then said, "Perhaps you came to propose marriage to Fatimah?"

"Yes," replied 'Ali.

The Prophet ﷺ smiled and said, "Welcome to the family." Then he asked 'Ali ؓ what **Mahr مَهْر Marriage Gift**, he had for Fatimah.

'Ali ؓ answered that he didn't have anything to give as a mahr. The Prophet ﷺ then reminded him that he had a shield which could be sold. So, 'Ali ؓ sold the shield to 'Uthman ؓ for 400 dirhams (silver coins). While 'Ali ؓ was rushing back to the masjid to see the Prophet ﷺ, 'Uthman ؓ came after him and told him to wait a minute. Ali ؓ stopped, and 'Uthman ؓ told him, "I am returning your shield to you as a present from me on your marriage to Fatimah."

'Ali ؓ and Fatimah ؓ were married, and the Prophet ﷺ himself performed the **Nikah نکاح**, or **Marriage**. The Blessed Prophet ﷺ prayed, "Oh Lord, bless them both, bless their house and bless their children." Life for the newlyweds was sweet yet difficult. To make their living, 'Ali ؓ worked as a water carrier, and Fatimah ؓ ground corn. One day, she said to her husband, "I've ground corn (so much so that) now my hands are blistered."

'Ali ؓ, who was also tired, replied, "I've carried water until my chest hurts."

Then 'Ali ؓ said, "Allah has given your father some captives of war, so go and ask him to give you one as a servant."

After thinking about it, she went to the Prophet ﷺ to ask. But she felt shy and didn't say what she really wanted. Later, she and 'Ali ؓ both went and asked together. The Prophet ﷺ replied that he had an obligation to help the poor Muslims first, so he couldn't grant their request.

Later that evening, the Prophet ﷺ came and visited them in their home and told them, "Shall I teach you something that is far better than what you asked me for? Words which Jibreel ؊ taught me? You are highly recommended to say after every Salah, **SubhanAllah سُبْحَانَ الله** 10 times, **Al hamdulillah الْحَمْدُلله** also 10 times, and then **Allahu Akbar الله أكْبَر** 10 times. Then, before going to bed at night, you are highly recommended to say each one 33 times." In later years, 'Ali ؓ recalled that from that day forward, he never forgot to say those words.

A Blessed Lady

Life was hard for the Prophet's ﷺ family in Al Madinah, not because Islam was growing, but because the Prophet ﷺ lived a very simple lifestyle. He often went hungry and preferred to give food to others first before taking any himself. Once, Fatimah brought him a loaf of bread, and he replied that it was the first food he had eaten in three days.

On another occasion, the Prophet ﷺ returned to Al Madinah from a journey and immediately went to the masjid to perform two rak'aat of prayer. Then he went to Fatimah's house to greet her. When she saw him, she began to cry. When the Prophet ﷺ asked her why she was crying, she replied, "I see you, Messenger of Allah, and your color is pale, and your clothes are worn out."

"Fatimah," he said, "don't cry. Allah has sent your father with a mission that He will make affect every house on the face of the Earth, whether it be in a town, village or tent. It will bring either glory or humiliation (on those who accept or reject it) until (Allah's) mission is finished, just as surely as nightfall always comes." Fatimah ؓ shared in the joys and sorrows of the Muslim community. She and 'Ali ؓ were blessed with three beloved children, Hassan, Hussain and the little Zaynab. Although the duties of motherhood took up much of her time, she participated fully in the life and needs of the community.

In Al Madinah, she helped take care of the poor Muslims who lived in the masjid. After the Battle of Uhud, she acted as a doctor for the wounded. During the Battle of the Ditch, she recruited many other women to cook for the Muslim soldiers and led the prayer at her own prayer station.

Fatimah ؓ also accompanied the Muslims when they made 'Umrah to Makkah, just before the Treaty of Hudaibiyah. She also marched, along with many other Muslim women, when the Muslim army finally took over Makkah from the idol-worshippers. Imagine her happiness at being able to see her old neighborhood where she and her sisters grew up with their beloved mother, Khadijah ؓ.

After a few more years, the Blessed Prophet ﷺ became ill. He told Fatimah ؓ that Angel Jibreel ؊ had recited the entire Qur'an with him twice that year, whereas he had always done it once in previous years. This, the Prophet ﷺ explained, made him feel that perhaps his mission was coming to a close. If you remember, as the Prophet ﷺ continued to grow weaker, he whispered to Fatimah ؓ that he wasn't going to recover from his illness, so she cried. Then he told her that she would be the first of his family to join him in Paradise after he died, so she laughed.

Five months after the Blessed Prophet ﷺ died, Fatimah ؓ woke up looking unusually happy. That afternoon, she called her friend Salma to help her take a bath and dress her in a new outfit. She asked Salma to help put her bed in the courtyard of her home, and then requested her to send for her husband, 'Ali ؓ.

When 'Ali ؓ came, he was shocked and full of worry when he saw her lying in the middle of the courtyard in bed. He rushed to her side and asked her what was wrong.

"I have an appointment today with the Messenger of Allah," she replied.

'Ali ؓ cried tears of grief and she tried hard to comfort him. She told him to take good care of their children and asked that she be buried without any extra special ceremony. She looked up at the sky, and then closed her eyes and entered an eternal sleep. She was less than 30 years old. May Allah ﷻ bless her and give her the best reward in Jannah! Ameen!

The Story of Salman the Persian

If a person's heart is searching, no amount of material wealth or pleading can hold him down. This truth is spectacularly illustrated in the life of one of the most interesting of the Sahaba: Salman al Faresi. The word **Faresi** فَارِسِيّ means **Persian**. He was from Persia, which refers to modern-day Iran.

He began life as a Zoroastrian, which is a follower of an ancient religion of Persia, and he later accepted Christianity. However, when he heard the message of Islam, he set out to search for its source. This story will inspire all who seek the truth all over the world. Salman's tale is told here in his own words, as he told it to others.

A map of Persia, which is modern-day Iran.

Salman Al Faresi - My Story

I grew up in the town of Jai in Persia, near the city of Asfahan. My father was the chief of the village. He was the richest person there and had the biggest home of all.

Ever since I was a boy, I remember my father loving me more than he did anyone else. And as time went by, his love for me became so strong that he developed an intense fear of losing me or of having something bad happen to me. So he made me stay at home, a virtual prisoner!

(Having nothing much else to do) I became devoted to the religion of Zoroaster and eventually became custodian of the household fire, which we worshipped daily. My duty was to make sure that the flame remained burning and that it did not go out for even a single hour, day or night.

My father had a huge estate which yielded many varieties of crops. He managed the estate himself and carefully calculated the harvest. One day, while he was occupied with his duties as chief of the village, he called to me and said, "My son, as you can tell, I'm too busy to go out to the estate just now. So you go and take care of matters there for me today."

Off I went, but on my way back from the estate, I happened to pass by a Christian church. The sound of the people's voices inside attracted my attention. I didn't know anything about Christianity or about the followers of this or any other religion. This was because my father had always kept me in the house sheltered from people.

When I heard the melodic voices of the Christians, I stopped and entered the building to see what they were doing. I was impressed by the way they were praying and felt myself drawn to their faith.

"By God," I said, "this faith is better than what we have. I will stay here and not leave them until the sun sets." So I stayed and talked with the priest, who told me that the Christian religion originated in Syria.

There I remained the entire day and did not return to my father's home. When I finally did reach home later that night, my father met me and asked what had delayed me. I told him about my meeting with the Christians and how I was impressed by their faith. He became upset and said, "My son, there is nothing good in that religion. Your religion, and the religion of your forefathers, is better." "No, their religion is better than ours," I insisted.

My father became dismayed and feared that I would leave our ancestral faith. So he locked me up in the house and put a chain on my ankle. I managed, however, to send a message to the Christians, asking them to inform me of any caravan going to Syria that I might travel with.

The Escape to Syria

Before long, they contacted me and told me of a caravan that would soon be headed in that direction. I managed to unchain myself, and, concealing my true identity, accompanied the caravan to Syria. When I arrived there, I asked who was the highest person in the Christian religion and was directed to the bishop of a local church. When I gained an audience with him, I explained my story and said, "I want to become a Christian, and I would like to become your servant so I can learn from you and pray with you."

The bishop agreed, and I entered the church in his service. I soon found out, however, that this man was corrupt. He would order his followers to give him money to use in charitable causes while holding out the promise of blessings for them. But when they gave money in the cause of God, he would take most of it for himself and give only a little to the poor and needy.

In this way he amassed a vast fortune. Then, when the bishop died and the Christians gathered to bury him, I told them of his corrupt doings. At their request, I showed them where he kept their stolen donations. When they saw the large jars filled with gold and silver, they cried, "By God, we will never bury him." Instead, they nailed his body on a cross and threw stones at it.

I stayed on, though, and continued to serve the person who replaced him. The new bishop was a spiritual man who longed for the Hereafter. He would worship Allah day and night. I became greatly devoted to him and spent a long time in his company. But alas, he was very old and passed away, leaving me alone again.

So I set out to find a new priest I could serve and learn from. I traveled to Mosul, Nisibus and many other cities and served many important men. Some were good in character; others were less than virtuous. Finally, I came into the service of a wise priest in the city of Ammuriyah, Palestine. He told me about a new prophet whom God was going to choose, and he would be in the land of the Arabs.

He gave me some signs by which I might recognize him. First, he would have a reputation for strict honesty. Next, he would accept charity but would never use it himself, he would give it away. But if given a gift for himself, he would take it. Also, he would have a birth mark between his shoulders.

He also added that the city where I would find him would be filled with date-palm groves. Hearing the news of a new prophet filled me with longing and delight. How I wished I could serve a man whom God Himself had given guidance to. With all haste, I gathered my meager supplies and looked for a way into the land of the Arabs.

From Slave to Sahaba

A group of Arabs from the tribe of Kalb were passing through the city. I asked them to take me with them to their land in return for whatever money I had. They agreed and I paid them.

When we reached Wadi al Qura (a place half-way between Al Madinah and Syria), they broke the deal and sold me into slavery. A Jewish trader bought me. I worked as a servant for him but eventually he sold me to a nephew of his who belonged to the tribe of Banu Quraytha.

This nephew took me with him to Yathrib, the city of palm groves, which is how the priest at Ammuriyah had described it. At that time, the Prophet ﷺ was inviting his people in Makkah to accept Islam, but I did not hear anything about him then because of the harsh duties that slavery brought upon me.

When the Prophet ﷺ reached Yathrib after his Hijrah from Makkah, I was working at the top of a date-palm tree belonging to my master, who was sitting under the tree. A nephew of his came up and said, "May Allah declare war on the Aws and the Khazraj (the two main Arab tribes of Yathrib). By Allah, they are even now gathering at Quba to meet a man who has today come from Makkah and who claims he is a prophet. I passed by the crowd."

I felt hot flashes as soon as I heard those words, and I began to shiver so violently that I was afraid that I might fall on my master. I quickly climbed down from the tree and spoke to my master's nephew.

"What did you say?" I asked, "Repeat the news for me."

My master became very angry at my insolence, and he hit me hard. "What does it matter to you? Go back to what you were doing!" he shouted.

That night, I took some dates that I had gathered, and went to the place where the Prophet ﷺ was staying. I walked up to him and said, "I have heard that you are a righteous man and that you have Companions with you who are strangers and are in need. Here is something from me as charity. I see that you are more deserving of it than others."

The Prophet ﷺ asked his Companions to have them, but he himself didn't eat any of them. So a few days later, I gathered some more dates. When the Prophet ﷺ was leaving Quba for Al Madinah, I went to him and said, "I noticed that you didn't eat any of the dates I gave in charity. These, however, are a gift for you especially." Of this gift of dates, both he and his Companions ate.

When I saw that he wouldn't take charity for himself, but only shared in the gift when I said it was for him, I became very excited. A few days later, I saw him attending a funeral. I came up behind him, and I saw the birthmark on his back where his shirt was parted.

All the signs were true! So I told the Prophet ﷺ my story and begged to be allowed to serve him and to follow his teachings. But I was a slave, I explained, and could not buy my freedom.

The Holy Prophet ﷺ then told me that he would buy my freedom from the Jew and that I was a seeker of truth. Elated, I returned to my master to await my promised freedom.

The next day, when the Prophet ﷺ came with some of his Companions, he offered to pay the Jew a sum of money to free me. The Jew agreed, but then added a condition that I had to plant a whole grove full of palm trees (300 trees in all) before the deal would go through.

I cried to the Messenger of Allah, "How can I pay this heavy price?" He merely told me, "Don't worry about it. Allah will manage things for you."

Imagine how my shock turned to joy! The following day, the Prophet ﷺ returned with a whole crowd of his Companions, who all worked together to plant an entire grove! The Prophet ﷺ placed each baby tree in the ground with his own hands, after his Companions dug the holes. My freedom was secured, and I became a Companion of Allah's Last Messenger on Earth.

From that day on, whenever I met anyone new, and they asked me whose son I was, I would always reply, "I am Salman, the son of Islam, from the children of Adam."

Abu Dharr ﷺ from the Tribe of Ghifar

Islam teaches that the truth must be spread to all. The Qur'an offers the best advice on how to give da'wah, and the Blessed Prophet ﷺ explained how it should be done.

The story of Abu Dharr ﷺ, from the tribe of Ghifar, is one of the many real-life examples of how an everyday person put this into effect. Though he was just a young man from a poor family in a place called the Waddan Valley, Abu Dharr ﷺ lived a very full life. Known for his great courage and practical nature, he had already decided from an early age that idol-worship was foolish.

When he heard that there was a prophet in the distant city of Makkah, he wasted no time in asking his brother Anis to go and gather more information about him. He said, "Go to Makkah and get whatever news you can about this man. He claims to be a prophet and to receive revelation that comes to him from heaven. Listen to some of his words and come back and repeat them to me."

Anis went to Makkah and met the Prophet ﷺ as instructed. He listened to what he had to say. Then he returned to Abu Dharr ﷺ, who met him and anxiously asked for news of the Prophet ﷺ.

"I have seen a man," reported Anis, "who calls people to noble qualities, and there is no mere poetry in what he says."

"What do people say about him?" asked Abu Dharr ﷺ.

"They say he is a magician, a fortune-teller or a poet."

"My curiosity isn't satisfied. I'm not finished with this matter. Will you look after my family while I go out and examine this Prophet's mission myself?"

"Yes. But beware of the Makkans."

The Encounter with 'Ali ﷺ

On his arrival in Makkah, Abu Dharr ﷺ immediately felt very apprehensive and decided to exercise great caution. The Quraysh were noticeably angry over the Muslim's verbal attacks on their idols. Abu Dharr ﷺ heard of the terrible violence they were inflicting on the followers of the Prophet ﷺ, though he wasn't surprised. He therefore refrained from asking anyone about Muhammad ﷺ, not knowing whether that person might be a friend or an enemy.

At nightfall, he lay down in the courtyard of the Ka'bah. 'Ali bin Abi Talib ﷺ passed by him and, realizing that he was a stranger, asked him to come to his house. Abu Dharr ﷺ spent the night with him and returned to the courtyard in the morning. He took his water pouch and bag containing provisions. He had asked no questions, and no questions were asked of him.

Abu Dharr ﷺ spent the following day without getting to meet the Prophet ﷺ. In the evening, he went to the courtyard of the Ka'bah to sleep, and 'Ali ﷺ again passed by him and said, "Isn't it time that a man knows his house?"

Abu Dharr ﷺ accompanied him and stayed at his house a second night. Again, no one asked the other about anything.

On the third night, however, 'Ali ﷺ asked him, "Aren't you going to tell me why you came to Makkah?"

"Only if you will take it upon yourself to guide me to what I seek." 'Ali ﷺ agreed and Abu Dharr ﷺ said, "I came to Makkah from a distant place seeking a meeting with the new prophet and to listen to what he has to say."

'Ali's face filled with happiness as he said, "By Allah, he is really the Messenger of Allah." Then he went on telling Abu Dharr ﷺ more about the Prophet ﷺ and his teachings.

Finally, he said, "When we get up in the morning, follow me wherever I go. If I see anything that I'm afraid of for your sake, I will stop as if to pass water. If I continue, follow me until you enter where I enter."

Abu Dharr ﷺ hardly slept a wink the rest of the night because of his intense longing to see the Prophet ﷺ and listen to the words of revelation. In the morning, he followed closely in 'Ali's footsteps until they were in the presence of the Prophet ﷺ.

"Assalamu 'Alayka yaa Rasulullah," said Abu Dharr ﷺ, greeting him with the words 'Peace be upon you, O Messenger of Allah.' "Wa 'alayka assalamullahi wa rahmatuhu wa barakaatuhu," replied the Prophet ﷺ, telling him 'And on you be the peace of Allah, His mercy and His blessing.'

Abu Dharr ﷺ was, thus, the first person to greet the Prophet ﷺ with the greeting of peace. After that, the greeting spread and came into general use. The Prophet, peace be on him, welcomed Abu Dharr ﷺ and invited him to Islam. He recited some of the Qur'an for him. Before long, Abu Dharr ﷺ declared the Shahadah, and entered the new faith. He was among the first people to accept Islam. Now Abu Dharr ﷺ will continue the story of what happened next in his own words.

My Adventure in Da'wah — Abu Dharr al Ghifari 🙵

After (accepting Islam), I stayed with the Prophet 🙵 in Makkah, and he taught me Islam and how to recite the Qur'an. Then he said to me, "Don't tell anyone in Makkah about your acceptance of Islam. I'm afraid they might kill you."

"By Him in whose hands is my soul, I shall not leave Makkah until I go to the courtyard of the Ka'bah and proclaim the call of Truth in the midst of the Quraysh," I said.

The Prophet 🙵 remained silent. I went to the courtyard of the Ka'bah. The leaders of the Quraysh were sitting and talking. I went in their midst and called out at the top of my voice, "O people of Quraysh, I declare that there is no God but Allah and that Muhammad is the Messenger of Allah."

My words had an immediate affect on them. They jumped up and said, "Get this one who has left his religion!"

They pounced on me and began to beat me mercilessly. They clearly meant to kill me. But 'Abbas bin 'Abdul Muttalib, the uncle of the Prophet 🙵, recognized me. He rushed into the middle of the angry men and bent over me to protect me from them. He told them, "Ruin to you! Would you kill a man from the Ghifar tribe, and this while your caravans must pass through their territory?" They then released me.

I went back to the Prophet 🙵, upon whom be peace, and when he saw my condition, he said, "Didn't I tell you not to announce your acceptance of Islam?"

"Messenger of Allah," I said. "It was a need I felt in my soul, and I fulfilled it."

"Go to your people," he commanded, "and tell them what you have seen and heard. Invite them to Allah. Maybe Allah will bring them good through you and reward you through them. And when you hear that I have come out in the open, then return to me."

I left and went back to my people. My brother came up to me and asked, "What have you done?" I told him that I had become a Muslim and that I believed in the truth of Muhammad's teachings.

"I'm not against your faith. In fact, I'm now a Muslim and a believer too," he announced.

Then we both went to our mother and invited her to Islam.

"I do not have any dislike towards your religion. I accept Islam also," she said.

The Advice of Abu Darda' 🙵

The Blessed Prophet 🙵 once observed that Islam is about giving good advice to each other. Some of the best advice for how we are to live our lives comes from people who learned their Islam from the Prophet 🙵 himself.

One of the most thoughtful Companions of the Blessed Prophet 🙵 was Abu Darda 🙵. He accepted Islam after his best friend smashed his idol to bits showing him that idols were false. Although Abu Darda 🙵 was mad at first, he quickly saw that a god made of wood was no god at all! Once he was a Muslim, he began to get restless in his quest for knowledge. He studied the Qur'an and thought about its meaning. After a while, he stopped opening up his store regularly.

A friend asked him why he wasn't doing much business lately, and Abu Darda 🙵 replied, "I was a merchant before my pledge to the Messenger of Allah. When I became a Muslim, I wanted to combine my business with my 'ibadah, but I didn't achieve what I wanted. So I left off business and have moved more towards 'ibadah."

"By the One Who holds my soul," he went on, "I want to open a shop near the door of the masjid so I won't miss any Salah. Then, I can buy and sell and make a little profit every day."

In later years, Abu Darda 🙵 was asked to marry his daughter to Yazid, the son of Mu'awiyah, who was very rich. Instead, Abu Darda 🙵 married his daughter to a poor Muslim who had very good morals. When people asked him why he didn't marry his daughter to the rich Yazid, Abu Darda 🙵 replied, "What would you think of my daughter if she had servants, and lived in the glamour of a palace? What would happen to her (Islamic) lifestyle then?"

His wisdom was perhaps best demonstrated when he went walking one day, as was his usual practice. Along the way, he noticed a crowd of people beating and insulting a man. When he asked someone why the man was being beaten, someone replied that the man had committed a big sin.

Abu Darda 🙵 stopped the people and said, "If you were walking and saw the man trapped in the bottom of a well, what would you do?"

They answered that they would probably help him out. So Abu Darda 🙵 said, "Then don't insult and beat him. Instead, admonish him and help him understand that what he did was wrong. Then, praise Allah 🙵 Who has saved you from committing the same sin."

One person asked, "But don't you hate him?"

Abu Darda answered, "I only hate what he has done, and if he stops doing it, then he is my brother."

Upon hearing this, the man who had been beaten began to cry, and he announced to everyone that he was truly sorry to Allah 🙵 for what he did.

The Great Wisdom

From that day onward, this family of believers went out tirelessly, inviting the Ghifar to Allah﷾ and did not flinch from their purpose. Eventually, a large number became Muslims, and the Salat Al Jum'uah was instituted among them.

Abu Dharr﷠ remained in his country home, and then returned to Makkah when the persecution of the idol-worshippers was at its peak. He remained in Makkah for a little while until after the Prophet ﷺ had gone to Al Madinah.

When he arrived in Al Madinah at last, he asked the Prophet ﷺ if he could be in his personal service. The Prophet ﷺ agreed and was pleased with his companionship and service. He sometimes showed preference to Abu Dharr﷠ above others, and whenever he met him, he would pat him and smile.

When the Prophet ﷺ led the Muslim army on the expedition to Tabuk, everyone except the hypocrites came along. One evening, while the army was making camp on the road, the Prophet ﷺ and the Sahaba saw a single man walking towards them from out of the desert.

Some people asked, "Who could that man be coming on foot alone?" The Blessed Prophet ﷺ answered, "It must be Abu Dharr." When the man came within close sight, the Prophet ﷺ remarked, "May Allah have mercy on Abu Dharr. He is a loner. He walks alone. He will die alone and be raised up alone on the Day of Judgement." (Al Hakem)

فقال النبي ﷺ: «رَحِمَ اللهُ أبا ذَرٍّ، يَمْشي وَحْدَهُ وَيَموتُ وَحْدَهُ وَيُبْعَثُ وَحْدَهُ». رواه الحَاكِم

When he reached the camp, Abu Dharr﷠ explained that he was running late because his camel refused to move and had to resume his journey on foot. The Prophet ﷺ told him, "You are one of those I miss very much. For every step you have walked, Allah has forgiven one of your sins."

One day many years later, a man visited Abu Dharr﷠ and began looking at the contents of his house. After searching for a while, he found it quite bare and empty. He asked Abu Dharr﷠, "Where are your possessions?"

"We have a house over there in the next life," said Abu Dharr﷠, "to which we send the best of our possessions."

The man understood what he meant and said, "But you must have some possessions as long as you are living in this world."

"The owner of this world will not leave us in it," replied Abu Dharr﷠.

During the rule of Khalifa 'Uthman﷠, Abu Dharr﷠ became critical of how so many people were gathering wealth and living a life of luxury. He lived out his last days in a small village, in a simple house. His last dying wish to his wife and her maid was to be prepared in the sheets of burial when he passed away and to be taken to the side of the road.

There, his wife was to ask the first person who passed by to help her bury his body. She was to announce, "This is the body of Abu Dharr, the Companion of the Messenger of Allah. Help us bury him." When he passed away a few days later, his wife carried out his request and took his wrapped body to the roadside. A short time later, a group of riders passed by led by a famous Sahaba named 'Abdallah bin Mas'ud﷠. Abu Dharr's wife declared her message to them, and the announcement brought tears to the eyes of the men. 'Abdallah bin Mas'ud﷠ said, "The Messenger of Allah was right when he remarked, 'He walks alone, will die alone and will be raised alone on the Day of Judgement.'" The group of men then buried him in silent sorrow. Then they moved on.

Hasan Al Basri was asked, 'What is the secret behind your piety and asceticism?'
He replied, 'Four things:
1. I know that no one else can take my livelihood, so my heart is content.
2. I know that no one will perform good deeds on my behalf, so I perform them myself.
3. I know that Allah always sees me, so I feel embarrassed to sin in front of Him.
4. I know death awaits me, so I am preparing to meet my Lord.

جَاءَ رجُلٌ إلى الحَسَن البَصري رحمَهُ الله يسأله: ما سِرُّ زُهدَكَ في الدنيا يا إمام؟

فقال أربعة أشياء:

١. عَلِمتُ أن رزقي لا يأخذهُ غيرِي فاطمئن قلبيُّ.

٢. وعَلِمتُ أن عمَلي لا يقومُ به غيري فاشتغلت به وحدي.

٣. وعَلِمتُ أن الله مطلعٌ علَيَّ فاستحييت أن يراني على معصيةٍ.

٤. وعَلِمتُ أن الموت ينتظرُني فأعددتُ الزادَ للقاء ربي.

A Very Clever Woman

Asma', the daughter of Abu Bakr, is one of the most celebrated women in Islamic history. She was among the earliest people to accept Islam, and she devoted herself to the success of the Islamic cause with all her strength and ability.

Asma' was one of the few people who knew about the Prophet's plan to migrate to Al Madinah. She packed a food bag and a water jug for the Prophet and her father, but could find nothing to tie it with. She decided to use the extra cloth of her dress-belt, and her father suggested she tear it into two strips. She earned the nickname, Woman with the Two Belts.

After most of the other Muslims had left Makkah for Al Madinah, she remained behind for a little while longer.

Asma's quick-thinking in difficult situations was remarkable. When her father left Makkah, he took all his wealth, amounting to some 6,000 gold coins and did not leave any for his family. Abu Quhafah, Abu Bakr's old, blind and unbelieving father, heard of his departure. He went to Asma's house and said to her, "I hear that he left you without money and has all but abandoned you."

"No, grandfather," replied Asma'. "Actually, he left us a lot of money."

Then she took some pebbles and put them on a small shelf in the wall where they used to put money. She threw a cloth over the heap and took the hand of her grandfather and said, "See how much money he left us?"

In so doing Asma' aimed to calm the fears of the old man and keep him from giving them anything of his own small resources. This was because she didn't want to receive any help from an idol-worshipper even if it was her own grandfather.

When the final emigration from Makkah to Al Madinah took place, Asma' was pregnant. She did not let her pregnancy, or the prospect of a long and difficult journey, delay her from leaving.

As soon as she reached Quba, on the outskirts of Al Madinah, she gave birth to a son. She named him 'Abdallah. The Muslims shouted, "Allahu Akbar" and "La ilaha ill Allah," in happiness, because he was the first child to be born to the Muhajirun in Al Madinah.

Asma's Nobility

Asma' became known for her fine and noble qualities and for the keenness of her intelligence. She was also an extremely generous person.

Her son, 'Abdallah, once said of her, "I have never seen two women more generous than my aunt, 'Aishah, and my mother, Asma'. But their generosity was expressed in different ways. My aunt would accumulate one thing after another until she had gathered what she felt was sufficient and then distributed it all to those in need. My mother, on the other hand, would not keep anything even for the next day."

Asma's mother, Qutaylah, once came to visit her in Al Madinah. She was not a Muslim yet, and was divorced from her father. Her mother brought her gifts of raisins and seeds. Asma' at first refused to admit her into her house or accept the gifts. She sent someone to ask 'Aishah and the Prophet of the legitimacy in her attitude towards her mother. 'Aishah, as advised by the Prophet, replied that she should certainly admit her to her house and accept the gifts. (60: 8-9)

Courage in Tough Times

Asma' lived to be about 100 years old, and survived through the terrible time of civil wars in the Muslim world. Her son, 'Abdallah, would later become a martyr during the Ummayid period. These were the days when Muslims were fighting each other for control of the Ummah.

Many Muslims supported 'Abdallah as the most fit for the job of khalifa. But the Ummayids were rival Muslims who were based in Syria. They had more powerful armies and wanted 'Abdul Malik bin Marwan to be the khalifa. In addition, they were willing to shed Muslim blood to get their man in power.

When 'Abdallah went to his old and blind mother for advice, the following conversation took place:

"Assalaamu alaikum, Mother."

"Wa 'alaikum salaam, 'Abdallah," she replied. "What is it that brings you here at this hour, while boulders from General Hajjaj's catapults are raining down on your soldiers in the masjid of the Ka'bah and shaking the houses of Makkah?"

"I came to seek your advice," he said.

"To seek my advice?" she asked in astonishment. "About what?"

"The people have deserted me out of fear of Hajjaj or are being tempted by what he has to offer. Even my own children and family have left me. There is only a small group of men with me now, and however strong and steadfast they are, they can only resist for an hour or two more. Messengers of the Banu Umayah are even now negotiating with me, offering to give me whatever worldly possessions I want if I just put down my arms and swear allegiance to 'Abdul Malik. What do you think?"

She replied, "It's your decision, 'Abdallah, and you know yourself better. If you think you're right and that you're standing up for the truth, then persevere and fight on as your companions who were killed under your flag showed perseverance. But if you desire the world, what a miserable soul you are. You would destroy yourself and you would destroy your men."

"But I'll probably be killed today, there's no doubt about that."

"That's better for you than surrendering yourself to Hajjaj voluntarily and letting some slaves of the Ummayid's play with your head."

"I'm not afraid of death. I'm only afraid that they'll mutilate my body."

"There's nothing after death that a man should fear. Skinning does not cause any pain to the slaughtered sheep."

'Abdallah's face brightened as he said, "What a blessed mother! Blessed be your noble qualities! I have come to you at this hour to hear what I have heard. Allah knows that I haven't weakened or given up. He is witness over me that I haven't stood up for what I have out of love for this world and its attractions, but only out of anger for the sake of Allah. His limits have been breached. Here am I, going to what is pleasing to you. So if I'm killed, don't feel bad for me but commend me to Allah."

"I will feel bad for you," spoke the aging but determined Asma' 🌸, "only if you are killed in a useless and unjust cause."

"Be assured that your son has not supported an unjust cause nor committed any bad deed, nor done any injustice to a Muslim or a non-Muslim and that there is nothing better in his sight than the pleasure of Allah The Greatest. I do not say this to cover myself. Allah knows that I've only said it to make your heart firm."

"Al hamdulillah that Allah has made you act according to what He likes and according to what I like. Come close to me, my son, so I can smell and feel your body, for this might be my last meeting with you."

'Abdallah knelt before her. She hugged him and kissed him. Her hands began to squeeze his body when suddenly she withdrew them and asked, "What is this that you're wearing?"

"This is my armor."

"This, my son, is not the dress of one who desires martyrdom. Take it off. That will make your movements lighter and quicker. Wear a long robe instead, so that if you are killed, your body will not be exposed."

'Abdallah took off his armor and put on the robe. As he left for the center of town to join the fighting, he said, "Mother, don't deprive me of your dua'."

Raising her hands in supplication, she prayed, "My Lord, have mercy on him for his staying up for long hours and his loud crying in the darkness of the night while other people slept. My Lord, have mercy on his hunger and his thirst, on his travels from Al Madinah and Makkah while he fasted. My Lord, bless his good conduct to his mother and his father."

"My Lord, I give him to Your cause and I am pleased with whatever You decide for him. Grant me, for his sake, the reward of those who are patient."

At the end of the day, 'Abdallah lay dead. 'Abdallah was a victim of fitna, or 'a tragic conflict,' between Muslims. Just over 10 days later, his mother joined him. May Allah🌸 have mercy on her soul, and grant her the finest rewards for her *emaan* and strength of character. Ameen.

Bilal bin Rabaah 🕮

Among the most well-known Companions of the Blessed Prophet 🕮 was Bilal bin Rabaah 🕮. His example set forth the shining truth of the equality of all people. He lived in a place where racism dominated and where a man was judged by the color of his skin.

Bilal 🕮 was the child of an African slave named Rabaah. People of African ancestry were often looked down upon by the idol-worshipping Arabs. Although skin color doesn't make one human different from another, this lesson wasn't known by the people of the world at that time.

Allah 🕮 made all human beings with the same inner components: a soul, feelings and the capacity for good and evil. When Bilal 🕮, who was also a slave, heard about Islam, he saw it as humanity's chance to be released from the bonds of ignorance.

Because of his choice to accept Islam, he was endured horrible torture. After Bilal 🕮 declared that he was a Muslim, the man who owned him, Umayya bin Khalaf, was furious. He believed a slave had no right to worship anything except what his master told him. He ordered Bilal 🕮 to be whipped and to be pressed under heavy stones.

Once he asked some local teenage boys to take Bilal 🕮 out and beat him. They drove Bilal 🕮 out onto the hot plains and tormented him. Through all his suffering, Bilal 🕮 kept repeating over and over, the following phrase, "Only One! Only One!" His emaan never faltered, and the idol-worshippers could not break his hold on Islam. When Abu Bakr 🕮 heard about what was happening to Bilal 🕮, he offered to buy him from his master. The disgusted Umayya sold him, and Abu Bakr 🕮 promptly freed his Muslim brother.

Bilal 🕮 later killed Umayya in the Battle of Badr. He went on to become a great warrior, scholar and teacher. He even had the honor of being the first man to call Muslims to prayer. The Blessed Prophet 🕮 even named Bilal 🕮 as one of his special compassionate Companions, whom Allah 🕮 granted to be with him in his mission.

Bilal 🕮 was also one of the first seven people to publicly accept Islam. As you have learned before, after the Blessed Prophet 🕮 passed away, Bilal 🕮 vowed to never say the athan again. In later years, he dedicated his entire life to jihad and marched with the Muslim armies in Syria. Bilal 🕮 was there when the victorious Muslims captured Jerusalem. 'Umar bin al Khattab 🕮 traveled from Al Madinah to Jerusalem to capture the city himself, upon the request of the city leaders.

After establishing the peace treaty with the leaders of the city, 'Umar 🕮 asked to see the site of the ancient temple of Prophet Sulayman 🕮. The temple had been destroyed by the Romans more than 600 years earlier. When 'Umar was taken to the location, he asked Bilal 🕮 to say the athan, given that they were standing in a holy place.

Bilal 🕮 agreed. When his powerful and full voice rang out over the city, all the Muslims who hadn't heard his sweet call for years stood in silence. When Bilal 🕮 returned to 'Umar 🕮 and the Sahaba around him, he found them in tears.

The only other time he said the athan again was when he was visiting Al Madinah, about five years later. He went to the grave of the Prophet 🕮, and then sat down in tears, remembering all the times he had with his beloved guide and friend.

Suddenly, he felt a pat on his shoulders. He turned around to find Hassan and Hussain, the grandsons of the Blessed Prophet 🕮, looking at him eagerly. A smile spread across his face, and he stood up and hugged them warmly.

Bilal 🕮 stayed with them through the night, talking about and remembering the old times. They finally asked him if he would say the athan for them at Fajr, which was fast approaching. For the sake of the grandsons of the Prophet 🕮, he immediately agreed and accompanied them to the masjid.

When the people heard Bilal's 🕮 voice carry over the morning sky, they were stunned. Everyone recognized the voice they hadn't heard for many years. Throngs of people rushed to the masjid to see him. Many cried as a flood of memories of the Blessed Prophet 🕮 returned.

The Prophet 🕮 once remarked about Bilal 🕮, "How worthy is Bilal! Only good believers try to follow his steps. Bilal 🕮 is the chief of all mu'athins, and mu'athins will be the most fortunate people on the Day of Judgement."

Chapter 17
Fiqh and Shari'ah

Shari'ah: The Islamic Way

The word **Shari'ah** شَرِيعَة **Islamic Law** literally means a straight path or 'an endless supply of water.' It is the term used to describe the rules of the deen ordained for us by Allah. When you live your life the Islamic way, you are following the Shari'ah. In more practical terms, the Shari'ah includes all the limits of Islam. What is allowed is called **Halal** حَلال, and what is forbidden is called **Haram** حَرَام. What is allowed, but not recommended to do, is called **Makruh** مَكْرُوه.

Then We have put you (O Muhammad) on a (plain) way of (Our) commandment [like the one which We commanded Our Messengers before you (i.e. legal ways and laws of the Islamic Monotheism)]. So follow you that (Islamic Monotheism and its laws), and follow not the desires of those who know not. Surat Al Jaathiyah (The Crouching) 45: 18

Allah's عَزَّوَجَلَّ Limits		
Halal	*Makruh*	*Haram*
Any object or action that is permissible to use or engage in or that is approved of by the Qur'an or by the expressed or silent approval of the Prophet ﷺ.	Any action not forbidden but that seems to push the limits of the Halal standard.	Any action forbidden by the Qur'an or the Prophet ﷺ. Any action that goes against the spirit of Islam.

﴿ثُمَّ جَعَلْنَاكَ عَلَىٰ شَرِيعَةٍ مِّنَ ٱلْأَمْرِ فَٱتَّبِعْهَا وَلَا تَتَّبِعْ أَهْوَآءَ ٱلَّذِينَ لَا يَعْلَمُونَ﴾ سُورَةُ الجاثية 45:18

The Shari'ah is meant for our own protection. For example, drinking alcohol, which is very common in non-Muslim societies, is in fact bad for people. Although a sip of red wine may be good for your heart, no one stops at just a sip. Instead, many people get drunk. That is because alcohol is a mind-numbing and addictive substance. Therefore, Allah has forbidden it.

They ask you about wine and gambling. Say, "In both there is great sin, and some benefits for people. And their sin is greater than their benefit." Surat Al Baqarah (The Cow) 2: 219

﴿يَسْأَلُونَكَ عَنِ ٱلْخَمْرِ وَٱلْمَيْسِرِ قُلْ فِيهِمَآ إِثْمٌ كَبِيرٌ وَمَنَٰفِعُ لِلنَّاسِ وَإِثْمُهُمَآ أَكْبَرُ مِن نَّفْعِهِمَا﴾ سُورَةُ البَقَرة 2:219

The word **Hudood** حُدود **limits of Allah** means the edge of the border between acceptable actions and bad deeds, which we do not want to stray into.

These are the limits set by Allah. Whoever obeys Allah and His Messenger, He will admit him to gardens beneath which rivers flow, where he will live forever. That is a great success. Whoever disobeys Allah and His Messenger and transgresses the limits set by Him, He shall admit him to the Fire, where he will remain forever. For him there is a humiliating punishment. Surat An-Nisa' (The Women) 4:13-14

﴿تِلْكَ حُدُودُ ٱللَّهِ وَمَن يُطِعِ ٱللَّهَ وَرَسُولَهُ يُدْخِلْهُ جَنَّٰتٍ تَجْرِي مِن تَحْتِهَا ٱلْأَنْهَٰرُ خَٰلِدِينَ فِيهَا وَذَٰلِكَ ٱلْفَوْزُ ٱلْعَظِيمُ﴾ ﴿وَمَن يَعْصِ ٱللَّهَ وَرَسُولَهُ وَيَتَعَدَّ حُدُودَهُ يُدْخِلْهُ نَارًا خَٰلِدًا فِيهَا وَلَهُ عَذَابٌ مُّهِينٌ﴾ سُورَةُ النِّساء 4:13-14

The operating principle of Islam is pretty simple: everything is allowed unless it is forbidden by the standards of the Qur'an or the Sunnah. (59:7 & 7:157)

The Blessed Prophet Muhammad ﷺ said once, "Allah has given you certain duties to perform, so don't neglect them. He has defined certain limits, so don't go beyond them. He has forbidden some things, so don't do them. And He has kept silent about some things, out of mercy for you, and not because of forgetfulness, so don't ask questions about them." (Al-Daraqutni)

عَنْ رَسُولِ اللهِ ﷺ : «إِنَّ اللهَ فَرَضَ فَرَائِضَ فَلَا تُضَيِّعُوهَا، وَحَدَّ حُدُودًا فَلَا تَعْتَدُوهَا، وَحَرَّمَ أَشْيَاءَ فَلَا تَنْتَهِكُوهَا، وَسَكَتَ عَنْ أَشْيَاءَ رَحْمَةً لَكُمْ غَيْرَ نِسْيَانٍ، فَلَا تَبْحَثُوا عَنْهَا». حَدِيثٌ حَسَنٌ، رَوَاهُ الدَّارقُطنِيُّ وغَيْرُهُ

Understanding the Way

The Shari'ah is the ideal path for us to follow. We learn what the Shari'ah contains from two primary sources: the Qur'an and the Sunnah. The Prophet ﷺ told us in his Farewell Sermon to hold on to these two sources.

All the major issues regarding our beliefs, others' rights, and what is good and bad to do, are covered in these two primary sources. Sometimes, however, people have different interpretations about what an ayah or a hadith means. Other times, there are situations where we need to find a clear-cut answer to a new issue facing us. What is the Islamic position on cloning, for example?

To help us overcome these hurdles, Muslims have developed a very detailed legal system in which complex issues can be studied, compared with known Islamic teachings and then evaluated. This science is known as **Fiqh** فقه. In the famous answer Mu'ath bin Jabal ﷺ gave to the Prophet ﷺ before leaving for Yemen, he listed three things he would use to conduct legal affairs: Qur'an, Sunnah and Reason.

Thus, we can say that the Shari'ah is the path of living Islam, and fiqh is the explanation of how to live Islam better. Even then, there will still be disagreements. But generally, most opinions fall under the four main schools of thought. Each school has its own particular methods of research and interpretation. This is not a problem, though, because it is the active pursuit of reason and knowledge that the Blessed Prophet ﷺ encouraged.

The Tools of Fiqh

The main tool developed by the Scholars of Islamic knowledge utilizes an important principle called **Ijtehad** اجتهاد **Independent Reasoning**. For example, if we wanted to determine the direction of the Qiblah while on the moon (a possibility of the future), a scholar would first look in the Qur'an and the Sunnah to find an answer.

It is not for a believer, man or woman, when Allah and His Messenger have decreed a matter that they should have any option in their decision. And whoever disobeys Allah and His Messenger, he has indeed strayed in to a plain error. Surat Al Ahzab (The Confederates) 33:36

﴿وَمَا كَانَ لِمُؤْمِنٍ وَلَا مُؤْمِنَةٍ إِذَا قَضَى اللَّهُ وَرَسُولُهُ أَمْرًا أَن يَكُونَ لَهُمُ الْخِيَرَةُ مِنْ أَمْرِهِمْ وَمَن يَعْصِ اللَّهَ وَرَسُولَهُ فَقَدْ ضَلَّ ضَلَالًا مُّبِينًا﴾ سُورَةُ الأَحزاب:36:33

If he or she doesn't find the answer there, then the next source would be the rulings and writings of the Sahaba. This is because the Sahaba learned directly from the Blessed Prophet ﷺ and dealt with many new issues. Their **Ijmaa'** إجماع **Agreement** on the subject would weigh heavily.

If there was still no answer, the scholar would then think about the issue. Then, guided by Islamic principles, he or she will arrive at a solution. This is called **Qiyas** قياس **Analogy**. When a decision is made by a prominent scholar or other responsible scholars, a **Fatwa** فتوى **Official Legal Proclamation** is announced. Their verdicts are the scholars' best attempts at answering a difficult issue.

A fatwa is not to be considered as binding for all time, however. This is because later scholars may understand an issue better as more facts come to light. In that case, new fatwas can be issued. It is strongly recommended for Muslims to listen to fatwas, and to take them seriously, because Islam teaches us to consult and follow people of knowledge. (16:43)

Have there been scholars who made mistakes and issued wrong fatwas? Of course, because they are only human. The Blessed Prophet ﷺ once mentioned that a scholar who tries their best, but makes a mistake, still gets a reward from Allah ﷻ for at least trying. If there is a fatwa that was issued that seems a little weak, it is the duty of Muslims in general to challenge it and arrive at the best answer possible.

The Islamic legal sciences are able to meet any new issue they come up against, because Islam is a way of life that can be lived in any time, any place, and any reality. Islamic Fiqh is a growing, transforming, and adaptive institution.

Whether we are stuck on our changing planet, colonize the stars or go back into a more primitive mode of civilization, Muslims will never be confused as to how to relate our way of life to the environment we live in. This is because Islam is based on the eternal principles of Allah ﷻ.

The Blessed Prophet Muhammad ﷺ said, "Whoever goes out seeking knowledge, then he is in Allah's cause until he returns." (At-Tirmidhi)

قَالَ رَسُولُ اللهِ ﷺ : «مَنْ خَرَجَ فِي طَلَبِ الْعِلْمِ فَهُوَ فِي سَبِيلِ اللهِ حَتَّى يَرْجِعَ». رَوَاهُ التِّرْمِذِيّ

Following the Shari'ah in Daily Life

Islam is a way of life that can be adapted to any time or place. This is proven everyday when millions of Muslims from every race, ethnic group and country, arise from their beds and live as believers in Allah. The path we follow, the 'Shari'ah,' contains the commandments of Allah and His Messenger about the best way to live our everyday lives. The source for this information is the Qur'an and the Sunnah.

If we face an issue that requires more help to answer, a scholar can do 'ijtehad,' or 'independent reasoning,' to arrive at an Islamically acceptable solution. The tools of ijtehad are: Qur'an, Sunnah, *ijmaa'* and *qiyas*.

In the early days of Islam, some concerned Muslims wanted to make the Shari'ah easier for the common people to follow. Not everyone had the time to study the Qur'an and the Sunnah, nor were most people qualified to do ijtehad. In addition, new Muslims needed a simplified list of the do's and dont's of Islam.

So the 'Olama'a made it their mission in life to study the Shari'ah in detail and explain it to the people. There were many people engaged in this activity, both men and women. They worked tirelessly and wrote many books explaining the laws of Islam, the duties of people, halal and haram issues and much more.

Some of these scholars were persecuted by evil rulers and spent time in jail for speaking out against tyrants. Most, however, were able to travel freely and spread their knowledge of Shari'ah far and wide. Al-Hasan Al-Basri said, "The ink of a scholar is more noble than the blood of a martyr." This was a powerful incentive for people to study and promote learning.

The Five Major Scholars

The five scholars that most Muslims recognize and follow today are: Imam Abu Hanifa, Imam Anas bin Malik, Imam Ash-Shafi'i, Imam Ahmad bin Hanbal and Imam Ja'far As Sadeq. Each of them gained many students who continued their work and developed fiqh into highly organized bodies of knowledge that are still consulted to this day.

It must be remembered that these scholars were trying to gain a better understanding of Islam. They were not inventing anything new in the deen. For example, Imam Malik did not want people to follow him, or any other person, in place of following the Qur'an and the Sunnah. He is quoted as saying, "The word of any person other than the Prophet is sometimes accepted and sometimes rejected."

Each of these scholars also knew they were not perfect. Imam Ash-Shafi'i once said, "My opinion is correct, with the possibility of it being wrong. An opinion different from mine is wrong, with the possibility that it is correct." By stating this, the imam recognized that others may understand things better than him.

Each of the scholars were teachers and instructors. Although there were many other scholars working in the field of fiqh and Shari'ah, these five gained the most popularity. The students of these scholars continued and expanded their work after they passed away. They formed what we might call 'intellectual clubs,' where the spirit of the founding scholar was used as the inspiration for the techniques, reasoning or methods of Islamic study that were developed.

In other words, the founding scholar taught his students whatever he knew. Then those students became teachers and passed on what they had learned to students after them. All along the way, new knowledge was added, and the people involved in that particular association of teachers and students became known as a **Madhab مَذْهَب School of Thought**.

Schools of Thought Today

Presently there are five main madhahib (plural of madhab) in the world: Maliki, Hanifi, Shafi'i, Hanbali and Ja'fari. Each is named after the founder of that madhab. Each madhab is based on the Qur'an and the Sunnah. They employ the tools of ijtehad to find solutions to new issues that arise. Though there are differences of opinion between them on some things, they all agree on the major issues.

In fact, the madhahib agree on about 85% of all issues. The differences are usually regarding concerns that are not foundational to the practice of Islam. For example, let's say a woman's husband disappears while traveling without a trace and is never heard from again. When can the woman safely remarry? When can the long lost man be safely declared deceased? There's no ayah or hadith covering such a situation.

According to one madhab, the waiting period is one year, while yet according to another, the period is 99 years. Although scholars use ijtehad they still may conclude with different answers. Thus, we can understand the nature of the differences between the various madhahib.

Unfortunately, some Muslims believe that the madhab they follow is the only way to live Islam. They look down on people who follow other madhahib and criticize them. This attitude is against Islam. Muslims should follow whatever methodology they choose, as long as it is in accordance with the Qur'an and the Sunnah.

Name of Scholar	Fact Sheet
Imam Ja'far As Sadeq	Lived: 699-765. Born in Al Madinah, Arabia. Renowned scholar and alchemist. Studied in Al Madinah and elsewhere. He is revered as an imam by the adherents of Shi'a Islam and as a renowned Islamic scholar and personality by Sunni Muslims.
Imam Abu Hanifa	Lived: 703-767. Born in Iraq. Studied in Al Madinah.
Imam Malik bin Anas	Lived: 717-801. Born in Al Madinah. Wrote the famous book "Al Muwatta" at the request of Khalifa Harun ar-Rasheed.
Imam Muhammad Ash-Shafi'i	Lived: 769-820. Born in Palestine. Studied in Al Madinah under Imam Malik bin Anas. Developed the basics of the methodology of Fiqh.
Imam Ahmad bin Hanbal	Lived: 778-855. Born in Baghdad. Studied in Al Madinah under Imam Ash-Shafi'i.

The founding scholars of these schools of thought did not think they were teaching a new outlook on Islam. They simply wanted to know more, and make it easier for Muslims to practice Islam. In fact, most of these scholars studied together to begin with. You can choose to follow a madhab if you wish, but you don't need to subscribe to one at all. It is helpful, however, to have some kind of fiqh books in your home to help guide you in your daily affairs.

The Blessed Prophet ﷺ oftentimes taught us many ways to do the same thing. This was a mercy for us. It gives us some choice in customizing our ''ibadah,' or 'service to Allah.' For example, At-Tahiyyat and At-Tashahud can be said in at least three different ways in the Salah, all of them similar and traceable to the Prophet ﷺ. Each madhab prefers one over the other, but some followers argue that there's only way to say it.

There are many such instances, and Muslims must be aware that Islam is a faith with many allowable methods. If it can be traced to the Qur'an and the Sunnah, then you are welcome to follow it. May Allah help us recognize the madhahib for what they are: useful tools for understanding how to live the Shari'ah. May He help us not to fall into the ignorance of believing that the madhahib are different religions unto themselves that must be followed. Ameen.

How Do We Deal With Differences?

"Islam teaches that wudu' is done this way," the man said confidently.

"But you're wrong," the younger man replied. "That's totally against the laws of Islam."

"But it says in a hadith that—" the older man started saying.

"That's a weak hadith!" the younger man interrupted.

"Oh yeah! What's your proof? I read in a book that the Blessed Prophet ﷺ said to—"

By this time, both men were fuming. The young man screamed, "I read in a book, too, that—"

But before he could finish his sentence, the older brother pushed him, and he pushed back. A fight would have ensued if some quick-thinking men nearby hadn't broken it up.

The two brothers eyed each other angrily and left in opposite directions. Those who remained just shook their heads in silence. Here were two brothers ready to fight over a minor difference of opinion.

And obey Allah and His Messenger, and do not dispute (with one another) lest you lose courage and your strength departs, and be patient. Surely, Allah is with those who are As-Sabirun (the patient).
Surat Al Anfaal (The Spoils of War) 8: 46

﴿وَأَطِيعُوا۟ ٱللَّهَ وَرَسُولَهُ وَلَا تَنَٰزَعُوا۟ فَتَفْشَلُوا۟ وَتَذْهَبَ رِيحُكُمْ وَٱصْبِرُوٓا۟ إِنَّ ٱللَّهَ مَعَ ٱلصَّٰبِرِينَ﴾ سُورَةُ الأنفال 8:46

The funny thing was they both could have been right. They just didn't know how to handle a difference of understanding. The Blessed Prophet ﷺ often remarked that Muslims are those who remain brothers even when they have a disagreement. He didn't mean that Muslims should argue about everything. Instead, he pointed out that if Muslims disagreed over something, then they must consult the Qur'an, the Sunnah and the righteous scholars. This will prevent them from fighting amongst themselves and from disliking each other.

On many occasions, Muslims have disagreed over what something means or what to do. The key is to follow the Islamic manners of how to deal with differences. We don't have to agree all the time, but we shouldn't fight over disagreements either.

For example, before the Battle of Uhud, the Muslims had to decide what to do. Some wanted to go out and fight, while others wanted to stay in the city and defend it from there. The Prophet ﷺ listened to both sides. In the end, he accepted the will of the majority, who wanted to go out and fight. People disagreed over the issue, but they united after a majority decision was taken.

Allah ﷻ gave us a formula for dealing with differences. He told us that the Qur'an is **Al Furqan** الْفُرْقَان, which means **the Standard**. A standard is something that we use to guide us towards the best beliefs, behaviors and actions. Further, Allah ﷻ instructed us to follow the example of the Blessed Prophet ﷺ.

If we have a disagreement, especially between one madhab and another, we must respect each other's opinions and present our evidence. In the end, even if neither side persuades the other, we must be courteous and respectful. If we find our position is wrong, then we should not stick with something that is not true. Simply say, "Al hamdulillah," and thank the brother or sister for helping you to understand the Shari'ah better.

Abu Hurayrah ﷺ narrated that the Messenger of Allah ﷺ said, "The Qur'an was revealed with five categories: Things lawful, things unlawful, clear and positive teachings, allegories, and stories. So hold lawful what is lawful for you and hold forbidden things forbidden. Act according to the clear and positive teachings, affirm your faith in the allegories and draw lessons from the stories."
(Al Baihaqi)

عَنْ أَبِي هُرَيْرَةَ ﷺ قَالَ: قَالَ رَسُولُ الله ﷺ: «إِنَّ الْقُرْآنَ نَزَلَ عَلَى خَمْسَةِ أَوْجُهٍ: حَلَالٍ، وَحَرَامٍ، وَمُحْكَمٍ، وَمُتَشَابِهٍ، وَأَمْثَالٍ، فَاعْمَلُوا بِالْحَلَالِ، وَاجْتَنِبُوا الْحَرَامَ، وَاتَّبِعُوا الْمُحْكَمَ، وَآمِنُوا بِالْمُتَشَابِهِ، وَاعْتَبِرُوا بِالْأَمْثَالِ». رَوَاهُ الْبَيْهَقِي

'Umar bin al Khattab ﷺ was once quoted as saying, "Allah ﷻ bless the person who makes me a gift of my own faults." The 'gift' is being able to realize and learn from one's mistakes. An arrogant person refuses to accept logic and never likes to listen to Allah's ﷻ guidance. In contrast, the Qur'an prefers those who are humble. It states: Those are the people whom Allah has blessed with bounties, the prophets from the progeny of Adam, and of those whom We caused to board (the Ark) along with Nuh, and from the progeny of Ibrahim and Isra'il (Jacob), and from those whom We guided and selected. When the verses of The Rahman (The All-Merciful) were recited before them, they used to fall down in Sajdah (prostration), while they were weeping. Surat Maryam (Mary) 19:58

﴿أُولَٰئِكَ الَّذِينَ أَنْعَمَ اللَّهُ عَلَيْهِم مِّنَ النَّبِيِّينَ مِن ذُرِّيَّةِ آدَمَ وَمِمَّنْ حَمَلْنَا مَعَ نُوحٍ وَمِن ذُرِّيَّةِ إِبْرَاهِيمَ وَإِسْرَائِيلَ وَمِمَّنْ هَدَيْنَا وَاجْتَبَيْنَا إِذَا تُتْلَىٰ عَلَيْهِمْ آيَاتُ الرَّحْمَٰنِ خَرُّوا سُجَّدًا وَبُكِيًّا۩﴾ سُورَةُ مَرْيَم ١٩:٥٨

'Umar bin al Khattab ﷺ went up to a person he disliked one day and told him to his face, "I don't like you." The person merely replied, "Are you going to take away my rights?" 'Umar ﷺ answered, "I don't like you, but I will respect your rights."

On another occasion, Khalid bin Walid ﷺ and Saad bin Waqqas ﷺ were having a heated argument. After Khalid ﷺ left, a friend of Saad's started saying bad things about Khalid ﷺ. Saad immediately stopped the man, and told him, "The disagreement between us does not affect the bond of our faith." Clearly, that is the best example for us to follow, in regards to dealing with differences among us.

The Blessed Prophet ﷺ said, "A rude and ill-tempered person shall not enter Paradise." (Abu Dawud)

قَالَ رَسُولُ الله ﷺ: «لَا يَدْخُلُ الْجَنَّةَ الْجَوَّاظُ وَلَا الْجَعْظَرِيُّ». رَوَاهُ أَبُو دَاوُد

The Blessed Prophet ﷺ said, "Fear Allah wherever you may be. Follow an evil deed with a good one, and you will erase it. Deal with people on the basis of good conduct." (At-Tirmidhi)

عَنْ رَسُولِ الله ﷺ قَالَ: «اتَّقِ اللهَ حَيْثُمَا كُنْتَ وَأَتْبِعِ السَّيِّئَةَ الْحَسَنَةَ تَمْحُهَا وَخَالِقِ النَّاسَ بِخُلُقٍ حَسَنٍ». رَوَاهُ التِّرْمَذِي

Anas bin Malik ﷺ narrated that the Blessed Prophet ﷺ said, "Don't be hostile to each other, or jealous or indifferent. Instead, be brothers as Allah's servants. No Muslim should avoid his brother for more than three days." (Al Bukhari)

عَنْ أَنَسِ بْنِ مَالِكٍ ﷺ، أَنَّ رَسُولَ الله ﷺ قَالَ: «لَا تَبَاغَضُوا، وَلَا تَحَاسَدُوا، وَلَا تَدَابَرُوا، وَكُونُوا عِبَادَ الله إِخْوَانًا، وَلَا يَحِلُّ لِمُسْلِمٍ أَنْ يَهْجُرَ أَخَاهُ فَوْقَ ثَلَاثِ لَيَالٍ». رَوَاهُ الْبُخَارِي

The Food Issue

You may wonder sometimes why certain foods are called 'haram' and others 'halal.' To put it simply, haram foods are forbidden foods because they contain ingredients that Allah﷾ has told people not to consume. Allah﷾ said, *People, eat from the world what is lawful and good. But don't follow in the ways of the Shaytan, because he is your declared enemy.* Surat Al Baqarah (The Cow) 2:168

﴿يَٰٓأَيُّهَا ٱلنَّاسُ كُلُوا۟ مِمَّا فِى ٱلْأَرْضِ حَلَٰلًا طَيِّبًا وَلَا تَتَّبِعُوا۟ خُطُوَٰتِ ٱلشَّيْطَٰنِ ۚ إِنَّهُۥ لَكُمْ عَدُوٌّ مُّبِينٌ﴾ سُورَةُ البَقَرَة 2:168

Halal foods are those that Allah﷾ has said are acceptable for people to eat. The basic rule is that something is halal, unless it has been deemed otherwise. Therefore, there are more foods that are halal than haram, even in our modern society.

These are the main foods, drink and substances that are considered haram from the Qur'an and Sunnah:
- Meat from swine
- Animals already dead before slaughtering is due to take place
- Animals killed or sacrificed in the name of others than Allah﷾
- Any intoxicating substances such as alcohol or hallucinogenic products (i.e. marijuana, cocaine, heroin, etc.)
- Blood and blood by-products
- Most carnivorous animals, birds of prey and land animals without external ears (i.e., snakes, reptiles, worms, insects etc.)

He has only forbidden you to eat dead meat, blood, pork, and food dedicated to idols in place of Allah. But if someone is forced to eat those things—without willfully disobeying nor going overboard—then there is no blame on them because Allah is the Forgiving and Merciful. Surat Al Baqarah (The Cow) 2:173

﴿إِنَّمَا حَرَّمَ عَلَيْكُمُ ٱلْمَيْتَةَ وَٱلدَّمَ وَلَحْمَ ٱلْخِنزِيرِ وَمَآ أُهِلَّ بِهِۦ لِغَيْرِ ٱللَّهِ ۖ فَمَنِ ٱضْطُرَّ غَيْرَ بَاغٍ وَلَا عَادٍ فَلَآ إِثْمَ عَلَيْهِ ۚ إِنَّ ٱللَّهَ غَفُورٌ رَّحِيمٌ﴾ سُورَةُ البَقَرَة 2:173

O you who believe! Wine, gambling, altars and divining arrows 49 are filth, made up by Satan. Therefore, refrain from it, so that you may be successful. Surat Al Ma'idah (The Table) 5:90

﴿يَٰٓأَيُّهَا ٱلَّذِينَ ءَامَنُوٓا۟ إِنَّمَا ٱلْخَمْرُ وَٱلْمَيْسِرُ وَٱلْأَنصَابُ وَٱلْأَزْلَٰمُ رِجْسٌ مِّنْ عَمَلِ ٱلشَّيْطَٰنِ فَٱجْتَنِبُوهُ لَعَلَّكُمْ تُفْلِحُونَ﴾ سُورَةُ المائدة 5:90

The trouble we have, living in our day and age, is that so many foods in the supermarket are processed foods. These processed foods are filled with chemicals and strange ingredients. Many are then radiated to make them resistant to spoilage while they sit on the store shelves for weeks, months or even years.

The source for many of these unusual ingredients is often from animals, in particular cows and pigs. For example, enzymes, a main ingredient for almost all cheeses and dairy products, are usually scraped out of dead cow or pig stomachs. Some cheeses may use plant-based or lab-created enzymes, however.

Many brands of flavored gelatins and marshmallows are made from collagen that is extracted from the skin and bones of animals—mostly cows and pigs. Dough conditioners and emulsifiers are often-times taken from pig and cow intestines, stomachs and other animal parts. If most people traced back the source of their foods, they might reconsider their diet.

The Best Foods

The best things for a Muslim to consume are fresh halal meats, fruits, grains, vegetables and fresh-baked breads and pastries. If you want to buy processed foods, then check the ingredients carefully. Don't buy things with lard (pig grease), enzymes (unless it says vegetable enzymes), monoglycerides and diglycerides (unless it says vegetable monoglycerides and diglycerides), or other strange ingredients, like Bone Phosphate-E542, Cochineal / Carmine- E120, E122, Gelatin, Glycerin- E422, L-Cysteine, Magnesium stearate, Rennet, Vanilla extract, whey, Emulsifiers(E470 TO E483), Dough conditioners, ShellacE904.

As Muslims, we place our trust in Allah﷾. If He has told us not to eat certain things, then it's for a good reason. Remember

Seafood is halal.

this phrase, "Allah✳ said it, the Prophet ﷺ lived it, and I will follow it."

If you have a favorite food, write to the company and ask for a complete list of ingredients and their sources. It is your right as a consumer to know these ingredients, thus, you will find that the companies will reply to your concerns. You can also look in a halal/haram food guide. However, these lists are being constantly revised, so contacting the company is usually a more accurate method. Remember, if you stay away from something in this life for Allah's✳ sake, He will reward you more than you can ever imagine.

The Meat of Ahl Al Kitab

Islam does teach that the meat slaughtered by the Ahl Al Kitab (People of the Book: Jews and Christians) is halal for us. (5:5) However, unless the meat at the supermarket is specifically labeled as such, there is no guarantee that it was slaughtered in accordance with the standards of those religions.

Currently, only animals killed according to kosher guidelines by observant Jews is similar to the standards in Islamic texts. Others, whether religious groups or federal organizations, have few guidelines that are humane, clean or sanitary. However, in Islam, there are guidelines that protect animals from cruelty and that ensure a clean, safe and sanitary method of slaughter. In contrast, the meat-packing industry today does not ensure the same protections and end results.

For example, blood is not always fully drained from slaughtered cows and chickens. Carcasses may lay around for hours before they are even processed, allowing ample time for germs and diseases to spread throughout the meat. In some cases, the bladder may become ruptured in the slaughtering process, causing urine to spill onto the meat. Slaughterhouse workers don't even make sure the animal dies a quick and painless death, as is required by Islam. Animals may be shocked or electrocuted to death, shot in the head with bullets or cut to pieces before they are even dead!

Modern-day slaughterhouse workers don't even mention Allah's✳ name when the animals are slaughtered. It becomes questionable, therefore, that modern-day slaughtering techniques qualify as halal. To be safe, it is better for a Muslim to preserve his or her health and way of life and only buy halal or kosher meat.

Dhabiha Meat

The method of slaughtering an animal according to Islam is called **Dhabiha** ذَبِيحَة. Dhabiha is a category that falls under 'halal,' and is preferred for Muslims. Dhabiha meat is slaughtered by a sharp knife, and the animals die with minimal pain. A worker is not allowed to slaughter one animal in front of another, nor starve them beforehand. They may not pack them cruelly in cages. Allah's✳ name must be mentioned at the time of slaughter, and the disease-ridden blood is drained out, making the meat more healthy and safe.

The Blessed Prophet ﷺ once said that whoever believes in Allah✳, practices Islam and eats halal food is a Muslim. Let's keep our tables pure, as we try to keep our hearts pure, too.

How to Stay on the Straight Path

An-Nu'man bin Bashir said, "I heard Allah's Messenger ﷺ saying, 'Both legal and illegal things are evident but in between them there are doubtful (suspicious) things and most of the people have no knowledge about them. So whoever saves himself from these suspicious things saves his religion and his honor. And whoever indulges in these suspicious things is like a shepherd who grazes (his animals) near the Hima (private pasture) of someone else and at any moment he is liable to get in it. (O people!) Beware! Every king has a Hima and the Hima of Allah on the earth is His illegal (forbidden) things. Beware! There is a piece of flesh in the body if it becomes good (reformed) the whole body becomes good but if it gets spoilt the whole body gets spoilt and that is the heart.'" (Al Bukhari)

عَنْ النُّعْمَانَ بْنِ بَشِيرٍ، يَقُولُ سَمِعْتُ رَسُولَ اللهِ ﷺ يَقُولُ: «الْحَلَالُ بَيِّنٌ وَالْحَرَامُ بَيِّنٌ، وَبَيْنَهُمَا مُشْتَبِهَاتٌ لَا يَعْلَمُهَا كَثِيرٌ مِنْ النَّاسِ، فَمَنْ اتَّقَى الْمُشْتَبِهَاتِ اسْتَبْرَأَ لِدِينِهِ وَعِرْضِهِ، وَمَنْ وَقَعَ فِي الشُّبُهَاتِ كَرَاعٍ يَرْعَى حَوْلَ الْحِمَى، يُوشِكُ أَنْ يُوَاقِعَهُ. أَلَا وَإِنَّ لِكُلِّ مَلِكٍ حِمًى، أَلَا إِنَّ حِمَى اللهِ فِي أَرْضِهِ مَحَارِمُهُ، أَلَا وَإِنَّ فِي الْجَسَدِ مُضْغَةً إِذَا صَلَحَتْ صَلَحَ الْجَسَدُ كُلُّهُ، وَإِذَا فَسَدَتْ فَسَدَ الْجَسَدُ كُلُّهُ، أَلَا وَهِيَ الْقَلْبُ». رَوَاهُ الْبُخَارِيُّ

The Need for Work

When Captain John Smith took over the Jamestown colony in Virginia in 1608, he found no one working and everyone hungry. He declared, "He that will not work shall not eat." Working is a fact of life. In fact, one of the most important activities of any human being is the gathering of resources. In ancient days, this may have consisted of collecting nuts and berries or putting aside supplies for the long winter ahead.

We are no longer in the Stone Age, but the hunt for resources lives on. Instead of gathering food directly from the land, we often go to places of work, where we can make money that we then exchange for supplies in stores.

Because this is the most time-consuming of all our pursuits, the potential exists for people to want to gain their money by less-than-fair means. Therefore, money and business transactions are the subject of a special section of the Shari'ah.

Truth in Business

We must make our money in an honest and fair fashion. If we do, Allah rewards our earnings with still more rewards and blessings. If we lie, cheat, steal or trick others, then our money can be the source of our ruin, in both this life and in the next.

You who believe! Don't consume other's property among yourselves by deception, but let there be among you trade and business with mutual good will. And don't destroy yourselves, for indeed Allah has been merciful to you. If anyone does injustice, We will soon throw them into the fire. That is easy for Allah. If you reject the worst sins you were forbidden to do, We will take out of you all your lowly deeds, and admit you to a gate of great honor. Surat An-Nisa' (The Women) 4:29-31

﴿يَٰٓأَيُّهَا ٱلَّذِينَ ءَامَنُوا لَا تَأْكُلُوٓا أَمْوَٰلَكُم بَيْنَكُم بِٱلْبَٰطِلِ إِلَّآ أَن تَكُونَ تِجَٰرَةً عَن تَرَاضٍ مِّنكُمْ وَلَا تَقْتُلُوٓا أَنفُسَكُمْ إِنَّ ٱللَّهَ كَانَ بِكُمْ رَحِيمًا﴾ ﴿وَمَن يَفْعَلْ ذَٰلِكَ عُدْوَٰنًا وَظُلْمًا فَسَوْفَ نُصْلِيهِ نَارًا وَكَانَ ذَٰلِكَ عَلَى ٱللَّهِ يَسِيرًا﴾ ﴿إِن تَجْتَنِبُوا كَبَآئِرَ مَا تُنْهَوْنَ عَنْهُ نُكَفِّرْ عَنكُمْ سَيِّـَٔاتِكُمْ وَنُدْخِلْكُم مُّدْخَلًا كَرِيمًا﴾ سُورَةُ النِّسَاء 4:29-31

Business must be conducted in a spirit of friendliness, and with fairness. We must not indulge in deceit, and we must use our profits wisely and not wastefully.

The Blessed Prophet once said, "The truthful and trustworthy business person will be in the company of the prophets, righteous people, and martyrs, on the Day of Judgement." (At-Tirmidhi)

عَنِ النَّبِيِّ ﷺ: «التَّاجِرُ الصَّدُوقُ الأَمِينُ مَعَ النَّبِيِّينَ وَالصِّدِّيقِينَ وَالشُّهَدَاءِ». رَوَاهُ التِّرْمِذِي

The Blessed Prophet once said, "The flesh and body that is fed on unlawful earnings shall not enter Paradise. Hellfire is more fitting for flesh that grows on the body out of haram earnings." (Ahmad)

قَالَ رَسُولُ الله ﷺ: «لَا يَدْخُلُ الْجَنَّةَ لَحْمٌ نَبَتَ مِنْ سُحْتٍ، النَّارُ أَوْلَى بِهِ». رَوَاهُ أَحْمَد

There are several ways of making money that Allah has forbidden. They include working with haram substances (such as alcohol or pork), taking **Riba ربا Interest-money**, unfair money-exchanging, gambling and using any dishonesty. The list also includes a type of stock transaction called 'futures-trading,' where you pay for the delivery of an item in the future, not knowing if you will gain or lose money on the deal.

Dealing in riba is practiced almost everywhere in the world today. Banks pay interest to account holders to get people to deposit money in their banks. The bank then turns around and lends the money it collects to others, and charges them interest, until the person or business pays the money back in full. The person receiving money from interest didn't work for it, and the one paying off a loan has to pay extra money back. If a person takes a loan, they were often poor to begin with, so it's a worse hardship to ask them to pay more.

Jabirﷺ said that, "The Prophetﷺ cursed the one who accepted riba, the one who paid it, the one who recorded it, and the one who witnessed it, saying they were all alike." (Muslim)

عَنْ جَابِرٍ ﷺ قَالَ:«لَعَنَ رَسُوْلُ اللهِ ﷺ آكِلَ الرِّبَا وَمُوكِلَهُ وَكَاتِبَهُ وَشَاهِدَيْهِ وَقَالَ هُمْ سَوَاءٌ». رَوَاهُمُسْلِمٌ

Almost any type of trade or business is a halal way to make money. The Blessed Prophetﷺ personally showed us, by his own example, how we can be the best business person. He was always fair, honest, and trustworthy.

The Blessed Prophetﷺ once said, "May Allah show mercy to the person who is kind when he sells, when he buys and when he makes a claim." (Al Bukhari)

قَالَ رَسُوْلُ اللهِ ﷺ : «رَحِمَ اللهُ رَجُلاً سَمْحًا إِذَا بَاعَ، وَ إِذَا اشْتَرَى، وَ إِذَا اقْتَضَى». رَوَاهُالْبُخَارِيُّ

Islamic Business Ethics

1. Halal Enterprises: A Muslim may only participate in a venture or occupation that does not engage in any haram practices or pursuits. Any business involving intoxicants, dealing with riba, dishonesty, swine products, futures speculation (futures markets), injustice or environmental abuse is strictly off-limits.

The Prophetﷺ said, "To earn a clean living is also a duty next to the main duties of emaan." (Al Baihaqi)

قَالَ رَسُوْلُ اللهِ ﷺ : « كَسْبُ الْحَلالِ فَرِيضَةٌ بَعْدَ الْفَرِيضَةِ». رَوَاهُالْبَيْهَقِي

2. Ready Compensation: Timely payment of employees or contractors must be made. Wages cannot be held for more than a reasonable time.

It was narrated from 'Abdallah bin 'Umarﷺ that the Messenger of Allahﷺ said, "Give the worker his wages before his sweat dries." (Ibn Majah)

عَنْ عَبْدِ اللهِ بْنِ عُمَرَ، قَالَ: قَالَ رَسُوْلُ اللهِ ﷺ :«أَعْطُوا الأَجِيرَ أَجْرَهُ قَبْلَ أَنْ يَجِفَّ عَرَقُهُ». رَوَاهُابْنُمَاجَه

3. Fair Dealing: A Muslim cannot seek to cheat partners, employees, contractors or others in the pursuit of his or her profits. Unfair burdens result in injustice. All important business dealings must have a written contract and witnesses. (2:282)

Abu Hurayrahﷺ narrated that the Prophetﷺ said, "(There are) three (types of persons to whom) Allah will neither speak to them on the Day of Resurrections, nor look at them (They are): (1) a man who takes a false oath that he has been offered for a commodity a price greater than what he has actually been offered; (2) and a man who takes a false oath after the 'Asr (prayer) in order to grab the property of a Muslim through it; (3) and a man who forbids others to use the remaining superfluous water. To such a man Allah will say on the Day of Resurrection, 'Today I withhold My Blessings from you as you withheld the superfluous part of that (water) which your hands did not create.'" (Al Bukhari)

عَنْ أَبِي هُرَيْرَةَ ﷺ، عَنِ النَّبِيِّ ﷺ قَالَ:«ثَلاَثَةٌ لاَ يُكَلِّمُهُمُ اللهُ يَوْمَ الْقِيَامَةِ وَلاَ يَنْظُرُ إِلَيْهِمْ رَجُلٌ حَلَفَ عَلَى سِلْعَةٍ لَقَدْ أَعْطَى بِهَا أَكْثَرَ مِمَّا أَعْطَى وَهُوَ كَاذِبٌ، وَرَجُلٌ حَلَفَ عَلَى يَمِينٍ كَاذِبَةٍ بَعْدَ الْعَصْرِ لِيَقْتَطِعَ بِهَا مَالَ امْرِئٍ مُسْلِمٍ، وَرَجُلٌ مَنَعَ فَضْلَ مَاءٍ فَيَقُولُ اللهُ يَوْمَ الْقِيَامَةِ، الْيَوْمَ أَمْنَعُكَ فَضْلِي، كَمَا مَنَعْتَ فَضْلَ مَا لَمْ تَعْمَلْ يَدَاكَ». رَوَاهُالْبُخَارِيُّ

4. Generosity: Kindness, graciousness, and a general sense of good-heartedness must prevail in business or work relations.

5. Continuous Improvement: Muslim workers and entrepreneurs must seek to reach new levels of excellence.

6. Open Dealing: In any transaction of goods, services, or information, the seller must provide complete details of any and all defects, or potential defects, to the buyer. One day, while in the market, the Blessed Prophetﷺ caught a grain merchant who tried to hide the poor quality of his product, and he admonished him.

7. Personal Responsibility: When money or position is entrusted to the Muslim worker or business owner, he or she must not seek to enrich himself at the expense of either his employer or stockholders while at the same time doing poorly in their service. Debts which lead to a bankruptcy must be answered equitably.

8. Efficient Use: Waste is strictly forbidden. Recycling, full exploitation of materials at hand and a strict process of accountability is a must. Pollution is also forbidden, as it corrupts the earth.

The Big Question

Many people wonder if they are allowed to have non-Muslim friends. Sometimes it is hard to find a clear answer from those around you. Thankfully, the Qur'an and Hadith are clear.

To begin with, Islam teaches that you can have non-Muslim friends, but there are a few conditions. When you consider what a real friend is, you will understand the wise guidance. Becoming friends with someone means making a personal commitment to share some of your time and to share fulfilling experiences.

The Holy Qur'an declares that a believer should never prefer a non-Muslim over a Muslim. If a person did so, then they would put themselves in danger of harming their faith. Therefore, we must realize that it is better to be with those who believe as we do. If you do choose to have some non-Muslim friends, you should make sure you have some Muslim friends also.

Keep your soul content with those who call on their Lord, morning and evening, seeking His face. Don't let your eyes go away from them, seeking the glittery things of this life, nor obey anyone whose heart We have allowed to forget Our remembrance. One who follows his own desires has gone beyond all bounds. Surat Al Kahf (The Cave) 18:28

﴿وَاصْبِرْ نَفْسَكَ مَعَ ٱلَّذِينَ يَدْعُونَ رَبَّهُم بِٱلْغَدَوٰةِ وَٱلْعَشِيِّ يُرِيدُونَ وَجْهَهُۥ وَلَا تَعْدُ عَيْنَاكَ عَنْهُمْ تُرِيدُ زِينَةَ ٱلْحَيَوٰةِ ٱلدُّنْيَا وَلَا تُطِعْ مَنْ أَغْفَلْنَا قَلْبَهُۥ عَن ذِكْرِنَا وَٱتَّبَعَ هَوَىٰهُ وَكَانَ أَمْرُهُۥ فُرُطًا﴾ سُورَةُ الْكَهْف 18:28

Thus, we see it's better to be around those who are more like us in their spiritual orientation. However, if we do choose to have non-Muslim friends, there are certain conditions which Islam places upon us. The first condition is that you do not become dependent on a non-Muslim. In other words, they should never hold power or authority over you. (60:1-2)

Don't let the believers take for protectors an unbeliever over a believer. If anyone does that, then there will be no help from Allah. (The only exception is) if it's a matter of safety. You must guard yourselves from them. Allah, Himself, cautions you and (remember that) the final end is with Allah. Surat Al 'Imran (The Family of 'Imran) 3:28

﴿لَّا يَتَّخِذِ ٱلْمُؤْمِنُونَ ٱلْكَـٰفِرِينَ أَوْلِيَآءَ مِن دُونِ ٱلْمُؤْمِنِينَ وَمَن يَفْعَلْ ذَٰلِكَ فَلَيْسَ مِنَ ٱللَّهِ فِي شَيْءٍ إِلَّآ أَن تَتَّقُوا۟ مِنْهُمْ تُقَىٰةً وَيُحَذِّرُكُمُ ٱللَّهُ نَفْسَهُۥ وَإِلَى ٱللَّهِ ٱلْمَصِيرُ﴾ سُورَةُ آلِ عِمْرَان 3:28

The word used in the Arabic text is **Awlia'a** أَوْلِيَاء which comes from the word **Wali** وَلِي protector. Allahﷻ says in this ayah to not take non-Muslims as protectors. Only reliable Muslims should have authority or power over you. (3:118-120) This is because, in the end, non-Muslims have their own way of life and it is natural for them to want their friends to follow their style. Therefore, they may not always respect your beliefs and may sometimes work against them, even if they don't mean to. (2:109)

The Jews and Christians will never be satisfied with you, unless you follow their ways. Tell them, "The guidance of Allah is the only guidance." If you followed their desires after the knowledge (of Islam) came to you, then you would find no protector or helper against Allah. Surat Al Baqarah (The Cow) 2:120

﴿وَلَن تَرْضَىٰ عَنكَ ٱلْيَهُودُ وَلَا ٱلنَّصَـٰرَىٰ حَتَّىٰ تَتَّبِعَ مِلَّتَهُمْ قُلْ إِنَّ هُدَى ٱللَّهِ هُوَ ٱلْهُدَىٰ وَلَئِنِ ٱتَّبَعْتَ أَهْوَآءَهُم بَعْدَ ٱلَّذِي جَآءَكَ مِنَ ٱلْعِلْمِ مَا لَكَ مِنَ ٱللَّهِ مِن وَلِيٍّ وَلَا نَصِيرٍ﴾ سُورَةُ الْبَقَرَة 2:120

The second condition is also very important, in that your non-Muslim friends should not ridicule or disrespect Islam. If they do, what kind of friend would they be to you? Can you imagine insulting their most cherished beliefs? (5:57)

You have already been given the command in the Book, that when you hear the signs of Allah being insulted or joked with, you are not to sit with them unless they start talking about something else. If you stayed with them while they were insulting Allah, then you would be like them. Allah will gather all the hypocrites and the unbelievers in Hell. *Surat An-Nisa' 4: 140*

﴿وَقَدْ نَزَّلَ عَلَيْكُمْ فِي ٱلْكِتَٰبِ أَنْ إِذَا سَمِعْتُمْ ءَايَٰتِ ٱللَّهِ يُكْفَرُ بِهَا وَيُسْتَهْزَأُ بِهَا فَلَا تَقْعُدُوا۟ مَعَهُمْ حَتَّىٰ يَخُوضُوا۟ فِي حَدِيثٍ غَيْرِهِ إِنَّكُمْ إِذًا مِّثْلُهُمْ إِنَّ ٱللَّهَ جَامِعُ ٱلْمُنَٰفِقِينَ وَٱلْكَٰفِرِينَ فِي جَهَنَّمَ جَمِيعًا﴾ سُورَةُ النِّسَاء 140:4

The third condition is that you must try your best to give them Islamic da'wah whenever the opportunity arises. (3:104) According to Islamic teachings, your intention when establishing new friendships should be to set an example of a good Muslim. Another reason should be to help them to discover the benefit and beauty of Islam. The fourth and final requirement is that you should prefer to have nice, believing Muslims as close friends, whenever possible. (4:144)

You want to constantly surround yourself with people who practice Islam the right way. People who may be nice, but live a lifestyle that clashes with Islamic teachings, such as drinking or dating, are not the best choice. Whether Muslim or not, choose your friends wisely.

To those who take unbelievers for protectors rather than believers, are they looking for honor or greatness from them? But all honor is with Allah. *Surat An-Nisa' (The Women) 4: 139*

﴿ٱلَّذِينَ يَتَّخِذُونَ ٱلْكَٰفِرِينَ أَوْلِيَآءَ مِن دُونِ ٱلْمُؤْمِنِينَ أَيَبْتَغُونَ عِندَهُمُ ٱلْعِزَّةَ فَإِنَّ ٱلْعِزَّةَ لِلَّهِ جَمِيعًا﴾ سُورَةُ النِّسَاء 139:4

Abu Hurayrah narrated that the Prophet said, "A person molds his way of life according to his friend. So you should be careful about who you make your friend." (Ahmad)

عَنْ أَبِي هُرَيْرَةَ، قَالَ: أَنَّ النَّبِيَّ ﷺ قَالَ: «الرَّجُلُ عَلَى دِينِ خَلِيلِهِ فَلْيَنْظُرْ أَحَدُكُمْ مَنْ يُخَالِلُ». رَوَاهُ أَحْمَد

Abu Sa'id narrated that the Messenger of Allah said, "Keep company only with the believers, and let your food be eaten only by the righteous." (At-Tirmidhi)

عَنْ أَبِي سَعِيدٍ، - أَنَّهُ سَمِعَ رَسُولَ اللهِ ﷺ يَقُولُ: «لَا تُصَاحِبْ إِلَّا مُؤْمِنًا وَلَا يَأْكُلْ طَعَامَكَ إِلَّا تَقِيٌّ». رَوَاهُ التِّرْمَذِي

The Prophet was reportedly asked, "Which of our companions are best?" He replied, "One whose appearance reminds you of God, and whose speech increases you in knowledge, and whose actions remind you of the hereafter." (At-Tirmidhi)

عَنِ ابْنِ عَبَّاسٍ، قَالَ: قِيلَ يَا رَسُولَ اللهِ أَيُّ جُلَسَائِنَا خَيْرٌ؟ قَالَ: «مَنْ ذَكَّرَكُمْ بِاللهِ مَنْظَرُهُ، وَزَادَ فِي عِلْمِكُمْ مَنْطِقُهُ، وَذَكَّرَكُمْ بِالْآخِرَةِ عِلْمُهُ». رَوَاهُ التِّرْمَذِي

Abu Musa narrated that the Messenger of Allah said, "The example of the good and evil companions is like a bearer of musk and a person blowing a pair of bellows. As for the musk bearer, he either gives you some, or you buy from him or at least you get a pleasant smell from him. As for the bellows blower he either gets your clothes burnt or you get an unpleasant smell from him." (Al Bukhari)

عَنْ أَبِي مُوسَى، قَالَ: قَالَ رَسُولُ اللهِ ﷺ: «مَثَلُ الْجَلِيسِ الصَّالِحِ، وَالْجَلِيسِ السَّوْءِ، كَمَثَلِ صَاحِبِ الْمِسْكِ، وَكِيرِ الْحَدَّادِ، لَا يَعْدَمُكَ مِنْ صَاحِبِ الْمِسْكِ، إِمَّا تَشْتَرِيهِ أَوْ تَجِدُ رِيحَهُ، وَكِيرُ الْحَدَّادِ يُحْرِقُ بَدَنَكَ أَوْ ثَوْبَكَ، أَوْ تَجِدُ مِنْهُ رِيحًا خَبِيثَةً». رَوَاهُ الْبُخَارِيُّ

Abu Hurayrah narrated that the Prophet said, "The believer is a mirror for the believer, and the believer is the brother of the believer. He safeguards his property for him and defends him from behind." (Al Baihaqi)

عَنْ أَبِي هُرَيْرَةَ، قَالَ: أَنَّ النَّبِيَّ ﷺ قَالَ: «الْمُؤْمِنُ مِرْآةُ الْمُؤْمِنِ، وَالْمُؤْمِنُ أَخُو الْمُؤْمِنِ، مِنْ حَيْثُ لَقِيَهُ يَكُفُّ عَنْهُ ضَيْعَتَهُ، وَيَحُوطُهُ مِنْ وَرَائِهِ». رَوَاهُ الْبَيْهَقِي

What to Look for in a Mate

The Islamic term for the wedding ceremony is **Nikah** نِكَاح. It is a very important event in the life of a young man and woman, and it affects the life of two different families.

And among His Signs is this, that He created for you wives from among yourselves, that you may find repose in them, and He has put between you affection and mercy. Verily, in that are indeed signs for a people who reflect. Surat Ar-Rum (The Romans) 30:21

﴿وَمِنْ ءَايَـٰتِهِۦٓ أَنْ خَلَقَ لَكُم مِّنْ أَنفُسِكُمْ أَزْوَٰجًا لِّتَسْكُنُوٓا۟ إِلَيْهَا وَجَعَلَ بَيْنَكُم مَّوَدَّةً وَرَحْمَةً إِنَّ فِى ذَٰلِكَ لَءَايَـٰتٍ لِّقَوْمٍ يَتَفَكَّرُونَ﴾ سُورَةُالرُّوم ٣٠:٢١

The Prophet ﷺ said, "A woman is married for four things, her wealth, her family status, her beauty and her religion. So you should marry the religious woman, otherwise you will be a loser." (Al Bukhari)

عَنِ النَّبِيِّ ﷺ قَالَ: «تُنْكَحُ الْمَرْأَةُ لِأَرْبَعٍ لِمَالِهَا وَلِحَسَبِهَا وَجَمَالِهَا وَلِدِينِهَا، فَاظْفَرْ بِذَاتِ الدِّينِ تَرِبَتْ يَدَاكَ». رَوَاهُالْبُخَارِيُّ

Unfortunately, some Muslims skip the inner beauty of taqwa and emaan that the Prophet ﷺ suggested to look for in a mate. Instead, people tend to focus on the outer beauty, wealth or status. Consequently, these people may end up in bad marriages in which greed and envy prevail. While there are many reasons that may cause a couple to divorce—many of which may be outside of the individual's control—sometimes it can be traced to these misplaced priorities.

In addition, using a person's race or ethnicity as the only factor in the selection of a spouse is undesirable. Islam counsels against it. Besides, any Muslim, regardless of their skin color or ethnic group, is equal in the Ummah of the Blessed Prophet Muhammad ﷺ.

The Blessed Prophet ﷺ said, "There is no superiority of an Arab over a non-Arab or a non-Arab over an Arab. And there is no superiority of a white over a black or a black over a white, except with God-consciousness." (Ahmad)

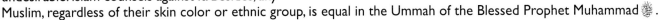

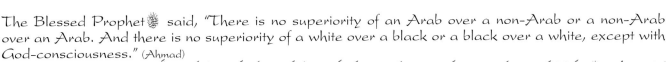

قَالَ رَسُولُ الله ﷺ : «لَا فَضْلَ لِعَرَبِيٍّ عَلَى عَجَمِيٍّ، وَلَا لِعَجَمِيٍّ عَلَى عَرَبِيٍّ، وَلَا لِأَبْيَضَ عَلَى أَسْوَدَ، وَلَا لِأَسْوَدَ عَلَى أَبْيَضَ: إِلَّا بِالتَّقْوَى». رَوَاهُأَحمَد

Therefore, it is best to look for taqwa, or genuine awareness of Allah ﷻ, before looking for wealth or anything else. After these priorities have been established and clearly agreed upon by everyone involved, the search for the spouse begins.

The Setting of the Agreement

Once a prospective spouse has been identified, usually there are a lot of behind-the-scenes meetings and discussions. The parents contact each other and discuss the matter, then the young man and woman are approached with the idea of meeting each other. If they both agree to meet, then a formal affair is arranged, such as a dinner, where they can meet without being the center of attention.

The prospective bride and groom can see each other, talk together and get to know each other for days, weeks, even months. There should be a chaperone nearby, however, to keep things properly within the limits of Allah ﷻ.

The Blessed Prophet ﷺ said, "When an (unmarried) man and woman are together, the third with them is Shaytan." (At-Tirmidhi)

عَنِ النَّبِيِّ ﷺ : «لَا يَخْلُوَنَّ رَجُلٌ بِامْرَأَةٍ إِلَّا كَانَ ثَالِثُهُمَا الشَّيْطَانُ». رَوَاهُالتِّرْمَذِيّ

If the man and woman agree to marry, then there is a formal engagement announced, and a wedding date is set.

According to the Prophet ﷺ, no one can be forced to marry someone they are not interested in. The Prophet ﷺ specifically mentioned the importance of obtaining the female's decision in the matter. This was overlooked in the culture at that time and continues to be ignored in many cultures, even today. It must be a free choice for both parties. Only then can the wedding be performed.

The nikah should be a simple one. According to the hadith of the Prophet ﷺ, "The best wedding is the one with the least amount of burden." (Al Baihaqi)

عَنْ عَائِشَةَ ﵂، قَالَ النَّبِيُّ ﷺ: «إِنَّ أَعْظَمَ النِّكَاحِ بَرَكَةً، أَيْسَرُهُ مَؤُونَةً». رواه البيهقي

Islam does not support the practice of having extravagant and expensive affairs. An imam, or an equally knowledgeable Muslim, typically performs the ceremony. The bride is represented by her **Wali** وَلِيّ **Protective Guardian.** Usually this is her father, brother or uncle. The groom also has someone who acts on his behalf, much like a best man.

A marriage contract is written beforehand, both by the bride and the groom. In the wedding contract, each side lists what they expect from the marriage. For example, the details of how the bride expects to be treated in the marriage, wedding vows or even a prenuptial agreement clause can be included, along with any other stipulations that she chooses.

In Islam, the groom is obligated to present his bride with a **Mahr** مَهْر **Dowry** to the wife. It is not the other way around. An example of where Muslims mix up this Islamic requirement is through a custom practiced in Southeast Asia, where the bride's family offers a dowry to the family of the husband; yet, this is not the Islamic way at all.

> Abu Hurayrah ﵁ reported that the Blessed Prophet ﷺ said, "The worst food is from a Walimah in which only the rich are invited and not the poor. Whoever refuses an invitation (to a dinner-party) disobeys Allah and His Messenger." (Agreed upon))
>
> عَنْ أَبِي هُرَيْرَةَ ﵁، قَالَ: قَالَ رَسُولُ اللهِ ﷺ: «بِئْسَ الطَّعَامُ طَعَامُ الْوَلِيمَةِ يُدْعَى إِلَيْهَا الْأَغْنِيَاءُ، وَيُتْرَكُ الْفُقَرَاءُ». مُتَّفَقٌ عَلَيْهِ

The mahr can consist of anything the bride desires, whether it's some amount of money, jewelry, a house or other item. The husband is not allowed to ever take her mahr away, but the wife can allow the husband to pay it to her over time. Some men need time to pay the mahr, if it's very high, or if the groom is not well-off.

And give women their mahr as a free gift, but if they forgive any of it of their own good pleasure, accept it and enjoy it with gladness. Surat An-Nisa' (The Women) 4:4

﴿وَءَاتُواْ ٱلنِّسَآءَ صَدُقَٰتِهِنَّ نِحْلَةً فَإِن طِبْنَ لَكُمْ عَن شَيْءٍ مِّنْهُ نَفْسًا فَكُلُوهُ هَنِيٓـًٔا مَّرِيٓـًٔا﴾ سُورَةُ النِّسَاءِ 4:4

Both parties will sign the contract, and then the actual nikah will starts. The imam begins by confirming publicly that both sides have agreed to marry, and then the amount of the mahr is announced.

Next, the imam reads the nikah khutbah. This describes the purpose of marriage and how Allah ﷻ made it to be the trust of men and women to abide faithfully in love and fairness to each other. One of the beautiful ayaat that is often read is: *O men, fear your Lord who created you from a single soul, and from it created its match, and spread many men and women from the two. Fear Allah in whose name you ask each other (for your rights), and fear (the violation of the rights of) the womb-relations. Surely, Allah is watchful over you.* Surat An-Nisa' (The Women) 4:1

﴿يَٰٓأَيُّهَا ٱلنَّاسُ ٱتَّقُواْ رَبَّكُمُ ٱلَّذِي خَلَقَكُم مِّن نَّفْسٍ وَٰحِدَةٍ وَخَلَقَ مِنْهَا زَوْجَهَا وَبَثَّ مِنْهُمَا رِجَالًا كَثِيرًا وَنِسَآءً وَٱتَّقُواْ ٱللَّهَ ٱلَّذِي تَسَآءَلُونَ بِهِۦ وَٱلْأَرْحَامَ إِنَّ ٱللَّهَ كَانَ عَلَيْكُمْ رَقِيبًا﴾ سُورَةُ النِّسَاءِ 4:1

Following the nikah is a joyous celebration called a **Walimah** وَلِيمَة **Reception,** where friends and family celebrate the birth of the new marriage.

Literature Selection
The Best Marriage Gift

Adapted from *Companions of the Prophet*
Compiled by 'Abdul Wahid Hamid

Rumaysa bint Milhan was one of the first women in Al Madinah to accept Islam. Her husband, who was an idol-worshipper, was on a trip at the time and didn't know about his wife's decision. When he returned home, he noticed that his wife seemed invigorated and full of excitement. When he asked her why, she answered that she accepted the Message of Prophet Muhammad ﷺ and gave up idol-worshipping.

Her husband didn't like what she did and he became angry. When he found out she was teaching their young son, Anas, how to say the Shahadah, his rage peaked and he became abusive.

One day, her husband left the house on some errand but was ambushed by an enemy that he had a feud with. He was killed in the attack. Everyone was upset, but Rumaysa was not terribly upset. She vowed to never marry again unless her son approved.

A few months later, a local man named Abu Talha wanted to marry her. He knew she was a Muslim while he wasn't, but he didn't care if they had different beliefs. He went to her house and asked to marry her.

She refused on the grounds that he was an unbeliever. Abu Talha was shocked! He couldn't believe that any woman would turn him down, because he was very rich. So Abu Talha asked her if she wanted some gold and silver as gifts first.

She shook her head, "No" and said, "I swear to Allah that if you accept Islam, I would be pleased to have you as my husband, without giving me any gold or silver. I'll consider your acceptance of Islam as my wedding gift."

Abu Talha, who had an expensive and beautiful idol made of wood, became worried about leaving his old ways. While he was thinking, Rumaysa asked him, "Don't you know that the idol you worship grew from the ground?"

Abu Talha nodded, "Yes."

Then she continued, "Don't you feel stupid worshipping part of a tree, while you use the rest of it for fuel to bake your bread or to warm yourself? Accept Islam and I'll be pleased to take you as my husband."

Abu Talha thought about it and asked, "Who will teach me about Islam?"

Rumaysa replied, "I will. Say that there is no god but Allah and that Muhammad is His Messenger. Then, go to your house and break your idol and throw it away."

Abu Talha left and reflected upon what she had told him. When he realized his idol was something stupid to worship, he broke it. Then rushed back to her smiling and declared himself a Muslim. Anas approved, and they were married.

Muslims would later say that there was no better marriage gift than that of Rumaysa, because she had given Islam as her marriage gift.

Chapter 18
Islam in Society

The Best Habits

One quality that makes humans different from all other living creatures is our ability to modify our behavior. A person can be taught to eat with his fingers or with a fork, just as a person can learn to stay up all night and sleep during the day. The best habits are those that are the most beneficial to us as humans. Obviously, it wouldn't be good to hit yourself in the head with a stick when you meet someone. Similarly it would probably be a bad idea to always pour swamp water in your bathtub.

Many societies have tried to set standards for behaviors and manners at the personal and social level. The Chinese bow slightly to each other when they meet; some South American Indian tribes have the custom of washing each other's hair, and Americans are taught not to put their elbows on the dinner table.

For Muslims, our **Adab آداب Good Manners** relate directly to our character, or **Akhlaq أَخْلاق**. The adab that we follow was not developed over many centuries. Rather, one man taught us everything about how to be good to others and good to ourselves. It was none other than Prophet Muhammad ﷺ who taught us the finest mode of civilization that ever existed. By following his great example, our akhlaq becomes refined and full of social graces.

The challenge now is to learn what adab entails and then to put it into practice. Nearly every Muslim knows that they should say "السَّلامُ عَلَيْكُم" (Peace be to you) when they meet each other. But this is just one small part of the many manners we should make a part of our daily life. The Blessed Prophet ﷺ is our model, and his path is the best to follow.

You have indeed in the Messenger of Allah, a beautiful pattern (of conduct), for any whose hope is in Allah and the Last Day and who remember Allah much. Surat Al Ahzab (The Confederates) 33:21

﴿لَقَدْ كَانَ لَكُمْ فِي رَسُولِ اللَّهِ أُسْوَةٌ حَسَنَةٌ لِّمَن كَانَ يَرْجُوا اللَّهَ وَالْيَوْمَ الْآخِرَ وَذَكَرَ اللَّهَ كَثِيرًا﴾ سُورَةُ الأحزاب 21:33

The great lady 'Aishah ﷺ was once asked what the Blessed Prophet's ﷺ manners were like. She gave a very interesting reply. She said, "His manners were the Qur'an."

Manners for Greeting

Our adab comes from the Qur'an and Sunnah. Any cultural practices that one follows must not go against these two sources. Islamic teachings must come first if we are to be true believers. When two Muslims meet each other, after exchanging the greetings of peace, they should shake hands. The Blessed Prophet ﷺ said the better one is the one who lets his hand go last.

The Prophet ﷺ said, "Those who are nearest to Allah are those who are the first to give a greeting." (Abu Dawud)

قَالَ رَسُولُ اللهِ ﷺ: «إِنَّ أَوْلَى النَّاسِ بِاللهِ مَنْ بَدَأَهُمْ بِالسَّلَامِ». رَوَاهُ أبو داود

The greeting of Islam, **Peace be to you** السلام عليكم, has a special significance for us. The word 'peace' is the highest and most honored term. Allah ﷻ says about it: 'Peace!' is a word from a Merciful Lord. Surat Ya-sin 36:58

﴿سَلَامٌ قَوْلًا مِّن رَّبٍّ رَّحِيمٍ﴾ سُورَةُ يس 58:36

Therefore it is the best word for people to use between each other. If a small group comes to a larger group, the rule is that the smaller group should greet the larger one first. If some people are sitting down, they should not stand up if someone comes to join them. The Blessed Prophet ﷺ didn't even like people to get up for him!

A younger person should greet an older person first. When a greeting is given, the reply should be something equal to or better than that. For example, if someone says, "السَّلامُ عَلَيْكُم," you can reply with **And you have peace** وَعَلَيْكُمُ السَّلامُ, which is an equal greeting. Or you can improve upon it by saying **Peace be upon you and Allah's mercy** السَّلامُ عَلَيْكُم وَرَحْمَةُ اللهِ, or **Peace be upon you and Allah's mercy and blessings** السَّلامُ عَلَيْكُم وَرَحْمَةُ اللهِ وَبَرَكَاتُهُ.

Respect for People

Islam teaches us to have regard for others. If we don't treat all people with respect, then we lack adab. The Blessed Prophet ﷺ said, Nothing is heavier in the scales of good deeds than good behavior. (At-Tirmidhi)

عَنِ النَّبِيِّ ﷺ قَالَ: «مَا شَيْءٌ أَثْقَلُ فِي مِيزَانِ الْمُؤْمِنِ يَوْمَ الْقِيَامَةِ مِنْ خُلُقٍ حَسَنٍ وَ إِنَّ اللهَ لَيَبْغَضُ الْفَاحِشَ الْبَذِيءَ». رَوَاهُ التِّرْمِذِيُّ

The Blessed Prophet ﷺ said, The best of you are those with the best character. (Al Bukhari)

قَالَ رَسُولُ اللهِ ﷺ: «إِنَّ خِيَارَكُمْ أَحَاسِنُكُمْ أَخْلَاقًا». رَوَاهُ الْبُخَارِيُّ

With regards to elderly people, we are supposed to treat them with kindness and respect. Think about it, they have lived much longer than you, and they've already gone through trials and struggles you have yet to experience. And in the case of your parents, they spent a lot of time and effort raising you.

The Blessed Prophet ﷺ declared, "Whenever a young person honors an old person because of their age, then Allah will give him or her somebody to honor them when they are old themselves." (At-Tirmidhi)

قَالَ رَسُولُ اللهِ ﷺ: «مَا أَكْرَمَ شَابٌّ شَيْخًا لِسِنِّهِ إِلَّا قَيَّضَ اللهُ لَهُ مَنْ يُكْرِمُهُ عِنْدَ سِنِّهِ». رَوَاهُ التِّرْمِذِيُّ

Allah ﷻ commands us to address our parents in kindness and not to lose patience with them or insult them if they frustrate us. He said, Your Lord has decreed that you worship none but Him, and do good to parents. If any one of them or both of them reach old age, do not say to them: uff (a word or expression of anger or contempt) and do not scold them, and address them with respectful words, And submit yourself before them in humility out of compassion, and say, "My Lord, be merciful to them as they have brought me up in my childhood." Surat Al Isra' (The Journey by Night) 17:23-24

﴿وَقَضَىٰ رَبُّكَ أَلَّا تَعْبُدُوٓا۟ إِلَّآ إِيَّاهُ وَبِٱلْوَٰلِدَيْنِ إِحْسَٰنًا إِمَّا يَبْلُغَنَّ عِندَكَ ٱلْكِبَرَ أَحَدُهُمَآ أَوْ كِلَاهُمَا فَلَا تَقُل لَّهُمَآ أُفٍّ وَلَا تَنْهَرْهُمَا وَقُل لَّهُمَا قَوْلًا كَرِيمًا﴾
﴿وَٱخْفِضْ لَهُمَا جَنَاحَ ٱلذُّلِّ مِنَ ٱلرَّحْمَةِ وَقُل رَّبِّ ٱرْحَمْهُمَا كَمَا رَبَّيَانِي صَغِيرًا﴾ سُورَةُ الإِسرا 17:23-24

Guests are also to be treated well. When a person invites another to their house, food should be served, and the guest should be made to feel welcome and at home.

Abu Hurayrah ﷺ narrated that Allah's Messenger ﷺ said, "Let him who believes in Allah and the Last Day speak good, or keep silent; and let him who believes in Allah and the Last Day be generous to his neighbor; and let him who believes in Allah and the Last Day be generous to his guest." (Al Bukhari and Muslim)

عَنْ أَبِي هُرَيْرَةَ ﷺ أَنَّ رَسُولَ اللهِ ﷺ قَالَ: «مَنْ كَانَ يُؤْمِنُ بِاللهِ وَالْيَوْمِ الْآخِرِ فَلْيَقُلْ خَيْرًا أَوْ لِيَصْمُتْ، وَمَنْ كَانَ يُؤْمِنُ بِاللهِ وَالْيَوْمِ الْآخِرِ فَلْيُكْرِمْ جَارَهُ وَمَنْ كَانَ يُؤْمِنُ بِاللهِ وَالْيَوْمِ الْآخِرِ فَلْيُكْرِمْ ضَيْفَهُ». رَوَاهُ الْبُخَارِيُّ وَمُسْلِمٌ

For their part, the guest should not try to take advantage of his or her host. The Blessed Prophet ﷺ advised us, in another saying, that the guest should not overstay his welcome. Guests should respect the privacy, home and family of the host.

Basic Respect

Islam teaches that there are some types of behavior that are not good. A Muslim is not allowed to spy on another Muslim, for example. And if we hear gossiping, we should refrain from joining the conversation and walk away. (49:12) Finally, we are not allowed to tease each other or call each other hurtful names. Allah ﷻ said, O you who believe, no men should ever scoff at other men. Maybe, the latter are better than the former. Nor should women (ever scoff) at other women. Maybe, the latter women are better than the former ones. And do not find fault with one another, nor call one another with bad nicknames. Bad is the name of sinfulness after embracing Faith. If anyone does not repent, then such people are the wrongdoers. Surat Al Hujrat (The Rooms) 49:11

﴿يَٰٓأَيُّهَا ٱلَّذِينَ ءَامَنُوا۟ لَا يَسْخَرْ قَوْمٌ مِّن قَوْمٍ عَسَىٰٓ أَن يَكُونُوا۟ خَيْرًا مِّنْهُمْ وَلَا نِسَآءٌ مِّن نِّسَآءٍ عَسَىٰٓ أَن يَكُنَّ خَيْرًا مِّنْهُنَّ وَلَا تَلْمِزُوٓا۟ أَنفُسَكُمْ وَلَا تَنَابَزُوا۟ بِٱلْأَلْقَٰبِ بِئْسَ ٱلِٱسْمُ ٱلْفُسُوقُ بَعْدَ ٱلْإِيمَٰنِ وَمَن لَّمْ يَتُبْ فَأُو۟لَٰٓئِكَ هُمُ ٱلظَّٰلِمُونَ﴾ سُورَةُ الْحُجُرات 49:11

If two Muslims fall to fighting, we must break it up and solve the problem. (49:9-10) No cursing or foul language should be used, and we must all present ourselves as dignified, refined and decent human beings. (33:58) These are examples of akhlaq in a Muslim.

The Muslim Family

Islam in the Family

O you who believe! Save yourselves and your families from a fire whose fuel is men and the stone (of idols). Surat At-Tahrim (The Prohibition) 66:6

﴿يَٰٓأَيُّهَا ٱلَّذِينَ ءَامَنُوا۟ قُوٓا۟ أَنفُسَكُمْ وَأَهْلِيكُمْ نَارًا وَقُودُهَا ٱلنَّاسُ وَٱلْحِجَارَةُ﴾ سُورَةُ التَّحْرِيمِ 66:6

Islam is the way of life—guidance from the Creator to us. It is concerned with our personal life, our social life as well as our family life. If Islam teaches that it is wrong to steal, shouldn't it also teach us how family members should behave with each other and shouldn't it explain their rights? In the Islamic family structure, both the father and mother are considered equal partners.

The structure of the Muslim family can best be summed up in the following hadith: 'Abdallah bin 'Umar reported that the Blessed Prophet once said, "Every one of you is a shepherd and is responsible for his flock. The leader of the people is a guardian and is responsible for his subjects: a man is the guardian of his family and is responsible for his subjects, a woman is the guardian of her husband's home and of his children and is responsible for them, and the slave of a man is a guardian of his master's property and is responsible for it. Surely, everyone of you is a shepherd and responsible for his flock." (Muslim)

عَنِ ابْنِ عُمَرَ، عَنِ النَّبِيِّ ﷺ قَالَ: «أَلَا كُلُّكُمْ رَاعٍ وَكُلُّكُمْ مَسْئُولٌ عَنْ رَعِيَّتِهِ فَالْأَمِيرُ الَّذِي عَلَى النَّاسِ رَاعٍ وَهُوَ مَسْئُولٌ عَنْ رَعِيَّتِهِ وَالرَّجُلُ رَاعٍ عَلَى أَهْلِ بَيْتِهِ وَهُوَ مَسْئُولٌ عَنْهُمْ وَالْمَرْأَةُ رَاعِيَةٌ عَلَى بَيْتِ بَعْلِهَا وَوَلَدِهِ وَهِيَ مَسْئُولَةٌ عَنْهُمْ وَالْعَبْدُ رَاعٍ عَلَى مَالِ سَيِّدِهِ وَهُوَ مَسْئُولٌ عَنْهُ أَلَا فَكُلُّكُمْ رَاعٍ وَكُلُّكُمْ مَسْئُولٌ عَنْ رَعِيَّتِهِ». رَوَاهُ مُسْلِمٌ

The Duties of the Husband

The husband is considered the protector and leader of the home, but at the same time, Islam says he is not a dictator. (4:34) The wife's opinions should carry as much weight as his own. They must decide things together by mutual consultation.

The husband is expected to provide the financial resources of the family. Although the wife can have a career of her own, she doesn't have to spend a dime of her own money on the family if she doesn't want to. However, if the husband makes very little money, it is noble on her part to help in the paying of the bills.

The husband also has the responsibility of maintaining the safety of the family. He must protect them from danger and ensure that the wife and children can live without fear and poverty to the best of his ability.

'Abdallah bin 'Amr narrated that, the Blessed Prophet once said, "The Lord's pleasure is in the parent's pleasure, and the Lord's anger is in the parent's anger." (At-Tirmidhi)

عَنْ عَبْدِاللهِ بْنِ عَمْرٍو، عَنِ النَّبِيِّ ﷺ قَالَ: «رِضَا اللهِ فِي رِضَا الْوَالِدَيْنِ, وَسَخَطُ اللهِ فِي سَخَطِ الْوَالِدَيْنِ». رَوَاهُ التَّرْمَذِي

Again, this is assuming that the father is following Islam sincerely and teaching it to his children with some wisdom.

Duties of the Wife

The wife is the major caregiver in the home. She must nurture the children, with the husband's help, so that they become good Muslims and well-mannered people. The wife can work and have a career if she chooses, as long as she understands that raising her children is her priority. If there are no relatives to help raise the children right, it is best for her to stay home for at least a few years to put them on the right path of Islam.

A man came to the prophet and said, "'O Messenger of Allah! I intend to go on a military expedition, but I have come to ask your advice.' He said, 'Is your mother alive?' He said 'Yes.' He said, 'Then stay with her, for the garden is under her feet.'" (An-Nasa'i)

عَنْ مُحَمَّدِ بْنِ طَلْحَةَ، - وَهُوَ ابْنُ عَبْدِاللهِ بْنِ عَبْدِالرَّحْمَنِ - عَنْ أَبِيهِ، طَلْحَةَ عَنْ مُعَاوِيَةَ بْنِ جَاهِمَةَ السُّلَمِيِّ، أَنَّ جَاهِمَةَ، جَاءَ إِلَى النَّبِيِّ صلى الله عليه وسلم فَقَالَ: «يَا رَسُولَ اللهِ أَرَدْتُ أَنْ أَغْزُوَ وَقَدْ جِئْتُ أَسْتَشِيرُكَ. فَقَالَ: هَلْ لَكَ مِنْ أُمٍّ. قَالَ نَعَمْ. قَالَ: فَالْزَمْهَا فَإِنَّ الْجَنَّةَ تَحْتَ رِجْلَيْهَا». رَوَاهُ النَّسَائِي

The mother is the most loved person in the home, even three times more than the father, according to a hadith of the Blessed Prophet.

Abu Hurayrah👤 reported that "a person came to Allah's Messenger👤 and said, 'Who among the people is most deserving of a fine treatment from my hand?' He said, 'Your mother.' He again said, 'Then who (is the next one)?' He said, 'Again it is your mother (who deserves the best treatment from you).' He said, 'Then who (is the next one)?' He (the Holy Prophet) said, 'Again, it is your mother.' He (again) said, 'Then who?' Thereupon he said, 'Then it is your father.'" (Muslim)

عَنْ أَبِي هُرَيْرَةَ، قَالَ: «جَاءَ رَجُلٌ إِلَى رَسُولِ اللهِ ﷺ فَقَالَ مَنْ أَحَقُّ النَّاسِ بِحُسْنِ صَحَابَتِي قَالَ: أُمُّكَ. قَالَ ثُمَّ مَنْ قَالَ: ثُمَّ أُمُّكَ. قَالَ ثُمَّ مَنْ قَالَ: ثُمَّ أُمُّكَ. قَالَ ثُمَّ مَنْ قَالَ: ثُمَّ أَبُوكَ» رَوَاهُ مُسْلِمٌ

Children, according to another hadith, are even forbidden to disobey their mothers. The Blessed Prophet👤 said, "Allah has indeed forbidden you to disobey your Mothers." (Al Bukhari)

عَنِ النَّبِيِّ ﷺ قَالَ: «إِنَّ اللهَ حَرَّمَ عَلَيْكُمْ عُقُوقَ الْأُمَّهَاتِ». رَوَاهُ الْبُخَارِيُّ

Islam teaches the equality of men and women. Both are equal in the sight of Allah👤 and one is not more valuable to Allah👤 than the other. Although Allah👤 did give men the position of 'head of the family,' it doesn't mean that men get more attention from Allah👤. Allah👤 said, *For Muslim men and Muslim women, for believing men and believing women, for devout men and devout women, for patient men and patient women, for humble men and humble women, for charitable men and charitable women, for fasting men and fasting women, for chaste men and chaste women, and for men and women who engage in the praise of Allah—for them Allah has prepared forgiveness and a great reward.* Surat Al Ahzab (The Confederates) 33:35

﴿إِنَّ الْمُسْلِمِينَ وَالْمُسْلِمَاتِ وَالْمُؤْمِنِينَ وَالْمُؤْمِنَاتِ وَالْقَانِتِينَ وَالْقَانِتَاتِ وَالصَّادِقِينَ وَالصَّادِقَاتِ وَالصَّابِرِينَ وَالصَّابِرَاتِ وَالْخَاشِعِينَ وَالْخَاشِعَاتِ وَالْمُتَصَدِّقِينَ وَالْمُتَصَدِّقَاتِ وَالصَّائِمِينَ وَالصَّائِمَاتِ وَالْحَافِظِينَ فُرُوجَهُمْ وَالْحَافِظَاتِ وَالذَّاكِرِينَ اللَّهَ كَثِيرًا وَالذَّاكِرَاتِ أَعَدَّ اللَّهُ لَهُمْ مَغْفِرَةً وَأَجْرًا عَظِيمًا﴾ سُورَةُ الْأَحْزَابِ 33:35

The Rights and Duties of Children

Children have rights and duties in Islam. It is their right to be raised as Muslims, with good manners and to be educated. It is their duty to obey their parents in everything they can, as long as it isn't haram.

The Blessed Prophet👤 once advised children, "Obey your parents and treat them kindly, for if you do, then your own children will be obedient and kindly to you." (At-Tabarani)

قَالَ رَسُولُ اللهِ ﷺ: «بَرُّوا آبَاءَكُمْ تَبَرَّكُمْ أَبْنَاؤُكُمْ، وَعِفُّوا تَعِفَّ نِسَاؤُكُمْ». رَوَاهُ الطَّبَرَانِيُّ

On another occasion he remarked👤, "Among all sins, for any sin that He wants to, Almighty Allah may postpone the punishment until the Day of Judgement except disobedience of parents, because Allah Most High punishes the person who is disobedient to his (or her) parents before death right in this world." (Al Baihaqi)

قَالَ رَسُولُ اللهِ ﷺ: «كُلُّ الذُّنُوبِ يَغْفِرُ اللهُ مِنْهَا مَا يَشَاءُ إِلَّا عُقُوقَ الْوَالِدَيْنِ، فَإِنَّهُ يُعَجِّلُ لِصَاحِبِهِ فِي الْحَيَاةِ قَبْلَ الْمَمَاتِ». رَوَاهُ الْبَيْهَقِيُّ

The Blessed Prophet👤 spelled out the rights of children and stressed their rights often, as the following sayings confirm:
- "There is no one who has three daughters, or three sisters, and he treats them well, except that he enters paradise." (At-Tirmidhi)

قَالَ رَسُولُ اللهِ ﷺ: «لَا يَكُونُ لِأَحَدِكُمْ ثَلَاثُ بَنَاتٍ أَوْ ثَلَاثُ أَخَوَاتٍ فَيُحْسِنُ إِلَيْهِنَّ إِلَّا دَخَلَ الْجَنَّةَ». رَوَاهُ التِّرْمِذِيُّ

- "There is no gift that a father gives his son more virtuous than good manners." (At-Tirmidhi)

قَالَ رَسُولُ اللهِ ﷺ: «مَا نَحَلَ وَالِدٌ وَلَدًا مِنْ نَحْلٍ أَفْضَلَ مِنْ أَدَبٍ حَسَنٍ». رَوَاهُ التِّرْمَذِيُّ

- "He is not one of us who is not kind to children." (Al Bukhari)

قَالَ رَسُولُ اللهِ ﷺ: «إِنَّهُ مَنْ لَا يَرْحَمْ لَا يُرْحَمْ». رَوَاهُ الْبُخَارِيُّ

Extended Family

While it is not always possible to live this way, ideally, Muslim families would have extended family members living nearby. A home where the parents, grandparents and children live together, or at least in the same neighborhood, is the most valued in many Muslim cultures. If possible, it helps to have aunts, uncles and cousins nearby to create a strong support network in times of difficulty and happiness.

'Aishah﷜ narrated that the Messenger of Allahﷺ said, "The best of you are those who are best to their families, and I am best to my family." (At-Tirmidhi)

عَنْ أُمِّ الْمُؤْمِنِينَ عَائِشَةَ﷜ قَالَتْ قَالَ رَسُولُ اللهِ ﷺ: «خَيْرُكُمْ خَيْرُكُمْ لِأَهْلِهِ وَأَنَا خَيْرُكُمْ لِأَهْلِي». رَوَاهُ التِّرْمَذِيُّ

Therefore, we must study how he ﷺ interacted with his family and try to do the same ourselves.

There is indeed a good model for you in the Messenger of Allah - for the one who has hope in Allah and the Last Day, and remembers Allah profusely. Surat Al Ahzab (The Confederates) 33:21

﴿لَقَدْ كَانَ لَكُمْ فِي رَسُولِ اللَّهِ أُسْوَةٌ حَسَنَةٌ لِمَنْ كَانَ يَرْجُواْ اللَّهَ وَالْيَوْمَ الْآخِرَ وَذَكَرَ اللَّهَ كَثِيرًا﴾ سُورَةُ الْأَحْزَابِ 33:21

Abu Usayd Malik bin Rabi'ah as-Sa'idi narrated, 'While we were with the Messenger of Allah! a man of Banu Salmah came to Him and said, 'Messenger of Allah is there any kindness left that I can do to my parents after their death?' He replied: 'Yes, you can invoke blessings on them, forgiveness for them, carry out their final instructions after their death, join ties of relationship which are dependent on them, and honour their friends.'" (Abu Dawud)

عَنْ أَبِي أُسَيْدٍ، مَالِكِ بْنِ رَبِيعَةَ السَّاعِدِيِّ قَالَ بَيْنَا نَحْنُ عِنْدَ رَسُولِ اللهِ ﷺ إِذْ جَاءَهُ رَجُلٌ مِنْ بَنِي سَلِمَةَ فَقَالَ: «يَا رَسُولَ اللهِ هَلْ بَقِيَ مِنْ بِرِّ أَبَوَيَّ شَيْءٌ أَبَرُّهُمَا بِهِ بَعْدَ مَوْتِهِمَا؟ قَالَ: نَعَمْ الصَّلَاةُ عَلَيْهِمَا وَالِاسْتِغْفَارُ لَهُمَا وَإِنْفَاذُ عَهْدِهِمَا مِنْ بَعْدِهِمَا وَصِلَةُ الرَّحِمِ الَّتِي لَا تُوصَلُ إِلَّا بِهِمَا وَإِكْرَامُ صَدِيقِهِمَا». رَوَاهُ أَبُو دَاوُدَ

Grandparents and the elderly are also highly respected. They are to be looked upon with love and affection and cared for when they become weaker with age. It is better to take care of your elderly parents and grandparents in your home, instead of sending them to a retirement home. Sometimes, though, they may need professional care that requires such housing situations.

Abu Hurayrah﷜ reported that the Blessed Prophet ﷺ said, "'May his nose be rubbed in dust,' then he repeated it twice more, 'Who found one or both of his parents approaching old age, but failed to enter Paradise (for not serving them).'" (Muslim)

عَنْ أَبِي هُرَيْرَةَ﷜، قَالَ قَالَ رَسُولُ اللهِ ﷺ: «رَغِمَ أَنْفُهُ ثُمَّ رَغِمَ أَنْفُهُ ثُمَّ رَغِمَ أَنْفُهُ قِيلَ مَنْ يَا رَسُولَ اللهِ قَالَ: مَنْ أَدْرَكَ وَالِدَيْهِ عِنْدَ الْكِبَرِ أَحَدَهُمَا أَوْ كِلَيْهِمَا ثُمَّ لَمْ يَدْخُلِ الْجَنَّةَ». رَوَاهُ مُسْلِمٌ

Women Have Always Struggled

Women have always had to struggle for **Equality** مُساواة in male-dominated societies. Sometimes cultural or national customs are to blame for the unfair **Discrimination** تَمييز that women have to face, while other times misapplication of religion is responsible. Every culture and nation has had to deal with this issue. Some have been more successful at finding fair solutions than others.

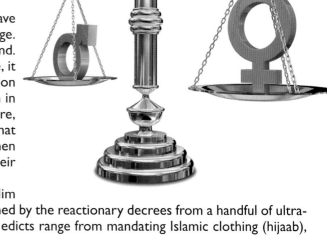

Over the last 100 years, women in many Western nations have been able to gain rights in inheritance, education, and voting privilege. However, women in much of the rest of the world have lagged behind. This is also a problem in the Muslim world, but as we shall see, it is not the fault of religion, but a problem of the misinterpretation of Islamic Law and its intentional misapplication. Muslim women in classical Muslim civilizations were granted all these rights and more, centuries before Western women fought bitterly for them. What they have gained, we have lost, and the struggle of Muslim women today is to regain what Allahﷻ has promised with regards to their equal status in the life of the community.

Indeed, the perception in the world today is that Muslim women have the least rights and liberties. This view is strengthened by the reactionary decrees from a handful of ultra-conservative, culturally-based Muslim groups and figures. These edicts range from mandating Islamic clothing (hijaab), to more serious indignities such as forbidding women to work, drive a car or even acquire an education.

Are these restrictions rooted in religion or in long-held local customs and prejudices that have nothing to do with Islam? The real story of women in the early era of Islam is one of progressive liberation and elevated status. It was for this reason that women were the strongest supporters of the Prophet's ﷺ mission. If women in some countries today are not enjoying the full rights bestowed upon them by Islam, it is not due to the religion, but to uneducated individuals who use religion selectively to maintain their dominance or mask their own powerlessness or ignorance.

Islam Teach Equality

Many people in the modern world believe Islam teaches that women are second-class citizens. Some point to the many backward customs that exist in the Muslim world as proof that the religion is to blame for discrimination against women. Muslim women who have escaped the backward lifestyle of their home countries are often held up by women's rights groups as examples of bravery who stood up to their cultures and were liberated.

This is a powerful narrative, and opens some serious issues . Clearly the inequality and oppression are rooted, not in the religion, but in the local cultures that are often opposed to Islamic teachings or ignorant of what Islam actually teaches about equality and women's rights.

The Qur'an acknowledges and warns that people often like to do whatever they want, regardless of what Allahﷻ revealed. This following ayah in the Qur'an frequently repeated to explain why people place culture over the teachings of Allahﷻ.

When it is said to them, "Come to what Allah hath revealed; come to the Messenger". They say, "Enough for us are the ways we found our fathers following." Is it so, even though their forefathers knew nothing, and had no guidance either? Surat Al Ma'idah (The Table) 5:104

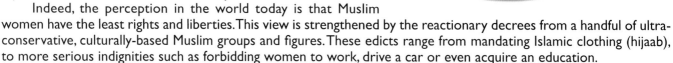

﴿وَإِذَا قِيلَ لَهُمْ تَعَالَوْا إِلَىٰ مَآ أَنزَلَ ٱللَّهُ وَإِلَى ٱلرَّسُولِ قَالُوا حَسْبُنَا مَا وَجَدْنَا عَلَيْهِ ءَابَآءَنَآ أَوَلَوْ كَانَ ءَابَآؤُهُمْ لَا يَعْلَمُونَ شَيْئًا وَلَا يَهْتَدُونَ﴾ سُورَةُ الْمَائِدَة 5:104

Indeed, the Holy Qur'an lays out the case for women's equality in several ways. For example, look at the verse below:

"O people! Reverence your Lord Who created you from a single soul and created of like nature its mate and from those two He scattered countless men and women. Reverence Allah through Whom you demand your mutual [rights] and [reverence] the wombs [of mothers that bore you] for Allah ever watches over you." Surat An-Nisa' (The Women) 4:1

﴿يَٰٓأَيُّهَا ٱلنَّاسُ ٱتَّقُوا۟ رَبَّكُمُ ٱلَّذِى خَلَقَكُم مِّن نَّفْسٍ وَٰحِدَةٍ وَخَلَقَ مِنْهَا زَوْجَهَا وَبَثَّ مِنْهُمَا رِجَالًا كَثِيرًا وَنِسَآءً وَٱتَّقُوا۟ ٱللَّهَ ٱلَّذِى تَسَآءَلُونَ بِهِۦ وَٱلْأَرْحَامَ إِنَّ ٱللَّهَ كَانَ عَلَيْكُمْ رَقِيبًا﴾ سُورَةُ النِّسَاءِ 4:1

Females were created from the same spiritual material as males and because we are all born of a woman, women are clearly due respect.

The Prophet ﷺ once said, "Truly, women are the twin-halves of men." (Abu Dawud)

عَنْ رَسُولِ اللهِ ﷺ أَنَّهُ قَالَ: «نَعَمْ إِنَّمَا النِّسَاءُ شَقَائِقُ الرِّجَالِ». رَوَاهُ أَبُو دَاوُد

In the Prophet's ﷺ time, a Muslim woman went to the masjid and wanted clarification on the rights of women. It seemed to her and many other women that the verses of the Qur'an in general spoke about men. Sometime later Allah ﷻ revealed the following verse, on her account, that laid out specifically that women are the equal of men in the sight of Allah ﷻ and that they have general equality in society. Here is what Allah ﷻ said, For men and women who have surrendered (their wills to Allah), for men and women who believe, for men and women who are devout, for men and women who are honest, for men and women who are patient, for men and women who are humble, for men and women who donate to charity, for men and women who fast, for men and women who guard their sexuality, and for men and women who remember Allah often - for them Allah has prepared forgiveness and a great reward. Surat Al Ahzab (The Confederates) 33: 35

﴿إِنَّ ٱلْمُسْلِمِينَ وَٱلْمُسْلِمَٰتِ وَٱلْمُؤْمِنِينَ وَٱلْمُؤْمِنَٰتِ وَٱلْقَٰنِتِينَ وَٱلْقَٰنِتَٰتِ وَٱلصَّٰدِقِينَ وَٱلصَّٰدِقَٰتِ وَٱلصَّٰبِرِينَ وَٱلصَّٰبِرَٰتِ وَٱلْخَٰشِعِينَ وَٱلْخَٰشِعَٰتِ وَٱلْمُتَصَدِّقِينَ وَٱلْمُتَصَدِّقَٰتِ وَٱلصَّٰئِمِينَ وَٱلصَّٰئِمَٰتِ وَٱلْحَٰفِظِينَ فُرُوجَهُمْ وَٱلْحَٰفِظَٰتِ وَٱلذَّٰكِرِينَ ٱللَّهَ كَثِيرًا وَٱلذَّٰكِرَٰتِ أَعَدَّ ٱللَّهُ لَهُم مَّغْفِرَةً وَأَجْرًا عَظِيمًا﴾ سُورَةُ الأَحْزَاب 33:35

Muslim Women Have a Voice in Society

Do Muslim women have secular and political rights beyond spiritual rights? The Prophet ﷺ established the political rights of women by including them in the swearing of oaths, the equivalent of the democratic vote in ancient Arabian society. The first political leaders that followed after the death of the Prophet ﷺ also accepted the oaths of women, and even appointed women to important government posts. As Khalifa, 'Umar al Khattab ﷺ appointed Shifa bint 'Abdallah as market inspector for the city of Al Madinah.

Islam has never taught that women should be denied a political voice, and in Muslim countries one finds that women often vote freely, regardless of whether the political system is functioning well or not. In some countries where women seem to lack rights, the men in general also lack rights. The destructive nature of unstable societies, civil wars, political corruption, overpopulation, foreign invasions or meddling—these internal disasters deny the rights of everyone, and, often times, women bear the brunt of the turmoil.

So as we can see, Islam does not teach that women are inferior in religion or in political rights. Their rights are guaranteed by the Qur'an, but are they practiced in the society? Do the leaders respect those rights? Does the culture respect those rights? Or does culture ignore or misinterpret those rights? Do current presidents, kings, husbands, fathers and brothers follow the religion as did the first Muslims, or are they "following what their ancestors did?" These are questions that need addressing. It is the modern struggle of Muslim women to take back their God given rights.

Some Rights of Muslim Women

As we have seen, the tenets of Islam do not oppress women. The teachings of Prophet Muhammad ﷺ call upon men to respect the rights of all women. Men are called upon to be the protectors and primary providers of the family, in addition to safeguarding their rights.

Men are caretakers of women, since Allah has made some of them excel the others, and because of the wealth they have spent. So, the righteous women are obedient, (and) guard (the property and honor of their husbands) in (their) absence with the protection given by Allah. As for women of whom you fear rebellion, convince them, and leave them apart in beds, and beat them. Then, if they obey you, do not seek a way against them. Surely, Allah is the Highest, the Greatest. Surat An-Nisa' (The Women) 4:34

﴿ٱلرِّجَالُ قَوَّٰمُونَ عَلَى ٱلنِّسَآءِ بِمَا فَضَّلَ ٱللَّهُ بَعْضَهُمْ عَلَىٰ بَعْضٍ وَبِمَآ أَنفَقُواْ مِنْ أَمْوَٰلِهِمْ فَٱلصَّٰلِحَٰتُ قَٰنِتَٰتٌ حَٰفِظَٰتٌ لِّلْغَيْبِ بِمَا حَفِظَ ٱللَّهُ وَٱلَّٰتِي تَخَافُونَ نُشُوزَهُنَّ فَعِظُوهُنَّ وَٱهْجُرُوهُنَّ فِي ٱلْمَضَاجِعِ وَٱضْرِبُوهُنَّ فَإِنْ أَطَعْنَكُمْ فَلَا تَبْغُواْ عَلَيْهِنَّ سَبِيلًا إِنَّ ٱللَّهَ كَانَ عَلِيًّا كَبِيرًا﴾ سُورَةُ النِّسَاء 4:34

This doesn't mean that women are weak or are incapable of defending or supporting themselves. Islamic history teems with stories of wealthy, strong, and resilient women. On the contrary, Islam elevates women by freeing them from the obligatory responsibilities of men. According to some Islamic scholars, women are not even required to do housework. (Any work they do is considered a charity on their part.) Prophet Muhammad ﷺ worked alongside his Companions and his wives, even assisting them in the housework.

Islam envisions the primary role of women as wives and mother. While fulfilling those duties they also have the right to work, own businesses and seek education. Allah ﷻ commands equal rights with differing responsibilities. An apple and an orange are both fruits, but they have different qualities that are complimentary and important in their own right. Allah ﷻ endowed each gender with unique characteristics that make each one excel at some things more than another, while both share some of each other's strengths, as well. Whereas the so-called 'modern' world envisions endless conflict between men and women, with each trying to copy the other, Islam allows each gender to be true to itself while respecting there is a lot of overlap, or things they can do equally well. "Women are the twin halves of men…" said the Prophet ﷺ.

Islamic Law contains dozens of laws for the protection of women's rights. Among these are the following:

- A woman's property, including her marriage dowry, cannot be seized by her husband. Allah ﷻ said, *If you want to take a wife in place of the one (you have), and you have given her plenty of wealth, then do not take any of it back. Would you take it through imputation and open sin? Surat An-Nisa' (The Women) 4:20*

﴿وَإِنْ أَرَدتُّمُ ٱسْتِبْدَالَ زَوْجٍ مَّكَانَ زَوْجٍ وَءَاتَيْتُمْ إِحْدَىٰهُنَّ قِنطَارًا فَلَا تَأْخُذُواْ مِنْهُ شَيْئًا أَتَأْخُذُونَهُ بُهْتَٰنًا وَإِثْمًا مُّبِينًا﴾

سُورَةُ النِّسَاء 4:20

- Women cannot be denied the right to an education.

- Ruining a woman's reputation is a criminal act. Allah ﷻ said, *Why did they (the accusers) not bring four witnesses to prove this? So, as they did not bring the witnesses, they are the liars in the sight of Allah. Surat An-Noor (The Light) 24:13*

﴿لَّوْلَا جَآءُو عَلَيْهِ بِأَرْبَعَةِ شُهَدَآءَ فَإِذْ لَمْ يَأْتُواْ بِٱلشُّهَدَآءِ فَأُوْلَٰئِكَ عِندَ ٱللَّهِ هُمُ ٱلْكَٰذِبُونَ﴾ سُورَةُ النُّور 24:13

- Forced marriage is prohibited.
  The Prophet ﷺ said, "A virgin should not be married till she is asked for her consent; and the matron should not be married till she is asked whether she agrees to marry or not." It was asked, "O Allah's Apostle! How will she (the virgin) express her consent?" He said, "By keeping silent." (Al Bukhari)

قَالَ قَالَ رَسُولُ اللهِ ﷺ: «لَا تُنْكَحُ الْبِكْرُ حَتَّى تُسْتَأْذَنَ، وَلَا الثَّيِّبُ حَتَّى تُسْتَأْمَرَ، فَقِيلَ: يَا رَسُولَ اللهِ، كَيْفَ إِذْنُهَا؟، قَالَ: إِذَا سَكَتَتْ». رَوَاهُ الْبُخَارِيُّ

- Women can file legal suits in court and provide sole testimony on their behalf. Allah ﷻ said, *And the fifth (oath) that Allah's curse be on him if he*

is one of the liars. And it will remove the punishment from the woman if she swears four oaths by Allah that he (the accuser husband) is certainly one of the liars. And the fifth (oath) that Allah's wrath be on her if he is one of the truthful. Had it not been for the grace of Allah upon you, and His mercy, and (had it not been) that Allah is Most-Relenting, All-Wise, (you would have faced severe hardships). *Surat An-Noor (The Light) 24:7-10*

﴿وَٱلْخَٰمِسَةَ أَنَّ لَعْنَتَ ٱللَّهِ عَلَيْهِ إِن كَانَ مِنَ ٱلْكَٰذِبِينَ﴾﴿وَيَدْرَؤُاْ عَنْهَا ٱلْعَذَابَ أَن تَشْهَدَ أَرْبَعَ شَهَٰدَٰتِ بِٱللَّهِ إِنَّهُۥ لَمِنَ ٱلْكَٰذِبِينَ﴾﴿وَٱلْخَٰمِسَةَ أَنَّ غَضَبَ ٱللَّهِ عَلَيْهَآ إِن كَانَ مِنَ ٱلصَّٰدِقِينَ﴾﴿وَلَوْلَا فَضْلُ ٱللَّهِ عَلَيْكُمْ وَرَحْمَتُهُۥ وَأَنَّ ٱللَّهَ تَوَّابٌ حَكِيمٌ﴾ سُورَةُ النُّور 24:7-10

- Women can initiate divorce. Allah ﷻ said, *If a woman fears ill treatment or aversion from her husband, then, there is no sin on them in entering into a compromise between them. Compromise is better. Avarice is made to be present in human souls. If you do good and fear Allah, then, Allah is All-Aware of what you do. Surat An-Nisa' (The Women) 4:128*

﴿وَإِنِ ٱمْرَأَةٌ خَافَتْ مِنۢ بَعْلِهَا نُشُوزًا أَوْ إِعْرَاضًا فَلَا جُنَاحَ عَلَيْهِمَآ أَن يُصْلِحَا بَيْنَهُمَا صُلْحًا وَٱلصُّلْحُ خَيْرٌ وَأُحْضِرَتِ ٱلْأَنفُسُ ٱلشُّحَّ وَإِن تُحْسِنُواْ وَتَتَّقُواْ فَإِنَّ ٱللَّهَ كَانَ بِمَا تَعْمَلُونَ خَبِيرًا﴾ سُورَةُ النِّسَاء 4:128

- Women can receive custody of young children after divorce. (2:233)
- Child support is mandatory. (2:233)
- Women must be paid a dowry that is under their control. (4:4)
- Women receive equal pay for equal work. (4:32)
- Women can pledge themselves and politically vote. (60:12)

The list goes on and further covers so many areas that it rivals current Western laws regarding women's status and rights. From the Islamic standpoint, the liberation of women is not accomplished by rejecting of religion but actually by implementing it.

Addressing the Misconceptions

It is easy to list the rights of Muslim women and say that they are not being respected by this or that group or culture, but it is quite another thing to deal with some of the more misunderstood situations directly. These issues include arranged marriages, genital mutilation, spousal abuse, honor killings, the right to travel unchaperoned, dress requirements, divorce rights, polygamy and others.

We will give a brief explanation of each of these in turn. Just know that there is more information and proof from the Qur'an, ahadith and practices of the early Muslims that support the rights of women. Unfortunately, the simple fact is that Muslims in general often do not understand these issues and continue to follow the dictates of culture rather than following the example of the Prophet ﷺ and his followers.

1. Arranged Marriages

Arranged marriages are not a new invention. Every society throughout history has at one time implemented this practice and continues to practice it to one degree or another. It is a useful method for bringing marriage-minded people together. Online matchmaking is merely the newest incarnation of this practice. Islam does not require arranged marriages and forbids forcing anyone into it. There are ahadith and much scholarly discussion about this. Muslim cultures often forsake Islam in a great many things, just as people of other faiths ignore their teachings when it comes down to following their own desires. When a forced marriage case was brought before him, the Prophet ﷺ allowed the girl to cancel the marriage if she wished.

2. Female Circumcision

This procedure is practiced today in many cultures and among many different religions in Africa and the Middle East including Christians. It was also practiced among some of the desert Arabs before the advent of Islam. It is an unknown practice among the majority of the Muslims of the world today.

There is but one hadith related to female circumcision in which the Prophet ﷺ neither approved nor disapproved but advised if doing so, not to cut deeply. Neither he, his Companions, nor any of the mainstream community engage in it.

However, communities that follow culture do continue the practice. Due to ignorance, there is danger of female circumcision becoming genital mutilation in which many women suffer greatly throughout their lives from the after affects of the cutting.

3. Spousal Abuse

This is one of the most misunderstood issues in Islam. Allah﷾ said, *As for women of whom you fear rebellion, convince them, and leave them apart in beds, and beat them. Then, if they obey you, do not seek a way against them. Surely, Allah is the Highest, the Greatest. Surat An-Nisa' (The Women) 4:34*

﴿وَٱلَّٰتِي تَخَافُونَ نُشُوزَهُنَّ فَعِظُوهُنَّ وَٱهۡجُرُوهُنَّ فِي ٱلۡمَضَاجِعِ وَٱضۡرِبُوهُنَّ فَإِنۡ أَطَعۡنَكُمۡ فَلَا تَبۡغُواْ عَلَيۡهِنَّ سَبِيلًا إِنَّ ٱللَّهَ كَانَ عَلِيًّا كَبِيرًا﴾ سُورَةُ النِّسَاء 34:4

Allah﷾ gives advice to men about what to do when a wife becomes a bitter foe in the marriage. The word for defiant foe is 'nushooz' and covers malicious gossiping against the spouse, enemy-like behavior and aggression. Islam seeks to keep the family intact as much as possible, so the verse tells men to try talking to the wife first, then sleeping apart, and finally, if nothing else works, to do "daraba." The word daraba has several meanings. One of the meanings is 'strike,' another is 'to strike out from' as in 'to go away' or 'separate from.' When the verse was revealed in Al Madinah after some of the male Muslim refugees complained to the Prophet ﷺ that their wives were becoming too outspoken like the local women, the men took it as permission to smack their wives. The next day the women went to the Prophet ﷺ to complain about being abused, and the Prophet ﷺ became very angry with the men who had misinterpreted what was meant. He publicly told them NOT to beat their wives and that any man who did so is the worst. So how did he interpret daraba? When he was having trouble with his own wives one year, he talked to them, then moved out of his house into a friend's apartment, and finally offered them a divorce, i.e. to separate from them. So the Qur'an, when interpreted by the Prophet's ﷺ own pronouncements and the Sunnah forbids spousal abuse, and instead offers divorce as the final solution to a marriage that cannot be saved. Of the scholars who prefer the interpretation of physically 'striking' their defiant wives instead of 'striking out from them,' they have ruled, according to the example of Ibn 'Abbas, that the 'strike' can only be a one-time slap with a toothbrush or handkerchief. That's a way of saying, "I've reached my last bit of patience: time for a divorce." So in either case, the third option is–divorce! Muslim cultures where abuse is prevalent are going against the teachings and good sense of Islam, and following only what they want to follow.

4. Honor Killings

The practice of 'honor' killing is prevalent all over the world, including among some Muslims, among Catholics in Latin America and also among Hindus in India. If a girl brings 'shame' on the family (i.e. refusing arranged marriage, rape, seen with non-related boys) she is killed by the male relatives. This is an unknown practice in the Islamic religion. There is no proof for it as neither the Prophet ﷺ nor early Muslims engaged in it. It was prevalent in areas that the Muslims conquered and was a practice never fully abandoned by the new converts. Muslim scholars and leaders have repeatedly declared it forbidden, yet some ignorant and tribal Muslims accept and promote it because it is part of the culture. It is murder, plain and simple.

5. The Right to Travel Unchaperoned

This understanding is based on a misreading of verse (33:33) which asks the Prophet's ﷺ wives to avoid going out if possible. Allah﷾ said, *Remain in your homes, and do not display (your) beauty as it used to be displayed in the days of earlier ignorance; and establish Salah, and pay Zakah, and obey Allah and His messenger. Allah only intends to keep (all sorts of) filth away from you, O members of the family (of the prophet), and to make you pure through a perfect purification. Surat Al Ahzab (The Confederates) 33:33*

﴿وَقَرۡنَ فِي بُيُوتِكُنَّ وَلَا تَبَرَّجۡنَ تَبَرُّجَ ٱلۡجَٰهِلِيَّةِ ٱلۡأُولَىٰ وَأَقِمۡنَ ٱلصَّلَوٰةَ وَءَاتِينَ ٱلزَّكَوٰةَ وَأَطِعۡنَ ٱللَّهَ وَرَسُولَهُۥ إِنَّمَا يُرِيدُ ٱللَّهُ لِيُذۡهِبَ عَنكُمُ ٱلرِّجۡسَ أَهۡلَ ٱلۡبَيۡتِ وَيُطَهِّرَكُمۡ تَطۡهِيرًا﴾ سُورَةُ الأحزاب 33:33

This was advice for the Prophet's ﷺ wives, who were

often sought out by people seeking knowledge of the Prophet's ﷺ habits at home. The verse, which contains several pieces of advice, begins by telling the wives that they "are not like other women," and so whatever is said in the verse does NOT apply to regular women. Ordinary women in the Prophet's ﷺ time and for many centuries beyond did not remain in their homes as a matter of policy, for many needed to work (and they were frequently in the public sphere— even in the masaajid, and there is voluminous evidence from the traditions, biographical literature and history books to demonstrate this. Save for the harsh rulings of some modern extremists and the assumptions of certain rustics, who mistake long-standing cultural practices for religion, the general opinion of most mainstream scholars is that women can hold jobs, go to the masjid and go to school, even as they can go out for other needs. The practice of total seclusion is actually a pre-Islamic custom from the Persian Empire.

The Prophet ﷺ said, "You (women) have been allowed to go out for your needs." (Muslim)

عَنْ عَائِشَةَ ﵂ ، عَنِ النَّبِيِّ ﷺ : «قَدْ أُذِنَ أَنْ تَخْرُجْنَ فِي حَاجَتِكُنَّ». رَوَاهُ مُسْلِمٌ

6. Dress Requirements

Both Muslim women and men have dress requirements. Women were endowed with physical attributes that are attractive to men. This is part of Allah's ﷻ great design to continue the propagation of the world. Women are warned to not flaunt themselves outside the home as it attracts the attention of unsavory men and disturbs the harmony in marriage. Women can dress however they wish in the home and have few dress requirements when they are among other women. Allah ﷻ honors a woman by asking her to cover so that she is appreciated for her intellect, personality and character. Islam seeks to liberate women from being judged solely on looks by men or women. This concept is not new in Islam. All other religions, including Judaism, Christianity, Hinduism, Sikhism, Buddhism and others, have guidelines of modesty for the dress of the believers. The dress requirement serves initially as a means of identification. A woman dressed modestly is recognized as a believer. Secondly it serves to minimize harassment. Dress requirement is merely one aspect. The addition of the Muslim behavioral code is necessary to be truly effective.

O Prophet, tell your wives and your daughters and the women of the believers to bring down over themselves [part] of their outer garments. That is more suitable that they will be known and not be abused. And ever is Allah Forgiving and Merciful. Surat Al Ahzab (The Confederates) 33:59

﴿يَا أَيُّهَا النَّبِيُّ قُل لِّأَزْوَاجِكَ وَبَنَاتِكَ وَنِسَاءِ الْمُؤْمِنِينَ يُدْنِينَ عَلَيْهِنَّ مِن جَلَابِيبِهِنَّ ذَٰلِكَ أَدْنَىٰ أَن يُعْرَفْنَ فَلَا يُؤْذَيْنَ وَكَانَ اللَّهُ غَفُورًا رَّحِيمًا﴾

سُورَةُ الْأَحْزَابِ 33:59

7. Divorce Rights

A woman can initiate divorce and is asked to return her dowry in order to be released from the marriage unless the husband is guilty of abuse. Women receive custody of their children until the children reach the age of puberty. (see *Shari'ah: The Islamic Law* by 'Abdur Rahman). If a man wishes for divorce, he must ask for the divorce a total of three times. The first time initiates a mandatory three-month waiting period. He must declare "I divorce you" once a month for three months. During that time the couple lives in separate rooms. This allows a cooling-off period to resolve differences and the opportunity to reconcile. Finally, a wife who is divorced receives child support and a living stipend until she remarries, and the husband is not allowed to take back any of her property or dowry.

8. Women "Half" of Men

The charge that a woman's testimony is only half of a man's arises from a Qur'anic verse (2:282) that references business contracts. The writing of contracts addressed in the Qur'an requires the witness of only one man but two women. It is further explained that if one woman forgets the details, the second is a witness to remind her. Men often have the upper hand and the position of power. The need of a second female witness protects the validity of the contract against trickery, bribery or any other deceit or coercion. In this and all other testimony, a woman's word is accepted as equal to that of a man.

9. Inheritance

The Qur'an is very explicit about inheritance rites and percentages. Verses that address this topic (4:11-12) are so detailed that a lawyer is often needed to apply the formulas for all of the heirs. Women inherit a share that is one half that of the man's. In the Muslim family men are required as a religious obligation to support the family. The earnings or assets of a woman who inherits from her family or works outside the home, are her own and are considered sadaqah or charity if she uses them to help support the family unit. At the time of marriage, the man must pay a dowry to the woman that is agreed upon by her and her family Men pay mandatory alimony and palimony, while no such requirement is on women. A man also must support his unmarried sisters and his mother if his father dies. So although a woman receives half the inheritance to keep for herself, a man is obligated to spend on all those around him.

10. Polygamy in Islam

A Muslim man is allowed to marry up to four wives. In Pre-Islamic times there was no limit in Arabia to the number of wives a man could take. Verses revealed in the Qur'an restricted marriage to a maximum of four. Polygamy was prominent in the past in Judaism and Christianity and is still practiced among some sects of Mormonism and other groups. At the same time, the Qur'an orders that a man considering multiple marriages must be fair in his equal treatment of all wives in terms of finances and time. If equality cannot be accomplished, then the man is asked to marry only one. (4:4) In practice, the majority of marriages in the Muslim world are monogamous. Allah﷾ in His Mercy and foreknowledge of events provides plans that will suit mankind in all times and all places. In the event of war, there is normally a shortage of men. Only a limited number of women can find husbands and have no support system financial or otherwise. In the West, multiple marriages offers a solution to adultery where wife and mistress often both suffer loss. Some women suffering from a debilitating condition cannot find a suitable match. Some may be barren. With the possibility of multiple wives, women are given choices other than divorce or being put aside in favor of a another wife. Some women are also blessed with other talents to pursue careers who would otherwise be incapable to adequately support all the family needs on a full time basis. Islam provides a solution for all situations.

Islam enshrines the basic rights of women in a variety of ways. If particular Muslim cultures do not respect these rights, or misinterpret them in the worst way possible, it is wrong and the sins will be on those who disobey Allah's﷾ perfect religion. One of the struggles of the Muslim community in modern times is to educate ourselves about the truth of Islamic teachings, and also to oppose wrong practices. The struggle for liberation among Muslim women that Allah﷾ intended begins with Islam, the Qur'an and the way and practice of the Prophet ﷺ.

Literature Selection
Khadijah bint Khuwaylid ﷺ

By Noor Saadeh

You will not recognize the name of the woman I chose to write about as the most influential woman in my life. Khadijah bint Khuwaylid ﷺ, Khadijah ﷺ daughter of Khuwaylid, lived over 1,400 years ago. Her story shatters present-day and historical stereotypes of a woman's role in society while affirming the attributes of noble and altruistic women everywhere.

History has little record of her prior to her fortieth year. We do know that she was a business woman, twice married and twice widowed. She successfully continued her late husband's business in the male-dominated world of trade.

Khadijah ﷺ refused the many nobles and notables who offered marriage. An upright and honest young employee, named Muhammad ﷺ, however, caught her attention. Breaking all customs of the day, She proposed marriage. She was 15 years his senior.

So began a remarkable love story. Their business grew as did their family. She bore Muhammad ﷺ six children, quite remarkable for a woman well past forty. In a polygamous society, she enjoyed a loving and faithful monogamous relationship with her husband. They lived a quiet and satisfied life, surrounded by their children. Both were renowned for their charity and kindness.

In later years, she supported her husband's meditative retreats in a nearby mountain cave. He returned one night from his reflections in a great state of agitation. She listened in astonishment as he related a story that is now so well-known to Muslims around the world.

Khadijah ﷺ immediately accepted the fantastic story Muhammad ﷺ told her of an angel that appeared to him announcing his Prophethood. The wisdom of years and knowledge of her husband's character left no doubt as to the truthfulness of his story. Khadijah ﷺ stood in solidarity with her husband and became the first Muslim, announcing her acceptance of the message of Islam that Muhammad ﷺ proclaimed.

Their peaceful lives would be forever altered. Harassment and terror awaited those who swore allegiance to monotheism. The idol-worshipping tribal clans of Arabia did everything in their power to wipe out this new and dangerous idea. Khadijah ﷺ was a constant source of help and comfort to Muhammad ﷺ in the difficulties they faced. All of her wealth was spent in spreading the message, sheltering and assisting those who had embraced Islam.

After years of persecution, the Muslims were turned out of their homes and sent into exile in the harsh desert climate. For three years the small Muslim community lived a life of hardship and deprivation, suffering from hunger and exposure. For Khadijah ﷺ, now 65, the years of boycott took their toll. In the following year, which Muhammad ﷺ named the 'Year of Sorrow,' Khadijah ﷺ died.

Muhammad's ﷺ honor and service to the memory of Khadijah ﷺ are legendary. In his own words, "She believed in me when no one else did; she accepted Islam when people rejected it; and she helped and comforted me when there was no one else to lend a helping hand."

In Islamic traditions, Khadijah ﷺ, along with Mary the Mother of Jesus, is counted among the most righteous of all women in history. Khadijah's ﷺ story dispels stereotypes not only of Muslim women, but of women everywhere and serves as an inspiration to us all.

Societies Out of Control

Everyone talks about how Muslims form one Ummah, but what does that mean? What does it mean to have an Islamic society and social system?

Do Muslim countries have an Islamic social system? Sadly, this is not the case in most Muslim-majority countries. Just because you have 10, 10,000, 1,000,000 Muslims living in a place, doesn't mean they are living according to Islam. In fact, many so-called Muslim countries provide us with few role models. So, how can we define what our Islamic society should look like? You know the answer. All we have to do is learn about Muslims who lived true to their beliefs in former times and then put their values into practice.

You could look at the model of Al Madinah during the Prophet's time and gain the most valuable insight. Then you could look at the growth and vitality of the Muslim Ummah for the next thousand years and get a pretty good idea of what an Islamic society entails.

Characteristics of an Islamic Society

To begin with, the law of the land is the Shari'ah of Allah. The khalifa of the Islamic nation, implements the Shari'ah in society. The people try to follow it as best they can in order to save their souls in the Hereafter.

All people are equal before the law and no one gets any special treatment. People greet each other with the greetings of peace and do their best to avoid committing haram acts. People would feel ashamed to litter and reluctant to pick a fight or harm others.

When someone is in need, people help him or her. When it's prayer time, the shops and businesses close for a little while. During Ramadan, the streets are filled with people going to Tarawih Salah. During the 'Eid holidays, people are celebrating with great fun and fanfare.

Hospitals are affordable, and schools are available for everyone to learn. Criminals are punished as they deserve. The army protects the people from attacks by outside enemies rather than oppressing the people like so many armies do today. No one goes hungry. Widows and orphans are supported by the community with fairness and compassion. (4:36) Hajj time is treated as a solemn occasion, and the Hujjaj are congratulated and asked about their wonderful journey when they return.

Children are taught to love Allah and the Messenger and to respect their elders with due deference. Men are taught to respect women, and women are taught to guard their modesty. Abusing one's wife or child is rare, and those guilty of it are punished severely. Women are allowed to hold any jobs they wish and also hold to leadership positions in such roles as judges, administrators, teachers, doctors and scholars. People do not fear that if they lose their jobs they will be ruined, because Zakah money is available for the unemployed.

All these things may sound like a tall order, but if you read your Qur'an, hadith and history books, you'll see that they are the foundation of an Islamic society. They were all implemented, in one form or another, in various Muslim communities throughout history. If something can be done once, it can be done again. Muslims lost their way as the Blessed Prophet predicted they would.

The Blessed Prophet Muhammad said, "By Allah, I don't fear poverty for you, but that worldly possessions may be given to you as lavishly as they were to your predecessors. You may incline towards the delights of the world as they did, and it may destroy you as it destroyed them." (Al Bukhari and Muslim)

Al Masjid An-Nabawi.

عَنِ النَّبِيِّ ﷺ قَالَ: «وَاللهِ مَا الْفَقْرَ أَخْشَى عَلَيْكُمْ، وَلَكِنِّي أَخْشَى أَنْ تُبْسَطَ عَلَيْكُمُ الدُّنْيَا كَمَا بُسِطَتْ عَلَى مَنْ قَبْلَكُمْ، فَتَنَافَسُوهَا كَمَا تَنَافَسُوهَا، وَتُهْلِكَكُمْ كَمَا أَهْلَكَتْهُمْ» رَوَاهُ الْبُخَارِيُّ وَمُسْلِم

How Do We Become Great Again?

Muslims dream of establishing the power of Islam in the world. Muslims of all backgrounds agree that the Islamic system is the best for humanity in this life. Even non-Muslim writers, such as Bertrand Russel and Napoleon, have recognized that the Islamic system is the best for the ordering of human affairs. But how do we regain what our ancestors lost so long ago? How do we once again build our Ummah into a shining example for all people to follow?

Some people believe it will only happen if we become secular, or non-religious, and adopt so-called 'modern' values. Others think we must build up current Muslim countries or have revolutions there. Still others say it will only happen when the non-Muslim world destroys itself from the inside, like the Roman empire did. Who has the answer? Everyone has an opinion, so what should you and I do to contribute to the rebirth of the Islamic World?

For all their talk, most political thinkers have forgotten the most important truth of all. (3:186) In all their secret meetings, shouting matches and plans for sweeping Muslim glory, they failed to start from square one. That is, victory comes from Allah﷽ and not from our wishes. (61:8-9)

When we look at the model of the Blessed Prophet Muhammad ﷺ, we find that the first 13 years of his mission were devoted to building a core of dedicated followers. After this training period, they would go through anything they had to for Allah﷽ and the Prophet ﷺ. (5:105)

People were approached with the call of Islam in the street, in the marketplace, in homes, at parties, on hills and in the city center. Those who embraced the message were taught to respect and love each other as brothers and sisters, and they formed one spiritual block.

Then, when the dominant society could no longer stand the existence of righteous people in their midst, the Muslim community relocated to a more friendly environment where Islam was the governing system. There, Islam flowered into a civilization with traditions, laws, customs, holidays, manners and substance. Islam became a nation. Importantly, all this could have only happened with strong, dedicated followers.

The first phase was known as the Makkan Period. During this period, the people delivering the message of Islam were persecuted, but proclaimed it to any who would listen. The second time period is known as the Madinan Period. After the Muslims migrated to Al Madinah, Islam grew in strength and then was able to become a self-sustaining force. The reason it was so strong was because it had strong people behind it. That was the key.

We can't just look at past Muslim civilizations either and think that that's what we need to re-create. When it comes down to it, many of the leaders in later Muslim history were not practicing Muslims. Do we want to remake the same old corrupt empire-model in the coming centuries? Of course not.

We want the ideal of Al Madinah for the next generations. But we will never get it without the struggle of the Makkan period. To illustrate this truth, look at the Muslim countries. They are full of Muslims, but the countries are far from Islamic. (3:179) If all we needed was a lot of Muslims living together, then those countries would be the **Dar as Salam** دَارُ السَّلام **Land of Peace**. But they're not. According to the Qur'an, not every Muslim is a believer. We need believers, whose faith is unwavering under any circumstance.

We cannot hope to build an Islamic nation on the backs of people who are hypocrites, weak in their emaan or just plain lazy. Allah﷽ even mentions that some people only serve Him if times are good, but then run away if things get tough. In fact, there are some Muslim countries where the people actually oppose the implementation of Shari'ah-based laws because they love their alcohol and illicit relations too much. You can't build a solid wall with bricks made of soft mud.

There was an interesting remark made by a scholar some time ago. He said, "The only thing that can reform Muslims today is the same thing that made them great before (following the Qur'an)."

In other words, we must build our character, build our emaan, build our taqwa and then truly surrender to Allah﷽ completely. Why shouldn't we do that? Our lives are shorter than the blinking of an eye. We have so little time to understand why we're here. What's wrong with insuring the eternal happiness of our soul? Like Allah﷽ says, *Do not lose heart and do not grieve, and you are the upper-most if you are believers.* Surat Al 'Imran 3:139

﴿وَلَا تَهِنُوا وَلَا تَحْزَنُوا وَأَنتُمُ الْأَعْلَوْنَ إِن كُنتُم مُّؤْمِنِينَ﴾ سُورَةُ آلِ عِمران 3:139

Indeed, only when we produce a generation of people who actually fear the Day of Judgement, and love to be closer to the Prophet's example, will we be able to make Islam dominant on Earth. This means we have to sweep away the old ideas from our minds. No longer can we view Qur'anic education as a punishment with a stick. No longer can we consider the masjid a place to hang out with people of the same ethnic group. No longer can we hold backward regional cultures as more important than Islamic culture.

Allah﷽ has said He will not change our condition until we change our hearts. (13:11) If we wish to change our condition and to receive the aid of Allah﷽, then we must become true believers again. (3:200) Islam only lives when there are people who believe in it and who practice it. (3:190-194)

Literature Selection
Father, May I Have a Ring?

Adapted from *God-Oriented Life*
Compiled by Wahiduddin Khan

Once, 'Umar bin Al Khattab, who was the second Khalifa, was notified of some valuables that had come into the treasury from the tax collections. When he was asked what should be done with them, 'Umar replied, "I'm busy right now, remind me about this in a few days when you see that I'm free."

A few days later, 'Umar was reminded again, so he went to the treasury and had the gold and silver plates and ornaments brought out for counting.

When he saw all the sparkling things, he recited the following ayah of the Qur'an: *Men are tempted by the love of women and children, of piled up treasures of gold and silver, and of fine horses, cattle and lands.*
Surat Al 'Imran (The Family of 'Imran) 3:14

﴿زُيِّنَ لِلنَّاسِ حُبُّ ٱلشَّهَوَٰتِ مِنَ ٱلنِّسَآءِ وَٱلْبَنِينَ وَٱلْقَنَٰطِيرِ ٱلْمُقَنطَرَةِ مِنَ ٱلذَّهَبِ وَٱلْفِضَّةِ وَٱلْخَيْلِ ٱلْمُسَوَّمَةِ وَٱلْأَنْعَٰمِ وَٱلْحَرْثِ ذَٰلِكَ مَتَٰعُ ٱلْحَيَوٰةِ ٱلدُّنْيَا وَٱللَّهُ عِندَهُ حُسْنُ ٱلْمَآبِ﴾ سُورَةُ آلِ عِمْران 3:14

Then 'Umar said, "We can't help rejoicing in something that tempts us. O Lord, may we spend it rightly. So protect us from its evil."

Just then, one of 'Umar's own sons, 'Abdul Rahman, came along and asked his father if he could have a ring out of the treasures there.

'Umar remembered what he had just said, and addressed his son saying, "Go to your mother. She will feed you barley soup."

It was thus that 'Umar gave him nothing. (It was reported by Ahmad.)

The Prophet ﷺ said, "There will come a time upon humanity when nothing will remain of Islam except its name only, and nothing will remain of the Qur'an except its ritual. The masaajid will be full, but will be lacking in guidance. The learned people will be the worst under the sky, and trouble will come from them and go back to them." (Al Baihaqi)

عَنِ النَّبِيِّ ﷺ قَالَ: «يُوشِكُ أَنْ يَأْتِي عَلَى النَّاسِ زَمَانٌ لَا يَبْقَى مِنَ الإِسْلَامِ إِلَّا اسْمُهُ، وَلَا يَبْقَى مِنَ القُرْآنِ إِلَّا رَسْمُهُ، مَسَاجِدُهُمْ عَامِرَةٌ وَهِيَ خَرَابٌ مِنَ الهُدَى، عُلَمَاؤُهُمْ شَرُّ مَنْ تَحْتَ أَدِيمِ السَّمَاءِ، مِنْ عِنْدِهِمْ تَخْرُجُ الفِتْنَةُ وَفِيهِم تَعُودُ». رواه البَيْهَقي

Religious and Political Systems

How would you describe the political system of Islam? Is it a democracy, a theocracy, a plutocracy or a monarchy? If you try to use one of these man-made labels, you will always fall short of the answer.

In many countries today, the governments are usually secular democracies—that is, a government where the people make all their own laws and elect leaders with no relation to any revealed wisdom or Divine Guidance. Some countries are constitutional monarchies, but monarchs have only a fraction of the power they once held hundreds of years ago. England is a good example because its queen is just a figure head. She is a symbol and has no real power. The elected members of Parliament make all the laws.

In most Western countries, religion is supposed to be kept separate from the government. In the United States, this practice is called 'the separation of church and state.' This principle means that the government will not be influenced by any religious teachings, nor will it support any religion at all. At the same time, it will not try to suppress any religion either.

Christianity and Politics

Because early Christians disputed among themselves, their faith never held together as a unified system. Every Christian country has its own kind of Christianity that is distinct from the other. (3:187-188) The biggest three sects of Christianity are the Catholic, Protestant and Orthodox churches. They have been disagreeing for centuries over religious issues.

Historically, whenever a country has tried to mix its local brand of Christianity with politics, disaster has soon followed. The officially-sanctioned priests have hunted down and persecuted all those Christians who belonged to other religious sects. For example, you may have studied the Spanish Inquisition, the French Huguenot Struggle or the Salem Witch Trials. Even scientists were sometimes arrested, such as Galileo, and books were burned. The masses were kept uneducated and ignorant, easily controlled by The Church for most of Western history.

Because of this corruption, by the middle of the 1700's, nearly every Christian country had pushed the power of their churches out of the government. They chose to have all their laws created by the public, or by their representatives, and to not let religion play any further role in the affairs of state. Consequently, science was able to grow, the people were better educated and the leaders of the countries could get down to the business of building states without interference from religious fanatics.

Colonial Impact on Muslim Countries

But what about Islam? Did the same results occur when Muslims intertwined Islam with politics? Was Islam ever against education or science or freedom of religion? The answer to all these questions is a big "No." The way of life known as Islam is a complete system. It was revealed by the Creator of the Universe as a guide for people to live by. This being the case, Islam provides answers for individuals, families, societies and governments. There is no separation of masjid and state, because the goal of the Islamic state is the establishment of the Deen of Allah.

By contrast, the goal of many Western countries, guided by a mix of secularism and ethno-religious nationalism, is the dominance of their nations over others and the gathering of riches. "Survival of the fittest" and "might makes right" are their implicit mottoes.

Muslims know that Allah is the Supreme Being in the Universe; therefore, His laws and commandments must form the basis for all human affairs. If we don't follow Allah's commandments, but still call ourselves Muslims, then we are hypocrites, like the followers of many other religions today. Surely, there are many hypocrites among Muslims today, and most Muslim countries are governed by people who try to suppress the free practice of Islam.

Some of this can be attributed to the history of many Muslim countries, in which Western nations invaded and occupied Muslim lands about 300 years ago. During the era of colonialism, European countries took over the Muslim world and divided it up. Muslims were forced to follow un-Islamic political systems.

To reinforce the permanence of this change, the colonialists raised a group of local people in every land who would be their loyal servants. The money and power tempted these Muslims away from practicing Islam, and instead they started 'loving' many of the non-Islamic practices. Then, when the colonialists were finally forced to leave the Muslim lands, these now-corrupt Muslims assumed control and continued the same political system that the outsiders brought.

Although Muslim lands may have been freed of direct control from colonialist powers, they have never been truly free. This is because the men trained by the colonialists simply moved into power and maintained the same un-Islamic system. Thus, we see that the Muslim countries have not yet returned to being Islamic nations.

Islam and Politics

What would a real Islamic system look like today? In an Islamic political system, the leader or khalifa, is the head of the whole Ummah, not just of one country or another. He should be elected by the community and is in charge of establishing Islam and justice on the Earth. (2:30) He must not ask for the position, nor can it be given to someone merely because their father was a khalifa before them. Hereditary rule of the Islamic state is haram in Islam.

The Blessed Prophetﷺ declared, "Do not ask for the position of leader, for if you are given it after asking for it, you will be left to carry it out for yourself. But if you are given leadership without asking for it, you will be helped (by Allah) to carry out its duties." (An-Nasa'i)

قَالَ رَسُولُ اللهِ ﷺ : «لَا تَسْأَلِ الإِمَارَةَ فَإِنَّكَ إِنْ أُعْطِيتَهَا عَنْ مَسْأَلَةٍ وُكِلْتَ إِلَيْهَا وَ إِنْ أُعْطِيتَهَا عَنْ غَيْرِ مَسْأَلَةٍ أُعِنْتَ عَلَيْهَا». رَوَاهُ النَّسَائِي

The khalifa, however, is not a dictator and must consult with the representatives of the community. This **body of representatives** is known as the **Majlis Ash-Shura** مَجْلِسُ الشُّورَى. The members of the Shura should also get elected and confirmed by the community. This is the Sunnah of the Blessed Prophet ﷺ.

Next, the Muslim community will have a judicial system in which a highly educated judge, known as **Qadi** قَاضِي, will administer justice. Scholars of Fiqh and Shari'ah assist in the application of the law.

The basis of the legal and political system is the Shari'ah of Allahﷻ. Its main sources are the Qur'an and the Sunnah. While the Shura is free to make laws for everyday life, there will be certain things that are eternal Islamic principles that must remain unchanged. On those things that have no apparent answer in the Qur'an and the Sunnah, people deliberate over the issues and come up with laws (ijtehad) that reflect the spirit of Islam.

For example, Allahﷻ gave us the law that Zakah must be paid to help the needy. The government can't change this law, because Allahﷻ made it. However, Allahﷻ didn't say anything about speed limits on the roads or immigration laws. In those instances, Muslim scholars would work out laws that are fair and safe. The Majlis Ash-Shura and khalifa could then approve it.

The duty of Muslim citizens is to be loyal to the Islamic State, to live as good Muslims, to approve of good and oppose wrong-doing and to answer the call of their leader if he needs them. (4:59)

The Blessed Prophet ﷺ said, "A Muslim must hear and obey, both in what he likes and in what he dislikes, so long as he is not commanded to perform an act of disobedience to Allah, in which case he must neither hear nor obey." (Al Bukhari & Muslim)

قَالَ رَسُولُ اللهِ ﷺ : «عَلَى الْمَرْءِ الْمُسْلِمِ السَّمْعُ وَالطَّاعَةُ فِيمَا أَحَبَّ وَ كَرِهَ إِلَّا أَنْ يُؤْمَرَ بِمَعْصِيَةٍ فَإِنْ أُمِرَ بِمَعْصِيَةٍ فَلَا سَمْعَ وَ لَا طَاعَةَ». رَوَاهُ الْبُخَارِي وَمُسْلِم

Non-Muslims who are living in an Islamic state and are loyal citizens of the country and pay their **Jizyah** جِزْيَة **Taxes** have equal rights with Muslims and have the right to practice their religion. No one can be persecuted, and no one can be forced to change their beliefs. (2:256) In fact, the historians of the world recognize that Islamic civilizations have been the most tolerant and fair out of all the world's civilizations. There has never been anything like the Inquisition, the Holocaust or the Soviet collectivization famine, in all of Muslim history.

The principles of the Islamic legal and political system are well developed. They have been studied and implemented for centuries. Even when some traditional Muslim empires and territories were ruled by kings and princes who falsely called themselves khulafa,' the Islamic Shari'ah was still used to one degree or another to oppose their abuses of power.

Examples of how this system was implemented throughout Muslim history are many. Once we become educated in the authentic system of Islam, we must try to establish it somewhere. This is our mission. Some Muslims say they want to establish it, but then they commit haram and violent acts in the process. We must not follow their example.

Basics of an Islamic Government

Judicial Branch

Title: Qadi.
Qualifications: Muslim, male or female, well grounded in the principles of Fiqh and Shari'ah.
Selected: Appointed by the khalifa in consultation with the Majlis Ash-Shura.
Job: To dispense justice, to make decisions about legal issues and to rule on the actions of the khalifa and the Majlis Ash-Shura. A council of Fiqh scholars may advise here.

Executive Branch

Title: Khalifa or Amir ul Mu'mineen.
Qualifications: Muslim, male, over 40 years old, of good standing and recognized knowledge and ability.
Selected: Chosen by vote of either the people directly or by their representatives.
Job: To implement the Shari'ah, manage the affairs of government and lead the Ummah in all its political affairs.
Term: Can be for life or a set period. Majlis Ash-Shura determines this time period. Un-Islamic behavior is grounds for removal or impeachment.

Representative Branch

Title: Majlis Ash-Shura.
Qualifications: A body of elected representatives chosen by the community. Can be male or female, must be Muslim and of recognized knowledge and ability.
Selected: By vote.
Job: To advise the khalifa, represent the people, approve or disapprove of the leader's decisions and remove him from office if he deviates from the Shari'ah.

The best example to follow is that of the Messenger of Allah ﷺ, the Sahaba and those righteous people throughout Muslim history who followed Islam sincerely.

Our Role in Creating a Real Islamic State

The Blessed Prophet ﷺ once said that when we see a wrong being committed, we must try to change it with our own hands. If we can't do that, then we must at least speak out against it. And if we can't do that, then we should at least feel bad about it in our hearts. The Prophet ﷺ then added that the third option was the weakest level of emaan.

If we want to establish a real Islamic state based on justice and equality for all people, then we must first build our emaan to the level of being so motivated that we have no choice but to take action. Otherwise, we will continue to flounder, and our communities will move aimlessly.

Blessed is the One Who sent down the Standard (the Qur'an) to His servant, so it can be a warning to all creatures. The control of space and the Earth belongs to Him. He has not given birth to any son, nor does He have any partner in His control. He is the One Who created all things and made them properly measured. Surat Al Furqan (The Criterion) 25:1-2

﴿تَبَارَكَ ٱلَّذِي نَزَّلَ ٱلْفُرْقَانَ عَلَىٰ عَبْدِهِۦ لِيَكُونَ لِلْعَٰلَمِينَ نَذِيرًا﴾ ﴿ٱلَّذِي لَهُۥ مُلْكُ ٱلسَّمَٰوَٰتِ وَٱلْأَرْضِ وَلَمْ يَتَّخِذْ وَلَدًا وَلَمْ يَكُن لَّهُۥ شَرِيكٌ فِى ٱلْمُلْكِ وَخَلَقَ كُلَّ شَيْءٍ فَقَدَّرَهُۥ تَقْدِيرًا﴾ سُورَةُ ٱلْفُرْقَانِ 25:1-2

The Blessed Prophet ﷺ said, "Whoever obeys me, obeys Allah. Whoever disobeys me, disobeys Allah. Whoever obeys my amir, obeys me. Whoever disobeys my amir, disobeys me." (Al Bukhari)

قَالَ رَسُولُ اللهِ ﷺ: «مَنْ أَطَاعَنِي فَقَدْ أَطَاعَ اللهَ، وَمَنْ عَصَانِي فَقَدْ عَصَى اللهَ، وَمَنْ أَطَاعَ أَمِيرِي فَقَدْ أَطَاعَنِي، وَمَنْ عَصَى أَمِيرِي فَقَدْ عَصَانِي». رَوَاهُ الْبُخَارِيّ

Literature Selection

How Do I Live Islam Today?

The Blessed Prophet Muhammad ﷺ once said that there will come a time when the struggle to live like a good Muslim will be so hard that it will be like holding a hot coal in your hand. It's not always easy to live in the full spirit of Islam when the world is dominated by people who follow their every whim, right or wrong, and who call you towards sinful living.

Indeed, whenever someone makes a stand for truth, justice, morality and an honest, clean living, the people in the society around them attack them mentally, verbally and sometimes physically. The problem has become so difficult that even in traditionally Muslim countries, the true followers of Islam are often discriminated against by un-Islamic governments, simply because they assert that Islam is the true path to follow for success in both worlds.

But it cannot be said that we are the only people who have lived in difficult times. In every age, and in every society, there have been temptations, worries, social problems and people who would try to steer us from the straight way of submission to Allah's ﷻ will. Shaytan has never rested, and he has ways of getting at the best of us through our weaknesses.

One famous Muslim writer, Imam Abu Hamid Muhammad Al Ghazzali, also knew what it was like to live in a world full of temptations and stumbling blocks on the road to true and sincere taqwa (awareness of Allah ﷻ). He was born in the year 1058 in the city of Tus in the Middle East. At that time, the Muslim world was expanding and growing. Muslim lands were not under the control of non-Muslims, nor were the leaders particularly bad.

Imam Al Ghazzali should have had an easy time being a good Muslim in such a situation. But, because of human shortcomings found within us all, he saw that his own society was filled with un-Islamic temptations and that men were motivated more by the delights of the world than by the delights of faith. Even Imam Al Ghazzali had a crisis of faith trying to understand how a person could be a sincere believer in such a situation.

After withdrawing from society for a while to think, he returned with the answers he had sought. He successfully identified the thorny path that the sincere believer must follow, and wrote a book entitled *Ihya 'Uloom Ad-Deen* إحْياء عُلوم الدّين *The Reawakening of Knowledge of the Deen* and helped millions of Muslims, even up to our present day, see how to live as a true Muslim in a world full of temptation and distraction. The following reading selection is Imam Al Ghazzali's analysis of the difficult path towards true peace that everyone who wants to submit to Allah ﷻ must pass through.

The Allegory of the Seven Valleys

by Imam Abu Hamid Al Ghazzali

Know, my brothers and sisters, that 'ibadah, or 'service for Allah,' is the fruit of knowledge, the benefit of life and the currency of the righteous. It's the aim and object of people of noble aspirations having sharp inward understanding. It's their reason for being and their everlasting paradise. "I am your Creator," says Allah in the Qur'an. "Serve Me. You will have your payback and your efforts will be rewarded."

'Ibadah, then, is essential for people, but at the same time it is filled with difficulties and hardships. It has stumbling blocks and pitfalls in its tortuous path, which is haunted by cut-throats and goblins, while helpers are scarce and friends are few. But this path of 'ibadah must be dangerous, for as the Blessed Prophet ﷺ says, "Paradise is surrounded by sufferings and covered by trials, while Hell is surrounded by easy things and unlimited enjoyment of passions."

The poor human! He is weak; his responsibilities are heavy; times are hard, and life is short. But because the journey from here to the hereafter is unavoidable, if he neglects taking the necessary supplies for the trip, he will be sure to perish. Think over the importance of the situation and the seriousness of our condition. By Allah, our condition is sorry indeed, for many are called, but few are chosen.

When I realized that the path of 'ibadah was so difficult and dangerous, I wrote certain books. Chiefly among them, *Ihya Uloom-id Deen*, in which I pointed out the ways and means of getting over those difficulties, facing the dangers boldly and crossing the path with success. But certain people, who didn't see what I was trying to do in my writings, failed to understand the meaning and purpose of it. They not only rejected the book, but treated it in a manner unbecoming of a Muslim.

But I was not discouraged. These were the same types of people who used to ridicule the Holy Qur'an, calling it, 'The Stories of the Ancients.' Nor was I offended by them. I felt pity on them because they didn't know what they were doing to themselves. I hate conflicts even now, but I feel I must do something for them. So out of compassion for my brothers and sisters, I prayed to Allah to enlighten me on the subject (of difficulty in living the deen) in a new manner.

Listen, then, and know that the first thing which awakens a person from the sleep of forgetfulness, and turns him towards the straight path, is Allah's grace, which stirs the mind to think the following thoughts:

"I am the receiver of so many gifts—life, power, reason, speech—and I find myself mysteriously protected from so many troubles and disasters. Who is my benefactor? Who is my savior? I must be grateful to Him in a fitting manner; otherwise, the gifts might be taken away, and I will be finished off forever! These gifts reveal their purpose, like tools in the hands of an artist, and the world appears to me like a beautiful picture leading my thoughts towards the painter."

These thoughts take the awakened person into the Valley of Knowledge where the Messenger of Allah ﷺ leads the way and tells him:

"The Benefactor is the One Who has no partner with Him. He is your Creator Who is everywhere, though you can't see Him, Whose commandments must be obeyed both inwardly and outwardly. He has decided that good will be rewarded and evil will be punished. The choice is now yours, because you are held responsible for your actions. Seek knowledge from teachers who fear Allah with an unshakable conviction."

When the Valley of Knowledge is crossed, a person then prepares for 'ibadah but his guilty conscience assaults him, saying, "How can you knock at the door of Heaven (when you are so filled with bad ways and behavior)? Away with the immorality and bad deeds first!"

The poor sinner then falls down into the Valley of Repentance, when suddenly a voice is heard crying, "Repent, repent! For your Lord is forgiving!"

He asks for repentance sincerely and cries to His Lord for mercy. He now takes heart and rises up with joy and proceeds further on the path. Then he enters into a Valley Full of Stumbling Blocks, chief of which are four in number:

1) The tempting world,
2) The attractive people,
3) The old enemy Shaytan, and finally,
4) The weak inner-self.

So let him have four weapons he can use to defeat the four main enemies. These four are:
1) Choosing a simple lifestyle.
2) Avoiding mixing with all sorts of people.
3) Fighting the old enemy, Shaytan, with increased learning.
4) Controlling the inner-self with the overseer of taqwa.

Let it be remembered that these four weapons, themselves, have to face four other psychological troubles. They are:
1) Worrying over money due to living a simple lifestyle.
2) Doubts and anxieties about our private affairs disturbing our peace of mind.
3) Worry, hardship and embarrassment, because of not meeting new people all the time. Indeed, when a person wishes to serve Allah☝, Shaytan attacks him openly and secretly from all sides!
4) Unpleasant happenings and unexpected suffering come out of nowhere.

These psychological worries throw the poor traveler into the Valley of Trials and Troubles. In this plight, let a person protect himself by:
1) Dependence on Allah☝ in the matter of his earnings.
2) Calling for His help when he finds himself helpless.
3) Patience in suffering.
4) Joyous submission to His Will.

Crossing this fearful Valley of Trials and Troubles makes a person think that the path will not be easy, but to his amazement, he finds that 'ibadah is boring, prayers are mechanical and contemplation has no pleasure. He is lazy, depressed, gloomy and stupid. Puzzled and perplexed, he now enters into the Thundering Valley. The lightning flash of Hope dazzles his sight, and he falls down trembling when he hears the deafening sound of the Thunder of Fear.

His eyes, brimming with tears, imitate the clouds; his pure thoughts flash with the lightning. In a moment, the mystery of Human Responsibility, with its rewards for good actions and punishment for wicked deeds, was solved. Afterwards, his 'ibadah will not be just lip service, and his daily work will not be just drudgery. Soaring on high, he will go forward on the wings of Hope and Fear.

With a light heart and in a happy mood, he now proceeds further until suddenly the Abysmal Valley presents its dreadful sight. Looking deep into why he does things, he finds that people who do good are motivated, either by the desire to show off to their fellow people, or they are simply trying to impress themselves.

On one side of the Abysmal Valley he sees the ten-headed monster of hypocrisy lurking, and on the other side he sees the bewitching Pandora of Conceit with her box open. In despair, he doesn't know what to do, when suddenly, the Angel of Sincerity emerges from the depths of his heart and takes him by the hand and carries him through the valley.

While expressing his thanks for the mercy of Allah☝, he proceeds further until the thought of Allah's☝ numerous favors to his unworthy self, and his inability to do full justice in giving thanks, overwhelms him.

And thus he enters into the Valley of Hymns where, mortal as he is, he tries his best to sing the songs of praise to the ever lasting Allah☝. The Invisible Hand of Divine Mercy then opens the door to the Garden of Love. He is ushered inside with his body and soul, because both had played their part directly or indirectly. Here ends the journey. The servant of Allah☝ now lives among his fellow travelers, but his heart lives in contemplation of Allah, waiting to carry out the last order, *O soul at peace! Return to your Creator well-pleased and well pleasing. Then enter among My Servants, and enter into My Paradise.*
Surat Al Fajr (The Dawn) 89:27-30

﴿يَا أَيَّتُهَا النَّفْسُ الْمُطْمَئِنَّةُ﴾ ﴿ارْجِعِي إِلَى رَبِّكِ رَاضِيَةً مَرْضِيَّةً﴾ ﴿فَادْخُلِي فِي عِبَادِي﴾ ﴿وَ ادْخُلِي جَنَّتِي﴾ سُورَةُ الفَجْر 89: 27 - 30

Reference
Section

Where Do Muslims Live?

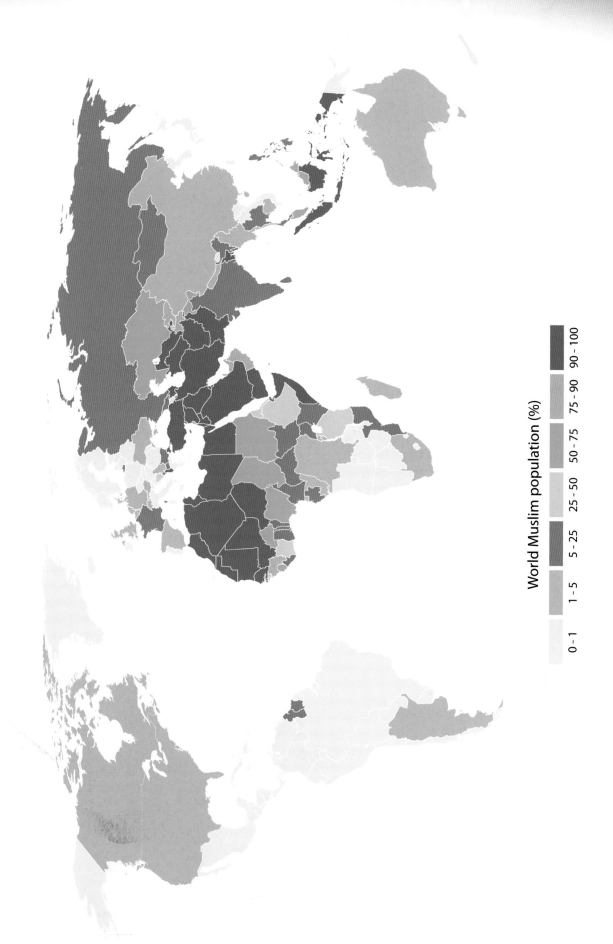

World Muslim population (%)

| 0 - 1 | 1 - 5 | 5 - 25 | 25 - 50 | 50 - 75 | 75 - 90 | 90 - 100 |

Books for Converts and Those Interested in Islam

Islam in General
- Minhaj Al-Muslim (The Muslim's Path): Abu Bakr Jabir Al-Jaza'iry
- The Beautiful Commands of Allah: Ruqaiyyah Waris Maqsood
- Al Tawhid: Ismail Raji Al-Faruqi
- Islamic Creed Series (Set of 8 Books): 'Umar S. al-Ashqar
- What Everyone Needs to Know about Islam: John L. Esposito
- Understanding Islam: Jerald F. Dirks
- Let Us Be Muslims: Sayyid Abul Ala Mawdudi
- Islam Today: Akbar S. Ahmed
- What Everyone Should Know About Islam and Muslims: Suzanne Haneef
- Islam The Straight Path Author: John L. Esposito
- The Everything Understanding Islam Book-A complete guide to Muslim beliefs, practices, and culture Author: Christine Huda Dodge
- Essential Message of Islam: Muhammad Yunus and Ashfaque Ullah
- Islam in Focus Author: Hammudah 'Abd al 'Ali
- A Basic Dictionary of Islam Author: Ruqaiyyah Waris Maqsood
- Islam Author: Ismail Raji Al-Faruqi
- Islam its Meaning and Message: Author: Khurshid Ahmad
- The Complete Idiot's Guide to Understanding Islam: Yahiya Emerick
- The Most Beautiful Names of Allah: Samira Fayyad Khawaldeh

Comparative Religion and Current Issues:
- What You Weren't Taught In Sunday School: Jerald F. Dirks
- The Cross and the Crescent: Jerald F. Dirks
- Problems Muslims Face in Today's World: Isa M. Tofte
- Struggling to Surrender: Some Impressions of an American Convert to Islam: Jeffrey Lang
- What I Believe: Tariq Ramadan
- Losing My Religion: A Call for Help: Jeffrey Lang
- Living Islam Treading the Path of Ideal: Ruqaiyyah Waris Maqsood
- A Young Muslim's Guide to the Modern World: Seyyed Hossein Nasr
- Why Islam? لماذا الإسلام؟: K. Sherman
- From MTV to Mecca: How Islam Inspired My Life Author: Kristiane Backer
- Islam - A Thousand Years of Faith and Power Author: Jonathan Bloom and Sheila Blair

Adab - Manners
- Muslim Character : An American-English Translation of Muhammad al-Ghazali's Khuluq al-Muslim
- The Ideal Muslim Society As defined in the Qur'an and Sunnah Living Islam: Muhammad Ali Al-Hashimi
- Treading the Path of Ideal: Ruqaiyyah Waris Maqsood
- Reclaim Your Heart: Yasmin Mogahed
- Morals and Manners in Islam (A Guide To Islamic Adab): Marwan Ibrahim Al-Kaysi

Learn Arabic:
http://www.noorart.com/shop_by_age/learn_arabic_adults_books_2

Pillars of Islam
- Salat Guide Made Simple: Mohammad Thompson
- Salaat the Islamic Prayer from A to Z: Mamdouh N. Mohamed
- The Muslim Prayer Encyclopedia: Ruqaiyyah Waris Maqsood
- A Simple Guide to Muslim Prayer: Muhammad Mahmud Al-Sawwat
- Zakat Calculation: Mushfiqur Rahman

Prophet Muhammad

- When the Moon Split: Safi Ar-Rahman Al-Mubarakfoury
- The Prophet Muhammad - A Role Model for Muslim Minorities
- Daily Wisdom - Sayings of the Prophet Muhammad: Abdur Raheem Kidwai
- Who Is Muhammad: Khurram Murad
- Remembrance and Prayer The Way Of Prophet Muhammad: Muhammad Al-Ghazali
- In the Footsteps of the Prophet: Tariq Ramadan
- Muhammad(ﷺ) His Life Based on the Earliest Sources: Martin Lings
- The Sealed Nectar: Safi Ar-Rahman Al-Mubarakfour
- The Life of the Last Prophet: Yusuf Islam
- Critical Lives: Muhammad(ﷺ): Yahiya Emerick
- Muhammad Man and Prophet: Adil Salahi
- Muhammad: His Character and Conduct: Adil Salahi
- A Day with the Prophet: Ahmad Von Deffner
- The Prophet Muhammad: The Best of All Husbands: Dr. Ghazi aShammari

The Holy Qur'an

http://www.noorart.com/shop_by_age/holy_quran_adults_books

Prophets

- Stories of the Prophets: Ismaeel Ibn Katheer
- Prophets Models for Humanity: Alia N. Athar

Du'a - Supplication

- The Accepted Whispers (English Translation of Munajaat-e-Maqbul): Maulana Ashraf Ali Thanvi
- Daily Wisdom: Islamic Prayers & Supplications: Abdur Raheem Kidwai
- Don't be Sad: Aaidh ibn Abdullah al-Qarni
- Living in Allah's Presence: Aspects of Islamic Spirituality: Abdur Rashid Siddiqui

Women in Islam

- Great Women of Islam: Mahmood Ahmad Ghadanfar
- Woman In Islam: Aisha Lemu and Fatima Heeren
- Tajweed Made Easy: Ruqaiyyah Islam

Family and Marriage

- The Muslim Marriage Guide: Ruqaiyyah Waris Maqsood
- Marriage and Family Building in Islam: Muhammad Abdul Bari
- Family Leadership (Qawamah): Dr. Mohamed Rida Beshir
- Before the Wedding: Munira Lekovic Ezzeldine

Ahadith

- Authentication of Hadith - Redefining the Criteria: Israr Ahmad Khan
- Summarized Sahih Al-Bukhari: Imam Bukhari
- English Translation of Sahih Muslim (7 Books): Imam Abul-Husain Muslim
- Riyad-us-Saliheen (2 Books): Imam Al-Nawawi
- Forty Hadith: Assad Nimer Busool
- The Hadith for Beginners: Dr. Muhammad Zubayr Siddiqi
- An-Nawawi's Forty Hadith

Islamic History and Civilization

- Islamic Civilization : It's Foundational Beliefs and Principles: Sayyid Abul Ala Mawdudi
- A Journey Through Islamic History: Yasminah Hashim & Dr M A J Beg
- Muslim Contributions to World Civilization: M. Basheer Ahmed & Syed A. Ahsani & Dilnawaz A. Siddiqui
- The House of Wisdom: How the Arabs Transformed Western Civilization Author: Jonathan Lyons
- Lost History: The Enduring Legacy of Muslim Scientists, Thinkers, and Artists Author: Michael Hamilton Morgan
- A Vanished World: Muslims, Christians, and Jews in Medieval Spain Author: Chris Lowney
- How Islam Created The Modern World Author: Mark Graham
- Winning the Hearts & Souls Author: Hafiz Ibn Kathir
- Studies in Islamic Civilization: The Muslim Contribution to the Renaissance Author: Ahmed Essa and Othman Ali
- 1001 Inventions: The Enduring Legacy of Muslim Civilization Author: Professor Salim T.S. Al-Hassani
- Stories from Islamic History: Sayyed Abul Hasan Ali NadwiThe History of Islam: 3 Volumes: Akbar Shah Najeebabadi
- Companions of the Prophet: 2 Books Author: Abdul Wahid Hamid
- Heroes of Islam Author: Prof. Mahmoud Esma'il Sieny
- A History of the Prophets of Islam: 2 Volumes Author: Suzanne Haneef
- Lost Islamic History - Reclaiming Muslim Civilisation from the Past: Firas Alkhateeb
- The Stories of the Sahaba (5 books): Noura Durkee
- Men & Women around the Messenger(ﷺ): Sa'd Yusuf Abu Aziz

Six Transliterated Suwar

About Transliterations

The easiest way to memorize a surat of the Qur'an to read in your salah, if you have not yet mastered the Arabic script, is to pronounce it in the letters and sounds of the language you speak. If you don't know how to read Arabic text at all, then a transliteration is highly useful.

All Muslims learn at least a few surahs in Arabic. It is important for Muslims to pray in the same language, because it builds commonalty amongst Muslims all over the world. No matter which country you find yourself in, whether it's China or Brazil, you will feel at home with Muslims there, even if you don't know the local language.

Also, Allah revealed His final Message in the language of Arabic. If we desire to really know what Allah wants for us, then we will need to know the original language. If we rely only on translations, we run the danger of someone translating something wrong, and following it out of ignorance. Accurate knowledge comes from greater learning!

We have listed six short surahs here, in their transliterated form. Remember that this is only a bridge for you to use until you can read the Arabic text on your own. This should be a goal of every conscientious Muslim. May Allah bless you in your efforts!

Before reciting any surat or ayah, you should say first,
A'oodhu billahimina Shaytanir Rajeem.
Bismillahir Rahmanir Raheem.

أَعوذُ بِاللهِ مِنَ الشَّيْطانِ الرَّجِيم
بِسْمِ اللهِ الرَّحْمَنِ الرَّحِيم

I seek Allah's protection from the rejected Shaytan.
In the Name of Allah, The Most Gracious, The Most Merciful

بِسْمِ ٱللَّهِ ٱلرَّحْمَٰنِ ٱلرَّحِيمِ

﴿قُلْ أَعُوذُ بِرَبِّ ٱلنَّاسِ ۞ مَلِكِ ٱلنَّاسِ ۞ إِلَٰهِ ٱلنَّاسِ ۞ مِن شَرِّ ٱلْوَسْوَاسِ ٱلْخَنَّاسِ ۞ ٱلَّذِي يُوَسْوِسُ فِي صُدُورِ ٱلنَّاسِ ۞ مِنَ ٱلْجِنَّةِ وَٱلنَّاسِ ۞﴾

سُورَةُ النَّاسِ 114: 1-6

Surat An-Naas
(The People) Surat114

Bismi Allahi Ar-Rahmani Ar-Rahim

Qul aʹoothu birabbi annas
Maliki annas
Ilahi annas
Min sharri alwaswasi alkhannas
Allathee yuwaswisu fee sudoori annas
Mina aljinnati wannas

In the Name of Allah, the Most Caring and the Most Kind

Say, "I want to be protected by the Lord of people, the King of people and the God of people, from the evil whispers put into the minds of people by jinn and other bad people." (1-6)

بِسْمِ ٱللَّهِ ٱلرَّحْمَٰنِ ٱلرَّحِيمِ

﴿قُلْ أَعُوذُ بِرَبِّ ٱلْفَلَقِ ۞ مِن شَرِّ مَا خَلَقَ ۞ وَمِن شَرِّ غَاسِقٍ إِذَا وَقَبَ ۞ وَمِن شَرِّ ٱلنَّفَّٰثَٰتِ فِي ٱلْعُقَدِ ۞ وَمِن شَرِّ حَاسِدٍ إِذَا حَسَدَ ۞﴾ سُورَةُ الفَلَقِ 113: 1-5

Surat Al Falaq
(The Dawn) Surat113

Bismi Allahi Ar-Rahmani Ar-Rahim

Qul aʹoothu birabbi alfalaq
Min sharri ma khalaq
Wamin sharri ghasiqin ithawaqab
Wamin sharri annaffathatifee alʹuqad
Wamin sharri hasidin itha hasad

In the Name of Allah, the Most Caring and the Most Kind

Say (this prayer): "I want to be safe with the Lord of the Sunrise from (any) danger He made in the world, and from the danger of coming darkness, and from the danger of evil magic and from the danger of jealous people when they are jealous." (1-5)

بِسْمِ اللَّهِ الرَّحْمَٰنِ الرَّحِيمِ

﴿قُلْ هُوَ اللَّهُ أَحَدٌ ۝ اللَّهُ الصَّمَدُ ۝ لَمْ يَلِدْ وَلَمْ يُولَدْ ۝ وَلَمْ يَكُن لَّهُ كُفُوًا أَحَدٌ ۝﴾

سُورَةُ الإِخْلَاصِ 112:1-4

Surat al Ikhlaas
(Pure Faith) Surat112

Bismi Allahi Ar-Rahmani Ar-Rahim

Qul huwa Allahu ahad
Allahu assamad
Lam yalid walam yoolad
Walam yakun lahu kufuwan ahad

In the Name of Allah, the Most Caring and the Most Kind

Declare: "Say Allah is one. Allah was never born. And He will never die. He has no parents. He has no child. And no one is anything like Him." (1-4)

بِسْمِ اللَّهِ الرَّحْمَٰنِ الرَّحِيمِ

﴿إِذَا جَاءَ نَصْرُ اللَّهِ وَالْفَتْحُ ۝ وَرَأَيْتَ النَّاسَ يَدْخُلُونَ فِي دِينِ اللَّهِ أَفْوَاجًا ۝ فَسَبِّحْ بِحَمْدِ رَبِّكَ وَاسْتَغْفِرْهُ ۚ إِنَّهُ كَانَ تَوَّابًا ۝﴾ سُورَةُ النَّصْرِ 110:1-3

Surat An-Nasr
(Assistance) Surat110

Bismillahir Rahmanir Raheem.

Itha jaa nasru Allahi walfath
Waraayta annasa yadkhuloona fee deeni Allahi afwaja
Fasabbih bihamdi rabbika wastaghfirhu
innahu kana tawwaba

In the Name of Allah, the Most Caring and the Most Kind

Declare: "When Allah's help comes and you win the contest, and when you see people becoming Muslims everywhere, then you should glorify and praise your Lord and ask Him to forgive you for any bad deeds you did. He really loves to forgive." (1-3)

بِسْمِ اللَّهِ الرَّحْمَٰنِ الرَّحِيمِ

﴿وَالْعَصْرِ ۝ إِنَّ الْإِنسَانَ لَفِي خُسْرٍ ۝ إِلَّا الَّذِينَ ءَامَنُوا وَعَمِلُوا الصَّالِحَاتِ وَتَوَاصَوْا بِالْحَقِّ وَتَوَاصَوْا بِالصَّبْرِ ۝﴾

سُورَةُ الْعَصْرِ 103: 1-3

Surat Al 'Asr
(The Ages) Surat103

Bismillahir Rahmanir Raheem.

Wal 'asr
Inna al-insana lafee khusr
Illa allatheena amanoo
wa'amiloo assalihati
watawasaw bilhaqqi
watawasaw bissabr

In the Name of Allah, the Most Caring and the Most Kind

Declare: "The passing of time shows that people are really in a bad way. Everyone is going to lose except those people who teach each other how to be truthful and how to be patient." (1-3)

بِسْمِ اللَّهِ الرَّحْمَٰنِ الرَّحِيمِ

﴿أَرَءَيْتَ الَّذِي يُكَذِّبُ بِالدِّينِ ۝ فَذَٰلِكَ الَّذِي يَدُعُّ الْيَتِيمَ ۝ وَلَا يَحُضُّ عَلَىٰ طَعَامِ الْمِسْكِينِ ۝ فَوَيْلٌ لِّلْمُصَلِّينَ ۝ الَّذِينَ هُمْ عَن صَلَاتِهِمْ سَاهُونَ ۝ الَّذِينَ هُمْ يُرَاءُونَ ۝ وَيَمْنَعُونَ الْمَاعُونَ ۝﴾ سُورَةُ الْمَاعُونَ 107: 1-7

Surat al 'Ma'un
(Small Kindnesses) Surat107

Bismillahir Rahmanir Raheem.

Ara aiyt al ladhee yukadh dhebu bid deen?
Fa dhaalikal ladhee yadu' ul yateem.
Wa laa yahuddu 'alaa ta'aamil miskeen.
Fa waiylul lil musalleen.
Al ladheenahum 'an sawlatehim saahoon.
Al ladheenahum yuraa-un.
Wa yamna 'oonal ma'oon.

In the Name of Allah, the Most Caring and the Most Kind

Declare: "Have you ever seen a person who denies the (Islamic) way of life (and the Judgment to come)? He's the one who pushes the orphan aside and doesn't support the feeding of the poor. So ruined are the people who pray, but who are careless about their prayers; whose prayers are only for show, and who refuse to share even the smallest amount of kindness." (1-7)

Selected Sayings of
the Blessed Prophet ﷺ

About the Hadith

The Blessed Prophet Muhammad's ﷺ 'recorded actions, sayings, and approvals', which are called *'hadith'*, are the second most important written record of Islam after the Qur'an. The Qur'an, itself, instructs us to listen to the words of the Prophet, as well as its own words. (33:36) The Qur'an provides the major guidelines of Islam, while the Prophet's sayings give us the specific details of how to live as a Muslim.

The Blessed Prophet ﷺ discouraged people from writing his sayings in the earliest days of his mission, so that his words would not be mixed up with the ayaat of the Qur'an. After this danger was eliminated by the extensive study and memorizing of the Qur'an, the Prophet ﷺ relaxed his disapproval of recording his sayings, and then many people did record them.

After the Prophet ﷺ passed away, the Sahaba began to write larger collections of the sayings they had heard directly from the Blessed Prophet. Those who could not write, told their children and grandchildren what the Prophet ﷺ had said and taught. Then they would write it down.

Many scholars, in later years, devoted their entire lives to the collection and preservation of the sayings of the Prophet ﷺ. They would research the origin of every reported saying of the Prophet ﷺ for accuracy. They developed an entire system for ensuring only accurate and truthful hadith were included in their collections.

The six main collections of the Prophet's sayings are named after the six scholars who produced them. They are called the 'Saha Sitta', or 'Reliable Six'. They are listed as follows: Al Bukhari, Muslim, Abu Dawood, At-Tirmidhi, An-Nasa'i and Ibn Majah.

Other lesser known collections were compiled by Ahmad, Al Baihaqi, Daraqutni and others. The collection known as *Al Muwatta* by Imam Malik is also popular. For a good selection of hadith from all six collections in one compilation, there are two collections entitled *Riyadh as Saliheen* and *Mishkat ul Masabih*. They are widely available.

All of the following hadith are taken from one of these *sahih*, or reliable, collections. They have been arranged by subject.

True Intentions

'Umar reports that the Messenger of Allah said:
Actions will be judged according to intentions, and every one shall have what he intended. So if someone migrates for the sake of Allah and His Messenger, then that is what his migration will be counted for. But if someone migrates for a worldly benefit, or to marry a person, then that is what his migration will be counted for. (Al Bukhari & Muslim)

~*~*~*~*~*~

Signs of Faith

Abu Umama reports:
Someone asked the Messenger of Allah: "What is emaan?"
He replied, "When doing good makes you feel pleasure, and doing wrong makes you feel terrible, then you are a believer."
Then he asked Allah's Messenger, "What is a sin?"
He replied, "When something bothers your conscience, give it up." (Ahmad)

~*~*~*~*~*~

The Burden of Age

Anas reports that the Messenger of Allah said:
The older a person gets, the more his desire for two things increases: the desire for wealth and long life. (Al Bukhari & Muslim)

~*~*~*~*~*~

Measurement

'Ali reports that the Messenger of Allah said:
"Everyone of you has their place in Hell or Paradise already known."
Someone asked, "Messenger of Allah, should we then count on what has already been decided for us and abandon our actions?"
He replied, "Continue to act, because things come easy for those (whose nature is) made for them; good actions come easy for (one who) does good, and evil actions come easy for (one who is) unfortunate."
He recited this ayah: "As for the one who donates, reveres (His Lord), and witnesses to the truth, We facilitate for him (the way to ease). But as for he who is greedy, and thinks himself in need of nothing, and rejects the good, We facilitate for him (the way to hardship)." Surat Al Layl (The Night) 92:5-10 (Al Bukhari & Muslim)

~*~*~*~*~*~

True Success

'Abdullah reports that the Messenger of Allah said:
"The successful person is one who has accepted Islam, has been provided with enough to live on, and has been made content by Allah for what He has given him." (Muslim)

The Basis of Belief

'Ali reports that the Messenger of Allah said:
"No servant is a true believer unless he affirms faith in these four doctrines: that there is no god but Allah, and that I am His Messenger He sent with the truth, and he believes in the fact of death, a life after death, and in Qadr (the measurement of life's course)." (At-Tirmidhi & Ibn Majah)

~*~*~*~*~*~

Life is a Journey

Uthman ibn Affan reports that once, while he was standing by a grave and crying so much that his beard became wet, someone asked him, "You don't cry over discussions of Paradise and Hell, but you are crying over a grave?"

Uthman replied that he had heard the Messenger of Allah say, "Surely, the grave is the first step in the journey towards the next life. If one finds salvation (at this stage), then the succeeding stages become easy for him. If one doesn't find salvation there, then what follows becomes very difficult."

Allah's Messenger also said: "I have never seen a site more horrible than that of the grave." (At-Tirmidhi and Ibn Majah)

~*~*~*~*~*~

A Better Way

'Umar reports that the Messenger of Allah said:
"If you would put your faith completely in Allah, He would provide for your needs in the same way He provides for the birds. They go out in the morning with their stomachs empty, and return in the evening with their stomachs full." (At-Tirmidhi)

~*~*~*~*~*~

A Warner

Abu Hurairah reports that the Messenger of Allah said:
"My example is that of a man who built a fire. When it blazed brightly, moths, and insects were attracted and fell into it. And though the man tried hard to keep them away, they thwarted him and dove in. This I do, I struggle to hold you back from the fire, but you leap right into it." (Al Bukhari)

~*~*~*~*~*~

The Amount of Virtue

Abu Hurairah reports that the Messenger of Allah said:
"You live in a blessed time, one in which anyone who abandons just one tenth of what is now required courts destruction. But after this will come a time when whoever follows just one tenth of what is now required will be saved." (At-Tirmidhi)

Light Lodgings

Abu Hurairah reports that the Messenger of Allah said:
"It is a part of the excellence of a person's practice of self-surrender (Islam), that he discards what is of no use to him either in this world or in the next." (At-Tirmidhi)

~*~*~*~*~*~

Human Nature

Abu Musa reports that the Messenger of Allah said:
"The heart is like a feather in the desert: the wind blows it to and fro." (Ahmad)

~*~*~*~*~*~

The Forest for the Trees

Al Mustaurid narrated that the Messenger of Allah said:
"By Allah, this world compared to the next is like dipping your fingertip into the sea. Consider what you bring out." (Muslim)

~*~*~*~*~*~

Envy Only These

'Abdullah narrated that the Messenger of Allah said:
"Don't wish to be like anybody except in two cases: The case of a person who Allah gave wealth to, and he or she spends it in the right way; and the case of a person who Allah gave spiritual knowledge to, and he or she gives their rulings by it and teach it to others." (Al Bukhari)

~*~*~*~*~*~

Real Admiration

Abu Umama reports that the Messenger of Allah said:
"The most enviable of my friends, in my reckoning, is the believer with few possessions who finds his pleasure in prayer, who performs well in the service of his Lord and obeys Him in secret, who is anonymous among men and is not pointed out among people, and whose supply is just enough which contents him."

He then snapped his fingers and said, "His death will come quickly, few women will mourn him, and he will leave only a little." (At-Tirmidhi and Ibn Majah)

~*~*~*~*~*~

Everything has a Proper Use

Abu Sa'eed reports that the Messenger of Allahﷺ said:
"Among the fears I have for you after I am gone are the beauty and distraction of the world which you will receive."
Then someone asked, "Messenger of Allahﷺ, can something that is good produce evil?"
He remained silent, causing those present to think he was receiving revelation. He then wiped the sweat off (his brow) and called to the man who asked the question in an approving way. Then he said, "Allahﷻ does not produce evil. Among the plants the spring rain produces are some which are poisonous, or nearly fatal to all but the type of animal that can feed on it. It eats, and when it is full it faces the sun. When it has dunged and urinated, it returns and eats. This wealth is green and sweet. But he who accepts it wrongly is like a glutton, and it will be evidence against him on the Day of Resurrection." (Al Bukhari and Muslim)

The Reality of Life

Abu Hurairahﷺ reports that the Messenger of Allahﷺ said:
"A person may say, 'My wealth. My property,' but his real property consists of only three things: What he eats, what he has worn and torn, and what he gives away (in charity), and so acquires. Everything else is left to others when he departs." (Muslim)

~*~*~*~*~*~

You Can Take Something With You

Abu Hurairahﷺ reports that the Messenger of Allahﷺ said:
"When a person dies, his deeds come to an end, except for three things: a continuing charity, knowledge which still gives benefit, and a righteous child who prays for him." (Muslim)

~*~*~*~*~*~

A Dangerous Lock

Sahl ibn Sa'd reports that the Messenger of Allahﷺ said:
"Wealth consists of a variety of treasures, and those treasures have keys. Blessed be he whom Allahﷻ has made a key for good and a lock for evil, but woe to he whom Allahﷻ has made a key for evil and a lock for good." (Ibn Majah)

~*~*~*~*~*~

Our Purpose

A'ishahﷺ reports that the Messenger of Allahﷺ said:
"The world is the dwelling of the one who has no dwelling, and the property of the one who has no property. For he who has no intelligence acquires possessions." (Ahmad & Al Baihaqi)

Where Our True Concern Lies

Abu Hurairah reports that the Messenger of Allah 🕮 said:
When a person dies, the Angels ask what he has sent ahead, but the children of Adam ask what he has left behind. (Al Baihaqi)

~*~*~*~*~*~

Focus on Life

Amr reports that the Messenger of Allah 🕮 said:
"Get a hold of five things before five things happen: your youth before old age, your health before sickness, your riches before poverty, your leisure before business, and your life before your death." (At-Tirmidhi)

~*~*~*~*~*~

Life is Temporary

Ibn Mas'ud reports that the Messenger of Allah 🕮 said:
"Whoever loves his present life, does damage to his hereafter, and whoever loves his hereafter, does damage to his present life. So prefer what is lasting to what is fleeting." (Ahmad & Al Baihaqi

~*~*~*~*~*~

A Sign of Wisdom

Abu Khalid report that the Messenger of Allah 🕮 said:
"When you see a person who is not possessed by worldly things and who says little, draw near to him, for he has been given wisdom." (Al Baihaqi)

~*~*~*~*~*~

Reality of it All

Abu Hurairah reports the Messenger of Allah 🕮 said:
"This world is the believer's prison and the unbeliever's paradise." (Muslim)

~*~*~*~*~*~

Greed

Sahl ibn Sa'd reports that someone asked the Messenger of Allah 🕮 how he can be loved by Allah 🕮 and by people at the same time. He replied: "Don't desire the world and Allah 🕮 will love you; don't desire the possessions of other people and they will love you." (At-Tirmidhi & Ibn Majah)

Orientation

Anas reported that the Messenger of Allahﷺ asked some people: "Can anyone walk in water without getting his feet wet?" They answered in the negative.

Then he said, "So too, this is the condition of the worldly-oriented man; he cannot avoid making mistakes." (Al Baihaqi)

Never Forget Allah's﷾ Blessings

Abu Hurairah reports the Messenger of Allahﷺ said:
"When you see someone who is better off than you, look at one who is not as well off as you. Doing this will keep you from despising the blessings Allah﷾ has given you." (Muslim)

Good Counsel

Abu Ayyub Al Ansari reports that someone went to the Messenger of Allahﷺ and asked him for some brief advice.
He replied: "When you stand for prayer, pray as if it were your last. Don't say anything you will have to make an excuse for tomorrow, and resolve to give up all hopes of what people possess." (Ahmad and Al Baihaqi)

Dual Fortune

Suhaib ibn Sinan reports that the Messenger of Allahﷺ said:
"How excellent is a believer's situation, unlike all others, because there is good in everything that happens to him. If he is prosperous, he thanks Allah﷾, which is good; and if misfortune befalls him, he endures it with perseverance, and that is best for him." (Muslim)

Allah's﷾ Mercy is Boundless

Abu Hurairah reports that the Messenger of Allahﷺ said:
"Allah﷾ has divided mercy into a hundred parts, out of which he retains ninety-nine parts with Him, and has sent the one remaining to earth. From this one part emaanates all the compassion that the whole of creation shows towards each other. So much so, that an animal will lift her hoof above her young lest it should get hurt." (Al Bukhari)

~*~*~*~*~*~

Endless Forgiveness

Anas reports that the Messenger of Allah ﷺ said:
"Allah ﷻ, the Exalted has declared: 'Child of Adam! Indeed, I will continue to forgive you as long as you call upon Me and hope for My forgiveness; whatever your sins may be, I care not. Child of Adam, even if your sins should pile up as high as the sky and you asked for My forgiveness, I would forgive you. Child of Adam, if you came to Me with an Earth full of sins and met Me, not holding anything as My equal, I would come to you with that much forgiveness.'" (At-Tirmidhi)

~*~*~*~*~*~

Poverty and Character

Anas reports that the Messenger of Allah ﷺ said:
"Allah ﷻ, grant me the life of a poor man, cause me to die as a poor man, and resurrect me in the company of the poor."

When A'ishah ؓ asked him why he said that, he replied, "Because they will enter Paradise forty years before the rich, so never turn a poor person away. A'ishah ؓ, even if you can only give a half a date, give it. If you love the poor and let them come near you, A'ishah ؓ, Allah ﷻ will bring you near to Him." (At-Tirmidhi and Al Baihaqi)

~*~*~*~*~*~

Allah ﷻ May Hide Our Faults

Ibn 'Umar reports that the Messenger of Allah ﷺ said:
"A believer will approach his Lord on the Day of Judgment and will be covered with His mercy.

(Allah ﷻ) will ask him about his sins saying, 'Do you remember such and such a sin?'

"He will answer, 'O Lord, I do remember.'
"Then Allah ﷻ will say, 'I kept it secret for you in the world, and I pardon you for it today.'

"Then the record of his good deeds will be given to him." (Al Bukhari and Muslim)

Selected

Hadith Qudsi

The term 'Hadith Qudsi' means, 'Holy Saying'. In addition to the Qur'an, Allah﷾ revealed specific teachings to the Prophet Muhammadﷺ, peace be upon him, which he then repeated to others. Although Hadith Qudsi are considered to be the direct words of Allah﷾, as is the Qur'an, they are not held to the same level, and are outside the established text of the Qur'an.

On the other hand, they are held in higher estimation than the Blessed Prophet's own hadith, because the word of Allah﷾ is always higher than any human being's words. The sayings of the Prophetﷺ are his explanations of revelation, and his discussions about how to perform the rituals. Therefore, you can see that the Hadith Qudsi occupy a middle ground between the Qur'an and the regular sayings of the Prophet.

There are over a hundred of these Hadith Qudsi spread throughout the main collections of the Prophetic sayings. Here, we provide a sampling of some of the more well-known ones. Remember that even though these are not Qur'anic texts, they are, nonetheless, to be revered and studied with full awareness of our responsibility to our Creator. It is He who spoke these words to the Prophet, who faithfully transmitted them to us, word-for-word.

Hadith Qudsi

Allah﷾ said, "I am as My servant thinks I am. I am with him when he makes mention of Me. If he mentions Me to himself, I mention him to Myself. If he mentions Me in an assembly, I mention him in a better assembly. If he comes an arm's length closer to Me, I come a yard's length closer to him. If he comes to Me walking, I go to him in a rush."

Allah﷾ said, "The son of Adam denied Me, and he had no right to do so. And he reviled Me, and he had no right to do so. As for his denying Me, it is his saying, '(Allah﷾) will not remake me as He made me at first' - and the initial creation [of him] is no harder for Me than the remaking of him! As for his reviling Me, it is his saying, 'Allah﷾ has taken to Himself a son,'- while I am the One, the Everlasting Refuge. I beget not nor was I begotten, and there is no one comparable to Me."

A Sahaba reported, "The Messenger of Allahﷺ (peace be upon him) led the Fajr prayer for us at al-Hudaybiyah, following a rainfall during the night. When the Prophetﷺ finished, he faced the people and said to them, 'Do you know what your Lord has said?' They answered, 'Allah﷾ and his Messengerﷺ know best.'

(The Prophetﷺ answered that Allah﷾ said), "This morning, one of My servants became a believer in Me, and one a disbeliever. As for the one who said, 'We have been given rain by virtue of Allah﷾ and His mercy', that one is a believer in Me, and a disbeliever in the (supposed power of the) stars; and as for the one who said, 'We have been given rain by such-and-such a star', that one is a disbeliever in Me, and a believer in the stars.'"

Allah﷾ said, "I am so self-sufficient that I am in no need of having an associate. Therefore, whoever does an action for someone else's sake, as well as Mine, will have that action renounced by Me and it will be attributed to the one whom he associated with Me."

Abu Hurairah said, "A prayer performed by someone who has not recited the Essence of the Quran (Surat Al Fatihah (The Opening)) during it is deficient (and he repeated the word three times), incomplete." Someone asked Abu Hurayrah, "[Even though] we're behind the imam?"

He answered, "Recite it to yourself, for I have heard the Prophetﷺ say, 'Allah﷾ has said, 'I have divided prayer between Myself and My servant into two halves, and My servant shall have what he has asked for.

When the servant says, 'Alhamdulillahi rabbil alameen,' Allah﷾ says, 'My servant has praised Me.' And when he says, 'Ar rahmanir raheem,' Allah﷾ says, 'My servant has extolled Me,' and when he says, 'Maaliki yawmid deen,' Allah﷾ says, 'My servant has glorified Me and My servant has submitted to My power.'

And when he says, 'Eyyaka na'budu wa eyyaka nasta'een,' He says, 'This is between Me and My servant, and My servant shall have what he has asked for.' And when he says, 'Ihdinas siratal mustaqim, siratal ladhina an 'amta 'alayhim. Ghayril maghdoobi 'alayhim wa lad dawl-leen,' He says, This is for My servant, and My servant shall have what he has asked for.'"

Allah﷾ said, "Spend (on charity), Oh son of Adam, and I shall spend on you."

A man from among those who were before you was called to account. Nothing in the way of good was found for him except that he used to have dealings with people and, being well-to-do, he would order his servants to let off the man in difficult circumstances [from repaying his debt]. He (the Prophet ﷺ) said that Allah﷾ said, "We are worthier than you of doing that (of being so generous). Let him off."

The Prophet ﷺ said, "Allah﷾ has written down the good deeds and the bad ones. Then He explained it [by saying that] he who has intended a good deed and has not done it, Allah﷾ writes it down with Himself as a full good deed, but if he has intended it and has done it, Allah﷾ writes it down with Himself as from 10 good deeds to seven hundred times, or many times over. But if he has intended a bad deed and has not done it, Allah﷾ writes it down with Himself as a full good deed, but if he has intended it and has done it, Allah﷾ writes it down as one bad deed."

Allah﷾ said, "O My servants, I have forbidden oppression for Myself, and have made it forbidden amongst you, so do not oppress each another. O My servants, all of you are astray except for those I have guided, so seek guidance of Me and I shall guide you. O My servants, all of you are hungry except for those I have fed, so seek food of Me and I shall feed you.

"O My servants, all of you are naked except for those I have clothed, so seek clothing of Me and I shall clothe you. O My servants, you sin by night and by day, and I forgive all sins, so seek forgiveness of Me and I shall forgive you. O My servants, you will not be able to achieve any harm against Me so as to harm Me, and you will not be able to achieve benefitting Me so as to benefit Me. O My servants, if the first of you and the last of you, the human of you and the jinn of you, were to be as pious as the most pious heart of any one man of you, that would not increase My kingdom in anything.

"O My servants, if the first of you and the last of you, the human of you and the jinn of you, were to be as wicked as the most wicked heart of any one man of you, that would not decrease My kingdom in anything. O My servants, if the first of you and the last of you, the human of you and the jinn of you, were to rise up in one place and make a request of Me, and were I to give everyone what he requested, that would not decrease what I have, any more that a needle decreases the sea if put into it.

"O My servants, it is but your deeds that I reckon up for you and then pay you back for, so let him who finds good offer good praise of Allah﷾, and let him who finds other than that blame no one but himself."

Allah﷾ said, "O son of Adam, I fell ill and you didn't visit Me." (The person) will ask, ' O Lord, and how should I visit You when You are the Lord of the worlds?'

(I) will answer, 'Didn't you know that My servant So-and-so had fallen ill and you didn't visit him? Didn't you know that if you had visited him, you would have found Me with him?'

"O son of Adam, I asked you for food and you didn't feed Me."

(The person) will ask, 'O Lord, and how should I feed You, when You are the Lord of the worlds?'

(I) will say, 'Didn't you know that My servant So-and-so asked you for food and you didn't feed him? Didn't you know that if you had fed him you, would surely have found (the reward for doing it) with Me?'

"O son of Adam, I asked you to give Me drink and you didn't give Me a drink. (The person) will say, 'O Lord, how should I give You a drink, when You are the Lord of the worlds?'

(I) will say, 'My servant So-and-so asked you to give him a drink and you didn't give him a drink. If you would have given him a drink you, would have surely found that (reward) with Me.'"

The Prophet ﷺ said, "Don't let anyone bring himself down."

The people asked, "O Messenger of Allah ﷺ, how can any one of us bring himself down?"

He answered, "(When a person) finds a matter concerning Allah ﷻ about which he should say something, and he does not say [it], so Allah ﷻ says to him on the Day of Resurrection, 'What prevented you from saying something about such-and-such and such-and-such?' '(The person) will answer, '[It was] out of fear of people.' Then (Allah ﷻ) will say, 'Rather, it is I whom you should more properly fear.'"

Allah ﷻ said, "Whoever shows hatred to someone devoted to Me, I shall be at war with him. My servant doesn't draw nearer to Me with anything more loved by Me than the religious duties I have enjoined upon him, and My servant continues to draw near to Me with extra-meritorious works so that I shall love him."

"When I love him, I am his hearing with which he hears, his seeing with which he sees, his hand with which he strikes, and his foot with which he walks. If he were to ask [something] of Me, I would surely give it to him, and if he were to ask Me for refuge, I would surely grant him it. I do not hesitate about anything as much as I hesitate about [seizing] the soul of My faithful servant: he hates death and I hate hurting him."

Allah ﷻ said, "Truly of those devoted to Me, the one I most favor is a believer who is of little means and much given to prayer, who has been particular in the worship of his Lord and has obeyed Him inwardly, who was obscure among people and not pointed out, and whose sustenance was just sufficient to provide for him, yet he bore this patiently." Then the Prophet ﷺ rapped his hand and said, "Death will come quickly to him, his mourners will be few, and his estate will be small."

There was amongst those before you a man who had a wound. He was in [such] anguish that he took a knife and made with it a cut in his hand, and the blood did not cease to flow till he died. Allah ﷻ the Almighty said, "My servant has himself acted ahead of Me; I have forbidden him Paradise."

A man sinned greatly against himself, and when death came to him he charged his sons, saying: "When I have died, burn me, then crush me and scatter [my ashes] into the sea, for, by Allah ﷻ, if my Lord takes possession of me, He will punish me in a manner in which He has punished no one [else]." So they did that to him. Then (Allah ﷻ) said to the Earth, "Produce what you have taken," and there he was! And He said to him: "What induced you to do what you did?" He said "Being afraid of You, O my Lord," and because of that (Allah ﷻ) forgave him.

Selected Index